PERL
BY EXAMPLE

THIRD EDITION

ISBN 0-13-028251-0

9 780130 282514

90000

PRENTICE HALL PTR
OPEN SOURCE TECHNOLOGY SERIES

- ▶ APACHE WEB SERVER ADMINISTRATION AND E-COMMERCE HANDBOOK
  Scott Hawkins

- ▶ LINUX DESK REFERENCE, SECOND EDITION
  Scott Hawkins

- ▶ INTEGRATING LINUX AND WINDOWS
  Mike McCune

- ▶ LINUX ASSEMBLY LANGUAGE PROGRAMMING
  Bob Neveln

- ▶ LINUX SHELLS BY EXAMPLE
  Ellie Quigley

- ▶ PERL BY EXAMPLE, THIRD EDITION
  Ellie Quigley

- ▶ UNIX SHELLS BY EXAMPLE, THIRD EDITION
  Ellie Quigley

- ▶ LINUX: RUTE USER'S TUTORIAL AND EXPOSITION
  Paul Sheer

- ▶ REAL WORLD LINUX SECURITY: INTRUSION PREVENTION, DETECTION, AND RECOVERY
  Bob Toxen

PERL
BY EXAMPLE

THIRD EDITION

ELLIE QUIGLEY

Prentice Hall PTR
Upper Saddle River, New Jersey 07458
www.phptr.com

Library of Congress Cataloging in Publication Data

Quigley, Ellie.
    Perl by example / Ellie Quigley--3rd ed.
        p. cm. -- (Prentice Hall PTR open source technology series)
    ISBN 0-13-028251-0
    1. Perl (Computer program language) I. Title. II. Series.

QA76.73.P22 Q53 2001
005.13'3--dc21

                                              2001036458

Editorial/Production Supervision: *Vanessa Moore*
Cover Design Director: *Jerry Votta*
Cover Designer: *Nina Scuderi*
Manufacturing Manager: *Maura Zaldivar*
Marketing Manager: *Bryan Gambrel*
Acquisitions Editor: *Mark Taub*
Editorial Assistant: *Sarah Hand*
Project Coordinator: *Anne R. Garcia*

© 2002 Prentice Hall PTR
Prentice-Hall, Inc.
Upper Saddle River, New Jersey 07458

The publisher offers discounts on this book when ordered in bulk quantities.
For more information, contact:

> Corporate Sales Department
> Prentice Hall PTR
> 1 Lake Street
> Upper Saddle River, NJ   07458
> Phone: 800-382-3419; FAX: 201-236-7141
> E-mail: corpsales@prenhall.com

Printed in the United States of America
10   9   8   7

ISBN 0-13-028251-0

Pearson Education Ltd.
Pearson Education Australia PTY, Limited
Pearson Education Singapore, Pte. Ltd
Pearson Education North Asia Ltd.
Pearson Education Canada, Ltd.
Pearson Educación de Mexico, S.A. de C.V.
Pearson Education — Japan
Pearson Education Malaysia, Pte. Ltd.
Pearson Education, Upper Saddle River, New Jersey

To the memory of my husband and best friend, Guy Sterling Quigley.

TABLE OF CONTENTS

CHAPTER 3

GETTING A HANDLE ON PRINTING 21

CHAPTER 4

WHAT'S IN A NAME 41

CHAPTER 5

WHERE'S THE OPERATOR? .101

CHAPTER 6

IF ONLY,
UNCONDITIONALLY, FOREVER 133

CHAPTER 7

REGULAR EXPRESSIONS—
PATTERN MATCHING 163

CHAPTER 8

GETTING CONTROL—REGULAR EXPRESSION METACHARACTERS 197

CHAPTER 9

GETTING A HANDLE ON FILES 249

CHAPTER 10

HOW DO SUBROUTINES FUNCTION? 289

CHAPTER 11

MODULARIZE IT, PACKAGE IT, AND SEND IT TO THE LIBRARY! 323

CHAPTER 12

DOES THIS JOB REQUIRE A REFERENCE? 355

CHAPTER 13

BLESS THOSE THINGS!
(OBJECT-ORIENTED PERL) 379

CHAPTER 14

THOSE MAGIC TIES, DBM STUFF,
AND THE DATABASE HOOKS 435

CHAPTER 15

INTRODUCTION TO PERL DATABASE PROGRAMMING 459

CHAPTER 16

INTERFACING WITH THE SYSTEM 499

CHAPTER 17

REPORT WRITING WITH PICTURES 583

CHAPTER 18

SEND IT OVER THE NET AND SOCK IT TO 'EM! 599

CHAPTER 19

CGI AND PERL: THE HYPER DYNAMIC DUO 631

APPENDIX A

PERL BUILT-INS, PRAGMAS, MODULES, AND THE DEBUGGER 735

APPENDIX B

SOME HELPFUL SCRIPTS. 783

APPENDIX C

AN OBJECT-ORIENTED PERL/CGI PROGRAM. 809

APPENDIX D

HTML DOCUMENTS: A BASIC INTRODUCTION 821

PREFACE

Last week, I was teaching *Perl* at the UCSC[1] extension in Santa Clara, California to a group of professionals coming from all around the Bay Area. I always ask at the beginning of the class, "and so why do you want to learn Perl?". The responses vary from, "Our company has an auction site on the Web and I'm the webmaster. I need to maintain the CGI programs that process our orders, " or "I work in a genetics research group at Stanford and have to deal with tons of data . . . we're looking for the gene that causes arteriosclerosis . . . oh and I heard that if I learn Perl, I won't have to depend on programmers to do this," or "I work at a local bank and we use Perl to interface with our big Oracle databases," or "I'm a UNIX/NT system administrator and our boss has decided that all future admin scripts should be written in Perl," or "I'm designing a Web page for my wife who wants to do Taro card readings for profit," or "I just got laid off and heard that it's an absolute must to have Perl on my resume." And I am always amazed at the variety of people who show up: engineers, scientists, geneticists, meteorologists, managers, salespeople, programmers, techies, hardware guys, students, stockbrokers, administrators of all kinds, librarians, authors, bankers, artists—you name it. Perl does not exclude anyone. Perl is for everyone and it runs on everything.

No matter who you are, I think you'll agree, a picture is worth a thousand words, and so is a good example. *Perl by Example* is organized to teach you Perl from scratch with examples of complete succinct programs. Each line of a script example is numbered, and important lines are highlighted in bold. The output of the program is then displayed with line numbers corresponding to the script line numbers. Following the output is a separate explanation for each of the numbered lines. The examples are small and to the point for the topic at hand. Since the backbone of this book was used as a student guide to a Perl course, the topics are modularized. Each chapter builds on the previous one with a minimum of forward referencing and a logical progression from one topic to the next. There are exercises at the end of the chapters. You will find all of the examples on the CD at the back of the book. They have been thoroughly tested on a number of major platforms.

Perl by Example is not just a beginner's guide, but a complete guide to Perl. It covers many aspects of what Perl can do, from regular expression handling, to formatting reports, to interprocess communication. It will teach you about Perl and, in the process, a lot about

---

1. University of California, Santa Cruz.

UNIX and Windows. Since Perl was originally written on and for UNIX systems, some UNIX knowledge will greatly accelerate your learning path, but it is not assumed that you are by any means a guru. Anyone reading, writing, or just maintaining Perl programs can greatly profit from this text. Topics such as networking, system calls, IPC, and CGI are designed to save the time it takes to figure out how the functions work, what libraries are needed, the correct syntax, etc. This third edition also covers Perl objects, references, and CGI, as well as a new chapter to show you how to use the popular *CGI.pm* module by Lincoln Stein.

Perl has a rich variety of functions for handling strings, arrays, the system interface, networking, and more. In order to understand how these functions work, background information concerning the hows, whys, and what fors is provided before demonstrating functional sample programs. This eliminates constantly wading through manual pages and other books to understand what is going on, what the arguments mean, and what the function actually does.

The appendices contain a complete list of functions and definitions, command line switches, special variables, popular modules, the Perl debugger; a fully functional, object-oriented CGI program; some other helpful scripts; and a helpful HTML tutorial.

I have been teaching now for the past 30 years and am committed to understanding how people learn. Having taught Perl now for over eight years, all over the world, I find that many new Perlers get frustrated when trying to teach themselves how to program. I found that most people learn best from succinct little examples and practice. So I wrote a book to help myself learn and to help my students, and now to help you. As Perl has grown, so have my books. This latest third edition, includes information for those using Windows as well as different flavors of UNIX. In my book you will not only learn Perl, you will also save yourself a great deal of time. At least that's what my students and readers have told me. You be the judge.

Acknowledgments

Please acknowledge the following great people for their huge contribution to my third edition. With highest praise, honors, and exhaltations, I dub thee knights of the highest order:

Deac Lancaster, my true friend and colleague, for his expertise in creating the much-needed database chapter (see Chapter 15) from a course that he has developed and taught, spending hours of his time and patience to help me as he has always done and probably always will—an incredibly generous and true scholar, thank you Deacy once again for your generous contibutions to this new edition.

Charles Dalsass, my smart and energetic nephew, for sharing his object-oriented CGI program (see Appendix C) that he developed for his very successful Web company, neptune.com, based in Boston. He carefully catalogued and annotated his modules for the rest of us, giving the book a peek at a real-world program and providing a fully developed tool for others doing the same kind of work. He's a true master at what he does.

Nick Main, my brother (no nepotism here) and fellow teaching colleague, who, over the past five years, has contributed much to the labs and exercises in my books and shared ideas on how to improve this edition. He has spent hours talking on the phone to me about Perl issues and remedies and has been the most stable force in keeping me focused on this project.

Mike Malione, fellow Perl teaching colleague who put together the CD—and what a professional job he has done! Every example and exercise, tested and tried on multiple platforms, an incredible job with precision and total dedication. He spent many hours working out all these examples and labs, and went way beyond the line of duty. Many many thanks to Mike!

Many thanks go to Joan Murray, who gets me all those Perl jobs for the U.S. Navy down in Monterrey, and keeps me amused with her great wit. For this book, she supplied an invaluable HTML tutorial (see Appendix D), which she has used in her own classes and has kindly offered to share with my readers.

And then there is Vanessa Moore! It's nice to have a gal on the project and especially one who really knows her stuff. It was her editing, formatting, proofing, etc., that made the book. She gives this new edition a real professional, polished look, just as she did with my UNIX and Linux shell books. And she's great under pressure, never seems to fold or get mad. I feel very honored to have her working on my book. She truly has that magic touch in turning a lump of coal into a diamond.

Now how should we thank Mark Taub, the editor-in-chief? Should he be praised for being a real pressure cooker? Should we praise a man who is relentless in thinking these books are possible, who knows how to talk a person into doing another project before the last one is even finished, who soft talks impossible deadlines, who makes a person feel that he can conquer the world, and quietly achieves his goal, always with a subtle sense of humor? Should we praise a person who sends curt little e-mails and voicemails reminding us that it is due NOW! Well, I guess when it's all over and the book is on the shelf looking all professional and pretty, I would have to say, "Thank you Mark, for all of it. When can I start my next book?"

Of course, none of this would have been possible without the contributions of the Perl pioneers—Larry Wall, Randall Schwartz, and Tom Christiansen. Their books are must reading and include *Learning by Perl* by Randall Schwartz and *Perl Programming* by Larry Wall, Tom Christiansen, and Jon Orwant.

And last, but certainly not least, a huge thanks to all the students, worldwide, who have done all the real troubleshooting and kept the subject alive.

THE PRACTICAL EXTRACTION AND REPORT LANGUAGE

1.1   What Is Perl?

Perl officially stands for The Practical Extraction and Report Language, but according to Larry Wall, the creator of Perl, those who love it refer to Perl as the Pathologically Eclectic Rubbish Lister. Perl is really much more than a practical reporting language or eclectic rubbish lister, though, as you'll soon see. Perl is a free, interpreted language maintained and enhanced by a core development team called the Perl Porters. It is used primarily as a scripting language and runs on a number of platforms. Although designed for the UNIX operating system, Perl is renowned for its portability and comes bundled with most operating systems, including RedHat Linux, Windows, Solaris, FreeBSD, Windows, Macintosh, and more. The examples in this book were created on systems running Solaris, Linux, and Win32. Perl makes programming easy, flexible, and fast. Those who use it, love it. And those who use it range from experienced programmers to novices with little computer background at all. The number of users is growing at a phenomenal rate.

Perl's heritage is UNIX. Perl scripts are functionally similar to UNIX *awk*, *sed*, shell scripts, and *C* programs. Shell scripts consist primarily of UNIX commands; Perl scripts do not. Whereas *sed* and *awk* are used to edit and report on files, Perl does not require a file in order to function. Whereas *C* has none of the pattern matching and wildcard metacharacters of the shells, *sed,* and *awk*, Perl has an extended set of characters. Perl was originally written to manipulate text in files, extract data from files, and write reports, but through continued development, it can now manipulate files, processes, and perform many networking tasks, and has become the de facto scripting language for common gateway interface (CGI) scripts, those programs that Web developers use to process forms.

1.2   Who Uses Perl?

Because Perl has built-in functions for easy manipulation of processes and files, and because Perl is portable (i.e., it can run on a number of different platforms), it is especially popular with system administrators who often oversee one or more systems of different types. The phenomenal growth of the World Wide Web has greatly increased interest in Perl, which is now the most popular language for writing CGI scripts to generate dynamic pages for processing forms. Perl is also drawing the attention of programmers, database administrators, scientists, geneticists, and simply curious users who like to keep up with the times.

Anyone can use Perl, but it is easier to learn if you are already experienced in writing UNIX shell scripts or *C* programs (or programs derived from *C*, such as *C++* and *Java*). For these people, the migration to Perl will be relatively easy. For those who do not program in *C* or any of the shells, the learning curve might be a little steeper, but after learning Perl, there may be no reason to ever use anything else. If you understand Perl, the UNIX shells and the *C* language will probably be much easier for you to learn.

If you are familiar with UNIX utilities such as *awk*, *grep*, *sed*, and *tr*, you know that they don't share the same syntax; the options and arguments are handled differently, and the rules change from one utility to the other. If you are a shell programmer, you usually go through the grueling task of learning a variety of utilities, shell metacharacters, regular expression metacharacters, quotes, and more quotes, etc. Also, shell programs are limited and slow. To perform more complex mathematical tasks, interprocess communication, and handle binary data, for example, you may have to turn to a higher-level language such as *C*, *C++*, or *Java*. If you know *C*, you also know that searching for patterns in files and interfacing with the operating system to process files and execute commands are not always easy tasks.

Perl integrates the best features of shell programming, *C*, and the UNIX utilities *awk*, *grep*, *sed*, and *tr*. Because it is fast and not limited to chunks of data of a particular size, many system administrators and database administrators are switching from the traditional shell scripting to Perl. *C++* and *Java* programmers can enjoy the object-oriented features added in Perl 5, including the ability to create reusable, extensible modules. Now Perl can be generated in other languages, and other languages can be embedded in Perl.

You don't have to know everything about Perl to start writing scripts. This book will help you get a good jump-start on Perl, and you will quickly see some of its many capabilities and advantages. Then you can decide how far you want to go with Perl. If nothing else, I think you'll find that Perl is fun!

1.3 Which Perl?

Perl has been through a number of revisions. There are two major versions of Perl: Perl 4 and Perl 5. The last version of Perl 4 was Perl 4, patchlevel 36 (Perl 4.036), released in 1992, making it ancient. Perl 5.000, introduced in the fall of 1994, was a complete rewrite of the Perl source code that optimized the language and introduced objects and many other features. Despite these changes, Perl 5 remains highly compatible with the previous releases. Examples in this book have been tested using both versions, and where there are differences, they are noted. As of this writing, the current version of Perl is 5.6.1.

For a history of Perl source releases, go to

www.perldoc.com/perl5.6/pod/perlhist.html

1.4 Where to Get Perl

Go to *www.perl.com/CPAN-local/ports* to find out more about what's available for your platform. Perl is available from a number of sources, including the Internet, e-mail, UUCP, and UUNET. There are a number of Web sites and FTP sites. The primary source for Perl distribution is CPAN, the Comprehensive Perl Archive Network (*www.cpan.org*). Although the master CPAN site is at FUNET, the Finnish University NETwork, the largest U.S. repository for Perl information is at the University of Florida at *ftp.cis.ufl.edu* in a directory named */pub/perl*.

If you want to install Perl quickly and easily, ActivePerl is a complete, self-installing distribution of Perl based on the standard Perl sources. It is distributed online at the ActiveState site (*www.activestate.com*) and is available for Linux, Solaris, and Windows operating systems. The complete ActivePerl package contains the binary of the core Perl distribution and complete online documentation.

Here are some significant Web sites to help you find more information about Perl:

- The Perl home page: *www.perl.com*
- The ActivePerl home page: *www.activestate.com*
- The Yahoo Perl page:
  www.yahoo.com/computers_and_internet/programming_languages/perl

Figure 1.1   The Perl home page.

1.4.1   What Version Do I Have?

To obtain your Perl version and patch level and some copyright information, type the following line shown in Example 1.1 (the dollar sign is the shell prompt):

EXAMPLE 1.1

```
1   $ perl -v
2   This is perl, v5.6.0 built for MSWin32-x86-multi-thread
    (with 1 registered patch, see perl -V for more detail)
3   Copyright 1987-2000, Larry Wall
4   Binary build 613 provided by ActiveState Tool Corp.
    http://www.ActiveState.com
    Built 12:36:25 Mar 24 2000
5   Perl may be copied only under the terms of either the Artistic
    License or the GNU General Public License, which may be found in
    the Perl 5.0 source kit.
      Complete documentation for Perl, including FAQ lists, should be
    found on this system using man perl or perldoc perl. If you have
    access to the Internet, point your browser to www.perl.com/, the
    Perl home page.
```

EXPLANATION

1   This version of Perl is 5.6.0.

3   Larry Wall, the author of Perl, owns the copyright.

4   This build was obtained from ActiveState.

5   Perl may be copied under the terms specified by the Artistic License or GNU. Perl is distributed under GNU, the Free Software Foundation, meaning that Perl is free.

EXAMPLE 1.2

```
C:\>perl -V
Summary of my perl5 (revision 5 version 6 subversion 0)
   configuration:
  Platform:
   osname=MSWin32, osvers=4.0, archname=MSWin32-x86-multi-thread
   uname=''
   config_args='undef'
   hint=recommended, useposix=true, d_sigaction=undef
   usethreads=undef use5005threads=undef useithreads=define
   usemultiplicity=define
   useperlio=undef d_sfio=undef uselargefiles=undef
   use64bitint=undef use64bitall=undef uselongdouble=undef
   usesocks=undef
```

EXAMPLE 1.2 (CONTINUED)

```
Compiler:
  cc='cl', optimize='-O1 -MD -DNDEBUG', gccversion=
  cppflags='-DWIN32'
  ccflags ='-O1 -MD -DNDEBUG -DWIN32 -D_CONSOLE -DNO_STRICT
  -DHAVE_DES_FCRYPT -DPERL_IMPLICIT_CONTEXT -DPERL_IMPLICIT_SYS
  -DPERL_MSVCRT_READFIX'
  stdchar='char', d_stdstdio=define, usevfork=false
  intsize=4, longsize=4, ptrsize=4, doublesize=8
  d_longlong=undef, longlongsize=8, d_longdbl=define,
  longdblsize=10
  ivtype='long', ivsize=4, nvtype='double', nvsize=8,
  Off_t='off_t', lseeksize=4
  alignbytes=8, usemymalloc=n, prototype=define
Linker and Libraries:
  ld='link', ldflags ='-nologo -nodefaultlib -release
  -libpath:"C:\Perl\lib\CORE"  -machine:x86'
  libpth="C:\Perl\lib\CORE"
  libs=  oldnames.lib kernel32.lib user32.lib gdi32.lib
  winspool.lib  comdlg32.lib advapi32.lib shell32.lib ole32.lib
  oleaut32.lib  netapi32.lib uuid.lib wsock32.lib mpr.lib winmm.lib
  version.lib odbc32.lib odbccp32.lib msvcrt.lib
  libc=msvcrt.lib, so=dll, useshrplib=yes, libperl=perl56.lib
Dynamic Linking:
  dlsrc=dl_win32.xs, dlext=dll, d_dlsymun=undef, ccdlflags=' '
  cccdlflags=' ', lddlflags='-dll -nologo -nodefaultlib -release
  -libpath:"C:\Perl\lib\CORE"  -machine:x86'

Characteristics of this binary (from libperl):
  Compile-time options: MULTIPLICITY USE_ITHREADS
    PERL_IMPLICIT_CONTEXT PERL_IMPLICIT_SYS

  Locally applied patches:
        ActivePerl Build 620
  Built under MSWin32
  Compiled at Oct 31 2000 18:31:05
  @INC:
    C:/Perl/lib
    C:/Perl/site/lib
```

1.5   **What Is CPAN?**

CPAN (the Comprehensive Perl Archive Network) is a Web site that houses all the free Perl material you will ever need, including documentation, FAQs, modules and scripts, binary distributions and source code, and announcements. CPAN is mirrored all over the world and you can find the nearest mirror at

> *www.perl.com/CPAN*
> *www.cpan.org*

CPAN is the place you will go if you want to find modules to help you with your work. The CPAN search engine will let you find modules under a large number of categories. Modules are discussed in Chapter 11, "Modularize It, Package It, and Send It to the Library."

1.6   **Perl Documentation**

The standard Perl distribution comes with complete online documentation called *man* pages, which provide help for all the standard utilities. (The name derives from the UNIX *man* [manual] pages.) Perl has divided its *man* pages into categories. If you type the following at your command line prompt:

```
man perl
```

you will get a list of all the sections by category. So, if you want help on how to use Perl's regular expresssions, you would type

```
man perlre
```

and if you want help on subroutines, you would type

```
man perlsub
```

The Perl categories are listed as follows, with the following sections available only in the online reference manual:

perlbot	Object-oriented tricks and examples
perldebug	Debugging
perldiag	Diagnostic messages
perldsc	Data structures: intro
perlform	Formats
perlfunc	Built-in functions
perlipc	Interprocess communication
perllol	Data structures: lists of lists

perlmod	Modules
perlobj	Objects
perlop	Operators and precedence
perlpod	Plain old documentation
perlre	Regular expressions
perlref	References
perlsock	Extension for socket support
perlstyle	Style guide
perlsub	Subroutines
perltie	Objects hidden behind simple variables
perltrap	Traps for the unwary
perlvar	Predefined variables

If you are trying to find out how a particular library module works, you can use the *perldoc* command to get the documentation. For example, if you want to know about the *CGI.pm* module, type at the command line

```
perldoc CGI
```

and the documentation for the *CGI.pm* module will be displayed. If you type

```
perldoc English
```

the documentation for the *English.pm* module will be displayed.

Perl 5.6.1 allows you to search for information from the *man* pages by using the name of the *man* page as a command (like *grep*), followed by the pattern you are searching for. For example, *perlvar hash* will search for the term *hash* in the *perlvar* section of the man pages whereas *perlfunc printf* will search for the pattern *printf* in the *perlfunc* section.

2

PERL SCRIPTS

2.1   Perl at the Command Line

Although most of your work with Perl will be done in scripts, Perl can also be executed at the command line for simple tasks such as testing a function, a print statement, or simply testing Perl syntax. Perl has a number of command line switches, also called command line options, to control or modify its behavior. The switches listed below are not a complete list (see Appendix A), but will demonstrate a little about Perl syntax at the command line.

When working at the command line you will see a shell prompt. The shell is called a "command interpreter." UNIX shells such as *Korn* and *bash* display a default *$* prompt and *C* shell displays a *%* prompt. The UNIX, Linux, anad Mac OS shells are quite similar in how they parse the command line. By default, if you are using Windows 95, 98, or 2000, the MS-DOS shell is called *command.com* and if you are using Windows NT, the command shell is a console application residing in *cmd.exe*. It too displays a *$* prompt.[1] The Win32 shells have their own way of parsing the command line. Since most of your Perl programming will be done in script files, you will seldom need to worry about the shell's interaction, but when a script interfaces with the operating system, problems will occur unless you are aware of what commands you have and how the shell executes them on your behalf.

2.1.1   The *-e* Switch

The *-e* switch allows Perl to **execute** Perl statements at the command line instead of from a script. This is a good way to test simple Perl statements before putting them into a script file.

---

1. It is possible that your command line prompt has been customized to contain the current directory, history number, drive number, etc.

EXAMPLE 2.1

```
1   $ perl -e 'print "hello dolly\n";'     # UNIX
    hello dolly
2   $ perl -e "print qq/hello dolly\n/;"   # Windows
    hello dolly
```

EXPLANATION

1   Perl prints the string *hello dolly* to the screen followed by a newline \n. The dollar sign (*$*) is the UNIX shell prompt. The single quotes surrounding the Perl statement protect it from the UNIX shell when it scans and interprets the command line.

2   At the MS-DOS prompt, Perl statements must be enclosed in double quotes. The *qq* construct surrounding *hello dolly* is another way Perl represents double quotes. For example, *qq/hello/* is the same as *"hello"*. An error is displayed if you type the following at the MS-DOS prompt:

```
$ perl -e 'print "hello dolly\n";'
Can't find string terminator "" anywhere before EOF at -e line 1.
```

2.1.2   The *-n* Switch

If you need to print the contents of a file or search for a line that contains a particular pattern, the *-n* switch is used to implicitly loop through the file one line at a time. Like *sed* and *awk*, Perl uses powerful pattern-matching techniques for finding patterns in text. Only specified lines from the file are printed when Perl is invoked with the *-n* switch.

Reading from a File.   The *-n* switch allows you to loop through a file whose name is provided at the command line. The Perl statements are enclosed in quotes and the file or files are listed at the end of the command line.

EXAMPLE 2.2

```
(The Text File)
1   $ more emp.first
    Igor Chevsky:6/23/83:W:59870:25:35500:2005.50
    Nancy Conrad:6/18/88:SE:23556:5:15000:2500
    Jon DeLoar:3/28/85:SW:39673:13:22500:12345.75
    Archie Main:7/25/90:SW:39673:21:34500:34500.50
    Betty Bumble:11/3/89:NE:04530:17:18200:1200.75
```

EXAMPLE 2.2 (CONTINUED)

```
2   $ perl -ne 'print;' emp.first     # Windows: use double quotes
    Igor Chevsky:6/23/83:W:59870:25:35500:2005.50
    Nancy Conrad:6/18/88:SE:23556:5:15000:2500
    Jon DeLoar:3/28/85:SW:39673:13:22500:12345.75
    Archie Main:7/25/90:SW:39673:21:34500:34500.50
    Betty Bumble:11/3/89:NE:04530:17:18200:1200.75
3   $ perl -ne 'print if /^Igor/;' emp.first
    Igor Chevsky:6/23/83:W:59870:25:35500:2005.50
```

EXPLANATION

1   The text file *emp.first* is printed to the screen. Perl uses this filename as a command line argument.

2   Perl prints all the lines in the file *emp.first* by implicitly looping through the file one line at a time. Windows users should enclose the statement in double quotes instead of single quotes.

3   Perl uses **regular expression** metacharacters to specify what patterns will be matched. The pattern, *Igor*, is placed within forward slashes and preceded by a caret (^). The caret is called a "beginning of line anchor." Perl prints only lines beginning with the pattern *Igor*. Windows users should enclose the statement in double quotes instead of single quotes.

Reading from a Pipe.   Since Perl is just another program, the output of commands can be piped to Perl, and Perl output can be piped to other commands. Perl will use what comes from the pipe as input, rather than a file. The *-n* switch is needed so that Perl can loop through the input coming in from the pipe.

EXAMPLE 2.3

```
(UNIX)
1   $ date | perl -ne 'print "Today is $_";'
2   Today is Mon Mar 12 20:01:58 PDT 2001

(Windows^a)
3   $ date /T | perl -ne "print qq/Today is $_/;"
4   Today is Mon 03/12/2001
```

a. Windows NT supports the */T* argument to the *date* command, but Windows 95 and 98 do not.

EXPLANATION

1   The output of the UNIX *date* command is piped to Perl and stored in the *$_* variable. The quoted string *Today is* and the contents of the *$_* variable will be printed to the screen followed by a newline.

2   The output illustrates that today's date was stored in the *$_* variable.

3   The Windows NT *date* command takes */T* as an option that produces today's date. That ouput is piped to Perl and stored in the *$_* variable. The double quotes are required around the print statement. (See Example 2.1.)

Perl can take its input from a file and send its output to a file using standard I/O redirection.

EXAMPLE 2.4

```
1   $ perl -ne 'print;' < emp.first
    Igor Chevsky:6/23/83:W:59870:25:35500:2005.50
    Nancy Conrad:6/18/88:SE:23556:5:15000:2500
    Jon DeLoar:3/28/85:SW:39673:13:22500:12345.75
    Archie Main:7/25/90:SW:39673:21:34500:34500.50
    Betty Bumble:11/3/89:NE:04530:17:18200:1200.75
2   $ perl -ne 'print' emp.first > emp.temp
```

EXPLANATION

1   Perl's input is taken from a file called *emp.first*. The output is sent to the screen. For Windows users, enclose the statement in double quotes instead of single quotes.

2   Perl's input is taken from a file called *emp.first*, and its output is sent to the file *emp.temp*. For Windows users, enclose the statement in double quotes instead of single quotes.

2.1.3   The *-c* Switch

The *-c* switch is used to check the Perl syntax without actually executing the Perl commands. If the syntax is correct, Perl will tell you so. It is a good idea to always check scripts with the *-c* switch. This is especially important with CGI scripts written in Perl, because error messages that are normally sent to the terminal screen are sent to a log file instead.

EXAMPLE 2.5

```
1   $ perl -ne 'print if /Igor;'      # Windows: use double quotes
    Search pattern not terminated at -e line 1.
2   $ perl -ce 'print if /Igor/;'
    -e syntax OK
```

EXPLANATION

1   The pattern *Igor* is supposed to be enclosed in forward slashes, but one of the forward slashes is missing. With the *-c* switch, Perl will complain if it finds syntax errors while compiling. For Windows users, enclose the statement in double quotes instead of single quotes.

2   After correcting the previous problem, Perl lets you know that the syntax is correct. For Windows users, enclose the statement in double quotes instead of single quotes.

2.2   Script Setup

Perl scripts are similar to shell, *sed*, and *awk* scripts in appearance. They consist of a list of Perl statements and declarations. Statements are terminated with a semicolon (*;*). Since only subroutines and report formats require declarations, they will be discussed when those topics are presented. Variables can be created anywhere in the script and, if not initialized, automatically get a value of 0 or "null," depending on their context.

Unlike *awk* and *sed*, where a sequence of commands is executed for each line of input, Perl executes each command just once. Therefore, when working with input files, you must either use an explicit loop in the script to repeat the command through the file, or use the *-n* switch to implicitly loop through the file.

2.3   The Script

2.3.1   Startup

UNIX.   If the **first line** of the script contains the *#!* symbols (called the *shbang* line) followed by the full pathname of the file where your version of the Perl executable resides, this tells the kernel what program is interpreting the script. An example of the startup line might be

```
#!/usr/bin/perl
```

It is extremely important that the path to the interpreter is entered correctly after the *shbang* (*#!*). Perl may be installed in different directories on different systems. Most Web servers will look for this line when invoking CGI scripts written in Perl. Any inconsistency will cause a fatal error.

If the *shbang* line is the first line of the script, you can execute the script directly from the command line by its name. If the *shbang* is not the first line of the script, the UNIX shell will try to interpret the program as a shell script and the first line will be interpreted as a comment line. (See "Executing the Script" on page 16 for more on how to execute Perl programs.)

Windows. Win32 platforms don't provide the *shbang* syntax or anything like it.[2] For Windows 2000 and Windows NT 4.0[3] you can associate a Perl script with extensions such as *.pl* or *.plx* and then run your script directly from the command line. At the command line prompt or from the system control panel, you can set the *PATHEXT* environment variable to the name of the extension that will be associated with Perl scripts. At the command line, to set the environment variable, type

```
SET PATHEXT=.pl;%PATHEXT%
```

At the control panel, to make the association permanent, do the following:

1. Go to the Start menu.
2. Select Settings.
3. Select Control Panel.
4. In the control panel, click on the System icon.
5. Click on Advanced.
6. Click on Environment Variables.
7. Click on New.
8. Type *PATHEXT* in the Variable Name box.
9. In the Variable Value box, type the extension you want, followed by a semicolon and *%PATHEXT%*.
10. OK the setting.

From now on when you create a Perl script, append its name with the extension you have chosen, such as *myscript.pl* or *myscript.plx*. Then the script can be executed directly at the command line by just typing the script name without the extension. (See "Executing the Script" on page 16 for more on script execution.)

---

2. Although Win32 platforms don't ordinarily require the *shbang* line, the Apache Web server does, so you will need the *shbang* line if you are writing CGI scripts that will be executed by Apache.

3. File association does not work on Windows 95 unless the program is started from the Explorer window.

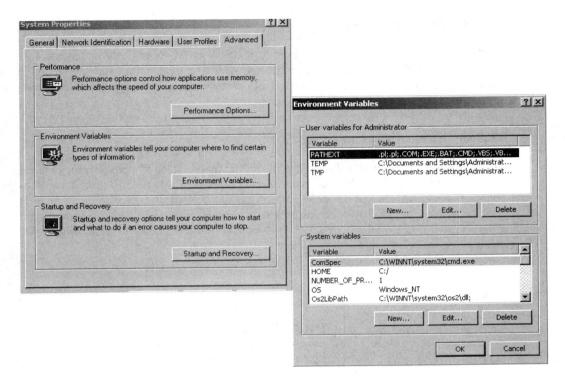

Figure 2.1 Setting the *PATHEXT* environment variable.

2.3.2 Comments

Comments are statements that allow you to insert documentation in your Perl script with no effect on the execution of the program. They are used to help you and other programmers maintain and debug scripts. Perl does not understand the *C* language comments /* and */.

EXAMPLE 2.6

```
1   # This is a comment
2   print "hello";  # And this is a comment
```

EXPLANATION

1   Comments, as in UNIX shell, *sed*, and *awk* scripts, are lines preceded with the pound sign (*#*) and can continue to the end of the line.

2   Comments can be anywhere on the line. Here the comment follows a valid Perl *print* statement.

2.3.3   Perl Statements

Perl executable statements make up most of the Perl script. As in *C*, the statement is an expression, or series of expressions, terminated with a semicolon. Perl statements can be simple or compound and there are a variety of operators, modifiers, expressions, and functions that make up a statement.

2.3.4   Executing the Script

The Perl script can be executed at the command line directly if the *#!* startup line is included in the script file and the script has execute permission (See Example 2.7.) or, if using Windows, filename association has been set as discussed in "Startup" on page 13. If the *#!* is not the first line of the script, you can execute a script by passing the script as an argument to the Perl program. Perl will then compile your script using its own internal form. If you have syntax errors, Perl will let you know.

To execute a script at either the UNIX or MS-DOS prompt, type

```
$ perl scriptname
```

2.3.5   Sample Script (UNIX, Windows)

The following example illustrates the four parts of a Perl script:

1. The startup line (UNIX)
2. Comments
3. The executable statements in the body of the script
4. The execution of the script

EXAMPLE 2.7

```
      $ cat first.perl        (UNIX display contents)
1     #!/usr/bin/perl
2     # My first Perl script
3     print "Hello to you and yours!\n";

4     $ perl -c first.perl    # The $ is the shell prompt
      first.perl syntax OK

5     $ chmod +x first.perl

6     $ first.perl or ./first.perl
7     Hello to you and yours!
```

EXPLANATION

1   The startup line tells the shell where Perl is located.

2   A comment describes information the programmer wants to convey about the script.

3   An executable statement includes the *print* function.

4   The *-c* switch is used to check for syntax errors.

5   The *chmod* command turns on execute permission.

6   The script is executed. If you get "Command not found" (or a similar message), precede the script name with a period and a forward slash.

7   The string *Hello to you and yours!* is printed on the screen.

EXAMPLE 2.8

```
    $ type first.perl      (MS-DOS display contents)
1   # No startup line; This is a comment.
2   # My first Perl script
3   print "Hello to you and yours!\n";

4   $ perl first.perl
5   Hello to you and yours!
```

EXPLANATION

1   The startup line with *#!* is absent. It is not necessary when using Windows. If using ActiveState you create a batch file with a utility called *pl2bat*.

2   This is a descriptive line; a comment explains that the startup line is missing.

3   An executable statement includes the *print* function.

4   The Perl program takes the script name as an argument and executes the script. The script's output is printed.

Win32 and the *pl2bat* Utility.   ActiveState provides another method for executing Perl scripts directly at the command line. It converts a Perl script into a batch file that can be executed on DOS-like operating systems. The *pl2bat* utility, *pl2bat.bat,* is found in the standard distribution of ActiveState Perl under the */bin* directory. To read the documentation, type the following at the MS-DOS prompt:

```
perlfunc pl2bat
```

EXAMPLE 2.9

```
1   $ pl2bat first.perl first.perl.bat
    pl2bat.bat: first.perl.bat has already been converted to a batch
    file!

2   $ ./first.perl
    It's great to see you again!

3   $ cat first.perl.bat
    @rem = '--*-Perl-*--
    @echo off
    if "%OS%" == "Windows_NT" goto WinNT
    perl -x -S "%0" %1 %2 %3 %4 %5 %6 %7 %8 %9
    goto endofperl
    :WinNT
    perl -x -S "%0" %*
    if NOT "%COMSPEC%" == "%SystemRoot%\system32\cmd.exe"
        goto endofperl
    if %errorlevel% == 9009 echo You do not have Perl in your PATH.
    if errorlevel 1
        goto script_failed_so_exit_with_non_zero_val 2>nul
    goto endofperl
    @rem ';
    #!perl
    #line 15
    print "Hello to you and yours!\n";

    _ _END_ _
    :endofperl
```

EXPLANATION

1   The *pl2bat* utility provided with the ActiveState distribution of Perl will create a batch file called *first.bat* from the Perl source file, *first.pl*.

2   The Perl script can now be executed directly at the command line without using an extension.

3   This is the batch file that was generated from the *pl2bat* utility.

EXERCISE 1
Getting with It Syntactically

1. At the command line prompt, write a Perl statement that will print

   Hello world!!
   Welcome to Perl programming.

2. Execute another Perl command that will print the contents of the *datebook* file. (The file is found on the accompanying CD.)

3. Execute a Perl command that will display the version and patch information of the Perl distribution you are currently using.

GETTING A HANDLE
ON PRINTING

3.1   The Filehandle

By convention, whenever your program starts execution, the shell opens three predefined streams called *stdin, stdout,* and *stderr.* All three of these streams are connected to your terminal by default.

    stdin is the place where input comes from, the terminal keyboard; *stdout* is where output normally goes, the screen; and *stderr* is where errors from your program are printed, also the screen.

    Perl inherits *stdin, stdout,* and *stderr* from the shell. Perl does not access these streams directly, but gives them names called *filehandles*. Perl accesses the streams via the filehandle. The filehandle for *stdin* is called *STDIN*; the filehandle for *stdout* is called *STDOUT*; and the filehandle for *stderr* is called *STDERR*. Later we'll see how you can create your own filehandles, but for now we'll stick with the defaults.

    The *print* and *printf* functions by default send their output to the *STDOUT* filehandle.

3.2   Words

When printing a list of words to *STDOUT*, it is helpful to understand how Perl views a word. Any unquoted word must start with an alphanumeric character. It can consist of other alphanumeric characters and an underscore. Perl words are case sensitive. If a word is unquoted, it could conflict with words used to identify filehandles, labels, and other reserved words. If the word has no special meaning to Perl, it will be treated as if surrounded by single quotes.

3.2.1   Quotes

Quoting rules affect almost everything you do in Perl, especially when printing a string of words. Strings are normally delimited by either a matched pair of double or single quotes. When a string is enclosed in single quotes, all characters are treated as literals. When a string is enclosed in double quotes, however, **almost** all characters are treated as literals with the exception of those characters that are used for variable substitution and special escape sequences. We will look at the special escape sequences in this chapter and discuss quoting and variables in Chapter 4, "What's in a Name."

Perl uses some characters for special purposes, such as the dollar sign (*$*), the at sign (*@*), and the percent sign (*%*). If these special characters are to be treated as literal characters, they may be preceded by a backslash (\) or enclosed within single quotes (' '). The backslash is used to quote a single character rather than a string of characters.

3.2.2 Literals (Constants)

When assigning literal values[1] to variables or printing literals, the literals can be represented numerically as integers in decimal, octal, hexadecimal, or as floats in floating point or scientific notation.

Strings enclosed in double quotes may contain string literals, such as \n for the newline character, \t for a tab character, or \e for an escape character. String literals are alphanumeric (**and only alphanumeric**) characters preceded by a backslash.[2] They may be represented in decimal, octal, hexadecimal, or as control characters.

Perl also supports special literals for representing the current script name, the line number of the current script, and the logical end of the current script.

Since you will be using literals with the *print* and *printf* functions, let's see what these literals look like. (For more on defining constants, see the "constant" pragma in Appendix A.)

Numeric Literals.   Literal numbers can be represented as positive or negative integers in decimal, octal, or hexadecimal (see Table 3.1). Floats can be represented in floating point notation or scientific notation. Octal numbers contain a leading *0* (zero), hex numbers a leading *0x* (zero and x), and numbers represented in scientific notation contain a trailing *E* followed by a negative or positive number representing the exponent.

Table 3.1   Numeric Literals

Example	*Description*
12345	Integer
0b1101	Binary
0x456fff	Hex
0777	Octal
23.45	Float
.234E–2	Scientific notation

---

1. Literals may also be called constants, but the Perl experts prefer the term "literal," so in deference to them we'll use the term "literal."

2. UNIX utilities, such as *sed* and *grep,* allow characters other than alphanumerics after the backslash; e.g., \<, \(.

String Literals.   Like shell strings, Perl strings are normally delimited by either single or double quotes. Strings containing string literals, also called **escape sequences**, are delimited by double quotes for backslash interpretation (see Table 3.2).

Table 3.2   String Literals

Escape Sequences	*Descriptions (ASCII Name)*
\t	Tab
\n	Newline
\r	Carriage return
\f	Form feed
\b	Backspace
\a	Alarm/bell
\e	Escape
\033	Octal character
\xff	Hexadecimal character
\c[	Control character
\l	Next character is converted to lowercase
\u	Next character is converted to uppercase
\L	Next characters are converted to lowercase until \E is found
\U	Next characters are converted to uppercase until \E is found
\Q	Backslash all following non-alphanumeric characters until \E is found
\E	Ends upper- or lowercase conversion started with \L or \U
\\	Backslash

Special Literals.   Perl's special literals _ _LINE_ _ and _ _FILE_ _ are used as separate words and will **not** be interpreted if quoted. They represent the current line number of your script and the name of the script, respectively. These special literals are equivalent to the predefined special macros used in the *C* language.

The _ _END_ _ special literal is used in scripts to represent the logical end of the file. Any trailing text following the _ _END_ _ literal will be ignored, just as if it had been commented. The control sequences for end of input in UNIX is *<Ctrl>-d* (\004) and *<Ctrl>-z* (\032) in MS-DOS; both are synonyms for _ _END_ _.

The _ _*DATA*_ _ special literal is used as a filehandle to allow you to process textual data from within the script instead of from an external file.

Note: There are two underscores on either side of the special literals (see Table 3.3).

Table 3.3   Special Literals

Literal	Description
_ _*LINE*_ _	Represents the current line number
_ _*FILE*_ _	Represents the current filename
_ _*END*_ _	Represents the logical end of the script; trailing garbage is ignored
_ _*DATA*_ _	Represents a special filehandle
_ _*PACKAGE*_ _	Represents the current package; default package is *main*

3.3   The *print* Function

The *print* function prints a string or a list of comma-separated words to the Perl filehandle *STDOUT*. If successful, the print function returns 1; if not, it returns 0.

The string literal \n adds a newline to the end of the string. It can be embedded in the string or treated as a separate string. In order to interpret backslashes, Perl, like the shell, requires that escape sequences like \n are enclosed in double quotes.

EXAMPLE 3.1

```
(The Script)
1   print "Hello", "world", "\n";
2   print "Hello world\n";

(Output)
1   Helloworld
2   Hello world
```

EXPLANATION

1   Each string passed to the *print* function is enclosed in double quotes and separated by a comma. To print whitespace, the whitespace must be enclosed within the quotes. The \n escape sequence must be enclosed in double quotes for it to be interpreted as a newline character.

2   The entire string is enclosed in double quotes and printed to standard output.

EXAMPLE 3.2

```
(The Script)
1   print Hello, world, "\n";

(Output)
1   No comma allowed after filehandle at ./perl.st line 1
```

EXPLANATION

1   If the strings are not quoted, the filehandle *STDOUT* must be specified or the *print* function will treat the first word it encounters as a filehandle (i.e., the word *Hello* would be treated as a filehandle). The comma is not allowed after a filehandle; it is used only to separate strings that are to be printed.

EXAMPLE 3.3

```
(The Script)
1   print STDOUT Hello, world, "\n";

(Output)
1   Helloworld
```

EXPLANATION

1   The filehandle *STDOUT* must be specified if strings are not quoted. The \n must be double quoted if it is to be interpreted.
Note: There is **no** comma after *STDOUT*.

3.3.1   Printing Literals

Now that you know what the literals look like, let's see how they are used with the *print* function.

Printing Numeric Literals

EXAMPLE 3.4

```
(The Script)
    #!/usr/bin/perl
    # Program to illustrate printing literals
1   print "The price is $100.\n";
2   print "The price is \$100.\n";
3   print "The price is \$",100, ".\n";
4   print "The binary number is converted to: ",0b10001,".\n";
5   print "The octal number is converted to: ",0777,".\n";
6   print "The hexadecimal number is converted to: ",0xAbcF,".\n";
7   print "The unformatted number is ", 14.56, ".\n";


(Output)
1   The price is .
2   The price is $100.
3   The price is $100.
4   The binary number is converted to: 17.
5   The octal number is converted to: 511.
6   The hexadecimal number is converted to: 43983.
7   The unformatted number is 14.56.
```

EXPLANATION

1   The string *The price is $100* is enclosed in double quotes. The dollar sign is a special Perl character. It is used to reference scalar variables (see Chapter 4, "What's in a Name"), not money. Therefore, since there is no variable called *$100*, nothing prints. Since single quotes protect all characters from interpretation, they would have sufficed here, or the dollar sign could have been preceded with a backslash. But when surrounded by single quotes, the \n will be treated as a literal string rather than a newline character.

2   The backslash quotes the dollar sign, so it is treated as a literal.

3   To be treated as a numeric literal, rather than a string, the number *100* is a single word. The dollar sign must be escaped even if it is not followed by a variable name. The \n must be enclosed within double quotes if it is to be interpreted as a special string literal.

4   The number is represented as a binary number because of the leading *0b* (zero and b). The decimal value is printed.

5   The number is represented as an octal value because of the leading *0* (zero). The decimal value is printed.

6   The number is represented as a hexadecimal number because of the leading *0x* (zero and x). The decimal value is printed.

7   The number, represented as *14.56*, is printed as is. The *print* function does not format output.

Printing String Literals

EXAMPLE 3.5

```
(The Script)
    #!/usr/bin/perl
1   print "***\tIn double quotes\t***\n";  # Backslash interpretation
2   print '%%%\t\tIn single quotes\t\t%%%\n'; # All characters are
                                             # printed as literals

3   print "\n";

(Output)
1   ***     In double quotes         ***
2   %%%\t\tIn single quotes\t\t%%%\n
3
```

EXPLANATION

1   When a string is enclosed in double quotes, backslash interpretation is performed.
The \t is a string literal and produces a tab; the \n produces a newline.
2   When enclosed within single quotes, the special string literals \t and \n are not interpreted. They will be printed as is.
3   The newline \n must be enclosed in double quotes to be interpreted. A "\n" produces
a newline.

EXAMPLE 3.6

```
(The Script)
    #!/usr/bin/perl
1   print "\a\t\tThe \Unumber\E \LIS\E ",0777,".\n";

(Output)
1   (BEEP)        The NUMBER is 511.
```

EXPLANATION

1   The \a produces an alarm or beep sound, followed by \t\t (two tabs). \U causes the
string to be printed in uppercase until \E is reached or the line terminates. The string
number is printed in uppercase until the \E is reached. The string *is* is to be printed
in lowercase, until the \E is reached, and the decimal value for octal *0777* is printed,
followed by a period and a newline character.

Printing Special Literals

EXAMPLE 3.7

```
(The Script)
    #!/usr/bin/perl
    # Program, named literals.perl, written to test special literals
1   print "We are on line number ", _ _LINE_ _, ".\n";
2   print "The name of this file is ",_ _FILE_ _,".\n";
3   _ _END_ _
    And this stuff is just a bunch of chitter-chatter that is to be
    ignored by Perl.
    The _ _END_ _ literal is like Ctrl-d or \004.ᵃ

(Output)
1   We are on line number 3.
2   The name of this file is literals.perl.
```

a.   See the -x switch in Appendix A for discarding leading garbage.

EXPLANATION

1   The special literal _ _LINE_ _ cannot be enclosed in quotes if it is to be interpreted. It holds the current line number of the Perl script.
2   The name of this script is *literals.perl*. The special literal _ _FILE_ _ holds the name of the current Perl script.
3   The special literal _ _END_ _ represents the logical end of the script. It tells Perl to ignore any characters that follow it.

EXAMPLE 3.8

```
(The Script)
    #!/usr/bin/perl
    # Program, named literals.perl2,
    # written to test special literal _ _DATA_ _
1   print <DATA>;
2   _ _DATA_ _
    This line will be printed.
    And so will this one.

(Output)
This line will be printed.
And so will this one.
```

EXPLANATION

1   The *print* function will display whatever text is found under the special literal _ _DATA_ _. Because the special literal _ _DATA_ _ is enclosed in angle brackets, it is treated as a filehandle opened for reading. The *print* function will display lines as they are read by *<DATA>*.

2   This is the data that is used by the *<DATA>* filehandle. (You could use _ _END_ _ instead of _ _DATA_ _ to get the same results.)

3.3.2   The *warnings* Pragma and the *-w* Switch

The *-w* switch is used to warn you about the possibility of using future reserved words and a number of other problems that may cause problems in the program. Larry Wall says in the Perl 5 *man* pages, "Whenever you get mysterious behavior, try the *-w* switch! Whenever you don't get mysterious behavior, try the *-w* switch anyway."

You can either use the *-w* switch as a command line option to Perl, as

```
perl -w <scriptname>
```

or after the *shbang* line in the Perl script, such as

```
#!/usr/bin/perl -w
```

A pragma is a special Perl module that hints to the compiler about how a block of statements should be compiled. You can use this type of module to help control the way your program behaves. Starting with Perl version 5.6.0, *warnings.pm* was added to the standard Perl library; similar to the *-w* switch, it is a pragma that allows you to control the types of warnings printed.

In your programs, add the following line under the *#!* line or, if not using the *#!* line, at the top of the script:

```
use warnings;
```

This enables all possible warnings. To turn off warnings, simply add as a line in your script

```
no warnings;
```

This disables all possible warnings for the rest of the script.

EXAMPLE 3.9

```
(The Script)
    #!/usr/bin/perl
    # Scriptname: warnme
1   print STDOUT Ellie, what\'s up?;
```

```
(Output) (At the Command Line)
$ perl -w warnme
  Unquoted string "what" may clash with future reserved word at warnme line 3.
  Backslash found where operator expected at warnme line 3, near "what\"
  Syntax error at warnme line 3, near "what\"
  Can't find string terminator "'" anywhere before EOF at warnme line 3.
```

EXPLANATION

1   Among many other messages, the -w switch (see Appendix A) prints warnings about ambiguous identifiers such as variables that have only been used once, improper conversion of strings and numbers, etc. Since the string *Ellie* is not quoted, Perl could mistake it for a reserved word or an undefined filehandle. The rest of the error message results from having an unmatched quote in the string.

EXAMPLE 3.10

```
(The Script)
    #!/usr/bin/perl
    # Scriptname: warnme
1   use warnings;
2   print STDOUT Ellie, what\'s up?;
```

```
(Output)
Unquoted string "what" may clash with future reserved word at warnme line 3.
Backslash found where operator expected at warnme line 3, near "what\"
Syntax error at warnme line 3, near "what\"
Can't find string terminator "'" anywhere before EOF at warnme line 3.
```

EXPLANATION

In Perl versions 5.6 and later, the *warnings* pragma is used instead of the -w switch. The *use* function allows you to use modules located in the standard Perl library. The *warnings* pragma sends warnings about ambiguous identifiers. Since the string *Ellie* is not quoted, Perl could mistake it for a reserved word or an undefined filehandle. The compiler complains because the string is not terminated with a closing quote.

3.3.3   The *strict* Pragma and Words

Another pragma we will mention now is the *strict* pragma. If your program disobeys the restrictions placed on it, it won't compile. If there is a chance that you might have used "bare," i.e., unquoted, words[3] as in the example above, the *strict* pragma will catch you and your program will abort. The *strict* pragma can be controlled by giving it various arguments. (See Appendix A for complete list.)

EXAMPLE 3.11

```
(The Script)
    #!/usr/bin/perl
    # Program: stricts.test
    # Script to demonstrate the strict pragma
1   use strict "subs";
2   $name = Ellie;              # Unquoted word Ellie
3   print "Hi $name.\n";

(Output)
$ stricts.test
    Bareword "Ellie" not allowed while "strict subs" in use at
      ./stricts.test line 5.
    Execution of stricts.test aborted due to compilation errors.
```

EXPLANATION

1   The *use* function allows you to use modules located in the standard Perl library. When the *strict* pragma takes *subs* as an argument, it will catch any bare words found in the program while it is being internally compiled. If a bare word is found, the program will be aborted with an error message.

3.4   The *printf* Function

The *printf* function prints a formatted string to the selected filehandle, the default being *STDOUT*. It is like the *printf* function used in the *C* and *awk* languages. The return value is *1* if *printf* is successful and *0* if it fails.

The *printf* function consists of a quoted control string that may include format specifications. The quoted string is followed by a comma and a list of comma-separated arguments, which are simply expressions. The format specifiers are preceded by a % sign. For each % sign and format specifier, there must be a corresponding argument. (See Tables 3.4 and 3.5.)

Placing the quoted string and expressions within parentheses is optional.

---

3. Putting quotes around a word is like putting clothes on the word—take off the quotes, and the word is "bare."

EXAMPLE 3.12

```
printf("The name is %s and the number is %d\n", "John", 50);
```

EXPLANATION

1   The string to be printed is enclosed in double quotes. The first format specifier is *%s*. It has a corresponding argument, *John*, positioned directly to the right of the comma after the closing quote in the control string. The *s* following the percent sign is called **a conversion character**. The *s* means *string* conversion will take place at this spot. In this case *John* will replace the *%s* when the string is printed.

2   The *%d* format specifies that the decimal (integer) value *50* will be printed in its place within the string.

Table 3.4   Format Specifiers

Conversion	Definition
%b	Unsigned binary integer
%c	Character
%d, i	Decimal number
%e	Floating point number in scientific notation
%E	Floating point number in scientific notation using capital *E*
%f, %F	Floating point number
%g	Floating point number using either *e* or *f* conversion, whichever takes the least space
%G	Floating point number using either *e* or *f* conversion, whichever takes the least space
%ld, %D	Long decimal number
%lu, %U	Long unsigned decimal number
%lo, %O	Long octal number
%p	Pointer (hexadecimal)
%s	String
%u	Unsigned decimal number
%x	Hexadecimal number
%X	Hexadecimal number using capital *X*
%lx	Long hexidecimal number
%%	Print a literal percent sign

Flag modifiers are used after the % to further define the printing; for example, *%-20s* represents a 20-character left-justfified field.

Table 3.5   Flag Modifiers

Conversion	Definition
%-	Left-justification modifier
%#	Integers in octal format are displayed with a leading *0*; integers in hexadecimal form are displayed with a leading *0x*
%+	For conversions using *d*, *e*, *f*, and *g*, integers are displayed with a numeric sign, + or -
%0	The displayed value is padded with zeros instead of whitespace
%number	Maximum field width; for example, if number is *6*, as in *%6d*, maximum field width is six digits
%.number	Precision of a floating point number; for example, *%.2f* specifies a precision of two digits to the right of the decimal point and *%8.2* represents a maximum field width of eight, where one of the characters is a decimal point followed by two digits after the decimal point

When an argument is printed, the place where the output is printed is called the **field**, and the **width** of the field is the number of characters contained in that field. The width of a field is specified by a percent sign and a number representing the maximum field width, followed by the conversion character; for example, *%20s* is a right-justified 20-character string; *%-25s* is a left-justified 25-character string; and *%10.2f* is a right-justified 10-character floating-point number, where the decimal point counts as one of the characters and the precision is two places to the right of the decimal point. If the argument exceeds the maximum field width, *printf* will not truncate the number, but your formatting may look bad. If the number to the right of the decimal point is truncated, it will be rounded up; for example, if the formatting instruction is *%.2f*, the corresponding argument, *56.555555*, would be printed as *56.6*.

EXAMPLE 3.13

```
(The Script)
    #!/usr/bin/perl
1   printf "Hello to you and yours %s!\n","Sam McGoo!";
2   printf("%-15s%-20s\n", "Jack", "Sprat");
3   printf "The number in decimal is %d\n", 45;
4   printf "The formatted number is |%10d|\n", 100;
5   printf "The number printed with leading zeros is |%010d|\n", 5;
```

EXAMPLE 3.13 (CONTINUED)

```
 6   printf "Left-justified the number is |%-10d|\n", 100;
 7   printf "The number in octal is %o\n",15;
 8   printf "The number in hexadecimal is %x\n", 15;
 9   printf "The formatted floating point number is |%8.2f|\n",
         14.3456;
10   printf "The floating point number is |%8f|\n", 15;
11   printf  "The character is %c\n", 65;

(Output)
 1   Hello to you and yours Sam McGoo!
 2   Jack                    Sprat
 3   The number in decimal is 45
 4   The formatted number is |       100|
 5   The number printed with leading zeros is |0000000005|.
 6   Left-justified the number is |100       |
 7   The number in octal is 17
 8   The number in hexadecimal is f
 9   The formatted floating point number is |   14.35|
10   The floating point number is |15.000000|
11   The character is A
```

EXPLANATION

1   The quoted string contains the *%s* format conversion specifier. The string *Sam Magoo* is converted to a string and replaces the *%s* in the printed output.
2   The string *Jack* has a field width of 15 characters and is left-justified. The string *Sprat* has a field width of 20 characters and is also left-justified. Parentheses are optional.
3   The number *45* is printed in decimal format.
4   The number *100* has a field width of 10 and is right-justified.
5   The number *5* has a field width of 10, is right-justified, and is preceded by leading zeros rather than whitespace. If the modifier *0* is placed before the number representing the field width, the number printed will be padded with leading zeros if it takes up less space than it needs.
6   The number *100* has a field width of 10 and is left-justified.
7   The number *15* is printed in octal.
8   The number *15* is printed in hexadecimal.
9   The number *14.3456* is given a field width of eight characters. One of them is the decimal point; the fractional part is given a precision of two decimal places. The number is then rounded up.
10 The number *15* is given a field width of eight characters, right-justified. The default precision is six decimal places to the right of the decimal point.
11 The number *65* is converted to the ASCII character *A* and printed.

3.4.1   The *sprintf* Function

The *sprintf* function is just like the *printf* function except it allows you to assign the formatted string to a variable. *sprintf* and *printf* use the same conversion tables (Tables 3.4 and 3.5). Variables are discussed in Chapter 4, "What's in a Name."

EXAMPLE 3.14

```
(The Script)
1   $string = sprintf("The name is: %10s\nThe number is: %8.2f\n",
                        "Ellie", 33);
2   print "$string";

(Output)
2   The name is:      Ellie
    The number is:    33.00
```

EXPLANATION

1   The *sprintf* function follows the same rules as *printf* for conversion of characters, strings, and numbers. The only real difference is that *sprintf* allows you to store the formatted output in a variable. In this example, the formatted output is stored in the scalar variable *$string*. The \n inserted in the string causes the remaining portion of the string to be printed on the next line. Scalar variables are discussed in Chapter 4, "What's in a Name." Parentheses are optional.

2   The value of the variable is printed showing the formatted output produced by *sprintf*.

3.4.2   Printing Without Quotes—The *here document*

The Perl *here document* is derived from the UNIX shell *here document*. It allows you to quote a whole block of text enclosed between words called terminators. From the first terminator to the last terminator, the text is quoted, or you could say "from *here* to *here*" the text is quoted. The *here document* is a line-oriented form of quoting, requiring the << operator followed by an initial terminating word and a semicolon. There can be no spaces after the << unless the terminator itself is quoted. If the terminating word is not quoted or double quoted, variable expansion is performed. If the terminating word is singly quoted, variable expansion is not performed. Each line of text is inserted between the first and last terminating word. The final terminating word must be on a line by itself, with no surrounding whitespace.

Perl, unlike the shell, does not perform command substitution (backquotes) in the text of a *here document*. Perl, on the other hand, does allow you to execute commands in the *here document* if the terminator is enclosed in backquotes.

Here documents are used extensively in CGI scripts for enclosing large chunks of HTML tags for printing.

EXAMPLE 3.15

```
(The Script)
1    $price=1000;    # A variable is assigned a value.
2    print <<EOF;
3    The consumer commented, "As I look over my budget, I'd say
4    the price of $price is right. I'll give you \$500 to start."\n
5    EOF

6    print <<'FINIS';
     The consumer commented, "As I look over my budget, I'd say
7    the price of $price is too much.\n I'll settle for $500."
8    FINIS

9    print << x 4;
     Here's to a new day.
     Cheers!
10
     print "\nLet's execute some commands.\n";
     # If terminator is in backquotes, will execute OS commands
11   print <<`END`;
     echo Today is
     date
     END
```

```
(Output)
3    The consumer commented, "As I look over my budget, I'd say
     the price of 1000 is right. I'll give you $500 to start."
6    The consumer commented, "As I look over my budget, I'd say
     the price of $price is too much. \n I'll settle for $500."
9    Here's to a new day.
     Cheers!
     Here's to a new day.
     Cheers!
     Here's to a new day.
     Cheers!
     Here's to a new day.
     Cheers!
11   Let's execute some commands.
     Today is
     Fri Oct 27 12:48:36 PDT 2000
```

EXPLANATION

1 A scalar variable, *$price*, is assigned the value *1000*.
2 Start of *here document*. *EOF* is the terminator. The block is treated as if in double quotes. If there is any space preceding the terminator, then enclose the terminator in double quotes, such as *"EOF"*.
3 All text in the body of the *here document* is quoted as though the whole block of text were surrounded by double quotes.
4 The dollar sign has a special meaning when enclosed in double quotes. Since the text in this *here document* is treated as if in double quotes, the variable has special meaning here as well. The *$* is used to indicate that a scalar variable is being used. The value of the variable will be interpreted. If a backslash preceeds the dollar sign, it will be treated as a literal. If special backslash sequences are used, such as *\n*, they will be interpreted.
5 End of *here document* marked by matching terminator, *EOF*.
6 By surrounding the terminator, *FINIS*, with single quotes, the text that follows will be treated literally turning off the meaning of any special characters such as the dollar sign or backslash sequences.
7 Text is treated as if in single quotes.
8 Closing terminator marks the end of the *here document*.
9 The value *x 4* says that the text within the *here document* will be printed four times. The *x* operator is called the *repetition operator*. There must be a **blank line** at the end of the block of text, so that the *here document* is terminated.
10 The blank line is required here to end the *here document*.
11 The terminator is enclosed in backquotes. The shell will execute the commands between `END` and *END*. This example includes UNIX commands. If you are using another operating system, such as Windows or Mac OS, the commands must be compatible with that operating system.

***Here Documents* and CGI.** The following program is called a CGI (common gateway interface) program, a simple Perl program executed by a Web server rather by the shell. It is just like any other Perl script with two exceptions:

1. There is a line called the MIME line (e.g., *Content-type: text/html*) that describes what kind of content will be sent back to the browser.

2. The document consists of text embedded with HTML tags, the language used by browsers to render text in different colors, fonts faces, types, etc. Many CGI programmers take advantage of the *here document* to avoid using the *print* function for every line of the program.

CGI programs are stored in a special directory called *cgi-bin,* which is normally found under the Web server's root directory. See Chapter 19, "CGI and Perl: The Hyper Dynamic Duo" for a complete discussion of CGI.

To execute the following script, you will start up your Web browser and type in the Location box: *http://servername/cgi-bin/scriptname*.[4] See Figure 3.1.

EXAMPLE 3.16

```
    #!/bin/perl
    # The HTML tags are embedded in the here document to avoid using
    # multiple print statements
1   print <<EOF;        # here document in a CGI script
2   Content-type: text/html
3
4   <HTML><HEAD><TITLE>Town Crier</TITLE></HEAD>
    <H1><CENTER>Hear ye, hear ye, Sir Richard cometh!!</CENTER></H1>
    </HTML>
5   EOF
```

EXPLANATION

1   The *here document* starts here. The terminating word is *EOF*. The *print* function will receive everything from *EOF* to *EOF*.
2   This line tells the browser that the type of content that is being sent is text mixed with HTML tags. This line **must** be followed by a blank line.
4   The body of the document consists of text and HTML tags.
5   The word *EOF* marks the end of the *here document*.

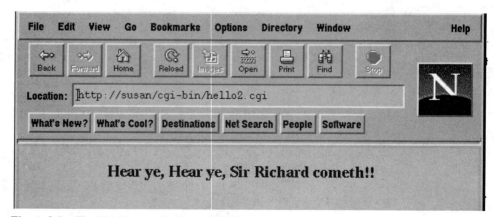

Figure 3.1   The Web browser in Example 3.16.

---

4. You must supply the correct server name for your system, and the correct filename. Some CGI files must have a *.cgi* or *.pl* extension.

EXERCISE 2
A String of Perls

1. Write a Perl script called *literals* that will print the following:

```
$ perl literals
Today is Mon Mar12 12:58:04 PDT 2001
The name of this PERL SCRIPT is literals.
Hello. The number we will examine is 125.5.
The NUMBER in decimal is 125.
The following number is taking up 20 spaces and is right justified.
|                 125|
              The number in hex is 7d
              The number in octal is 175
The number in scientific notation is 1.255000e+02
The unformatted number is 125.500000
The formatted number is 125.50
My boss just said, "Can't you loan me $12.50 for my lunch?"
I flatly said, "No way!"
Good-bye (Makes a beep sound)
```

Note: The words PERL SCRIPT and NUMBER are capitalized by using string literal escape sequences.

What command line option would you use to check the syntax of your script?

2. Add to your literals script a *here document* to print:

Life is good with Perl.
I have just completed my second exercise!

WHAT'S IN A NAME

4.1 About Perl Variables

4.1.1 Types

Variables are data items whose values may change throughout the run of the program, whereas literals or constants remain fixed. Perl variables are of three types: scalar, array, and associative array (more commonly called hashes). A scalar variable contains a single value, an array variable contains an ordered list of values indexed by a positive number, and a hash contains an unordered set of key/value pairs indexed by a string (the key) that is associated with a corresponding value. (See "Scalars, Arrays, and Hashes" on page 49.)

4.1.2 Scope and the Package

The scope of a variable determines where it is visible in the program. In Perl scripts, the variable is visible to the entire script (i.e., global in scope), and can be changed anywhere within the script.

The Perl sample programs you have seen in the previous chapters are compiled internally into what is called a **package**, which provides a **namespace** for variables. Almost all variables are **global** within that package. A global variable is known to the whole package and, if changed anywhere within the package, the change will permanently affect the variable. The default package is called *main*, similar to the *main()* function in the *C* language. Such variables in *C* would be classified as **static**. At this point, you don't have to worry about naming the *main* package or the way in which it is handled during the compilation process. The only purpose in mentioning packages now is to let you know that the scope of variables in the *main* package, your script, is global. Later, when we talk about the *our, local,* and *my* functions in packages, you will see that it is possible to change the scope and namespace of a variable.

41

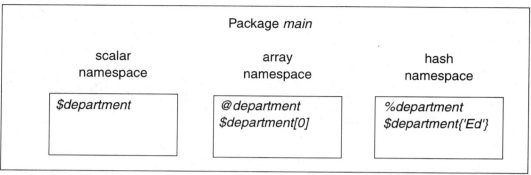

Figure 4.1   Namespaces for scalars, lists, and hashes in package *main*.

4.1.3   Naming Conventions

Unlike *C* or *Java*, Perl variables don't have to be declared before being used. They spring to life just by the mere mention of them. Variables have their own namespace in Perl. They are identified by the "funny characters" that precede them. Scalar variables are preceded by a *$* sign, array variables are preceded by an @ sign, and hash variables are preceded by a % sign. Since the "funny characters" indicate what type of variable you are using, you can use the same name for a scalar, array, or hash and not worry about a naming conflict. For example, *$name*, *@name*, and *%name* are all different variables; the first is a scalar, the second is an array, and the last is a hash.[1]

Since reserved words and filehandles are not preceded by a special character, variable names will not conflict with reserved words or filehandles. Variables are **case sensitive**. The variables named *$Num*, *$num*, and *$NUM* are all different.

If a variable starts with a letter, it may consist of any number of letters (an underscore counts as a letter) and/or digits. If the variable does not start with a letter, it must consist of only one character. Perl has a set of special variables (e.g., *$_*, *$^*, *$.*, *$1*, *$2*, etc.) that fall into this category. (See "Special Variables" on page 764 in Appendix A.) In special cases, variables may also be preceded with a single quote, but only when packages are used.

An uninitialized variable will get a value of zero or null, depending on whether its context is numeric or string.

4.1.4   Assignment Statements

The assignment operator, the equal sign (=), is used to assign the value on its right-hand side to a variable on its left-hand side. Any value that can be "assigned to" represents a named region of storage and is called an *lvalue*.[2] Perl reports an error if the operand on the left-hand side of the assignment operator does not represent an *lvalue*.

---

1. Using the same name is allowed, but not recommended; it makes reading too confusing.
2. The value on the left-hand side of the equal sign is called an *lvalue*, and the value on the right-hand side an *rvalue*.

When assigning a value or values to a variable, if the variable on the left-hand side of the equal sign is a scalar, Perl evaluates the expression on the right-hand side in a scalar context. If the variable on the left of the equal sign is an array, then Perl evaluates the expression on the right in an array context. (See "Scalars, Arrays, and Hashes" on page 49.)

A simple statement is an expression terminated with a semicolon.

FORMAT

```
variable=expression;
```

EXAMPLE 4.1

```
(The Script)
    # Scalar, array, and hash assignment
1   $salary=50000;                    # Scalar assignment
2   @months=('Mar', 'Apr', 'May');    # Array assignment
3   %states= (                        # Hash assignment
        CA => 'California',
        ME => 'Maine',
        MT => 'Montana',
        NM => 'New Mexico',
            );
4   print "$salary\n";
5   print "@months\n";
6   print "$months[0], $months[1], $months[2]\n";
7   print "$states{CA}, $states{NM}\n";
8   print $x + 3, "\n";               # $x just came to life!
9   print "***$name***\n";            # $name is born!


(Output)
4   50000
5   Mar Apr May
6   Mar, Apr, May
7   California, New Mexico
8   3
9   ******
```

EXPLANATION

1   The scalar variable *$salary* is assigned the numeric literal *50000*. (See "Scalar Variables" on page 49.)

2   The array *@months* is assigned the comma-separated list, *Mar, Apr, May*. The list is enclosed in parentheses and each list item is quoted. (See "Arrays" on page 52.)

EXPLANATION (CONTINUED)

3 The hash, *%states*, is assigned a list consisting of a set of strings separated either by a digraph symbol (=>) or a comma.[a] The string on the left is called the *key*.[b] The string to the right is called the *value*. The *key* is associated with its *value*. (See"Hashes" on page 60.)

4 The value of the scalar, *$salary*, is printed, followed by a newline.

5 The *@months* array is printed. The double quotes preserve spaces between each element.

6 The individual elements of the array, *@months*, are scalars and are thus preceded by a dollar sign (*$*). The array index starts at zero.

7 The *key* elements of the hash, *%states*, are enclosed in curly braces (*{}*). The associated *value* is printed. Each *value* is a single value, a scalar. The *value* is preceded by a dollar sign (*$*).

8 The scalar variable, *$x*, is referenced for the first time. Because the number *three* is added to *$x*, the context is numeric. *$x* has an initial value of *zero*.

9 The scalar variable, *$name*, is referenced for the first time. The context is string and the initial value is null.

a. The comma can be used in both Perl 4 and Perl 5. The => symbol was introduced in Perl 5.
b. The => operator, unlike the comma, causes the key to be quoted, but if the key consists of more than one word, then it must be quoted.

4.1.5 Quoting Rules

Since quoting affects the way in which variables are interpreted, this is a good time to review Perl's quoting rules. Perl quoting rules are similar to shell quoting rules. This may not be good news to shell programmers, who find using quotes frustrating, to say the least. It is often difficult to determine which quotes to use, where to use them, and how to find the culprit if they are misused; in other words, it's a real debugging nightmare.[3] For those of you who fall into this category, Perl offers an alternate method of quoting.[4]

Perl has three types of quotes and all three types have a different function. They are **single quotes**, **double quotes**, and **backquotes**.

The backslash (\) behaves like a set of single quotes but can be used only to quote a single character.

A pair of single or double quotes may delimit a string of characters. Quotes will either allow the interpretation of special characters or protect special characters from interpretation, depending on the kind of quotes you use.

Single quotes are the "democratic" quotes. All characters enclosed within them are treated equally; in other words, there are no special characters. But the double quotes dis-

---

3. Barry Rosenberg, in his book *KornShell Programming Tutorial,* has a chapter titled "The Quotes From Hell."
4. Larry Wall, creator of Perl, calls his alternate quoting method "syntactic sugar."

criminate. They treat some of the characters in the string as special characters. The special characters include the *$* sign, the @ symbol, and escape sequences such as \t and \n.

When backquotes surround an operating system command, the command will be executed by the shell. This is called **command substitution**. The output of the command will either be printed as part of a *print* statement or assigned to a variable. If you are using Windows, Linux, or UNIX, the commands enclosed within backquotes must be supported by the particular operating system and will vary from system to system.

No matter what kind of quotes you are using, they **must** be matched. Because the quotes mark the beginning and end of a string, Perl will complain about a *"Might be a multiline runaway string"* or *"Execution of quotes aborted…"*, or *"Can't find string terminator anywhere before EOF…"* and fail to compile, if you forget one of the quotes.

Double Quotes.   Double quotes must be matched unless embedded within single quotes or preceded by a backslash.

When a string is enclosed in double quotes, scalar variables (preceded with a *$*) and arrays (preceded by the @ symbol) are interpolated (i.e., the value of the variable replaces the variable name in the string). Hashes (preceded by the % sign) are **not** interpolated within the string enclosed in double quotes.

Strings that contain string literals (e.g., \t, \n) must be enclosed in double quotes for backslash interpretation.

A single quote may be enclosed in double quotes, as in, *"I don't care!"*

EXAMPLE 4.2

```
(The Script)
    # Double quotes
1   $num=5;
2   print "The number is $num.\n";
3   print "I need \$5.00.\n";
4   print "\t\tI can't help you.\n";

(Output)
2   The number is 5.
3   I need $5.00.
4       I can't help you.
```

EXPLANATION

1   The scalar variable *$num* is assigned the value *5*.
2   The string is enclosed in double quotes. The value of the scalar variable is printed. The string literal, \n, is interpreted.
3   The dollar sign (*$*) is printed as a literal dollar sign when preceded by a backslash; in other words, variable substitution is ignored.
4   The special literals \t and \n are interpreted when enclosed within double quotes.

Single Quotes.   If a string is enclosed in single quotes, it is printed literally (what you see is what you get).

If a single quote is needed within a string, then it can be embedded within double quotes or backslashed. If double quotes are to be treated literally, they can be embedded within single quotes.

EXAMPLE 4.3

```
(The Script)
    # Single quotes
1   print 'I need $100.00.', "\n";
2   print 'The string literal, \t, is used to represent a tab.', "\n";
3   print 'She cried, "Help me!"', "\n";

(Output)
1   I need $100.00.
2   The string literal, \t, is used to represent a tab.
3   She cried, "Help me!"
```

EXPLANATION

1   The dollar sign is interpreted literally. In double quotes, it would be interpreted as a scalar. The \n is in double quotes in order for backslash interpretation to occur.
2   The string literal, \t, is not interpreted to be a tab, but is printed literally.
3   The double quotes are protected when enclosed in single quotes (i.e., they are printed literally).

Backquotes.   UNIX/Windows[5] commands placed within backquotes are executed by the shell, and the output is returned to the Perl program. The output is usually assigned to a variable or made part of a *print* string. When the output of a command is assigned to a variable, the context is scalar (i.e., a single value is assigned).[6] In order for command substitution to take place, the backquotes cannot be enclosed in either double or single quotes. (Make note UNIX shell programmers, backquotes cannot be enclosed in double quotes as in shell programs.)

---

5.   If using other operating systems, such as DOS or Mac OS 9.1 and below, the OS commands available for your system will differ.

6.   If output of a command is assigned to an array, the first line of output becomes the first element of the array, the second line of output becomes the next element of the array, and so on.

EXAMPLE 4.4

```
(The Script)
    # Backquotes and command substitution
1   print "The date is ", `date`ᵃ;        # Win32 users: `date /T`
2   print "The date is `date`", ".\n"; # Backquotes treated literally
3   $directory=`pwd`;                     # Win32 users: `cd`
4   print "\nThe current directory is $directory.";

(Output)
1   The date is Mon Jun 26 17:27:49 PDT 2001.
2   The date is `date`.
4   The current directory is /home/jody/ellie/perl.
```

a. Windows 95+ users: don't use the *date* command. It does not behave the same way as the UNIX *date* command. Windows 2000 and NT support many traditional UNIX commands, including the *date* command, with different options.

EXPLANATION

1   The UNIX *date* command will be executed by the shell, and the output will be returned to Perl's *print* string. The output of the *date* command includes the newline character.
2   Command substitution will not take place when the backquotes are enclosed in single or double quotes.
3   The scalar variable *$dir*, including the newline, is assigned the output of the UNIX *pwd* command (i.e., the present working directory).
4   The value of the scalar, *$dir*, is printed to the screen.

Perl's Alternative Quotes.   Perl provides an alternate form of quoting—the *q*, *qq*, *qx* and *qw* constructs.

- The *q* represents single quotes.
- The *qq* represents double quotes.
- The *qx* represents backquotes.
- The *qw* represents a quoted list of words. (See "Arrays" on page 52.)

Table 4.1   Alternative Quoting Constructs

Quoting Construct	*What It Represents*
q/Hello/	'Hello'
qq/Hello/	"Hello"
qx/date/	`date`
@list=qw/red yellow blue/;	@list=('red', 'yellow', 'blue');

The string to be quoted is enclosed in **forward slashes**, but alternate delimiters can be used for all four of the *q* constructs. A single character or paired characters can be used:

q/Hello/
q#Hello#
q{Hello}
q[Hello]
q(Hello)

EXAMPLE 4.5

```
(The Script)
    # Using alternative quotes
1   print 'She cried, "I can\'t help you!"',"\n";    # Clumsy
2   print qq/She cried, "I can't help you!" \n/;     # qq for double
                                                     # quotes
3   print qq/I need $5.00\n/;  # Really need single quotes
                               # for a literal dollar sign to print
4   print q/I need $5.00\n/;   # What about backslash interpretation?
5   print qq/\n/, q/I need $5.00/,"\n";
6   print q!I need $5.00!,"\n";
7   print "The present working directory is ", `pwd`;
8   print qq/Today is /, qx/date/;ª
9   print "The hour is ", qx{date +%H};

(Output)
1   She cried, "I can't help you!"
2   She cried, "I can't help you!"
3   I need .00
4   I need $5.00\n
5   I need $5.00
6   I need $5.00
7   The present working directory is /home/jody/ellie/perl
8   Today is Mon Jun 26 17:29:34 PDT 2001
9   The hour is 17
```

a. Windows NT users: *date /T*.

EXPLANATION

1   The string is enclosed in single quotes. This allows the conversational quotes to be printed as literals. The single quote in *can\'t* is quoted with a backslash so that it will also be printed literally. If it were not quoted, it would be matched with the first single quote. The ending single quote would then have no mate and, alas, the program would either tell you you have a runaway quote, or search for its mate until it reached the end of file unexpectedly.

2   The *qq* construct replaces double quotes. The forward slashes delimit the string.

3   Because the *qq* is used, the dollar sign (*$*) in *$5.00* is interpreted as a scalar variable with a null value. The *.00* is printed. (This is not the way to handle your money!)

4   The single *q* replaces single quotes. The *$5* is treated as a literal. Unfortunately, so is the *\n*. Backslash interpretation does not take place within single quotes.

5   The *\n* is double quoted with the *qq* construct, the string *I need $5.00* is single quoted with the *q* construct, and old-fashioned double quotes are used for the second *\n*.

6   An alternative delimiter, the exclamation point (*!*), is used with the *q* construct (instead of the forward slash) to delimit the string.

7   The string *The present working directory is* is enclosed in double quotes; the UNIX command *pwd* is enclosed in backquotes for command substitution.

8   The *qq* construct quotes *Today is*; the *qx* construct replaces the backquotes used for command substitution.

9   Alternative delimiters, the curly braces, are used with the *qx* construct (instead of the forward slash). The output of the UNIX *date* command is printed.

4.2   Scalars, Arrays, and Hashes

Now that we have discussed the basics of Perl variables (types, visibility, funny characters, etc.), we can look at them in more detail and without (or, should I say, with less) confusion about the quoting mechanism, and how quoting affects variable interpretation.

4.2.1   Scalar Variables

Scalar variables hold a single number or string and are preceded by a dollar sign (*$*). Perl scalars need a preceding dollar sign whenever the variable is referenced, even when the scalar is being assigned a value. If you are familiar with shell programs, using the dollar sign when making assignments may seem a little strange at first.

Assignment.   When making an assignment, the value on the right-hand side of the equal sign is evaluated as a single value (i.e., its context is scalar). A quoted string, then, is considered a single value even if it contains a number of words.

EXAMPLE 4.6

```
1   $number=150;
2   $name="Jody Savage";
```

EXPLANATION

1   The numeric literal, *150*, is assigned to the scalar variable *$number*.
2   The string literal *Jody Savage* is assigned to the scalar *$name* as a single string.

Curly Braces.   If a scalar variable is surrounded by curly braces (*{}*), the scalar is shielded from any characters that may be appended to the variable.

EXAMPLE 4.7

```
(The Script)
1   $var="net";
2   print "${var}work\n";

(Output)
2   network
```

EXPLANATION

1   The value, *net*, is assigned to the scalar variable *$var*.
2   The curly braces surrounding the variable insulate it from the string *work* that has been appended to it. Without the curly braces, nothing would be printed because a variable called *$varwork* has not been defined.

EXAMPLE 4.8

```
(The Script)
    # Initializing scalars and printing their values
1   $num = 5;
2   $friend = "John Smith";
3   $money = 125.75;
4   $now = `date`;            # Backquotes for command substitution
5   $month="Jan";
6   print "$num\n";
7   print "$friend\n";
8   print "I need \$$money.\n";        # Protecting our money
9   print qq/$friend gave me \$$money.\n/;
10  print qq/The time is $now/;
11  print "The month is ${month}uary.\n";    # Curly braces shield
                                             # the variable
```

EXAMPLE 4.8 (CONTINUED)

```
(Output)
6   5
7   John Smith
8   I need $125.75.
9   John Smith gave me $125.75.
10  The time is Jan 27 09:34:41 PDT 2001.
11  The month is January.
```

EXPLANATION

1　The scalar *$num* is assigned the numeric literal, *5*.
2　The scalar *$friend* is assigned the string literal, *John Smith*.
3　The scalar *$money* is assigned the numeric floating point literal, *125.75*.
4　The scalar *$now* is assigned the output of the UNIX *date* command.
5　The scalar *$month* is assigned *Jan*.
6　The value of the scalar *$num* is printed.
7　The value of the scalar *$friend* is printed.
8　The quoted string is printed. The backslash allows the first dollar sign (*$*) to be printed literally; the value of *$money* is interpolated within double quotes, and its value printed.
9　The Perl *qq* construct replaces double quotes. The string to be quoted is enclosed in forward slashes. The value of the scalar *$friend* is interpolated; a literal dollar sign precedes the value of the scalar interpolated variable, *$money*.
10　The quoted string is printed. The *$now* variable is interpolated.
11　As with the UNIX shell, curly braces can be used to shield the variable from characters that are appended to it. *January* will be printed.

The *defined* Function. If a scalar has neither a valid string nor a valid numeric value, it is undefined. The *defined* function allows you to check for the validity of a variable's value. It returns 1 if the variable has a value, and null if it does not. The function is also used to check the validity of arrays, subroutines, and null strings.

EXAMPLE 4.9

```
$name="Tommy";
print "OK \n" if defined $name;
```

The *undef* Function. This function *undefines* an already defined variable. It releases whatever memory that was allocated for the variable. The function returns the undefined value. This function also releases storage associated with arrays and subroutines.

EXAMPLE 4.10

```
undef $name;
```

The $_ Scalar Variable.   The $_ is a ubiquitous little character. Although it is very useful in Perl scripts, it is often not seen. It is used as the default pattern space for searches and to hold the current line. When used as a pattern space for searches, it behaves like *sed*. When used to hold the current line, it is like the *$0* variable in *awk*.

EXAMPLE 4.11

```
1   $ᵃ perl -ne 'print' emp.names
2   $ perl -ne 'print $_' emp.names
    Steve Blenheim
    Betty Boop
    Igor Chevsky
    Norma Cord
    Jon DeLoach
    Karen Evich
```

a. Windows users: Use double quotes in these examples; e.g., *perl -ne "print" emp.names*

EXPLANATION

1   The *-n* switch allows you to implicitly loop through the file. Since the *$_* is a default used to hold the current line of the *emp.names* file, it is not required in the *print* statement. The output is the same as in the next example.
2   This example is equivalent to the first example. This time the *$_* is used explicitly to hold the current line, even though it is not necessary.

4.2.2 Arrays

When you have a collection of similar data elements, it is easier to use an array than to create a separate variable for each of the elements. The array name allows you to associate a single variable name with a list of data elements. Each of the elements in the list is referenced by its name and a subscript (also called an index).

Perl, unlike *C*-like languages, doesn't care whether the elements of an array are of the same data type. They can be a mix of numbers and strings. To Perl, an array is a named list containing an ordered set of scalars. The name of the array starts with an @ sign. The subscript follows the array name and is enclosed in square brackets (*[ ]*). Subscripts are simply integers and start at zero.

Assignment.   If the array is initialized, the elements are enclosed in parentheses, and each element is separated by a comma. The list is parenthesized due to the lower precedence of the comma operator over the assignment operator. Elements in an array are simply scalars.

Perl 5 introduced the *qw* construct for creating a list (similar to *qq*, *q*, and *qx*). The items in the list are treated as singly quoted words.

EXAMPLE 4.12

```
1    @name=("Guy", "Tom", "Dan",  "Roy");
2    @list=(2..10);
3    @grades=(100, 90, 65, 96, 40, 75);
4    @items=($a, $b, $c);
5    @empty=();
6    $size=@items;
7    @mammals = qw/dogs cats cows/;
8    @fruit = qw(apples pears peaches);
```

EXPLANATION

1   The array @*name* is initialized with a list of four string literals.
2   The array @*list* is assigned numbers ranging from *2* through *10*. (See Example 4.14.)
3   The array @*grades* is initialized with a list of six numeric literals.
4   The array @*items* is initialized with the values of three scalar variables.
5   The array @*empty* is assigned a null list.
6   The array @*items* is assigned to the scalar variable *$size*. The value of the scalar is the number of elements in the array (in this example, *3*).
7   The *qw* (quote word) construct is followed by a delimiter of your choice. Each of the words in the list is treated as a singly quoted word. The list is terminated with a closing delimiter. This example could be written:

```
@mammals = ( 'cats', 'dogs', 'cows' );
```

8   The *qw* construct accepts paired characters *( )*, *{ }*, *< >*, and *[ ]*, as optional delimeters.

Special Scalars and Array Assignment.   The special scalar variable *$#arrayname* returns the number of the last subscript in the array. Since the array subscripts start at zero, this value is one less than the array size. The *$#arrayname* variable can also be used to shorten or truncate the size of the array.

The *$[* variable is the current array base subscript, zero. Its value can be changed so that the subscript starts at 1 instead of 0, but changing this value is discouraged by Larry Wall.

EXAMPLE 4.13

```
1    $indexsize=$#grades;
2    $#grades=3;
3    $#grades=$[ - 1;
4    @grades=();
```

EXPLANATION

1   The scalar variable *$indexsize* is assigned the value of the last subscript in the *@grades* array.
2   The last subscript in the array has been shortened to *3*.
3   The array base subscript, starting at zero, has been decremented by one. This will truncate the entire array to a null or empty list; this is the same as *@grades=()*;
4   The *@grades* array is assigned a null list creating an empty list.

The Range Operator and Array Assignment.   The .. operator, called the **range** operator, when used in an array context, returns an array of values starting from the left value to the right value, counting by ones.

EXAMPLE 4.14

```
1    @digits=(0 .. 10);
2    @letters=( 'A' .. 'Z' );
3    @alpha=( 'A' .. 'Z', 'a' .. 'z' );
4    @n=( -5 .. 20 );
```

EXPLANATION

1   The array *@digits* is assigned a list of numbers, *0* through *10*.
2   The array *@letters* is assigned a list of capital letters, *A* through *Z*.
3   The array *@alpha* is assigned a list of uppercase and lowercase letters.
4   The array *@n* is assigned a list of numbers, *–5* through *20*.

Accessing Elements.   To reference the individual elements in an array, each element is considered a scalar (preceded by a dollar sign), and the subscripts start at zero. The subscripts are positive whole numbers. For example, In the array *@names,* the first element in the array is *$name[0]*, the next element is *$name[1]*, and so forth.

EXAMPLE 4.15

```
(The Script)
     # Populating an array and printing its values
1    @names=('John', 'Joe', 'Jake');      # @names=qw/John Joe Jake/;
2    print @names, "\n";  # prints without the separator
3    print "Hi $names[0], $names[1], and $names[2]!\n";
4    $number=@names;          # The scalar is assigned the number
                              # of elements in the array
5    print "There are $number elements in the \@names array.\n";
6    print "The last element of the array is $names[$number - 1].\n";
7    print "The last element of the array is $names[$#names].\n";
                              # Remember, the array index starts at zero!!
8    @fruit = qw(apples pears peaches plums);
9    print "The first element of the \@fruit array  is $fruit[0];
          the second element is $fruit[1].\n";
10   print "Starting at the end of the array; @fruit[-1, -3]\n";

(Output)
2    JohnJoeJake
3    Hi John, Joe, and Jake!
5    There are 3 elements in the @names array.
6    The last element of the array is Jake.
7    The last element of the array is Jake.
9    The first element of the @fruit array is apples; the second
     element is pears.
10   Starting at the end of the array: plums pears
```

EXPLANATION

1   The @*names* array is initialized with three strings: *John*, *Joe*, and *Jake*.
2   The entire array is printed to *STDOUT*. The space between the elements is not printed.
3   Each element of the array is printed, starting with subscript number zero.
4   The scalar variable $*number* is assigned the array @*names*. The value assigned is the number of elements in the array @*names*.
5   The number of elements in the array @*names* is printed.
6   The last element of the array is printed. Since subscripts start at zero, the number of elements in the array decremented by one evaluates to the number of the last subscript.
7   The last element of the array is printed. The $#*names* value evaluates to the number of the last subscript in the array. This value used as a subscript will retrieve the last element in the @*names* array.
8   The *qw* construct allows you to create an array of singly quoted words without enclosing the words in quotes or separating the words with commas. The delimiter is any pair of non-alphanumeric characters. (See "Perl's Alternative Quotes" on page 47.)

EXPLANATION (CONTINUED)

9 The first two elements of the @*fruit* array are printed.
10 With a negative offset as a subscript, the elements of the array are selected from the end of the array. The last element (*$fruit[-1]*) is *plums* and the third element from the end (*$fruit[-3]*) is *pears*. Note that when both index values are within the same set of brackets, as in @*fruit[-1,-3]*, the reference is to a list, not a scalar; that is why the @ symbol precedes the name of the array, rather than the *$*.

Array Slices.   When the elements of one array are assigned the values from another array, the resulting array is called an **array slice**.

If the array on the right-hand side of the assignment operator is larger than the array on the left-hand side, the unused values are discarded. If it is smaller, the values assigned are undefined. As indicated in the following example, the array indices in the slice do not have to be consecutively numbered; each element is assigned the corresponding value from the array on the right-hand side of the assignment operator.

EXAMPLE 4.16

```
(The Script)
    # Array slices
1   @names=('Tom', 'Dick', 'Harry', 'Pete' );
2   @pal=@names[1,2,3];  # slice -- @names[1..3] also O.K.
3   print "@pal\n\n";

4   ($friend[0], $friend[1], $friend[2])=@names;    # Array slice
5   print "@friend\n";

(Output)
3   Dick Harry Pete

5   Tom Dick Harry
```

EXPLANATION

1 The array @*names* is assigned the elements *'Tom'*, *'Dick'*, *'Harry'*, and *'Pete'*.
2 The array @*pal* is assigned the elements *1*, *2*, and *3* of the @*names* array. The elements of the @*names* array are sliced out and stored in the @*pal* array.
3 The @*friend* array is created by taking a slice from the @*names* array, i.e., elements *0*, *1*, and *2*.

EXAMPLE 4.17

```
(The Script)
    # Array slices
1   @colors=('red','green','yellow','orange');
2   ($c[0], $c[1],$c[3], $c[5])=@colors;  # The slice
3   print "**********\n";
4   print @colors,"\n";  # Prints entire array, but does
                         # not separate elements quoted
5   print "@colors,\n";  # Prints the entire array with
                         # elements separated
6   print "**********\n";
7   print $c[0],"\n";    # red
8   print $c[1],"\n";    # green
9   print $c[2],"\n";    # undefined
10  print $c[3],"\n";    # yellow
11  print $c[4],"\n";    # undefined
12  print $c[5],"\n";    # orange
13  print "**********\n" ;
14  print "The size of the \@c array is ", $#c + 1,".\n";

(Output)
3   **********
4   redgreenyelloworange
5   red  green yellow orange
6   **********
7   red
8   green
9
10  yellow
11
12  orange
13  **********
14  The size of the @c array is 6.
```

EXPLANATION

1 The array @*colors* is assigned the elements *'red'*, *'green'*, *'yellow'*, and *'orange'*.
2 An array slice is created, consisting of four scalars, *$c[0]*, *$c[1]*, *$c[3]*, and *$c[5]*. Note: The subscripts in the array slice are not numbered consecutively.
3 A row of stars is printed, just for clarity.
4 The elements are not separated when printed.
5 When the array is enclosed in double quotes, the whitespace between elements is preserved.
6 Another row of stars is printed.
7 The first element of the array slice, *red*, is printed.

EXPLANATION (CONTINUED)

8 The second element of the array slice, *green*, is printed.
9 The third element of the array slice is undefined. Its value is null because it was not assigned a value.
10 The fourth element of the array slice, *yellow*, is printed.
11 The fifth element of the array slice is undefined.
12 The sixth element of the array slice, *orange*, is printed.
13 Another row of stars is printed.
14 Even though some of the elements of the @*c* array are undefined, the size of the array indicates that the elements exist.

Multidimensional Arrays—Lists of Lists. Multidimensional arrays are sometimes called **tables** or **matrices**. They consist of rows and columns and can be represented with multiple subscripts. In a two-dimensional array, the first subscript represents the row and the second subscript represents the column.

In Perl, each row in a two-dimensional array is enclosed in square brackets. The row is an unnamed list. An unnamed list is called an **anonymous** array, and contains its own elements. The arrow operator, also called an **infix** operator, can be used to get the individual elements of an array. There is an implied –> between adjacent brackets. (Anonymous variables will be discussed in detail in Chapter 12, "Does this Job Require a Reference?")

EXAMPLE 4.18

```
(The Script)
    # A two-dimensional array consisting of 4 rows and 3 columns
1   @matrix=( [ 3 , 4, 10 ],    # Each row is an unnamed list
             [ 2,  7, 12 ],
             [ 0,  3,  4 ],
             [ 6,  5,  9 ],
           ) ;
2   print "@matrix\n";
3   print "Row 0, column 0 is $matrix[0][0].\n";
                # can also be written - $matrix[0]->[0]
4   print "Row 1, column  0 is $matrix[1][0].\n";
                # can also be written - $matrix[1]->[0]
5   for($i=0; $i < 4; $i++){
6      for($x=0; $x < 3; $x++){
7         print "$matrix[$i][$x] ";
      }
      print "\n";
   }
```

EXAMPLE 4.18 (CONTINUED)

```
(Output)
2   ARRAY(0xbf838) ARRAY(0xc7768) ARRAY(0xc77a4) ARRAY(0xc77e0)
3   Row 0, column 0 is 3.
4   Row 1, column 0 is 2.
7   3 4 10
    2 7 12
    0 3 4
    6 5 9
```

EXPLANATION

1   The array @*matrix* is assigned four unnamed or anonymous arrays. Each of the arrays has three values.

2   The addresses of the four anonymous arrays are printed. To access the individual elements of an anonymous array, double subscripts or the arrow operator must be used.

3   The first element of the first anonymous array in the @*matrix* array is printed. The –> is called the **arrow** or **infix** operator. It is used to dereference array and hash references. $*matrix[0][0]* or $*matrix[0]–>[0]* is the first element of the first row, where subscripts start at zero.

4   The second row, first element of the @*matrix* is printed. $*matrix[1]–>[0]* is another way to say $*matrix[1][0]*.

5   The outer *for* loop will iterate through each of the rows, starting at row zero. After the first iteration of the loop, the second *for* loop is entered.

6   The inner *for* loop iterates faster than the outer loop. Each element of a row is printed and then control returns to the outer *for* loop.

7   Print each element in the matrix. The first index represents the row, and the second index represents the column.

EXAMPLE 4.19

```
(The Script)
    # A list of lists
1   @record=( "Adams",   [2, 1, 0, 0],
2             "Edwards", [1, 0, 3, 2],
              "Howard",  [3 ,3 ,2, 0],
          );
3   print "In the first game $record[0] batted $record[1]->[0].\n";
4   print "In the first game $record[2] batted $record[3]->[0].\n";
5   print "In the first game $record[4] batted $record[5]->[0].\n";

(Output)
3   In the first game Adams batted 2.
4   In the first game Edwards batted 1.
5   In the first game Howard batted 3.
```

EXPLANATION

1   *@record* is a six-element array consisting of three anonymous arrays, each of which
    is enclosed in brackets. *Adams* is the first element of the array; *[2, 1, 0, 0]* is the
    second element of the array, etc.

2   *Edwards* is the third element of the *@record* array.

3   When printing the first element, the subscript is 0. When printing the value of the
    second array, the anonymous array in brackets, two subscripts are required. The –>
    operator is not necessary. It is implied if not used. In the example, the –> is used to
    show that it can be placed only between adjacent brackets.

    For example, *$record–>[1]–>[0]* would be incorrect. *$record[1][0]* is fine with-
    out the arrow operator.

4   The third element of *@record* is printed. The first element of the anonymous array
    (fourth element of the *@record* array) is printed.

5   The fifth element of *@record* is printed. The first element of the anonymous array
    (sixth element of the *@record* array) is printed.

4.2.3   Hashes

An associative array, more commonly called a **hash**, consists of one or more pairs of scalars—either strings, numbers, or Booleans. The first set of scalars is associated with the second set of scalars. The first string in the pair of strings is called the **key**, and the second
string is called the **value**. Whereas arrays are ordered lists with numeric indices starting at
0, hashes are unordered lists with string indices randomly distributed.

Assignment.   A hash must be defined before the elements can be referenced. Since a hash
consists of pairs of values, indexed by the first element of each pair, if one of the elements
in a pair is missing within the array definition, the association of the keys and their respective values will be affected. When assigning keys and values, make sure that you have a key
associated with its corresponding value. When indexing a hash, curly braces are used
instead of square brackets.

EXAMPLE 4.20

```
1   %seasons=(Sp => 'Spring',
              Su => 'Summer',
              F  => 'Fall',
              W  => 'Winter'
             );
2   %days=(Mon => 'Monday',
           Tue => 'Tuesday'
           Wed => undef,
          );
3   $days{'Wed'}="Wednesday";
4   $days{5}="Friday";
```

EXPLANATION

1. The hash *%seasons* is assigned keys and values. Each key and value is separated by the digraph operator, =>. The string *Sp* is the key with a corresponding value of *Spring*; the string *Su* is the key for its corresponding value *Summer*, etc. It is not necessary to quote the key if it is a single word.

2. The hash *%days* is assigned keys and values. The third key, *Wed*, is assigned *undef*. The *undef* function evaluates to a null string.

3. Individual elements of a hash are scalars. The key *Wed* is assigned the string value *Wednesday*. The index is enclosed in curly braces.

4. The key *5* is assigned the string value *Friday*. Note: the keys do not have any consecutive numbering order and the pairs can consist of numbers and/or strings.

Accessing Elements. When accessing the values of a hash, the subscript consists of the key enclosed in curly braces. Perl provides a set of functions to list the keys, values, and each of the elements of the hash. (See "Array Functions" on page 72.)

Due to the internal hashing techniques used to store the keys, Perl does not guarantee the order in which an entire hash is printed.

EXAMPLE 4.21

```
(The Script)
    # Assigning keys and values to a hash
1   %department = (
2                   Eng => 'Engineering',  # Eng is the key,
                                           # Engineering is the value
                    M   => 'Math',
                    S   => 'Science',
                    CS  => 'Computer Science',
                    Ed  => 'Education',
3                   );
4   $department = $department{'M'};
5   $school = $department{'Ed'};
6   print "I work in the $department section\n" ;
7   print "Funds in the $school department are being cut.\n";
8   print qq/I'm currently enrolled in a $department{CS} course.\n/;
9   print qq/The department hash looks like this:\n/;
10  print %department, "\n";   # The printout is not in the expected
                               # order due to internal hashing

(Output)
6   I work in the Math section
7   Funds in the Education department are being cut.
8   I'm currently enrolled in a Computer Science course.
9   The department hash looks like this:
10  SScienceCSComputer ScienceEdEducationMMathEngEngineering
```

EXPLANATION

1 The hash is called *%department*. It is assigned keys and values.
2 The first key is the string *Eng*, and the value associated with it is *Engineering*.
3 The closing parenthesis and semicolon end the assignment.
4 The scalar *$department* is assigned *Math*, the value associated with the *M* key.
5 The scalar *$school* is assigned *Education*, the value associated with the *Ed* key.
6 The quoted string is printed; the scalar *$department* is interpolated.
7 The quoted string is printed; the scalar $school is interpolated.
8 The quoted string and the value associated with the *CS* key are printed.
9 The quoted string is printed.
10 The entire hash is printed with keys and values packed together, and not in the expected order.

Hash Slices.   A hash slice is a list of hash keys whose corresponding values are assigned to another list of keys. The list consists of the hash name preceded by the @ symbol. The list of hash keys is enclosed in curly braces.

EXAMPLE 4.22

```
(The Script)
    # Hash slices
1   %officer= (NAME=>"Tom Savage",
              SSN=>"510-22-3456",
              DOB=>"05/19/66"
              );

2   @info=qw(Marine Captain 50000);
3   @officer{'BRANCH', 'TITLE', 'SALARY'}=@info;
    # This is a hash slice
4   @sliceinfo=@officer{'NAME','BRANCH','TITLE'};
    # This is also a hash slice
5   print "The new values from the hash slice are: @sliceinfo\n\n";
    print "The hash now looks like this:\n";
6   foreach $key ('NAME', 'SSN', 'DOB', 'BRANCH', 'TITLE', 'SALARY'){
7       printf "Key: %-10sValue: %-15s\n", $key, $officer{$key};
    }

(Output)
5   The new values from the hash slice are: Tom Savage Marine Captain

    The hash now looks like this:
7   Key: NAME          Value: Tom Savage
    Key: SSN           Value: 510-22-3456
    Key: DOB           Value: 05/19/66
    Key: BRANCH        Value: Marine
    Key: TITLE         Value: Captain
    Key: SALARY        Value: 50000
```

EXPLANATION

1   The hash *%officer* is assigned keys and values.
2   The array *@info* is assigned three values.
3   This is an example of a hash slice. The hash *officer* is assigned an array (*@info*) of values *Marine*, *Captain*, and *50000* to the corresponding keys, *BRANCH*, *TITLE*, *SALARY*. The name of the hash is prepended with an @ symbol because it is a list of keys that will receive its corresponding values from another list, *@info*.
4   The hash slice is used in the assignment to create an array called *@sliceinfo*. The array will consist of the hash values associated with keys *NAME, BRANCH,* and *TITLE*.
5   The values created by the hash slice are printed.
6   The *foreach* loop is used to iterate through the list of keys.
7   The keys and their corresponding values are printed. On line 3, the new key/value pairs were created by the slice.

Hashes of Hashes.   More complex data structures can be created in Perl 5. For example, a hash can contain another hash. It is like a record that contains records. The nested hash has no name. It is an anonymous hash and can be dereferenced with the arrow operator. Each of the keys in the named hash contains a value which is itself another hash. This anonymous hash consists of its own key/value pairs.

EXAMPLE 4.23

```
(The Script)
    # Nested hashes
                                              values
                      keys        key    value    key    value
1   %students=( Math    => { Joe  => 100,  Joan => 95 },
               Science => { Bill => 85,   Dan  => 76 }
          );
2   print "On the math test Joan got ";
3   print qq/$students{Math}->{Joan}.\n/;
4   print "On the science test Bill got ";
5   print qq/$students{Science}->{Bill}.\n/;

(Output)
3   On the math test Joan got 95.
5   On the science test Bill got 85.
```

EXPLANATION

1   The hash *%students* consists of two keys, *Math* and *Science*. The values associated
    with those keys are enclosed in curly braces. The value contains a set of nested keys
    and values. The value for the *Math* key contains two nested keys, *Joe* and *Joan*, with
    their respective values, *100* and *95*. The value for the *Science* key contains two nested
    keys, *Bill* and *Dan*, with their respective values, *85* and *76*. The nested keys and val-
    ues are in an unnamed or anonymous hash.
3   The arrow (infix) operator, –>, allows you to access the anonymous nested hash val-
    ue of the *%students* hash.

EXAMPLE 4.24

```
(The Script)
    # Anonymous arrays as keys in a hash
1   %grades=(Math     => [ 90, 100, 94 ],
            Science => [ 77, 87, 86 ],
            English => [ 65, 76, 99, 100 ],
            );
2   print %grades, "\n";
3   print "The third math grade is: $grades{Math}->[2]\n";
4   print "All of the science grades are: @{$grades{Science}}\n";

(Output)
2   EnglishARRAY(0x8a65128)ScienceARRAY(0x8a650b0)MathARRAY(0x8a6f134)
3   The third math grade is: 94
4   All of the science grades are: 77 87 86
```

EXPLANATION

1   The hash *%grades* is assigned keys and values. The values are an unnamed list of
    numbers. Perl knows that this is an anonymous list because it is enclosed in square
    brackets. The anonymous arrays are stored at a memory location that can be accessed
    by using the arrow notation.
2   The values of each key are printed as hexadecimal addresses preceded by the data
    type *ARRAY* stored at that location.
3   The third element of the first list is retrieved by placing an arrow after the hash key,
    Math, that points to the index of the anonymous array. Since indices start at zero,
    $grades{Math}–>[2] references the third element of the array.
4   To access the entire list of *Science* grades, the key/value pair is enclosed in curly
    braces and prepended with an @ symbol.

Array of Hashes.   An array can contain nested hashes. It's like an array of records. Each of the elements of the array is an anonymous hash with a set of keys and corresponding values.

EXAMPLE 4.25

```
(The Script)
    # An array of hashes
1   @stores=( { Boss =>"Ari Goldberg",
                Employees => 24,
                Registers => 10,
                Sales => 15000.00,
              },
2             { Boss =>"Ben Chien",
                Employees => 12,
                Registers => 5,
                Sales => 3500.00,
              },
    );
3   print "The number of elements in the array: ",
4       $#stores + 1, "\n";   # The number of the last subscript + 1

5   for($i=0; $i< $#stores + 1; $i++){
6       print $stores[$i]->{"Boss"},"\n";   # Access an array element
        print $stores[$i]->{"Employees"},"\n";
        print $stores[$i]->{"Registers"},"\n";
        print $stores[$i]->{"Sales"},"\n";
        print "-" x 20 ,"\n";
    }

(Output)
3   The number of elements in the array: 2
6   Ari Goldberg
    24
    10
    15000
    --------------------
    Ben Chien
    12
    5
    3500
    --------------------
```

1   The array @*stores* contains two hashes, one for *Ari Goldberg*'s store and one for *Ben Chien*'s store. Each of the elements of the array is a hash.

2   This is the second element of the @*stores* array. It is a hash.

4   *$#stores* evaluates to the number of the last subscript in the @*stores* array. Since subscripts start at *0*, by adding *1* we get the number of elements in the array, which is *2*.

6   To access a value in one of the elements of the array, first the number of the index is specified and then the key into the hash. The arrow operator is not required here but it makes the program a little more readable.

4.3   Reading from *STDIN*

The three filehandles *STDIN*, *STDOUT*, and *STDERR*, as you may recall, are names given to three predefined streams, *stdin*, *stdout*, and *stderr*. By default, these filehandles are associated with your terminal. When printing output to the terminal screen, *STDOUT* is used. When printing errors, *STDERR* is used. When assigning user input to a variable, *STDIN* is used.

The Perl <> input operator encloses the *STDIN* filehandle so that the next line of standard input can be read from the terminal keyboard and assigned to a variable. Unlike the shell and *C* operations for reading input, Perl retains the newline on the end of the string when reading a line from standard input. If you don't want the newline, then you have to explicitly remove it or "chomp" it off (see "The chop and chomp Functions" on page 67).

4.3.1   Assigning Input to a Scalar Variable

When reading input from the filehandle *STDIN*, if the context is scalar, one line of input is read, including the newline, and assigned to a scalar variable as a single string.

EXAMPLE 4.26

```
(The Script)
    # Getting a line of input from the keyboard.
1   print "What is your name?  ";
2   $name = <STDIN>;
3   print "What is your father's name? ";
4   $paname=<>;
5   print "Hello respected one, $paname";
```

EXAMPLE 4.26 (CONTINUED)

```
(Output)
1   What is your name? Isabel
3   What is your father's name? Nick
5   Hello respected one, Nick
```

EXPLANATION

1   The string *What is your name?* is sent to *STDOUT*, which is the screen by default.
2   The input operator <> (called the diamond operator) surrounding *STDIN* reads one line of input and assigns that line and its trailing newline to the scalar variable *$name*. When input is assigned to a scalar, characters are read until the user presses the Enter key.
3   The string is printed to *STDOUT*.
4   If the input operator is empty, the next line of input is read from *STDIN* and the behavior is identical to line 2, except input is assigned to *$paname*.

4.3.2 The *chop* and *chomp* Functions

The *chop* function removes the last character in a scalar variable and the last character of each word in an array. Its return value is the character it chopped. *Chop* is used primarily to remove the newline from the line of input coming into your program, whether it is *STDIN*, a file, or the result of command substitution. When you first start learning Perl, the trailing newline can be a real pain!

The *chomp* function was introduced in Perl 5 to remove the last character in a scalar variable and the last character of each word in a array **only if** that character is the newline (or, to be more precise, the character that represents the input line separator, initially defined as a newline and stored in the *$/* variable). It returns the number of characters it chomped. Using *chomp* instead of *chop* protects you from inadvertently removing some character other than the newline.

EXAMPLE 4.27

```
(The Script)
    # Getting rid of the trailing newline. Use chomp instead of chop.
1   print "Hello there, and what is your name? ";
2   $name = <STDIN>;
3   print "$name is a very high class name.\n";
4   chop($name);   # Removes the last character no matter what it is.
5   print "$name is a very high class name.\n\n";
6   chop($name);
```

EXAMPLE 4.27 (CONTINUED)

```
7    print "$name has been chopped a little too much.\n";
8    print "What is your age?  ";
9    chomp($age=<STDIN>);  # Removes the last character if
                           # it is the newline.
10   chomp($age);          # The last character is not removed
                           # unless a newline.
11   print "For $age, you look so young!\n";
```

(Output)
```
1    Hello there, and what is your name? Joe Smith
3    Joe Smith
     is a very high class name.
5    Joe Smith is a very high class name.

7    Joe Smit has been chopped a little too much.

8    What is your age? 25
11   For 25, you look so young!
```

EXPLANATION

1   The quoted string is printed to the screen, *STDOUT*, by default.
2   The scalar variable is assigned a single line of text typed in by the user. The <> operator is used for read operations. In this case, it reads from *STDIN*, which is your keyboard, until the carriage return is pressed. The newline is included in the text that is assigned to the variable *$name*.
3   The value of *$name* is printed. Note that the newline breaks the line after *Joe Smith*, the user's input.
4   The *chop* function removes the last character of the string assigned to *$name*. The character that was chopped is returned.
5   The string is printed again after the *chop* operation. The last character was removed (in this case, the newline).
6   This time *chop* will remove the last character in *Joe Smith*'s name, i.e., the *h* in *Smith*.
7   The quoted string is printed to *STDOUT*, indicating that the last character was removed.
9   The user input is first assigned to the variable *$age*. The trailing newline is chomped. The character whose value is stored in the special variable, *$/*, is removed. This value is by default the newline character. The number of characters chomped is returned. Because of the low precedence of the equal (=) operator, parentheses ensure that the assignment occurs before the *chomp* function chomps.
10 The second *chomp* will have no effect. The newline has already been removed and *chomp* removes only the newline. It's safer than using *chop*.
11 The chomped variable string is printed.

4.3.3 The *read* Function

The *read* function[7] allows you to read a number of bytes into a variable from a specified filehandle. If reading from standard input, the filehandle is *STDIN*. The *read* function returns the number of bytes that were read.

FORMAT

```
number_of_bytes = read(FILEHANDLE,buffer,how_many_bytes);
```

EXAMPLE 4.28

```
(The Script)
    # Reading input in a requested number of bytes
1   print "Describe your favorite food in 10 bytes or less.\n";
    print "If you type less than 10 characters, press Ctrl-d on a
    line by itself.\n";
2   $number=read(STDIN, $favorite, 10);
3   print "You just typed: $favorite\n";
4   print "The number of bytes read was $number.\n";

(Output)
1   Describe your favorite food in 10 bytes or less.
    If you type less than 10 characters, press Ctrl-d on a line by
    itself.
    apple pie and ice cream            <-user input
3   You just typed: apple pie
4   The number of bytes read was 10.
```

EXPLANATION

1 The user is asked for input. If he types less than 10 characters, he should press <Ctrl>-d to exit.

2 The *read* function takes three arguments: the first argument is *STDIN*, the place from where the input is coming; the second argument is the scalar *$favorite*, where the input will be stored; and the third argument is the number of characters (bytes) that will be read.

3 The 10 characters read in are printed. The rest of the characters were discarded.

4 The number of characters (bytes) actually read was stored in *$number* and is printed.

---

7. The *read* function is similar to the *fread* function in the *C* language.

4.3.4   The *getc* Function

The *getc* function gets a single character from the keyboard or from a file. At EOF, *getc* returns a null string.

FORMAT

```
getc(FILEHANDLE)
getc FILEHANDLE
getc
```

EXAMPLE 4.29

```
(The Script)
    # Getting only one character of input
    print "Answer y or n   ";
1   $answer=getc;      # Gets one character from stdin
2   $restofit=<>;      # What remains in the input buffer is
                       # assigned to $restofit
3   print "$answer\n";
4   print "The characters left in the input buffer were:
            $restofit\n";

(Output)
1   Answer  y or n   yessirreebob <ENTER>
3   y
4   The characters left in the input buffer were: essirreebob
```

EXPLANATION

1   Only one character is read from the input buffer by *getc* and stored in the scalar *$answer*.
2   The characters remaining in the input buffer are stored in *$restofit*. This clears the input buffer. Now, if you ask for input later in the program, you will not be picking up those characters that were left hanging around in the buffer.
3   The character that was read in by *getc* is printed.
4   The characters stored in *$restofit* are displayed.

4.3.5   Assigning Input to an Array

When reading input from the filehandle *STDIN*, if the context is an array, then each line is read with its newline and is treated as a single list item, and the read is continued until you press <Ctrl>-d (in UNIX) or <Ctrl>-z (in Windows) for end of file (EOF). Normally, you will not assign input to an array because it could eat up a large amount of memory or because the user of your program may not realize that he should press <Ctrl>-d or <Ctrl>-z to stop reading input.

EXAMPLE 4.30

```
(The Script)
    # Assigning input to an array
1   print "Tell me everything about yourself.\n ";
2   @all = <STDIN>;
3   print "@all";
4   print "The number of elements in the array are: ",
           $#all + 1, ".\n";
5   print "The first element of the array is:
    $all[0]";


(Output)
1   Tell me everything about yourself.
2   OK. Let's see I was born before computers.
    I grew up in the 50s.
    I was in the hippie generation.
    I'm starting to get bored with talking about myself.
    <Ctrl>-d
3   OK. Let's see I was born before computers.
    I grew up in the 50s.
    I was in the hippie generation.
    I'm starting to get bored with talking about myself.
4   The number of elements in the array are: 4.
5   The first element of the array is:
    OK. Let's see I was born before computers.
```

EXPLANATION

1   The string *Tell me everything about yourself.* is printed to *STDOUT*.
2   The input operator <> surrounding *STDIN* reads input lines until <Ctrl>-d, EOF, is reached. (For Windows users, use <Ctrl>-z instead of <Ctrl>-d.) Each line and its trailing newline are stored as a list element of the array *@all*.
3   The user input is printed to the screen after the user presses <Ctrl>-d or <Ctrl>-z.
4   The $# construct lets you get the last subscript or index value in the array. By adding *1* to $#all, the size of the array is obtained; i.e., the number of lines that were read.
5   $all[0] is the first element of the array which evaluates to the first line of input from the user. Each line read is an element of the array.

4.3.6   Assigning Input to a Hash

EXAMPLE 4.31

```
(The Script)
    # Assign input to a hash
1   $course_number=101;
2   print "What is the name of course 101?";
3   chomp($course{$course_number} = <STDIN>);
4   print %course, "\n";

(Output)
2   What is the name of course 101? Linux Administration
4   101Linux Administration
```

EXPLANATION

1   The scalar variable *$course_number* is assigned the value *101*.
2   The string *What is the name of course 101?* is printed to *STDOUT*.
3   The name of the hash is *%course*. We are assigning a value to one of the hash elements. The key is *$course_number* enclosed in curly braces. The *chomp* function will remove the newline from the value assigned by the user.
4   The new array is printed. It has one key and one value.

4.4   Array Functions

Arrays can grow and shrink. The Perl array functions allow you to insert or delete elements of the array from the front, middle, or end of the list.

4.4.1   The *chop* and *chomp* Functions (with Lists)

The *chop* function chops off the last character of a string and returns the chopped character, usually for removing the newline after input is assigned to a scalar variable. If a list is chopped, *chop* will remove the last letter of each string in the list.

The *chomp* function removes the last character of each element in a list if it ends with a newline and returns the number of newlines it removed.

FORMAT

```
chop(LIST)
chomp(LIST)
```

EXAMPLE 4.32

```
(In the Script)
    # Chopping and chomping a list
1   @line=("red", "green", "orange");
2   chop(@line);     # Chops the last character off each
                     # string in the list
3   print "@line";
4   @line=( "red", "green", "orange");
5   chomp(@line);    # Chomps the newline off each string in the list
6   print "@line";

(Output)
3   re gree orang
6   red green orange
```

EXPLANATION

1   The array *@line* is assigned list elements.
2   The array is chopped. The *chop* function chops the last character from each element of the array.
3   The chopped array is printed.
4   The array *@line* is assigned elements.
5   The *chomp* function will chop off the newline character from each word in the array. This is a safer function than *chop*.
6   Since there were no newlines on the end of the words in the array, it was not chomped.

4.4.2   The *exists* Function

The *exists* function returns **true** if an array index (or hash key) has been defined, and **false** if it has not.

FORMAT

```
exists $ARRAY[index];
```

EXAMPLE 4.33

```
    #!/usr/bin/perl
1   @names = qw(Tom Raul Steve Jon);
2   print "Hello $names[1]\n", if exists $names[1];
3   print "Out of range!\n", if not exists $names[5];

(Output)
2   Hello Raul
3   Out of range!
```

EXPLANATION

1   An array of names is assigned to *@names*.
2   If the index, *1*, is defined, the *exists* function returns true and the string is printed.
3   If the index, *5*, does not exist (and in this example it doesn't) then the string *Out of range!* is printed.

4.4.3 The *delete* Function

The *delete* function allows you to remove a value from an element of an array, but not the element itself. The value deleted is simply undefined.

4.4.4 The *grep* Function

The *grep* function evaluates the expression (*EXPR*) for each element of the array (*LIST*). The return value is another array consisting of those elements for which the expression evaluated as true. As a scalar value, the return value is the number of times the expression was true (i.e., the number of times the pattern was found).

FORMAT

```
grep(EXPR,LIST)
```

EXAMPLE 4.34

```
(The Script)
    # Searching for patterns in a list
1   @list = (tomatoes, tomorrow, potatoes, phantom, Tommy);
2   $count = grep( /tom/i, @list);
    @items= grep( /tom/i, @list);
    print "Found items: @items\nNumber found: $count\n";

(Output)
4   Found items: tomatoes tomorrow phantom Tommy
    Number found: 4
```

EXPLANATION

1   The array *@list* is assigned list elements.
2   The *grep* function searches for the regular expression *tom*. The *i* turns off case sensitivity. When the return value is assigned to a scalar, the result is the number of times the regular expression was matched.
3   *grep* again searches for the regular expression *tom*. The *i* turns off case sensitivity. When the return value is assigned to an array, the result is a list of the matched items.

4.4.5 The *join* Function

The *join* function joins the elements of an array into a single string and separates each element of the array with a given delimiter—the opposite of *split* (see "The split Function" on page 83). It can be used after the *split* function has broken a string into array elements. The expression *DELIMITER* is the value of the delimiter that will separate the array elements. The *LIST* consists of the array elements.

FORMAT

```
join(DELIMITER, LIST)
```

EXAMPLE 4.35

```
(The Script)
    # Joining each elements of a list with colons
1   $name="Joe Blow";
    $birth="11/12/86";
    $address="10 Main St.";
2   print join(":", $name, $birth, $address ), "\n";

(Output)
2   Joe Blow:11/12/86:10 Main St.
```

EXPLANATION

1   A string is assigned to a scalar.
2   The *join* function joins the three scalars using a colon delimiter and the new string is printed.

EXAMPLE 4.36

```
(The Script)
    # Joining each element of a list with a newline
1   @names=('Dan','Dee','Scotty','Liz','Tom');
2   @names=join("\n", sort(@names));
3   print @names,"\n";

(Output)
3   Dan
    Dee
    Liz
    Scotty
    Tom
```

EXPLANATION

1   The array @*names* is assigned a list.
2   The *join* function will *join* each word in the list with a newline (\n) after the list has
    been sorted alphabetically.
3   The sorted list is printed with each element of the array on a line of its own.

4.4.6 The *map* Function

The *map* function maps each of the values in an array to an expression or block, returning
another array with the results of the mapping. This is easier to demonstrate in an example
than to describe in words.

FORMAT

```
map EXPR, LIST;
map {BLOCK} LIST;
```

EXAMPLE 4.37

```
(The Script)
    # Mapping a list to an expression
1   @list=(0x53,0x77,0x65,0x64,0x65,0x6e,012);
2   @words = map chr, @list;
3   print @words;
4   @n = (2, 4, 6, 8);
5   @n = map $_ * 2 + 6, @n;
6   print "@n\n";

(Output)
3   Sweden
6   10 14 18 22
```

EXPLANATION

1   The array @*list* consists of six hexadecimal numbers and one octal number.
2   The *map* function maps each item in @*list* to its corresponding *chr* (character) value
    and returns a new list.
3   The new list is printed. Each numeric value was converted with the *chr* function to a
    character corresponding to its ASCII value.
4   The array @*n* consists of a list of integers.
5   The *map* function evaluates the expression for each element in the @*n* array and re-
    turns the new list to @*n*, resulting from the evaluation.
6   The results of the mapping are printed.

EXAMPLE 4.38

```
(The Script)
    # Map using a block
1   open(FH, "datebook.master") or die;
2   @lines=<FH>;
3   @fields = map { split(":") } @lines;
4   foreach $field (@fields){
5       print $field,"\n";
    }


(Output)
5   Sir Lancelot
    837-835-8257
    474 Camelot Boulevard, Bath, WY 28356
    5/13/69
    24500

    Tommy Savage
    408-724-0140
    1222 Oxbow Court, Sunnyvale, CA 94087
    5/19/66
    34200

    Yukio Takeshida
    387-827-1095
    13 Uno Lane, Asheville, NC 23556
    7/1/29
    57000

    Vinh Tranh
    438-910-7449
    8235 Maple Street, Wilmington, VT 29085
    9/23/63
    68900
```

EXPLANATION

1   The *datebook.master* file is opened for reading from the *FH* filehandle. Each line consists of colon-separated fields terminated by a newline.

2   The contents of the file are read and assigned to *@lines*. Each line of the file is an element of the array.

3   The *map* function uses the block format. The *split* function splits up the array at colons, resulting in a list where each field becomes an element of the array.

4   The *foreach* loop iterates through the array, assigning each element, in turn, to *$field*.

5   The display demonstrates the results of the mapping. Before mapping, the line was:
    Sir Lancelot:837-835-8257:474 Camelot Boulevard, Bath, WY 28356:5/13/69:24500

4.4.7 The *pack* and *unpack* Functions

The *pack* and *unpack* functions have a number of uses. These functions are used to pack a list into a binary structure and then expand the packed values back into a list. When working with files, you can use these functions to create uuencoded files, relational databases, and binary files.

The *pack* function converts a list into a scalar value that may be stored in machine memory. The *TEMPLATE* is used to specify the type of character and how many characters will be formatted. For example, the string *c4* or *cccc* packs a list into 4 unsigned characters and *a14* packs a list into a 14-byte ASCII string, null padded. The *unpack* function converts a binary formatted string into a list, and puts a string back into Perl format.

See also "The pack and unpack Functions" on page 531 for an example.

Table 4.2   The Template *pack* and *unpack*—Types and Values

Template	Description
a	An ASCII string (null padded)
A	An ASCII string (space padded)
b	A bit string (low-to-high order, like *vec*)
B	A bit string (high-to-low order)
c	A signed *char* value
C	An unsigned *char* value
d	A double-precision float in the native format
f	A single-precision float in the native format
h	A hexadecimal string (low nybble first, to high)
H	A hexadecimal string (high nybble first)
i	A signed integer
I	An unsigned integer
l	A signed long value
L	An unsigned long value
n	A short in "network" (big-endian) order
N	A long in "network" (big-endian) order
p	A pointer to a null-terminated string
P	A pointer to a structure (fixed-length string)
q	A signed 64-bit value
Q	An unsigned 64-bit value

Table 4.2   The Template *pack* and *unpack*—Types and Values *(continued)*

Template	Description
s	A signed short value (16-bit)
S	An unsigned short value (16-bit)
u	A uuencoded string
v	A short in "VAX" (little-endian) order
V	A long in "VAX" (little-endian) order
w	A BER compressed unsigned integer in base 128, high bit first
x	A null byte
X	Back up a byte
@	Null fill to absolute position

4.4.8   The *pop* Function

The *pop* function pops off the last element of an array and returns it. The array size is subsequently decreased by one.

FORMAT

```
pop(ARRAY)
pop ARRAY
```

EXAMPLE 4.39

```
(In Script)
      # Removing an element from the end of a list
1   @names=("Bob", "Dan", "Tom", "Guy");
2   print "@names\n";
3   $got = pop(@names);      # Pops off last element of the array
4   print "$got\n";
5   print "@names\n";

(Output)
2   Bob Dan Tom Guy
4   Guy
5   Bob Dan Tom
```

EXPLANATION

1   The @*name* array is assigned list elements.
2   The array is printed.
3   The *pop* function removes the last element of the array and returns the popped item.
4   The *$got* scalar contains the popped item, *Guy*.
5   The new array is printed.

4.4.9   The *push* Function

The *push* function pushes values onto the end of an array, thereby increasing the length of the array.

FORMAT

```
push(ARRAY, LIST)
```

EXAMPLE 4.40

```
(In Script)
    # Adding elements to the end of a list
1   @names=("Bob", "Dan", "Tom", "Guy");
2   push(@names, "Jim", "Joseph", "Archie");
3   print "@names \n";

(Output)
2   Bob Dan Tom Guy Jim Joseph Archie
```

EXPLANATION

1   The array @*names* is assigned list values.
2   The *push* function pushes three more elements onto the end of the array.
3   The new array has three more elements appended to it.

4.4.10   The *shift* Function

The *shift* function shifts off and returns the first element of an array, decreasing the size of the array by one element. If *ARRAY* is omitted, then the *ARGV* array is shifted, and, if in a subroutine, the @_ array is shifted.

FORMAT

```
shift(ARRAY)
shift ARRAY
shift
```

EXAMPLE 4.41

```
(In Script)
    # Removing elements from front of a list
1   @names=("Bob", "Dan", "Tom", "Guy");
2   $ret  = shift @names;
3   print "@names\n";
4   print "The item shifted is $ret.\n";

(Output)
3   Dan Tom Guy
4   The item shifted is Bob.
```

EXPLANATION

1   The array @*names* is assigned list values.
2   The *shift* function removes the first element of the array and returns that element to the scalar *$ret*, which is *Bob*.
3   The new array has been shortened by one element.

4.4.11   The *splice* Function

The *splice* function removes and replaces elements in an array. The *OFFSET* is the starting position where elements are to be removed. The *LENGTH* is the number of items from the *OFFSET* position to be removed. The *LIST* consists of new elements that are to replace the old ones.

FORMAT

```
splice(ARRAY, OFFSET, LENGTH, LIST)
splice(ARRAY, OFFSET, LENGTH)
splice(ARRAY, OFFSET)
```

EXAMPLE 4.42

```
(The Script)
    # Splicing out elements of a list
1   @colors=("red", "green", "purple", "blue", "brown");
2   print "The original array is @colors\n";
3   @discarded = splice(@colors, 2, 2);
4   print "The elements removed after the splice are: @discarded.\n";
5   print "The spliced array is now @colors.\n";

(Output)
2   The original array is red green purple blue brown
4   The elements removed after the splice are: purple blue.
5   The spliced array is now red green brown.
```

EXPLANATION

1   An array of five colors is created.
2   The original array is printed.
3   The *splice* function will delete elements starting at offset 2 (offset is initially 0), re-move the two elements, *purple* and *blue,* and return the removed elements to another array named *@discarded.*
4   The splice removed elements *purple* and *blue* and returned them to *@discarded,* starting at element *$colors[2],* with a length of 2 elements.
5   The array *@colors* has been spliced. *purple* and *blue* were removed.

EXAMPLE 4.43

```
(The Script)
    # Splicing and replacing elements of a list
1   @colors=("red", "green", "purple", "blue", "brown");
2   print "The original array is @colors\n";
3   @lostcolors=splice(@colors, 2, 3, "yellow", "orange");
4   print "The removed items are @lostcolors\n";
5   print "The spliced array is now @colors\n";

(Output)
2   The original array is red green purple blue brown
4   The removed items are purple blue brown
5   The spliced array is now red green yellow orange
```

1 An array of five colors is created.
2 The original array is printed.
3 The *splice* function will delete elements starting at offset 2 (offset is initially 0) and remove the next three elements. The removed elements (*purple*, *blue*, and *brown*) are stored in @*lostcolors*. The colors *yellow* and *orange* will replace the ones that were removed.
4 The values that were removed are stored in @*lostcolors* and printed.
5 The new array, after the splice, is printed.

4.4.12 The *split* Function

The *split* function splits up a string (*EXPR*) by some delimiter (whitespace by default) and returns an array. The first argument is the delimiter, and the second is the string to be split. The Perl *split* function can be used to create fields when processing files, just as you would with *awk*. If a string is not supplied as the expression, the *$_* string is split.

The *DELIMITER* statement matches the delimiters that are used to separate the fields. If *DELIMITER* is omitted, the delimiter defaults to whitespace (spaces, tabs, or newlines). If the *DELIMITER* doesn't match a delimiter, *split* returns the original string. You can specify more than one delimiter using the regular expression metacharacter [ ]. For example, [+\t:] represents zero or more spaces, or a tab, or a colon.

LIMIT specifies the number of fields that can be split. If there are more than *LIMIT* fields, the remaining fields will all be part of the last one. If the *LIMIT* is omitted, the *split* function has its own *LIMIT*, which is one more than the number of fields in *EXPR*. (See the *-a* switch for auto split mode, in Appendix A.)

```
split("DELIMITER",EXPR,LIMIT)
split(/DELIMITER/,EXPR,LIMIT)
split(/DELIMITER/,EXPR)
split("DELIMITER",EXPR)
split(/DELIMITER/)
split
```

```
(The Script)
    # Splitting a scalar on whitespace and creating a list
1   $line="a b c d e";
2   @letter=split(' ',$line);
3   print "The first letter is $letter[0]\n";
4   print "The second letter is $letter[1]\n";
```

EXAMPLE 4.44 (CONTINUED)

```
(Output)
3    The first letter is a
4    The second letter is b
```

EXPLANATION

1   The scalar variable *$line* is assigned the string *a b c d e*.
2   The value in *$line* (scalar) is a single string of letters. The *split* function will split the string using whitespace as a delimiter. The *@letter* array will be assigned the individual elements *a*, *b*, *c*, *d*, and *e*. Using single quotes as the delimiter is **not** the same as using the regular expression */ /*. The ' ' resembles *awk* in splitting lines on whitespace. Leading whitespace is ignored. The regular expression */ /* includes leading whitespace, creating as many null initial fields as there are whitespaces.
3   The first element of the *@letter* array is printed.
4   The second element of the *@letter* array is printed.

EXAMPLE 4.45

```
(The Script)
   # Splitting up $_
1  while(<DATA>){
2      @line=split(":");        # or split (":", $_);
3      print "$line[0]\n";
   }


_ _DATA_ _
Betty Boop:245-836-8357:635 Cutesy Lane, Hollywood, CA 91464:6/23/23:14500
Igor Chevsky:385-375-8395:3567 Populus Place, Caldwell, NJ 23875:6/18/68:23400
Norma Corder:397-857-2735:74 Pine Street, Dearborn, MI 23874:3/28/45:245700
Jennifer Cowan:548-834-2348:583 Laurel Ave., Kingsville, TX 83745:10/1/35:58900
Fred Fardbarkle:674-843-1385:20 Park Lane, Duluth, MN 23850:4/12/23:78900


(Output)
Betty Boop
Igor Chevsky
Norma Corder
Jennifer Cowan
Fred Fardbarkle
```

EXPLANATION

1   The *$_* variable holds each line of the file *DATA* filehandle; the data being processed is below the _ _*DATA*_ _ line. Each line is assigned to *$_*. *$_* is also the default line for *split*.
2   The *split* function splits the line, (*$_*), using the *:* as a delimiter and returns the line to the array, *@line*.
3   The first element of the *@line* array, *line[0]*, is printed.

EXAMPLE 4.46

```
(The Script)
    # Splitting up $_ and creating an unnamed list
    while(<DATA>){
1       ($name,$phone,$address,$bd,$sal)=split(":");
2       print "$name\t $phone\n" ;
    }

_ _DATA_ _
Betty Boop:245-836-8357:635 Cutesy Lane, Hollywood, CA 91464:6/23/23:14500
Igor Chevsky:385-375-8395:3567 Populus Place, Caldwell, NJ 23875:6/18/68:23400
Norma Corder:397-857-2735:74 Pine Street, Dearborn, MI 23874:3/28/45:245700
Jennifer Cowan:548-834-2348:583 Laurel Ave., Kingsville, TX 83745:10/1/35:58900
Fred Fardbarkle:674-843-1385:20 Park Lane, Duluth, MN 23850:4/12/23:78900

(Output)
2   Betty Boop         245-836-8357
    Igor Chevsky       385-375-8395
    Norma Corder       397-857-2735
    Jennifer Cowan     548-834-2348
    Fred Fardbarkle    674-843-1385
```

EXPLANATION

1   Perl loops through the *DATA* filehandle one line at a time. Each line of the file is stored in the *$_* variable. The *split* function splits each line, using the colon as a delimiter.
2   The array consists of five scalars, *$name*, *$phone*, *$address*, *$bd*, and *$sal*. The values of *$name* and *$phone* are printed.

EXAMPLE 4.47

```
(The Script)
    # Many ways to split a scalar to create a list
1   $string= "Joe Blow:11/12/86:10 Main St.:Boston, MA:02530";
2   @line=split(":", $string);      # The string delimiter is a colon
3   print @line,"\n";
4   print "The guy's name is $line[0].\n";
5   print "The birthday is $line[1].\n\n";

6   @str=split(":", $string, 2);
7   print $str[0],"\n";  # The first element of the array
8   print $str[1],"\n";  # The rest of the array because limit is 2
9   print $str[2],"\n";  # Nothing is printed

10  @str=split(":", $string);     # Limit not stated will be one more
                                  # than total number of fields
11  print $str[0],"\n";
12  print $str[1],"\n";
13  print $str[2],"\n";
14  print $str[3],"\n";
15  print $str[4],"\n";
16  print $str[5],"\n";

17  ( $name, $birth, $address )=split(":", $string);
            # Limit is implicitly 4, one more than
            # the number of fields specified
18  print $name , "\n";
19  print $birth,"\n";
20  print $address,"\n";


(Output)
3   Joe Blow11/12/8610 Main St.Boston, MA02530
4   The guy's name is Joe Blow.
5   The birthday is 11/12/86.

7   Joe Blow
8   11/12/86:10 Main St.:Boston, MA:02530
9

11  Joe Blow
12  11/12/86
13  10 Main St.
14  Boston, MA
15  02530
16
18  Joe Blow
19  11/12/86
20  10 Main St.
```

2 The scalar *$string* is split at each colon.
6 The delimiter is a colon. The limit is 2.
10 *LIMIT*, if not stated, will be one more than total number of fields.
17 *LIMIT* is implicitly 4, one more than the number of fields specified.

4.4.13 The *sort* Function

The *sort* function sorts and returns a sorted array. If *SUBROUTINE* is omitted, the sort is in string comparison order. If *SUBROUTINE* is specified, the first argument to *sort* is the name of the subroutine followed by a list of integers. The subroutine returns an integer less than, equal to, or greater than 0. The values are passed to the subroutine by reference and are received by the special variables, *$a* and *$b*, not the normal @_ array.

FORMAT

```
sort(SUBROUTINE LIST)
sort(LIST)
sort SUBROUTINE LIST
sort LIST
```

EXAMPLE 4.48

```
(The Script)
    # Sorting a list
1   @string=(1, 5, 9.5, 10, 1000, a, B, z);
2   @string_sort=sort(@string);
3   print "@string_sort\n";
4   sub numeric { $a <=> $b ; }
5   @number_sort=sort numeric -10, 0, 5, 9.5, 10, 1000;
6   print "@number_sort.\n";

(Output)
3   1 10 1000 5 9.5 B a z
6   -10, 0, 5, 9.5, 10, 1000
```

EXPLANATION

1   The @*string* array will contain a list of items to be sorted.
2   The *sort* function performs a string (ASCII) sort on the items.
3   The sorted string is printed.
4   A subroutine, *numeric,* is defined. The special variables, $a and $b, replace the @_
    in the subroutine and are used with the comparison operator. $a and $b receive the
    numeric values to be sorted.
5   The *sort* function performs a numeric sort by calling the subroutine *numeric* and
    passing a list of numbers. These values are passed by reference.

EXAMPLE 4.49

```
(The Script)
    # Sorting numbers with an unamed subroutine
1   @sorted_numbers= sort {$a <=> $b} (3,4,1,2);
2   print "The sorted numbers are: @sorted_numbers", ".\n";

(Output)
2   The sorted numbers are: 1 2 3 4.
```

EXPLANATION

1   The *sort* function is given an unnamed subroutine, also called an **inline function**, to
    sort a list of numbers passed as arguments. The variables $a and $b are used to com-
    pare the numbers for the numeric sort. $a and $b are special Perl variables, not user-
    defined. The sorted numeric list is returned at stored in the array @*sorted_numbers.*
2   The sorted list is printed.

4.4.14   The *reverse* Function

The *reverse* function reverses the elements in an array, so that if the values appeared in
descending order, now they are in ascending order, and so on.

FORMAT

```
reverse(LIST)
reverse LIST
```

EXAMPLE 4.50

```
(In Script)
    # Reversing the elements of an array
1   @names=("Bob", "Dan", "Tom", "Guy");
2   print "@names \n";
3   @reversed=reverse(@names),"\n";
4   print "@reversed\n";

(Output)
2   Bob Dan Tom Guy
4   Guy Tom Dan Bob
```

EXPLANATION

1   The array @*names* is assigned list values.
2   The original array is printed.
3   The *reverse* function reverses the elements in the list and returns the reversed list. The array @*names* is not changed. The reversed items are stored in @*reversed*.
4   The reversed array is printed.

4.4.15   The *unshift* Function

The *unshift* function prepends *LIST* to the front of the array.

FORMAT

```
unshift(ARRAY, LIST)
```

EXAMPLE 4.51

```
(In Script)
    # Putting new elements at the front of a list
1   @names=("Jody", "Bert", "Tom") ;
2   unshift(@names, "Liz", "Daniel");
3   print "@names\n";

(Output)
3   Liz Daniel Jody Bert Tom
```

EXPLANATION

1   The array @*names* is assigned three values, *Jody, Bert,* and *Tom.*
2   The *unshift* function will prepend *Liz* and *Daniel* to the array.
3   The @*names* array is printed.

4.5   Hash (Associative Array) Functions

4.5.1   The *keys* Function

The *keys* function returns, in random order, an array whose elements are the keys of a hash (see "The values Function" on page 91, and "The each Function" on page 91).

FORMAT

```
keys(ASSOC_ARRAY)
keys ASSOC_ARRAY
```

EXAMPLE 4.52

```
(In Script)
        # The keys function returns the keys of a hash
1    %weekday= (
                '1'=>'Monday',
                '2'=>'Tuesday',
                '3'=>'Wednesday',
                '4'=>'Thursday',
                '5'=>'Friday',
                '6'=>'Saturday',
                '7'=>'Sunday',
            );
2    foreach $key ( keys(%weekday) ){print "$key ";}
     print "\n";
3    foreach $key ( sort keys(%weekday) ){print "$key ";}
     print "\n";

(Output)
2    7 1 2 3 4 5 6
3    1 2 3 4 5 6 7
```

EXPLANATION

1   The hash *%weekday* is assigned keys and values.
2   For each value in *%weekday*, call the *keys* function to get the key. Assign the key value to the scalar *$key* and print it in random order.
3   Now the keys are sorted and printed.

4.5.2   The *values* Function

The *values* function returns, in random order, an array consisting of all the values of a hash.

FORMAT

```
values(ASSOC_ARRAY)
values ASSOC_ARRAY
```

EXAMPLE 4.53

```
(In Script)
    # The values function returns the values in a hash
1   %weekday= (
                '1'=>'Monday',
                '2'=>'Tuesday',
                '3'=>'Wednesday',
                '4'=>'Thursday',
                '5'=>'Friday',
                '6'=>'Saturday',
                '7'=>'Sunday',
                );
2   foreach $value ( values(%weekday)){print "$value";}
    print "\n";

(Output)
2   Monday Tuesday Wednesday Thursday Friday Saturday Sunday
```

EXPLANATION

1   The hash *%weekday* is assigned keys and values.
2   For each value in *%weekday,* call the *values* function to get the value associated with
    each key. Assign that value to the scalar, *$value*, and print it to *STDOUT*.

4.5.3   The *each* Function

The *each* function returns, in random order, a two-element array whose elements are the *key*
and the corresponding *value* of a hash.

FORMAT

```
each(ASSOC_ARRAY)
```

EXAMPLE 4.54

```
(In Script)
#! /usr/bin/perl
# The each function retrieves both keys and values from a hash
1   %weekday=(
                'Mon' => 'Monday',
                'Tue' => 'Tuesday',
                'Wed' => 'Wednesday',
                'Thu' => 'Thursday',
                'Fri' => 'Friday',
                'Sat' => 'Saturday',
                'Sun' => 'Sunday',
            );
2   while(($key,$value)=each(%weekday)){
3       print "$key = $value\n";
    }

(Output)
3   Sat = Saturday
    Fri = Friday
    Sun = Sunday
    Thu = Thursday
    Wed = Wednesday
    Tue = Tuesday
    Mon = Monday
```

EXPLANATION

1   The hash *%weekday* is assigned keys and values.
2   The *each* function returns each key and its associated *value* of the *%weekday* hash. They are assigned to the scalars *$key* and *$value*, respectively.
3   The keys and values are printed, but in an unordered way.

4.5.4 The *delete* Function

The *delete* function deletes a value from a hash. The deleted value is returned if successful.[8]

FORMAT

```
delete $ASSOC_ARRAY{KEY}
```

---

8. If a value in an *%ENV* hash is deleted, the environment is changed. (See "The %ENV Hash" on page 96.)

EXAMPLE 4.55

```
(In Script)
    #!/usr/bin/perl
1   %employees=(
                "Nightwatchman" => "Joe Blow",
                "Janitor" => "Teddy Plunger",
                "Clerk" => "Sally Olivetti",
                );

2   $layoff=delete $employees{"Janitor"};
    print "We had to let $layoff go.\n";
    print "Our remaining staff includes: ";
    print "\n";
    while(($key, $value)=each(%employees)){
        print "$key: $value\n";
    }

(Output)
We had to let Teddy Plunger go.
Our remaining staff includes:
Nightwatchman: Joe Blow
Clerk: Sally Olivetti
```

EXPLANATION

1 A hash is defined with three key/value pairs.
2 The *delete* function deletes an element from the specified hash by specifying the key. *Janitor* is the key. Both key and value are removed.
3 The hash value associated with the key *Janitor* is removed and returned. The value *Teddy Plunger* is returned and assigned to the scalar *$layoff*.

4.5.5 The *exists* Function

The *exists* function returns true if a hash key (or array index) has been defined, and false if not.

FORMAT

```
exists $ASSOC_ARRAY{KEY}
```

EXAMPLE 4.56

```
   #!/usr/bin/perl
1  %employees=( "Nightwatchman" => "Joe Blow",
               "Janitor" => "Teddy Plunger",
               "Clerk" => "Sally Olivetti",
             );

2  print "The Nightwatchman exists.\n" if exists
          $employees{"Nightwatchman"};
3  print "The Clerk exists.\n" if exists $employees{"Clerk"};
4  print "The Boss does not exist.\n" if not exists
   $employees{"Boss"};

(Output)
2  The Nightwatchman exists.
3  The Clerk exists.
4  The Boss does not exist.
```

EXPLANATION

1 A hash is defined with three key/value pairs.
2 If a key *"Nightwatchman"* has been defined, the *exists* function returns true.
3 If a key *"Clerk"* has been defined, the exists function returns true.
4 If the key *"Clerk"* does **not** exist, the return value of the *exists* function is reversed.

4.6   More Hashes

4.6.1   Loading a Hash from a File

EXAMPLE 4.57

```
(The Database)
   1 Steve Blenheim
   2 Betty Boop
   3 Igor Chevsky
   4 Norma Cord
   5 Jon DeLoach
   6 Karen Evich

(The Script)
   #!/usr/bin/perl
   # Loading an Hash from a file.
1  open(NAMES,"emp.names") || die "Can't open emp.names: $!\n";
2  while(<NAMES>){
3      ( $num, $name )= split(' ', $_, 2);
4      $realid{$num} = $name;
   }
5  close NAMES;
```

EXAMPLE 4.57 (CONTINUED)

```
6   while(1){
7       print "Please choose a number from the list of names? ";
8       chomp($num=<STDIN>);
9       last unless $num;
10      print $realid{$num},"\n";
    }
```

```
(Output)
7   Please choose a number from the list of names? 1
10  Steve Blenheim
    Number for which name? 4
    Norma Cord
    Number for which name? 5
    Jon DeLoach
    Number for which name? 2
    Betty Boop
    Number for which name? 6
    Karen Evich
    Number for which name? 8
    Number for which name? 3
    Igor Chevsky
    Number for which name?
    <Ctrl>-d or <Ctrl>-z (Exit the program)
```

EXPLANATION

1   A file called *emp.names* is opened for reading via the *NAMES* filehandle.
2   A line at a time is read from the file via the *while* loop.
3   The line just read in, *$_*, is split into two fields with whitespace (spaces, tabs, and newline) as the delimiter. After splitting up the *$_* line, the *split* function returns a list, *$num* and *$name* (consisting of both the first and last name).
4   An hash called *%realid* is created on the fly with *$num* as the key and *$name* as the value associated with that key. Each time through the loop, a new key/value pair is added to *%realid*.
5   The filehandle is closed.
6   The *while* loop is re-entered.
7   The user is asked for a number to be associated with a name.
8   The number is read from standard input (the keyboard) as the user types it, and is assigned to *$num* and *chomp*ed.
9   The loop exits if *$num* does not have a value.
10 The "name" value, *$name*, associated with the "number" key, *$num*, from the *%realid* hash is printed.

4.6.2 Special Hashes

The %ENV Hash.   The *%ENV* hash contains the environment variables handed to Perl from the parent process, e.g., a shell or a Web server. The key is the name of the environment variable, and the value is what was assigned to it. If you change the value of *%ENV*, you will alter the environment for your Perl script and any processes spawned from it.

EXAMPLE 4.58

```
(In Script)
   #!/usr/bin/perl
1  foreach $key (keys(%ENV){
2      print "$key\n";
   }
3  print "\nYour login name $ENV{'LOGNAME'}\n";
4  $pwd=$ENV{'PWD'};
5  print "\n", $pwd, "\n";
   }


(Output)
2  OPENWINHOME
   MANPATH
   FONTPATH
   LOGNAME
   USER
   TERMCAP
   TERM
   SHELL
   PWD
   HOME
   PATH
   WINDOW_PARENT
   WMGR_ENV_PLACEHOLDER

3  Your login name is ellie

5  /home/jody/home
```

EXPLANATION

1   Iterate through the *foreach* loop to get the keys of the *%ENV* hash.
2   Print the key value.
3   Print the value of the key *LOGNAME*.
4   Assign the value of the key *PWD* to *$pwd*.
5   Print the value of *$pwd*.

The %*SIG* Hash.   The %*SIG* hash allows you to set signal handlers for signals. If, for example, you press <Ctrl>-C when your program is running, that is a signal, identified by the name, *SIGINT.* (See UNIX manual pages for a complete list of signals.) The default action of *SIGINT* is to interrupt your process. The signal handler is a subroutine that is automatically called when a signal is sent to the process. Normally, the handler is used to perform a clean-up operation or to check some flag value before the script aborts. (All signal handlers are assumed to be set in the main package.)

The %*SIG* array only contains values for signals set within the Perl script.

EXAMPLE 4.59

```
(In Script)
    #!/usr/bin/perl
1   sub handler{
2       local($sig) = @_;   # First argument is signal name
        print "Caught SIG$sig -- shutting down\n";
        exit(0);
    }
4   $SIG{'INT'} = 'handler';   # Catch <Ctrl>-c
    print "Here I am!\n";
5   sleep(10);
6   $SIG{'INT'}='DEFAULT';
```

EXPLANATION

1   *handler* is the name of the subroutine. The subroutine is defined.
2   *$sig* is a local variable and will be assigned the signal name.
3   When the *SIGINT* signal arrives, this message will appear, and the script will exit.
4   The value assigned to the key *INT* is the name of the subroutine, *handler.* When the signal arrives, the handler is called.
5   The *sleep* function gives you 10 seconds to press <Ctrl>-c to see what happens.
6   The default action is restored. The default action is to abort the process.

The %*INC* Hash.   The %*INC* hash contains the entries for each filename that has been included via the *do* or *require* functions. The **key** is the filename; the **value** is the location of the actual file found.

4.6.3   Context

In summary, the way that Perl evaluates variables—the "funny" characters—depends on how the variables are being used; they are evaluated by context, either scalar or list.

If the value on the left-hand side of an assignment statement is a scalar, then the expression on the right-hand side is evaluated in a scalar context; whereas if the value on the left-hand side is an array, the right-hand side is evaluated in a list context.

See "Reading from STDIN" on page 66 for a good review of how context is handled. You'll see examples throughout the rest of this book where context plays a major role.

EXERCISE 3
The Funny Characters

1. Write a script called *foods* that will ask the user for his favorite foods. Ask for at least five foods. The list of foods will be stored in a scalar. (At this time you have no way to check how many foods are entered. Don't worry about this.)
   a. Split the scalar and create an array.
   b. Print the array.
   c. Print each of the elements of the array.
   d. Print the number of elements in the array.

2. Create an array slice from three elements of the *food* array and print the values. Write a script called *elective* that will contain a hash.
   a. The keys will be code numbers—*2CPR2B, 1UNX1B, 3SH414, 4PL400*.
   b. The values will be course names, *C Language, Intro to UNIX, Shell Programming, Perl Programming*.
   c. Print the entire array.
   d. Ask the user to type the code number for the course he plans to take this semester and print a line resembling the following:

   You will be taking Shell Programming this semester.

3. Write a script called *tellme* that will print out the names, phones, and salaries of all the people in the *datebook* file. To execute, type at the command line

   tellme datebook

   Output should resemble the following:

   Salary: 14500
   Name: Betty Boop
   Phone: 245–836–8357

4. Modify your *elective* script to produce output resembling that appearing below. The user will be asked to enter registration information and to select an EDP number from a menu. The course name will be printed. It doesn't matter if the user types in the EDP number with upper- or lowercase letters. A message will confirm the user's address and thank him for enrolling.

   Output should resemble the following:

   REGISTRATION INFORMATION FOR SPRING QUARTER
   Today's date is Wed Apr 19 17:40:19 PDT 2000

Please enter the following information:
Your full name: Fred Z. Stachelin
What is your Social Security Number (xxx–xx–xxxx): 004–34–1234
Your address:
   Street: 1424 Hobart St.
   City, State, Zip: Chico, CA 95926

"EDP" NUMBERS AND ELECTIVES:

1UNX1B | Intro to UNIX
_____

4PL400 | Perl Programming
_____

2CPR2B | C Programming
_____

3SH414 | Shell Programming
_____

What is the EDP number of the course you wish to take? 4pl400
The course you will be taking is "Perl Programming".

Registration confirmation will be sent to your address at
   1424 HOBART ST.
   CHICO, CA 95926

Thank you, Fred, for enrolling.

5. Given the array: *@names=qw(Nick Susan Chet Dolly Bill),* write a statement that would
   a. Replace *Susan* and *Chet* with *Ellie*, *Beatrice*, and *Charles*.
   b. Remove *Bill* from the array.
   c. Add *Lewis* and *Izzy* to the end of the array.
   d. Remove *Nick* from the beginning of the array.
   e. Reverse the array.
   f. Add *Archie* to the beginning of the array.
   g. Sort the array.

6. Write a script called *findem* that will
   a. Assign the contents of the *datebook* file to an array. (File is on the CD.)
   b. Ask the user for the name of a person to find. Use the built-in *grep* function to find the elements of the array that contain the person and number of times that person is found in the array. The search will ignore case.
   c. Use the *split* function to get the current phone number.

d. Use the *splice* function to replace the current phone number with the new phone number, or use any of the other built-in array functions to produce output that resembles the following:

Who are you searching for? Karen
What is the new phone number for Karen? 530-222-1255
Karen's phone number is currently 284-758-2857.

Here is the line showing the new phone number:
Karen Evich:530-222-1255:23 Edgecliff Place, Lincoln, NB 92086:7/25/53:85100

Karen was found in the array 3 times.

5

WHERE'S THE OPERATOR?

5.1 About Perl Operators

An **operator** manipulates data objects called **operands**. The operands can be strings, numbers, or a combination of both. Data objects can be manipulated in a number of ways by the large number of operators provided by Perl. Operators are symbols that produce a result based on some rules. Most of the Perl operators are borrowed from the *C* language, although Perl has some additional operators of its own.[1]

5.2 Mixing Data Types

If you have operands of mixed types (i.e., numbers and strings), Perl will make the appropriate conversion by testing whether the operator expects a number or a string for an operand. This is called **overloading** the operator.

    If the operator is a numeric operator, such as an arithmetic operator, and the operand(s) is a string, Perl will convert the string to a decimal floating point value. If there is leading whitespace or trailing non-numeric characters, they will be ignored, and if a string cannot be converted to a number, it will be converted to zero. Likewise, if Perl encounters a string operator and the operand(s) is numeric, Perl will treat the number as a string.

---

1. The operators can be symbols or words. Perl 5 functions can be used as operators if the parentheses are omitted.

Table 5.1   How Strings Are Converted to Numbers

String	→ Converts to →	Number
"123 go!"		*123*
"hi there"		*0*
"4e3"		*4000*
"-6**3xyz"		*–6*
" .456!!"		*0.456*
"x.1234"		*0*
"0xf"		*0*

EXAMPLE 5.1

```
(The Script)
1   $x = "    12hello!!" + "4abc\n";
2   print "$x";
3   print "\n";

4   $y = ZAP . 5.5;
5   print "$y\n";

(Output)
2   16
5   ZAP5.5
```

EXPLANATION

1   The plus sign (+) is a numeric operator. The strings *"   12hello!!"* and *"4abc\n"* are converted to numbers (leading whitespace and trailing non-numeric characters are removed) and addition is performed. The result is stored in the scalar *$x*.

2   The scalar *$x* is printed.

3   Since the \n was stripped from the string *4\n* in order to convert it to a number, another \n is needed to get the newline in the printout.

4   The period (.), when surrounded by whitespace, is a string operator. It concatenates two strings. The number *5.5* is converted to a string and concatenated to the string *ZAP*.

5   The value of the scalar *$y* is printed.

5.3 Precedence and Associativity

When an expression contains a number of operators and operands, and the result of the operation is potentially ambiguous, the order of precedence and associativity tells you how the compiler evaluates such an expression. **Precedence** refers to the way is which the operator binds to its operand. The multiplication operator binds more tightly to its operands than the addition operator, so it is of higher precedence, whereas the assignment operators are low in precedence and thus bind loosely to their operands.[2] Parentheses are of the highest precedence and are used to control the way an expression is evaluated. When parentheses are nested, the expression contained within the innermost set of parentheses is evaluated first.

Associativity refers to the order in which an operator evaluates its operands: left to right, in no specified order, or right to left.

In the following example, how is the expression evaluated? Is addition, multiplication, or division done first? And in what order—right to left or left to right?

EXAMPLE 5.2

```
(The Script)
1   $x = 5 + 4  * 12 / 4;
2   print "The result is  $x\n";

(Output)
2   The result is 17
```

EXPLANATION

1   The order of associativity is from left to right. Multiplication and division are of a higher precedence than addition and subtraction, and addition and subtraction are of higher precedence than assignment. To illustrate this, we'll use parentheses to group the operands as they are handled by the compiler. In fact, if you want to force precedence, use the parentheses around the expression to group the operands in the way you want them evaluated.

```
$x = (5 + ( ( 4 * 12 ) / 4));
```

2   The expression is evaluated and the result is printed to *STDOUT*.

Table 5.2 summarizes the rules of precedence and associativity for the Perl operators. The operators on the same line are of equal precedence. The rows are in order of highest to lowest precedence.

---

2. An easy rule to remember precedence: **P**lease **E**xcuse **M**y **D**ear **A**unt **S**ally, which stands for **P**arentheses, **E**xponentiation, **M**ultiplication, **D**ivision, **A**ddition, and **S**ubstraction.

Table 5.2   Precedence and Associativity

Operator	Description	Associativity
() [ ] { }	Function call, array subscripts	Left to right
–>	De-referencing operator	Left to right
++ – –	Auto increment, decrement	None
**	Exponentiation	Right to left
! ~ \ + –	Logical *not*, bitwise *not*, backslash, unary plus, unary minus	Right to left
=~ !~	Match and not match	Left to right
* / % x	Multiply, divide, modulus, string repetition	Left to right
+ – .	Add, subtract, string concatenation	Left to right
<< >>	Bitwise left shift, right shift	Left to right
-r -w -x -o etc.	Named unary operators; e.g., file test operators	None
< <= > >= lt le gt ge	Numeric and string tests, e.g., less than, greater than, etc.	None
== != <=> eq ne cmp	Numeric and string tests, e.g., equal to, not equal to, etc.	None
&	Bitwise *and*	Left to right
| ^	Bitwise *or*, exclusive *or* (*xor*)	Left to right
&&	Logical *and*	Left to right
||	Logical *or*	Left to right
..	Range operator	None
? :	Ternary, conditional	Right to left
= += -= *= /= %=	Assignment	Right to left
, =>	Evaluate left operand, discard it, and evaluate right operand	Left to right
not	Synonym for ! with lower precedence	Right
and	Synonym for &&	Left to right
or xor	Synonym for ||, ^	Left to right

5.3.1   Assignment Operators

The = sign is an assignment operator. The value on the right-hand side of the equal sign is assigned to the variable on the left-hand side. Table 5.3 illustrates assignment and shortcut assignment statements borrowed from the *C* language.

Table 5.3   Assignment Operators

Operator	Example	Meaning
=	$var = 5;	Assign 5 to $var
+=	$var += 3;	Add 3 to $var and assign result to $var
−=	$var -= 2;	Subtract 2 from $var and assign result to $var
.=	$str.="ing";	Concatenate *ing* to $str and assign result to $str
*=	$var *= 4;	Multiply $var by 4 and assign result to $var
/=	$var /= 2;	Divide $var by 2 and assign result to $var
**=	$var **= 2;	Square $var and assign result to $var
%=	$var %= 2;	Divide $var by 2 and assign remainder to $var
x=	$str x= 20;	Repeat value of $str 20 times and assign result to $str
<<=	$var <<= 1;	Left-shift bits in $var one position and assign result to $var
>>=	$var>>= 2;	Right-shift bits in $var two positions and assign result to $var
&=	$var &= 1;	One is bitwise-*AND*ed to $var and the result is assigned to $var
|=	$var |= 2;	Two is bitwise-*OR*ed to $var and the result is assigned to $var
^=	$var ^= 2;	Two is bitwise-exclusive *OR*ed to $var and the result is assigned to $var

EXAMPLE 5.3

```
(The Script)
    #!/usr/bin/perl
1   $name="Dan";
    $line="*";
    $var=0;          # Assign 0 to var

2   $var += 3;       # Add 3 to $var; same as $var=$var+3
    print  "\$var += 3 is $var \n";

3   $var -= 1;       # Subtract 1 from $var
    print "\$var -= 1 is $var\n";
```

EXAMPLE 5.3 (CONTINUED)

```
4    $var **= 2;          # Square $var
     print "\$var squared is $var\n";

5    $var %= 3;           # Modulus
     print "The remainder of \$var/3 is $var\n";

6    $name .= "ielle";   # Concatenate string "Dan" and "ielle"
     print "$name is the girl's version of Dan.\n";

7    $line x= 10;         # Repetition; print 10 stars
     print "$line\n";

8    printf "\$var is %.2f\n", $var=4.2 + 4.69;

(Output)
2    $var += 3 is 3
3    $var -=1 is 2
4    $var squared is 4
5    The remainder of $var/3 is 1
6    Danielle is the girl's version of Dan.
7    **********
8    $var is 8.89
```

EXPLANATION

1 Values on the right-hand side of the equal sign are assigned to scalar variables on the left-hand side of the equal sign.
2 The shortcut assignment operator, +=, adds three to the scalar $var. This is equivalent to $var = $var + 3;
3 The shortcut assignment operator, -=, subtracts one from the scalar $var. This is equivalent to $var = $var – 1;
4 The shortcut assignment operator, **, squares the scalar $var. This is equivalent to $var = $var ** 2;
5 The shortcut assignment modulus operator, %, yields the integer amount that remains after the scalar $var is divided by three. The operator is called the modulus operator or remainder operator. The expression $var% = 3 is equivalent to $var = $var % 3;
6 The shortcut assignment operator, ., concatenates the string "ielle" to the string value of the scalar, $name. This is equivalent to $name = $name . "ielle"
7 The repetition operator takes two operands. The operand on the right is the number of times that the string operand on the left is repeated. The value of the scalar $line, an asterisk (*), is repeated ten times.
8 The *printf* function is used to format and print the result of the addition of two floating point numbers.

5.3.2   Relational Operators

Relational operators are used to compare operands. The result of the comparison is either **true** or **false**. Perl has two classes of relational operators: one set that compares numbers and another that compares strings.

The expression *(5 > 4 > 2)* will produce a syntax error because there is no associativity. (See Table 5.2.)

Numeric.   Table 5.4 contains a list of numeric relational operators.

Table 5.4   Relational Operators and Numeric Values

Operator	Example	Meaning
>	$x > $y	$x is greater than $y
>=	$x >= $y	$x is greater than or equal to $y
<	$x < $y	$x is less than $y
<=	$x <= $y	$x is less than or equal to $y

EXAMPLE 5.4

```
(The Script)
    $x = 5;
    $y = 4;
1   $result = $x > $y;
2   print "$result\n";

3   $result = $x < $y;
4   print $result;

(Output)
2   1
4   0
```

EXPLANATION

1   If *$x* is greater than *$y*, the value *1* (true) is returned and stored in *$result*; otherwise *0* (false) is returned.
2   Since the expression was true, the value of *$result*, *1*, is printed to *STDOUT*.
3   If *$x* is less than *$y*, the value *1* (true) is returned and stored in *$result;* otherwise *0* (false) is returned.
4   Since the expression was false, the value of *$result*, *0*, is printed to *STDOUT*.

String.   The string relational operators evaluate their operands (strings) by comparing the ASCII value of each character in the first string with the corresponding character in the second string. The comparison includes trailing whitespace.

If the first string contains a character that is of a higher or lower ASCII value than the corresponding character in the second string, the value *1* is returned; otherwise *0* is returned.

Table 5.5 contains a list of relational string operators.

Table 5.5   Relational Operators and String Values

Operator	*Example*	*Meaning*
gt	$str1 gt $str2	$str1 is greater than $str2
ge	$str1 ge $str2	$str1 is greater than or equal to $str2
lt	$str1 lt $str2	$str1 is less than $str2
le	$str1 le $str2	$str1 is less than or equal to $str2

EXAMPLE 5.5

```
(The Script)
1   $fruit1 = "pear";
2   $fruit2 = "peaR";
3   $result = $fruit1 gt $fruit2;
4   print "$result\n";

5   $result = $fruit1 lt $fruit2;
6   print "$result\n";

(Output)
4   1
6   0
```

EXPLANATION

1   The scalar *$fruit1* is assigned the string value *pear*.
2   The scalar *$fruit2* is assigned the string value *peaR*.
3   When lexographically comparing each of the characters in *$fruit1* and *$fruit2*, all of the characters are equal until the *r* and *R* are compared. The ASCII value of the lowercase *r* is 114 and the ASCII value of the uppercase *R* is 82. Since 114 is greater than 82, the result of evaluating the strings is *1* (true); i.e., *pear* is greater than *peaR*.
4   Since the expression was true, the value of *$result*, *1*, is printed to *STDOUT*.
5   This is the reverse of #3. The ASCII value of uppercase *R* (82) is less than the value of the lowercase *r* (114). The result of evaluating the two strings is *0* (false); i.e., *pear* is less than *peaR*.
6   Since the expression was false, the value of *$result*, *0*, is printed to *STDOUT*.

5.3.3 Equality Operators

The equality operators evaluate numeric operands and string operands. (See Tables 5.6 and 5.7.)

Numeric.   The numeric equality operators evaluate their operands (numbers) by comparing their numeric values. If the operands are equal, *1* (true) is returned; if the operands are not equal, *0* (false) is returned.

The numeric comparison operator evaluates its operands, returning a *–1* if the first operand is less than the second operand, *0* if the numbers are equal, or *1* if the first operand is greater than the second.

Table 5.6   Equality Operators and Numeric Values

Operator	Example	Meaning
==	$num1 == $num2	$num1 is equal to $num2
!=	$num1 != $num2	$num1 is not equal to $num2
<=>	$num1 <=> $num2	$num1 is compared to $num2 with a signed return; *1* if $num1 isgreater than $num2, *0* if $num1 is equal to $num2, and *–1* if $num1 is less than $num2

EXAMPLE 5.6

```
(The Script)
    $x = 5;
    $y = 4;
1   $result = $x == $y;
2   print "$result\n";

3   $result = $x != $y;
4   print "$result\n";

5   $result = $x <=> $y;
6   print "$result\n";

7   $result = $y <=> $x;
8   print "$result\n";

(Output)
2   0
4   1
6   1
8   -1
```

EXPLANATION

1. If $x is equal to $y, the value *1* (true) is returned and stored in $result; otherwise, *0* (false) is returned.
2. Since the expression was not true, the value of $result, *0*, is printed to *STDOUT*.
3. If $x is not equal to $y, the value *1* (true) is returned and stored in $result; otherwise, *0* (false) is returned.
4. Since the expression was true, the value of $result, *1*, is printed to *STDOUT*.
5. The scalars, $x and $y, are compared. If $x is greater than $y, *1* is returned; if $x is equal to $y, *0* is returned; if $x is less than $y, a signed *–1* is returned.
6. Since $x is greater than $y, the value of $result, *1*, is printed to *STDOUT*.
7. The scalars, $x and $y, are compared. If $y is greater than $x, *1* is returned; if $x is equal to $y, *0* is returned; if $y is less than $x, a signed *–1* is returned.
8. Since $x is less than $y, the value of $result, *–1*, is printed to *STDOUT*.

String. The string equality operators evaluate their operands (strings) by comparing the ASCII value of each character in the first string with the corresponding character in the second string. The comparison includes trailing whitespace.

If the first string contains a character that is of a higher ASCII value than the corresponding character in the second string, the value *1* is returned; if the strings are equal, *0* is returned; if the first string character has a lesser ASCII value than the corresponding character in the second string, *–1* is returned. (See Table 5.7.)

Table 5.7 Equality Operators and String Values

Operator	Example	Meaning
eq	$str1 eq $str2	$str1 is equal to $str2
ne	$str1 ne $str2	$str1 is not equal to $str2
cmp	$str1 cmp $str2	$str1 is compared to $str2, with a signed return

EXAMPLE 5.7

```
(The Script)
1   $str1 = "A";
    $str2 = "C";
    $result = $str1 eq $str2;
    print "$result\n";

2   $result = $str1 ne $str2;
    print "$result\n";

3   $result = $str1 cmp $str2;
    print "$result\n";

4   $result = $str2 cmp $str1;
    print "$result\n";

5   $str1 = "C";        # Now both strings are equal
6   $result = $str1 cmp $str2;
    print "$result\n";

(Output)
1   0
2   1
3   -1
4   1
6   0
```

EXPLANATION

1   The scalar *$str1* is assigned the value *A* and scalar *$str2* is assigned the value *C*. If *$str1* is **equal** to *$str2*, the value *1* (true) is returned, assigned to *$result*, and printed.

2   If *$str1* is **not equal** to *$str2*, the value *1* (true) is returned, assigned to *$result*, and printed.

3   If *$str1* is compared with *$str2* (i.e., an ASCII comparison is made on each character), and all characters are the same, the value *0* is returned and assigned to *$result*. If *$str1* is greater than *$str2*, the value *1* is returned, and if *$str1* is less than *$str2*, *–1* is returned. In this example, *$str1* is less than *$str2*. The value of *$result* is printed.

4   In this example, we reverse the order of comparison. Since *$str2* is greater than *$str1*, the result is *1*. The value of *$result* is printed.

5   *$str1* is assigned *C*. It has the same value as *$str2*.

6   Now *$str1* and *$str2* are equal. Since all of the characters are the same, the value *0* is returned and assigned to *$result*. The value of *$result* is printed.

EXAMPLE 5.8

```
(The Script)
    # Don't use == when you should use eq!
1   $x = "yes";
    $y = "no";
    print "\nIs yes equal to no? If so, say 1; if not say 'null'.\n";
2   print "The result is: ",$x == $y,"\n";      # Should be $x eq $y

(Output)
1   Is yes equal to no? If so, say 1; if not say 'null'.
2   The result is: 1
```

EXPLANATION

1   The scalars *$x* and *$y* are assigned string values *yes* and *no*, respectively.
2   The numeric equality operator, ==, is being used incorrectly to test the equality of
    two strings. The strings are converted to numbers. Since the characters are non-
    numeric, the result is to convert each string to *0* (zero). *0* is equal to *0*, resulting in *1*
    (true). The string equality operator *eq* should have been used in this test.

5.3.4   Logical Operators (Short-Circuit Operators)

The short-circuit operators evaluate their operands, from left to right, testing the truth or fal-
sity of each operand in turn. There is no further evaluation once a true or false condition is
satisfied. Unlike *C*, the short-circuit operators do not return *0* (false) or *1* (true), but rather
the **value** of the last operand evaluated. These operators are most often used in conditional
statements. (See Chapter 6, "If Only, Unconditionally, Forever.")

If the expression on the left-hand side of the *&&* evaluates to *0*, the expression is false
and *0* is returned. If the expression on the left-hand side of the operator evaluates to true
(non-zero), the right-hand side is evaluated and its value is returned.

The logical operators can also be represented as *and*, *or*, or *not*, but the precedence for
them is **lower**. See Table 5.2 on page 104. If the expression on the left-hand side of the ||
operator is evaluated as true (non-zero), the value of the expression is returned. If the value
on the left-hand side of the || is false, the value of the expression on the right-hand side of
the operator is evaluated, and its value is returned.

A list of logical operators can be found in Table 5.8.

Table 5.8   Logical Operators (Short-Circuit Operators)

Operator	*Alternate Form*	*Example*	*Meaning*
&&	*and*	*$x **&&** $y*	If *$x* is true, evaluate *$y* and return *$y*
		*$x **and** $y*	If *$x* is false, evaluate *$x* and return *$x*
||	*or*	*$x || $y*	If *$x* is true, evaluate *$x* and return *$x*
		*$x **or** $y*	If *$x* is false, evaluate *$y* and return *$y*
	xor	*$x **xor** $y*	True if *$x **or** $y* is true, but not both
!	*not*	*! $x*	Not *$x*; true if *$x* is not true
		***not** $x*	

EXAMPLE 5.9

```
(The Script)
    #!/usr/bin/perl
    # Short-circuit operators
1   $num1=50;
2   $num2=100;
3   $num3=0;

4   print $num1 && $num3, "\n";    # result is 0
5   print $num3 && $num1, "\n";    # result is 0
6   print $num1 && $num2, "\n";    # result is 100
7   print $num2 && $num1, "\n\n";  # result is 50

8   print $num1 || $num3, "\n";    # result is 50
9   print $num3 || $num1, "\n";    # result is 50
10  print $num1 || $num2, "\n";    # result is 50
11  print $num2 || $num1, "\n";    # result is 100

(Output)
4   0
5   0
6   100
7   50
8   50
9   50
10  50
11  100
```

EXPLANATION

1   The scalar *$num1* is assigned the value *50*.
2   The scalar *$num2* is assigned the value *100*.
3   The scalar *$num3* is assigned the value *0*.
4   Since the expression to the left of the *&&* operator, *$num1*, is non-zero (true), the expression to the right of the *&&*, *$num3*, is returned.
5   Since the expression to the left of the *&&* operator, *$num3*, is zero (false), the expression *$num3* is returned.
6   Since the expression to the left of the *&&* operator, *$num1*, is true (true), the expression on the right-hand side of the *&&* operator, *$num2*, is returned.
7   Since the expression to the left of the *&&* operator, *$num2*, is true (true), the expression on the right-hand side of the *&&* operator, *$num1*, is returned.
8   Since the expression to the left of the *||* operator, *$num1*, is non-zero (true), the expression *$num1* is returned.
9   Since the expression to the left of the *||* operator, *$num3*, is zero (false), the expression to the right of the *||* operator, *$num1*, is returned.
10 Since the expression to the left of the *||* operator, *$num*1, is non-zero (true), the expression *$num1* is returned.
11 Since the expression to the left of the *||* operator, *$num2*, is non-zero (true), the expression *$num2* is returned.

5.3.5   Logical Word Operators

These logical operators are of lower precedence than the short-circuit operators, but basically work the same way and make the program easier to read and they also short-circuit. In addition to the short-circuit operators, the *xor* (exclusive *or*) operator has been added to the logical word operators.

EXAMPLE 5.10

```
    # Examples using the word operators
1   $num1=50;
    $num2=100;
    $num3=0;
    print "\nOutput using the word operators.\n\n";
2   print "\n$num1 and $num2: ",($num1 and $num2);, "\n";
3   print "\n$num1 or $num3: ", ($num1 or $num3), "\n";
4   print "\n$num1 xor $num3: ",($num1 xor $num3), "\n";
5   print "\nnot $num3: ", not $num3;
    print "\n";
```

EXAMPLE 5.10 (CONTINUED)

```
(Output)
    Output using the word operators.

2   50 and 100: 100

3   50 or 0: 50

4   50 xor  0: 1

5   not 0: 1
```

EXPLANATION

1   Initial values are assigned to $num1, $num2, and $num3.
2   The *and* operator evaluates its operands. $num1 and $num2 are both true, resulting in the value of the last expression evaluated, *100*. Since *100* is a non-zero value, the expression is true.
3   The *or* operator evaluates its operands. $num1 is true. The word operators also short-circuit, so that if the first expression is true, there is no need to continue evauating. The result returned is *50*, which is true.
4   The exclusive *xor* operator evaluates both its operands. It does not short-circuit. If one of the operands is *true*, then the expression is true and *1* is returned; if both sides are either true or false, the result is false.
5   The logical *not* operator evaluates the operand to the right; if it is true, false is returned, if false, true is returned.

EXAMPLE 5.11

```
    # Precedence with word operators and short-circuit operators
    $x=5;
    $y=6;
    $z=0;
1   $result=$x && $y && $z;          # Precedence of = lower than &&
    print "Result: $result\n";

2   $result2 = $x and $y and $z;   # Precedence of = higher than and
    print "Result: $result2\n";

3   $result3 = ( $x and $y and $z );
    print "Result: $result3\n";

(Output)
1   Result: 0
2   Result: 5
3   Result: 0
```

EXPLANATION

1. The logical short-circuit operators evaluate each of the expressions and return the value of the last expression evaluated. The value *0* is assigned to *$result*. Since *&&* is higher in precedence than the equal sign, the logical operators evaluated their expressions first.
2. The word operators are used here, but they are lower in precedence than the equal sign. The first expression to the right of the equal sign is assigned to *$result2*.
3. By adding parentheses to the expression on the right-hand side of the equal sign, that expression is evaluated first and the result assigned to *$result3*.

5.3.6 Arithmetic Operators

Perl's arithmetic operators are listed in Table 5.9.

Table 5.9 Arithmetic Operators

Operator	Example	Meaning
+	$x + $y	Addition
−	$x − $y	Subtraction
*	$x * $y	Multiplication
/	$x / $y	Division
%	$x % $y	Modulus
**	$x ** $y	Exponentiation

EXAMPLE 5.12

```
(The Script)
1   printf "%d\n", 4 * 5 / 2;
2   printf "%d\n", 5 ** 3;
3   printf "%d\n", 5 + 4 - 2 * 10;
4   printf "%d\n", (5 + 4 - 2 ) * 10;
5   printf "%d\n", 11 % 2;
```

EXAMPLE 5.12 (CONTINUED)

```
(Output)
1    10
2    125
3    -11
4    70
5    1
```

EXPLANATION

1   The *printf* function formats the result of arithmetic expression in decimal. Multiplication and division are performed. Operators are of the same precedence, left to right associativity. Same as: *(4 * 5) / 2*

2   The *printf* function formats the result of arithmetic expression in decimal. The exponentiation operator cubes its operand, *5*, same as 5^3.

3   The *printf* function formats the result of arithmetic expression in decimal. Since the multiplication operator is of higher precedence than the addition and subtraction operators, multiplication is performed first, left to right associativity. Same as: *5 + 4 – (2 * 10)*

4   The *printf* function formats the result of arithmetic expression in decimal. Since the parentheses are of highest precedence, the expression enclosed in parentheses is calculated first.

5   The *printf* function formats the result of arithmetic expression in decimal. The modulus operator produces the remainder after performing division on its operands. (See "The printf Function" on page 31.)

5.3.7   Autoincrement and Autodecrement Operators

The autoincrement operator and autodecrement operators are taken straight from the *C* language (see Table 5.10). The autoincrement operator adds one to the value of a variable and the autodecrement operator subtracts one from the value of a variable. When used with a single variable, these operators are just a shortcut for the traditional method of adding and subtracting one. However, if used in an assignment statement or if combined with other operators, the end result depends on the placement of the operator. (See Table 5.11.)

Table 5.10   Autoincrement and Autodecrement Operators

Example	*Description*	*Equivalence*
++x	Pre-increment	$x = $x + 1$
$x++	Post-increment	$x = $x + 1$
--x	Pre-decrement	$x = $x – 1$
$x--	Post-decrement	$x = $x – 1$

Table 5.11   Autoincrement and Autodecrement Operators and Assignment

Example	*Description*	*Equivalence*	*Result*
If $y is 0 and $x is 0: $y = $x++;	Assign the value of $x to $y, then increment $x	$y = $x; $x = $x + 1;	$y is 0 $x is 1
If $y is 0 and $x is 0: $y = ++$x;	Increment $x, then assign $x to $y	$x = $x + 1; $y = $x;	$x is 1 $y is 1
If $y is 0 and $x is 0: $y = $x--;	Assign the value of $x to $y, then decrement $x	$y = $x; $x = $x - 1;	$y is 0 $x is -1
If $y is 0 and $x is 0: $y = --$x;	Decrement $x, then assign $x to $y	$x = $x - 1; $y = $x;	$x is -1 $y is -1

EXAMPLE 5.13

```
(The Script)
    #!/usr/bin/perl
1   $x=5; $y=0;
2   $y=++$x;      # Add one to $x first; then assign to $y
3   print "Pre-increment:\n";
4   print "y is $y\n";
5   print "x is $x\n";
6   print  "---------------------\n";
7   $x=5;
8   $y=0;
9   print "Post-increment:\n";
10  $y=$x++;      # Assign value in $x to $y; then add one to $x
11  print "y is $y\n";
12  print "x is $x\n";

(Output)
3   Pre-increment:
4   y is 6
5   x is 6

    ---------------------
9   Post-increment
11  y is 5
12  x is 6
```

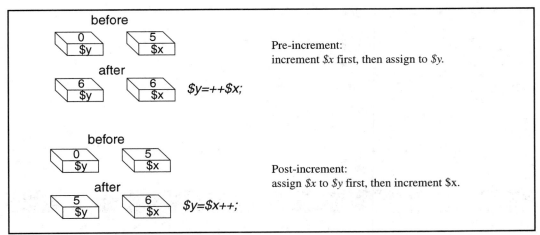

Figure 5.1 Pre- and post-increment operators.

5.3.8 Bitwise Logical Operators

When you're ready to manipulate integer values at the bit level, the bitwise logical operators are used. The bitwise operators are binary operators and manipulate their operands in terms of the internal binary representation of those operands. A bit-by-bit comparison is made on each of the corresponding operands, producing its result as the binary value (see Tables 5.12 and 5.13).

Table 5.12 Bitwise Logical Operators

Operator	*Example*	*Meaning*
&	$x & $y	Bitwise *and*
|	$x | $y	Bitwise *or*
^	$x ^ $y	Bitwise exclusive *or*
<<	$x << 1	Bitwise left shift, integer multiply by two
>>	$x >> 1	Bitwise right shift, integer divide by two

Table 5.13 Resulting Values of Bitwise Operators

$x	$y	$x & $y	$x | $y	$x ^ $y
0	0	0	0	0
0	1	0	1	1
1	0	0	1	1
1	1	1	1	0

EXAMPLE 5.14

```
(The Script)
1   print 5 & 4,"\n";          # 101 & 100
2   print 5 & 0,"\n";          # 101 & 000
3   print 4 & 0,"\n";          # 100 & 000
4   print 0 & 4,"\n";          # 000 & 100
5   print "=" x 10,"\n";       # print 10 equal signs
6   print 1 | 4,"\n";          # 001 & 100
7   print 5 | 0,"\n";          # 101 | 000
8   print 4 | 0,"\n";          # 100 | 000
9   print 0 | 4,"\n";          # 000 | 100
    print "=" x 10,"\n";       # print 10 equal signs
10  print 5 ^ 4,"\n";          # 101 ^ 100
11  print 5 ^ 0,"\n";          # 101 ^ 000
12  print 4 ^ 0,"\n";          # 100 ^ 000
13  print 0 ^ 4,"\n";          # 000 ^ 100

(Output)
1   4
2   0
3   0
4   0
5   ==========
6   5
7   5
8   4
9   4
    ==========
10  1
11  5
12  4
13  4
```

EXPLANATION

1 *5* bitwise *and*ed to *4* results in *000* binary, *4* decimal.
2 *5* bitwise *and*ed to *0* results in *000* binary, *0* decimal.
3 *4* bitwise *and*ed to *0* results in *000* binary, *0* decimal.
4 *0* bitwise *and*ed to *4* results in *000* binary, *0* decimal.
5 The *x* operator tells the *print* function to print 10 equal signs.
6 *1* bitwise *or*ed to *4* results in *101* binary, *5* decimal.
7 *5* bitwise *or*ed to *0* results in *101* binary, *5* decimal.
8 *4* bitwise *or*ed to *0* results in *100* binary, *4* decimal.
9 *0* bitwise *or*ed to *4* results in *100* binary, *4* decimal.
10 *5* bitwise exclusively *or*ed to *4* results in *001* binary, *1* decimal.
11 *5* bitwise exclusively *or*ed to *0* results in *101* binary, *5* decimal.
12 *4* bitwise exclusively *or*ed to *0* results in *100* binary, *4* decimal.
13 *0* bitwise exclusively *or*ed to *4* results in *100* binary, *4* decimal.

EXAMPLE 5.15

```
(The Script)
    #!/usr/bin/perl
    # Convert a number to binary
1   while (1) {
2      $mask = 0x80000000;        # 32-bit machine
3      printf("Enter an unsigned integer: ");
4      chomp($num=<STDIN>);
5      printf("Binary of %x hex is: ", $num);
6      for ($j = 0; $j < 32; $j++) {
7          $bit = ($mask & $num) ? 1 : 0;
8          printf("%d", $bit);
9          if ($j == 15)){
10             printf("--");
           }
11      $mask /=2;                 # $mask >>= 1;  not portable
       }
       printf("\n");
    }
```

EXAMPLE 5.15 (CONTINUED)

```
(Output)
Enter an unsigned integer: 1
Binary of 1 hex is: 0000000000000000--0000000000000001
Enter an unsigned integer: 5
Binary of 5 hex is: 0000000000000000--0000000000000101
Enter an unsigned integer: 10
Binary of a hex is: 0000000000000000--0000000000001010
Enter an unsigned integer: 12
Binary of c hex is: 0000000000000000--0000000000001100
Enter an unsigned integer: 15
Binary of f hex is: 0000000000000000--0000000000001111
Enter an unsigned integer: 200
Binary of c8 hex is: 0000000000000000--0000000011001000
```

EXPLANATION

1   This little program introduces some constructs that have not yet been discussed. It is presented here as an example of using bitwise operations to perform a real task (in this case, to convert a number to binary and print it). The first line starts a loop that will continue until the user presses <Ctrl>-c (UNIX) or <Ctrl>-z (Windows).

2   The scalar is set to the hexadecimal value representing 32 zeros. This program works on a machine with a 32-bit word.

3   The user is asked to type in an integer.

4   The number is assigned and the newline is *chomp*ed.

5   The *printf* will print the value of the number in hexadecimal notation.

6   The *for* loop will iterate 32 times, once for each bit.

7   The value of *$mask* is bitwise *and*ed to *$num*. If the result is *1*, *1* will be assigned to *$bit*; otherwise, *0* is assigned. (See "Conditional Operators" below.)

8   The value of *$bit* is printed.

9   If the value of *$j* is *15* (the loop has iterated 16 times) a double underscore is printed.

11 The value of *$mask* is divided by 2. This has the same effect as shifting the bits to the right once, but will not try to shift the sign bit if one exists.

5.3.9   Conditional Operators

The conditional operator is another taken from the *C* language. It requires three operands, thus it is often called a **ternary** operator. It is used as a shortcut for the *if/else* construct.

FORMAT

```
conditional expression ? expression : expression
```

EXAMPLE 5.16

```
$x ? $y : $z
```

EXPLANATION

If x is true, y becomes the value of the expression. If x is false, z becomes the value of the expression.

EXAMPLE 5.17

```
(The Script)
    print "What is your age? ";
2   chomp($age=<STDIN>);

3   $price=($age > 60 ) ? 0 : 5.55;
4   printf "You will pay \$%.2f.\n", $price;

(Output)
1   What is your age? 44
4   You will pay $5.55.

(Output)
1   What is your age? 77
4   You will pay $0.00.
```

EXPLANATION

1 The string *What is your age?* is printed to *STDOUT*.
2 The input is read from the terminal and stored in the scalar *$age*. The newline is *chomp*ed.
3 The scalar *$price* is assigned the result of the conditional operator. If the age is greater than *60*, the price is assigned the value to the right of the question mark (*?*). Otherwise, the value after the colon (*:*) is assigned to the scalar *$price*.
4 The *printf* function prints the formatted string to *STDOUT*.

EXAMPLE 5.18

```
(The Script)
1   print "What was your grade? ";
2   $grade = <STDIN>;
3   print $grade > 60 ? "Passed.\n" : "Failed.\n";

(Output)
1   What was your grade? 76
3   Passed.

(Output)
1   What was your grade? 34
3   Failed.
```

EXPLANATION

1 The user is asked for input.
2 The input is assigned to the scalar *$grade*.
3 The *print* function takes as its argument the result of the conditional expression. If the grade is greater than *60*, *Passed.* is printed; otherwise, *Failed.* is printed.

5.3.10 Range Operator

The range operator is used in both scalar and array context. In a scalar context, the value returned is a Boolean, *1* or *0*. In an array context, it returns a list of items starting on the left side of the operator and counting by ones until the value on the right-hand side is reached.

EXAMPLE 5.19

```
1   $ perl -ne 'if ( 1 .. 3 ){print}' emp.names
    Steve Blenheim
    Betty Boop
    Igor Chevsky
2   $ perl -e 'print 0 .. 10,"\n";'
    0 1 2 3 4 5 6 7 8 9 10
3   $ perl -e '@alpha=('A' .. 'Z') ; print "@alpha";'
    A B C D E F G H I J K L M N O P Q R S T U V W X Y Z
4   perl -e '@a=('a'..'z', 'A'..'Z') ; print "@a\n";'
    a b c d e f g h i j k l m n o p q r s t u v w x y z A B C D E F G H
    I J K L M N O P Q R S T U V W X Y Z
5   perl -e '@n=( -5 .. 20 ) ; print "@n\n";'
    -5 -4 -3 -2 -1 0 1 2 3 4 5 6 7 8 9 10 11 12 13 14 15 16 17 18 19 20
```

EXPLANATION

1   The first three lines of the file *emp.names* are printed. As long as the expression evaluates true, the lines are printed. The context is scalar and Boolean.

2   Print the numbers *0* to *10* to *STDOUT*.

3   Create an array called *@alpha* and store all uppercase letters in the array in the range from *A* to *Z*. The context is array. Print the array.

4   Create an array called *@alpha* and store all lowercase letters in one list and all uppercase letters in another list. Print the array.

5   Create an array called *@n* and store all numbers in the range between *–5* and *20*. Print the array.

5.3.11   Special String Operators and Functions

There are a number of operations that can be performed on strings. For example, the concatenation operator joins two strings together, and the string repetition operator concatenates as many copies of its operand as specified.

Perl also supports some special functions for manipulating strings (see Table 5.14). The *substr* function returns a substring found within an original string, starting at a byte offset in the original string and ending with the number of character positions to the right of that offset. The *index* function returns the byte offset of the first character of a substring found within the original string. The *length* function returns the number of characters in a given expression.

Table 5.14   String Operations

Example	*Meaning*
$str1 . $str2	Concatenate strings *$str1* and *$str2*
$str1 x $num	Repeat *$str1*, *$num* times
substr ($str1, $offset, $len)	Substring of *$str1* at *$offset* for *$len* bytes
index ($str1, $str2)	Byte offset of string *$str2* in string *$str1*
length (EXPR)	Returns the length in characters of expression, *EXPR*
rindex($str, $substr, POSITION)	Returns the position of the last occurrence of *$substr* in *$str*. If the *POSITION* is specified, start looking there. If *POSITION* is not specified, start at the end of the string.
chr(NUMBER)	Returns the character represented by that *NUMBER* in the ASCII character set. For example, *chr(65)* is the letter *A*.
lc($str)	Returns a lowercase string
uc($str)	Returns an uppercase string

EXAMPLE 5.20

```
(The Script)
    #!/usr/bin/perl
1   $x="pop";
2   $y="corn";
3   $z="*";
4   print $z x 10, "\n";                # Print 10 stars
5   print $x . $y, "\n";                # Concatenate "pop" and "corn"
6   print $z x 10, "\n";                # Print 10 stars
7   print (($x . $y ." " )  x 5 );      # Concatenate "pop" and "corn"
                                        # and print 5 times
8   print "\n";
9   print uc($x . $y), "!\n";           # Convert string to uppercase

(Output)
4   **********
5   popcorn
6   **********
7   popcorn popcorn popcorn popcorn popcorn
9   POPCORN!
```

EXPLANATION

1   The scalar *$x* is assigned *pop*.
2   The scalar *$y* is assigned *corn*.
3   The scalar *$z* is assigned ***.
4   The string *** is concatenated ten times and printed to *STDOUT*.
5   The value of *$x*, string *pop*, and the value of *$y*, string *corn*, are concatenated and printed to *STDOUT*.
6   The value of *$x*, string ***, is concatenated ten times and printed to *STDOUT*.
7   The strings *pop* and *corn* are concatenated five times and printed to *STDOUT*.
8   Print a newline to *STDOUT*.
9   The *uc* function converts and returns the string in uppercase. The *lc* function will convert a string to lowercase.

EXAMPLE 5.21

```
(The Script)
1   $line="Happy New Year";
2   print substr($line, 6, 3),"\n";        # Offset starts at zero
3   print index($line, "Year"),"\n";
4   print substr($line, index($line, "Year")),"\n";
5   substr($line, 0, 0)="Fred, ";
```

EXAMPLE 5.21 (CONTINUED)

```
6   print $line,"\n";
7   substr($line, 0, 1)="Ethel";
8   print $line,"\n";
9   substr($line, -1, 1)="r to you!";
10  print $line,"\n";
11  $string="I'll eat a tomato tomorrow.\n";
12  print rindex($string, tom), "\n";
```

(Output)
```
2   New
3   10
4   Year
5   Fred, Happy New Year
7   Ethelred, Happy New Year
8   Ethelred, Happy New Year to you!
9   18
```

EXPLANATION

1   The scalar $line is assigned *Happy New Year*.

2   The substring *New* of the original string *Happy New Year* is printed to *STDOUT*. The offset starts at byte zero. The beginning of the substring is position *6*, the *N*, and the end of the substring is three characters to the right of *N*. The substring *New* is returned.

3   The *index* function returns the first position in the string where the substring is found. The substring *Year* starts at position 10. Remember, the byte offset starts at 0.

4   The *substr* and *index* functions are used together. The *index* function returns the starting position of the substring *Year*. The *substr* function uses the return value from the *index* function as the starting position for the *substring*. The *substring* returned is *Year*.

5   The substring *Fred* is inserted at starting position, byte *0*, and over length *0* of the scalar $line; i.e., at the beginning of the string.

6   The new value of $line is printed to *STDOUT*.

7   The substring *Ethel* is inserted at starting position, byte *0*, and over length *1* of the scalar $line.

8   The new value of $line, *Ethelred, Happy New Year* is printed to *STDOUT*.

9   The substring, *r to you!* is appended to the scalar $line starting at the end (*−1*) of the substring, over one character.

10 The new value of $line, *Ethelred, Happy New Year to you!* is printed to *STDOUT*.

11 The $string scalar is assigned.

12 The *rindex* function finds the index of the **rightmost** substring, *tom*, and returns the index position where it was found the substring. That position, *18*, is the number of characters starting at the zero-ith position from the beginning of the string; in other words, the position where *tom* begins in the substring *tomorrow*.

5.3.12 Generating Random Numbers

When looking for a good description of random number generation on the Web, one of the related categories is *Games>Gambling>Lotteries>Ticket Generators*. Games and lotteries depend on the use of random number generation, and so do more sophisticated programs such as cryptographic protocols that use unpredictable encrypted keys to ensure security when passing information back and forth on the Web.

Random numbers produced by programs are called **pseudorandom** numbers. As described in an article by Ian Goldberg and David Wagner concerning Web security, truly random numbers can only be found in nature, such as the rate of decay of a radioactive element. Apart from using external sources, computers must generate these numbers themselves, but since compuers are deterministic, these numbers will not be truly random.[3] Perl programs that need to generate pseudorandom numbers can use the built-in *rand* function described below.

5.3.13 The *rand/srand* Functions

The *rand* function returns a pseudorandom fractional number between 0 and 1. If *EXPR* has a positive value, *rand* returns a fractional number between 0 and *EXPR*. The *srand* function sets the random number seed for the *rand* function, but is no longer required if you are using a version of Perl greater than 5.004. A seed is a random number itself that is fed to the random number generator as the starting number from which new random numbers are produced. The *rand* function is given a seed and, using a complex algorithm, produces random numbers within some range. If the same seed is fed to the *rand* function, the same series of numbers will be produced. A different seed will produce a different series of random numbers. The default seed value used to be the time of day, but now a more unpredictable number is selected for you by Perl.

FORMAT

```
rand(EXPR)
rand EXPR
rand

srand(EXPR)
srand EXPR
```

3. Goldberg, I., and Wagner, D., "Randomness and the Netscape Browser. How Secure is the World Wide Web?," *Dr. Dobb's Journal, http://www.ddj.com/articles/1996/9601h/9601h.html.*

EXAMPLE 5.22

```
(The Script)
     #!/usr/bin/perl
1    $num=10;
2    srand(time|$$);  # Seed rand with the time or'ed to
                       # the pid of this process
3    while($num){     # srand not necessary in versions 5.004 and above
4        $lotto = int(rand(10)) + 1;
                       # Returns a random number between 1 and 10
5        print "The random number is $lotto\n";
         sleep 3;
         $num--;
     }

(Output)
5    The random number is 5
     The random number is 5
     The random number is 7
     The random number is 8
     The random number is 1
     The random number is 5
     The random number is 4
     The random number is 4
     The random number is 4
     The random number is 6
```

EXPLANATION

1   The value of *$num* will be used in the *while* loop on line 7 which will iteratate 10 times.
2   The *srand* function sets the seed for the *rand* function to a unique starting point, the return value of the built-in *time* function bitwise *or*ed to the process identification number of this Perl program (*$$*).
3   The *while* loop will iterate 10 times.
4   The *rand* function will return an integer value between 1 and 10, inclusive. The value will be assigned to *$lotto*.
5   The value of the random number is printed.

EXAMPLE 5.23

```
(The Script)
   #!/usr/bin/perl
1  $x=5 ;      # Starting point in a range of numbers
2  $y=15;      # Ending point

   # Formula to produce random numbers between 5 and 15 inclusive
   # $random = int(rand($y - $x + 1)) + $x;
   # $random = int(rand(15 - 5 + 1)) + 5

3  while(1){
4      print int(rand($y - $x + 1)) + $x , "\n";
5      sleep 1;
   }

(Output)
15
14
5
10
11
6
12
6
7
10
6
8
6
15
11
```

EXPLANATION

1   The scalar $x is assigned the starting value in the range of numbers produced by the *rand* function.

2   The scalar $y is assigned the ending value of the range of numbers produced by the *rand* function.

3   An infinite *while* loop is started. To exit, the user must type <Ctrl>-d (UNIX) or <Ctrl>-z (Windows).

4   The *rand* function is given a formula that will produce random integer values in the range 1 to 15, inclusive.

5   The *sleep* function causes the program to pause for 1 second.

EXERCISE 4
Operator, Operator

1. Print the average of three floating point numbers with a precision of two decimal places.

2. What are two other ways that you could write
   $x = $x + 1;

3. Write the following expression using a shortcut:
   $y = $y + 5;

4. Square the number 15 and print the result.

5. What would the following program print?
   $a = 15;
   $b = 4;
   $c = 25.0;
   $d = 3.0;
   printf ("4 + c / 4 * d = %f\n", 4 + $c / 4 * $d);
   printf ("a / d * a + c = %.2f\n", $a / $d * $a + $c);
   printf ("%d\n", $result = $c / 5 – 2);
   printf ("%d = %d + %f\n", $result = $b + $c, $b, $c);
   printf ("%d\n", $result == $d);

6. Given the values of $a=10, $b=3, $c=7, and $d=20, print the value of $result:
   a. $result = ($a >= $b) && ($c < $d);
      print "$result\n";
   b. $result = ($a >= $b) and ($c < $d);
      print "$result\n";
   c. $result = ($a < $b) || ($c <= $d);
      print "$result\n";
   d. $result=($a < $b) or ($c <= $d);
      print "$result\n";
   e. $result = $a % $b;

7. Write a program called *convert* that converts a Fahrenheit temperature to Celsius using the following formula.
   C = (F – 32) / 1.8

8. Create an array of five sayings:
   "An apple a day keeps the doctor away"
   "Procrastination is the thief of time"
   "The early bird catches the worm"
   "Handsome is as handsome does"
   "Too many cooks spoil the broth"

Each time you run your script, a random saying will be printed. Hint: the index of the array will be the random number generated.

IF ONLY, UNCONDITIONALLY, FOREVER

6.1 Control Structures, Blocks, and Compound Statements

So far, we have seen script examples that are linear in structure, that is, simple statements that are executed one after the other. Control structures, such as branching and looping statements, allow the flow of the program's control to change depending on some conditional expression.

The decision-making constructs (*if, if/else, if/elsif/else, unless*, etc.) contain a control expression that determines whether a block of statements will be executed. The looping constructs (*while, for, foreach*) allow the program to repetitively execute a statement block until some condition is satisfied.

A compound statement or block consists of a group of statements surrounded by curly braces. The block is syntactically equivalent to a single statement and usually follows an *if, else, while*, or *for* construct. But unlike *C*, where curly braces are not always required, Perl requires them even with one statement when that statement comes after the *if, else, while*, etc. The conditional modifiers, discussed in Chapter 7, "Regular Expressions—Pattern Matching," can be used when a condition is evaluated within a **single** statement.

6.2 Decision Making—Conditional Constructs

6.2.1 *if* and *unless* Statements

The *if* and *unless* constructs are followed by an expression surrounded by parentheses and followed by a block of one more statements. The block is always enclosed in curly braces.

An *if* statement is a conditional statement. It allows you to test an expression and, based on the results of the test, make a decision. The expression is enclosed in parentheses, and Perl, unlike *C*, evaluates the expression in a string context. If the string is non-null, the expression is *true*; if it is null, the expression is *false*. If the expression is a numeric value,

133

it will be converted to a string and tested. If the expression is evaluated to be *true* (non-null), the next statement block is executed; if the condition is *false* (null), Perl will ignore the block associated with the expression and go onto the next executable statement within the script.

The *unless* statement is constructed exactly the same as the *if* statement; the results of the test are simply reversed. If the expression is evaluated to be *false*, the next statement block is executed; if the expression is evaluated to be *true*, Perl will ignore the block of statements controlled by the expression.

The *if* Construct.   The *if* statement consists of the keyword *if*, followed by a conditional expression, followed by a block of one or more statements enclosed in curly braces. Each statement within the block is terminated with a semicolon (*;*). The block of statements collectively is often called a **compound statement**.

FORMAT

```
if (Expression) {Block}
if (Expression) {Block} else {Block}
if (Expression) {Block} elsif (Expression)
   {Block}... else {Block}
```

EXAMPLE 6.1

```
(The Script)
1    $num1 = 1;
2    $num2 = 0;

3    $str1 = "hello";
4    $str2 = "";        # Null string

5    if ($num1) {print "TRUE!\n"; $x++;}      # $x and $y were
                                              # initially assigned zero
6    if ($num2) {print "FALSE! \n";$y++;}  # never execute this block
7    if ($str1) {print "TRUE AGAIN!\n";}
8    if ($str2) {print "FALSE AGAIN!\n";}
9    if ($num1 != $num2) {print "Not Equal!\n";}

(Output)
5    TRUE!
7    TRUE AGAIN!
9    Not Equal!
```

EXPLANATION

1   The scalar *$num1* is assigned the number *1*, which will be converted to "1".
2   The scalar *$num2* is assigned the number *0*, which will be converted to "0".
3   The scalar, *$str1*, is assigned the string *hello*.
4   The scalar *$str2* is assigned the null string.
5   Since the value of *$num1* is not a null string, equating to true, the block of statement(s) is executed; *$x* is incremented.
6   Since the value of *$num2* is the null string, false, the block of statement(s) is not executed.
7   Since the value of *$str1* is not a null string, the block of statement(s) is executed.
8   Since the value of *$str2* is an empty string, the block of statement(s) is not executed.
9   Since *$num1* is not equal to *$num2*, the expression is true and the block of statement(s) is executed.

The *if/else* Construct.   Another form of the *if* statement is the *if/else* construct. This construct allows for a two-way decision. If the first conditional expression following the *if* keyword is true, the block of statements following the *if* are executed. Otherwise, if the conditional expression following the *if* keyword is false, control branches to the *else* and the block of statements following the *else* are executed. The *else* statement is never an independent statement. It must follow an *if* statement. When the *if* statements are nested within other *if* statements, the *else* statement is associated with the closest previous *if* statement.

FORMAT

```
if (Expression)
      {Block}
else
      {Block}
```

EXAMPLE 6.2

```
(The Script)
1   print "What version of the operating system are you using? ";
2   chomp($os = <STDIN>);
3   if ($os > 2.2) {print "Most of the bugs have been worked
                          out!\n";}
4   else {print "Expect some problems.\n";}

(Output)
1   What version of the operating system are you using?  2.4
3   Most of the bugs have been worked out!

(Output)
1   What version of the operating system are you using?  2.0
4   Expect some problems.
```

EXPLANATION

1   The user is asked for input.
2   The newline is removed.
3   If the value of *$os* is greater than *2.2*, the block enclosed in curly braces is executed.
4   If *$os* is not greater than *2.2*, this block is executed.

The *if/elsif/else* Construct.   Yet another form of the *if* statement is the *if/else/elsif* construct. This construct provides a multiway decision structure. If the first conditional expression following the *if* keyword is true, the block of statements following the *if* is executed. Otherwise, the first *elsif* statement is tested. If the conditional expression following the first *elsif* is false, the next *elsif* is tested, etc. If all of the conditional expressions following the *elsif*'s are false, the block after the *else* is executed; this is the default action.

FORMAT

```
if (Expression1)
     {Block}
elsif (Expression2)
     {Block}
elsif (Expression3)
     {Block}
else
     {Block}
```

EXAMPLE 6.3

```
(The Script)
1   $hour = (localtime)[2];
2   if ($hour >= 0 && $hour < 12){print "Good-morning!\n";}
3   elsif ($hour == 12){print "Lunch time.\n";}
4   elsif ($hour > 12 && $hour < 17) {print "Siesta time.\n";}
5   else {print "Goodnight. Sweet dreams.\n";}

(Output)
4   Siesta time
```

EXPLANATION

1   The scalar *$hour* is set to the current hour. The *localtime* built-in function returns the hour, the third element of the array of time values.
2   The *if* statement tests whether the value of *$hour* is greater than or equal to *0* and less than *12*. The result of the evaluation is true, so the block following the control expression is executed (i.e., the *print* statement is executed).

3   If the first *if* test is false, this expression is tested. If the value of *$hour* is equal to *12*, the *print* statement is executed.

4   If the previous *elsif* test failed, and this *elsif* expression evaluates to true, the *print* statement will be executed.

5   If none of the above statements are true, the *else* statement, the default action, is executed.

6.2.2   The *unless* Construct

The *unless* statement is similar to the *if* statement, except that the control expression after the *unless* is tested for the reverse condition; that is, if the conditional expression following the *unless* is false, the statement block is executed.

The *unless/else* and *unless/elsif* behave in the same way as the *if/else* and *if /elsif* statements with the same reversed test as previously stated.

FORMAT

```
unless (Expression) {Block}
unless (Expression) {Block} else {Block}
unless (Expression) {Block} elsif (Expression)
    {Block}... else {Block}
```

EXAMPLE 6.4

```
(The Script)
1    $num1 = 1;
2    $num2 = 0;

3    $str1 = "hello";
4    $str2 = "";       # Null string

5    unless ($num1) {print "TRUE!\n"; $x++;}
                     # Never execute this block
6    unless ($num2) {print "FALSE! \n"; $y++;}
7    unless ($str1) {print "TRUE AGAIN!\n";}
8    unless ($str2) {print "FALSE AGAIN!\n";}
9    unless ($num1 == $num2) {print "Not Equal!\n";}
                     # unless modifier and simple statement

(Output)
6    FALSE!
8    FALSE AGAIN!
9    Not Equal!
```

Chapter 6 • If Only, Unconditionally, Forever

EXPLANATION

1   The scalar *$num1* is assigned the number *1*, which will be converted to "1".
2   The scalar *$num2* is assigned the number *0*, which will be converted to "0".
3   The scalar *$str1* is assigned the string *hello*.
4   The scalar *$str2* is assigned the null string.
5   Since the value of *$num1* is not an empty string, in other words, it is true; the block of statement(s) **is not** executed.
6   Since the value of *$num2* is an empty string, or, in other words it is false; the block of statement(s) **is** executed; *$y* is incremented.
7   Since the value of *$str1* is not an empty string, the block of statement(s) **is not** executed.
8   Since the value of *$str2* is an empty string, or false, the block of statement(s) **is** executed.
9   Since the expression being tested evaluates to false, the block of statement(s) is executed.

EXAMPLE 6.5

```
(The Script)
    #!/bin/perl
    # Scriptname: excluder
1   while(<>){
2       ($name, $phone) = split(/:/);
3       unless($name eq "barbara"){
            $record = "$name\t$phone";
4           print "$record";
        }
    }
5   print "\n$name has moved from this district.\n";
```

```
(Output)
$ excluder names
igor chevsky        408-123-4533
paco gutierrez      510-453-2776
ephram hardy        916-235-4455
james ikeda         415-449-0066
barbara kerz        207-398-6755
jose santiago       408-876-5899
tommy savage        408-876-1725
lizzy stachelin     415-555-1234

barbara has moved from this district.
```

6.3   Loops

Loops are used to execute a segment of code repeatedly. Perl's basic looping constructs are

> *while*
> *until*
> *for*
> *foreach*

Each loop is followed by a block of statements enclosed in curly braces.

6.3.1   The *while* Loop

The *while* statement executes the block as long as the control expression after the *while* is true. An expression is *true* if it evaluates to *non–zero* (non-null); *while(1)* is always true and loops forever. An expression is *false* if it evaluates to *zero* (null); *while(0)* is false and never loops.

Often the *while* statement is used to loop through a file. (See "Reading from the Filehandle" on page 252.)

FORMAT

```
while(Expression)  {Block}
```

EXAMPLE 6.6

```
(The Script)
    #!/usr/bin/perl
1   $num = 0;                       # Initialize $num
2   while($num < 10){       # Test expression
    # Loop quits when expression is false or 0

3   print "$num ";
4       $num++;     # Update the loop variable $num; increment $num
5       }
6   print "\nOut of the loop.\n";

(Output)
3   0 1 2 3 4 5 6 7 8 9
6   Out of the loop.
```

EXPLANATION

1   The scalar *$num* is initialized. The initialization takes place before entering the loop.
2   The test expression is evaluated. If the result is true, the block of statements in curly braces is executed.
4   The scalar *$num* is incremented. If not, the test expression would always yield a true value, and the loop would never end.

EXAMPLE 6.7

```
(The Script)
    #!/usr/bin/perl
1   $count = 1;        # Initialize variables
    $beers = 10;
    $remai = $beers;
    $where = "on the shelf";
2   while ($count <= $beers) {
        if($remain == 1){print "$remain bottle of beer $where ." ;}
        else {print "$remain bottles of beer $where $where .";}
        print " Take one down and pass it all around.\n";
        print "Now ", $beers - $count , " bottles of beer $where!\n";

3       $count++;
4       $remain--;
5       if($count > 10){print "Party's over. \n";}
    }
    print "\n";
```

EXAMPLE 6.7 (CONTINUED)

```
(Output)
10 bottles on the shelf on the shelf. Take one down and pass it all around.
Now 9 bottles of beer on the shelf!
9 bottles on the shelf on the shelf. Take one down and pass it all around.
Now 8 bottles of beer on the shelf!
8 bottles on the shelf on the shelf. Take one down and pass it all around.
Now 7 bottles of beer on the shelf!
7 bottles on the shelf on the shelf. Take one down and pass it all around.
Now 6 bottles of beer on the shelf!
6 bottles on the shelf on the shelf. Take one down and pass it all around.
Now 5 bottles of beer on the shelf!
5 bottles on the shelf on the shelf. Take one down and pass it all around.
Now 4 bottles of beer on the shelf!
4 bottles on the shelf on the shelf. Take one down and pass it all around.
Now 3 bottles of beer on the shelf!
3 bottles on the shelf on the shelf. Take one down and pass it all around.
Now 2 bottles of beer on the shelf!
2 bottles on the shelf on the shelf. Take one down and pass it all around.
Now 1 bottle of beer on the shelf!
1 bottle of beer on the shelf on the shelf. Take one down and pass it all around.
Now 0 bottles of beer on the shelf!
Party's over.
```

EXPLANATION

1   The scalars $count, $beers, $remain, and $where are initialized.
2   The *while* loop is entered; the control expression is tested and evaluated.
3   The scalar $count is incremented.
4   The scalar $remain is decremented.
5   When the value of $count is greater than *10*, this line is printed.

6.3.2 The *until* Loop

The *until* statement executes the block as long as the control expression after the *until* is false or zero. When the expression evaluates to true (non-zero), the loop exits.

FORMAT

```
until(Expression) {Block}
```

EXAMPLE 6.8

```
(The Script)
    #!/usr/bin/perl
1   $num = 0;        # initialize
2   until($num == 10){
        # Test expression; loop quits when expression is true or 1
3       print "$num ";
4       $num++;    # Update the loop variable $num; increment $num
5   }
6   print "\nOut of the loop.\n";

(Output)
3   0 1 2 3 4 5 6 7 8 9
6   Out of the loop.
```

EXPLANATION

1   The scalar *$num* is initialized. The initialization takes place before entering the loop.
2   The test expression is evaluated. If the result is false, the block of statements in curly braces is executed. When *$num* is equal to *10*, the loop exits.
4   The scalar *$num* is incremented. If not, the test expression would always yield a false value, and the loop would never end.

EXAMPLE 6.9

```
(The Script)
    #!/usr/bin/perl
1   print "Are you o.k.? ";
2   chomp($answer = <STDIN>);
3   until ($answer eq "yes"){
4       sleep(1);
5       print "Are you o.k. yet? ";
6       chomp($answer = <STDIN>);
7   }
8   print "Glad to hear it!\n";

(Output)
1   Are you o.k.? n
1   Are you o.k. yet? nope
1   Are you o.k. yet? yup
1   Are you o.k. yet? yes
8   Glad to hear it!
```

EXPLANATION

1 The user is asked an initial question.
2 The user's response is taken from standard input and stored in the scalar $answer. The newline is *chomp*ed.
3 The *until* loop checks the expression enclosed in parentheses, and if the value of $answer is not exactly equal to the string *yes*, the block following the expression will be entered. When $answer evaluates to *yes*, the loop exits and control begins at line 8.
4 If the value of $answer is not equal to *yes*, this line will be executed; in other words, the program will pause for one minute (*sleep 1*). This gives the user time before being asked the question again.
5 The user is asked again if he is okay.
6 The user's response is read again from *STDIN* and stored in $answer. This line is very important. If the value of $answer never changes, the loop will go on forever.
7 The closing curly brace marks the end of the block connected to the *until* loop. Control will returned to line 3 and the expression will be tested again. If the value of $answer is *yes*, control will go to line 8; otherwise, the statements in the block will be re-executed.
8 When the loop exits, this line is executed; in other words, when the value of $answer is equal to *yes*.

The *do/while* and *do/until* Loops. The *do/while* or *do/until* loops evaluate the conditional expression for true and false just as in the *while* and *until* loop statements. However, the expression is not evaluated until after the block is executed at least once.

FORMAT

```
do {Block} while (Expression);
do {Block} until (Expression);
```

EXAMPLE 6.10

```
(The Script)
    #!/usr/bin/perl
1   $x = 1;
2   do {
3       print "$x ";
4       $x++;
5   } while($x <= 10);
    print "\n";
6   $y = 1;
7   do{
8       print "$y " ;
9       $y++;
10  }until($y > 10);
```

EXAMPLE 6.10 (CONTINUED)

```
(Output)
3   1 2 3 4 5 6 7 8 9 10
8   1 2 3 4 5 6 7 8 9 10
```

EXPLANATION

1 The scalar *$x* is assigned the value *1*.
2 The *do/while* loop statement starts.
3 The block of statements is executed.
4 The scalar *$x* is incremented once.
5 The conditional expression following the *while* is evaluated. If true, the block of statements is executed again, and so on.
6 The scalar *$y* is assigned the value *1*.
7 The *do/until* loop statement starts.
8 The block of statements is executed.
9 The scalar *$y* is incremented once.
10 The conditional expression following the *until* is evaluated. If false, the block of statements is executed again, and so on.

6.3.3 The *for* Loop

The *for* statement is like the *for* loop in *C*. The *for* keyword is followed by three expressions separated by semicolons and enclosed within parentheses. Any or all of the expressions can be omitted, but the two semicolons cannot.[1] The first expression is used to set the initial value of variables, the second expression is used to test whether the loop should continue or stop, and the third expression updates the loop variables.

FORMAT

```
for (Expression1;Expression2;Expression3) {Block}
```

The above format is equivalent to the following *while* statement:

```
Expression1;
while (Expression2)
    {Block; Expression3};
```

---

1. The infinite loop can be written as: *for(;;)*

EXAMPLE 6.11

```
(The Script)
    #!/usr/bin/perl
1   for($i = 0; $i<10; $i++){    # Initialize, test, and increment $i
2       print "$i ";
    }
3   print "\nOut of the loop.\n";

(Output)
2   0 1 2 3 4 5 6 7 8 9
3   Out of the loop.
```

EXPLANATION

1   The *for* loop contains three expressions. In the first expression, the scalar $i is assigned the value *0*. This statement is executed just once. The second expression tests whether $i is less than *10*, and if so, the block statements are executed (i.e., the value of $i is printed). The last expression increments the value of $i by one. The second expression is again tested, and the block is executed, $i is incremented, and so on, until the test evaluates to false.

2   The value of $i is printed.

EXAMPLE 6.12

```
(The Script)
    #!/usr/bin/perl
    # Initialization, test, and increment, decrement of
    # counters is done in one step.
1   for ($count = 1, $beers = 10, $remain = $beers, $where = "on the shelf";
        $count <= $beers; $count++, $remain--){
2       if($remain == 1){
            print "$remain bottle of beer $where $where " ;
        }
        else{
            print "$remain bottles of beer $where $where.";
        }
        print " Take one down and pass it all around.\n";
        print "Now ", $beers - $count , " bottles of beer $where!\n";
3       if($count == 10 ){print "Party's over.\n";}
    }
```

EXAMPLE 6.12   (CONTINUED)

```
(Output)
10 bottles of beer on the shelf  on the shelf. Take one down and pass it all around.
Now 9 bottles of beer on the shelf!
9 bottles of beer on the shelf on the shelf. Take one down and pass it all around.
Now 8 bottles of beer on the shelf!
8 bottles of beer on the shelf on the shelf. Take one down and pass it all around.
Now 7 bottles of beer on the shelf!

  < continues >

2 bottles of beer on the shelf on the shelf. Take one down and pass it all around.
Now 1 bottle of beer on the shelf!
1 bottle of beer on the shelf on the shelf. Take one down and pass it all around.
Now 0 bottles of beer on the shelf!
Party's over.
```

EXPLANATION

1   The initialization of all scalars is done in the first expression of the *for* loop. Each initialization is separated by a comma, and the expression is terminated with a semicolon. The first expression is executed only once, when the loop starts. The second expression is the test. If it evaluates to true, the statements in the block are executed. After the last statement in the block is executed, the third expression is evaluated. The control is then passed to the second expression in the *for* loop, and so on.

2   The block is executed if the second expression in the *for* loop is evaluated as true.

3   This statement will be tested and, if the condition is true, the statement will be executed and control will go to the third expression within the *for* loop, incrementing *$count* for the last time.

6.3.4   The *foreach* Loop

If you are familiar with *C* shell programming, the Perl *foreach* loop is similar in appearance and behavior to the *C* shell *foreach* loop, but appearances can be deceiving and there are some obvious differences between the two constructs. So, read on.

The *foreach* loop iterates over each element in the parenthesized list, an array, assigning each element of the array to a scalar variable, one after the other, until the end of the list.

The *VARIABLE* is local to the *foreach* block. It will regain its former value when the loop is exited. Any changes made when assigning values to *VARIABLE* will, in turn, affect the individual elements of the array. If *VARIABLE* is not present, the *$_* special scalar variable is implicitly used.

FORMAT

```
foreach VARIABLE (ARRAY)
   {BLOCK}
```

EXAMPLE 6.13

```
(The Script)
   #!/usr/bin/perl
1  foreach $pal('Tom', 'Dick', 'Harry', 'Pete'){
2      print "Hi $pal!\n";
   }

(Output)
2  Hi Tom!
   Hi Dick!
   Hi Harry!
   Hi Pete!
```

EXPLANATION

1   The *foreach* is followed by the scalar *$pal* and a list of names. *$pal* points to each name in the list starting with *Tom*. You can think of *$pal* as an alias or reference for each item in the list. Each time the loop is entered, *$pal* goes to the next item in the list and gets that value. So, for example, after *Tom*, *Dick* is fetched, and then *Harry*, and so on until all list items have been used, at which time the loop exits.

2   Each time through the loop, the value referenced by *$pal* is printed. (See Figure 6.1.)

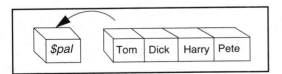

Figure 6.1   The *foreach* loop.

EXAMPLE 6.14

```
(The Script)
1  foreach $hour(1 .. 24){    # The range operator is used here
2      if($hour > 0 && $hour < 12) {print "Good-morning.\n";}
3      elsif($hour == 12) {print "Happy Lunch.\n";}
4      elsif($hour > 12 && $hour < 17) {print "Good afternoon.\n";}
5      else{print "Good-night.\n";}
   }
```

EXAMPLE 6.14   (CONTINUED)

```
(Output)
2    Good-morning.
     Good-morning.
     Good-morning.
     Good-morning.
     Good-morning.
     Good-morning.
     Good-morning.
     Good-morning.
     Good-morning.
     Good-morning.
     Good-morning.
3    Happy Lunch.
4    Good afternoon.
     Good afternoon.
     Good afternoon.
     Good afternoon.
5    Good-night.
     Good-night.
     Good-night.
     Good-night.
     Good-night.
     Good-night.
     Good-night.
     Good-night.
```

EXPLANATION

1   The list *(1 .. 24)* is a range of list items starting with *1* and ending with *24*. Each of those values are referenced in turn by the scalar *$hour*. The block is executed, and the next item in the list is assigned to *$hour*, and so on.
2   The scalar *$hour* is tested, and if the value is greater than *0* and less than *12*, the *print* statement is executed.
3   If the previous *elsif* statement is false, this statement is tested. If the scalar *$hour* is equal to *12*, the *print* statement is executed.
4   If the previous *elsif* statement is false, this statement is tested. If the scalar *$hour* is greater than *12* and less than *17*, the *print* statement is executed.
5   If all of the previous statements are false, the *else*, or default statement, is executed.

EXAMPLE 6.15

```
(The Script)
    #!/usr/bin/perl
1   $str = "hello";
2   @numbers = (1, 3, 5, 7, 9);
3   print "The scalar \$str is initially $str.\n";
4   print "The array \@numbers is initially @numbers.\n";
5   foreach $str(@numbers ){
6       $str += 5;
7       print "$str\n";
8   }
9   print "Out of the loop--\$str is $str.\n";
10  print "Out of the loop--The array \@numbers is now @numbers.\n";

(Output)
3   The initial value of scalar $str is "hello".
4   The array @numbers is initially 1 3 5 7 9.
7   6
    8
    10
    12
    14
9   Out of the loop--$str is hello.
10  Out of the loop--The array @numbers is now 6 8 10 12 14.
```

EXPLANATION

1   The scalar *$str* is assigned the string *hello*.

2   The array *@numbers* is assigned the list of numbers: 1, 3, 5, 7, and 9.

3   The *print* function prints the initial value of *$str* to *STDOUT*.

4   The *print* function prints the initial value of *@numbers* to *STDOUT*.

5   The *foreach* statement assigns, in turn, each element in the list to *$str*. The variable *$str* is local to the loop and references each item in the list so that whatever is done to *$str* will affect the array *@numbers*. When the loop exits, it will regain its former value.

6   Each time through the loop, the value referenced by *$str* is incremented by *5*.

7   The *print* function prints the new value of *$str* to *STDOUT*.

8   After exiting the loop, the original value of *$str* is printed to *STDOUT*.

9   After exiting the loop, the new and modified values of the *@number* array are printed to *STDOUT*.

EXAMPLE 6.16

```
(The Script)
    #!/usr/bin/perl
1   @colors = (red, green, blue, brown);
2   foreach(@colors){
3       print "$_ ";
4       $_="YUCKY";
    }
5   print "\n@colors\n";

(Output)
3   red green blue brown
5   YUCKY  YUCKY  YUCKY  YUCKY
```

EXPLANATION

1   The array @*colors* is initialized.
2   The *foreach* loop is not followed by an explicit variable, but it does have a list. Since the variable is missing, the *$_* special scalar is used implicitly.
3   *$_* is really a reference to the item in the list that is currently being evaluated. As each item of the list @*colors* is referenced by the *$_* variable, the value is printed to *STDOUT*.
4   The *$_* variable is assigned the string *YUCKY*. Each original element in the array @*colors* will be replaced permanently by the value *YUCKY*, in turn.
5   The @*color* array has really been changed. The *$_* variable is null, its value before entering the loop.

6.3.5   Loop Control

To interrupt the normal flow of control within a loop, Perl provides labels and simple control statements. These statements are used for controlling a loop when some condition is reached; that is, the control is transferred directly to either the bottom or the top of the loop, skipping any statements that follow the control statement condition.

Labels.   Labels are optional but can be used to control the flow of a loop. By themselves, labels do nothing. They are used with the loop control modifiers, listed below. A block by itself, whether or not it has a label, is equivalent to a loop that executes only **once**. If labels are capitalized, they will not be confused with reserved words.

FORMAT

```
LABEL: while (Expression){Block}
LABEL: while (Expression) {Block} continue{Block}
LABEL: for (Expression; Expression; Expression)
   {BLOCK}
LABEL: foreach Variable (Array){Block}
LABEL: {Block} continue {Block}
```

To control the flow of loops, the following simple statements may be used within the block:

```
next
next LABEL
last
last LABEL
redo
redo LABEL
goto LABEL
```

The *next* statement restarts the next iteration of the loop, skipping over the rest of the statements in the loop and re-evaluating the loop expression, like a C, *awk,* or shell *continue* statement. Since a block is a loop that iterates once, *next* can be used (with a *continue* block, if provided) to exit the block early.

The *last* statement leaves or breaks out of a loop and is like the *break* statement in C, *awk*, and shell. Since a block is a loop that iterates once, *last* can be used to break out of a block.

The *redo* statement restarts the block without evaluating the loop expression again.

The *continue block* is executed just before the conditional expression is about to be evaluated again.

The *goto* statement, although frowned upon by most programmers, is allowed in Perl programs. It takes a label as its argument and jumps to the label when the *goto* statement is executed. The label can be anywhere in your script but does not work when it appears inside a *do* statement or within a subroutine.

A Labeled Block Without a Loop.   A block is like a loop that executes once. A block can be labeled.

The *redo* statement causes control to start at the top of the innermost or labeled block without reevaluating the loop expression if there is one (similar to a *goto*).

EXAMPLE 6.17

```
(The Script)
     #!//usr/bin/perl
     # Program that uses a label without a loop and the redo statement
1    ATTEMPT: {
2    print "Are you a great person? ";
         chomp($answer = <STDIN>);
3        redo ATTEMPT unless $answer eq "yes";
     }


(Output)
2    Are you a great person? Nope
2    Are you a great person? Sometimes
2    Are you a great person? yes
```

EXPLANATION

1   The label is user defined. It precedes a block. It is as though you had named the block *ATTEMPT*.
2   The user is asked for input.
3   The *redo* statement restarts the block, similar to a *goto* statement, unless the *$answer* evaluates to *yes*.

EXAMPLE 6.18

```
(The Script)
     #!/usr/bin/perl
1    while(1){      # start an infinite loop

2        print "What was your grade? ";
         $grade = <STDIN>;

3        if($grade < 0 || $grade > 100){
             print "Illegal choice\n";
4            next; }      # start control at the beginning of
                          # the innermost loop
5        if($grade  > 89 && $grade < 101) {print "A\n";}
         elsif($grade > 79 && $grade < 90) {print "B\n";}
         elsif($grade > 69 && $grade < 80) {print "C\n";}
         elsif($grade > 59 && $grade < 70) {print "D\n";}
         else{print "You Failed."};
6        print "Do you want to enter another grade? (y/n) ";
         $choice = <STDIN>;
7        last  if $choice ne "y";      # break out of the innermost
                                       # loop if the condition is true

     }
```

EXAMPLE 6.18   (CONTINUED)

```
(Output)
2   What was your grade? 94
    A
6   Do you want to enter another grade (y/n)?  y
2   What was your grade? 66
    D
6   Do you want to enter another grade (y/n)?  n
```

EXPLANATION

1   Start an infinite loop.
2   Ask for user input.
3   Logical test. If the value of *$grade* is less than *0* or greater than *100*.
4   If the test yields *false*, control starts again at the beginning of the *while* loop.
5   Test each of the *if* conditional statements.
6   Ask for user input.
7   Break out of the innermost loop if the conditional modifier tests true.

EXAMPLE 6.19

```
(The Script)
1   ATTEMPT:{
2       print "What is the course number? ";
        chomp($number = <STDIN>);
        print "What is the course name? ";
        chomp($course = <STDIN>);

3       $department{$number} = $course;

        print "\nReady to quit? ";
        chomp($answer = <STDIN>);
4       if ("$answer" eq  "yes") {last;}
5       redo ATTEMPT;
    }
6   print "Program continues here.\n";

(Output)
2   What is the course number? 101
    What is the course name?  CIS342
3   Ready to quit? n
2   What is the course number? 201
    What is the course name? BIO211
```

EXAMPLE 6.19 (CONTINUED)

```
3    Ready to quit? n
2    What is the course number? 301
     What is the course name? ENG120
3    Ready to quit? yes
6    Program continues here.
```

EXPLANATION

1. The label *ATTEMPT* prepends the block. A block without a looping construct is like a loop that executes only once.
2. The script gets user input in order to fill an associative array. Both the key and value are provided by the user.
3. The hash *%department* is assigned a value.
4. If the user is ready to quit, the *last* statement sends the control out of the block.
5. The *redo* statement returns control to the top of the labeled block. Each of the statements is executed again.
6. After exiting the block (line 4), the program continues here.

Nested Loops and Labels.   A loop within a loop is a **nested loop**. The outside loop is initialized and tested, the inside loop then iterates completely through all of its cycles, and the outside loop starts again where it left off. The inside loop moves faster than the outside loop. Loops can be nested as deeply as you wish, but there are times when it is necessary to terminate the loop when some condition is met. Normally, if you use loop-control statements such as *next* and *last*, the control is directed to the innermost loop. There are times when it might be necessary to switch control to some outer loop. This is accomplished by using labels.

By prefixing a loop with a label, you can control the flow of the program with *last, next,* and *redo* statements. Labeling a loop is like giving the loop its own name.

EXAMPLE 6.20

```
(A Demo Script)
1   OUT: while(1){
2       < Program continues here >
3       MID: while(1){
4           if(<expression is true>) {last OUT;}
            < Program continues here >
5           INNER: while(1){
6               if(<expression is true>) {next OUT;}
                <Program continues here>
            }
        }
    }
7   print "Out of all loops.\n";
```

EXPLANATION

1   The *OUT* label is used to control this infinite *while* loop, if necessary. The label is followed by a colon and the loop statement.
2   The program code continues here.
3   The *MID* label is used to control this inner *while* loop, if necessary.
4   If the expression being evaluated is true, the *last* loop-control statement is executed, breaking from this loop, labeled *OUT*, all the way out to line 7.
5   The innermost *while* loop is labeled *INNER*.
6   This time the *next* statement with the *OUT* label causes loop control to branch back to line 1.
7   This statement is outside all of the loops and is where the *last* statement branches, if given the *OUT* label.

EXAMPLE 6.21

```
(The Script)
1   for($rows = 5; $rows >= 1; $rows--){
2       for($columns = 1; $columns <= $rows; $columns++){
3           printf "*";
4       }
5   print "\n";
6   }

(Output)
3   *****
    ****
    ***
    **
    *
```

EXPLANATION

1   The first expression in the outside loop initializes the scalar *$rows* to 5. The variable is tested. Since it is greater or equal to *1*, the inner loop starts.
2   The first expression in the inner loop initializes the scalar *$columns* to *1*. The scalar *$columns* is tested. The inner loop will iterate through all of its cycles. When the inner loop has completed, the outer loop will pick up where it left off; that is, *$rows* will be decremented, then tested, and if true, the block will be executed again, and so on.
3   This statement belongs to the inner *for* loop and will be executed for each iteration of the loop.
4   This curly brace closes the inner *for* loop.
5   The *print* statement is executed for each iteration of the outer *for* loop.
6   This curly brace closes the outer *for* loop.

When a label is omitted, the loop control statements, *next, last*, and *redo* reference the innermost loop. When branching out of a nested loop to an outer loop, labels may precede the loop statement.

EXAMPLE 6.22

(The Script)
```
    # This script prints the average salary of employees
    # earning over $50,000 annually
    # There are 5 employees. If the salary falls below $50,000
    # it is not included in the tally

1   EMPLOYEE: for($emp = 1,$number = 0; $emp <= 5; $emp++){
2       do{ print "What is the monthly rate for employee #$emp? ";
            print "(Type q to quit) ";
3           chomp($monthly = <STDIN>);
4           last EMPLOYEE if $monthly eq 'q';
5           next EMPLOYEE if (($year = $monthly * 12.00) <= 50000);
6           $number++;
7           $total_sal += $year;
            next EMPLOYEE;
8       }while($monthly ne 'q');
    }
9   unless($number == 0){
10      $average = $total_sal/$number;
11      print "There were $number employees who earned over \$50,000
                annually.\n";
        printf "Their average annual salary is \$%.2f.\n", $average;
        }
    else{
        print "None of the employees made over \$50,000\n";
    }
```

(Output)
```
2   What is the monthly rate for employee #1? (Type q to quit) 4000
2   What is the monthly rate for employee #2? (Type q to quit) 5500
2   What is the monthly rate for employee #3? (Type q to quit) 6000
2   What is the monthly rate for employee #4? (Type q to quit) 3400
2   What is the monthly rate for employee #5? (Type q to quit) 4500
11  There were 3 employees who earned over $50,000 annually.
    Their average annual salary is $64000.00.
```

EXPLANATION

1 The label *EMPLOYEE* precedes the outer loop. This loop keeps track of five employees.
2 The *do/while* loop is entered.
3 The script gets user input for the monthly salary.

EXPLANATION (CONTINUED)

4   If the user types *q*, the *last* control statement is executed and branching goes to the bottom of the outer loop, labeled *EMPLOYEE*.

5   The *next* control statement transfers execution to the top of the outer *for* loop labeled *EMPLOYEE*, if the condition is true.

6   The scalar *$number* is incremented.

7   The value of the scalar *$total_sal* is calculated.

8   The *next* control statement transfers execution to the top of the outermost *for* loop, labeled *EMPLOYEE*.

9   Unless the value of *$number* equals *0*, in the case that no one earned over $50,000, the block is entered.

10   The average annual salary is calculated.

11   The results are displayed.

The *continue* Block.   The *continue* block with a *while* loop preserves the correct semantics as a *for* loop, even when the *next* statement is used.

EXAMPLE 6.23

```
(The Script)
    #! /usr/bin/perl#
    # Example using the continue block
1   for($i = 1; $i <= 10; $i++){       # $i is incremented only once
2       if ($i == 5){
3           print "\$i == $i\n";
4           next;
        }
5       print "$i ";
    }

    print "\n"; print '=' x 35; print "\n";
# ---------------------------------------------------------

6   $i = 1;
7   while ($i <= 10){
8       if ($i == 5){
            print "\$i == $i\n";
9           $i++;     # $i must be incremented here or an
                      # infinite loop will start
10          next;
        }
```

EXAMPLE 6.23 (CONTINUED)

```
11      print "$i ";
12      $i++;              # $i is incremented again
   } # end while loop unclear ;page break

   print "\n"; print '=' x 35; print "\n";
   # -------------------------------------------------------
   # The continue block allows the while loop to act like a for loop
   $i = 1;
13 while ($i <= 10) {
14    if ($i == 5) {
15        print "\$i == $i\n";
16        next;
      }
17    print "$i ";
18 }continue {$i++; }      # $i is incremented only once

(Output)
1 2 3 4 $i == 5
6 7 8 9 10
===================================
1 2 3 4 $i == 5
6 7 8 9 10
===================================
1 2 3 4 $i == 5
6 7 8 9 10
```

EXPLANATION

1 The *for* loop is entered and will loop ten times.
2 If the value of *$i* is 5, the block is entered and . . .
3 . . . the value of *$i* is printed.
4 The *next* statement returns control back to the *for* loop. When control is returned to the *for* loop, the third expression is always evaluated before the second expression is tested. **Before** the second expression is tested, *$i* is incremented.
5 Each time through the loop, the value of *$i* is printed unless *$i* equals 5.
6 *$i* is initialized to 5.
7 The body of the *while* loop is entered if the expression tested is true.
8 If *$i* is equal to 5, the value of *$i* is displayed.
9 *$i* is incremented by one. If the *$i* is not incremented here, it will never be incremented and the program will go into an infinite loop.
10 The *next* statement causes control to start again at the top of the *while* loop, where the expression after *while* is evaluated.
11 The current value of *$i* is displayed.

EXPLANATION (CONTINUED)

11 After *$i* is incremented, control will go back to the top of the *while* loop and the expression will be tested again.

12 While *$i* is less than or equal to *10*, enter the loop body.

13 If *$i* is equal to *5*, the block is entered.

14 The current value of *$i* is displayed.

15 The *next* statement normally causes control to go back to the top of *while* loop, but because there is a *continue* block at the end of the loop, control will go into the *continue* block first and then back to the top of the *while* loop where the expression will be tested.

16 The value of *$i* is displayed.

17 The *continue* block is executed at the end of the *while* loop block, before the *next* statement returns control to the top of the loop or, if *next* is not executed, after the last statement in the loop block.

6.3.6 The Phoney Switch Statement

Perl does not have an official switch statement. A block (labeled or not) is equivalent to a loop that executes once, and loop control statements, such as *last*, *next*, and *redo*, can be used within this block to emulate *C*'s *switch/case* construct.

The *do* block executes the sequence of commands in the block and returns the value of the last expression evaluated in the block.

EXAMPLE 6.24

```
(The Script)
    #! /usr/bin/perl
1   $hour = 0;
2   while($hour < 24) {
3     SWITCH: {       # SWITCH is just a user-defined label
4         $hour < 12                    && do {  print "Good-morning!\n";
5                                                last SWITCH;};
6         $hour == 12               && do {  print "Lunch!\n";
                                             last SWITCH;};

7         $hour > 12 && $hour <= 17  && do {  print "Siesta time!\n";
                                             last SWITCH;};

8         $hour > 17                  && do {  print "Good night.\n";
                                             last SWITCH;};
      }  # End of block labeled SWITCH

9     $hour++;
    } # End of loop block
```

EXAMPLE 6.24 (CONTINUED)

```
(Output)
Good-morning!
Good-morning!
Good-morning!

<Output continues>

Good-morning!
Good-morning!
Good-morning!
Lunch!
Siesta time!
Siesta time!
Siesta time!
Siesta time!
Siesta time!
Good night.
Good night.
Good night.
Good night.
Good night.
```

EXPLANATION

1 The *$hour* scalar is assigned an initial value of *0* before entering the loop.
2 The *while* loop expression is evaluated.
3 The label *SWITCH* labels the block. It is simply a label, nothing more.
4 After entering the block, the expression is evaluated. The expression reads *if $hour is less than 12...*, the expression on the right of the *&&* is evaluated. This is a *do* block. Each of the statements within this block is executed in sequence. The value of the last statement evaluated is returned.
5 The last statement causes control to branch to the end of this block labeled *SWITCH* to line 8.
6 This statement is evaluated if the expression in the previous statement evaluates to false. The expression reads *if $hour is equal to 12...*
7 This statement is evaluated if the expression in the previous statement evaluates to false. The expression reads *if $hour is greater than 12 and also less than or equal to 17...*
8 If this statement is true, the *do* block is executed. The expression reads *if $hour is greater than 17...*
9 The *$hour* scalar is incremented once each time after going through the loop.

EXERCISE 5
What Are Your Conditions?

1. Physicists tell us that the lowest possible temperature is absolute zero. Absolute zero is –459.69 degrees Fahrenheit.
   a. Accept inputs from the user: a beginning temperature, an ending temperature, and an increment value (all Fahrenheit).
   b. Check for bad input: a temperature less than absolute zero and an ending temperature less than a beginning temperature. The program will send a message to *STDERR* if either condition is detected.
   c. Print a header showing: *"Fahrenheit   Celcius"*. Print all the values from the beginning to the ending temperature. Use a looping mechanism.
   The conversion formula is: C = (F – 32) / 1.8

   *Bonus: Make sure the user enters a number, either decimal or floating point; e.g., 5.5, .5, or 5.

CHAPTER

7

REGULAR EXPRESSIONS— PATTERN MATCHING

7.1   What Is a Regular Expression?

If you are familiar with UNIX utilities such as *vi, sed, grep*, and *awk*, you have met face-to-face with the infamous regular expressions and metacharacters used in delimiting search patterns. Well, with Perl, they're back!

What is a regular expression, anyway? A **regular expression** is really just a sequence or pattern of characters that is matched against a string of text when performing searches and replacements. A simple regular expression consists of a character or set of characters that matches itself. The regular expression is normally delimited by forward slashes.[1] The special scalar, *$_*, is the default search space where Perl does its pattern matching. *$_* is like a shadow. Sometimes you see it; sometimes you don't. Don't worry; all this will become clear as you read through this chapter.

EXAMPLE 7.1

```
1   /abc/
2   ?abc?
```

EXPLANATION

1   The pattern *abc* is enclosed in forward slashes. If searching for this pattern, for example, in a string or text file, any string that contained the pattern *abc* would be matched.

2   The pattern *abc* is enclosed in question marks. If searching for this pattern, only the first occurrence of the string is matched. (See the *reset* function in Appendix A.)

---

1. Actually, any character can be used as a delimiter. See Table 7.3 on page 189 and Example 7.12 on page 172.

7.2   Expression Modifiers and Simple Statements

A **simple statement** is an expression terminated with a semicolon. Perl supports a set of modifiers that allow you to further evaluate an expression based on some condition. A simple statement may contain an expression **ending** with a single modifier. The modifier and its expression are always terminated with a semicolon. When evaluating regular expressions, the modifiers may be simpler to use than the full-blown conditional constructs (discussed in Chapter 6, "If Only, Unconditionally, Forever").

The modifiers are

if
unless
while
until
foreach

7.2.1   Conditional Modifiers

The *if* Modifier.   The *if* modifier is used to control a simple statement consisting of two expressions. If *Expression1* is true, *Expression2* is executed.

FORMAT

```
Expression2 if Expression1;
```

EXAMPLE 7.2

```
(In Script)
1    $x = 5;
2    print $x  if $x == 5;

(Output)
5
```

EXPLANATION

1    $x is assigned 5. The value of $x is printed only if $x is equal to 5.
2   The *if* modifier must be placed at the end of a statement and, in this example, controls the *print* function. If the expression $x == 5 is true, then the value of $x is printed. It could be written *if ($x == 5) {print $x;}*.

EXAMPLE 7.3

```
(In Script)
1   $_ = "xabcy\n";
2   print if /abc/;     # Could be written: print $_ if $_ =~ /abc/;

(Output)
xabcy
```

EXPLANATION

1   The $_ scalar variable is assigned the string *xabcy*.
2   When the *if* modifier is followed directly by a regular expression, Perl assumes that the line being matched is $_, the default place holder for pattern matching. The value of $_, *xabcy*, is printed if the regular expression, *abc*, is matched anywhere in the string.[a] The expression could have been written as *if $_ =~ /abc/*. (The =~ match operator will be discussed at the end of this chapter.)

a. $_ is the also default output for the *print* function.

EXAMPLE 7.4

```
(In Script)
1   $_ = "I lost my gloves in the clover.";
2   print "Found love in gloves!\n" if /love/;
                    # Long form: if $_ =~ /love

(Output)
Found love in gloves!
```

EXPLANATION

1   The $_ is assigned the string *I lost my gloves in the clover.*
2   The regular expression, *love*, is matched in the $_ variable, and the string *Found love in gloves!* is printed; otherwise, nothing will be printed. The regular expression *love* is found in both *gloves* and *clover*. The search starts at the left-hand side of the string, so that matching *love* in *gloves* will produce the true condition before *clover* is reached. If $_ (or, for that matter, any other scalar) is used explicitly after the *if* modifier, then the =~ pattern matching operator is necessary when evaluating the regular expression.

EXAMPLE 7.5

```
(The Script)
1   while(<DATA>){
2       print if /Norma/;        # Print the line if it matches Norma
    }
3   _ _DATA_ _
    Steve Blenheim
    Betty Boop
    Igor Chevsky
    Norma Cord
    Jon DeLoach
    Karen Evich

(Output)
Norma Cord
```

EXPLANATION

1 The special *DATA* filehandle gets its input from the text after the _ _*DATA*_ _ token. When the *while* loop is entered, a line of input is stored in the *$_* scalar variable. The first line stored in *$_* is *Steve Blenheim*. The next time around the loop, *Betty Boop* is stored in *$_*, and this continues until all of the lines following the _ _*DATA*_ _ token are read and processed.

2 Only the lines containing the regular expression, *Norma*, are printed. *$_* is the default for pattern matching; it could also have been written as *print $_ if $_ =~ /Norma/;*.

3 The *DATA* filehandle gets its data from the lines that follow the _ _*DATA*_ _ token.

EXAMPLE 7.6

```
(The Script)
1   while(<DATA>){
2       if /Norma/ print;        # Wrong!
    }

3   _ _DATA_ _
    Steve Blenheim
    Betty Boop
    Igor Chevsky
    Norma Cord
    Jon DeLoach
    Karen Evich

(Output)
Execution of script aborted due to compilation errors.
```

EXPLANATION

1   The special *DATA* filehandle gets its input from the text after the _ _*DATA*_ _ token. The *while* loop iterates through each line of text. Each line of input is assigned to *$_*, the default scalar used to hold a line of input and to test pattern matches.
2   The modifier must be at the end of the expression, or a syntax error results. This statement should be *print if /Norma/* or *if(/Norma/) {print;}*.

The *unless* Modifier.   The *unless* modifier is used to control a simple statement consisting of two expressions. If *Expression1* is false, *Expression2* is executed. Like the *if* modifier, *unless* is placed at the end of the statement.

FORMAT

```
Expression2 unless Expression1;
```

EXAMPLE 7.7

```
(The Script)
1   $x=5;
2   print $x unless $x == 6;

(Output)
5
```

EXPLANATION

The *unless* modifier controls the *print* statement. If the expression *$x == 6* is false, then the value of *$x* is printed.

EXAMPLE 7.8

```
(The Script)
1   while(<DATA>){
2       print unless /Norma/;   # Print line if it doesn't match Norma
    }

3   _ _DATA_ _
    Steve Blenheim
    Betty Boop
    Igor Chevsky
    Norma Cord
    Jon DeLoach
    Karen Evich
```

EXAMPLE 7.5

```
(The Script)
1   while(<DATA>){
2       print if /Norma/;        # Print the line if it matches Norma
    }
3   _ _DATA_ _
    Steve Blenheim
    Betty Boop
    Igor Chevsky
    Norma Cord
    Jon DeLoach
    Karen Evich

(Output)
Norma Cord
```

EXPLANATION

1   The special *DATA* filehandle gets its input from the text after the _ _DATA_ _ token. When the *while* loop is entered, a line of input is stored in the *$_* scalar variable. The first line stored in *$_* is *Steve Blenheim*. The next time around the loop, *Betty Boop* is stored in *$_*, and this continues until all of the lines following the _ _DATA_ _ token are read and processed.

2   Only the lines containing the regular expression, *Norma*, are printed. *$_* is the default for pattern matching; it could also have been written as *print $_ if $_ =~ /Norma/;*.

3   The *DATA* filehandle gets its data from the lines that follow the _ _DATA_ _ token.

EXAMPLE 7.6

```
(The Script)
1   while(<DATA>){
2       if /Norma/ print;        # Wrong!
    }

3   _ _DATA_ _
    Steve Blenheim
    Betty Boop
    Igor Chevsky
    Norma Cord
    Jon DeLoach
    Karen Evich

(Output)
Execution of script aborted due to compilation errors.
```

EXPLANATION

1   The special *DATA* filehandle gets its input from the text after the _ _*DATA*_ _ token.
     The *while* loop iterates through each line of text. Each line of input is assigned to *$_*,
     the default scalar used to hold a line of input and to test pattern matches.
2   The modifier must be at the end of the expression, or a syntax error results. This
     statement should be *print if /Norma/* or *if(/Norma/) {print;}*.

The *unless* Modifier.   The *unless* modifier is used to control a simple statement consisting of two expressions. If *Expression1* is false, *Expression2* is executed. Like the *if* modifier, *unless* is placed at the end of the statement.

FORMAT

```
Expression2 unless Expression1;
```

EXAMPLE 7.7

```
(The Script)
1    $x=5;
2    print $x unless $x == 6;

(Output)
5
```

EXPLANATION

The *unless* modifier controls the *print* statement. If the expression *$x == 6* is false, then
the value of *$x* is printed.

EXAMPLE 7.8

```
(The Script)
1    while(<DATA>){
2        print unless /Norma/;    # Print line if it doesn't match Norma
     }

3    _ _DATA_ _
     Steve Blenheim
     Betty Boop
     Igor Chevsky
     Norma Cord
     Jon DeLoach
     Karen Evich
```

EXAMPLE 7.8 (CONTINUED)

```
(Output)
Steve Blenheim
Betty Boop
Igor Chevsky
Jon DeLoach
Karen Evich
```

EXPLANATION

1   The special *DATA* filehandle gets its input from the text after the _ _*DATA*_ _ token. The *while* loop is entered and the first line below the _ _*DATA*_ _ token is read in and assigned to *$_*, and so on.

2   All lines that don't contain the pattern *Norma* are matched and printed.

3   The *DATA* filehandle gets its data from the lines that follow the _ _*DATA*_ _ token.

7.2.3 Looping Modifiers

The *while* Modifier.   The *while* modifier repeatedly executes the second expression as long as the first expression is true.

FORMAT

```
Expression2 while Expression1;
```

EXAMPLE 7.9

```
(The Script)
1   $x=1;
2   print $x++,"\n" while $x != 5;

(Output)
1
2
3
4
```

EXPLANATION

Perl prints the value of *$x* while *$x* is not *5*.

The *until* Modifier.   The *until* modifier repeatedly executes the second expression as long as the first expression is false.

FORMAT

```
Expression2 until Expression1;
```

EXAMPLE 7.10

```
(The Script)
1   $x=1;
2   print $x++,"\n" until $x == 5;

(Output)
1
2
3
4
```

EXPLANATION

1   x is assigned an initial value of *1*.
2   Perl prints the value of x until x is equal to *5*. The variable x is set to one and then incremented. Be careful that you don't get yourself into an infinite loop.

The *foreach* Modifier.   The *foreach* modifier evaluates once for each element in its list, with $_ aliased to each element of the list, in turn.

EXAMPLE 7.11

```
(The Script)
1   @alpha=(a .. z, "\n");
2   print foreach @alpha;

(Output)
abcdefghijklmnopqrstuvwxyz
```

EXPLANATION

1   A list of lowercase letters is assigned to array *@alpha*.
2   Each item in the list is aliased to $_ and printed, one at a time, until there are no more items in the list.

7.3   **Regular Expression Operators**

The regular expression operators are used for matching patterns in searches and for replacements in substitution operations. The *m* operator is used for matching patterns and the *s* operator is used when substituting one pattern for another.

7.3.1   The *m* Operator and Matching

The *m* operator is used for matching patterns. The *m* operator is optional if the delimiters enclosing the regular expression are forward slashes (the forward slash is the default), but required if you change the delimiter. You may want to change the delimiter if the regular expression itself contains forward slashes (e.g., when searching for birthdays such as *3/15/93* or pathnames such as */usr/var/adm*).

FORMAT

```
/Regular Expression/      default delimiter
m#Regular Expression#      optional delimiters
m{regular expression}     pair of delimiters
```

Table 7.1   Matching Modifiers

Modifier	Meaning
i	Turn off case sensitivity.
m	Treat a string as multiple lines.
o	Only compile pattern once. Used to optimize the search.
s	Treat string as a single line when a newline is embedded.
x	Permit comments in a regular expression and ignore whitespace.
g	Match globally, i.e., find all occurrences. Return a list if used with an array context, or true or false if a scalar context.

EXAMPLE 7.12

```
1   m/Good morning/
2   /Good evening/
3   /\/usr\/var\/adm/
4   m#/usr/var/adm#
5   m(Good evening)
6   m'$name'
```

EXPLANATION

1   The *m* operator is not needed in this example since forward slashes delimit the regular expression.

2   The forward slash is the delimiter; therefore, the *m* operator is optional.

3   Each of the forward slashes in the search path is quoted with a backslash so that it will not be confused with the forward slash used for the pattern delimiter—a messy approach.

4   The *m* operator is required because the pound sign (#) is used as an alternative to the forward slash. The pound sign delimiter clarifies and simplifies the previous example.

5   If the opening delimiter is a parenthesis, square bracket, angle bracket, or brace, then the closing delimiter must be the corresponding closing character, such as *m(expression)*, *m[expression]*, *m<expression>*, or *m{expression}*.

6   If the delimiter is a single quote, then variable interpolation is turned off; in other words, *$name* is treated as a literal.

EXAMPLE 7.13

```
(The Script)
1   while(<DATA>){
2       print if /Betty/;        # Print the line if it matches Betty
    }

3   _ _DATA_ _
    Steve Blenheim
    Betty Boop
    Igor Chevsky
    Norma Cord
    Jon DeLoach
    Karen Evich

(Output)
Betty Boop
```

EXPLANATION

1   The special *DATA* filehandle gets its input from the text after the _ _*DATA*_ _ token. The *while* loop is entered and the first line after the _ _*DATA*_ _ token is read in and assigned to *$_*.
2   All lines that match the pattern *Betty* are matched and printed.
3   The *DATA* filehandle gets its data from the lines that follow the _ _*DATA*_ _ token.

EXAMPLE 7.14

```
(The Script)
1   while(<DATA>){
2       print unless /Evich/;     # Print line unless it matches Evich
    }
3   _ _DATA_ _
    Steve Blenheim
    Betty Boop
    Igor Chevsky
    Norma Cord
    Jon DeLoach
    Karen Evich

(Output)
Steve Blenheim
Betty Boop
Igor Chevsky
Norma Cord
Jon DeLoach
```

EXPLANATION

1   The special *DATA* filehandle gets its input from the text after the _ _*DATA*_ _ token. The *while* loop is entered and the first line from under the _ _*DATA*_ _ token is read in and assigned to *$_*.
2   All lines that don't match the pattern *Evich* are printed.
3   The *DATA* filehandle gets its data from the lines that follow the _ _*DATA*_ _ token.

EXAMPLE 7.15

```
(The Script)
1   while(<DATA>){
2       print if m#Jon#        # Print the line if it matches Jon
    }
3   _ _DATA_ _
    Steve Blenheim
    Betty Boop
    Igor Chevsky
    Norma Cord
    Jon DeLoach
    Karen Evich

(Output)
Jon DeLoach
```

EXPLANATION

1   The special *DATA* filehandle gets its input from the text after the _ _*DATA*_ _ token. The *while* loop is entered and the first line following the _ _*DATA*_ _ token is read in and assigned to *$_*.

2   The *m* (match) operator is necessary because the delimiter has been changed from the default forward slash to a pound sign (*#*). The line is printed if it matches *Jon*.

3   The *DATA* filehandle gets its data from the lines that follow the _ _*DATA*_ _ token.

EXAMPLE 7.16

```
(The Script)
1   while(<DATA>){
2       print if m(Karen E);    # Print the line if it matches Karen E
    }
3   $name="Jon";
4   $_=qq/$name is a good sport.\n/;
5   print if m'$name';
6   print if m"$name";

7   _ _DATA_ _
    Steve Blenheim
    Betty Boop
    Igor Chevsky
    Norma Cord
    Jon DeLoach
    Karen Evich
```

EXAMPLE 7.16 (CONTINUED)

```
(Output)
2    Karen Evich
5    <No output>
6    Jon is a good sport.
```

EXPLANATION

1   The special *DATA* filehandle gets its input from the text after the _ _*DATA*_ _ token. The *while* loop is entered and the first line below the _ _*DATA*_ _ token is read in and assigned to *$_*.

2   The *m* (match) operator is necessary because the delimiter has been changed from the default forward slash to a set of opening and closing parentheses. Other pairs that could be used are square brackets, curly braces, angle brackets, and single quotes. If single quotes are used, and the regular expression contains variables, the variables will not be interpolated. The line is printed if it matches *Karen E*.

3   The scalar *$name* is assigned *Jon*.

4   *$_* is assigned a string including the scalar *$name*.

5   When the matching delimiter is a set of single quotes, variables in the regular expression are not interpolated. The literal value *$name* is not found in *$_*; therefore, nothing is printed.

6   If double quotes enclose the expression, the variable *$name* will be interpolated. The string assigned to *$_* is printed if it contains *Jon*.

7   The *DATA* filehandle gets its data from the lines that follow the _ _*DATA*_ _ token.

The *g* Modifier—Global Match.   The *g* modifier is used to cause a global match; in other words, all occurrences of a pattern in the line are matched. Without the *g*, only the first occurrence of a pattern is matched. The *m* operator will return a list of the patterns matched.

FORMAT

```
m/search pattern/g
```

EXAMPLE 7.17

```
(The Script)
    #!/usr/bin/perl
1   $_ = "I lost my gloves in the clover, Love.";
2   @list=/love/g;
3   print "@list.\n";

(Output)
3   love love.
```

EXPLANATION

1   The *$_* scalar variable is assigned a string of text.
2   If the search is done with the *g* modifier, in an array context, each match is stored in the *@list* array. The regular expression *love* was found in the string twice, once in *gloves* and once in *clover*. *Love* is not matched since the *L* is uppercase.
3   The list of matched items is printed.

The *i* Modifier—Case Insensitivity.   Perl is sensitive to whether or not characters are upper- or lowercase when performing matches. If you want to turn off case sensitivity, an *i* (insensitive) is appended to the last delimiter of the match operator.

FORMAT

```
m/search pattern/i
```

EXAMPLE 7.18

```
1   $_ = "I lost my gloves in the clover, Love.";
2   @list=/love/gi;
3   print "@list.\n";

(Output)
3   love love Love.
```

EXPLANATION

1   The *$_* scalar variable is assigned the string.
2   This time the *i* modifier is used to turn off the case sensitivity. Both *love* and *Love* will be matched and assigned to the array *@list*.
3   The pattern was found three times. The list is printed.

Special Scalars for Saving Patterns. The $& special scalar is assigned the string that was matched in the last successful search. $` saves what was found preceding the pattern that was matched, and $' saves what was found after the pattern that was matched.

EXAMPLE 7.19

```
1    $_="San Francisco to Hong Kong\n";

2    /Francisco/;      # Save 'Francisco' in $& if it is found
3    print $&,"\n";

4    /to/;
5    print $`,"\n";     # Save what comes before the string 'to'

6    /to\s/;           # \s represents a space
7    print $', "\n";   # Save what comes after the string 'to'

(Output)
3    Francisco
5    San Francisco
7    Hong Kong
```

EXPLANATION

1 The $_ scalar is assigned a string.
2 The search pattern contains the regular expression, *Francisco*. Perl searches for this pattern in the $_ variable. If found, the pattern *Francisco* will be saved in another special scalar, $&.
3 The search pattern *Francisco* was successfully matched, saved in $&, and printed.
4 The search pattern contains the regular expression *to*. Perl searches for this pattern in the $_ variable. If the pattern *to* is matched, the string to the **left** of this pattern, *San Francisco*, is saved in the $` scalar (note the backquote).
5 The value of $` is printed.
6 The search pattern contains the regular expression *to\s* (*to* followed by a space; \s represents a space). Perl searches for this pattern in the $_ variable. If the pattern *to\s* is matched, the string to the **right** of this pattern, *Hong Kong*, is saved in the $' scalar (note the straight quote).
7 The value of $' is printed.

The *x* Modifier—The Expressive Modifier. The *x* modifier allows you to place comments within the regular expression and add whitespace characters (spaces, tabs, newlines) for clarity without having those characters interpreted as part of the regular expression; in other words, you can *express* your intentions within the regular expression.

EXAMPLE 7.20

```
1   $_="San Francisco to Hong Kong\n";
2   /Francisco        # Searching for Francisco
    /x;
3   print "Comments and spaces were removed and \$& is $&\n";

(Output)
3   Comments and spaces were removed and $& is Francisco
```

EXPLANATION

1   The *$_* scalar is assigned a string.
2   The search pattern consists of *Francisco* followed by a space, comment, and another space. The *x* modifier allows the additional whitespace and comments to be inserted in the pattern space without being interpreted as part of the search pattern.
3   The printed text illustrates that the search was unaffected by the extra spaces and comments. *$&* holds the value of what was matched as a result of the search.

7.3.2   The *s* Operator and Substitution

The *s* operator is used for substitutions. The substitution operator replaces the first regular expression pattern with the second. The delimiter can also be changed. The *g* modifier placed after the last delimiter stands for **global change** on a line. The return value from the *s* operator is the number of substitutions that were made. Without it, only the first occurrence of the pattern is affected by the substitution.

The special built-in variable *$&* gets the value of whatever was found in the search string.

FORMAT

```
s/old/new/;
s/old/new/i;
s/old/new/g;
s+old+new+g;
s(old)/new/;   s[old]{new};
s/old/expression to be evaluated/e;
s/old/new/ige;
s/old/new/x;
```

EXAMPLE 7.21

```
s/Igor/Boris/;
s/Igor/Boris/g;
s/norma/Jane/i;
s!Jon!Susan!;
s{Jon} <Susan>;
s/$sal/$sal * 1.1/e
s/dec/"Dec" . "ember"        # Replace "dec" or "Dec" with "December"
 /eigx;
```

Table 7.2 Substitution Modifiers

Modifier	Meaning
e	Evaluate the replacement side as an expression
i	Turn off case sensitivity
m	Treat a string as multiple lines[a]
o	Only compile pattern once. Used to optimize the search
s	Treat string as single line when newline is embedded
x	Allows whitespace and comments within the regular expression
g	Replace globally, i.e., find all occurrences

a. The *m*, *s*, and *x* options are defined only for Perl 5.

EXAMPLE 7.22

```
(The Script)
1   while(<DATA>){
2       s/Norma/Jane/;      # Substitute Norma with Jane
3       print;
    }
4   _ _DATA_ _
    Steve Blenheim
    Betty Boop
    Igor Chevsky
    Norma Cord
    Jon DeLoach
    Karen Evich
```

EXAMPLE 7.22 (CONTINUED)

```
(Output)
Steve Blenheim
Betty Boop
Igor Chevsky
Jane Cord
Jon DeLoach
Karen Evich
```

EXPLANATION

1   The special *DATA* filehandle gets its input from the text after the _ _*DATA*_ _ token. The *while* loop is entered and the first line after the _ _*DATA*_ _ token is read in and assigned to *$_*.

2   In lines where *$_* contains the regular expression *Norma*, the substitution operator, *s*, will replace *Norma* with *Jane* for the first occurrence of *Norma* on each line.

3   Each line will be printed, whether or not the substitution occurred.

4   The *DATA* filehandle gets its data from the lines that follow the _ _*DATA*_ _ token.

EXAMPLE 7.23

```
(The Script)
1   while($_= <DATA>){
2       print if s/Igor/Ivan/;      # Substitute Igor with Ivan
    }
3   _ _DATA_ _
    Steve Blenheim
    Betty Boop
    Igor Chevsky
    Norma Cord
    Jon DeLoach
    Karen Evich

(Output)
Ivan Chevsky
```

EXPLANATION

1   The special *DATA* filehandle gets its input from the text after the _ _*DATA*_ _ token. The *while* loop is entered and the first line following the _ _*DATA*_ _ token is read in and assigned to *$_*.

2   In lines where *$_* contains the regular expression *Igor*, the substitution operator, *s*, will replace *Igor* with *Ivan* for the first occurrence of *Igor* on each line. Only if the substitution is successful, will the line be printed.

3   The *DATA* filehandle gets its data from the lines that follow the _ _*DATA*_ _ token.

Changing the Substitution Delimiters.   Normally the forward slash delimiter encloses both the search pattern and the replacement string. Any non-alphanumeric character following the *s* operator can be used in place of the slash. For example, if a # follows the *s* operator, it must be used as the delimiter for the replacement pattern. If pairs of parentheses, curly braces, square brackets, or angle brackets are used to delimit the search pattern, any other type of delimiter may be used for the replacement pattern, such as *s(John) /Joe/*;

EXAMPLE 7.24

```
(The Script)
1    while(<DATA>){
2        s#Igor#Boris#;          # Substitute Igor with Boris
3        print;
     }
4    _ _DATA_ _
     Steve Blenheim
     Betty Boop
     Igor Chevsky
     Norma Cord
     Jon DeLoach
     Karen Evich


(Output)
Steve Blenheim
Betty Boop
Boris Chevsky
Norma Cord
Jon DeLoach
Karen Evich
```

EXPLANATION

1   The special *DATA* filehandle gets its input from the text after the _ _*DATA*_ _ token. The *while* loop is entered and the first line after the _ _*DATA*_ _ token is read in and assigned to $_.

2   The delimiter following the *s* operator has been changed to a pound sign (#). This is fine as long as all three delimiters are pound signs. The regular expression *Igor* is replaced with *Boris*.

3   The *DATA* filehandle gets its data from the lines that follow the _ _*DATA*_ _ token.

EXAMPLE 7.25

```
(The Script)
1    while(<DATA>){
2        s(Blenheim) {Dobbins};        # Substitute Blenheim with Dobbins
3        print;
     }
4    _ _DATA_ _
     Steve Blenheim
     Betty Boop
     Igor Chevsky
     Norma Cord
     Jon DeLoach
     Karen Evich


(Output)
Steve Dobbins
Betty Boop
Igor Chevsky
Norma Cord
Jon DeLoach
Karen Evich
```

EXPLANATION

1   The special *DATA* filehandle gets its input from the text after the _ _DATA_ _ token. The *while* loop is entered and the first line following the _ _DATA_ _ token is read in and assigned to $_.

2   The search pattern *Blenheim* is delimited with parentheses and the replacement pattern, *Dobbins*, is delimited with forward slashes.

3   The substitution is shown in the output when it is printed. *Blenheim* is replaced with *Dobbins*.

4   The *DATA* filehandle gets its data from the lines that follow the _ _DATA_ _ token.

The *g* Modifier—Global Substitution.   The *g* modifier is used to cause a global substitution; that is, all occurrences of a pattern are replaced on the line. Without the *g*, only the first occurrence of a pattern on each line is changed.

FORMAT

```
s/search pattern/replacement string/g;
```

EXAMPLE 7.26

```
(The Script)
# Without the g option
   (The Script)
1   while(<DATA>){
2       print if s/Tom/Christian/;   # First occurrence of Tom on each
                                      # line is replaced with Christian
    }
3   _ _DATA_ _
    Tom Dave Dan Tom
    Betty Tom Henry Tom
    Igor Norma Tom Tom

(Output)
Christian Dave Dan Tom
Betty Christian Henry Tom
Igor Norma Christian Tom
```

EXPLANATION

1   The special *DATA* filehandle gets its input from the text after the _ _*DATA*_ _ token. The *while* loop is entered and the first line following the _ _*DATA*_ _ token is read in and assigned to *$_*.
2   The **first** occurrence of *Tom* will be replaced with *Christian* for each line that is read.
3   The *DATA* filehandle gets its data from the lines that follow the _ _*DATA*_ _ token.

EXAMPLE 7.27

```
(The Script)
# With the g option
1   while(<DATA>){
2       print if s/Tom/Christian/g;   # All occurrences of Tom on each
                                       # line are replaced with Christian
    }
3   _ _DATA_ _
    Tom Dave Dan Tom
    Betty Tom Henry Tom
    Igor Norma Tom Tom

(Output)
Christian Dave Dan Christian
Betty Christian Dick Christian
Igor Norma Christian Christian
```

EXPLANATION

1   The special *DATA* filehandle gets its input from the text after the _ _*DATA*_ _ token.
    The *while* loop is entered and the first line after the _ _*DATA*_ _ token is read in and
    assigned to *$_*.

2   With the *g* option, the substitution is global. **Every** occurrence of *Tom* will be re-
    placed with *Christian* for each line that is read.

3   The *DATA* filehandle gets its data from the lines that follow the _ _*DATA*_ _ token.

The *i* Modifier—Case Insensitivity.   Perl is sensitive to upper- or lowercase characters
when performing matches. If you want to turn off case sensitivity, an *i* (insensitive) is
appended to the last delimiter of the match or substitution operator.

FORMAT

```
s/search pattern/replacement string/i;
```

EXAMPLE 7.28

```
(The Script)
    # Matching with the i option
1   while(<DATA>){
2       print if /norma cord/i;      # Turn off case sensitivity
    }
3   _ _DATA_ _
    Steve Blenheim
    Betty Boop
    Igor Chevsky
    Norma Cord
    Jon DeLoach
    Karen Evich


(Output)
Norma Cord
```

EXPLANATION

1   The special *DATA* filehandle gets its input from the text after the _ _*DATA*_ _ token.
    The *while* loop is entered and the first line following the _ _*DATA*_ _ token is read
    in and assigned to *$_*.

2   Without the *i* option, the regular expression */norma cord/* would not be matched be-
    cause all the letters are not lowercase in the lines that are read as input. The *i* option
    turns off the case sensitivity.

3   The *DATA* filehandle gets its data from the lines that follow the _ _*DATA*_ _ token.

EXAMPLE 7.29

```
(The Script)
1   while(<DATA>){
2       print if s/igor/Daniel/i;    # Substitute igor with Daniel
    }

3   _ _DATA_ _
    Steve Blenheim
    Betty Boop
    Igor Chevsky
    Norma Cord
    Jon DeLoach
    Karen Evich

(Output)
Daniel Chevsky
```

EXPLANATION

1   The special *DATA* filehandle gets its input from the text after the _ _*DATA*_ _ token. The *while* loop is entered and the first line after the _ _*DATA*_ _ token is read in and assigned to $_. Each time the loop is entered, the next line following _ _*DATA*_ _ is assigned to $_ until all the lines have been processed.

2   The regular expression in the substitution is also case-insensitive, owing to the *i* option. If *igor* or *Igor* (or any combination of upper- and lowercase) is matched, it will be replaced with *Daniel*.

3   The *DATA* filehandle gets its data from the lines that follow the _ _*DATA*_ _ token.

The *e* Modifier—Evaluating an Expression.   On the replacement side of a substitution operation, it is possible to evaluate an expression or a function. The search side is replaced with with the result of the evaluation.

FORMAT

```
s/search pattern/replacement string/e;
```

EXAMPLE 7.30

```
(The Script)
    # The e and g modifiers
1   while(<DATA>){
2       s/6/6 * 7.3/eg;        # Substitute 6 with product of 6 * 7.3

3       print;
    }
    __DATA__
    Steve Blenheim    5
    Betty Boop        4
    Igor Chevsky      6
    Norma Cord        1
    Jon DeLoach       3
    Karen Evich       66


(Output)
Steve Blenheim    5
Betty Boop        4
Igor Chevsky      43.8
Norma Cord        1
Jon DeLoach       3
Karen Evich       43.843.8
```

EXPLANATION

1   The special *DATA* filehandle gets its input from the text after the _ _DATA_ _ token. The *while* loop is entered and the first line following the _ _DATA_ _ token is read in and assigned to $_. Each time the loop is entered, the next line after _ _DATA_ _ is assigned to $_ until all the lines have been processed.

2   If the $_ scalar contains the number 6, the replacement side of the substitution is evaluated. In other words, the 6 is multiplied by *7.3* (*e* modifier); the product of the multiplication (*43.8*) replaces the number 6 each time the number 6 is found (*g* modifier).

3   Each line is printed. The last line contained two occurrences of 6 causing each 6 to be replaced with *43.8*.

EXAMPLE 7.31

```
(The Script)
    # The e modifier
1   $_=5;
2   s/5/6 * 4 - 22/e;
3   print "The result is: $_\n";

4   $_=1055;
5   s/5/3*2/eg;
6   print "The result is: $_\n";

(Output)
3   The result is: 2
6   The result is: 1066
```

EXPLANATION

1   The $_ scalar is assigned 5.

2   The s operator searches for the regular expression 5 in $_. The e modifier evaluates the replacement string as a numeric expression and replaces it with the result of the arithmetic operation, 6* 4 – 22, which results in 2.

3   The result of the evaluation is printed.

4   The $_ variable is assigned 1055.

5   The s operator searches for the regular expression 5 in $_. The e modifier evaluates the replacement string as a numeric expression and replaces it with the product of 3*2; i.e., every time 5 is found, it is replaced with 6. Since the substitution is global, all occurrences of 5 are replaced with 6.

6   The result of the evaluation is printed.

EXAMPLE 7.32

```
(The Script)
1   $_ = "knock at heaven's door.\n";
2   s/knock/"knock, " x 2  . "knocking"/ei;
3   print "He's $_;

(Output)
He's knock, knock, knocking at heaven's door.
```

EXPLANATION

1   The $_ variable is the string *knock at heaven's door.\n*;
2   The *s* operator searches for the regular expression *knock* in $_. The *e* modifier evaluates the replacement string as a string expression and replaces it with *knock x 2* (repeated twice), and concatenated (the dot operator) with the string *knocking*, ignoring case.
3   The resulting string is printed.

EXAMPLE 7.33

```
(The Script)
    # Saving in the $& special scalar
1   $_=5000;
2   s/$_/$& * 2/e;
3   print "The new value is $_\.n";

4   $_="knock at heaven's door.\n";
5   s/knock/"$&," x 2 . "$&ing"/ei;
6   print "He's $_;

(Output)
3   The new value is 10000.
6   He's knock,knock,knocking at heaven's door.
```

EXPLANATION

1   The $_ scalar is assigned *5000*.
2   The search string, *5000*, is stored in the $& variable. In the replacement side the expression is evaluated; in other words, the value of $& is multiplied by *2*. The new value is substituted for the original value. $_ is assigned the new value.
3   The resulting value is printed.
4   The $_ scalar is assigned the string, *knock at heaven's door.\n.*
5   If the search string (*knock*) is found, it is stored in the $& variable. In the replacement side the expression is evaluated. So, the value of $& (*knock*) is replicated twice and concatenated with $&ing (*knocking*). The new value is substituted for the original value. $_ is assigned the new value, and printed.

7.3.3   Pattern Binding Operators

The **pattern binding** operators are used to bind a matched pattern, substitution, or translation (see *tr* in Appendix A) to another scalar expression. In the previous examples, pattern searches were done implicitly (or explicitly) on the $_ variable, the default pattern space.

That is, each line was stored in the $_ variable when looping through a file. In the previous example, the $_ was assigned a value and used as the search string for the substitution. But what if you store a value in some variable other than $_?

Instead of

```
$_ = 5000;
```

you would write

```
$salary = 5000;
```

Then if a match or substitution is performed on *$salary*, instead of

```
print if /5/;  or  s/5/6;
```

you would write

```
print if $salary =~ /5/;  or  $salary =~ s/5/6/;
```

So, if you have a string that is not stored in the $_ variable and need to perform matches or substitutions on that string, then the pattern binding operators =~ or !~ are used. They are also used with the *tr* function for string translations.

The pattern matching operators are listed in Table 7.3.

FORMAT

```
Variable =~ /Expression/
Variable !~ /Expression/
Variable =~ s/old/new/
```

Table 7.3   Pattern Matching Operators

Example	*Meaning*
$name =~ /John/	True if *$name* contains pattern. Returns 1 for *true*, null for *false*.
$name !~ /John/	True if *$name* does not contain pattern.
$name =~ s/John/Sam/	Replace first occurrence of *John* with *Sam*.
$name =~ s/John/Sam/g	Replace all occurrences of *John* with *Sam*.
$name =~ tr/a–z/A–Z/	Translate all lowercase letters to uppercase.
$name =~ /$pal/	A variable can be used in the search string.

EXAMPLE 7.34

```
(The Script)
    # Using the $_ scalar explicitly
1   while($_=<DATA>){
2       print $_ if $_ =~ /Igor/;   # $_ holds the current input line
3   #   print if /Igor/;
        }
    _ _DATA_ _
    Steve Blenheim
    Betty Boop
    Igor Chevsky
    Norma Cord
    Jon DeLoach
    Karen Evich


(Output)
Igor Chevsky
```

EXPLANATION

1   The special *DATA* filehandle gets its input from the text after the _ _DATA_ _ token. The *while* loop is entered and the first line following the _ _DATA_ _ token is read in and assigned to *$_*. Each time the loop is entered the next line after _ _DATA_ _ is assigned to *$_* until all the lines have been processed.

2   If the regular expression */Igor/* is matched in the *$_* variable, the *print* function will print the value of *$_*. The =~ is only necessary here if the *$_* scalar is explicitly used as an operand.

3   If the =~ pattern matching operator is omitted, the default is to match on *$_*, and if the *print* function is given no arguments, the value of *$_* is also printed.

EXAMPLE 7.35

```
(The Script)
    #!/usr/bin/perl
1   $name="Tommy Tuttle";
2   print "Hello Tommy\n" if $name =~ /Tom/;
                                        # Prints Hello Tommy,if true
3   print "$name\n" if $name !~ /Tom/;  # Prints nothing if false

4   $name =~ s/T/M/;                    # Substitute first T with an M
5   print "$name.\n";
```

EXAMPLE 7.35 (CONTINUED)

```
6    $name="Tommy Tuttle";
7    print "$name\n" if $name =~ s/T/M/g;   # Substitute every T with M
8    print "What is Tommy's last name? ";
9    print "You got it!\n" if <STDIN> =~ /Tuttle/;
```

```
(Output)
2    Hello Tommy
5    Mommy Tuttle.
7    Mommy Muttle
8    What is Tommy's last name? Tuttle
9    You got it!
```

EXPLANATION

1 The scalar *$name* is assigned *Tommy Tuttle*.
2 The string *$name* is printed if *$name* contains the pattern *Tom*. The return value from a successful match is *1*.
3 The string *$name* is not printed if *$name* does **not** contain the pattern *Tom*. The return value from an unsuccessful match is null.
4 The first occurrence of the letter *T* in *$name* is replaced with the letter *M*.
5 *$name* is printed, reflecting the substitution.
6 *$name* is assigned *Tommy Tuttle*.
7 **All** occurrences of the letter *T* in *$name* are replaced with the letter *M*. The *g* at the end of the substitution expression causes a global replacement across the line.
8 User input is requested.
9 The user input (*<STDIN>*) is matched against the regular expression, *Tuttle*, and if there is a match, the *print* statement is executed.

EXAMPLE 7.36

```
(The Script)
1    $salary=50000;
2    $salary =~ s/$salary/$& * 1.1/e;
3    print "\$& is $&\n";
4    print "The salary is now \$$salary.\n";
```

```
(Output)
3    $& is 50000
4    The salary is now $55000.
```

EXPLANATION

1   The scalar *$salary* is assigned *50000.*
2   The substitution is performed on *$salary.* The replacement side evaluates the expression. The special variable *$&* holds the value found on the search side. To change the value in *$salary* after the substitution, the pattern matching operator **=~** is used. This binds the result of the substitution to the scalar $*salary.*
3   The *$&* scalar holds the value of what was found on the search side of the substitution.
4   The scalar *$salary* has been increased by *10%.*

EXAMPLE 7.37

```
(The Script)
    # Using split and pattern matching
1   while(<DATA>){
2       @line = split(":", $_);
3       print $line[0],"\n"  if $line[1] =~ /408-/
                             # Using the pattern matching operator
    }

4   _ _DATA_ _
    Steve Blenheim:415-444-6677:12 Main St.
    Betty Boop:303-223-1234:234 Ethan Ln.
    Igor Chevsky:408-567-4444:3456 Mary Way
    Norma Cord:555-234-5764:18880 Fiftieth St.
    Jon DeLoach:201-444-6556:54 Penny Ln.
    Karen Evich:306-333-7654:123 4th Ave.

(Output)
Igor Chevsky
```

EXPLANATION

1   The special *DATA* filehandle gets its input from the text after the _ _DATA_ _ token. The *while* loop is entered and the first line following the _ _DATA_ _ token is read in and assigned to *$_.* Each time the loop is entered, the next line from _ _DATA_ _ is assigned to *$_* until all the lines have been processed.
2   Each line from the file will be split at the colons and the value returned stored in an array, *@line.*
3   The pattern */408-/* is matched against the array element *$line[1].* If that pattern is matched in *$line[1],* the value of *$line[0]* is printed. Prints *Igor*'s name, *$line[0],* because his phone, *$line[1],* matches the *408* area code.
4   The text following _ _DATA_ _, is used as input by the special *DATA* filehandle.

EXAMPLE 7.38

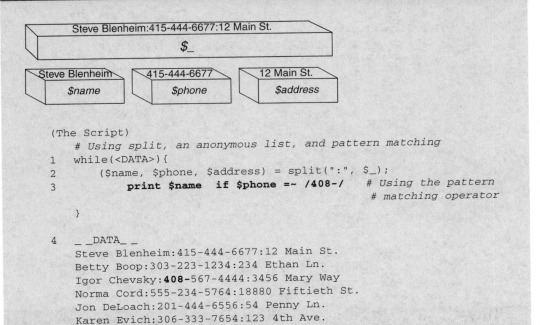

```
(The Script)
    # Using split, an anonymous list, and pattern matching
1   while(<DATA>){
2       ($name, $phone, $address) = split(":", $_);
3           print $name  if $phone =~ /408-/    # Using the pattern
                                                # matching operator

    }


4   _ _DATA_ _
    Steve Blenheim:415-444-6677:12 Main St.
    Betty Boop:303-223-1234:234 Ethan Ln.
    Igor Chevsky:408-567-4444:3456 Mary Way
    Norma Cord:555-234-5764:18880 Fiftieth St.
    Jon DeLoach:201-444-6556:54 Penny Ln.
    Karen Evich:306-333-7654:123 4th Ave.


(Output)
Igor Chevsky
```

EXPLANATION

1   The special *DATA* filehandle gets its input from the text after the _ _*DATA*_ _ token. The *while* loop is entered and the first line after the _ _*DATA*_ _ token is read in and assigned to $_. Each time the loop is entered, the next line following _ _*DATA*_ _ is assigned to $_ until all the lines have been processed.

2   Each line from the file will be split at the colons and the value returned stored in an anonymous list consisting of three scalars: *$name*, *$phone*, and *$address*. Using the anonymous list makes the program easier to read and manipulate than in the previous example where an array was used. With the array, you have make sure you get the right index number to represent the various fields, whereas the named scalars are straightforward.

3   The pattern */408-/* is matched against the *$phone* variable. If that pattern is matched in *$phone*, the value of *$name* is printed. *Igor*'s name is printed because his phone matches the *408* area code.

4   The text following _ _*DATA*_ _ is used as input by the special *DATA* filehandle.

EXAMPLE 7.39

```
(The Script)
1   while($inputline=<DATA>){
2       ($name, $phone, $address) = split(":", $inputline);
3           print $name   if $phone =~ /408-/    # Using the pattern
                                                 # matching operator
4           print $inputline if $name =~ /^Karen/;
5           print if /^Norma/;
    }


6   _ _DATA_ _
    Steve Blenheim:415-444-6677:12 Main St.
    Betty Boop:303-223-1234:234 Ethan Ln.
    Igor Chevsky:408-567-4444:3456 Mary Way
    Norma Cord:555-234-5764:18880 Fiftieth St.
    Jon DeLoach:201-444-6556:54 Penny Ln.
    Karen Evich:306-333-7654:123 4th Ave.

(Output)
3   Igor Chevsky
4   Karen Evich:306-333-7654:123 4th Ave.
5   < No output >
```

EXPLANATION

1   The special *DATA* filehandle gets its input from the text after the _ _DATA_ _ token. The *while* loop is entered and the first line after the _ _DATA_ _ token is read in and assigned to a user-defined variable, *$inputline*, rather than *$_*. Each time the loop is entered, the next line from _ _DATA_ _ is assigned to *$inputline* until all the lines have been processed.

2   Each line from the file, stored in *$inputfile*, will be split at the colons and the value returned stored in an anonymous list consisting of three scalars: *$name*, *$phone*, and *$address*.

3   The pattern */408-/* is matched against the *$phone* variable. If that pattern is matched in *$phone*, the value of *$name* is printed. Prints *Igor*'s name because his phone matches the *408* area code.

4   Each line is stored in *$inputline*, one after the other, until the end of the file is reached. The value of *$inputline* is displayed if it begins with the regular expression *Karen*.

5   Since the default line holder, *$_*, is no longer being used, nothing is assigned to it, and nothing is matched against it, or displayed. The lines are now being stored and matched in the user-defined variable, *$inputline*.

6   The text following _ _DATA_ _ is used as input by the special *DATA* filehandle.

(sample.file found on CD)
```
Tommy Savage:408-724-0140:1222 Oxbow Court, Sunnyvale,CA 94087:5/19/66:34200
Lesle Kerstin:408-456-1234:4 Harvard Square, Boston, MA 02133:4/22/62:52600
JonDeLoach:408-253-3122:123 Park St., San Jose, CA 94086:7/25/53:85100
Ephram Hardy:293-259-5395:235 Carlton Lane, Joliet, IL 73858:8/12/20:56700
Betty Boop:245-836-8357:635 Cutesy Lane, Hollywood, CA 91464:6/23/23:14500
William Kopf:846-836-2837:6937 Ware Road, Milton, PA 93756:9/21/46:43500
Norma Corder:397-857-2735:74 Pine Street, Dearborn, MI 23874:3/28/45:245700
James Ikeda:834-938-8376:23445 Aster Ave., Allentown, NJ 83745:12/1/38:45000
Lori Gortz:327-832-5728:3465 Mirlo Street, Peabody, MA 34756:10/2/65:35200
Barbara Kerz:385-573-8326:832 Ponce Drive, Gary, IN 83756:12/15/46:268500
```

1. Print all lines containing the pattern *Street*.

2. Print lines where the first name matches a *B* or *b*.

3. Print last names that match *Ker*.

4. Print phone numbers in the *408* area code.

5. Print Lori Gortz's name and address.

6. Print Ephram's name in capital letters.

7. Print lines that do not contain a *4*.

8. Change William's name to Siegfried.

9. Print Tommy Savage's birthday.

10. Print the names of those making over $40,000.

11. Print the names and birthdays of those people born in June.

12. Print the zip code for Massachusetts.

8

GETTING CONTROL— REGULAR EXPRESSION METACHARACTERS

8.1 Regular Expression Metacharacters

Regular expression metacharacters are characters that do not represent themselves. They are endowed with special powers to allow you to control the search pattern in some way (e.g., find the pattern only at the beginning of line, or at the end of the line, or only if it starts with an upper- or lowercase letter). Metacharacters lose their special meaning if preceded with a backslash (\). For example, the dot metacharacter represents any single character, but when preceded with a backslash is just a dot or period.

If you see a backslash preceding a metacharacter, the backslash turns off the meaning of the metacharacter, but if you see a backslash preceding an alphanumeric character in a regular expression, then the backslash means something else. Perl provides a simpler form of some of the metachacters, called **metasymbols**, to represent characters. For example, *[0–9]*, represents numbers in the range between 0 and 9, and \d represents the same thing. *[0–9]* uses the bracket metacharacter; \d is a metasymbol.

EXAMPLE 8.1

```
/^a...c/
```

EXPLANATION

This regular expression contains metacharacters. (See Table 8.1.) The first one is a caret (^). The caret metacharacter matches for a string only if it is at the beginning of the line. The period (.) is used to match for any single character, including whitespace. This expression contains three periods, representing any three characters. To find a literal period or any other character that does not represent itself, the character must be preceded by a backslash to prevent interpretation.

In Example 8.1, the regular expression reads: Search at the beginning of the line for an *a*, followed by any three single characters, followed by a *c*. It will match, for example: *abbbc, a123c, a c,* or *aAx3c* only if those patterns were found at the beginning of the line.

197

Table 8.1   Metacharacters

Metacharacter	What It Matches
Character Class: Single Characters and Digits	
.	Matches any character except a newline
[a–z0–9]	Matches any single character in set
[^a–z0–9]	Matches any single character **not** in set
\d	Matches one digit
\D	Matches a non-digit, same as [^0–9]
\w	Matches an alphanumeric (word) character
\W	Matches a non-alphanumeric (non-word) character
Character Class: Whitespace Characters	
\s	Matches a whitespace character such as spaces, tabs, and newlines
\S	Matches non-whitespace character
\n	Matches a newline
\r	Matches a return
\t	Matches a tab
\f	Matches a formfeed
\b	Matches a backspace
\0	Matches a null character
Character Class: Anchored Characters	
\b	Matches a word boundary (when not inside [ ])
\B	Matches a non-word boundary
^	Matches to beginning of line
$	Matches to end of line
\A	Matches the beginning of the string only
\Z	Matches the end of the string or line
\z	Matches the end of string only
\G	Matches where previous m//g left off

Table 8.1   Metacharacters *(continued)*

Metacharacter	*What It Matches*
Character Class: Repeated Characters	
x?	Matches 0 or 1 *x*
x*	Matches 0 or more occurrences of *x*
x+	Matches 1 or more occurrences of *x*
(xyz)+	Matches one or more patterns of *xyz*
x{m,n}	Matches at least *m* occurrences of *x* and no more than *n* occurrences of *x*
Character Class: Alternative Characters	
was|were|will	Matches one of *was*, *were*, or *will*
Character Class: Remembered Characters	
(string)	Used for backreferencing (see Examples 8.38 and 8.39)
1 or *$1*	Matches first set of parentheses[a]
2 or *$2*	Matches second set of parentheses
3 or *$3*	Matches third set of parentheses
Character Class: Miscellaneous Characters	
12	Matches that octal value, up to *377*
x811	Matches that hex value
cX	Matches that control character; e.g., *cC* is *<Ctrl>-C* and *cV* is *<Ctrl>-V*
e	Matches the ASCII ESC character, not backslash
E	Marks the end of changing case with *U*, *L*,or *Q*
l	Lowercase the next character only
L	Lowercase characters until the end of the string or until *E*
N	Matches that named character; e.g., *N{greek:Beta}*
p{PROPERTY}	Matches any character with the named property; e.g., *p{IsAlpha}/*
P{PROPERTY}	Matches any character without the named property

a. *1* and *$1* are called backreferences. They differ in that the *1* backreference is valid within a pattern, whereas the *$1* notation is valid within the enclosing block or until another successful search.

Table 8.1   Metacharacters *(continued)*

Metacharacter	What It Matches
\Q	Quote metacharacters until \E
\u	Titlecase next character only
\U	Uppercase until \E
\x{NUMBER}	Matches Unicode NUMBER given in hexadecimal
\X	Matches Unicode "combining character sequence" string
\/	Matches that metacharacter
\\	Matches a backslash

8.1.1   Metacharacters for Single Characters

If you are searching for a particular character within a regular expression, you can use the **dot** metacharacter to represent a single character or a **character class** that matches one character from a set of characters. In addition to the dot and character class, Perl has added some backslashed symbols (called **metasymbols**) to represent single characters. (See Table 8.2.)

Table 8.2   Metacharacters for Single Characters

Metacharacter	What It Matches
.	Matches any character except a newline
[a–z0–9_]	Matches any single character in set
[^a–z0–9_]	Matches any single character **not** in set
\d	Matches a single digit
\D	Matches a single non-digit; same as [^0–9]
\w	Matches a single alphanumeric (word) character; same as [a–z0–9_]
\W	Matches a single non-alphanumeric (non-word) character; same as [^a–z0–9_]

The Dot Metacharacter.   The dot (.) metacharacter matches any single character with the exception of the newline character. For example, the regular expression /a.b/ is matched if the string contains an *a*, followed by any one single character (except the \n), followed by *b*, whereas the expression /.../ matches any string containing at least three characters.

EXAMPLE 8.2

```
(The Script)
    # The dot metacharacter
1   while(<DATA>){
2       print "Found Norma!\n" if /N..ma/;
    }
    _ _DATA_ _
    Steve Blenheim 101
    Betty Boop 201
    Igor Chevsky 301
    Norma Cord 401
    Jonathan DeLoach 501
    Karen Evich 601


(Output)
Found Norma!
```

EXPLANATION

1   The special *DATA* filehandle gets its input from the text after the _ _DATA_ _ token. The *while* loop is entered and the first line following the _ _DATA_ _ token is read in and assigned to $_. Each time the loop is entered, the next line below _ _DATA_ _ is assigned to $_ until all the lines have been processed.

2   The string *Found Norma!\n* is printed only if the pattern found in $_ contains an uppercase *N*, followed by any two single characters, followed by an *m* and an *a*. It would find *Norma*, *No man*, *Normandy*, etc.

The *s* Modifier—The Dot Metacharacter and the Newline.   Normally, the dot metacharacter does not match the newline character, \n, because it matches only the characters within a string up until the newline is reached. The *s* modifier treats the line with embedded newlines as a single line, rather than a group of multiple lines, and allows the dot metacharacter to treat the newline character the same as any other character it might match. The *s* modifier can be used with both the *m* (match) and the *s* (substitution) operators.

EXAMPLE 8.3

```
(The Script)
    # The s modifier and the newline
1   $_ = "Sing a song of sixpence\nA pocket full of rye.\n";
2   print $& if /pence./s;
3   print $& if /rye\../s;
4   print if s/sixpence.A/twopence, a/s;

(Output)
2   pence
3   rye.
4   Sing a song of twopence, a pocket full of rye.
```

EXPLANATION

1   The *$_* scalar is assigned; it contains two newlines.
2   The regular expression, */pence./*, contains a dot metacharacter. The dot metacharacter does not match a newline character unless the *s* modifier is used. The *$&* special scalar holds the value the pattern found in the last successful search, i.e., *pence\n*.
3   The regular expression, */rye\../*, contains a literal period (the backslash makes the period literal), followed by the dot metacharacter that will match on the newline, thanks to the *s* modifier. The *$&* special scalar holds the value the pattern found in the last successful search, i.e., *rye.\n*.
4   The *s* modifier allows the dot to match on the newline character, *\n,* found in the search string. The newline will be replaced with a space.

The Character Class.   A character class represents **one** character from a set of characters. For example *[abc]* matches either an *a*, *b*, **or** *c*, and *[a–z]* matches one character from a set of characters in the range from *a* to *z*, and *[0–9]* matches one character in the range of digits between *0* to *9*. If the character class contains a leading caret (^), then the class represents any one character **not** in the set; for example, *[^a–zA–Z]* matches a single character **not** in the range from *a* to *z* or *A* to *Z*, and *[^0–9]* matches a single character not in the range between *0* and *9*.[1] To represent a number between 10 and 13, use *1[0–3]*, not *[10–13]*.

Perl provides additional symbols, **metasymbols**, to represent a character class. The symbols *\d* and *\D* represent a single digit and a single non-digit, respectively; they are the same as *[0–9]* and *[^0–9]*. Similarly, *\w* and *\W* represent a single word character and a single non-word character, respectively; they are the same as *[A–Za–z_0–9]* and *[^A–Za–z_0–9]*.

EXAMPLE 8.4

```
(From a Script)
1   while(<DATA>){
2       print if /[A-Z][a-z]eve/;
    }
    _ _DATA_ _
    Steve Blenheim 101
    Betty Boop 201
    Igor Chevsky 301
    Norma Cord 401
    Jonathan DeLoach 501
    Karen Evich 601

(Output)
Steve Blenheim 101
```

---

1. Don't confuse the caret inside square brackets with the caret used as a beginning of line anchor. See Table 8.7 on page 221.

EXPLANATION

1   The special *DATA* filehandle gets its input from the text after the _ _DATA_ _ token. The *while* loop is entered and the first line following the _ _DATA_ _ token is read in and assigned to $_. Each time the loop is entered, the next line after _ _DATA_ _ is assigned to $_ until all the lines have been processed.

2   The line $_ is printed only if $_contains a pattern matching one uppercase letter *[A–Z]*, followed by one lowercase letter *[a–z]*, and followed by *eve*.

EXAMPLE 8.5

```
(The Script)
    # The bracketed character class
1   while(<DATA>){
2       print if /[A-Za-z0-9_]/;
    }
    _ _DATA_ _
    Steve Blenheim 101
    Betty Boop 201
    Igor Chevsky 301
    Norma Cord 401
    Jonathan DeLoach 501
    Karen Evich 601


(Output)
Steve Blenheim 101
Betty Boop 201
Igor Chevsky 301
Norma Cord 401
Jonathan DeLoach 501
Karen Evich 601
```

EXPLANATION

1   The special *DATA* filehandle gets its input from the text after the _ _DATA_ _ token. The *while* loop is entered and the first line after the _ _DATA_ _ token is read in and assigned to $_. Each time the loop is entered, the next line from _ _DATA_ _ is assigned to $_ until all the lines have been processed.

2   The line $_ is printed only if it contains a pattern matching one alphanumeric word character, represented by the character class, *[A–Za–z0–9_]*. All lines are printed.

EXAMPLE 8.6

```
(The Script)
    # The bracket metacharacters and negation
1   while(<DATA>){
2       print if / [^123]0/; won't compile
    }
    _ _DATA_ _
    Steve Blenheim 101
    Betty Boop 201
    Igor Chevsky 301
    Norma Cord 401
    Jonathan DeLoach 501
    Karen Evich 601


(Output)
Norma Cord 401
Jonathan DeLoach 501
Karen Evich 601
```

EXPLANATION

1   The special *DATA* filehandle gets its input from the text after the _ _DATA_ _ token. The *while* loop is entered and the first line after the _ _DATA_ _ token is read in and assigned to *$_*. Each time the loop is entered, the next line from _ _DATA_ _ is assigned to *$_* until all the lines have been processed.

2   The line *$_* is printed only if *$_* contains a pattern matching one space, followed by one number **not** in the range between *1* and *3*, (not *1*, *2*, or *3*), followed by *0*.

EXAMPLE 8.7

```
(The Script)
    # The metasymbol, \d
1   while(<DATA>){
2       print if /6\d\d/; ncompile
    }
    _ _DATA_ _
    Steve Blenheim 101
    Betty Boop 201
    Igor Chevsky 301
    Norma Cord 401
    Jonathan DeLoach 501
    Karen Evich 601


(Output)
Karen Evich 601
```

EXPLANATION

1   The special *DATA* filehandle gets its input from the text after the _ _DATA_ _ token. The *while* loop is entered and the first line after the _ _DATA_ _ token is read in and assigned to *$_*. Each time the loop is entered, the next line from _ _DATA_ _ is assigned to *$_* until all the lines have been processed.

2   The line *$_* is printed only if it contains a pattern matching the number *6*, followed by two single digits. The metasymbol \d represents the character class *[0–9]*.

EXAMPLE 8.8

```
(The Script)
    # Metacharacters and metasymbols
1   while(<DATA>){
2       print if /[ABC]\D/; won't compile as is.
    }
    _ _DATA_ _
    Steve Blenheim 101
    Betty Boop 201
    Igor Chevsky 301
    Norma Cord 401
    Jonathan DeLoach 501
    Karen Evich 601

(Output)
Steve Blenheim 101
Betty Boop 201
Igor Chevsky 301
Norma Cord 401
```

EXPLANATION

1   The special *DATA* filehandle gets its input from the text after the _ _DATA_ _ token. The *while* loop is entered and the first line after the _ _DATA_ _ token is read in and assigned to *$_*. Each time the loop is entered, the next line from _ _DATA_ _ is assigned to *$_* until all the lines have been processed.

2   The line *$_* is printed only if *$_* contains a pattern matching an uppercase *A*, *B*, or *C*, *[ABC]*, followed by one single **non**-digit, \D. The metasymbol \D represents the character class *[^0–9]*; that is, a number **not** in the range between *0* and *9*.

EXAMPLE 8.9

```
(The Script)
    # The word metasymbols
1   while(<DATA>){
2       print if / \w\w\w\w \d/;
    }
 _ _DATA_ _
 Steve Blenheim 101
 Betty Boop 201
 Igor Chevsky 301
 Norma Cord 401
 Jonathan DeLoach 501
 Karen Evich 601


(Output)
Betty Boop 201
Norma Cord 401
```

EXPLANATION

1   The special *DATA* filehandle gets its input from the text after the _ _DATA_ _ token. The *while* loop is entered and the first line after the _ _DATA_ _ token is read in and assigned to $_. Each time the loop is entered, the next line from _ _DATA_ _ is assigned to $_ until all the lines have been processed.
2   The line $_ is printed only if it matches a pattern containing a space, followed by four alphanumeric word characters, \w, followed by a space and a digit, \d. The metasymbol \w represents the character class [A–Za–z0–9_].

EXAMPLE 8.10

```
(The Script)
    # The word metasymbols
1   while(<DATA>){
2       print if /\W\w\w\w\w\w\W/;
    }
 _ _DATA_ _
 Steve Blenheim 101
 Betty Boop 201
 Igor Chevsky 301
 Norma Cord 401
 Jonathan DeLoach 501
 Karen Evich 601
```

EXAMPLE 8.10 (CONTINUED)

```
(Output)
Betty Boop 201
Norma Cord 401
```

EXPLANATION

1   The special *DATA* filehandle gets its input from the text after the _ _DATA_ _ token. The *while* loop is entered and the first line after the _ _DATA_ _ token is read in and assigned to $_. Each time the loop is entered, the next line from _ _DATA_ _ is assigned to $_ until all the lines have been processed.

2   The line $_ is printed only if $_ matches a pattern containing a non-alphanumeric word character, followed by four alphanumeric word characters, \w, followed by another non-alphanumeric word character, \W. The metasymbol \W represents the character class *[^A–Za–z0–9_]*. Both *Boop* and *Cord* are four word characters surrounded by whitespace (non-alphanumeric characters).

The POSIX Character Class.   Perl 5.6 introduced the POSIX character classes. POSIX (the Portable Operating System Interface) is an industry standard used to ensure that programs are portable across operating systems. In order to be portable, POSIX recognizes that different countries or locales may vary in the way characters are encoded, the symbols used to represent currency, and how times and dates are represented. To handle different types of characters, POSIX added the bracketed character class of characters shown in Table 8.3 to regular expressions.

The class *[:alnum:]* is another way of saying *A–Za–z0–9*. To use this class, it must be enclosed in another set of brackets in order for it to be recognized as a regular expression. For example, *A–Za–z0–9*, by itself, is not a regular expression character class, but *[A–Za–z0–9]* is. Likewise, *[:alnum:]* should be written *[[:alnum:]]*. The difference between using the first form, *[A–Za–z0–9]* and the bracketed form, *[[:alnum:]]*, is that the first form is dependent on ASCII character encoding, whereas the second form allows characters from other languages to be represented in the class.

To negate one of the characters in the POSIX character class, the syntax is

```
[:^digit:]
[:^space:]
[:^word:]
```

Table 8.3   The Bracketed Character Class

Bracket Class	Meaning
[:alnum:]	Alphanumeric characters
[:alpha:]	Alphabetic characters
[:ascii]:	Any character with ordinal value between *0* and *127*
[:cntrl:]	Control characters
[:digit:]	Numeric characters, *0* to *9*, or \d
[:graph:]	Non-blank characters (not spaces, control characters, etc.) other than alphanumeric or punctuation characters
[:lower:]	Lowercase letters
[:print:]	Like *[:graph:]*, but includes the space character
[:punct:]	Punctuation characters
[:space:]	All whitespace characters (newlines, spaces, tabs); same as \s
[:upper:]	Uppercase letters
[:word:]	Any alphanumeric or underline characters[a]
[:xdigit:]	Allows digits in a hexadecimal number (*0–9a–fA–F*)

a.   This is a Perl extension, same as \w.

EXAMPLE 8.11

```
(In Script)
    # The POSIX character classes
1   require 5.6.0;
2   while(<DATA>){
3       print if /[[:upper:]][[:alpha:]]+ [[:upper:]][[:lower:]]+/;
    }
    _ _DATA_ _
    Steve Blenheim
    Betty Boop
    Igor Chevsky
    Norma Cord
    Jon DeLoach
    Betty Boop
    Karen Evich
```

EXAMPLE 8.11 (CONTINUED)

```
(Output)
Steve Blenheim
Betty Boop
Igor Chevsky
Norma Cord
Jon DeLoach
Betty Boop
Karen Evich
```

EXPLANATION

1 Perl version 5.6.0 (and above) is needed to use the POSIX character class.
2 The special *DATA* filehandle gets its input from the text after the _ _*DATA*_ _ token. The *while* loop is entered and the first line after the _ _*DATA*_ _ token is read in and assigned to *$_*. Each time the loop is entered, the next line following _ _*DATA*_ _ is assigned to *$_* until all the lines have been processed.
3 The regular expression contains POSIX character classes. The line is printed if *$_* contains one uppercase letter, *[[:upper:]]*, followed by one or more (+) alphabetic characters, *[[:alpha:]]*, followed by an uppercase letter, and one or more lowercase letters, *[[:lower:]]*. (The + is a regular expression metacharacter representing one or more of the previous characters and is discussed in "Metacharacters to Repeat Pattern Matches" on page 212.)

8.1.2 Whitespace Metacharacters

A whitespace character represents a space, tab, return, newline, or formfeed. The whitespace character can be represented literally, by pressing a <Tab> key or the spacebar, or by pressing the <Enter> key.

Table 8.4   Whitespace Metacharacters

Metacharacter	*What It Matches*
\s	Matches whitespace character, spaces, tabs, and newlines
\S	Matches non-whitespace character
\n	Matches a newline, the end of line character (012 UNIX, 015 Mac OS)
\r	Matches a return
\t	Matches a tab
\f	Matches a formfeed

EXAMPLE 8.12

```
(The Script)
    # The \s metasymbol and whitespace
1   while(<DATA>){
2      print if s/\s/*/g;       # Substitute all spaces with stars
    }
    _ _DATA_ _
    Steve Blenheim 101
    Betty Boop 201
    Igor Chevsky 301
    Norma Cord 401
    Jonathan DeLoach 501
    Karen Evich 601

(Output)
Steve*Blenheim*101*Betty*Boop*201*Igor*Chevsky*301*Norma*
*Cord*401*Jonathan*DeLoach*501*Karen*Evich*601
```

EXPLANATION

1   The special *DATA* filehandle gets its input from the text after the _ _DATA_ _ token. The *while* loop is entered and the first line after the _ _DATA_ _ token is read in and assigned to $_. Each time the loop is entered, the next line following _ _DATA_ _ is assigned to $_ until all the lines have been processed.

2   The line $_ is printed if it matches a pattern containing a whitespace character (space, tab, newline) \s. All whitespace characters are replaced with a *.

EXAMPLE 8.13

```
(The Script)
    # The \S metasymbol and non-whitespace
1   while(<DATA>){
2      print if s/\S/*/g;
    }
    _ _DATA_ _
    Steve Blenheim 101
    Betty Boop 201
    Igor Chevsky 301
    Norma Cord 401
    Jonathan DeLoach 501
    Karen Evich 601
```

EXAMPLE 8.13 (CONTINUED)

```
(Output)
***** ********* ***
***** **** ***
**** ******* ***
***** **** ***
******* ******* ***
***** ****** ***
```

EXPLANATION

1 The special *DATA* filehandle gets its input from the text after the _ _*DATA*_ _ token. The *while* loop is entered and the first line after the _ _*DATA*_ _ token is read in and assigned to *$_*. Each time the loop is entered, the next line following _ _*DATA*_ _ is assigned to *$_* until all the lines have been processed.

2 The line *$_* is printed if *$_* matches a pattern containing a non-whitespace character (**not** a space, tab, or newline), \S. This time all non-whitespace characters are replaced with a *. When a metasymbol is capitalized, it negates the meaning of the lowercase version of the metasybol; \d is a digit; \D is a non-digit.

EXAMPLE 8.14

```
(The Script)
    # Escape sequences, \n and \t
1   while(<DATA>){
2       print if s/\n/\t/;
    }
    _ _DATA_ _
    Steve Blenheim 101
    Betty Boop 201
    Igor Chevsky 301
    Norma Cord 401
    Jonathan DeLoach 501
    Karen Evich 601

(Output)
Steve Blenheim 101    Betty Boop 201    Igor Chevsky 301
Norma Cord 401    Jon DeLoach 501    Karen Evich 601
```

EXPLANATION

1   The special *DATA* filehandle gets its input from the text after the _ _DATA_ _ token. The *while* loop is entered and the first line after the _ _DATA_ _ token is read in and assigned to $_. Each time the loop is entered, the next line following _ _DATA_ _ is assigned to $_ until all the lines have been processed.

2   The regular expression contains the \n escape sequence, representing a single new-line character. The expression reads: Replace each newline with a tab (\t).

8.1.3 Metacharacters to Repeat Pattern Matches

In the previous examples, the metacharacter matched on a single character. What if you want to match on more than one character? For example, let's say you are looking for all lines containing names, and the first letter must be in uppercase—which can be represented as *[A–Z]*—but the following letters are lowercase and the number of letters varies in each name. *[a–z]* matches on a single lowercase letter. How can you match on one or more lowercase letters? Or zero or more lowercase letters? To do this you can use what are called **quantifiers**. To match on one or more lowercase letters, the regular expression can be written: */[a–z]+/* where the + sign means "one or more of the previous characters," in this case, one or more lowercase letters. Perl provides a number of quantifiers, as shown in Table 8.5.

Table 8.5 The Greedy Metacharacters

Metacharacter	*What It Matches*
x?	Matches 0 or 1 occurrences of *x*
(xyz)?	Matches 0 or 1 occurrences of pattern *xyz*
x*	Matches 0 or more occurrences of *x*
(xyz)*	Matches 0 or more occurrences of pattern *xyz*
x+	Matches 1 or more occurrences of *x*
(xyz)+	Matches 1 or more occurrences of pattern *xyz*
x{m,n}	Matches at least *m* occurrences of *x* and no more than *n* occurrences of *x*

The Greed Factor.   Normally, quantifiers are greedy; in other words, they match on the largest possible set of characters starting at the left-hand side of the string and searching to the right, look for the last possible character that would satisfy the condition. For example, given the following string:

```
$_="ab123456783445554437AB"
```

and the regular expression

```
s/ab[0-9]*/X/;
```

the search side would match

```
ab123456783445554437
```

All of this will be replaced with an *X*. After the substitution, *$_* would be

XAB

The asterisk (*) is a greedy metacharacter. It matches for zero or more of the preceding character. In other words, it attaches itself to the character preceding it. In the above example, the asterisk attaches itself to the character class *[0–9]*. The matching starts on the left, searching for *ab* followed by zero or more numbers in the range between *0* and *9*. The matching continues until the last number is found, in this example the number *7*. The pattern *ab* and all of the numbers in the range between *0* and *9* are replaced with a single *X*.

Greediness can be turned off so that instead of matching on the greatest number of characters, the match is made on the least number of characters found. This is done by appending a question mark after the greedy metacharacter. See Example 8.15.

EXAMPLE 8.15

```
(The Script)
    # The zero or one quantifier
1   while(<DATA>){
2       print if / [0-9]\.?/;
    }
    _ _DATA_ _
    Steve Blenheim 1.10
    Betty Boop .5
    Igor Chevsky 555.100
    Norma Cord 4.01
    Jonathan DeLoach .501
    Karen Evich 601

(Output)
Steve Blenheim 1.10
Igor Chevsky 555.100
Norma Cord 4.01
Karen Evich 601
```

EXPLANATION

1   The special *DATA* filehandle gets its input from the text after the _ _*DATA*_ _ token. The *while* loop is entered and the first line after the _ _*DATA*_ _ token is read in and assigned to *$_*. Each time the loop is entered, the next line following _ _*DATA*_ _ is assigned to *$_* until all the lines have been processed.

2   The regular expression contains the *?* metacharacter, representing zero or one of the preceding characters. The expression reads: Find a space, followed by a number between *0* and *9*, followed by either one literal period or no period at all.

EXAMPLE 8.16

```
(The Script)
    # The zero or more quantifier
1   while(<DATA>){
2       print if /\sB[a-z]*/;
    }
    _ _DATA_ _
    Steve Blenheim 1.10
    Betty Boop .5
    Igor Chevsky 555.100
    Norma Cord 4.01
    Jonathan DeLoach .501
    Karen Evich 601


(Output)
Steve Blenheim 1.10
Betty Boop .5
```

EXPLANATION

1   The special *DATA* filehandle gets its input from the text after the _ _*DATA*_ _ token. The *while* loop is entered and the first line after the _ _*DATA*_ _ token is read in and assigned to *$_*. Each time the loop is entered, the next line following _ _*DATA*_ _ is assigned to *$_* until all the lines have been processed.

2   The regular expression contains the * metacharacter, representing zero or more of the preceding character. The expression reads: Find a space, \s, followed by a *B*, and zero or more lowercase letters, *[a–z]**.

EXAMPLE 8.17

```
(The Script)
    # The dot metacharacter and the zero or more quantifier
1   while(<DATA>){
2       print if s/[A-Z].*y/Tom/;
    }
    _ _DATA_ _
    Steve Blenheim 101
    Betty Boop 201
    Igor Chevsky 301
    Norma Cord 401
    Jonathan DeLoach 501
    Karen Evich 601


(Output)
Tom Boop 201
Tom 301
```

EXPLANATION

1. The special *DATA* filehandle gets its input from the text after the _ _DATA_ _ token. The *while* loop is entered and the first line after the _ _DATA_ _ token is read in and assigned to $_. Each time the loop is entered, the next line following _ _DATA_ _ is assigned to $_ until all the lines have been processed.

2. The regular expression contains .*, where the * represents zero or more of the previous character. In this example, the previous character is the dot metacharacter which represents any character at all. This expression reads: Find an uppercase letter, *[A–Z]*, followed by zero or more of any character, .*, followed by the letter *y*. If there is more than one *y* on the line, the search will include all characters up until the **last** *y*. Both *Betty* and *Igor Chevsky* are matched. Note that the space in *Igor Chevsky* is included as one of the characters matched by the dot metacharacter.

EXAMPLE 8.18

```
(The Script)
    # The one or more quantifier
1   while(<DATA>){
2       print if /5+/;
    }
    _ _DATA_ _
    Steve Blenheim 1.10
    Betty Boop .5
    Igor Chevsky 555.100
    Norma Cord 4.01
    Jonathan DeLoach .501
    Karen Evich 601
```

EXAMPLE 8.18(CONTINUED)

```
(Output)
Betty Boop .5
Igor Chevsky 555.100
Jonathan DeLoach .501
```

EXPLANATION

1   The special *DATA* filehandle gets its input from the text after the _ _*DATA*_ _ token.
    The *while* loop is entered and the first line after the _ _*DATA*_ _ token is read in and
    assigned to *$_*. Each time the loop is entered, the next line following _ _*DATA*_ _ is
    assigned to *$_* until all the lines have been processed.

2   The regular expression contains the + metacharacter, representing one or more of the
    preceding characters. The expression reads: Find one or more repeating occurrence
    of the number *5*.

EXAMPLE 8.19

```
(The Script)
    # The one or more quantifier
1   while(<DATA>){
2       print if s/\w+/X/g;
    }
    _ _DATA_ _
    Steve Blenheim 101
    Betty Boop 201
    Igor Chevsky 301
    Norma Cord 401
    Jonathan DeLoach 501
    Karen Evich 601


(Output)
X X X
X X X
X X X
X X X
X X X
X X X
```

EXPLANATION

1   The special *DATA* filehandle gets its input from the text after the _ _*DATA*_ _ token.
    The *while* loop is entered and the first line after the _ _*DATA*_ _ token is read in and
    assigned to *$_*. Each time the loop is entered the next line following _ _*DATA*_ _ is
    assigned to *$_* until all the lines have been processed.

EXPLANATION (CONTINUED)

2   The regular expression contains \w followed by a + metacharacter, representing one or more alphanumeric word characters. For example, the first set of alphanumeric word characters is *Steve*, and *Steve* is replaced by an *X*. Since the substitution is global, the next set of alphanumeric characters, *Blenheim*, is replaced by an *X*. Lastly, the alphanumeric characters, *101*, are replaced by an *X*.

EXAMPLE 8.20

```
(The Script)
   # Repeating patterns
1  while(<DATA>){
2     print if /5{1,3}/;
   }
_ _DATA_ _
Steve Blenheim 1.10
Betty Boop .5
Igor Chevsky 555.100
Norma Cord 4.01
Jonathan DeLoach .501
Karen Evich 601


(Output)
Betty Boop .5
Igor Chevsky 555.100
Jonathan DeLoach .501
```

EXPLANATION

1   The special *DATA* filehandle gets its input from the text after the _ _DATA_ _ token. The *while* loop is entered and the first line after the _ _DATA_ _ token is read in and assigned to $_. Each time the loop is entered, the next line following _ _DATA_ _ is assigned to $_ until all the lines have been processed.

2   The regular expression contains the curly brace ({}) metacharacters, representing the number of times the preceding expression will be repeated. The expression reads: Find at least one occurrence of the pattern *5*, and as many as three in a row.

EXAMPLE 8.21

```
(The Script)
   # Repeating patterns
1  while(<DATA>){
2      print if /5{3}/;
   }
   _ _DATA_ _
   Steve Blenheim 1.10
   Betty Boop .5
   Igor Chevsky 555.100
   Norma Cord 4.01
   Jonathan DeLoach .501
   Karen Evich 601


(Output)
Igor Chevsky 555.100
```

EXPLANATION

1   The special *DATA* filehandle gets its input from the text after the _ _*DATA*_ _ token. The *while* loop is entered and the first line after the _ _*DATA*_ _ token is read in and assigned to $_. Each time the loop is entered, the next line following _ _*DATA*_ _ is assigned to $_ until all the lines have been processed.

2   The expression reads: Find three consecutive occurrences of the pattern *5*. This does not mean that the string must contain exactly three, and no more, of the number *5*. It just means that there must be **at least** three consecutive occurrences of the number *5*. If the string contained 5555555, the match would still be successful. To find exactly three occurrences of the number *5*, the pattern would have to be anchored in some way, either by using the ^ and $ anchors or by placing some other character before and after the three occurrences of the number *5*; for example, */^5{3}$/* or */5{3}898/* or */95{3}\.56/*.

EXAMPLE 8.22

```
(The Script)
   # Repeating patterns
1  while(<DATA>){
2      print if /5{1,}/;
   }
   _ _DATA_ _
   Steve Blenheim 1.10
   Betty Boop .5
   Igor Chevsky 555.100
   Norma Cord 4.01
   Jonathan DeLoach .501
   Karen Evich 601
```

EXAMPLE 8.22 (CONTINUED)

```
(Output)
Betty Boop .5
Igor Chevsky 555.100
Jonathan DeLoach .501
```

EXPLANATION

1   The special *DATA* filehandle gets its input from the text after the _ _DATA_ _ token. The *while* loop is entered and the first line after the _ _DATA_ _ token is read in and assigned to $_. Each time the loop is entered, the next line following _ _DATA_ _ is assigned to $_ until all the lines have been processed.

2   The expression reads: Find at least one or more consecutive occurrences of *5*.

Metacharacters That Turn Off Greediness.   By placing a question mark after a greedy quantifier, the greed is turned off and the search ends after the first match, rather than the last one.

EXAMPLE 8.23

```
(The Script)
    # Greedy and not greedy
1   $_="abcdefghijklmnopqrstuvwxyz";
2   s/[a-z]+/XXX/;
3   print $_, "\n";

4   $_="abcdefghijklmnopqrstuvwxyz";
5   s/[a-z]+?/XXX/;
6   print $_, "\n";

(Output)
3   XXX
6   XXXbcdefghijklmnopqrstuvwxyz
```

EXPLANATION

1   The scalar $_ is assigned a string of lowercase letters.

2   The regular expression reads: Search for one or more lowercase letters, and replace them with *XXX*. The + metacharacter is greedy. It takes as many characters as match the expression; i.e., it starts on the left-hand side of the string, grabbing as many lowercase letters as it can find until the end of the string.

3   The value of $_ is printed after the substitution.

EXPLANATION (CONTINUED)

4   The scalar $_ is assigned a string of lowercase letters.

5   The regular expression reads: Search for one or more lowercase letters, and, after finding the first one, stop searching and replace it with *XXX*. The *?* affixed to the + turns off the greediness of the metacharacter. The minimal number of characters are searched for.

6   The value of $_ is printed after the substitution.

Table 8.6   Turning Off Greediness

Metacharacter	*What It Matches*
x??	Matches 0 or 1 occurrences of *x*
(xyz)??	Matches 0 or 1 occurrences of pattern *xyz*
x?*	Matches 0 or more occurrences of *x*
(xyz)?*	Matches 0 or more occurrences of pattern *xyz*
x+?	Matches 1 or more occurrences of *x*
(xyz)+?	Matches 1 or more occurrences of pattern *xyz*
x{m,n}?	Matches at least *m* occurrences of *x* and no more than *n* occurrences of *x*
x{m}?	Matches at least *m* occurrences of *x*
x{m,}?	Matches at least *m* times

EXAMPLE 8.24

```
(The Script)
   # A greedy quantifier
1  $string="I got a cup of sugar and two cups of flour
          from the cupboard.";

2  $string =~ s/cup.*/tablespoon/;
3  print "$string\n";

   # Turning off greed
4  $string="I got a cup of sugar and two cups of flour
          from the cupboard.";
5  $string =~ s/cup.*?/tablespoon/;
6  print "$string\n";
```

EXAMPLE 8.24 (CONTINUED)

```
(Output)
3    I got a tablespoon
6    I got a tablespoon of sugar and two cups of flour from the
     cupboard.
```

EXPLANATION

1   The scalar *$string* is assigned a string containing the pattern *cup* three times.
2   The *s* (substitution) operator searches for the pattern *cup* followed by zero or more characters; that is, *cup* and all characters to the end of the line are matched and replaced with the string *tablespoon*. The .* is called a greedy quantifier because it matches for the largest possible pattern.
3   The output shows the result of a greedy substitution.
4   The scalar *$string* is reset.
5   This time the search is not greedy. By appending a question mark to the .*, the smallest pattern that matches *cup*, followed by zero or more characters, is replaced with *tablespoon*.
6   The new string is printed.

Anchoring Metacharacters.   Often, it is necessary to anchor a metacharacter so that it matches only if the pattern is found at the beginning or end of a line, word, or string. These metacharacters are based on a position just to the left or to the right of the character that is being matched. Anchors are technically called **zero-width assertions** because they correspond to positions, not actual characters in a string. For example, /^abc/ means find *abc* at the beginning of the line, where the ^ represents a position, not an actual character.

Table 8.7   Anchors (Assertions)

Metacharacter	*What It Matches*
^	Matches to beginning of line or beginning of string
$	Matches to end of line or end of a string
\A	Matches the beginning of the string only
\Z	Matches the end of the string or line
\z	Matches the end of string only
\G	Matches where previous *m//g* left off
\b	Matches a word boundary (when not inside *[ ]*)
\B	Matches a non-word boundary

EXAMPLE 8.25

```
(The Script)
    # Beginning of line anchor
1   while(<DATA>){
2       print if /^[JK]/;
    }
    _ _DATA_ _
    Steve Blenheim 1.10
    Betty Boop .5
    Igor Chevsky 555.100
    Norma Cord 4.01
    Jonathan DeLoach .501
    Karen Evich 601


(Output)
Jonathan DeLoach .501
Karen Evich 601.100
```

EXPLANATION

1 The special *DATA* filehandle gets its input from the text after the _ _DATA_ _ token. The *while* loop is entered and the first line after the _ _DATA_ _ token is read in and assigned to $_. Each time the loop is entered, the next line following _ _DATA_ _ is assigned to $_ until all the lines have been processed.

2 The regular expression contains the caret (^) metacharacter, representing the beginning of line anchor only when it is the first character in the pattern. The expression reads: Find a *J* or *K* at the beginning of the line. \A would produce the same result as the caret in this example. The expression /^[^JK]/ reads: Search for a non-*J* or non-*K* character at the beginning of the line. Remember that when the caret is within a character class, it negates the character class. It is only a beginning of line anchor when positioned **directly after** the opening delimiter.

EXAMPLE 8.26

```
(The Script)
    # End of line anchor
1   while(<DATA>){
2       print if /10$/;
    }
    _ _DATA_ _
    Steve Blenheim 1.10
    Betty Boop .5
    Igor Chevsky 555.10
    Norma Cord 4.01
    Jonathan DeLoach .501
    Karen Evich 601
```

EXAMPLE 8.26 (CONTINUED)

```
(Output)
Steve Blenheim 1.10
Igor Chevsky 555.10
```

EXPLANATION

1   The special *DATA* filehandle gets its input from the text after the _ _*DATA*_ _ token. The *while* loop is entered and the first line after the _ _*DATA*_ _ token is read in and assigned to *$_*. Each time the loop is entered, the next line following _ _*DATA*_ _ is assigned to *$_* until all the lines have been processed.

2   The regular expression contains the *$* metacharacter, representing the end of line anchor only when the *$* is the last character in the pattern. The expression reads: Find a *1* and a *0* followed by a newline.

EXAMPLE 8.27

```
(The Script)
    # Word anchors or boundaries
1   while(<DATA>){
2       print if /\bJon/;
    }
    _ _DATA_ _
    Steve Blenheim 1.10
    Betty Boop .5
    Igor Chevsky 555.100
    Norma Cord 4.01
    Jonathan DeLoach .501
    Karen Evich 601


(Output)
Jonathan DeLoach .501
```

EXPLANATION

1   The special *DATA* filehandle gets its input from the text after the _ _*DATA*_ _ token. The *while* loop is entered and the first line after the _ _*DATA*_ _ token is read in and assigned to *$_*. Each time the loop is entered, the next line following _ _*DATA*_ _ is assigned to *$_* until all the lines have been processed.

2   The regular expression contains the *\b* metacharacter, representing a word boundary. The expression reads: Find a word beginning with the pattern *Jon*.

EXAMPLE 8.28

```
(The Script)
    # Beginning and end of word anchors
1   while(<DATA>){
2       print if /\bJon\b/;
    }
    _ _DATA_ _
    Steve Blenheim 1.10
    Betty Boop .5
    Igor Chevsky 555.100
    Norma Cord 4.01
    Jonathan DeLoach .501
    Karen Evich 601


(Output)
<No output>
```

EXPLANATION

1   The special *DATA* filehandle gets its input from the text after the _ _*DATA*_ _ token. The *while* loop is entered and the first line after the _ _*DATA*_ _ token is read in and assigned to *$_*. Each time the loop is entered, the next line following _ _*DATA*_ _ is assigned to *$_* until all the lines have been processed.

2   The regular expression also contains the *\b* metacharacter, representing a word boundary. The expression reads: Find a word beginning and ending with *Jon*. Nothing is found.

The *m* Modifier.   The *m* modifier is used to control the behavior of the *$* and *^* anchor metacharacters. A string containing newlines will be treated as multiple lines. If the regular expression is anchored with the *^* metacharacter, and that pattern is found at the beginning of any one of the multiple lines, the match is successful. Likewise, if the regular expression is anchored by the *$* metacharacter (or *\Z*) at the end of any one of the multiple lines, and the pattern is found, it too will return a successful match. The *m* modifier has no effect with *\A* and *\z*.

EXAMPLE 8.29

```
(The Script)
    # Anchors and the m modifier
1   $_="Today is history.\nTomorrow will never be here.\n";
2   print if /^Tomorrow/;     # Embedded newline

3   $_="Today is history.\nTomorrow will never be here.\n";
4   print if /\ATomorrow/;    # Embedded newline

5   $_="Today is history.\nTomorrow will never be here.\n";
6   print if /^Tomorrow/m;

7   $_="Today is history.\nTomorrow will never be here.\n";
8   print if /\ATomorrow/m;

9   $_="Today is history.\nTomorrow will never be here.\n";
10  print if /history\.$/m;

(Output)
6   Today is history.
    Tomorrow will never be here.
10  Today is history.
    Tomorrow will never be here.
```

EXPLANATION

1   The $_ scalar is assigned a string with embedded newlines.
2   The ^ metacharacter anchors the search to the beginning of the line. Since the line does not begin with *Tomorrow,* the search fails and nothing is returned.
3   The $_ scalar is assigned a string with embedded newlines.
4   The \A assertion matches only at the beginning of a string, no matter what. Since the string does not begin with *Tomorrow,* the search fails and nothing is returned.
5   The $_ scalar is assigned a string with embedded newlines.
6   The *m* modifier treats the string as multiple lines, each line ending with a newline. In this example, the ^ anchor matches at the beginning of any of these multiple lines. The pattern /^*Tomorrow*/ is found in the second line.
7   The $_ scalar is assigned a string with embedded newlines.
8   The \A assertion only matches at the beginning of a string, no matter how many newlines are embedded, and the *m* modifier has no effect. Since *Tomorrow* is not found at the beginning of the string, nothing is matched.
9   The $_ scalar is assigned a string with embedded newlines.
10 The $ metacharacter anchors the search to the end of a line. With the *m* modifier, embedded newlines create multiple lines. The pattern /*history*\ .$/ is found at the end of the first line. This will also work with the \Z assertion, but not with \z.

Alternation.   Alternation allows the regular expression to contain alternative patterns to be matched. For example, the regular expression /*John\Karen\Steve*/ will match a line containing *John* or *Karen* or *Steve*. If *Karen, John,* or *Steve* are all on different lines, all lines are matched. Each of the alternative expressions is separated by a vertical bar (pipe symbol) and the expressions can consist of any number of characters, unlike the character class that only matches for one character; e.g., /*a\b\c*/ is the same as *[abc]*, whereas /*ab\de*/ cannot be represented as *[abde]*. The pattern /*ab\de*/ is either *ab* or *de* whereas the class *[abcd]* represents only **one** character in the set, *a*, *b*, *c*, or *d*.

EXAMPLE 8.30

```
(The Script)
    # Alternation: this, that, and the other thing
1   while(<DATA>){
2       print if /Steve|Betty|Jon/;
    }
    _ _DATA_ _
    Steve Blenheim
    Betty Boop
    Igor Chevsky
    Norma Cord
    Jonathan DeLoach
    Karen Evich


(Output)
2   Steve Blenheim
    Betty Boop
    Jonathan DeLoach
```

EXPLANATION

1   The special *DATA* filehandle gets its input from the text after the _ _DATA_ _ token. The *while* loop is entered and the first line after the _ _DATA_ _ token is read in and assigned to *$_*. Each time the loop is entered, the next line following _ _DATA_ _ is assigned to *$_* until all the lines have been processed.

2   The pipe symbol, |, is used in the regular expression to match on a set of alternative patterns. If any of the patterns *Steve, Betty,* or *Jon,* are found, the match is successful.

Grouping or Clustering.   If the regular expression pattern is enclosed in parentheses, a subpattern is created. Then, for example, instead of the greedy metacharacters matching on zero, one, or more of the previous single character, they can match on the previous subpattern. Alternation can also be controlled if the patterns are enclosed in parentheses. This process of grouping characters together is also called **clustering** by the Perl wizards.

EXAMPLE 8.31

```
(The Script)
    # Clustering or grouping
1   $_=qq/The baby says, "Mama, Mama, I can say Papa!"\n/;
2   print if s/(ma|pa)+/goo/gi;

(Output)
The baby says, "goo, goo, I can say goo!"
```

EXPLANATION

1   The $_ scalar is assigned the doubly quoted string.
2   The regular expression contains a pattern enclosed in parentheses, followed by a +
    metacharacter. The parentheses group the characters that are to be controlled by the
    + metacharacter. The expression reads: Find one or more occurrences of the pattern
    ma or *pa* and replace that with *goo*.

EXAMPLE 8.32

```
(The Script)
    # Clustering or grouping
1   while(<DATA>){
2       print if /\s(12){3}$/;    # Print lines matching exactly 3
                                  # consecutive occurrences of 12 at
                                  # the end of the line

    }
    _ _DATA_ _
    Steve Blenheim    121212
    Betty Boop        123
    Igor Chevsky      123444123
    Norma Cord        51235
    Jonathan DeLoach123456
    Karen Evich       121212456

(Output)
Steve Blenheim   121212
```

EXPLANATION

1   The special *DATA* filehandle gets its input from the text after the _ _DATA_ _ token.
    The *while* loop is entered and the first line after the _ _DATA_ _ token is read in and
    assigned to $_. Each time the loop is entered, the next line following _ _DATA_ _ is
    assigned to $_ until all the lines have been processed.
2   The pattern *12* is grouped in parentheses. It is controlled by the quantifier *{3}*, i.e., a
    row of exactly *3* occurrences of *12* at the end of the line ($) will be matched.

EXAMPLE 8.33

```
The Script)
    # Clustering or grouping
1   $_="Tom and Dan Savage and Ellie Main are cousins.\n";
2   print if s/Tom|Ellie Main/Archie/g;

3   $_="Tom and Dan Savage and Ellie Main are cousins.\n";
4   print if s/(Tom|Ellie) Main/Archie/g;

(Output)
2   Archie and Dan Savage and Archie are cousins.
4   Tom and Dan Savage and Archie are cousins.
```

EXPLANATION

1   The *$_* scalar is assigned the string.
2   If either the pattern *Tom* or the pattern *Ellie Main* are matched in *$_*, both patterns will be replaced with *Archie*.
3   The *$_* scalar is assigned the string.
4   By enclosing *Tom* and *Ellie* in parentheses, the alternative now becomes either *Tom Main* or *Ellie Main*. Since the pattern *Ellie Main* is the only one matched in *$_*, *Ellie Main* is replaced with *Archie*.

EXAMPLE 8.34

```
(The Script)
    # Clustering and anchors
1   while(<DATA>){
2       # print if /^Steve|Boop/;
3       print if /^(Steve|Boop)/;
    }
_ _DATA_ _
Steve Blenheim
Betty Boop
Igor Chevsky
Norma Cord
Jonathan DeLoach
Karen Evich


(Output)
Steve Blenheim
```

EXPLANATION

1   The special *DATA* filehandle gets its input from the text after the _ _DATA_ _ token. The *while* loop is entered and the first line after the _ _DATA_ _ token is read in and assigned to *$_*. Each time the loop is entered, the next line following _ _DATA_ _ is assigned to *$_* until all the lines have been processed.

2   This line has been commented. It would print any line that begins with *Steve* and any line containing the pattern *Boop*. The beginning of line anchor, the caret, only applies to the pattern *Steve*.

3   The line will be printed if it begins with either *Steve* or *Boop*. The parentheses group the two patterns so that the beginning of line anchor, the caret, applies to both patterns *Steve* and *Boop*. It could also be written as */(^Steve|^Boop)/*.

Remembering or Capturing.   If the regular expression pattern is enclosed in parentheses, a subpattern is created. The subpattern is saved in special numbered scalar variables, starting with *$1*, then *$2*, and so on. These variables can be used later in the program and will persist until another successful pattern match occurs, at which time they will be cleared. Even if the intention was to control the greedy metacharacter or the behavior of alternation as shown in the previous example, the subpatterns are saved as a side effect.[2]

EXAMPLE 8.35

```
(The Script)
    # Remembering subpatterns
1   while(<DATA>){
2       s/([Jj]on)/$1athan/;        # Substitute Jon or jon with
                                     # Jonathan or jonathan

3       print;
    }
_ _DATA_ _
Steve Blenheim
Betty Boop
Igor Chevsky
Norma Cord
Jon DeLoach
Karen Evich
```

_____

2. It is possible to prevent a subpattern from being saved.

EXAMPLE 8.35 (CONTINUED)

```
(Output)
Steve Blenheim
Betty Boop
Igor Chevsky
Norma Cord
Jonathan DeLoach
Karen Evich
```

EXPLANATION

1   The special *DATA* filehandle gets its input from the text after the _ _*DATA*_ _ token. The *while* loop is entered and the first line after the _ _*DATA*_ _ token is read in and assigned to *$_*. Each time the loop is entered, the next line following _ _*DATA*_ _ is assigned to *$_* until all the lines have been processed.

2   The regular expression contains the pattern *Jon* enclosed in parentheses. This pattern is captured and stored in a special scalar, *$1*, so that it can be *remembered*. If a second pattern is enclosed in parentheses, it will be stored in *$2*, and so on. The numbers are represented on the replacement side as *$1*, *$2*, *$3*, and so on. The expression reads: Find *Jon* or *jon* and replace either with *Jonathan* or *jonathan*, respectively. The special numbered variables are cleared after the next successful search is performed.

EXAMPLE 8.36

```
(The Script)
    # Remembering multiple subpatterns
1   while(<DATA>){
2       print if s/(Steve) (Blenheim)/$2, $1/;
```

```
    }
    _ _DATA_ _
    Steve Blenheim
    Betty Boop
    Igor Chevsky
    Norma Cord
    Jonathan DeLoach
    Karen Evich

(Output)
Blenheim, Steve
```

EXPLANATION

1   The special *DATA* filehandle gets its input from the text after the _ _DATA_ _ token. The *while* loop is entered and the first line after the _ _DATA_ _ token is read in and assigned to *$_*. Each time the loop is entered, the next line following _ _DATA_ _ is assigned to *$_* until all the lines have been processed.

2   The regular expression contains two patterns enclosed in parentheses. The first pattern is captured and saved in the special scalar *$1* and the second pattern is captured and saved in the special scalar *$2*. On the replacement side, since *$2* is referenced first, *Blenheim* is printed first, followed by a comma, and then by *$1*, which is *Steve* (i.e., the effect is to reverse *Steve* and *Blenheim)*.

EXAMPLE 8.37

```
(The Script)
   # Reversing subpatterns
1  while(<>){
2      s/([A-Z][a-z]+)\s([A-Z][a-z]+)/$2, $1/;
                                   # Reverse first and last names

3      print;
   }
_ _DATA_ _
Steve Blenheim
Betty Boop
Igor Chevsky
Norma Cord
Jon DeLoach
Karen Evich

(Output)
Blenheim, Steve
Boop, Betty
Chevsky ,Igor
Cord, Norma
De, JonLoach        # Whoops!
Evich, Karen
```

EXPLANATION

2   This regular expression also contains two patterns enclosed in parentheses. In this example, metacharacters are used in the pattern matching process. The first pattern reads: Find an uppercase letter followed by one or more lowercase letters. A space follows the remembered pattern. The second pattern reads: Find an uppercase letter followed by one or more lowercase letters. The patterns are saved in *$1* and *$2*, respectively, and then reversed on the replacement side. Note the problem that arises with the last name *DeLoach*. That is because *DeLoach* contains **both** uppercase and lowercase letters after the first uppercase letter in the name. To allow for this case, the pattern should be *s/([A–Z][a–z]+)\s([A–Z][A–Za–z]+)/$2, $1/*.

EXAMPLE 8.38

```
(The Script)
    # Metasymbols and subpatterns
1   while(<DATA>){
2       s/(\w+)\s(\w+)/$2, $1/;      # Reverse first and last names
3       print;
    }

    _ _DATA_ _
    Steve Blenheim
    Betty Boop
    Igor Chevsky
    Norma Cord
    Jon DeLoach
    Betty Boop

(Output)
Blenheim, Steve
Boop, Betty
Chevsky, Igor
Cord, Norma
DeLoach, Jon
Boop, Betty
```

EXPLANATION

1   The special *DATA* filehandle gets its input from the text after the _ _DATA_ _ token. The *while* loop is entered and the first line after the _ _DATA_ _ token is read in and assigned to *$_*. Each time the loop is entered, the next line following _ _DATA_ _ is assigned to *$_* until all the lines have been processed.

2   The regular expression contains two subpatterns enclosed in parentheses. The \w+ represents one or more word characters. The regular expression consists of two parenthesized subpatterns (called **backreferences**) separated by a space (\s). Each subpattern is saved in *$1* and *$2*, respectively. *$1* and *$2* are used in the replacement side of the substitution to reverse the first and last names.

EXAMPLE 8.39

```
(The Script)
   # Backreferencing
1  while(<DATA>){
2      ($first, $last)=/(\w+) (\w+)/;    # Could be: (\S+) (\S+)/
3      print "$last, $first\n";
   }
   _ _DATA_ _
   Steve Blenheim
   Betty Boop
   Igor Chevsky
   Norma Cord
   Jon DeLoach
   Betty Boop


(Output)
Blenheim, Steve
Boop, Betty
Chevsky, Igor
Cord, Norma
DeLoach, Jon
Boop, Betty
```

EXPLANATION

1   The special *DATA* filehandle gets its input from the text after the _ _*DATA*_ _ token. The *while* loop is entered and the first line after the _ _*DATA*_ _ token is read in and assigned to $_. Each time the loop is entered, the next line following _ _*DATA*_ _ is assigned to $_ until all the lines have been processed.

2   The regular expression contains two patterns enclosed in parentheses. The \w+ represents one or more word characters. The regular expression consists of two parenthesized patterns (called backreferences). The return value is an array of all the backreferences. Each word is assigned to *$first* and *$last*, respectively.

3   The values of the variables are printed for each line of the file.

EXAMPLE 8.40

```
(The Script)
    # The greedy quantifier
1   $string = "ABCdefghiCxyzwerC YOU!";
2   $string = ~s/.*C/HEY/;
3   print "$string", "\n";
```

```
(Output)
HEY YOU!
```

EXPLANATION

1 The scalar *$string* is assigned a string containing a number of the pattern *C*.
2 The search side of the substitution, */.*C/*, reads: Find the largest pattern that contains any number of characters ending in *C*. This search is greedy. It will search from left to right until it reaches the last *C*. The string *HEY* will replace what was found in *$string*.
3 The new string is printed showing the result of the substitution.

EXAMPLE 8.41

```
(The Script)
    # Backreferencing and greedy quantifiers
1   $string = "ABCdefghiCxyzwerC YOU!";
2   $string = ~s/(.*C)(.*)/HEY/; # Substitute the whole string with
    HEY
3   print $1, "\n";
4   print $2, "\n";
5   print "$string\n";
```

```
(Output)
3   ABCdefghiCxyzwerC
4   YOU!
5   HEY
```

EXPLANATION

1 The scalar *$string* is assigned the string.
2 The */*.*C/* regular expression is enclosed in parentheses. The pattern found will be stored in the *$1* special variable. Whatever is left will be stored in *$2*.
3 The largest possible pattern was stored in *$1*. It is printed.
4 The remainder of the string was stored in *$2*. It is printed.
5 The entire string was replaced with *HEY* after the substitution.

EXAMPLE 8.42

```
(The Script)
    # Backreferencing and greed
1   $fruit = "apples pears peaches plums";
2   $fruit =~ /(.*)\s(.*)\s(.*)/;
3   print "$1\n";
4   print "$2\n";
5   print "$3\n";
    print "-" x 30, "\n";
6   $fruit="apples pears peaches plums";
7   $fruit =~ /(.*?)\s(.*?)\s(.*?)\s/;    # Turn off greedy quantifier
8   print "$1\n";
9   print "$2\n";
10  print "$3\n";


(Output)
3   apples pears
4   peaches
5   plums
    ------------------------------
8   apples
9   pears
10  peaches
```

EXPLANATION

1   The scalar *$fruit* is assigned the string.

2   The string is divided into three remembered substrings, each substring enclosed within parentheses. The .* metacharacter sequence reads zero or more of any character. The * always matches for the largest possible pattern. The largest possible pattern would be the whole string. However, there are two whitespaces outside of the parentheses that must also be matched in the string. What is the largest possible pattern that can be saved in *$1* and still leave two spaces in the string? The answer is *apples pears*.

3   The value of *$1* is printed.

4   The first substring was stored in *$1*. *peaches plums* is what remains of the original string. What is the largest possible pattern (.*) that can be matched and still have one whitespace remaining? The answer is *peaches*. *peaches* will be assigned to *$2*. The value of *$2* is printed.

5   The third substring is printed. *plums* is all that is left for *$3*.

6   The scalar *$fruit* is assigned the string again.

EXPLANATION (CONTINUED)

7   This time a question mark follows the greedy quantifier (*). This means that the pattern saved will be the minimal, rather than the maximal, number of characters found. *apples* will be the minimal numbers of characters stored in *$1*, *pears* the minimal number in *$2*, and *peaches* the minimal number of characters in *$3*. The \s is required or the minimal amount of characters would be zero, since the * means zero or more of the preceding character.

8   The value of *$1* is printed.

9   The value of *$2* is printed.

10 The value of *$3* is printed.

Turning Off Capturing.   When the only purpose is to use the parentheses for grouping, and you are not interested in saving the subpatterns in *$1*, *$2*, or *$3*, the special *?:* metacharacter can be used to suppress the capturing of the subpattern.

EXAMPLE 8.43

```
(In Script)
1   $_ = "Tom Savage and Dan Savage are brothers.\n";
2   print if /(?:D[a-z]*|T[a-z]*) Savage/;     # Perl will not capture
                                               # the pattern

3   print $1,"\n";      # $1 has no value

(Output)
2   Tom Savage and Dan Savage are brothers.
3   <Nothing is printed>
```

EXPLANATION

1   A string is assigned to the _$ scalar.

2   The *$_* scalar is assigned a string.

3   The *?:* turns off capturing when a pattern is enclosed in parentheses. In this example, alternation is used to search for any of two patterns. If the search is successful, the value of *$_* is printed, but whichever pattern is found, it will not be captured and assigned to *$1*.

4   Without the *?:*, the value of *$1* would be *Tom* since it is the first pattern found. *?:* says "Don't save the pattern when you find it." Nothing is saved and nothing is printed.

Metacharacters that Look Ahead and Behind.   Looking ahead and looking behind in a string for a particular pattern gives you further control of a regular expression.

With a positive look ahead, Perl looks forward or ahead in the string for a pattern (*?=pattern*) and if that pattern is found, will continue pattern matching on the regular expression. A negative look ahead looks ahead to see if the pattern (*?!pattern*) is **not** there, and if it is not, finishes pattern matching.

With a positive look behind, Perl looks backwards in string for a pattern (*?<=pattern*) and if that pattern is found, will then continue pattern matching on the regular expression. A negative look behind looks behind in the string to see if a pattern (*?<!pattern*) is not there, and if it is not, finishes the matching.

Table 8.8   Look Around Assertions

Metacharacter	*What It Matches*
/PATTERN(?=pattern)/	Positive look ahead
/PATTERN(?!pattern)/	Negative look ahead
(?<=pattern)/PATTERN/	Positive look behind
(?<!pattern)/PATTERN/	Negative look behind

EXAMPLE 8.44

```
(The Script)
    # A positive look ahead
1   $string = "I love chocolate cake and chocolate ice cream.";
2   $string =~ s/chocolate(?= ice)/vanilla/;
3   print "$string\n";

4   $string="Tomorrow night Tom Savage and Tommy Johnson will leave
            for vacation.";
5   $string =~ s/Tom(?=my)/Jere/g;
6   print "$string\n";

(Output)
3   I love chocolate cake and vanilla ice cream.
6   Tomorrow night Tom Savage and Jeremy Johnson will leave for
    vacation.
```

EXPLANATION

1   The scalar *$string* contains *chocolate* twice; the word *cake* follows the first occurrence of *chocolate* and the word *ice* follows the second occurrence.
2   This is an example of a **positive look ahead**. The pattern *chocolate* is followed by *(?=ice)* meaning, if *chocolate* is found, look ahead *(?=)* and see if *ice* is the next pattern. If *ice* is found just ahead of *chocolate*, the match is successful and *chocolate* will be replaced with *vanilla*.
3   After the substitution on line 2, the new string is printed.
4   A string of text consisting of three words starting with *Tom* is assigned to the scalar *$string*.
5   The pattern is matched if it contains *Tom*, only if *Tom* is followed by *my*. If the positive look ahead is successful, then *Tom* will be replaced with *Jere* in the string.
6   After the substitution on line 5, the new string is printed. *Tommy* has been replaced with *Jeremy*.

EXAMPLE 8.45

```
(The Script)
    # A negative look ahead
1   while(<DATA>){
2       print if /^\w+\s(?![BC])/;
    }
    _ _DATA_ _
    Steve Blenheim
    Betty Boop
    Igor Chevsky
    Norma Cord
    Jon DeLoach
    Karen Evich


(Output)
Jon DeLoach
Karen Evich
```

EXPLANATION

1   The special *DATA* filehandle gets its input from the text after the _ _DATA_ _ token. The *while* loop is entered and the first line after the _ _DATA_ _ token is read in and assigned to *$_*. Each time the loop is entered, the next line following _ _DATA_ _ is assigned to *$_* until all the lines have been processed.
2   The regular expression means: Search at the beginning of the line for one or more word characters (\w+), followed by a space (\s), and look ahead for any character that is **not** a *B* or *C*. This is called a **negative look ahead**.

EXAMPLE 8.46

```
(The Script)
    # A positive look behind
1   $string = "I love chocolate cake, chocolate milk,
            and chocolate ice cream.";
2   $string =~ s/(?<= chocolate) milk/ candy bars/;
3   print "$string\n";

4   $string = "I love coffee, I love tea, I love the boys
            and the boys love me.";
5   $string =~ s/(?<=the boys) love/ don't like/;
6   print "$string\n";

(Output)
3   I love chocolate cake, chocolate candy bars, and chocolate ice
    cream.
6   I love coffee, I love tea, I love the boys and the boys don't
    like me.
```

EXPLANATION

1. The scalar *$string* is assigned a string with three different occurrences of *chocolate*.
2. The pattern in parentheses is called a **positive look behind,** meaning that Perl looks **backward** in the string to make sure that this pattern occurs. If the pattern *milk* is found, Perl will look back in the string to see if it is preceded by *chocolate* and, if so, *milk* will be replaced with *candy bars*.
3. The string is printed after the substitution.
4. This is another example of a positive look behind. Perl looks backwards in the string for the pattern *the boys*, and if the pattern is found, the regular expression *love* will be replaced with *don't like*.

EXAMPLE 8.47

```
(The Script)
    # A negative look behind
1   while(<DATA>){
2       print if /(?<!Betty) B[a-z]*/;
    }
    _ _DATA_ _
    Steve Blenheim
    Betty Boop
    Igor Chevsky
    Norma Cord
    Jon DeLoach
    Karen Evich
```

EXAMPLE 8.47 (CONTINUED)

```
(Output)
Steve Blenheim
```

EXPLANATION

1   The special *DATA* filehandle gets its input from the text after the _ _DATA_ _ token. The *while* loop is entered and the first line after the _ _DATA_ _ token is read in and assigned to *$_*. Each time the loop is entered, the next line following _ _DATA_ _ is assigned to *$_* until all the lines have been processed.

2   The pattern in parentheses is called a **negative look behind**, meaning that Perl looks **backward** in the string to make sure that this pattern does not occur. Any line that contains the letter *B*, followed by zero or more lowercase letters, *[a–z]**, will be printed, as long as the pattern behind it is **not** *Betty*.

8.1.4   The *tr* or *y* Function

The *tr* function (similar to the UNIX *tr* command) translates characters, in a one-on-one correspondence, from the characters in the search string to the characters in the replacement string. *tr* returns the number of characters that it replaced. The *tr* function does not interpret regular expression metacharacters, but allows a dash to represent a range of characters. The letter *y* can be used in place of *tr*. This strangeness comes from UNIX, where the *sed* utility has a *y* command to translate characters, similar to the UNIX *tr*. This illustrates the role UNIX has played in the development of Perl.

The *d* option deletes the search string.

The *c* option complements the search string.

The *s* option is called the squeeze option. Multiple occurrences of characters found in the search string are replaced by a single occurrence of that character (e.g., you may want to replace multiple tabs with single tabs). See Table 8.9 for a list of modifiers.

FORMAT

```
tr/search/replacement/
tr/search/replacement/d
tr/search/replacement/c
tr/search/replacement/s
y/search/replacement/        (same as tr; uses same modifiers)
```

Table 8.9 *tr* Modifiers

Modifier	Meaning
d	Delete characters
c	Complement the search list
s	Squeeze out multiple characters to single character

EXAMPLE 8.48

```
(The Input Data)
    Steve Blenheim 101
    Betty Boop 201
    Igor Chevsky 301
    Norma Cord 401
    Jon DeLoach 501
    Karen Evich 601

(Lines from a Script)
1   tr/a-z/A-Z/;print;

(Output)
STEVE BLENHEIM  101
BETTY BOOP  201
IGOR CHEVSKY  301
NORMA CORD  401
JON DELOACH  501
KAREN EVICH  601


2   tr/0-9/:/; print;

(Output)
Steve Blenheim :::
Betty Boop :::
Igor Chevsky :::
Norma Cord :::
Jon DeLoach :::
Karen Evich :::
```

EXAMPLE 8.48   (CONTINUED)

```
3   tr/A-Z/a-c/;print;
```

```
(Output)
cteve blenheim 101
betty boop 201
cgor chevsky 301
corma cord 401
con cecoach 501
caren cvich 601
```

```
4   tr/ /#/; print;
```

```
(Output)
Steve#Blenheim#101
Betty#Boop#201
Igor#Chevsky#301
Norma#Cord#401
Jon#DeLoach#501
Karen#Evich#601
```

```
5   y/A-Z/a-z/;print;
```

```
(Output)
steve blenheim 101
betty boop 201
igor chevsky 301
norma cord 401
jon deloach 501
karen evich 601
```

EXPLANATION

1   The *tr* function makes a one-on-one correspondence between each character in the search string with each character in the replacement string. Each lowercase letter will be translated to its corresponding uppercase letter.

2   Each number will be translated to a colon.

3   The translation is messy here. Since the search side represents more characters than the replacement side, all letters from *D* to *Z* will be replaced with a *c*.

4   Each space will be replaced with pound signs (#).

5   The *y* is a synonym for *tr*. Each uppercase letter is translated to its corresponding lowercase letter.

The *tr* Delete Option.   The *d* (delete) option removes all characters in the search string not found in the replacement string.

EXAMPLE 8.49

```
1   tr/ //; print;

(Output)
1 Steve Blenheim
2 Betty Boop
3 Igor Chevsky
4 Norma Cord
5 Jon DeLoach
6 Karen Evich

2   tr/ //d;print;

(Output)
1SteveBlenheim
2BettyBoop
3IgorChevsky
4NormaCord
5JonDeLoach
6KarenEvich
```

EXPLANATION

1   In this example, the translation does not take place as it would if you were using *sed* or *vi*.
2   The *d* option is required to delete each space when using the *tr* function.

The *tr* Complement Option.   The *c* (complement) option complements the search string; that is, it translates each character not listed in this string to its corresponding character in the replacement string.

EXAMPLE 8.50

```
1   tr/0-9/*/; print;
```

(Output)
Steve Blenheim
Betty Boop
Igor Chevsky
Norma Cord
Jon DeLoach
Karen Evich

```
2   tr/0-9/*/c; print;
```

(Output)
```
1*****************2*************3***************4*************5****
*********6*************
```

EXPLANATION

1   Without the *c* option, *tr* translates each number to an asterisk (*).
2   With the *c* option, *tr* translates each character that is **not** a number to an asterisk (*); this includes the newline character.

The *tr* Squeeze Option.   The *s* (squeeze) option translates all characters that are repeated to a single character.

EXAMPLE 8.51

```
(The Text File)
1   while (<DATA>){
        tr/:/:/s;
        print;
    }
    _ _DATA_ _
    1:::Steve Blenheim
    2::Betty Boop
    3:Igor Chevsky
    4:Norma Cord
    5:::::Jon DeLoach
    6:::Karen Evich
```

EXAMPLE 8.51   (CONTINUED)

```
(Output)
1:Steve Blenheim
2:Betty Boop
3:Igor Chevsky
4:Norma Cord
5:Jon DeLoach
6:Karen Evich
```

EXPLANATION

1   Multiple colons are translated (squeezed) into single colons.

8.2   Unicode

For every character, Unicode specifies a unique identification number that remains consistent across applications, languages, and platforms.

With the advent of the Internet, it became obvious that the ASCII coding for characters was insufficient if the whole world were to be included in transferring data from one Web site to another without corrupting the data. The ASCII sequence of characters consists of only 256 (one-byte) characters and could hardly accommodate languages like Chinese and Japanese, where a given symbol is drawn from a set of thousands of characters.

The Unicode standard is an effort to solve the problem by creating new characters sets, called UTF8 and UTF16, where characters are not limited to one byte. UTF8, for example, allows two bytes that can hold up to 65,536 characters, and each character has a unique number. To remove ambiguity, any given 16-bit value would always represent the same character, thereby allowing for consistent sorting, searching, displaying and editing of text. According to the Unicode Consortium,[3] Unicode has the capacity to encode over one million characters, which is sufficient to encompass all the world's written languages. Further, all symbols are treated equally, so that all characters can be accessed without the need for escape sequences or control codes.

---

3. The Unicode Consortium is a non-profit organization founded to develop, extend, and promote use of the Unicode standard. For more information on Unicode and the Unicode Consortium, go to *http://www.unicode.org/unicode/standard/whatisunicode.html.*

8.2.1   Perl and Unicode

The largest change in Perl 5.6 was to provide UTF8 Unicode support. By default, Perl represents strings internally in Unicode and all the relevant built-in functions (*length*, *reverse*, *sort*, *tr*) now work on a character-by-character basis instead of on a byte-by-byte basis. Two new Perl pragmas are used to turn Unicode settings on and off. The *utf8* pragma turns on the Unicode settings and loads the required character tables, while the *bytes* pragma refers to the old byte meanings, reading one byte at a time.

When *utf8* is turned on, you can specify string literals in Unicode using the \x{N} notation, where N is a hexadecimal character code such as \x{395}.

Unicode also provides support for regular expressions and matching characters based on Unicode properties, some of which are defined by the Unicode standard and some by Perl. The Perl properties are composites of the standard properties; in other words, you can now match any uppercase character in any language with \p{IsUpper}. For more information, go to *http://www.perl.com/pub/a/2000/04/whatsnew.html*.

Table 8.10 is a list of Perl's composite character classes. If the *p* in \p is capitalized, the meaning is a negation; so, for example, \p{IsASCII} represents an ASCII character, whereas \P{IsASCII} represents a non-ASCII character.

Table 8.10   *utf8* Composite Character Classes

utf8 Property	Meaning
\p{IsASCII}	ASCII character
\p{Cntrl}	Control character
\p{IsDigit}	A digit between 0 and 9
\p{IsGraph}	Alphanumeric or punctuation character
\p{IsLower}	Lowercase letter
\p{IsPrint}	Alphanumeric, punctuation character, or space
\p{IsPunct}	Any punctuation character
\p{IsSpace}	Whitespace character
\p{IsUpper}	Uppercase letter
\p{IsWord}	Alphanumeric word character or underscore
\p{IsXDigit}	Any hexadecimal digit

EXAMPLE 8.52

```
1   use utf8;
2   $chr = 11;
3   print "$chr is a digit.\n"if $chr =~ /\p{IsDigit}/;
4   $chr = "junk";
5   print "$chr is not a digit.\n"if $chr =~ /\P{IsDigit}/;
6   print "$chr is not a control character.\n"if $chr =
      ~ /\P{IsCntrl}/;
```

(Output)
3   *11 is a digit.*
5   *junk is not a digit.*
6   *junk is not a control character.*

EXPLANATION

1   The *utf8* pragma is used to turn on the Unicode settings.
2   Scalar *$chr* is assigned a number.
3   The Perl Unicode property *IsDigit* is used to check for number between *0* and *9*, the same as using *[0–9]*.
4   The string *junk* Scalar *$chr* is assigned.
5   The \p is now \P, causing the escape sequence to mean **not** a digit, the same as using *[^0–9]*. Since *junk* is not a digit, the condition is true.
6   The opposite of *junk* is not a control character.

EXERCISE 7
Is it *sed*, *awk*, or *grep*?
Give Perl Another Whirl!

```
(Sample file found on CD)
Tommy Savage:408-724-0140:1222 Oxbow Court, Sunnyvale,CA 94087:5/19/66:34200
Lesle Kerstin:408-456-1234:4 Harvard Square, Boston, MA 02133:4/22/62:52600
JonDeLoach:408-253-3122:123 Park St., San Jose, CA 94086:7/25/53:85100
Ephram Hardy:293-259-5395:235 Carlton Lane, Joliet, IL 73858:8/12/20:56700
Betty Boop:245-836-8357:635 Cutesy Lane, Hollywood, CA 91464:6/23/23:14500
Wilhelm Kopf:846-836-2837:6937 Ware Road, Milton, PA 93756:9/21/46:43500
Norma Corder:397-857-2735:74 Pine Street, Dearborn, MI 23874:3/28/45:245700
James Ikeda:834-938-8376:23445 Aster Ave., Allentown, NJ 83745:12/1/38:45000
Lori Gortz:327-832-5728:3465 Mirlo Street, Peabody, MA 34756:10/2/65:35200
Barbara Kerz:385-573-8326:832 Ponce Drive, Gary, IN 83756:12/15/46:268500
```

1. Print the city and state where Norma lives.

2. Give everyone a $250.00 raise.

3. Calculate Lori's age.

4. Print lines 2 through 6. (The $. variable holds the current line number.)

5. Print names and phone numbers of those in the 408 area code.

6. Print names and salaries in lines 3, 4, and 5.

7. Print a row of stars after line 3.

8. Change *CA* to *California*.

9. Print the file with a row of stars after the last line.

10. Print the names of the people born in March.

11. Print all lines that don't contain *Karen*.

12. Print lines that end in exactly five consecutive digits.

13. Print the file with the first and last names reversed.

GETTING A HANDLE
ON FILES

9.1   The User-Defined Filehandle

A **filehandle** is a name for a file, device, pipe, or socket. In Chapter 3, "Getting a Handle on Printing," we discussed the three default filehandles, *STDIN*, *STDOUT*, and *STDERR*. Perl allows you to create your own filehandles for input and output operations on files, devices, pipes, or sockets. A filehandle allows you to associate the filehandle name with a system file[1] and to use that filehandle to access the file.

9.1.1   Opening Files—The *open* Function

The *open* function lets you name a filehandle and the file you want to attach to that handle. The file can be opened for reading, writing, or appending (or both reading and writing) and the file can be opened to pipe data to or from a process. The *open* function returns a non-zero result if successful, and an undefined value if it fails. Like scalars, arrays, and labels, filehandles have their own namespace. So that they will not be confused with reserved words, the Perl wizards recommend that filehandle names be written in all uppercase letters. (See the *open* function in Appendix A.)

When opening text files on Win32 platforms, the \r\n (characters for return and newline) are translated into \n when text files are read from disk, and the ^Z character is read as an end-of-file marker (EOF). The following functions for opening files should work fine with text files, but will cause a problem with binary files. (See "Win32 Files" on page 257.)

9.1.2   Open for Reading

The following examples illustrate how to open files for reading. Even though the examples represent UNIX files, they will work the same way on Windows, Mac OS, etc.

---

1. A system file would be a UNIX, Win32, Macintosh file, etc. stored on the system's disk.

FORMAT

```
1    open(FILEHANDLE, "FILENAME");
2    open(FILEHANDLE, "<FILENAME");
2    open(FILEHANDLE);
3    open FILEHANDLE;
```

EXAMPLE 9.1

```
1    open(MYHANDLE, "myfile");
2    open (FH, "< /etc/passwd");
3    open (MYHANDLE);
```

EXPLANATION

1   The *open* function will create the filehandle *MYHANDLE*, and attach it to the system file *myfile*. The file will be opened for reading. Since a full pathname is not specified for *myfile*, it must be in the current working directory and you must have read permission to open it for reading.

2   The *open* function will create the filehandle *FH* and attach it to the system file */etc/passwd*. The file will be opened for reading, but this time the < symbol is used to indicatethe operation. The < symbol is not necessary, but may help clarify that this is a *read* operation. The full pathname is specified for *passwd*.

3   If *FILENAME* is omitted, the name of the filehandle is the same name as a scalar variable previously defined. The scalar variable has been assigned the name of the real file. In the example, the filename could have been defined as

```
$MYHANDLE = "myfile";
open(MYHANDLE);
```

The *open* function will create the filehandle *MYHANDLE* and attach it to the value of the variable, *$MYHANDLE*. The effect will be the same as the first example. The parentheses are optional.

Closing the Filehandle.   The *close* function closes the file, pipe, socket, or device attached to *FILEHANDLE*. Once *FILEHANDLE* is opened, it stays open until the script ends or you call the *open* function again. (The next call to *open* closes *FILEHANDLE* before reopening it.) If you don't explicitly close the file, when you reopen it this way, the line counter variable, *$.*, will not be reset. Closing a pipe causes the process to wait until the pipe is complete and reports the status in the *$!* variable (see "The *die* Function" on page 251). It's a good idea to explicitly close files and handles after you are finished using them.

FORMAT

```
close (FILEHANDLE);
close FILEHANDLE;
```

EXAMPLE 9.2

```
1   open(INFILE, "datebook");
    close(INFILE);
```

EXPLANATION

1   The user-defined filehandle *INFILE* will be closed.

The *die* Function.   In the following examples, the *die* function is used if a call to the *open* function fails. If Perl cannot open the file, the *die* function is used to exit the Perl script and print a message to *STDERR*, usually the screen.

If you were to go to your shell or MS-DOS prompt and type

```
cat junk   (UNIX)
```

or

```
$ type junk (DOS)
```

and if *junk* is a non-existent file, the following system error would appear on your screen:

```
cat: junk: No such file or directory    (UNIX)
The system cannot find the file specified.   (Windows)
```

The Perl special variable *$!* holds the value of the system error (see "Error Handling" on page 571) that occurs when you are unable to successfully open a file or execute a system utility. When used with the *die* function, this is very useful for detecting a problem with the filehandle before continuing with the execution of the script. (See use of *Carp.pm* discussed in Example 11.10 on page 343–344.)

EXAMPLE 9.3

```
(Line from Script)
1   open(MYHANDLE, "/etc/password) || die "Can't open: $!\n";
2   open(MYHANDLE, "/etc/password) or die "Can't open: $!\n";

(Output)
1   Can't open: No such file or directory

(Line from Script)
3   open(MYHANDLE, "/etc/password") || die "Can't open: ";

(Output)
3   Can't open: No such file or directory at ./handle line 3.
```

EXPLANATION

1   When trying to open the file */etc/password*, the *open* fails (it should be */etc/passwd*). The short-circuit operator causes its right operand to execute if the left operand fails. The *die* operator is executed. The string *Can't open:* is printed, followed by the system error *No such file or directory*. The \n suppresses any further output from the *die* function. All of *die*'s output is sent to *STDERR* after the program exits.

2   For readability, you may want to use the *or* operator instead of ||.

3   This is exactly like the first example, except that the \n has been removed from the string *Can't open:* . Omitting the \n causes the *die* function to append a string to the output, indicating the line number in the script where the system error occurred.

Reading from the Filehandle.   In Example 9.4, a file called *datebook* is opened for reading. Each line read is assigned, in turn, to *$_*, the default scalar that holds what was just read until the end of file is reached.

EXAMPLE 9.4

```
(The Text File: datebook)
    Steve Blenheim
    Betty Boop
    Lori Gortz
    Sir Lancelot
    Norma Cord
    Jon DeLoach
    Karen Evich

----------------------------------------------------------------
```

EXAMPLE 9.4   (CONTINUED)

```
(The Script)
    #!/usr/bin/perl
    # Open a file with a filehandle
1   open(FILE, "datebook") || die "Can't open datebook: $!\n";
2   while(<FILE>){
3       print  if /Sir Lancelot/;
4   }
5   close(FILE);

(Output)
3   Sir Lancelot
```

EXPLANATION

1   The *open* function will create a filehandle called *FILE* (opened for reading) and attach the system file *datebook* to it. If *open* fails because the file *datebook* does not exist, the *die* operator will print to the screen, *Can't open datebook: No such file or directory.*

2   The expression in the *while* loop is the filehandle *FILE*, enclosed in angle brackets. The angle brackets are the operators used for reading input. (They are not part of the filehandle name.) When the loop starts, the first line from the filehandle *FILE* will be stored in the *$_* scalar variable. (Remember the *$_* variable holds each line of input from the file.) If it has not reached end of file, the loop will continue to take a line of input from the file, execute statements 3 and 4, and continue until end of file is reached.

3   The default input variable *$_* is implicitly used to hold the current line of input read from the filehandle. If the line contains the regular expression *Sir Lancelot*, that line (stored in *$_*) is printed to *STDOUT*. For each loop iteration, the next line read is stored in *$_* and tested.

4   The closing curly brace marks the end of the loop body. When this line is reached, control will go back to the top of the loop (line 2) and the next line of input will be read from file; this process will continue until all the lines have been read.

5   After looping through the file, the file is closed by closing the filehandle.

EXAMPLE 9.5

```
(The Text File: datebook)
    Steve Blenheim
    Betty Boop
    Lori Gortz
    Sir Lancelot
    Norma Cord
    Jon DeLoach
    Karen Evich
-----------------------------------------------------------------
(The Script)
    #!/usr/bin/perl
    # Open a file with a filehandle
1   open(FILE, "datebook") || die "Can't open datebook: $!\n";
2   while($line = <FILE>){
3      print "$line" if  $line =~ /^Lori/;
4   }
5   close(FILE);

(Output)
3   Lori Gortz
```

EXPLANATION

1   The *datebook* file is opened for reading.
2   When the *while* loop is entered, a line is read from the file and stored in the scalar *$line*.
3   The value of the scalar *$line* is printed if it contains the pattern *Lori*, and *Lori* is at the beginning of the line.
4   When the closing brace is reached, control goes back to line 2, and another line is read from the file. The loop ends when the file has no more lines.
5   The file is closed by closing the filehandle.

EXAMPLE 9.6

```
(The Text File: datebook)
    Steve Blenheim
    Betty Boop
    Lori Gortz
    Sir Lancelot
    Norma Cord
    Jon DeLoach
    Karen Evich

-----------------------------------------------------------------
```

EXAMPLE 9.6 (CONTINUED)

```
(The Script)
   #!/usr/bin/perl
   # Open a file with a filehandle
1  open(FILE, "<datebook") || die "Can't open datebook: $!\n";
2  @lines = <FILE>;
3  print @lines;        # Contents of the entire file are printed
4  print "\nThe datebook file contains ", $#lines + 1,
          " lines of text.\n";
5  close(FILE);

(Output)
The datebook file contains 7 lines of text.
```

EXPLANATION

1 The *datebook* file is opened for reading. (The < read operator is not required.)
2 All of the lines are read from the file, via the filehandle, and assigned to *@lines*, where each line is an element of the array. The newline terminates each element.
3 The array *@lines* is printed.
4 The value of *$#lines* is the number of the last subscript in the array. By adding one to *$#lines*, the number of elements (lines) is printed. A *–1* offset, *$lines[–1]*, will also print the last line.

9.1.3 Open for Writing

To open a file for writing, the file will be created if it does not exist, and if it already exists, it must have write permission. If the file exists, its contents will be overwritten. The filehandle is used to access the system file.

FORMAT

```
1  open(FILEHANDLE, ">FILENAME");
```

EXAMPLE 9.7

```
1  open(MYOUTPUT, ">temp");
```

EXPLANATION

1 The user-defined filehandle *MYOUTPUT* will be used to send output to the file called *temp*. As with the shell, the redirection symbol directs the output from the default filehandle, *STDOUT*, to the *temp* file.

EXAMPLE 9.8

```
(The Script)
    #!/usr/bin/perl
    # Write to a file with a filehandle. Scriptname: file.handle
1   $file = "/home/jody/ellie/perl/newfile";
2   open(HANDOUT, ">$file") || die "Can't open newfile: $!\n";

3   print HANDOUT "hello world.\n";
4   print HANDOUT "hello world again.\n";

(At the Command Line)
5   $ perl file.handle
6   $ cat newfile

(Output)
3   hello world.
4   hello world, again.
```

EXPLANATION

1   The scalar variable *$file* is set to the full pathname of a UNIX file called *newfile*. The scalar will be used to represent the name of the UNIX file to which output will be directed via the filehandle. This example will work the same way with Windows, but if you use the backslash as a directory separator, either enclose the path in single quotes, or use two backslashes; e.g., *C:\\home\\ellie\\testing*.

2   The user-defined filehandle *HANDOUT* will change the default place to where output normally goes, *STDOUT*, to the file that it represents, *newfile*. The > symbol indicates that *newfile* will be created if it does not exist and opened for writing. If it does exist, it will be opened and any text in it will be **overwritten**, so be careful!

3   The *print* function will send its output to the filehandle, *HANDOUT*, instead of to the screen. The string *hello world.* will be written into *newfile* via the *HANDOUT* filehandle. The file *newfile* will remain open unless it is explicitly closed or the Perl script ends (see "Closing the Filehandle" on page 250).

4   The *print* function will send its output to the filehandle *HANDOUT* instead of to the screen. The string *hello world, again.* will be written into *newfile* via the *HANDOUT* filehandle. The operating system keeps track of where the last write occurred and will send its next line of output to the location immediately following the last byte written to the file.

5   The script is executed. The output is sent to *newfile*.

6   The contents of the file *newfile* are printed.

9.1.4   Win32 Files

Win32 distinguishes between text and binary files. If ^Z is found, the program may abort prematurely or have problems with the newline translation. When reading and writing Win32 binary files, use the *binmode* function to prevent these problems. The *binmode* function arranges for a specified filehandle to be read or written to in either binary (raw) or text mode. If the discipline argument is not specified, the mode is set to "raw." The discipline is either *:raw, :crlf, :text, :utf8,* or *:latin1*, etc.

FORMAT

```
binmode FILEHANDLE
binmode FILEHANDLE, DISCIPLINE
```

EXAMPLE 9.9

```
# This script copies one binary file to another.
# Note its use of binmode to set the mode of the filehandle.

1   $infile = "statsbar.gif";
2   open( INFILE, "<$infile" );
3   open( OUTFILE, ">outfile.gif" );

4   binmode( INFILE );        # Crucial for binary files!

5   binmode( OUTFILE );
    # binmode should be called after open() but before any I/O
    # is done on the filehandle.

6   while( read( INFILE, $buffer, 1024 ) ){
7        print OUTFILE $buffer;
    }

8   close(INFILE);
    close(OUTFILE);
```

EXPLANATION

1   The scalar *$infile* is assigned a *.gif* filename.
2   The file *statsbar.gif* is opened for reading and attached to the *INFILE* filehandle.
3   The file *outfile.gif* is opened for writing and assigned to the *OUTFILE* filehandle.
4   The *binmode* function arranges for the input file to be read as binary text.
5   The *binmode* function arranges for the output file to be written as binary text.
6   The *read* function reads 1024 bytes at a time, storing the input read in the scalar *$buffer*.
7   After the 1024 bytes are read in, they are sent out to the output file.
8   Both filehandles are closed. The result was that one binary file was copied to another binary file.

9.1.5 Open for Appending

To open a file for appending, the file will be created if it does not exist, and if it already exists, it must have write permission. If the file exists, its contents will be left intact, and the output will be appended to the end of the file. Again, the filehandle is used to access the file rather than accessing it by its real name.

FORMAT

```
1   open(FILEHANDLE, ">> FILENAME");
```

EXAMPLE 9.10

```
1   open(APPEND, ">> temp");
```

EXPLANATION

1   The user-defined filehandle *APPEND* will be used to append output to the file called *temp*. As with the shell, the redirection symbol directs the output from the default, standard out filehandle, *STDOUT*, to the *temp* file.

EXAMPLE 9.11

```
(The Text File)
$ cat newfile
hello world.
hello world, again.

(The Script)
    #!/usr/bin/perl
1   open(HANDLE, ">> newfile") ||
            die print "Can't open newfile: $!\n";
2   print HANDLE "Just appended \"hello world\"
            to the end of newfile.\n";

(Output)
$ cat newfile
hello world.
hello world, again.
Just appended "hello world" to the end of newfile.
```

EXPLANATION

1   The user-defined filehandle *HANDLE* will be used to send and append output to the file called *newfile*. As with the shell, the redirection symbol directs the output from the default filehandle, *STDOUT*, and appends the output to the file *newfile*. If the file cannot be opened because, for example, the write permissions are turned off, the *die* operator will print the error message, *Can't open newfile: Permission denied.*, and the script will exit.

2   The *print* function will send its output to the filehandle, *HANDLE*, instead of to the screen. The string, *Just appended "hello world" to the end of newfile*, will be written to end of *newfile* via the *HANDLE* filehandle.

9.1.6   The *select* Function

The *select* function sets the default **output** to the specified *FILEHANDLE* and returns the previously selected filehandle. All printing will go to the selected handle.

EXAMPLE 9.12

```
(The Script)
    #! /usr/bin/perl
1   open(FILEOUT,">newfile") || die "Can't open newfile: $!\n";
2   select(FILEOUT);        # Select the new filehandle for output
3   open (DB, "< datebook") || die "Can't open datebook: $!\n";
    while(<DB>){
4       print ;            # Output goes to FILEOUT, i.e., newfile
    }
5   select(STDOUT);        # Send output back to the screen
    print "Good-bye.\n";   # Output goes to the screen
```

EXPLANATION

1   *newfile* is opened for writing and assigned to the filehandle *FILEOUT*.

2   The *select* function assigns *FILEOUT* as the current default filehandle for output. The return value from the *select* function is the name of the filehandle that was closed (*STDOUT*) in order to select *FILEOUT*, the one that is now opened for writing.

3   The *DB* filehandle is opened for reading.

4   As each line is read into the *$_* variable from *DB*, it is then printed to the currently selected filehandle, *FILEOUT*. Notice that you don't have to name the filehandle.

5   By selecting *STDOUT*, the rest of the program's output will go to the screen.

9.1.7 File Locking with *flock*

To prevent two programs from writing to a file at the same time, you can lock the file so that you have exclusive access to it and then unlock it when you're finished using it. The *flock* function takes two arguments: a filehandle and a file locking operation. The operations are listed in Table 9.1.[2]

Table 9.1   File Locking Operations

Name	*Operation*	*What It Does*
lock_sh	1	Creates a shared lock
lock_ex	2	Creates an exclusive lock
lock_nb	4	Creates a non-blocking lock
lock_un	8	Unlocks an existing lock

Read permission is required on a file to obtain a shared lock, and write permission is required to obtain an exclusive lock. With operations 1 and 2, normally the caller requesting the file will block (wait) until the file is unlocked. If a non-blocking lock is used on a filehandle, an error is produced immediately if a request is made to get the locked file.[3]

EXAMPLE 9.13

```perl
    #!/bin/perl
    # Program that uses file locking -- UNIX
1   $LOCK_EX = 2;
2   $LOCK_UN = 8;

3   print "Adding an entry to the datafile.\n";
    print "Enter the name: ";
    chomp($name = <STDIN>);
    print "Enter the address: ";
    chomp($address = <STDIN>);

4   open(DB, ">>datafile") || die "Can't open: $!\n";

5   flock(DB, $LOCK_EX) || die ;          # Lock the file

6   print DB "$name:$address\n";

7   flock(DB, $LOCK_UN) || die;           # Unlock the file
```

2. File locking may not be implemented on non-UNIX systems.
3. *flock* may not work if the file is being accessed from a networked system.

EXPLANATION

1   The scalar is assigned the value of the operation that will be used by the *flock* function to lock the file. This operation is to block (wait) until an exclusive lock can be created.
2   This operation will tell *flock* when to unlock the file so that others can write to it.
3   The user is asked for the information to update the file. This information will be appended to the file.
4   The filehandle is opened for appending.
5   The *flock* function puts an exclusive lock on the file.
6   The data is appended to the file.
7   Once the data has been appended, the file is unlocked so that others can access it.

9.1.8   The *seek* and *tell* Functions

The *seek* Function.   Seek allows you to randomly access a file. The *seek* function is the same as the *fseek* standard I/O function in *C*. Rather than closing the file and then reopening it, the *seek* function allows you to move to some byte (not line) position within the file. The *seek* function returns *1* if successful, *0* otherwise.

FORMAT

```
seek(FILEHANDLE, BYTEOFFSET, FILEPOSITION);
```

The *seek* function sets a position in a file, where the first byte is 0. Positions are

0 = Beginning of the file
1 = Current position in the file
2 = End of the file

The offset is the number of bytes from the file position. A positive offset moves the position forward in the file; a negative offset moves the position backward in the file for position 1 or 2.

The *od* command lets you look at how the characters in a file are stored. This file was created on a Win32 platform; on UNIX systems the linefeed/newline is one character, \n.

```
$ od -c db
0000000000   S   t   e   v   e       B   l   e   n   h   e   i   m  \r  \n
0000000020   B   e   t   t   y       B   o   o   p  \r  \n   L       o   r   i
0000000040   G   o   r   t   z  \r  \n   S   i   r       L   a   n   c
0000000060   e   l   o   t  \r  \n   N   o   r   m   a       C   o   r   d
0000000100  \r  \n   J   o   n       D   e   L   o   a   c   h  \r  \n   K
0000000120   a   r   e   n       E   v   i   c   h  \r  \n
0000000134
```

EXAMPLE 9.14

```
(The Text File: db)
Steve Blenheim
Betty Boop
Lori Gortz
Sir Lancelot
Norma Cord
Jon DeLoach
Karen Evich

---------------------------------------------------------------

(The Script)
    # Example using the seek function
1   open(FH,"db") or die "Can't open: $!\n";
2   while($line=<FH>){          # Loop through the whole file
3       if ($line =~ /Lori/) { print "—$line—\n";}
    }
4   seek(FH,0,0);               # Start at the beginning of the file
5   while(<FH>){
6       print if /Steve/;
    }

(Output)
3   --Lori Gortz--
6   Steve Blenheim
```

EXPLANATION

1   The *db* file is assigned to the *FH* filehandle and opened for reading.
2   Each line of the file is assigned, in turn, to the scalar *$line* while looping through the file.
3   If $*line* contains *Lori*, the *print* statement is executed.
4   The *seek* function causes the file pointer to be positioned at the top of the file (position 0) and starts reading at byte 0, the first character. If you want to get back to the top of the file without using *seek*, then the filehandle must first be explicitly closed with the *close* function.
5   Starting at the top of the file, the loop is entered. The first line is read from the filehandle and assigned to *$_*, the default line holder.
6   If the pattern *Steve* is found in *$_*, the line will be printed.

EXAMPLE 9.15

```
(The Text File: db)
Steve Blenheim
Betty Boop
Lori Gortz
Sir Lancelot
Norma Cord
Jon DeLoach
Karen Evich

------------------------------------------------------------

(The Script)
1   open(FH, "db") or die "Can't open datebook: $!\n";
2   while(<FH>){
3       last if /Norma/;    # This is the last line that
                            # will be processed

    }
4   seek(FH,0,1) or die;    # Seeking from the current position
5   $line = <FH>;                 # This is where the read starts again
6   print "$line";
7   close FH;

(Output)
6   Jon DeLoach
```

EXPLANATION

1   The *db* file is opened for reading via the FH filehandle.
2   The *while* loop is entered. A line from the the file is read and assigned to *$_*.
3   When the line containing the pattern *Norma* is reached, the *last* function causes the loop to be exited.
4   The *seek* function will reposition the file pointer at the byte position 0 where the next read operation would have been performed in the file, position 1; in other words, the line right after the line that contained *Norma*. The byte position could be either a negative or positive value.
5   A line is read from the *db* file and assigned to the scalar *$line*. The line read is the line that would have been read just after the *last* function caused the loop to exit.
6   The value of *$line* is printed.

EXAMPLE 9.16

```
(The Script)
1   open(FH, "db") or die "Can't open datebook: $!\n";
2   seek(FH,-13,2) or die;
3   while(<FH>){
4       print;
    }

(Output)
4   Karen Evich
```

EXPLANATION

1   The *db* file is opened for reading via the *FH* filehandle.
2   The *seek* function starts at the end of the file (position 2) and backs up 13 bytes. The newline (\r\n), although not visible, is represented as the last two bytes in the line (Windows).
3   The *while* loop is entered and each line, in turn, is read from the filehandle *db*.
4   Each line is printed. By backing up 13 characters from the end of the file, *Karen Evich* is printed. Note the output of the *od -c* command and count back 13 characters from the end of the file.

```
0000000000    S   t   e   v   e       B   l   e   n   h   e   i   m  \r  \n
0000000020    B   e   t   t   y       B   o   o   p  \r  \n   L   o   r   i
0000000040        G   o   r   t   z  \r  \n   S   i   r       L   a   n   c
0000000060    e   l   o   t  \r  \n   N   o   r   m   a       C   o   r   d
0000000100   \r  \n   J   o   n       D   e   L   o   a   c   h  \r  \n   K
0000000120    a   r   e   n       E   v   i   c   h  \r  \n
0000000134
```

The *tell* Function.   The *tell* function returns the current byte position in the file and is used with the *seek* function to move to that position in the file. If *FILEHANDLE* is omitted, *tell* returns the position of the file last read.

FORMAT

```
tell(FILEHANDLE);
tell;
```

EXAMPLE 9.17

```
(The Text File: db)
Steve Blenheim
Betty Boop
Lori Gortz
Sir Lancelot
Norma Cord
Jon DeLoach
Karen Evich


-----------------------------------------------------------------


(The Script)
    #!/usr/bin/perl
    # Example using the tell function
1   open(FH,"db") || die "Can't open: $!\n";
2   while ($line = <FH>){        # Loop through the whole file
        chomp($line);
3       if ($line =~ /^Lori/){
4           $currentpos = tell;
5           print "The current byte position is $currentpos.\n";
6           print "$line\n\n";
        }
    }
7   seek(FH,$currentpos,0);      # Start at the beginning of the file
8   @lines = (<FH>);
9   print @lines;

(Output)
5   The current byte position is 40.
6   Lori Gortz

9   Sir Lancelot
    Norma Cord
    Jon DeLoach
    Karen Evich
```

EXPLANATION

1   The *db* file is assigned to the *FH* filehandle and opened for reading.

2   Each line of the file is assigned, in turn, to the scalar *$line* while looping through the file.

3   If the scalar *$line* contains the regular expression *Lori*, the *if* block is entered.

4   The *tell* function is called and returns the current byte position (starting at byte 0) in the file. This represents the position of the first character in the line that was just read in after the line containing *Lori* was processed.

EXPLANATION (CONTINUED)

5   The value in bytes is stored in *$currentpos*. It is printed. Byte position 40 represents the position where *Sir Lancelot* starts the line.

6   The line containing the regular expression *Lori* is printed.

7   The *seek* function will position the file pointer for *FH* at the byte offset, *$currentpos*, 40 bytes from the beginning of the file. Without *seek*, the filehandle would have to be closed in order to start reading from the top of the file.

8   The lines starting at offset 40 are read in and stored in the array *@lines*.

9   The array is printed, starting at offset 40.

9.1.9 Open for Reading and Writing

Table 9.2 Reading and Writing Operations

Symbol	Open For
+<	Read first, then write
+>	Write first, then read
+>>	Append first, then read

EXAMPLE 9.18

```
(The Script)
   # Scriptname: countem.pl
   # Open visitor_count for reading first, and then writing
1  open(FH, "+<visitor_count") ||
          die "Can't open visitor_count: $!\n";
2  $count = <FH>;              # Read a number from from the file
3  print "You are visitor number $count.";
4  $count++;
5  seek(FH, 0,0) || die;   # Seek back to the top of the file
6  print FH $count;          # Write the new number to the file
7  close(FH);
```

```
(Output)
(First run of countem.pl)
You are visitor number 1.

(Second run of countem.pl)
You are visitor number 2.
```

EXPLANATION

1   The file *visitor_count* is opened for reading first, and then writing. If the file does not exist or is not readable, *die* will cause the program to exit with an error message.

2   A line is read from the *visitor_count* file. The first time the script is executed, the number *1* is read in from *visitor_count* file and stored in the scalar *$count*.

3   The value of *$count* is printed.

4   The *$count* scalar is incremented by one.

5   The *seek* function moves the file pointer to the beginning of the file.

6   The new value of *$count* is written back to the *visitor_count* file. The number that was there is overwritten by the new value of *$count* each time the script is executed.

7   The file is closed.

EXAMPLE 9.19

```
(The Script)
   #!/usr/bin/perl
   # Open for writing first, then reading
   print "\n\n";
1  open(FH, "+>joker") || die;
2  print FH "This line is written to joker.\n";
3  seek(FH,0,0);           # Goto the beginning of the file
4  while(<FH>){
5      print;              # Reads from joker; the line is in $_
   }

(Output)
5  This line is written to joker.
```

EXPLANATION

1   The filehandle *FH* is opened for writing first. This means that the file *joker* will be created or, if it already exists, it will be truncated. Be careful not to mix up +< and +>.

2   The output is sent to *joker* via the *FH* filehandle.

3   The *seek* function moves the filepointer to the beginning of the file.

4   The *while* loop is entered. A line is read from the file *joker* via the *FH* filehandle and stored in *$_*.

5   Each line (*$_*) is printed after it is read until the end of the file is reached.

9.1.10   Open for Pipes

When using a **pipe** (also called a **filter**), a connection is made from one program to another. The program on the left-hand side of a pipe sends its output into a temporary kernel buffer. This program writes into the pipe. On the other side of the pipe is a program that is a reader. It gets its input from the buffer. Here is an example of a typical UNIX pipe:

```
who | wc -l
```

and an MS-DOS pipe:

```
dir /B | more
```

The output of the *who* command is sent to the *wc* command. The *who* command sends its output to the pipe; it writes to the pipe. The *wc* command gets its input from the pipe; it reads from the pipe. (If the *wc* command were not a reader, it would ignore what is in the pipe.) The output is sent to the *STDOUT*, the terminal screen. The number of people logged on is printed.

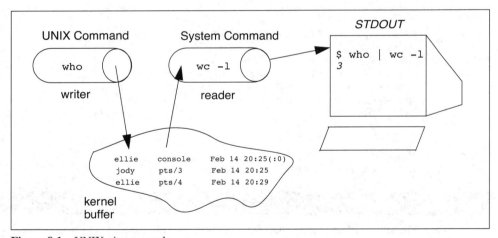

Figure 9.1   UNIX pipe example.

The Output Filter.   When creating a filehandle with the *open* function, you can open a filter so that the output is piped to a system command. The command is preceded by a pipe symbol (|) and replaces the filename argument in the previous examples. The output will be piped to the command and sent to *STDOUT*.

FORMAT

```
1   open(FILEHANDLE,|COMMAND);
```

EXAMPLE 9.20

```
(The Script)
    #!/bin/perl
    # Scriptname: outfilter (UNIX)
1   open(MYPIPE, "| wc -w");
2   print MYPIPE "apples pears peaches";
3   close(MYPIPE);


(Output)
3
```

EXPLANATION

1   The user-defined filehandle *MYPIPE* will be used to pipe output from the Perl script to the UNIX command *wc -w*, which counts the number of words in the string.

2   The *print* function sends the string *apples pears peaches* to the output filter filehandle *MYPIPE*; the string is piped to the *wc* command. Since there are three words in the string, the output *3* will be sent to the screen.

3   After you have finished using the filehandle, use the *close* function to close it. This guarantees that the command will complete before the script exits. If you don't close the filehandle, the output may not be flushed properly.

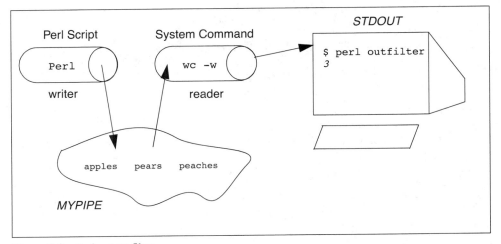

Figure 9.2   Perl output filter.

EXAMPLE 9.21

```
(The Script)
1   open(FOO, "| tr '[a-z]' '[A-Z]'");
2   print FOO "hello there\n";
3   close FOO;    # If you don't close FOO, the output may be delayed

(Output)
2   HELLO THERE
```

EXPLANATION

1   The user-defined filehandle *FOO* will be used to send output from your Perl script to the UNIX command *tr* which will translate lowercase letters to uppercase.

2   The *print* function sends the string *hello there* to the output filter filehandle *FOO*; that is, the string is piped to the *tr* command. The string, after being filtered, will be sent to the screen with all the characters translated to uppercase.

EXAMPLE 9.22

```
(The Text File)
$ cat emp.names
1 Steve Blenheim
2 Betty Boop
3 Igor Chevsky
4 Norma Cord
5 Jon DeLoach
6 Karen Evich

(The Script)
   #!/usr/bin/perl
1   open(FOO, "| sort  +1| tr '[a-z]' '[A-Z]'"); # Open output filter
2   open(DB, "emp.names");          # Open DB for reading
3   while(<DB>){ print FOO ; }
4   close FOO;

(Output)
2   BETTY BOOP
3   IGOR CHEVSKY
5   JON DELOACH
6   KAREN EVICH
4   NORMA CORD
1   STEVE BLENHEIM
```

EXPLANATION

1   The user-defined filehandle *FOO* will be used to pipe output to the UNIX command *sort* and the output of *sort* will be piped to the *tr* command. The *sort +1* command sorts on the second field, where fields are words separated by whitespace. The UNIX *tr* command translates lowercase letters into uppercase letters.

2   The *open* function creates the filehandle *DB* and attaches it to the UNIX file *emp.names*.

3   The expression in the *while* loop contains the filehandle *DB*, enclosed in angle brackets, indicating a read operation. The loop will read the first line from the *emp.names* file and store it in the *$_* scalar variable. The input line will be sent through the output filter, *FOO*, and printed to the screen. The loop will iterate until end of file is reached. Note that when the file is sorted by the second field, the numbers in the first column are no longer sorted.

4   The *close* function closes the filehandle *FOO*.

Sending the Output of a Filter to a File.   In the previous example, what if you had wanted to send the output of the filter to a file intead of to *STDOUT*? You can't send output to a filter and a filehandle at the same time, but you can redirect *STDOUT* to a filehandle. Since, later in the program, you may want *STDOUT* to be redirected back to the screen, you can first save it or simply reopen *STDOUT* to the terminal device by typing

```
open(STDOUT, ">/dev/tty");
```

EXAMPLE 9.23

```
    #!/usr/bin/perl
    # Program to redirect STDOUT from filter to a UNIX file
1   $| = 1;            # Flush buffers
2   $tmpfile = "temp";
3   open(DB, "data") || die qq/Can't open "data": $!\n/;
                                        # Open DB for reading
4   open(SAVED, ">&STDOUT") || die "$!\n";  # Save stdout
5   open(STDOUT, ">$tmpfile" ) || die "Can't open: $!\n";
6   open(SORT, "| sort +1") || die;         # Open output filter
7   while(<DB>){
8       print SORT;    # Output is first sorted and then sent to temp.
9   }
10  close SORT;
11  open(STDOUT, ">&SAVED") || die "Can't open";
12  print "Here we are printing to the screen again.\n";
                        # This output will go to the screen
13  rename("temp","data");
```

EXPLANATION

1 The *$|* variable guarantees an automatic flush of the output buffer after each *print* statement is executed. (See *autoflush* module in Appendix A.)
2 The scalar *$tmpfile* is assigned *temp* to be used later as an output file.
3 The UNIX *data* file is opened for reading and attached to the *DB* filehandle.
4 *STDOUT* is being copied and saved in another filehandle called *SAVED*. Behind the scenes, the file descriptors are being manipulated.
5 The *temp* file is being opened for writing and is assigned to the file descriptor normally reserved for *STDOUT*, the screen. The file descriptor for *STDOUT* has been closed and reopened for *temp*.
6 The output filter will be assigned to *SORT*. Perl's output will be sent to the UNIX *sort* utility.
7 The *DB* filehandle is opened for reading.
8 The output filehandle will be sent to the *temp* file after being sorted.
9 Close the loop.
10 Close the output filter.
11 Open the standard output filehandle so that output is redirected back to the screen.
12 This line prints to the screen because *STDOUT* has been reassigned there.
13 The *temp* file is renamed *data*, overwriting what was in *data* with the contents of *temp*.

Input Filter. When creating a filehandle with the *open* function, you can also open a filter so that input is piped **into** Perl. The command ends with a pipe symbol.

FORMAT

```
open(FILEHANDLE, COMMAND|);
```

EXAMPLE 9.24

```
  #!/bin/perl
  # Scriptname: infilter
1 open(INPIPE, "date |");      # Windows (2000/NT) use:  date /T
2 $today = <INPIPE> ;
3 print $today;
4 close(INPIPE);


(Output)
Sun Feb 18 14:12:44 PST 2001
```

EXPLANATION

1   The user-defined filehandle *INPIPE* will be used to pipe the output from the filter as input to Perl. The output of a UNIX *date* command will be used as input by your Perl script via the *INPIPE* filehandle. Windows 2000/NT users: use *date /T*.

2   The scalar *$today* will receive its input from the *INPIPE* filehandle; in other words, Perl reads from *INPIPE*.

3   The value of the UNIX *date* command was assigned to *$today* and is displayed.

4   After you have finished using the filehandle, use the *close* function to close it. This guarantees that the command will complete before the script exits. If you don't close the filehandle, the output may not be flushed properly.

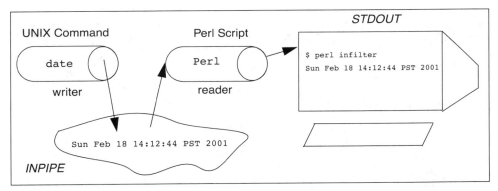

Figure 9.3   Perl input filter.

EXAMPLE 9.25

```
(The Script)
1   open(FINDIT, "find . -name 'perl*' -print |") ||
          die "Couldn't execute find!\n";
2   while($filename = <FINDIT>){
3       print $filename;
    }

(Output)
3   ./perl2
    ./perl3
    ./perl.man
    ./perl4
    ./perl5
    ./perl6
    ./perl7
    ./perlsub
    ./perl.arg
```

EXPLANATION

1   The output of the UNIX *find* command will be piped to the input filehandle *FINDIT*. When enclosed in angle brackets, the standard input will come from *FINDIT* instead of *STDIN*. If the open fails, the *die* operator will print *Couldn't execute find!* and exit the script.

2   The output from the UNIX *find* command has been piped into the filehandle *FINDIT*. For each iteration of the *while* loop, one line from the *FINDIT* filehandle will be assigned to the scalar variable, *$filename*.

3   The *print* function prints the value of the variable *$filename* to the screen.

EXAMPLE 9.26

```
(The Script)
    # Opening an input filter on a Win32 platform
1   open(LISTDIR, 'dir "C:\perl" |') || die;
2   @filelist = <LISTDIR>;
3   foreach $file (@filelist){
        print $file;
    }

(Output)
 Volume in drive C is 010599
 Volume Serial Number is 2237-130A

 Directory of C:\perl

03/31/1999  10:34p      <DIR>           .
03/31/1999  10:34p      <DIR>           ..
03/31/1999  10:37p                 30,366 DeIsL1.isu
03/31/1999  10:34p      <DIR>           bin
03/31/1999  10:34p      <DIR>           lib
03/31/1999  10:35p      <DIR>           html
03/31/1999  10:35p      <DIR>           eg
03/31/1999  10:35p      <DIR>           site
               1 File(s)         30,366 bytes
               7 Dir(s)     488,873,984 bytes free
```

9.2 Passing Arguments

9.2.1 The *ARGV* Array

How does Perl pass command line arguments to a Perl script? If you are coming from a *C, awk*, or *C* shell background, at first glance you might think, "Oh, I already know this!" Beware! There are some subtle differences. So again, read on.

Perl does store arguments in a special array called *ARGV*. The subscript starts at zero and, unlike *C* and *awk*, *ARGV[0]* does **not** represent the name of the program; it represents the name of the first word after the script name. Like the shell languages, the *$0* special variable is used to hold the name of the Perl script. Unlike the *C* shell, the *$#ARGV* variable contains the number of the last subscript in the array, **not** the number of elements in the array. The number of arguments is *$#ARGV + 1*. *$#ARGV* initially has a value of *–1*.

When *ARGV*, the filehandle, is enclosed in angle brackets, *<ARGV>*, the command line argument is treated as a filename. The filename is assigned to *ARGV* and the *@ARGV* array is shifted immediately to the left by one, thereby shortening the *@ARGV* array.

The value that is shifted off the *@ARGV* array is assigned to *$ARGV*. *$ARGV* contains the name of the currently selected filehandle.

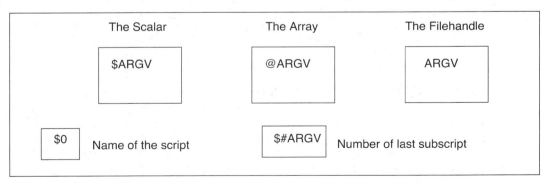

Figure 9.4 The many faces of *ARGV.*

EXAMPLE 9.27

```
(The Script)
    $!/usr/bin/perl
1   die "$0 requires an argument.\n" if $#ARGV < 0;
                            # Must have at least one argument
2       print "@ARGV\n";       # Print all arguments
3       print "$ARGV[0]\n";    # Print first argument
4       print "$ARGV[1]\n";    # Print second argument
5       print "There are ", $#ARGV + 1," arguments.\n";
                            # $#ARGV is the last subscript
6       print "$ARGV[$#ARGV] is the last one.\n";  # Print last arg

(Output)
    $ perl.arg
2   perl.arg requires an argument.

    $ perl.arg f1 f2 f3 f4 f5
2   f1 f2 f3 f4 f5
3   f1
4   f2
5   There are 5 arguments.
6   f5 is the last one.
```

EXPLANATION

1   If there are no command line arguments, the *die* function is executed and the script is terminated. The *$0* special variable holds the name of the Perl script, *perl.arg*.

2   The contents of the *@ARGV* array are printed.

3   The first argument, not the script name, is printed.

4   The second argument is printed.

5   The *$#ARGV* variable contains the number value of the last subscript. Since the subscript starts at zero, *$#ARGV + 1* is the total number of arguments, not counting the script name.

6   Since *$#ARGV* contains the value of the last subscript, *$ARGV[$#ARGV]* is the value of the last element of the *@ARGV* array.

9.2.2 *ARGV* and the Null Filehandle

When used in loop expressions and enclosed in the input angle brackets (<>), each element of the *ARGV* array is treated as a **special filehandle**. Perl shifts through the array, storing each element of the array in a variable *$ARGV*. A set of empty angle brackets is called the **null filehandle** and Perl implicitly uses each element of the *ARGV* array as a filehandle. When using the input operators <>, either with or without the keyword *ARGV*, Perl shifts through its arguments one at a time, allowing you to process each argument in turn. Once the *ARGV* filehandle has been opened, the arguments are shifted off one at a time, so that if they are to be used later, they must be saved in another array.

EXAMPLE 9.28

```
(The Text Files)
$ cat f1
Hello there. Nice day.
$ cat f2
Are you sure about that?
$ cat f3
This is it.
This is the end.

(The  Script)
1   while(<ARGV>) {print ;}
2   print "The value of \$ARGV[0] is $ARGV[0].\n";

(Output)
$ argv.test f1 f2 f3
Hello there. Nice day.
Are you sure about that?
This is it.
This is the end.
The value of $ARGV[0] is .
```

EXPLANATION

1   This will print the contents of all the files named at the command line. Once used, the argument is shifted off. The contents of *f1*, *f2*, and *f3* are read and then printed, respectively.

2   Since the arguments were all shifted off, *$ARGV[0]* has no value and, therefore, nothing is printed.

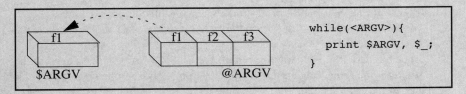

EXAMPLE 9.29

```
(The Text File: emp.names)
Steve Blenheim
Betty Boop
Igor Chevsky
Norma Cord
Jon DeLoach
Karen Evich

(The Script)
    # Scriptname: grab.pl
    # Program will behave like grep -- will search for a pattern
    # in any number of files.
1   if ( ($#ARGV  < 1 ) {die "Usage: $0 pattern filename(s) \n";}
2   $pattern = shift;
3   while($line = <ARGV>){
        print "$ARGV: $.:  $line" if $line =~ /$pattern/i;
        close(ARGV) if eof;
    }

(Output)
    $ grab.pl
1   Usage: grab.pl pattern filenames(s)
    $ grab.pl 'norma' db
2   db:5: Norma Cord
    $ grab.pl 'Sir Lancelot' db
3   db:4: Sir Lancelot
    $ grab.pl '^.... ' db
4   db:3: Lori Gortz
    $ grab.pl Steve d*
5   datebook.master:12: Johann Erickson:Stevensville, Montana
    datafile:8: Steven Daniels:496-456-5676:83755:11/12/56:20300
    db:1: Steve Blenheim
```

EXPLANATION

1   If there are no command line arguments, the *die* function is executed.
2   The first argument is shifted from the *@ARGV* array. This should be the pattern that will be searched for.
3   Since the first argument was shifted off the *@ARGV* array and assigned to the scalar *$pattern*, the remaining arguments passed in from the command line are assigned in turn to the *ARGV* filehandle. When the *while* loop is entered, a line is read and assigned to *$line*.

EXPLANATION (CONTINUED)

4   The *$ARGV* scalar holds the name of the file that is currently being processed. The *$.* variable holds the current line number. If the value in *$pattern* is matched, the filename where it was found, the number of the line where the pattern was found, and the line itself are printed. The *i* after the last delimiter in the pattern turns off case sensitivity.

5   When the file being processed reaches the end of file (EOF), the *ARGV* filehandle is closed. This causes the *$.* variable to be reset. If *ARGV* is not closed explicitly here, the *$.* variable will continue to increment and not be set back to *1* when the next file is read.

EXAMPLE 9.30

```
(The Script)
1   unless ($#ARGV == 0){die "Usage: $0 <argument>: $!";}
2   open(PASSWD, "etc/passwd") || die "Can't open: $!";
3   $username = shift(@ARGV);
4   while($pwline = <PASSWD>){
5       unless ($pwline =~ /$username:/){die "$username is not
                                              a user here.\n";}

    }
6   close PASSWD;
7   open(LOGGEDON, "who |" ) || die "Can't open: $!" ;
8   while($logged = <LOGGEDON> ){
        if ($logged =~ /$username/){$logged_on = 1; last;}
    }
9   close LOGGEDON;
    die "$username is not logged on.\n" if ! $logged_on;
    print "$username is logged on and running these processes.\n";
10  open(PROC, "ps -aux|") || die "Can't open: $! ";
    while($line = <PROC>){
        print "$line" if  $line =~ /$username:/;
    }
11  close PROC;
    print '*' x 80; "\n";
    print "So long.\n";
```

EXAMPLE 9.30 (CONTINUED)

```
(Output)
    $ checkon
1   Usage: checkon <argument>:  at checkon line 6.
    $ checkon joe
5   Joe is not a user here.
    $ checkon ellie
8   ellie is logged on and running these processes:
ellie   3825  6.4  4.5  212   464 p5 R    12:18     0:00 ps -aux
ellie   1383  0.8  8.4  360   876 p4 S    Dec 26 11:34 /usr/local/OW3/bin/xview
ellie   173   0.8 13.4 1932 1392 co S     Dec 20389:19 /usr/local/OW3/bin/xnews
ellie   164   0.0  0.0  100     0 co IW   Dec 20   0:00 -c
                < some of the output was cut to save space >
ellie   3822  0.0  0.0    0     0 p5 Z    Dec 20   0:00 <defunct>
ellie   3823  0.0  1.1   28   112 p5 S    12:18     0:00 sh -c ps -aux | grep '^'
ellie   3821  0.0  5.6  144   580 p5 S    12:18     0:00 /bin/perl checkon ellie
ellie   3824  0.0  1.8   32   192 p5 S    12:18     0:00 grep ^ellie
ellie   3815  0.0  1.9   24   196 p4 S    12:18     0:00 script checkon.tsc
*************************************************************************
```

EXPLANATION

1   This script calls for only one argument. If *ARGV* is empty (i.e., no arguments are passed at the command line), the *die* function is executed and the script exits with an error message. (Remember: *$#ARGV* is the number of the last subscript in the *ARGV* array and *ARGV[0]* is the first argument, not counting the name of the script, which is *$0*.) If more than one argument is passed, the script will also exit with the error message.

2   The */etc/passwd* file is opened for reading via the *PASSWD* filehandle.

3   The first argument is shifted from *@ARGV* and assigned to *$username*.

4   Each time the *while* loop is entered, a line of the */etc/passwd* file is read via the *PASSWD* filehandle.

5   The =~ is used to test if the first argument passed matches the *$username*. If a match is not found, the loop is exited.

6   The filehandle is closed.

7   The filehandle *LOGGEDON* is opened as an input filter. Output from the UNIX *who* command will be piped to the filehandle.

8   Each line of the input filter is tested. If the user is logged on, the scalar *$logged_on* is set to *1*, and the loop is exited.

9   The input filter is closed.

10   The filehandle *PROC* is opened as an input filter. Output from the UNIX *ps* command will be piped to the filehandle. Each line from the filter is read in turn and placed in the scalar *$line*. If *$line* contains a match for the user, that line will be printed to *STDOUT*, the screen.

11   The filter is closed.

9.2.3 The *eof* Function

The *eof* function can be used to test if end of file has been reached. It returns *1* if either the next read operation on a *FILEHANDLE* is at the end of the file or if the file was not opened. Without an argument, the *eof* function returns the *eof* status of the last file read. The *eof* function with parentheses can be used in a loop block to test the end of file when the last filehandle has been read. Without parentheses, each file opened can be tested for end of file.

FORMAT

```
eof(FILEHANDLE)
eof()
eof
```

EXAMPLE 9.31

```
(The Text File: emp.names)
Steve Blenheim
Betty Boop
Igor Chevsky
Norma Cord
Jon DeLoach
Karen Evich

(In Script)
1   open(DB, "emp.names") || die "Can't open emp.names: $!;
2   while(<DB>){
3       print if /Norma/ .. eof();        # .. is the range operator
    }

(Output)
Norma Cord
Jonathan DeLoach
Karen Evitch
```

EXPLANATION

1   The file *emp.names* is opened via the *DB* filehandle.
2   The *while* loop reads a line at a time from the filehandle *DB*.
3   When the line containing the regular expression *Norma* is reached, that line and all lines in the range from *Norma* until *eof* (the end of file) are printed.

EXAMPLE 9.32

```
(The Text Files)
$ cat file1
abc
def
ghi

$ cat file2
1234
5678
9101112

(The Script)
    #!/usr/bin/perl
    # eof.p script
1   while(<>){
2       print "$.\t$_";
3       if (eof){
            print "-" x 30, "\n";
4           close(ARGV);
        }
    }

(Output)
$ eof.p file1 file2
1   abc
2   def
3   ghi
------------------------------
1   1234
2   5678
3   9101112
------------------------------
```

EXPLANATION

1   The first argument stored in the *ARGV* array is *file1*. The null filehandle is used in the *while* expression. The file *file1* is opened for reading.

2   The $. variable is a special variable containing the line number of the currently opened filehandle. It is printed, followed by a tab, and then the line itself.

3   If end of file is reached, print a row of 30 dashes.

4   The filehandle is closed in order to reset the $. value back to *1* for the next file that is opened. When *file1* reaches end of file, the next argument, *file2*, is processed, starting at line 1.

9.2.4 The -i Switch—Editing Files in Place

The -i option is used to edit files in place. The files are named at the command line and stored in the @ARGV array. Perl will automatically rename the output file to the same name as the input file. The output file will be the selected default file for printing. To ensure that you keep a backup of the original file, you can specify an extension to the -i flag, such as -i.bak. The original file will be renamed *filename.bak*. The file must be assigned to the ARGV filehandle when it is being read from. Multiple files can be passed in from the command line and each one in turn will be edited in place.

EXAMPLE 9.33

```
(The Text File)
1   $ more names
    igor chevsky
    norma corder
    jennifer cowan
    john deloach
    fred fardbarkle
    lori gortz
    paco gutierrez
    ephram hardy
    james ikeda

(The Script)
2   #!/usr/bin/perl —i.bak
    # Scriptname: inplace

3     while(<ARGV>){     # Open ARGV for reading
4       tr/a-z/A-Z/;
5       print;     # Output goes to file currently being read in-place
6       close ARGV if eof;
    }

(Output)
7   $ inplace names
    $ more names
    IGOR CHEVSKY
    NORMA CORDER
    JENNIFER COWAN
    JOHN DELOACH
    FRED FARDBARKLE
    LORI GORTZ
    PACO GUTIERREZ
    EPHRAM HARDY
    JAMES IKEDA
```

EXAMPLE 9.33 (CONTINUED)

```
8   $ more names.bak
    igor chevsky
    norma corder
    jennifer cowan
    john deloach
    fred fardbarkle
    lori gortz
    paco gutierrez
    ephram hardy
    james ikeda
```

EXPLANATION

1   The contents of the original text file, called *names*, is printed.
2   The *-i* in-place switch is used with an extension. The *names* file will be edited in place and the original file will be saved in *names.bak*.
3   The *while* loop is entered. The *ARGV* filehandle will be opened for reading.
4   All lowercase letters are translated to uppercase letters in the file being processed (*tr* function).
5   The *print* function sends its output to the file being processed in place.
6   The *ARGV* filehandle will be closed when the end of file is reached. This makes it possible to reset line numbering for each file when processing multiple files or to mark the end of files when appending.
7   The *names* file has been changed, illustrating that the file was modified in place.
8   The *names.bak* file was created as a backup file for the original file. The original file has been changed.

9.3 File Testing

Like the shells, Perl provides a number of file test operators (see Table 9.3) to check for the various attributes of a file, such as existence, access permissions, directories, files, and so on. Most of the operators return *1* for true and "" (null) for false.

A single underscore can be used to represent the name of the file if the same file is tested more than once. The *stat* structure of the previous file test is used.

Table 9.3 File Test Operators[a]

Operator	Meaning
–r $file	True if $file is a readable file.
–w $file	True if $file is a writeable file.
–x $file	True if $file is an executable file.
–o $file	True if $file is owned by effective uid.
–e $file	True if file exists.
–z $file	True if file is zero in size.
–s $file	True if $file has non-zero size. Returns the size of the file in bytes.
–f $file	True if $file is a plain file.
–d $file	True if $file is a directory file.
–l $file	True if $file is a symbolic link.
–p $file	True if $file is a named pipe or *FIFO*.
–S $file	True if $file is a socket.
–b $file	True if $file is a block special file.
–c $file	True if $file is a character special file.
–u $file	True if $file has a setuid bit set.
–g $file	True if $file has a setgid bit set.
–k $file	True if $file has a sticky bit set.
–t $file	True if filehandle is opened to a tty.
–T $file	True if $file is a text file.
–B $file	True if file is a binary file.
–M $file	Age of the file in days since modified.
–A $file	Age of the file in days since last accessed.
–C $file	Age of the file in days since the inode changed.

a. If a filename is not provided, $_ is the default.

EXAMPLE 9.34

```
(At the Command Line)
1  $ ls -l perl.test
   -rwxr-xr-x  1 ellie          417 Apr 23 13:40 perl.test
2  $ ls -l afile
   -rws--x--x  1 ellie            0 Apr 23 14:07 afile

(In Script)
   #!/usr/bin/perl
   $file = perl.test;

3  print "File is readable\n" if -r  $file;
   print "File is writeable\n" if -w  $file;
   print "File is executable\n" if -x  $file;
   print "File is a regular file\n" if -f  $file;
   print "File is a directory\n" if -d  $file;
   print "File is text file\n" if -T $file;
   printf "File was last modified  %f days ago.\n", -M $file;
   print "File has been accessed in the last 12 hours.\n" if -M <= 12;
4  print "File has read, write, and execute set.\n"
            if  -r  $file && -w _ && -x _;
5  stat("afile");  # stat another file
   print "File is a set user id program.\n" if  -u _;
                   # underscore evaluates to last file stat'ed
   print "File is zero size.\n" if -z _;

(Output)
3  File is readable
   File is writeable
   File is executable
   File is a regular file
   *** No print out here because the file is not a directory ***
   File is text file
   File was last modified 0.000035 days ago.
   File has read, write, and execute set.
   File is a set user id program.
   File is zero size.
```

EXPLANATION

1   The permissions, ownership, file size, etc., on *perl.test* are shown.
2   The permissions, ownership, file size, etc., on *afile* are shown.
3   The *print* statement is executed if the file is readable, writeable, executable, etc.
4   Since the same file is checked for more than one attribute, an underscore is appended to the file test flag. The underscore references the *stat*[a] structure, an array that holds information about the file.
5   The *stat* function returns a 13-element array containing the statistics about a file. As long as the underscore is appended to the file test flag, the statistics for *afile* are used in the tests that follow.

a. Read more about the *stat* structure in Chapter 16, "Interfacing with the System."

EXERCISE 8
Getting a Handle on Things

Exercise A

1. Create a filehandle for reading from the *datebook* file (on the CD); print to another filehandle the names of all those who have a salary greater than $50,000.

2. Ask the user to input data for a new entry in the *datebook* file. (The name, phone, address, etc., will be stored in separate scalars.) Append the newline to the *datebook* file by using a user-defined filehandle.

Exercise B

1. Sort the *datebook* file by last names using a filter.

2. Create a filehandle with the *open* function that uses an input filter to list all the files in your current directory and will print only those files that are readable text files. Use the *die* function to quit if the *open* fails.

3. Rewrite the program to test if any of the files listed have been modified in the last 12 hours. Print the names of those files.

Exercise C

1. Create a number of duplicate entries in the *datebook* file. *Fred Fardbarkle*, for example, might appear five times, and *Igor Chevsky* three times, etc. If you're using the *vi* editor, just *yank* and *put* some of the entries.

   Write a program that will assign the name of the *datebook* file to a scalar and check to see if the file exists. If it does exist, the program will check to see if the file is readable and writeable. Use the *die* function to send any errors to the screen. Also tell the user when the *datebook* was last modified.

   The program will read each line of the *datebook* file giving each person a 10% raise in salary. If, however, the person appears more than once in the file (assume having the same first and last name means it is a duplicate), he will be given a raise the first time, but if he appears again, he will be skipped over. Send each line of output to a file called *raise*. The *raise* file should not contain any person's name more than once. It will also reflect the 10% increase in pay.

Display on the screen the average salary for all the people in the *datebook* file. For duplicate entries, print the names of those who appeared in the file more than once and how many times each appeared.

2. Write a script called *checking* that will take any number of filenames as command line arguments and will print the names of those files that are readable and write-able text files. The program will print an error message if there are no arguments, and exit.

10

HOW DO SUBROUTINES FUNCTION?

10.1 Subroutines/Functions

In addition to the large number of Perl functions already available, you can create your own functions or subroutines. Some languages distinguish between the term **function** and **subroutine**. Perl doesn't. If you say "subroutine," everyone will know you are talking about a "function," and if you say "function," everyone will know you are talking about a "subroutine."[1] Technically, a function is a block of code that returns a value, whereas a subroutine is a block of code that performs some task, but doesn't return anything. Perl subroutines and functions can do both, so we'll use the two terms interchangeably in this text.

So what are subroutines supposed to do? Subroutines allow you to break the program into one or more component parts, commonly called **modules**. This helps keep your program organized and easier to read and maintain.

Subroutines let you name a block of statements that may be executed any number of times to perform a given task, saving you the trouble of rewriting the same lines over and over again. For example, if you are getting the average of a list of numbers, you can call a subroutine that calculates and returns the average. Once written, the subroutine can be called as often as you like with different lists of numbers, thus saving you much time and energy.

A subroutine declaration consists of one or more statements that are not executed until the function is called. The scope of a variable or subroutine is where it is visible in the program. Subroutines are global and can be placed anywhere in the script, even in another file. When coming from another file, they are loaded into the script with either the *do*, *require*, or *use* keywords. All variables created within a subroutine or accessed by it are also global unless specifically made local with either the *local* or *my* functions.

---

1. You could even change the title of this chapter to, "How Do Functions Subroutine?" but some people might frown.

The subroutine is called either by prefixing the subroutine name with an ampersand (&), by prefixing the subroutine with the *do* function,[2] or by appending a set of empty parentheses to the subroutine name. If a forward reference is used, neither ampersands nor parentheses are needed to call the subroutine.

If a nonexistent subroutine is called, the program quits with an error message: *Undefined subroutine in "main::prog"* .... If you want to check whether the subroutine has been defined, you can do so with the built-in *defined* function.

The return value of a subroutine is the value of the last expression evaluated (either a scalar or an array). The *return* function can be used explicitly to return a value or to exit from the subroutine early due to the result of testing some condition.

If the call to the subroutine is made part of an expression, the returned value can be assigned to a variable, thus emulating a function call.

FORMAT

```
Subroutine declaration:
    sub subroutine_name;
Subroutine definition:
    sub subroutine_name { Block }
Subroutine call:
    do subroutine_name;
    &subroutine_name;
    subroutine_name();
    subroutine_name;
Subroutine call with parameters:
    &subroutine_name(parameter1, parameter2, ...)
    subroutine_name(parameter1, parameter2, ...)
```

10.1.1 Defining and Calling a Subroutine

A **declaration** simply announces to the Perl compiler that a subroutine is going to be defined in the program and may take specified arguments. Declarations are global in scope; in other words, they are visible no matter where you put them in the program, although it is customary to put declarations at the beginning or end of the program. A subroutine **definition** is a block of statements that follows the subroutine name. A subroutine that has not been explicitly declared, is declared at the same time it is defined.

   Declaration: *sub name_of_subroutine;*
   Definition: *sub name_of_subroutine { statement; statement; }*

A subroutine can be defined anywhere in your program or even in another file. The subroutine consists of the keyword *sub* followed by an opening curly brace, a set of statements, and ending in a closing curly brace. The subroutine and its statements are not executed until

2. The primary use of the *do* function was to include Perl subroutines from the Perl 4 library (e.g., *do'pwd.pl'*).

called. You can call a subroutine by preceding its name with an ampersand or by attaching a set of empty parentheses after its name, or by doing neither and calling it as a built-in function. If you call the subroutine with neither the ampersand nor parentheses, then you must declare it first.

EXAMPLE 10.1

```
(The Script)
1   sub greetme{ print "Welcome, Valkommen till, Bienvenue!\n";}
2   &greetme if defined &greetme;
3   print "Program continues....\n";
4   &greetme;
5   print "More program here.\n";
6   &bye;
7   sub bye{ print "Bye, adjo, adieu.\n"; }
8   &bye;

(Output)
2   Welcome, Valkommen till, Bienvenue!
3   Program continues....
4   Welcome, Valkommen till, Bienvenue!
5   More program here.
    Bye, adjo, adieu.
    Bye, adjo, adieu.
```

EXPLANATION

1   This is a subroutine definition consisting of the keyword *sub*, followed by the name of the subroutine, *greetme*, and a block of statements that will be executed when the subroutine is called. Officially, the subroutine name is preceded by an ampersand (&), but the only time you really need the ampersand is when calling the subroutine or when using its name to create a reference or as an argument to a function such as *defined*. This definition can be placed anywhere in your program, and will do nothing until it is called. In this example, there is only one *print* statement that will be executed when the function is called.

2   The subroutine *greetme* is called by placing an ampersand (&) in front of its name. The *defined* built-in function is used to check that the subroutine has been defined. When using the subroutine's name, the ampersand is required. When called, the program will jump into the subroutine and start executing the statements defined there, in this case, the *Welcome* statement.

3   After the subroutine is called, program execution starts at the line right after where it was called and continues from there.

4   The subroutine *greetme* is called again.

5   The program resumes execution after the subroutine exits on line 4.

6   The subroutine *bye* is called. The definition is found later on line 7.

7   Subroutine *bye* is defined. No matter where subroutines are placed, the compiler sees them.

8   Subroutine *bye* is called.

A Null Parameter List.   If the subroutine name is followed by parentheses (null parameter list), it can also be called without the ampersand.

EXAMPLE 10.2

```
#!/usr/bin/perl
1   $name = "Ellie";
2   print "Hello $name.\n";

3   bye();   # Without parens or an ampersand, bye would be a bare
             # word causing a warning message when -w is used.
4   sub bye{
5       print "Bye $name.\n";
    }
```

Forward Reference.   A forward reference announces to the compiler that the subroutine has been defined somewhere in the program. The ampersand is not needed to call a subroutine if it has been forward referenced.

EXAMPLE 10.3

```
    #!/usr/bin/perl
1   sub bye;  # Forward reference

    $name = "Ellie";
2   print "Hello $name.\n";

3   bye;       # Call subroutine without the ampersand

4   sub bye{
5       print "Bye $name\n";
    }
(Output)
2   Hello Ellie.
5   Bye Ellie
```

Scope of Variables.   **Scope** describes where a variable is visible in your program. Perl variables are global in scope. They are visible throughout the entire program, even in subroutines. If you declare a variable in a subroutine, it is visible to the entire program. If you change the value of an already existing variable from within a subroutine, it will be changed when you exit the subroutine. A local variable is private to the block, subroutine, or file where it is declared. You must use either the *local* or *my* built-in functions to create local variables since, by default, Perl variables are global in scope. (See "Call-by-Value with local and my" on page 296.)

EXAMPLE 10.4

```
(The Script)
    # Script: perlsub_sub2
    # Variables used in subroutines are global by default
1   sub bye{print "Bye $name\n"; $name = "Tom";}
                            # Subroutine definition
2   $name = "Ellie";
3   print "Hello to you and yours!\n";
4   &bye;
5   print "Out of the subroutine. Hello $name.\n";
                            # $name is now Tom

6   &bye;

(Output)
3   Hello to you and yours!
1   Bye Ellie
5   Out of the subroutine. Hello Tom.
1   Bye Tom
```

EXPLANATION

1   The subroutine *bye* is defined. Within the subroutine block, the variable *$name* is assigned the value *Tom*. *$name* is a global variable; in other words, it is visible throughout the program.[a]

2   Program execution starts here. Global variable *$name* is assigned the value *Ellie*.

3   This line is here just to show you the flow of execution.

4   The subroutine *&bye* is called. The program jumps into the subroutine on line 1. The value of *$name* is still *Ellie*. After the line *Bye, Ellie* is printed, and the variable *$name* is assigned a new value, *Tom*. The subroutine exits and the program resumes execution at line 5.

5   The value of the global variable *$name* was changed in subroutine.

6   The subroutine is called again. The value of *$name* is *Tom*.

a. We are assuming that the program was compiled into one package, *main*. For more on packages and scope, see Chapter 11, "Modularize It, Package It, and Send It to the Library!".

10.1.2 Passing Arguments

Call-by-Reference and the @_ Array.   Arguments, whether scalar values or arrays, are passed into the subroutine and stored in the @_ array. The @_ array is a local array whose values are implicit references to the actual parameters. If you modify the @_ array, you will modify the actual parameters. However, if you shift or pop off elements of the @_ array, you merely lose the reference to the actual parameters. (See "Call-by-Value with local and my" on page 296.)

When arrays or scalars are passed to a function or subroutine, the default in Perl is **call-by-reference**. The @_ is a special local array used for referencing the names of the formal arguments. Its values can be changed, thus changing the value of the actual parameters. The elements of the @_ array are *$_[0]*, *$_[1]*, *$_[2]*, and so on. If a scalar variable is passed, its value is the first element of the @_ array, *$_[0]*. Perl doesn't care if you don't use all the parameters passed, or if you have an insufficient number of parameters. If you shift or pop the @_ array, you merely lose your reference to the actual arguments. If you want to modify the global copy rather than the local @_ array, then you can use either **typeglobs** (symbolic references) or **pointers** (hard references). Hard references are discussed briefly in "Passing by Pointer" on page 310 and in more detail in Chapter 12, "Does This Job Require a Reference?".

EXAMPLE 10.5

```
(The Script)
    # Passing arguments
1   $first = "Charles";
    $last = "Dobbins";
2   &greeting($first, $last);
3   sub greeting{
4       print "@_", "\n";
5       print "Welcome to the club, $_[0] $_[1]!\n";
6   }

(Output)
4   Charles Dobbins
5   Welcome to the club, Charles Dobbins!
```

EXPLANATION

1   Scalars are assigned values.
2   The *greeting* subroutine is called with two parameters, *$first* and *$last*.
3   The subroutine is declared.
4   The parameters are stored in the @_ array, a local array that is created when the subroutine is entered and is removed when the subroutine exits. It contains references to the *$first* and *$last*.
5   The first two elements of the @_ array are printed. The individual elements are represented as scalars *$_[0]* and *$_[1]*.
6   The closing curly brace marks the end of the subroutine definition. @_ will disappear.

EXAMPLE 10.6

```
(The Script)
    # Program to demonstrate how @_ references values.
1   sub params{
2      print 'The values in the @_ array are ', "@_\n";
3      print "The first value is $_[0]\n";
4      print "The last value is ", pop(@_),"\n";
5      foreach $value( @_ ){
6          $value += 5;
           print "The value is $value", "\n";
       }
    }

    print "Give me 5 numbers : ";
7   @n = split(' ',<STDIN>);
8   &params(@n);
    print "Back in main\n";
9   print "The new values are @n \n";
```

```
(Output)
    Give me 5 numbers: 1 2 3 4 5
2   The values in the @_ array are 1 2 3 4 5
3   The first value is 1
4   The last value is 5
    The value is 6
    The value is 7
    The value is 8
    The value is 9
9   Back in main
10  The new values are 6 7 8 9 5
```

EXPLANATION

1   The subroutine *params* is defined.
2   The value of @_, the actual parameter list, is printed. @_ is a local array referencing any arguments passed to the subroutine.
3   The first value of the @_ array is printed.
4   The last element of the array is removed with the *pop* function and then printed.
5   The *foreach* loop assigns, in turn, to scalar *$value* each element of the @_ array.
6   Each element of the array is incremented by *5* and stored in the scalar *$value*.
7   After the user has typed five numbers, the *split* function returns an array consisting of each of the numbers read from *STDIN*.
8   The subroutine is called, passing the array as a parameter.
9   The values printed illustrate that those values changed in the function were really changed. The only value that wasn't changed is the last element of the original array. The reference to it was popped in line 4 of the subroutine.

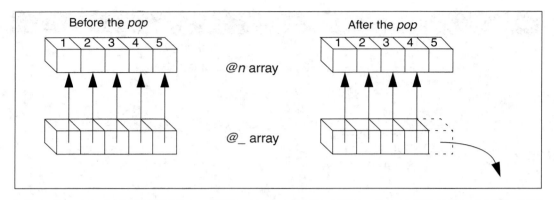

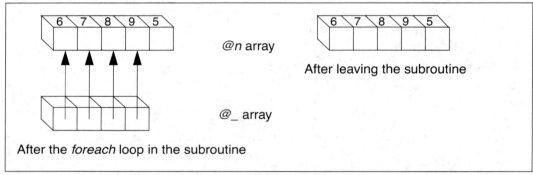

Figure 10.1   The @_ references the actual scalar parameters.

Call-by-Value with *local* and *my*.   When an argument is passed using a **call-by-value**, a copy of the value of the argument is sent to the subroutine. If the copy is modified, the original value is untouched. To make variables local, Perl provides two built-in functions: *local* and *my*.

The local Function

The *local* function is used to turn on call-by-value. Perl 5 introduced another function, called *my*, which further ensures the privacy of variables within a block.

The *local* function creates local variables from its list. Any variable declared with *local* is said to be dynamically scoped, which means it is visible from within the block where it was created and visible to any functions called from within this block or any blocks (or subroutines) nested within the block where it is defined. If a local variable has the same name as a global variable, the value of the global one is saved and a new local variable is temporarily created. When the local variable goes out of scope, the global variable becomes visible again with its original value(s) restored. After the last statement in a subroutine is executed, its local variables are discarded. It is recommended that all local variables be set at the beginning of the subroutine block.

EXAMPLE 10.7

```
(The Script)
1   $first=Per;
    $last=Lindberg;
2   &greeting( $first, $last ) ;      # Call the greeting subroutine
3   print "---$fname---\n" if defined $fname;   # $fname is local to
                                                 # sub greeting


    # Subroutine defined
    sub greeting{
4       local ($fname, $lname) = @_ ;
5       print "Welcome $fname!!\n";
    }

(Output)
3   <no output>
5   Welcome Per!!
```

EXPLANATION

1   The scalar variables are assigned values.
2   A call is made to the *greeting* subroutine. Two arguments are passed.
3   The *print* statement is not executed because *$fname* is not defined here. It was de-fined as a local variable in the subroutine. It is local to the *greeting* subroutine.
4   The *local* function takes a list of arguments from the @_ array and creates two local variables, *$fname* and *$lname*, from that list. The values in the local variables are copies of the values that were passed.
5   The *print* statement is executed. The contents of the local variable *$fname* are print-ed, which is a copy of what is in *$first*.

The my Function

The *my* function is used to turn on *call-by-value* and is said to be lexically scoped. This means that variables declared as *my* variables are visible from the point of declaration to the end of the innermost enclosing block. That block could be a simple block enclosed in curly braces, a subroutine, *eval*, or a file. A variable declared with the *my* function is created on a special scratch pad that is private to the block where it was created.[3]

Unlike the variables declared with the *local* function, any variables declared as *my* variables are visible only within the subroutine in which they are declared, not in any subrou-tines called from this subroutine. If more than one variable is listed, the list must be enclosed in parentheses. So, the subroutine in Example 10.7 could have been written as follows:

---

3. See Chapter 11 for more on the *my* variables.

```
sub greeting{
    my ($fname, $lname) = @_ ;
    print "Welcome $fname!!\n";
}
```

EXAMPLE 10.8

```
     (The Script)
     #  The scope of my variables
1    my $name = "Raimo";
2    print "$name\n";
3       {  # Enter block
4           print "My name is $name\n";
5           my $name = "Elizabeth";
6           print "Now name is $name\n";
7           my $love = "Christina";
8           print "My love is $love.\n";
9       }  # Exit block
10   print "$name is back.\n";
11   print "I can't see my love,$love, out here.\n";
```

```
(Output)
2   Raimo
5   My name is Raimo
6   Now name is Elizabeth
8   My love is Christina.
10  Raimo is back.
11  I can't see my love,, out here.
```

EXPLANATION

1 The *my* function is used to create a lexical variable *$name* assigned the value *Raimo*. The variable is visible from the place where it is created and within any inner blocks. It is placed on its own private scratch pad.
2 The value of the lexical variable is printed.
3 A new block is entered.
4 The lexical variable, *$name*, is still in scope; i.e., visible.
5 A new lexical variable is declared. It gets its own private scratch pad.
6 The new variable, *$name*, is visible and its value is printed.
7 Another lexical variable is declared within the block and given its private scratch pad.
8 The value of *$love, Christina*, is printed. It is visible within this block.
9 The block ends here. The *my* variables will go out of scope.
10 The value of the *$name* variable is now visible. *Raimo* is printed.
11 The *$love* variable has gone out of scope.

EXAMPLE 10.9

```
(The Script)
      # Difference between my and local
1     $friend = Louise;          # Global variables
2     $pal = Danny;
3     print "$friend and $pal are global.\n";

4     sub guests{
5         my $friend = Pat;
6         local $pal = Chris;
7         print "$friend and $pal are welcome guests.\n";
8         &who_is_it;            # Call subroutine
      }

9     sub who_is_it{
10        print "You still have your global friend, $friend, here.\n";
11        print "But your pal is now $pal.\n";
      }

12    &guests;                   # Call subroutine
13    print "Global friends are back: $friend and $pal.\n";

(Output)
3     Louise and Danny are global.
7     Pat and Chris are welcome guests.
10    You still have your global friend, Louise, here.
11    But your pal is now Chris.
12    Global friends are back: Louise and Danny.
```

EXPLANATION

1 The variable *$friend* is assigned a value, *Louise*. All variables are global within *main*.
2 The variable *$pal* is assigned a value, *Danny*. It is also global.
3 The values of the global variables are printed.
4 The subroutine *guests* is defined.
5 The *my* function localizes the scalar *$friend* to this subroutine.
6 The *local* function localizes the variable *$pal* to this and all subroutines called from here.
7 The *$friend* and the *$pal* variables are printed in the *guests* subroutine.
8 The subroutine *who_is_it* is called.
9 The subroutine *who_is_it* is defined.
10 In the subroutine *who_is_it*, the global variable *$friend(Louise)* is visible. The lexical variable *$friend (Pat)* is declared as a *my* variable in the calling subroutine and is not visible in this subroutine.

EXPLANATION (CONTINUED)

11 The *local* scalar variable *$pal (Chris)*, on the other hand, was defined in the *guests* subroutine and is still visible in this subroutine, *who_is_it*.

12 The *guests* subroutine is called.

13 After exiting the subroutines, the global variables are back in scope and their values printed.

Using the *strict* Pragma (*my* and *our*). A pragma is a module that triggers a compiler error if it detects something in your program it doesn't like. The *strict* pragma can be used to prevent the use of global variables in a program. When you use a global variable, even a variable declared with *local*, the compiler will complain if *strict* has been declared. Lexically scoped variables are allowed. They are variables that are declared with either the *my* or *our* built-in functions. The *our* built-in (Perl 5.6+) is used when you need a global variable but still want to use the *strict* pragma to protect from the accidental use of global variables elsewhere in the program. (For more information about *strict* and packages, see "The strict Pragma" on page 357.)

EXAMPLE 10.10

```
(The Script)
1   use strict "vars";
2   my $name = "Ellie";               # my (lexical) variables are okay
3   @friends = qw(Tom Stefan Bin Marie);
                                      # global variables not allowed
4   local $newspaper = "The Globe"; # local variables are not allowed
5   print "My name is $name and our friends are @friends.\n";

(Output)
3   Global symbol "@friends" requires explicit package name at
        rigid.pl line 3.
4   Global symbol "$newspaper" requires explicit package name at
        rigid.pl line 4.
    In string, @friends now must be written as \@friends at rigid.pl
        line 5, near "$name and our friends our @friends"
    Global symbol "@friends" requires explicit package name at
        rigid.pl line 5.
    Execution of rigid.pl aborted due to compilation errors.
```

EXPLANATION

1 The *strict* pragma is used with *vars* as its argument. This tells the compiler to complain if it spots any global variables. The *strict* module, *strict.pm*, is part of the standard Perl distribution.

2 The variable *$name* is a lexically scoped *my* variable, which means it is private to the block where it is created. The *strict* pragma likes *my* variables.

EXPLANATION (CONTINUED)

3   The array *@friends* is a global variable. The compiler will complain when it sees global variables as shown in line 3 of the output. By *explicit package name*, the message is saying that you can still use this global variable if you precede its name with the package name and two colons; in other words, *@main::friends* is acceptable.

4   Perl classifies variables declared with the *local* function as dynamically allocated global variables. The compiler again complains because the variable is not declared with *my*. To still use the local variable, explicit means *local $main::newspaper*.

5   Due to compiler errors, the program never gets this far.

EXAMPLE 10.11

```
(The Script)
1   use strict "vars";
2   my $name = "Ellie";          # All variables are lexical in scope
3   our @friends = qw(Tom Stefan Bin Marie);
4   our $newspaper = "The Globe";
5   print "$name and $friends[0] read the $newspaper.\n";

(Output)
5   Ellie and Tom read the The Globe.
```

EXPLANATION

1   The *strict* pragma is declared with *vars* as its argument. This tells the compiler to complain if it spots any global variables. The *strict* module, *strict.pm*, is part of the standard Perl distribution.

2   The variable *$name* is a lexically scoped *my* variable; in other words, it is private to the block where it is created. The *strict* pragma likes *my* variables.

3   An *our* variable (Perl 5.6.0+) is disguised as a lexically scoped variable[a] so the *strict* pragma overlooks it. This allows you to get away with using a global variable if you really need one.

4   The scalar is also an *our* variable. It is global and lexical, bypassing compiler warnings caused by the *strict* pragma.

5   The *print* function displays the values of the lexical variables.

a. Wall, L., Christianson, T., and Orwant, J., *Programming Perl,* 3rd ed., O'Reilly & Associates: Sebastopol, CA, 2000, p. 138.

10.1.3   Prototypes

A **prototype**, also described as a template, tells the compiler how many and what types of arguments the subroutine should get when it is called. It lets you treat your subroutine just like a Perl built-in function. The prototype is made part of a declaration and is handled at

compile time. To call subroutines that have been declared with a prototype, the ampersand
(&) must be omitted or the subroutine will be treated like a normal user-defined subroutine,
rather than a built-in, and the compiler will ignore the prototype.

Prototype: *(Perl 5.003+)*
```
    sub subroutine_name($$);   Takes two scalar arguments
    sub subroutine_name(\@);
    Argument must be an array, preceded with an @ symbol


    sub subroutine_name($$;@);
    Takes two scalar arguments and an optional array.
    Anything after the semi-colon is optional.
```

EXAMPLE 10.12

```
    # Filename: prototypes
    # Testing prototyping
1   my $a = 5;
    my $b = 6;
    my $c = 7;
2   @list = (100,200,300);
3   sub myadd($$){        # myadd requires two scalar arguments
        my($x, $y) = @_;
        print $x + $y,"\n";
    }
4   myadd($a, $b);        # Okay
5   myadd(5, 4);          # Okay
6   myadd($a, $b, $c);    # Too many arguments

(Output)
6   Too many arguments for main::myadd at prototypes line 14,
        near "$c)" Execution of prototypes aborted due to compilation
        errors.11
```

EXPLANATION

1   Three scalar variables are declared and assigned values.
2   The array *@list* is assigned values.
3   The subroutine *myadd* is prototyped. Two scalar values are expected as parameters.
    Any more or less will cause a compiler error.
4   The subroutine is passed two scalar variables. This is okay.
5   The subroutine is passed two numbers. This is okay.
6   The subroutine was prototyped to take two scalars, but three are being passed here.
    The compiler sends an error message.

EXAMPLE 10.13

```
    # Prototypes
1   sub mynumbs(@$;$);          # Declaration with prototype
2   @list = (1,2,3);
3   mynumbs(@list, 25);
4   sub mynumbs(@$;$){          # Match the prototypes
5      my ($scalar) = pop(@_);
6      my(@arr) = @_;
7      print "The array is: @arr","\n";
8      print "The scalar is $scalar\n";
    }
```

```
(Output)
7   The array is: 1 2 3
8   The scalar is: 25
```

EXPLANATION

1   This is a declaration with a prototype, asking for an array, a scalar, and an optional scalar. The semicolon is used to indicate that the argument is optional.
2   The array *@list* is assigned values.
3   The *mynumbs* subroutine is called with a list and a scalar value, *25*. Don't use an ampersand when calling prototyped subroutines.
4   The subroutine is defined. Even though the declaration of the subroutine on line 1 established the prototype, it must be repeated again here or the following error will appear:

   Prototype mismatch: sub main::mynumbs (@$;$) vs none at prototype line 19.

5   The last element from the *@_* array is popped off and assigned to *$scalar.*
6   The rest of the *@_* array is assigned to *@arr.*
7   The values of the array *@arr* are printed.
8   The value of *$scalar* is printed.

10.1.4   Return Value

The subroutine can act like a function if it is included in an assignment statement and its returned value is assigned to a variable, either scalar or array. The value returned is really the value of the last expression evaluated within the subroutine.

   The *return* function can also be used to return a specified value, or to return early from the subroutine based on some condition. If used outside a subroutine, the *return* function causes a fatal error. You could say that the *return* is to a subroutine what an *exit* is to a program. If you use the *exit* function in a subroutine, you will exit the entire program and return to the command line.

EXAMPLE 10.14

```
(The Script)
    #!/bin/perl
    sub MAX{
1       my($max) = shift(@_);
2       foreach $foo ( @_ ){
3           $max = $foo if $max < $foo;
            print $max,"\n";
        }
        print "------------------------------ \n";
4       $max;
    }
    sub MIN{
        my($min) = pop( @_ );
        foreach $foo ( @_ ) {
            $min = $foo if $min > $foo;
            print $min,"\n";
        }
        print "------------------------------ \n";
        return $min;
    }

5   my $biggest = &MAX (2, 3, 4, 10, 100, 1);
6   my $smallest = &MIN (200, 2, 12, 40, 2, 20);
7   print "The biggest is $biggest and the smallest is $smallest.\n";

(Output)
    3
    4
    10
    100
    100
    ------------------------------
    200
    2
    2
    2
    2
    ------------------------------
7   The biggest is 100 and the smallest is 2.
```

EXPLANATION

1   The scalar $max is assigned the value of the first element in the array, @_. The *my*
    function makes $max local to this subroutine. If $max is modified, the original copy
    is not affected.

2   For each element in the list, the loop will assign, in turn, an element of the list to the
    scalar $foo.

3   If *$max* is less than *$foo*, *$max* gets *$foo*.

4   Since the **last statement** executed in subroutine *MAX* is *$max*, the value of *$max* is
    returned and assigned to *$biggest* at line 5.

5   The scalar *$biggest* is assigned the value of the last expression in the *MAX* subrou-
    tine.

6   The scalar *$smallest* is assigned the return value from function *MIN*. The return func-
    tion is explicitly used in subroutine *MIN*.

10.1.5   Call-by-Reference—Aliases and Typeglobs

Definition.   A **typeglob** is an alias for a variable. An alias is just another name for a variable. It is called a **symbolic reference** and is analogous to a soft link in the UNIX file-
system. It is another name for all identifiers on the symbol table with the same name.
Aliases were used predominantly in Perl 4 programs as a mechanism to pass parameters by
reference and are still used in Perl 5 programs, although with the advent of hard references
(see Chapter 12, "Does This Job Require a Reference?"), the practice of using typeglobs
and aliases is not as widespread. Since there are a number of library routines that evolved
during the early years of Perl, where typeglobs are still often found, they will be covered
here. (To see an example of how hard references are used with subroutines, see "Passing by
Pointer" on page 310, and for a complete discussion see Chapter 12, "Does This Job
Require a Reference?".)

Passing by Reference with Aliases.   Aliases (or typeglobs) can be passed to functions to
ensure true call-by-reference so that you can modify the global copy of the variable rather
than the local copy stored in the @_ array. If you are passing an array or multiple arrays to
a subroutine, rather than copying the entire array into the subroutine, you can pass an alias
or a pointer. (See "Passing by Pointer" on page 310.) To create an alias for a variable, an
asterisk is prepended to the alias name, as in

```
*alias = *variable;
```

   The asterisk represents all of the funny characters that prefix variables, including subroutines, filehandles, and formats. Typeglobs produce a scalar value that represents all
objects with the same name; i.e., it "globs" onto all the symbols in the symbol table that
have that name.[4] It is your job to determine what symbol you want the alias to reference.
This is done by prepending the correct funny character to the alias name when you want to
access its underlying value. For example:

---

4. This is not the same as the globbing done for filename substitution, as in <*p**>.

Given: *alias* = *var*
Then: *$alias* refers to the scalar *$var*
           @*alias* refers to the array @*var*
           $alias{string} refers to an element of a hash %*var*

If a filehandle is passed to a subroutine, a typeglob can be used to make the filehandle local.

Perl 5 improved the alias mechanism so that the alias can now represent one funny character rather than all of them, and introduced an even more convenient method for passing by reference, the hard reference, or what you may recognize as a *C/update*-like pointer.

Making Aliases Private—*local* **versus** *my.*   The names of variables created with the *my* function are not stored on the symbol table but within a temporary scratch pad. The *my* function creates a new variable that is private to its block. Since typeglobs are associated with the symbol table of a particular package, they cannot be made private with the *my* function. To make typeglobs local, the *local* function must be used.

EXAMPLE 10.15

```
(The Script)
    #!/usr/bin/perl
1   $colors = "rainbow";
2   @colors = ("red", "green", "yellow" );
3   &printit(*colors);               # Which color is this?
4   sub printit{
5       local(*whichone) = @_;        # Must use local, not my with globs
6       print *whichone, "\n";        # The package is main
7       $whichone = "Prism of Light"; # Alias for the scalar
8       $whichone[0] = "PURPLE";      # Alias for the array
    }
9   print "Out of subroutine.\n";
10  print "\$colors is $colors.\n";
11  print "\@colors is @colors.\n";

Output)
6   *main::colors
9   Out of subroutine.
10  $colors is Prism of Light.
11  @colors is PURPLE green yellow.
```

EXPLANATION

1   The scalar $colors is assigned *rainbow*.
2   The array @*colors* is assigned three values: *red*, *green*, and *yellow*.
3   The *printit* subroutine is called. An alias for all symbols named *colors* is passed as a parameter. The asterisk creates the alias (typeglob).
4   The *printit* subroutine is defined.
5   The @_ array contains the alias that was passed. Its value is assigned with the local alias, *whichone*. *whichone* is now an alias for any *colors* symbol.
6   Attempting to print the value of the alias itself only tells you that it is in the *main* package and is a symbol for all variables, subroutines, and filehandles called *colors*.
7   The scalar represented by the alias is assigned a new value.
8   The array represented by the alias, the first element of the array, is assigned a new value.
9   Out of the subroutine.
10 Out of the subroutine, the scalar $colors has been changed.
11 Out of the subroutine, the array @*colors* has also been changed.

EXAMPLE 10.16

```
(The Script)
    # Revisiting Example 10.6 -- Now using typeglob
1   print "Give me 5 numbers: ";
2   @n = split(' ', <STDIN>);
3   &params(*n);

4   sub params{
5       local(*arr) = @_;
6       print 'The values of the @arr array are ', @arr, "\n";
7       print "The first value is $arr[0]\n";
8       print "the last value is ", pop(@arr), "\n";
9       foreach $value(@arr){
10          $value += 5;
11          print "The value is $value.\n";
        }
    }
    print "Back in main\n";
12  print "The new values are @n.\n";
```

EXAMPLE 10.16 (CONTINUED)

```
(Output)
1    Give me 5 numbers: 1 2 3 4 5
6    The values in the @arr array are 12345
7    The first value is 1
8    The last value is 5
11   The value is 6
     The value is 7
     The value is 8
     The value is 9
     Back in main
12   The new values are 6 7 8 9  <--- Look here. Got popped this time!
```

EXPLANATION

1 The user is asked for input.
2 The user input is *split* on whitespace and returned to the @*n* array.
3 The subroutine *params* is called. An alias for any *n* in the symbol table is passed as a parameter.
4 The *params* subroutine is defined.
5 In the subroutine, the alias was passed to the @_ array. This value is assigned to a local typeglob, **arr*.
6 The values in the @*arr* array are printed. Remember, @*arr* is just an alias for the array @*n*. It refers to the values in the @*n* array.
7 The first element in the array is printed.
8 The last element of the array is popped, not just the reference to it.
9 The *foreach* loop assigns, in turn, each element of the @*arr* array to the scalar $*value*.
10 Each element of the array is incremented by *5* and stored in the scalar, $*value*.
11 The new values are printed.
12 The values printed illustrate that those values changed in the function by the alias really changed the values in the @*n* array. See Example 10.6.

Passing Filehandles by Reference.   The only way to pass a filehandle directly to a subroutine is by reference. You can use typeglob to create an alias for the filehandle or use a hard reference. (See Chapter 12, "Does This Job Require a Reference?" for more on hard references.)

EXAMPLE 10.17

```
(The Script)
   #!/bin/perl
1  open(READMEFILE, "f1") || die;
2  &readit(*READMEFILE);      # Passing a filehandle to a subroutine
   sub readit{
3     local(*myfile) = @_;     # myfile is an alias for READMEFILE
4     while(<myfile>){
          print;
       }
    }
```

EXPLANATION

1   The *open* function opens the UNIX file *f1* for reading and attaches it to the *READMEFILE* handle.

2   The *readit* subroutine is called. The filehandle is aliased with typeglob and passed as a parameter to the subroutine.

3   The local alias *myfile* is assigned the value of *@_*; i.e., the alias that was passed into the subroutine.

4   The alias is another name for *READMEFILE*. It is enclosed in angle brackets, and each line from the filehandle will be read and then printed as it goes through the *while* loop.

Selective Aliasing and the Backslash Operator.   Perl 5 references allow you to alias a particular variable rather than all variable types with the same name. For example:

```
*array = \@array;
*scalar = \$scalar;
*hash = \%assoc_array;
*func = \&subroutine;
```

EXAMPLE 10.18

```
(The Script)
   # References and typeglob
1  @list = (1, 2, 3, 4, 5);
2  $list = "grocery";
3  *arr = \@list;        # *arr is a reference only to the array @list
4  print @arr, "\n";
5  print "$arr\n";        # Not a scalar reference
   sub alias{
6     local (*a) = @_;    # Must use local, not my
```

EXAMPLE 10.18 (CONTINUED)

```
7       $a[0] = 7;
8       pop @a;
    }
9  &alias(*arr);          # Call the subroutine
10 print "@list\n";
11 $num = 5;
12 *scalar = \$num;       # *scalar is a reference to the scalar $num
13 print "$scalar\n";

(Output)
4   1 2 3 4 5
5
10  7 2 3 4
13  5
```

EXPLANATION

1   The *@list* array is assigned a list of values.
2   The *$list* scalar is assigned a value.
3   The **arr* alias is another name for the array *@list*. **It is not an alias for any other type.**
4   The alias **arr* is used to refer to the array *@list*.
5   The alias **arr* does not reference a scalar. Nothing prints.
6   In the subroutine, the local alias **a* receives the value of the alias passed in as a parameter and assigned to the *@_* array.
7   The array is assigned new value via the alias.
8   The last value of the array is popped off via the alias.
9   The subroutine is called, passing the alias **arr* as a parameter.
10 The *@list* values are printed reflecting the changes made in the subroutine.
11 The scalar *$num* is assigned a value.
12 A new alias is created. **scalar* refers only to the scalar *$num*.
13 The alias is just another name for the scalar *$num*. Its value is printed.

10.1.6   Passing by Pointer

Definition.   A hard reference, commonly called a **pointer**, is a scalar variable that contains the address of another variable. The backslash operator (\) is used to create the pointer. When printing the value of the pointer, you not only see a hexadecimal address stored there, but also the data type of the variable that resides at that address.

For example, if you write

```
$p = \$name;
```

then *$p* will be assigned the address of the scalar *$name*. *$p* is a reference to *$name*. The value stored in *$p*, when printed, looks like *SCALAR(0xb057c)*.

Since pointers contain addresses, they can be used to pass parameters by reference to a subroutine; and, because the pointer is simply a scalar variable, not a typeglob, it can be made a private, lexical *my* variable.

```
my $arrayptr = \@array;       # creates a pointer to an array
my $scalarptr = \$scalar;     # creates a pointer to a scalar
my $hashptr = \%assoc_array;  # creates a pointer to a hash
my $funcptr = \&subroutine;   # creates a pointer to a subroutine
```

De-referencing the Pointer. If you print the value of the reference, you will see an address. If you want to go to that address and get the value stored there—i.e., de-reference the pointer—the pointer must be prefaced by two funny symbols: one is the dollar sign because the pointer itself is a scalar, and preceding that, the funny symbol representing the type of data it points to. For example, if *$p* is a reference to a scalar *$x*, then *$$p* will get the value of *$x*, and if *$p* is a reference to an array *@x*, then *@$p* would get the values in *@x*. In both examples, the reference *$p* is preceded by the funny symbol representing the data type of the variable it points to. When using more complex types, the arrow (infix) operator can be used. (See "References and Anonymous Variables" on page 360 for more on the arrow operator.). Table 10.1 shows examples of creating and de-referencing pointers.

Table 10.1 Creating and De-referencing Pointers

Assignment	Create a Reference	De-reference	De-reference with Arrow
$sca = 5;	*$p = \$sca;*	*print $$p;*	
@arr = (4,5,6);	*$p = \@arr;*	*print @$p;* *print $$p[0];*	*$p–>[0]*
%hash = (key => 'value');	*$p = \%hash;*	*print %$p;* *print $$p{key};*	*$p–>{key}*

EXAMPLE 10.19

```
(The Script)
    #!/bin/perl
1   $num = 5;
2   $p = \$num;         # The backslash operator means "adddress of"
3   print 'The address assigned $p is ', $p, "\n";
4   print "The value stored at that address is $$p\n"; .
```

```
(Output)
3   The address assigned $p is SCALAR(0xb057c)
4   The value stored at that address is 5
```

EXPLANATION

1   The scalar *$num* is assigned the value *5*.
2   The scalar *$p* is assigned the address of *$num*. The function of the backslash operator
    is to create the reference. *$p* is called either a **reference** or a **pointer** (the terms are
    interchangeable).
3   The address stored in *$p* is printed. Perl also tells you the data type is *SCALAR*.
4   To de-reference *$p*, another dollar sign is prepended to *$p*. This dollar sign tells Perl
    that you are looking for the value of the scalar that *$p* references, which is *$num*.

EXAMPLE 10.20

```
(The Script)
1    @toys = qw( Buzzlightyear Woody Thomas Pokemon );
2    $num = @toys;
3    %movies = ("Toy Story"=>"US",
               "Thomas"=>"England",
               "Pokemon"=>"Japan",
               );
4    $ref1 = \$num;         # Scalar pointer
5    $ref2 = \@toys;        # Array pointer
6    $ref3 = \%movies;      # Hash pointer
7    print "There are $$ref1 toys.\n";       # De-reference pointers
8    print "They are: @$ref2.\n";
9    while(($key, $value) = each ( %$ref3 )){
10      print "$key--$value\n";
     }
11   print "His favorite toys are $ref2->[0] and $ref2->[3].\n";
12   print "The Pokemon movie was made in $ref3->{Pokemon}.\n";
```

EXAMPLE 10.20 (CONTINUED)

```
(Output)
7    There are 4 toys.
8    They are: Buzzlightyear Woody Thomas Pokemon.
10   Thomas--England
     Pokemon--Japan
     Toy Story--US
11   His favorite toys are Buzzlightyear and Pokemon.
12   The Pokemon movie was made in Japan.
```

EXPLANATION

1   The array *@toys* is assigned a list.

2   The array *@toys* is assigned to the scalar variable *$num*, returning the number of elements in the array.

3   The hash *%movies* is assigned key/value pairs.

4   The reference *$ref1* is a scalar. It is assigned the address of the scalar *$num*. The backslash operator allows you to create the reference.

5   The reference *$ref2* is a scalar. It is assigned the address of the array *@toys*.

6   The reference *$ref3* is a scalar. It is assigned the address of the hash *%movies*.

7   The reference is de-referenced, meaning: Go to the address that *$ref1* is pointing to and print the value of the scalar stored there.

8   The reference is again de-referenced, meaning: Go to the address that *$ref2* is pointing to, get the array, and print it.

9   The built-in *each* function gets keys and values from the hash. The hash pointer, *$ref3*, is preceded by a percent sign; in other words, de-reference the pointer to the hash.

10 Key/value pairs are printed from the hash *%movies*.

11 De-reference the pointer and get the first element and the fourth elements of the array. To de-reference a pointer to an array, use the arrow (infix operator) and the subscript of the array element you are fetching. You could also use the form *$$ref2[0]* or *$$ref2[3]*, but it's not as easy to read or write.

12 The pointer is de-referenced using the arrow notation. Curly braces surround the hash key. You could also use the form *$$ref3{Pokemon}*.

EXAMPLE 10.21

```
(The Script)
    # Hard References (Pointers)
    # When assigning to a scalar, the backslash operator gets the
    # address of the variable
1   @list = (1, 2, 3, 4, 5);
2   $name = "Nicklas";
3   $ptr1 = \@list;      # $ptr1 is assigned the address of @list
4   $ptr2 = \$name;      # $ptr2 is assigned the address of $name

5   print q(The value of $ptr1 is: ), $ptr1, "\n";
6   print q(The array values $ptr1 is pointing at are: ), "@$ptr1\n";
7   print q(The value of $ptr2 is: ), $ptr2, "\n";
8   print q(The scalar value $ptr2 is pointing to is: ),$$ptr2, "\n";

9   &fun($ptr1, $ptr2);       # Call the subroutine; pass pointers

10  sub fun{
11      my ($arrayptr, $scalarptr) = @_;      # Use my, not local

12      print q(In subroutine: $arrayptr is: ), $arrayptr,"\n";
13      print q(In subroutine: $scalarptr is: ), $scalarptr, "\n";
14      $arrayptr->[0] = 7;        # Assign to the array with a pointer
15      pop @$arrayptr;            # Pop the array
16      $$scalarptr = "Andreas";   # Assign to the scalar with a
    pointer
17      print "$$scalarptr  @$arrayptr\n";
    }
    print "Out of subroutine.\n";
18  print "Now \@list is: @list\n";
19  print "Now \$name is $name\n";

(Output)
5   The value of $ptr1 is: ARRAY(0x8a62d80)
6   The array values $ptr1 is pointing at are: 1 2 3 4 5
7   The value of $ptr2 is: SCALAR(0x8a62df8)
8   The scalar value $ptr2 is pointing to is: Nicklas
12  In subroutine: $arrayptr is: ARRAY(0x8a62d80)
13  In subroutine: $scalarptr is: SCALAR(0x8a62df8)
17  Andreas   7 2 3 4
    Out of subroutine.
18  Now @list is: 7 2 3 4
19  Now $name is Andreas
```

EXPLANATION

1   The array @*list* is assigned values.

2   Scalar $*name* is assigned *Nicklas*.

3   The scalar variable, $*ptr1*, is assigned the address of the array @*list*. The backslash operator gets the address of a variable. Because $*ptr1* contains the address of array @*list*, $*ptr1* is said to point to @*list*. It is also called a hard reference because it contains the actual virtual address of where @*list* is stored in memory.

4   The variable $*ptr2* is assigned the address of the scalar $*name*.

5   The value of the pointer $*ptr1* is printed. The value stored there is not only the hexadecimal address of @*list*, but also its data type. Since @*list* is an array, the string *ARRAY* is printed, followed by its address.

6   The pointer $*ptr1* is de-referenced. It points to an array. Prepending $*ptr1* with an @ symbol tells Perl to go to the address that $*ptr1* holds and get the values from the array @*list*.

7   The value stored in the pointer $*ptr2* is a hexadecimal address. It is the address of $*name* and $*name* is a scalar, so $*ptr2* references or points to a scalar.

8   The pointer, $*ptr2*, is de-referenced. Since $*ptr* contains the address of $*name*, a scalar, it is de-referenced by prepending a $ to it, for example, $$*ptr2*. Stated simply, $*ptr2* is pointing to $*name*; go there and get the value in $*name*. *Niklas* is stored there.

9   The subroutine *fun* is called, with the two pointers as its parameters.

10   This is the subroutine declaration.

11   Two local scalars, $*arrayptr* and $*scalarptr*, are created. The first two values from the @_ are assigned to them, respectively. The values are addresses passed in as parameters from line 9.

12   In the subroutine, $*arrayptr* has the same address as $*ptr1*. The address was passed as a parameter to the subroutine, copied into the @_ array, and then into the *my* variable $*arrayptr*. The address of $*arrayptr* is printed.

13   In the subroutine, $*scalarptr* has the same address as $*ptr2*. The address was passed as a parameter to the subroutine, copied into the @_ array, and then into the *my* variable $*scalarptr*. The address of $*scalarptr* is printed.

14   The arrow notation is used to de-reference the pointer $*arrayptr*. The first element of the original array is assigned *7*; in other words, $*list[0]* is assigned *7* via the pointer.

15   The pointer $*arrayptr* is de-referenced. The *pop* function removes the last element of the array @*list* via the pointer.

16   The pointer to the scalar $*scalarptr* is de-referenced by prepending it with a $. Perl will go to that address and assign *Andreas* to the scalar $*name*.

17   Both pointers are de-referenced and the values to which they are pointing are printed.

18   After exiting the subroutine, the array @*list* is printed. The values have changed.

19   After exiting the subroutine, the array @*scalar* is printed. The values have changed.

EXAMPLE 10.22

```
(The Script)
    # This script demonstrates the use of hard references
    # when passing arrays. Instead of passing the entire
    # array, a hard reference (pointer) is passed.
    # The value of the last expression is returned.

1   my @list1 = (1 .. 100);
2   my @list2 = (5, 10, 15, 20);

3   print "The total is :  ", &addemup(\@list1, \@list2) , ".\n";
            # two pointers

4   sub addemup{
5       my($arr1, $arr2) = (shift, shift) ;      # The two pointers
                                                 # are shifted from @_

6       my $total = 0;
7       print $arr1, "\n" ;
8       print $arr2, "\n";
9       foreach $num(@$arr1){
10          $total1 += $num;
        }
11      foreach $num(@$arr2){
12          $total2 += $num;
        }

13  $total1 + $total2;     # The expression is evaluated and returned
    }

(Output)
7   ARRAY(0x8a62d68)
8   ARRAY(0x8a60f2c)
3   The total is:  5100.
```

EXPLANATION

1. The array *@list1* is assigned values between *1* and *100*.
2. The array *@list2* is assigned four values. Four values are assigned to the *@list2* array.
3. The *&addemup* subroutine is called with two arguments. The backslash is used to create the pointers. The addresses of *@list1* and *@list2* are being passed.
4. The subroutine *&addemup* is declared.
5. The *@_* array contains the two arguments just passed in. The arguments are shifted from the *@_* into *my* variables *$arr1* and *$arr2*. They are pointers.
6. *$total* is assigned an initial value of *0*.
7. The value of the pointer is printed. It points to the array *@list1*.

8 The value of the pointer is printed. It points to the array *@list2*.

9 The *foreach* loop is entered and, by using the de-referenced pointer, each element from *@list1* is assigned, in turn, to *$num* until all of the elements in the array have been processed.

10 Each value of *$num* is added on and assigned to the value in *$total1* until the loop ends.

11 The *foreach* loop is entered and, by using the de-referenced pointer, each element from *@list2* is assigned, in turn, to *$num* until all of the elements in the array have been processed.

12 Each value of *$num* is added on and assigned to the value in *$total2* until the loop ends.

13 The sum of *$total1* and *$total2* is returned to line 3, where it is passed as an argument to the *print* function and then printed.

10.1.7 Autoloading

The Perl 5 *AUTOLOAD* function lets you check to see if a subroutine has been defined. The *AUTOLOAD* subroutine is called whenever Perl is told to call a subroutine and the subroutine can't be found. The special variable $*AUTOLOAD* is assigned the name of the undefined subroutine.

The *AUTOLOAD* function can also be used with objects to provide an implementation for calling unnamed methods. (A **method** is an object-oriented name for a subroutine.)

EXAMPLE 10.23

```
(The Script)
    #!/bin/perl
1   sub AUTOLOAD{
2       my(@arguments) = @_;
3       $args = join(', ', @arguments);
4       print "$AUTOLOAD was never defined.\n" ;
5       print "The arguments passed were $args.\n";
    }

6   $driver = "Jody";
    $miles = 50;
    $gallons = 5;

7   &mileage($driver, $miles, $gallons);   # Call to an undefined
                                            # subroutine
(Output)
4   main::mileage was never defined.
5   The arguments passed were Jody, 50, 5.
```

EXPLANATION

1   The subroutine *AUTOLOAD* is defined.

2   The *AUTOLOAD* subroutine is called with the same arguments as would have been passed to the original subroutine called on line 7.

3   The arguments are joined by commas and stored in the scalar *$args*.

4   The name of the package and the subroutine that was originally called are stored in the *$AUTOLOAD* scalar. (For this example, *main* is the default package.)

5   The arguments are printed.

6   The scalar variables are assigned values.

7   The *mileage* subroutine is called with three arguments. Perl calls the *AUTOLOAD* function if there is a call to an undefined function, passing the same arguments as would have been passed in this example to the *mileage* subroutine.

EXAMPLE 10.24

```
    #!/bin/perl
    # Program to call a subroutine without defining it
1   sub AUTOLOAD{
2       my(@arguments) = @_;
3       my($package, $command) = split("::",$AUTOLOAD, 2);
4       return `$command @arguments`;    # Command substitution
    }

5   $day = date("+%D");       # date is an undefined subroutine
6   print "Today is $day.\n";
7   print cal(3,2003);    # cal is an undefined subroutine
```

```
(Output)
Today is 03/19/03.

        March 2003
   S   M  Tu  W  Th   F   S
                          1
   2   3   4  5   6   7   8
   9  10  11 12  13  14  15
  16  17  18 19  20  21  22
  23  24  25 26  27  28  29
  30  31
```

EXPLANATION

1   The subroutine *AUTOLOAD* is defined.
2   The *AUTOLOAD* subroutine is called with the same arguments as would have been passed to the original subroutine on lines 5 and 7.
3   The *$AUTOLOAD* variable is *split* into two parts by a double colon delimiter (*::*). The array returned consists of the package name and the name of the subroutine that was called.
4   The value returned is the name of the function called, which in the first case happens to be a UNIX command and its arguments. The backquotes cause the enclosed string to be executed as a UNIX command. Tricky!
5   The *date* function has never been defined. *AUTOLOAD* will pick its name and assign it to *$AUTOLOAD* in the *AUTOLOAD* function. The *date* function will pass an argument. The argument, *+%D*, is also an argument to the UNIX *date* command. It returns today's date.
6   The returned value is printed.
7   The *cal* function has never been defined. It takes two arguments. *AUTOLOAD* will assign *cal* to *$AUTOLOAD*. The arguments are *3* and *2003* assigned to *@arguments*. They will be passed to the *AUTOLOAD* function and used in line 4. After variable substitution, the backquotes cause the string to be executed. The UNIX command *cal 3 2003* is executed and the result returned to the *print* fucntion.

10.1.8   *BEGIN* and *END* Subroutines (Startup and Finish)

The *BEGIN* and *END* subroutines may remind UNIX programmers of the special *BEGIN* and *END* patterns used in the *awk* programming language. For *C++* programmers, the *BEGIN* has been likened to a constructor, and the *END* a destructor. The *BEGIN* and *END* subroutines are similar to both in functionality.

A *BEGIN* subroutine is executed immediately, before the rest of the file is even parsed. If you have multiple *BEGIN*s, they will be executed in the order they were defined.

The *END* subroutine is executed when all is done; that is, when the program is exiting, even if the *die* function caused the termination. Multiple *END* blocks are executed in reverse order.

The keyword *sub* is not necessary when using these special subroutines.

EXAMPLE 10.25

```
    #!/bin/perl
    # Program to demonstrate BEGIN and END subroutines
1   chdir("/stuff") || die "Can't cd: $!\n";
2   BEGIN{print "Welcome to my Program.\n"};
3   END{print "Bailing out somewhere near line ",__LINE__,
                                       " So long.\n"};
```

EXAMPLE 10.25 (CONTINUED)

```
(Output)
Welcome to my Program.
Can't cd: No such file or directory
Bailing out somewhere near line 5. So long.
```

EXPLANATION

1   An effort is made to change directories to /*stuff*. The *chdir* fails and the *die* is execut-
     ed. Normally, the program would exit immediately, but this program has defined an
     END subroutine. The *END* subroutine will be executed before the program dies.
2   The *BEGIN* subroutine is executed as soon as possible; that is, as soon as it has been
     defined. This subroutine is executed before anything else in the program happens.
3   The *END* subroutine is always executed when the program is about to exit, even if a
     die is called. The line printed is there just for you *awk* programmers.

10.1.9 The *subs* Function

The *subs* function allows you to predeclare subroutine names. Its arguments are a list of
subroutines. This allows you to call a subroutine without the ampersand or parentheses, and
to override built-in Perl functions.

EXAMPLE 10.26

```
     #!/bin/perl
     # The subs module
1    use subs qw(fun1 fun2 );

2    fun1;
3    fun2;

4    sub fun1{
         print "In fun1\n";
     }

5    sub fun2{
         print "In fun2\n";
     }

(Output)
In fun1
In fun2
```

EXPLANATION

1   The *subs* module is loaded (see "The use Function (Modules and Pragmas)" on page 339) into your program and given a list of subroutines.

2   *fun1* is called with neither an ampersand nor parentheses because it was in the *subs* list. The function is not defined until later.

3   *fun2* is also called before it is defined.

EXERCISE 9
I Can't Seem to Function Without Subroutines

1. Write a program called *tripper* that will ask the user the number of miles he has driven and the amount of gas he used. In the *tripper* script, write a subroutine called *mileage* that will calculate and return the user's mileage (miles per gallon). The number of miles driven and the amount of gas used will be passed as arguments. All variables should be *my* variables. Print the results. Prototype *tripper*.

2. Hotels are often rated by using stars to represent their score. A five-star hotel may have a king-size bed, a kitchen, and two TVs; a one-star hotel may have cockroaches and a leaky roof. Write a subroutine called *printstar* that will produce a histogram to show the star rating for hotels shown in the following hash. The *printstar* function will be given two parameters: the name of the hotel and the number of its star rating. (Hint: sort the hash keys into an array. Use a loop to iterate through the keys, calling the *printstar* function for each iteration.)

```
%hotels=("Pillowmint Lodge" => "5",
         "Buxton Suites"    => "5",
         "The Middletonian" => "3",
         "Notchbelow"       => "4",
         "Rancho El Cheapo" => "1",
         "Pile Inn"         => "2",
       );
```

```
(OUTPUT)
Hotel                      Category
-------------------------------------------
Notchbelow            |****       |
The Middletonian      |***        |
Pillowmint Lodge      |*****      |
Pile Inn              |**         |
Rancho El Cheapo      |*          |
Buxton Suites         |*****      |
-------------------------------------------
```

(Note that the hotel names have been sorted. Can you sort by stars?)

3. Write the *grades* program to take the course number and the name of a student as command line arguments. The course numbers are *CS101*, *CS202*, and *CS303*. The program will include three subroutines:

   a. Subroutine *ave* to calculate the overall average for a set of grades.

   b. Subroutine *highest* to get the highest grade in the set.

   c. Subroutine *lowest* to get the lowest grade in the set.

   Print the average, the highest score, and the lowest score. If there were any failures (average below 60), print the name, course number, and a warning to *STDERR* such as: *Be advised: Joe Blow failed CS202*. Send the name of the failing student and the course number to a file called *failures*. Sort the file by course number.

   Use the *AUTOLOAD* function to test that each of the subroutines has been defined.

MODULARIZE IT, PACKAGE IT, AND SEND IT TO THE LIBRARY!

11.1 Packages and Modules

11.1.1 An Analogy

Two boys each have a box of Lego building blocks. One set of Lego blocks will build a toy boat, the other a toy plane. The boys open their boxes and throw the contents on the floor, mixing them together. The Lego blocks are different shapes and colors. There are yellow square pieces, red triangular pieces, and blue rectangular pieces from both boxes, but now they are mixed up so that it is difficult to tell which Lego blocks should be used to build the toy boat or the toy plane. If the pieces had been kept in their separate boxes, this confusion never would have happened.

In Perl, the separate boxes are called packages, and the Lego blocks are called symbols; i.e., names for variables and constants. Keeping symbols in their own private packages makes it possible to include library modules and routines in your program without causing a conflict between what you named your variables and what they are named in the module or library file that you have included.

11.1.2 Definition

The bundling of data and functions into a separate namespace is termed **encapsulation** (to *C++* programmers, this is called a **class**, and to object-oriented Perl programmers it can also be called a class). The separate namespace is termed a **package**. A separate namespace means that Perl has a separate symbol table for all the variables in a named package. By default, the current package is called package *main*. All the example scripts up to this point are in package *main*. All variables are global within the package. The package mechanism allows you to switch namespaces, so that variables and subroutines in the package are private, even if they have the same name somewhere outside of the package. (See Figure 11.1.)

The scope of the package is from the declaration of the package to the end of the inner-most enclosing block, or until another package is declared. To reference a package variable in another package, the package name is prefixed by the funny character representing the data type of the variable, followed by two colons and the variable name. In Perl 4, an apostrophe is used instead of the colon.[1] (The double colons are reminiscent of the $C++$ scope resolution operator.) When referring to the *main* package, the name of the package can be eliminated.

Perl 5 extends the notion of packages to that of **modules**. A module is a package that is usually defined in a library and is reusable. Modules are more complex than simple packages. They have the ability to export symbols to other packages and to work with classes and methods. A module is a package stored in a file, where the basename of the file is given the package name appended with a *.pm* extension. The *use* function takes the module name as its argument and loads the module into your script.

```
$package'variable
$package::variable
$main::variable
$::variable
```

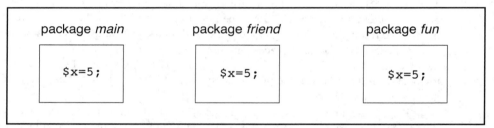

Figure 11.1   Each package has its own namespace (symbol table).

11.1.3   The Symbol Table

To compile a program, the compiler must keep track of all the names for variables, filehandles, directory handles, formats, and subroutines that are used. Perl stores the names of these symbols as keys in a hash table for each package. The name of the hash is the same name as the package. The values associated with the hash keys are the corresponding type-glob values. Perl actually creates separate pointers for each of the values represented by the same name. (See Figure 11.2.)

Each package has its own symbol table. Any time you use the package declaration, you switch to the symbol table for that package.

A variable assigned using the *local* function can be accessed in another package by using a :: to qualify it by package name. It is still within scope and accessible from the main symbol table.

---

1. The apostrophe is still acceptable in Perl 5 scripts as of version 5.003.

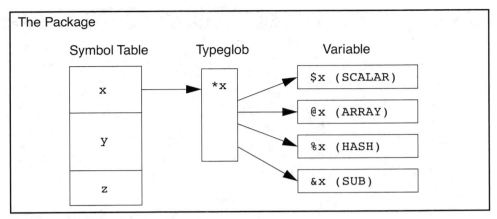

Figure 11.2   The package provides privacy.

The variables assigned using the *my* function are not accessible outside their own packages. They are not stored in a package symbol table, but are stored in a private scratch pad created for each subroutine called.

In the following example, you will notice that the *main* package not only stores symbols that are provided by the program, but also other symbols such as *STDIN, STDOUT, STDERR, ARGV, ARGVOUT, ENV,* and *SIG.* These symbols and special variables such as *$_* and *$!* are forced into package *main.* Other packages refer to these symbols unless qualified. Example 11.1 shows the contents of the symbol table for the *main* package.

EXAMPLE 11.1

```
(The Script)
    #!/bin/perl
    # Package main
1   use strict "vars";
2   use warnings;
3   our (@friends, @dogs, $key, $value);     # Declaring variables
4   my($name,$pal,$money);
5   $name = "Susanne";
6   @friends = qw(Joe Jeff Jan);
7   @dogs = qw(Guyson Lara Junior);
8   local $main::dude="Ernie";       # Keep strict happy
9   my $pal = "Linda";               # Not in the symbol table
10  my $money = 1000;
11  while(($key, $value) = each (%main::)){
                                 # Look at main's symbol table
        print "$key:\t$value\n";
    }
```

EXAMPLE 11.1 (CONTINUED)

```
(Output)
Name "main::dude" used only once: possible typo at packages line 10.
STDOUT:               *main::STDOUT
@:                    *main::@
ARGV:                 *main::ARGV
STDIN:                *main::STDIN
:                     *main::
dude:                 *main::dude
attributes:::         *main::attributes::
DB:::                 *main::DB::
key:                  *main::key
_<..\xsutils.c:       *main::_<..\xsutils.c
_<perllib.c:          *main::_<perllib.c
UNIVERSAL:::          *main::UNIVERSAL::
?:                    *main::?
value:                *main::value
DynaLoader:::         *main::DynaLoader::
?:                    *main::?
?ARNING_BITS:         *main::?ARNING_BITS
SIG:                  *main::SIG
Exporter:::           *main::Exporter::
Win32:::              *main::Win32::
warnings:::           *main::warnings::
BEGIN:                *main::BEGIN
stderr:               *main::stderr
INC:                  *main::INC
_:                    *main::_
":                    *main::"
DATA:                 *main::DATA
_<.\win32.c:          *main::_<.\win32.c
$:                    *main::$
stdout:               *main::stdout
IO:::                 *main::IO::
ENV:                  *main::ENV
dogs:                 *main::dogs
strict:::             *main::strict::
stdin:                *main::stdin
Carp:::               *main::Carp::
CORE:::               *main::CORE::
/:                    *main::/
0:                    *main::0
friends:              *main::friends
_<..\universal.c:     *main::_<..\universal.c
STDERR:               *main::STDERR
main:::               *main::main::
```

EXPLANATION

1 The *strict* pragma is turned on, barring any global variables.

2 The *warnings* pragma issues warnings if there are bare words, uninitialized variables, etc.

3 Lexically global *our* variables are declared. They will not be picked up as global variables by the *strict* pragma.

4 Lexically scoped *my* variables are declared.

5 The *my* variable, *$name*, is assigned *Susanne*.

6 The array *@friends* is assigned a list of names.

7 The array *@dogs* is assigned a list.

8 In order to keep the *strict* pragma from complaining, the *local* variable *$dude* must be fully qualified with the package name.

9 The lexically scoped *my* variable is assigned a value. This variable will not show up on the symbol table. It is stored in a special scratch pad within the block.

10 This *my* variable will also be absent from the symbol table.

11 The keys and values from the *main* symbol table are printed. The key is the name of the identifier and the value is the corresponding typeglob value.

EXAMPLE 11.2

```
(The Script)
    # Default package is main
1   @town = (Boston, Chico, Tampa);
2   $friend = Mary;

3   print "In main: \$friend is $friend\n";

4   package boy;            # Package declaration
5   $name = Steve;
6   print "In boy \$name is $name.\n";
7   $main::friend = Patricia;
8   print "In boy \@town is @::town\n";
9   package main;           # Package declaration
10  print "In main: \$name is $name\n";
11  print "In main: \$name is $boy::name\n";
12  print "In main: \$friend is $friend.\n";

(Output)
3   In main: $friend is Mary
6   In boy $name is Steve.
8   In boy @town is Boston Chico Tampa
10  In main: $name is
11  In main: $name is Steve
12  In main: $friend is Patricia
```

EXPLANATION

1   The default package is called *main*. In the *main* package an array, *@town*, is assigned values. *@town* is in *main*'s symbol table.
2   In package *main*, the scalar *$friend* is assigned *Mary*. *$friend* is in *main*'s symbol table.
3   The value of *$friend* is printed.
4   The package *boy* is declared. We now switch from the *main* package to the *boy* package. This package has its own symbol table. From this point on until the program ends or another package is declared, the *boy* package is in scope. Variables created in this package are global within itself, but are not part of the *main* package.
5   The scalar *$name* is assigned *Steve*.
6   The value in *$name* is printed.
7   To access the variable *$friend* in package *main*, first the dollar sign is prepended to the package name to indicate that the type of the variable is a scalar, followed by the name of the package, *main*, two colons, and the variable name, *friend*. This allows you to switch namespaces from within this package. *Patricia* is assigned to *main*'s variable *$friend*.
8   Since *main* is the default package, it is not necessary to use its name when switching namespaces. *@::town* tells Perl to switch namespaces back to the array *@town* in the *main* package.
9   Package *main* is declared. We will now switch back into the *main* package.
10   In the *main* package, *$name* is not defined.
11   The value of the variable *$name* from the *boy* package is printed.
12   The *$friend* scalar was changed in package *boy* because it was fully qualified with *main*'s package *main*, meaning that the program was temporarily switched to package *main* when this variable was assigned. Its value is printed.

EXAMPLE 11.3

```
(The Script)
    # Package declarations
1   $name = "Suzanne";      # These variables are in package main
2   $num = 100;
3   package friend;         # Package declaration
4   sub welcome {
5       print "Who is your pal? ";
6       chomp($name =<STDIN>);
7       print "Welcome $name!\n";
8       print "\$num is $num.\n";     # Unknown to this package
9       print "Where is $main::name?\n\n";
    }
10  package main;           # Package declaration; back in main
11  &friend::welcome;       # Call subroutine
12  print "Back in main package \$name is $name\n";
13  print "Switch to friend package, Bye ",$friend::name,"\n";
```

EXAMPLE 11.3   (CONTINUED)

```
14  print "Bye $name\n\n";

15  package birthday;        # Package declaration

16  $name = Beatrice;
17  print "Happy Birthday, $name.\n";
18  print "No, $::name and $friend::name, it is not your birthday!\n";
```

(Output)
```
5   Who is your pal? Tommy
7   Welcome Tommy!
8   $num is .
9   Where is Suzanne?

12  Back in main package $name is Suzanne
13  Switch to friend package, Bye Tommy
14  Bye Suzanne

17  Happy Birthday, Beatrice!!
18  No, Suzanne and Tommy, it is not your birthday!
```

EXPLANATION

1 Scalar *$name* is assigned *Suzanne* for the default package, *main*.
2 Scalar *$num* is assigned *100*.
3 Package *friend* is declared. It is in scope until line 10.
4 The subroutine *welcome* is defined within the *friend* package.
5 The user is asked for input.
6 *$name* is assigned a value. The package is *friend*.
7 The value of *$name* is printed.
8 The scalar *$num* was local to the *main* package; it's not defined here. Nothing is printed.
9 To access the *$name* variable from the *main* package, the name of the package, *main*, is followed by two colons and the variable name. Note that the $ precedes the package name, not the variable.
10 Out of the subroutine, the package *main* is declared.
11 The subroutine *welcome* cannot be called unless qualified by its package name.
12 *$name* is *Suzanne* in package *main*.
13 To access a variable from the package *friend*, the package has to precede the variable name. This causes a switch in namespaces.
14 *$name* is *Suzanne* in package *main*.
15 A new package called *birthday* is declared. It remains in effect until the block ends—in this case, when the script ends.
16 The *$name* variable in package *birthday* is assigned.
17 *$name* is *Beatrice* in package *birthday*.
18 In order to access variables from the previous packages, the package name and a double colon must precede the variable.

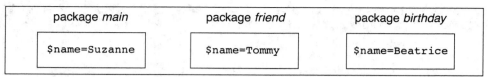

Figure 11.3   Packages create separate namespaces, as shown in Example 11.3.

11.2 The Standard Perl Library

The Perl distribution comes with a number of standard Perl library functions and packages. The Perl 4 library routines are procedural programs and their names end in a *.pl* extension. The Perl 5 modules end with a *.pm* extension. In Perl 5, the *.pm* files are called **modules**. The *.pm* files are modules written in two programming styles: procedural and object-oriented. The module filenames start with a capital letter. The *.pm* filenames starting with a lowercase letter are a special type of module, called a pragma. A **pragma** is a module that tells the compiler that certain conditions must be checked in a Perl program before it can run. Files that have no extension at all are subdirectories. They contain common modules that are divided into several *.pm* files; for example, the *Math* subdirectory contains *Big-Float.pm*, *BigInt.pm*, *Complex.pm*, and *Trig.pm*.

Here is a sample listing from the standard Perl 5 library:[2]

AnyDBM_File.pm	*Exporter.pm*	*Sys*	*complete.pl*	*open3.pl*
AutoLoader.pm	*ExtUtils*	*Term*	*constant.pm*	*ops.pm*
AutoSplit.pm	*Fatal.pm*	*Test*	*ctime.pl*	*overload.pm*
B	*Fcntl.pm*	*Test.pm*	*diagnostics.pm*	*perl5db.pl*
B.pm	*File*	*Text*	*dotsh.pl*	*perllocal.pod*
Benchmark.pm	*FileCache.pm*	*Thread*	*dumpvar.pl*	*ppm.pm*
ByteLoader.pm	*FileHandle.pm*	*Thread.pm*	*exceptions.pl*	*pwd.pl*
CGI	*FindBin.pm*	*Tie*	*fastcwd.pl*	*re.pm*
CGI.pm	*Getopt*	*Time*	*fields.pm*	*shellwords.pl*
CORE	*I18N*	*UNIVERSAL.pm*	*filetest.pm*	*sigtrap.pm*
CPAN	*IO*	*User*	*find.pl*	*stat.pl*
CPAN.pm	*IO.pm*	*XSLoader.pm*	*finddepth.pl*	*strict.pm*
Carp	*IPC*	*abbrev.pl*	*flush.pl*	*subs.pm*
Carp.pm	*Math*	*assert.pl*	*ftp.pl*	*syslog.pl*
Class	*Net*	*attributes.pm*	*getcwd.pl*	*tainted.pl*
Config.pm	*O.pm*	*attrs.pm*	*getopt.pl*	*termcap.pl*
Config.pm~	*Opcode.pm*	*auto*	*getopts.pl*	*timelocal.pl*
Cwd.pm	*POSIX.pm*	*autouse.pm*	*hostname.pl*	*unicode*
DB.pm	*POSIX.pod*	*base.pm*	*importenv.pl*	*utf8.pm*
Data	*Pod*	*bigfloat.pl*	*integer.pm*	*utf8_heavy.pl*
Devel	*SDBM_File.pm*	*bigint.pl*	*less.pm*	*validate.pl*
DirHandle.pm	*Safe.pm*	*bigrat.pl*	*lib.pm*	*vars.pm*
Dumpvalue.pm	*Search*	*blib.pm*	*locale.pm*	*warnings*
DynaLoader.pm	*SelectSaver.pm*	*bytes.pm*	*look.pl*	*warnings.pm*
English.pm	*SelfLoader.pm*	*bytes_heavy.pl*	*network.pl*	
Env.pm	*Shell.pm*	*cacheout.pl*	*newgetopt.pl*	
Errno.pm	*Socket.pm*	*charnames.pm*	*open.pm*	
Exporter	*Symbol.pm*	*chat2.pl*	*open2.pl*	

---

2. The pathname to the standard Perl library is determined at the time Perl is installed. This can be assigned either a default value or a pathname designated by the person installing Perl.

11.2.1   The *@INC* Array

The special array *@INC* contains the directory path to where the library routines are
located. To include directories not in the *@INC* array, you can use the *-I* switch[3] at the command line, or set the *PERL5LIB* environment variable to the full pathname. Normally, this
variable is set in one of your shell initialization files, either *.login* or *.profile* if using UNIX.
See Figure 11.4 if using Windows.

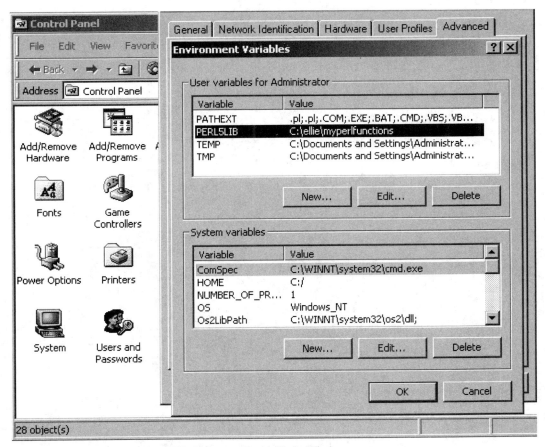

Figure 11.4   Setting the *PERL5LIB* environment variable in Windows.

---

3. See Table A.18 in Appendix A for a description of the *-I* switch.

EXAMPLE 11.4

```
1  $ perl -V  (UNIX command line)
   Summary of my perl5 (5.0 patchlevel 5 subversion 2)
   configuration:
 Platform:
   osname=solaris, osvers=2.6, archname=sun4-solaris
   uname='sunos 5.6 generic_105181-06 sun4u sparc sunw,ultra-1 '
   hint=recommended, useposix=true, d_sigaction=define
   usethreads=undef useperlio=undef d_sfio=undef
 Compiler:
   cc='gcc', optimize='-O', gccversion=2.8.1
   cppflags='-I/usr/local/include'
   ccflags ='-I/usr/local/include'
   stdchar='unsigned char', d_stdstdio=define, usevfork=false
   intsize=4, longsize=4, ptrsize=4, doublesize=8
   d_longlong=define, longlongsize=8, d_longdbl=define,
       longdblsize=16 alignbytes=8, usemymalloc=y,
       prototype=define
 Linker and Libraries:
   ld='gcc', ldflags =' -L/usr/local/lib'
   libpth=/usr/local/lib /lib /usr/lib /usr/ccs/lib
   libs=-lsocket -lnsl -ldb -ldl -lm -lc -lcrypt
   libc=/lib/libc.so, so=so, useshrplib=false, libperl=libperl.a
 Dynamic Linking:
   dlsrc=dl_dlopen.xs, dlext=so, d_dlsymun=undef, ccdlflags=' '
   cccdlflags='-fPIC', lddlflags='-G -L/usr/local/lib'
 Characteristics of this binary (from libperl):
   Built under solaris
   Compiled at Jan  2 1999 04:29:40
 @INC:

2  /usr/local/lib/perl5/5.00502/sun4-solaris
   /usr/local/lib/perl5/5.00502
   /usr/local/lib/perl5/site_perl/5.005/sun4-solaris
   /usr/local/lib/perl5/site_perl/5.005

3  $ perl -e 'print "@INC\n"'     (UNIX)
   /usr/local/lib/perl5/5.00502/sun4-solaris
   /usr/local/lib/perl5/5.00502
   /usr/local/lib/perl5/site_perl/5.005/sun4-solaris
   /usr/local/lib/perl5/site_perl/5.005
```

EXPLANATION

1   Perl with the -V option displays version, configuration, and library information.
2   The @INC array contains the directories where the Solaris (UNIX) libraries are located. Those pathnames with the word *site* or *solaris* are for Solaris-specific library routines and modules. */usr/local/lib/Perl5/5.00502* is where the standard Perl library resides. The pathnames containing the word *site* are site-specific and contain library routines that have been downloaded for this particular site or architecture. Some of the site-specific routines come with the standard distribution.
3   The values in the @INC array contain a list of all the directories that Perl will search when looking for library routines.

EXAMPLE 11.5

```
1   $ perl -V (Windows)
    Summary of my perl5 (revision 5 version 6 subversion 0)
    configuration:
Platform:
    osname=MSWin32, osvers=4.0,
        archname=MSWin32-x86-multi-thread
    uname=''
    config_args='undef'
    hint=recommended, useposix=true, d_sigaction=undef
usethreads=undef use5005threads=undef useithreads=define
    usemultiplicity=define
    useperlio=undef d_sfio=undef uselargefiles=undef
    use64bitint=undef use64bitall=undef uselongdouble=undef
    usesocks=undef
Compiler:
    cc='cl.exe', optimize='-O1 -MD -DNDEBUG', gccversion=
    cppflags='-DWIN32'
    ccflags='-O1 -MD -DNDEBUG -DWIN32 -D_CONSOLE -DNO_STRICT
        -DHAVE_DES_FCRYPT -DPERL_IMPLICIT_CONTEXT
        -DPERL_IMPLICIT_SYS -DPERL_MSVCRT_READFIX'
    stdchar='char', d_stdstdio=define, usevfork=false
    intsize=4, longsize=4, ptrsize=4, doublesize=8
    d_longlong=undef, longlongsize=8, d_longdbl=define,
        longdblsize=10
    ivtype='long', ivsize=4, nvtype='double', nvsize=8,
        Off_t='off_t', lseeksize=4
    alignbytes=8, usemymalloc=n, prototype=define
```

EXAMPLE 11.5 (CONTINUED)

```
Linker and Libraries:
  ld='link', ldflags ='-nologo -nodefaultlib -release -machine:x86'
  libpth="c:\Perl\lib\core"
libs=oldnames.lib kernel32.lib user32.lib gdi32.lib winspool.lib
      comdlg32.lib advapi32.lib shell32.lib ole32.lib
      oleaut32.lib  netapi32.lib uuid.lib wsock32.lib mpr.lib
      winmm.lib  version.lib odbc32.lib odbccp32.lib msvcrt.lib
  libc=c:\Perl\lib\core\PerlCRT.lib, so=dll, useshrplib=yes,
  libperl=perl56.lib
Dynamic Linking:
  dlsrc=dl_win32.xs, dlext=dll, d_dlsymun=undef, ccdlflags=' '
  cccdlflags=' ', lddlflags='-dll -nologo -nodefaultlib
      -release -machine:x86'
Characteristics of this binary (from libperl):
  Compile-time options: MULTIPLICITY USE_ITHREADS
      PERL_IMPLICIT_CONTEXT PERL_IMPLICIT_SYS
Locally applied patches:
  ActivePerl Build 613
Built under MSWin32
Compiled at Mar 24 2000 12:36:25
@INC:
  c:/Perl/lib
  c:/Perl/site/lib
  .

2  C: \>  perl -e "print @INC"   (Windows)
   C:/Perl/libC:/Perl/site/lib.
```

EXPLANATION

1 Perl with the -V option displays version, configuration, and library information.
2 At the Windows command line prompt, the @INC array is printed. The first element in the colon-separated path is *libC*, the standard Perl library, and the second element is */Perl/site/lib* where Windows-specific library functions are stored.

Setting the *PERL5LIB* Environment Variable.   If you are using UNIX/Linux operating systems, to add new path elements to the @INC array, the *PERL5LIB* environment variable can be set in your startup initialization files.

In *.login* for the *C* and *TC* shells:
```
setenv PERL5LIB "directory path"
```

In *.profile* for the *Bourne*, *Korn*, and *Bash* shells:
```
PERL5LIB="directory path"; export PERL5LIB
```

If you are using Windows, go to the *Start* menu, then to *Settings*, then *System Properties*, then *Environment Variables*, and finally *New*. Refer back to Figure 11.4.

To give your own library routines precedence over those in listed in the *@INC* array, you can put the following line in your program:

```
unshift(@INC,".");
```

Unshift causes the . to be prepended to the *@INC* array, making your present working directory the first element in the search path. If your library is in a different directory, use its full pathname, rather than the dot.

11.2.2   Packages and *.pl* Files

Most of the library routines found in the standard Perl library ending in *.pl* were written in the days of Perl 4. They consisted of subroutines contained within a package. The library files are still available and widely used.

The *require* Function.   In order to include and execute routines from the standard Perl library[4] or Perl code from any other file, the *require* function is used, which is similar to the C *#include* statement. The *require* function checks to see if the library has already been included, unlike the *eval* and the *do* functions, which are older methods for including files. Without an argument, the value of *$_* is included. If the *@INC* array does not have the correct path to the library, the *require* will fail with a message like the following:

Can't locate pwd.pl in @INC at package line 3.

The *require* function loads files into the program during runtime. The *@INC* array is also updated at runtime.

FORMAT

```
require (Expr)
require Expr
require
```

Including Standard Library Routines.   To see an example of a library routine in Perl's library, the *pwd.pl* routine (written by Larry Wall) is shown in Example 11.6. The *pwd* package consists of two subroutines that update the *PWD* environment variable after the *chdir* function has been executed. The value of *$ENV{PWD}* is the present working directory.

---

4. To include UNIX system calls from the standard C library, see "The syscall Function and the h2ph Script" on page 563.

Notice that in the following Perl library function, the package *pwd* is declared before the subroutines are defined, thus placing the rest of the file within the *pwd* package. All variables belong to the package. The **names** of the subroutines are explicitly switched to package *main*. They may be called from your *main* package, but the variables remain local to the *pwd* package. (The apostrophe is used here instead of the two colons to switch namespaces. The apostrophe is the Perl 4 symbol for switching namespaces.)

The following example is a sample *.pl* routine from Perl's standard library.

EXAMPLE 11.6

```
  (The pwd package)
     #
1  # Usage:
2  #    require "pwd.pl";
   #    &initpwd;
   #    ...
   #    &chdir($newdir);
3  package pwd;
4  sub main'initpwd {
       if ($ENV{'PWD'}) {
       local($dd,$di) = stat('.');
       local($pd,$pi) = stat($ENV{'PWD'});
       return if $di == $pi && $dd == $pd;
   }
   chop($ENV{'PWD'} = 'pwd');
   }
5  sub main'chdir {
       local($newdir) = shift;
       if (chdir $newdir) {
           if ($newdir =~ m#^/#) {
               $ENV{'PWD'} = $newdir;
           }
           else {
               local(@curdir) = split(m#/#,$ENV{'PWD'});
               @curdir = '' unless @curdir;
               foreach $component (split(m#/#, $newdir)) {
                   next if $component eq '.';
                   pop(@curdir),next if $component eq '..';
               }
               $ENV{'PWD'} = join('/',@curdir) || '/';
           }
       }
       else {
           0;
       }              # Return value
   }

6  1;      <--- Looky here!
```

EXPLANATION

1   The usage message tells you how you're supposed to use this package.
2   In the usage message, you are being told to be sure to require the file, *pwd.pl*. The two subroutines that will be called are *initpwd* and *chdir*. The *chdir* function requires an argument, which is a directory name.
3   The package *pwd* is declared. This is the only package in the file.
4   The subroutine *initpwd* is defined. Notice that its name is qualified as a symbol for the *main* package. This means that when you call *initpwd* from your *main* package, you won't have to mention the package *pwd* at all.
5   The *chdir* subroutine is defined.
6   The *1* is required at the end of this package for the *require* function. If the last expression evaluated in this file is not true, the *require* function will not load the file into your program.

The following example uses a library routine in the script.

EXAMPLE 11.7

```
(The Script)
    #!/bin/perl
1   require "ctime.pl";
2   require "pwd.pl";
3   &initpid;              # Call the subroutine
4   printf "The present working directory is %s\n", $ENV{PWD};
5   &chdir "../..";
6   printf "The present working directory is %s\n", $ENV{PWD};
7   $today=&ctime(time);
8   print "$today";

(Output)
4   The present working directory is /home/jody/ellie/perl
6   The present working directory is /home/jody
8   Wed  Mar 14 11:51:59 2001
```

EXPLANATION

1   The *ctime.pl* Perl standard library function is included here.
2   The *pwd.pl* Perl standard library function is included.
3   The *initpid* subroutine is called for the *pwd.pl* function. It initializes the value of *PWD*.
4   The present value of the environment variable *PWD* is printed.
5   A call to *chdir* changes the present working directory.
6   The present updated value of the environment variable *PWD* is printed.
7   Today's date is set in a human readable format by the subroutine *ctime*, from *ctime.pl*.
8   Today's date is printed in its new format.

Using Perl to Include Your Own Library.   The following example shows you how to create your own library functions and include them into a Perl script with the *require* function. When including user-defined routines or adding routines to a library, make sure to include *1;* (a non-zero value) as the last line of the routine.

EXAMPLE 11.8

```
(The midterms Script)
    #!/bin/perl
    # Program name: midterms
    # This program will call a subroutine from another file
1   unshift(@INC, "/home/jody/ellie/perl/mylib");
2   require "average.pl";
    print "Enter your midterm scores.\n";
    @scores=split(' ', <STDIN>);
3   printf "The average is %.1f.\n", $average=&ave(@scores);
    # The ave subroutine is found in a file called average.pl
-------------------------------------------------------------
4   $ cd mylib            # Directory where library is located
-------------------------------------------------------------

(The Script)
5   $ cat average.pl    # File where subroutine is defined
    # Average a list of grades
6   sub ave {
7       my(@grades)=@_;
        my($num_of_grades)=$#grades + 1;
        foreach $grade ( @grades ){
            $total=$total + $grade;
        }
8       $total/$num_of_grades;   # What gets returned
    }
9   1; # Make sure the file returns true or require will not succeed!
```

EXPLANATION

1   The *unshift* function prepends the *@INC* array with the pathname to your custom library, *mylib*.
2   The *require* function first checks the *@INC* array to get a listing of all directories in which it will search for the *.pl* file. The *require* function includes the Perl function *average.pl*.
3   The *ave* function is called and returns a value to be stored in the scalar *$average*.
4   We will change directories to *mylib* from the command line. The dollar sign is the shell prompt.
5   Now we look at the contents of the file *average.pl*.

EXPLANATION (CONTINUED)

6 The subroutine *ave* is defined.
7 It will accept a list of grades as parameters. The list is made local with the *my* function.
8 The expression is evaluated and returned.
9 This statement evaluates to true and is located at the end of the file. The *require* function needs a true return value in order to load this file when asked.

11.2.3 Modules and *.pm* Files

When using one of the modules (those files ending in *.pm*) provided in the standard Perl library, you must first make sure the *@INC* array contains the full pathname to your library distribution and that you include the *use* function with the module name.

If you are trying to find out how a particular library module works, you can use the *perldoc* command to get the documentation. (The *perldoc* command does not work for *.pl* files from the library.) For example, if you want to know about the *CGI.pm* module, type at the command line

```
perldoc CGI
```

and the documentation for the *CGI.pm* module will be displayed. If you type

```
perldoc English
```

the documentation for the *English.pm* module will be displayed.

The *use* Function (Modules and Pragmas). The *use* function allows Perl modules and pragmas to be imported into your program at **compile** time. The *use* function will not import a module if the module's filename does not have the *.pm* extension. The *require* function does the same thing, but does not do imports, and loads the module at **runtime**.

A **module** is a file in a library that behaves according to certain set of conventions. The modules in the standard Perl library are suffixed with the *.pm* extension. They can also be found in subdirectories. For example, the module *Bigfloat.pm* is found in a subdirectory called *Math*. To use a module found in a subdirectory, the directory name is followed by two colons and the name of the module, such as *Math::Bigfloat.pm*.

A **pragma**, spelled in lowercase letters, is a warning to the compiler that your program should behave in a certain way and, if it doesn't, the program will abort. Some common pragmas are *lib, strict, subs*, and *diagnostics*. For a list of modules and pragmas, see Tables A.3 and A.4 in Appendix A.

In object-oriented terminology, subroutines are called **methods**. If you receive diagnostics using the term *method*, for now just think of methods as glorified subroutines. Many of the modules in the library use object-oriented Perl. The modules discussed in this chapter do not require any understanding of objects. For a complete discussion on how to use the object-oriented modules, see Chapter 13, "Bless Those Things! (Object-Oriented Perl)".

FORMAT

```
use Module;
use Module ( list );
use Directory::Module;
use pragma (list);
no pragma;
```

The _Exporter_ Module.   In the export/import business, someone exports his goods and the someone who imports them is waiting on the other side. Let's say a wine maker in California has four great-tasting wines in his cellar, and he decides to export three of the wines to buyers, but keep the best one for himself. So he creates an export list and tacks it to the wall of his cellar and, when the buyer comes, the buyer selects only those wines on the export list. The buyer is the importer. There's nothing preventing the importer from taking all four of the wines, but if he follows the guidelines of the export list, he will take only those listed.

When you use a Perl module, you are like the buyer. You import symbols (subroutines and variables) from the export list, provided by the module. You can take what's on the list by default, or you can ask for specific symbols from the list, or you can even exclude some or all of the symbols on the list. The business of exporting and importing is really just a way of getting symbols into the namespace of your program package so that you don't have to fully qualify all the imported names with the module package name and two colons, such as _&Module::fun1_. What you import can be listed after the _use_ directive, such as _use Module qw(fun1 fun2);_

The _Exporter.pm_ module found in the standard Perl library supplies the necessary semantics for modules to be able to export symbols for variables or subroutines. The _Exporter.pm_ module is an object-oriented module that functions as a class. Other modules inherit from the _Exporter_ class the ability to export symbols. (See Chapter 13 for more on object-oriented programs.) Inherited classes must be listed in the _@ISA_ array.

```
require Exporter;
our @ISA=qw(Exporter);[5]
```

The names listed in the _@EXPORT_ array are by default switched into the namespace of the program using the module; the names on the _@EXPORT_OK_ array are added to the user's namespace only if requested. The _@EXPORT_FAIL_ array lists those symbols that cannot be exported. If the module is imported with _use_ and parentheses are added to the module name, as in _use Module()_, none of the symbols are exported to the module. Table 11.1 describes the exporting modules and the users of the modules.

---

5. Note that the _Exporter_ module is not enclosed in double quotes when used as an argument to _require_ and that _.pm_ is missing. This tells the compiler two things: if for example, the module is _Math::BigFloat_ that will be translated to _Math/BigFloat_, and if there are indirect method calls within the module, they will be treated as object-oriented method calls, not ordinary subroutine calls.

Table 11.1   Exporting Symbols

The Exporting Module	*What It Means*	
package Testmodule;	Package declaration.	
require Exporter;	Use the *Exporter.pm* module to export symbols from package to package.	
our @ISA = qw(Exporter);	@ISA contains the names of base classes needed to do the exporting.	
our @EXPORT = qw($x @y z);	Symbols in this list are automatically exported to the user of this module.	
our @EXPORT_OK = qw(fun b c);	Symbols in this list are exported only if requested by the user of this module.	
our @EXPORT_FAIL=qw(fun3 e);	These symbols are not to be exported.[a]	
our %EXPORT_TAGS= (group1 => [qw(a b c)], group2=> [qw($x @y %c)]);	The key *group1* represents the symbols *a*, *b*, and *c* (function names), collectively; *group2* represents the symbols *$x*, *@y*, and *%c*, collectively.	
The Importing Module	*What It Means*	
use Testmodule;	*Testmodule* is loaded.	
use Testmodule qw(fun2);	*Testmodule* is loaded; *fun2* is imported.	
use Testmodule();	*Testmodule* is loaded, no symbols imported.	
use Testmodule qw (:group1 !:group2);	*Testmodule* imports symbols from *group1* (See:*%EXPORT_TAGS* hash, above) but not symbols from *group2*.	
use Testmodule qw(:group1 !fun2);	*Testmodule* imports symbols from *group1* not the symbol *fun2*.	
use Testmodule qw(/^fu/);	*Testmodule* imports symbols whose names start with *fu*.	
SomeModule.pm	*User of the Module*	
package SomeModule.pm;	use *SomeModule*;	*# functions and variables automatically*
use Exporter;	&*a*;	*# imported from the @EXPORT array*
our @ISA = qw(Exporter);	&*b*;	
our @EXPORT=qw(a b c);	&*c*;	
sub a { }	&*SomeModule::d*;	*# d isn't on the @EXPORT list;*
sub b { }		*# its name must be fully defined*
sub c { }		
sub d { }		
1;		
package SomeModule.pm;	*use SomeModule qw(a c);*	*# must ask for symbols*
use Exporter;	&*a*;	*# or they won't be imported*
our @ISA = qw(Exporter);	&*c*;	
our @EXPORT_OK=qw(a b c);	&*SomeModule::c*;	*# must fully qualify names of symbols*
sub a { }	*SomeModule::d*;	*# not asked for from @EXPORT_OK list*
sub b { }		
sub c { }		
sub d { }		
1;		

a. Variables have the funny symbol preceding their name; subroutines don't have a funny symbol. *a*, *b*, and *c* refer to subroutines with those names.

Using a Perl 5 Module from the Standard Perl Library.   The following module, *English.pm*, provides aliases for built-in variables such as *$_* and *$/*. For any variables that are also part of the *awk* programming language, there are both long and short English names for the variable. For example, the number of the current record is represented and *$.* in Perl and NR in awk. The English names are either *$RS* (*awk*) or *$INPUT_RECORD_SEPARATOR* (Perl).

EXAMPLE 11.9

```
(The Script)
    #!/usr/bin/perl
1   use English;     # Use English words to replace
                     # special Perl variables
2   print "The pid is $PROCESS_ID.\n";
3   print "The pid is $PID.\n";
4   print "The real uid $REAL_USER_ID.\n";
5   print "This version of perl is $PERL_VERSION.\n";

(Output)
2   The pid is 948.
3   The pid is 948.
4   The real uid 9496.
5   5.6.0.
```

EXPLANATION

1   The *English.pm* module is loaded in at compile time with the *use* directive.
2   The process id number of this process is printed.
3   The *$PID* variable is the same as *$PROCESS.ID*.
4   The real user id for the user of this program is printed.
5   The version of Perl is 5.6.0.

The following example is a sample *.pm* file from Perl's standard library.

EXAMPLE 11.10

```
(A Module from the Standard Perl Library)ᵃ
1   package Carp;
    # This package implements handy routines
    # for modules that wish to throw
    # exceptions outside of the current package
2   require Exporter;
3   @ISA = Exporter;
4   @EXPORT = qw(confess croak carp);
5   sub longmess {
6       my $error = shift;
        my $mess = "";
        my $i = 2;
        my ($pack,$file,$line,$sub);
        while (($pack,$file,$line,$sub) = caller($i++)) {
            $mess .= "\t$sub " if $error eq "called";
            $mess .= "$error at $file line $line\n";
            $error = "called";
        }
    $mess || $error;
    }
    sub shortmess {
        my $error = shift;
        my ($curpack) = caller(1);
        my $i = 2;
        my ($pack,$file,$line,$sub);
        while (($pack,$file,$line,$sub) = caller($i++)) {
            return "$error at $file line $line\n"
                        if $pack ne $curpack;
        }
    longmess $error;
    }
7   sub confess { die longmess @_; }
8   sub croak { die shortmess @_; }
9   sub carp { warn shortmess @_; }
```

a. The *Carp.pm* module has been rewritten and is much larger with an additional function, called *cluck*, but this version is used because it is easier to see how the exporting of subroutines works.

EXPLANATION

1   This is the package declaration. The package is named after the file it resides in, *Carp.pm*. The functions *carp, croak,* and *confess* generate error messages such as *die* and *warn*. The difference is that with *carp* and *croak*, the error is reported at the line in the calling routine where the error was invoked, whereas *confess* prints out the stack backtrace showing the chain of subroutines that was involved in generating the error. It prints its message at the line where it was invoked.

2   The *Exporter* module is required so that subroutines and variables can be made available to other programs.

3   The *@ISA* array contains the names of packages this module will use. Perl implements inheritance by listing other modules this package will use in the *@ISA* array.

4   The *@EXPORT* array lists the subroutines from this module that will be exported by default to any program using this module. The subroutines *confess, croak,* and *carp* are now available to you if you want to use this module. Since *longmess* and *shortmess* are not on the list to be exported, you cannot directly use these subroutines.

5   This is a subroutine definition for this module.

6   The error message provided as an argument to *confess* is passed here and shifted into the *$error* scalar.

7   The definition for subroutine *confess* is to call *die* with the return value of *longmess*.

8   The definition for subroutine *croak* is to call *die* with the return value of *shortmess*.

9   The definition for subroutine *carp* is to call *warn* with the return value of *shortmess*.

EXAMPLE 11.11

```
(Using a Module from the Standard Perl Library in a Script)
    #!/bin/perl
1   use Carp qw(croak);

2   print "Give me a grade: ";
    $grade = <STDIN>;
3   try($grade);       # Call subroutine

4   sub try{
5       my($number)=@_;
6       croak "Illegal value: " if $number < 0 || $number > 100;
    }

(Output)
2   Give me a grade: 200
6   Illegal value:  at expire line 13
        main::try called at expire line 8
```

EXPLANATION

1   The *Carp* module is imported into the current package, *main*. Only the subroutine *croak* will be allowed in this program. Using either *confess* or *carp* will produce an error message.

2   The user is asked for input.

3   The subroutine *try* is called and passed the scalar $*grade*.

4   The *if* subroutine *try* is defined.

5   The argument passed in is assigned to $*number*.

6   The *croak* function is called with an error message. The program will die if the value of $*number* is not in the range between *0* and *100*. The error message reports the line where the program died as well as the name of the package, subroutine name, and the number of the line where the subroutine was invoked.

Using Perl to Create Your Own Module.   The following example illustrates how to create a module in a separate *.pm* file and use the module in another program. Although this module itself looks like any other package, it must additionally include the *Exporter* module, the *@ISA* array, and the *@EXPORT* array in order for it to really behave as a module. The ability to export specific symbols to other programs and to import other modules is what differentiates a module from a *.pl* file. To see a skeletal module for creating modules for CPAN, see "Creating Extensions and Modules for CPAN with the h2xs Tool" on page 350.

EXAMPLE 11.12

```
(The Me.pm Module)
1    package Me;
2    use strict;  use warnings;
3    require 5.6;        # Make sure we're a version of Perl no
                         # older than 5.6
4    require Exporter;   # Exporter.pm allows routines to be imported
                         # by others
5    our @ISA=qw(Exporter); # ISA is a list of packages needed
                            # by this package
6    our @EXPORT_OK=qw(hello goodbye );  # List of your subroutines
                                         # to export

7    sub hello {my($name)=shift;
         print "Hi there, $name.\n"; }
8    sub goodbye {my($name)=shift;
         print "Good-bye $name.\n";}
9    sub do_nothing {print "Didn't print anything.
                          Not in EXPORT list\n";}

     1;
```

EXAMPLE 11.12 (CONTINUED)

```
#!/usr/bin/perl
# Program name: main.perl
10  use lib ("/home/ellie/Module");    # A pragma to update @INC.
11  use Me  qw(hello goodbye);         # Import package
12  &hello (Daniel);
13  &goodbye (Steve);
14  &do_nothing;          # This was not on the Export list
                          # in Me.pm so cannot be imported unless
                          # explicitly with &Me::do_nothing
(Output)
12  Hi there, Daniel.
13  Good-bye Steve.
14  Undefined subroutine &main::do_nothing
```

EXPLANATION

1 The file is called *Me.pm*. It contains a package of the same name without the extension. The *Me* package is declared.

2 The *strict* pragma bars global variables and the *warnings* pragma issues the appropriate warnings.

3 The *require* is used to make sure that the Perl version being used is not less than 5.003. If it is, the script will abort.

4 The *Exporter* module is a special Perl module that allows the *use* function to import subroutines called **methods** from a particular module.

5 The *@ISA* array lists any packages containing subroutines (methods) that will be used by this package. This is how Perl implements inheritance from one module to another. (See Chapter 13, "Bless Those Things! (Object-Oriented Perl)".)

6 The *@EXPORT* array lists all subroutines (methods) that can be exported by default. The *@EXPORT_OK* array lists subroutines (methods) that can be exported if the user of the module requests them in his *use* statement. If he doesn't ask, he won't get them. Those subroutines on the export list are *hello* and *goodbye,* defined below.

7 The subroutine *hello* is defined.

8 The subroutine *goodbye* is defined.

9 The subroutine *do_nothing* is defined. Note: this subroutine is not on the export list; that is, it is not in the *@EXPORT_OK* arrray.

10 The *lib* pragma tells the compiler to update the *@INC* array at compile time. It is the same as saying: *BEGIN{ require "/home/ellie/Module"; import Module;}*

11 The *use* function causes Perl to include the *Me.pm* module into this package.

12 The subroutine *hello* is called with an argument. This subroutine was imported.

13 The subroutine *goodbye* is called with an argument. It was also imported.

14 This subroutine was not imported. It was not on the export list (*@EXPORT*) in *Me.pm*. An error message is printed indicating that package main does not recognize this subroutine. If the explicit package name, *&Me::goodbye,* is given, the subroutine can be imported.

11.2.4 Modules from CPAN

CPAN (the Comprehensive Perl Archive Network) is the central repository for a collection of hundreds of Perl modules. To find the CPAN mirror closest to you, go to *http://www.perl.com/CPAN*.

Perl modules that depend upon each other are bundled together by name, author, and category. These modules can be found under the CPAN *modules* directory or by using the CPAN search engine under *http://search.cpan.org*. If you need to install these modules, the CPAN documentation gives you easy-to-follow instructions. The Web pages shown below display how the information is catalogued and a gives partial list of the modules.

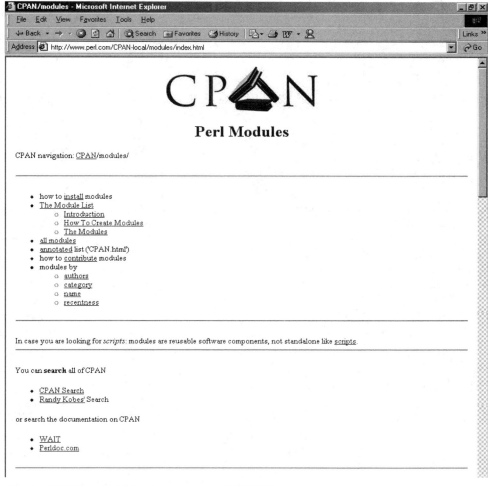

Figure 11.5 The Perl Modules page at the CPAN Web site.

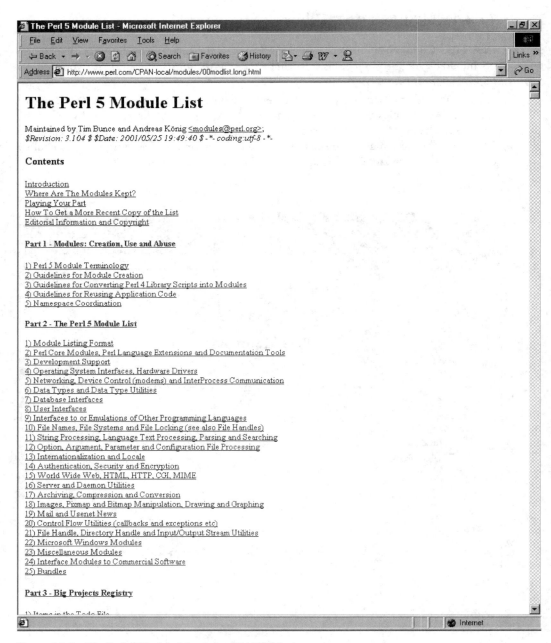

The Perl 5 Module List - Microsoft Internet Explorer

File   Edit   View   Favorites   Tools   Help

⇐ Back ▾ ⇒ ▾ ⊗ ⬚ ⬚ | ⬚ Search ⬚ Favorites ⬚ History | ⬚▾ ⬚ ⬚ ▾ ⬚   Links »

Address ⬚ http://www.perl.com/CPAN-local/modules/00modlist.long.html   ⬚ ⬚ Go

The Perl 5 Module List

Maintained by Tim Bunce and Andreas König <modules@perl.org>;
*$Revision: 3.104 $ $Date: 2001/05/25 19:49:40 $ - *- coding:utf-8 - *-*

Contents

Introduction
Where Are The Modules Kept?
Playing Your Part
How To Get a More Recent Copy of the List
Editorial Information and Copyright

Part 1 - Modules: Creation, Use and Abuse

1) Perl 5 Module Terminology
2) Guidelines for Module Creation
3) Guidelines for Converting Perl 4 Library Scripts into Modules
4) Guidelines for Reusing Application Code
5) Namespace Coordination

Part 2 - The Perl 5 Module List

1) Module Listing Format
2) Perl Core Modules, Perl Language Extensions and Documentation Tools
3) Development Support
4) Operating System Interfaces, Hardware Drivers
5) Networking, Device Control (modems) and InterProcess Communication
6) Data Types and Data Type Utilities
7) Database Interfaces
8) User Interfaces
9) Interfaces to or Emulations of Other Programming Languages
10) File Names, File Systems and File Locking (see also File Handles)
11) String Processing, Language Text Processing, Parsing and Searching
12) Option, Argument, Parameter and Configuration File Processing
13) Internationalization and Locale
14) Authentication, Security and Encryption
15) World Wide Web, HTML, HTTP, CGI, MIME
16) Server and Daemon Utilities
17) Archiving, Compression and Conversion
18) Images, Pixmap and Bitmap Manipulation, Drawing and Graphing
19) Mail and Usenet News
20) Control Flow Utilities (callbacks and exceptions etc)
21) File Handle, Directory Handle and Input/Output Stream Utilities
22) Microsoft Windows Modules
23) Miscellaneous Modules
24) Interface Modules to Commercial Software
25) Bundles

Part 3 - Big Projects Registry

1) Items in the Todo File

⬚   ⬚ Internet

Figure 11.6   The Perl 5 Module List at the CPAN Web site.

ActivePerl, available for the Linux, Solaris, and Windows operating systems, contains
Perl, the Perl Package Manager (for installing packages of CPAN modules), and complete
online help. PPM allows you to access package repositories and install new packages or
update old ones you already have with relative ease.

Go to *www.activestate.com/ppmpackages/5.6* to access the ActiveState Package repository.

The *Cpan.pm* Module.   The *Cpan.pm* module allows you to query, download, and build
Perl modules from CPAN sites. It runs in both interactive and batch mode and is designed
to automate the installation of Perl modules and extensions. The modules are fetched from
one or more of the mirrored CPAN sites and unpacked in a dedicated directory. To learn
more about this module, at your system command line, type

```
$ perldoc Cpan
```

to read the following:

```
NAME
    CPAN - query, download and build perl modules from CPAN sites

SYNOPSIS
  Interactive mode:

    perl -MCPAN -e shell;

  Batch mode:

    use CPAN;

    autobundle, clean, install, make, recompile, test

DESCRIPTION
    The CPAN module is designed to automate the make and install of perl
    modules and extensions. It includes some searching capabilities and
    knows how to use Net::FTP or LWP (or lynx or an external ftp client)
    to fetch the raw data from the net.

    Modules are fetched from one or more of the mirrored CPAN
    (Comprehensive Perl Archive Network) sites and unpacked in a
    dedicated directory.

    The CPAN module also supports the concept of named and versioned
    *bundles* of modules. Bundles simplify the handling of sets of related
    modules. See Bundles below.

    The package contains a session manager and a cache manager. There is no
    status retained between sessions. The session manager keeps track of
    what has been fetched, built and installed in the current session. The
    cache manager keeps track of the disk space occupied by the make
    processes and deletes excess space according to a simple FIFO
    mechanism.
```

> *For extended searching capabilities there's a plugin for CPAN*
> *available, the CPAN::WAIT manpage. 'CPAN::WAIT' is a full-text search*
> *engine that indexes all documents available in CPAN authors*
> *directories. If 'CPAN::WAIT' is installed on your system, the*
> *interactive shell of <CPAN.pm> will enable the 'wq', 'wr', 'wd', 'wl',*
> *and 'wh' commands which send queries to the WAIT server that has been*
> *configured for your installation.*

<continues>

Creating Extensions and Modules for CPAN with the *h2xs* Tool.   The *h2xs* tool is a standard application that comes with the regular Perl distribution. It creates a directory and a set of skeleton files to use when creating a module or adding *C* language extensions. To get a full description, type at your system prompt

```
$ perldoc h2xs
```

EXAMPLE 11.13

```
1   $ h2xs -A -n Exten.dir
    Writing Exten.dir/Exten.dir.pm
    Writing Exten.dir/Exten.dir.xs
    Writing Exten.dir/Makefile.PL
    Writing Exten.dir/test.pl
    Writing Exten.dir/Changes
    Writing Exten.dir/MANIFEST


2   $ cd Exten.dir

3   $ ls

4   $ more Exten.dir.pm
    package Exten.dir;

    require 5.005_62;
    use strict;
    use warnings;

    require Exporter;
    require DynaLoader;

    our @ISA = qw(Exporter DynaLoader);

    # Items to export into caller's namespace by default.
    # Note: do not export names by default without
    # a very good reason. Use EXPORT_OK instead.
    # Do not simply export all your public
    # functions/methods/constants.

    # This allows declaration use Exten.dir ':all';
    # If you do not need this, moving things directly
    # into @EXPORT or @EXPORT_OK will save memory.
```

EXAMPLE 11.13 (CONTINUED)

```
our %EXPORT_TAGS = ( 'all' => [ qw() ] );

our @EXPORT_OK = ( @{ $EXPORT_TAGS{'all'} } );

our @EXPORT = qw();
our $VERSION = '0.01';

bootstrap Exten.dir $VERSION;

# Preloaded methods go here.

1;
__END__
# Below is stub documentation for your module. You'd better edit
it!

=head1 NAME

Exten.dir - Perl extension for blah blah blah

=head1 SYNOPSIS

use Exten.dir;
blah blah blah

=head1 DESCRIPTION

Stub documentation for Exten.dir, created by h2xs. It looks like
the author of the extension was negligent enough to leave the
stub unedited.

Blah blah blah.

=head2 EXPORT

None by default.

=head1 AUTHOR

A. U. Thor, a.u.thor@a.galaxy.far.far.away

=head1 SEE ALSO

perl(1).

=cut
```

EXPLANATION

1   The *h2xs* tool creates a subdirectory (this one is called *Exten.dir*) consisting of six files that will be used in the creation of a CPAN-style module. Before creating a module for CPAN, you should go to *www.cpan.org/modules/00modlist.long.html* to make sure someone else hasn't already written it, which could save you some work.

2   We change into the new directory created by *h2xs*.

3   This is a listing of the files created by *h2xs* (not shown). The *MANIFEST* file contains a list of all files just created in this directory, and where any additional files should be listed that will be distributed with the module. The *Makefile.PL* file generates a *Makefile*. *Exten.dir.pm* is the skeletal module which will contain extensions, and *Exten.dir.xs* will contain the *XSUB* routines for loading *C* extensions.

4   This is the skeleton module used to help set up the module correctly.

EXERCISE 10
I Hid All My Perls in a Package

1. Write a script called *myATM*.

2. In the *myATM* script, declare a package called *Checking*.
   It will contain a global *my* variable called *balance* set to *0*.
   It will contain four subroutines:
   a. *get_balance*
   b. *set_balance*
   c. *deposit*
   d. *withdraw*

3. In package *main* (in the same file), create a *here document* that will produce the following output:

   1) Deposit
   2) Withdraw
   3) Current Balance
   4) Exit

   Ask the user to select one of the menu items. Until he selects number *4*, the program will go into a loop to redisplay the menu and wait for the user to select another transaction.

   The subroutines will be called in the *main* package without qualifying the *Checking* package name with double colons.

If the user chooses number *4*, before the program exits, print today's date and the current balance to a file called *register*.

Could you print the value of the balance without calling the *get_balance* subroutine?

4. Rewrite the *Checking* package so that it gets the balance from the file *register* if the file exists; otherwise it will start at a zero balance. Each time the program exits, save the current balance and the time and date in the *register* file.

EXERCISE 11
Pack It up and Take It to the Library

1a. In Exercise 8 of Chapter 10, you wrote a program called *tripper* that contained a subroutine called *mileage*. It asked the user the number of miles he drove and the amount of gas he used. The subroutine was to calculate and return the user's mileage (miles per gallon). The arguments passed to the subroutine are the number of miles driven and the amount of gas used. These values are assigned to *my* variables. If you haven't written the *tripper* program, now is a good time to do so.

b. If the input is a non-number, a negative number, or zero for the amount of gas, use the *croak* function to print the error message.

Now create a directory called *myfunctions*. Change to that directory and create a file called *mileage.pl*. Put the subroutine *mileage* in the file *mileage.pl*.

c. In your *tripper* script, update the *@INC* array and use the *require* function to include the *mileage* subroutine. (Be sure that the last line after the closing curly brace of the subroutine is *1*.)

2. Move the *Checking* package from the *myATM* script (Exercise 10 above) into a file called *Checking.pm*. Use the *Checking* package in the *myATM* script.

12

DOES THIS JOB
REQUIRE A REFERENCE?

12.1 What Is a Reference?

12.1.1 Symbolic versus Hard References

Definition. A **reference** is a variable that **refers** to another one. A **symbolic reference** is a variable that **names** another variable. A **typeglob** is a type of symbolic reference, just another name or alias for a variable. (Typeglobs were discussed in Chapter 10, "How Do Subroutines Function?".) A **hard reference** is a scalar variable that holds the address of another type of data. It is similar to a **pointer** found in *C* and *Pascal*. In fact, the terms reference and pointer are interchangeable in Perl. This chapter will focus on hard references.

A Perl variable resides in a symbol table and holds **only one** hard reference to its underlying value. Its value may be as simple as a single number, or as complex as a hash. There may be other hard references that point to the same value, but the variable that actually holds the value is unaware of them. A symbolic reference, on the other hand, actually names another variable, rather than just pointing to a value.[1]

---

1. Wall, L., *Programming Perl*, O'Reilly & Associates: Sebastopol, CA, 1996, p. 244.

EXAMPLE 12.1

```
        #!/bin/perl
        # Program using symbolic references
        # use strict "refs";

1       $language="English";                # Hard reference
2       $english="Brooklyn";
3       print "Your native tongue is $language. \n";

4       print "But you speak with a ${$language} accent.\n";
                                            # Symbolic reference
        print "-------------------------\n";

5       print qq/What's wrong with a $english accent.\n/;

6       eval "\$$language=British ;";   # Symbolic reference

7       print "Why don't you try a $english accent? \n";

(Output)
3       Your native tongue is English.
4       But you speak with a Brooklyn accent.
        -------------------------
5       What's wrong with a  Brooklyn accent.
7       Why don't you try a British accent?
```

EXPLANATION

1   The scalar *$language* is assigned the value string *English*. The name *language* is stored in the symbol table along with a hard reference to its value *English*.

2   The scalar *$english* is assigned the string *Brooklyn*.

3   The value of *$language* is printed.

4   The variable *${$language}* is evaluated to *Brooklyn*. This is a symbolic reference. *$language*, one variable, is evaluated to *English*. The second dollar sign causes another variable, *$english*, to be evaluated to its underlying value *Brooklyn*. One variable has referenced another.

5   The value of the *$english* scalar is printed.

6   The *eval* function evaluates the statement as if in a separate little Perl program. The first dollar sign is escaped. *$language* will be evaluated to its value, *English*. The literal dollar sign, prepended to the result of the evaluation, leaves *$english=British* as the statement.

7   After the *eval*, the value of *$english* is *British*. It is printed.

The *strict* **Pragma.**   To protect yourself from inadvertently using symbolic references in a program, use the *strict* pragma with the *refs* argument. This causes Perl to check that symbolic references are **not** used in the program. Here, we re-execute the previous example using the *strict* pragma.

EXAMPLE 12.2

```
      #!/bin/perl
      # Program using symbolic references
1     use strict "refs";

      $language = "English";          # Hard reference
      $english = "Brooklyn";

2     print "Your native tongue is $language. \n";

3     print "But you speak with a ${$language} accent.\n";
                                    # Symbolic reference
      print "------------------------\n";

      print qq/What's wrong with a  $english accent.\n/;

4     eval "\$$language = British ;";  # Symbolic reference

      print "Why don't you try an $english accent? \n";
```

(Output)
2   *Your native tongue is English.*
3   *Can't use string ("English") as a SCALAR ref while "strict refs"*
     in use at symfile line 10

EXPLANATION

1   The *strict* pragma ensures that the program uses only hard references and, if it doesn't, will abort during compilation and print an error message as shown in the output of this script.
3   This is line number 10 in the script. The program died at this point because of the first use of a symbolic reference, *${$language}*.
4   This line also includes a symbolic reference, but is never reached because the program had already aborted because of the use of the *strict* pragma.

12.1.2 Hard References

A **hard reference** is a scalar that holds the address of another data type. A variable that is assigned an address can also be called a **pointer** because it points to some other address or to another reference. This type of reference can point to a scalar, array, associative array, or a subroutine. The pointer was introduced in Perl 5 to give you the ability to create complex data types such as arrays of arrays, arrays of hashes, hashes of hashes, etc. In all of the examples where typeglobs were used, we can now opt for pointers instead. Pointers provide a way to pass parameters to subroutines by reference.

The Backslash Operator.   The backslash unary operator is used to create a hard reference, similar to the & used in *C and C++* to get the "address of." In the following example, *$p* is the reference. It is assigned the address of the scalar, *$x*.

```
$p = \$x;
```

An example of hard references from the Perl *man* page *perlref*:

```
$scalarref = \$foo;        # reference to scalar $foo
$arrayref  = \@ARGV;       # reference to array @ARGV
$hashref   = \%ENV;        # reference to hash %ENV
$coderef   = \&handler;    # reference to subroutine handler
$globref   = \*STDOUT;     # reference to typeglob STDOUT
$reftoref  = \$scalarref;  # reference to another reference
                                 (pointer to pointer, ugh)
```

De-referencing the Pointer.   If you print the value of a reference (or pointer), you will see an address. If you want to go to that address and get the value stored there — that is, de-reference the pointer — the pointer must be preceded by two "funny" symbols. The first is the dollar sign, because the pointer itself is a scalar, and preceding that goes the funny symbol representing the type of data to which it points. When using more complex types, the arrow (infix) operator can be used.

EXAMPLE 12.3

```
(The Script)
    #!/bin/perl
1   $num=5;
2   $p = \$num;        # $p gets the address of $num
3   print 'The address assigned $p is ', $p, "\n";
4   print "The value stored at that address is $$p\n";

(Output)
3   The address assigned $p is SCALAR(0xb057c)
4   The value stored at that address is 5
```

EXPLANATION

1   The scalar *$num* is assigned the value 5.
2   The scalar *$p* is assigned the address of *$num*. This is the function of the backslash operator. *$p* is called either a reference or a pointer; the terms are interchangeable.
3   The address stored in *$p* is printed. Perl also tells you the data type is *SCALAR*.
4   To de-reference *$p*, another dollar sign is prepended to *$p*. This dollar sign tells Perl that you are looking for the value of the scalar that *$p* references, i.e., *$num*.

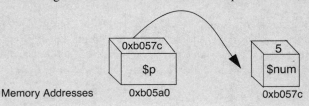

EXAMPLE 12.4

```
    #!/bin/perl
1   @toys = qw(Buzz Lightyear Woody Thomas Barney);
2   $num = @toys;
3   $ref1 = \$num;
4   $ref2 = \@toys;
5   print "There are $$ref1 toys.\n"; # de-reference pointers
6   print "They are: @$ref2.\n";
7   print "His favorite toy is $ref2->[0].\n";

(Output)
5   There are 4 toys.
6   They are: Buzzlightyear Woody Thomas Barney.
7   His favorite toy is Buzzlightyear.
```

EXPLANATION

1   The array *@toys* is assigned a list.
2   The array *@toys* is assigned to the scalar variable *$num* returning the number of elements in the array.
3   The pointer *$ref1* is a scalar. It is assigned the address of the scalar *$num*. The backslash operator allows you to create the pointer.
4   The pointer *$ref2* is a scalar. It is assigned the address of the array *@toys*.
5   The pointer is de-referenced, meaning: Go to the address that *$ref1* is pointing to and print the value of the scalar stored there.
6   The pointer is again de-referenced, meaning: Go to the address that *$ref2* is pointing to, get the array, and print it.
7   De-reference the pointer and get the first element of the array that it points to. This could also be written as *$$ref2[0]*.

12.1.3   References and Anonymous Variables

It is not necessary to name a variable to create a reference (pointer) to it. If a variable or subroutine has no name, it is called **anonymous**. If an anonymous variable or subroutine is assigned to a scalar, then the scalar is a reference to that subroutine.

The **arrow operator** (–>), also called the **infix operator**, is used to de-reference the reference to anonymous arrays and hashes. Although not really necessary, the arrow operator makes the program easier to read.

Anonymous Arrays.   Anonymous array elements are enclosed in square brackets (*[]*). These square brackets are not to be confused with the square brackets used to subscript an array. Here they are used as an expression to be assigned to a scalar. The brackets will not be interpolated if enclosed within quotes. The arrow (infix) operator is used to de-ref the individual elements of the array.

EXAMPLE 12.6

```
(The Script)
    #!/bin/perl
1   my $arrayref = [ 'Woody', 'Buzz', 'Bo', 'Mr. Potato Head' ];
2   print "The value of the reference, \$arrayref is ",
                                    $arrayref, "\n";
    # All of these examples de-reference $arrayref
3   print "$arrayref->[3]", "\n";
4   print $$arrayref[3], "\n";
5   print ${$arrayref}[3], "\n";
6   print "@{$arrayref}", "\n";


(Output)
2   The value of the reference, $arrayref is ARRAY(0x8a6f134)
3   Mr. Potato Head
4   Mr. Potato Head
5   Mr. Potato Head
6   Woody Buzz Bo Mr. Potato Head
```

EXPLANATION

1   The anonymous array elements are assigned to the array reference *$arrayref*.
2   The array reference contains the data type and the hexadecimal address of the anonymous array.
3   The fourth element of the array is printed. The pointer variable, *$arrayref*, is followed by the arrow operator pointing to the index value that will be retrieved.
4   The arrow operator is not really needed here. Instead, the element could have been accessed by the last two methods in lines 4 and 5.
6   The entire array is printed after de-referencing the pointer. Curly braces are required.

Anonymous Hashes.   An **anonymous hash** is created by using curly braces (*{}*). You can mix array and hash composers to produce complex data types. These braces are not the same braces that are used when subscripting a hash. The anonymous hash is assigned to a scalar reference.

EXAMPLE 12.7

```
(The Script)
    #!/bin/perl
1   my $hashref = { Name=>"Woody",
                    Type=>"Cowboy"
                  };
2   print $hashref->{Name}, "\n\n";
3   print keys %$hashref, "\n";
4   print values %$hashref, "\n";

(Output)
2   Woody

3   NameType
4   WoodyCowboy
```

EXPLANATION

1   The anonymous hash contains a set of key/value pairs enclosed in curly braces. The anonymous hash is assigned to the reference *$hashref*.
2   The hash pointer, *$hashref*, uses the arrow operator to de-reference the hash. The key, *Name*, is associated with the value, *Woody*.
3   The *keys* function returns all the keys in the anonymous hash via the reference (pointer).
4   The *values* function returns all the values in the anonymous hash via the reference (pointer).

12.1.4   Nested Data Structures

The ability to create references (pointers) to anonymous data structures lends itself to more complex types. For example, you can have hashes nested in hashes, or arrays of hashes, or arrays of arrays, etc.

Just as with simpler references, the anonymous data structures are de-referenced by prepending the reference with the correct funny symbol that represents its data type. For example, if *$p* is a pointer to a scalar you can write *$$p*, and if *$p* is a pointer to an array you could write *@$p* to de-reference the array or *$$p[0]* to get the first element of the array. You can also de-reference a pointer by treating it as a block. *$$p[0]* could also be written *${$p}[0]* or *@{p}[0..3]*. Sometimes the braces are used prevent ambiguity and sometimes they are necessary so that the funny character de-references the correct part of the structure.

Lists of Lists.   A list may contain another list or set of lists, most commonly used to create a mulitdimensional array. A reference is assigned an anonymous array containing another anonymous array in Examples 12.8 and 12.9.

EXAMPLE 12.8

```
    #!/bin/perl
    # Program to demonstrate a reference to a list with a
    # nested list
1   my $arrays = [ '1', '2', '3', [ 'red', 'blue', 'green' ]];
2   for($i=0;$i<3;$i++){
3       print $arrays->[$i],"\n";
    }

4   for($i=0;$i<3;$i++){
5       print $arrays->[3]->[$i],"\n";
    }
6   print "@{$arrays}\n";
7   print "--@{$arrays->[3]}--", "\n";

(Output)
3   1
    2
    3
5   red
    blue
    green

6   1 2 3 ARRAY(0x8a6f134)
7   --red blue green--
```

EXPLANATION

1   *$arrays* is a reference (pointer) to a four-element array that contains another anonymous three-element array whose elements are *red*, *blue*, and *green*.
2   The *for* loop is used to get the values of the first array, consisting of elements *1*, *2*, and *3*.
3   The arrow operator is used here to de-reference *$arrays*.
4   The second *for* loop is used to iterate through the nested anonymous array. Since this array is the fourth element of the first array, starting at subscript 0, the first index is *3* and the second index references each of its elements.
5   Each of the elements (*red, blue, green*) of the nested anonymous array are printed.
6   By prepending the @ symbol to the block containing the reference, the elements of the anonymous array are retrieved and printed. The third element of the array is a reference (pointer) to another anonymous hash. Its address is printed.
7   The second nested array is de-referenced and printed.

EXAMPLE 12.9

```
(The Script)
    #!/bin/perl
    # Program to demonstrate a pointer to a two-dimensional array.
1   my $matrix = [
                   [ 0, 2, 4 ],
                   [ 4, 1, 32 ],
                   [ 12, 15, 17 ]
                 ] ;

2   print "Row 3 column 2 is $matrix->[2]->[1].\n";

3   print "De-referencing with two loops.\n";

4   for($x=0;$x<3;$x++){
5       for($y=0;$y<3;$y++){
6           print "$matrix->[$x]->[$y] ";
        }
        print "\n\n";
    }
    print "\n";
7   print "De-referencing with one loop.\n";
8   for($i = 0; $i < 3; $i++){
9       print "@{$matrix->[$i]}", "\n\n";
    }
10  $p=\$matrix;      # Reference to a reference
11  print "De-referencing a reference to a reference.\n"
12  print ${$p}->[1][2], "\n";


(Output)
2   Row 3 column 2 is 15.
3   De-referencing with two loops.
6   0 2 4
    4 1 32
    12 15 17

7   De-referencing with one loop.
9   0 2 4
    4 1 32
    12 15 17

11  De-referencing a reference to a reference.
12  32
```

EXPLANATION

1 The reference (pointer) *$matrix* is assigned an anonymous array of three anonymous arrays, that is, a two-dimensional array (list of lists).

2 The arrow operator is used to access the first element of the array. An arrow is implied between adjacent subscript brackets and is not needed. It could have been written as *$matrix–>[2][1]*.

4 The outer *for* loop is entered. This will iterate through the rows of the array.

5 The inner *for* loop is entered. This loop iterates through the columns of the array.

6 Each element of the two-dimensional array is printed via the reference (pointer).

8 This time only one *for* loop will be used to print out the contents of the matrix.

9 The block format is used to de-reference the pointer. All elements of each list are printed.

10 *$p* is a reference assigned another reference, *$matrix*. This is more commonly called a pointer to a pointer.

12 If you want to access the array elements—that is, de-reference *$p*—an additional dollar sign is needed, one for *p* and one for *matrix*. The arrow is implied between the adjacent subscripts; for example, this line could have been written *$p–>[1]–>[2]*.

Array of Hashes.   A list may contain a hash or a set of hashes. In Example 12.10, a reference is assigned an anonymous array containing two anonymous hashes.

EXAMPLE 12.10

```
1    my $petref = [    { name=>"Rover",
                         type=>"dog",
                         owner=>"Mr. Jones",
                       },
2                      { name=>"Sylvester",
                         type=>"cat",
                         owner=>"Mrs. Black",
                       }
3                    ];

4    print "The first pet's name is $petref->[0]->{name}.\n";
     print "Printing an array of hashes.\n";
5    for($i=0; $i<2; $i++){
6       while(($key,$value)=each %{$petref->[$i]} ){
7           print "$key -- $value\n";
        }
        print "\n";
     }
     print "Adding a hash to the array.\n";
```

EXAMPLE 12.10 (CONTINUED)

```
8   push @{$petref},{owner =>"Mrs. Crow", name=>"Tweety",
                     type=>"bird"};

9   while(($key,$value)=each %{$petref->[2]}){
10     print "$key -- $value\n";
    }
```

(Output)
```
4   The first pet's name is Rover.
    Printing an array of hashes.
7   owner -- Mr. Jones
    type -- dog
    name -- Rover

    owner -- Mrs. Black
    type -- cat
    name -- Sylvester

    Adding a hash to the array.
10  type -- bird
    owner -- Mrs. Crow
    name -- Tweety
```

EXPLANATION

1   The reference (pointer) *$petref* is assigned the address of an anonymous array containing two anonymous hashes.
2   This is the second element of the list, an anonymous hash with its key/value pairs.
3   This is the closing square bracket for the anonymous array.
4   The pointer, *$petref*, is used to de-reference the list, first by selecting the zeroth element of the array and, with the arrow operator, selecting the key in the hash. The value associated with the key, *name*, is displayed.
5   The *for* loop is entered to iterate through the list.
6   The *while* loop is entered. Each time through the loop, a key and a value are extracted from the hash pointed to by *$petref–>[$i]*, and assigned to *$key* and *$value*, respectively.
7   The key/value pairs are displayed.
8   A new hash is pushed onto the array, *@{$petref}*, with the *push* function.
9   The *while* loop is entered. Each time through the loop, a key and a value are extracted from the hash pointed to by *$petref–>[0]*, and assigned to *$key* and *$value*, respectively. The new hash that was pushed on will be displayed.
10 After de-referencing *$petref*, the second element of the array, *$petref–>[0]*, is de-referenced and each of the key/value pairs of the nested hash is displayed.

Hash of Hashes.   A hash may contain another hash or a set of hashes. In Example 12.11, a reference is assigned an anonymous hash consisting of two keys, each of which is associated with a value that happens to be another hash (consisting of its own key/value pairs).

EXAMPLE 12.11

```
    #!/bin/perl
    # Program to demonstrate a hash containing anonymous hashes.
1   my $hashref = {
2                 Math => {                        # key
                           Anna => 100,
                           Hao => 95,              # values
                           Rita => 85,
                          },
3                 Science => {                     # key
                             Sam => 78,
                             Lou => 100,           # values
                             Vijay =>98,
                            },
4                };
5   print "Anna got $hashref->{Math}->{Anna} on the Math test.\n";
6   $hashref->{Science}->{Lou}=90;
7   print "Lou's grade was changed to $hashref->{Science}->{Lou}.\n";
8   print "The nested hash of Math students and grades is:\n";
9   print %{$hashref->{Math}}, "\n";   # Prints the nested hash, Math

10  foreach $key (keys %{$hashref}){
11      print "Outer key: $key \n";
12      while(($nkey,$nvalue)=each(%{$hashref->{$key}})){
13          printf "\tInner key: %-5s -- Value: %-8s\n",
                                   $nkey,$nvalue;
        }
    }


(Output)
5   Anna got 100 on the Math test.
7   Lou's grade was changed to 90.
8   The nested hash of Math students and grades is:\n
    Rita85Hao95Anna100
11  Outer key: Science
13  Inner key: Lou   -- Value: 90
    Inner key: Sam   -- Value: 78
    Inner key: Vijay -- Value: 98
11  Outer key: Math
13  Inner key: Rita  -- Value: 85
    Inner key: Hao   -- Value: 95
    Inner key: Anna  -- Value: 1005
    Anna got 100 on the Math test.
```

EXPLANATION

1   The anonymous hash is defined. It consists of two hash keys, *Math* and *Science*, whose values are themselves a hash (key/value pair). The address of the hash is assigned to *$hashref*. *$hashref* is a hard reference (pointer).

2   *Math* is the key for its value, a nested hash.

3   *Science* is the key for its value, also a nested hash.

4   This is the closing curly brace of the anonymous hash.

5   To access Anna's grade, first the key *Math* is de-referenced, followed by the arrow operator, and the nested key *Anna*. The second arrow is not necessary, but may make the construct easier to follow. In fact, you don't need to use the arrow operator at all. This could have been written as *$$hashref{Math}{Anna}*.

6   Using the *$hashref* reference, you can also change or add new values to the hash. Lou's grade is changed.

7   The new grade is printed by de-referencing *$hashref*.

8, 9   The nested hash, *Math*, is printed by enclosing the reference *$hashref->Math* in curly braces prepended by a %. The % represents the unnamed hash, both keys and values.

10   The *foreach* loop iterates through the list (produced by the *keys* function) of outer keys in the anonymous hash.

11   Each of the outer keys is printed.

12   Since each of the outer keys is associated with a value that happens to be another hash, the reference, *$hashref*, is de-referenced by placing *$hashref->{$key}* in a block prepended by a percent sign.

13   The nested keys and their associated values are printed.

Hash of Hashes with Lists of Values.   A hash may contain nested hash keys associated with lists of values. In Example 12.12, a reference is assigned two keys associated with values that are also keys into another hash. The nested hash keys are, in turn, associated with an anonymous list of values.

EXAMPLE 12.12

```
(The Script)
    # A hash with nested hash keys and anonymous arrays of values
1   my $hashptr = { Teacher=>{Subjects=>[ qw(Science Math English)]},
                    Musician=>{Instruments=>[ qw(piano flute harp)]},
                  };
                  # Teacher and Musician are keys.
                  # The values consist of nested hashes.
2   print $hashptr->{Teacher}->{Subjects}->[0],"\n";
3   print "@{$hashptr->{Musician}->{Instruments}}\n";

(Output)
2   Science
3   piano flute harp
```

EXPLANATION

1   The pointer $hashptr is assigned an anonymous hash consisting of two keys, *Teacher* and *Musician*. The values for *Teacher* consist of another anonymous hash with a key, *Subjects*, associated with an anonymous array of values, *Science*, *Math*, and *English*. The key, *Musician*, also consists of an anonymous hash with a key, *Instruments*, associated with an anonymous array of values, *piano*, *flute*, and *harp*.

2   To de-reference the pointer, the arrow operator is used to separate the nested keys. The final arrow refers to the first element of the array of values associated with *Subjects*, *Science*.

3   To get all the values from the anonymous array associated with the key, the @ symbol proceeds the pointer and its nested keys, each key separated with the arrow operator. If a variable has no name, you can replace its name with a block preceded by the symbol for the correct data type. Here, the curly braces enclosing the entire structure allow you to de-reference the whole block as an array.

12.1.5   References and Subroutintes

Anonymous Subroutines.   An anonymous subroutine is created by using the keyword *sub* without a subroutine name. The expression is terminated with a semicolon.

EXAMPLE 12.13

```
(The Script)
    #!/bin/perl
1   my $subref = sub { print @_ ; };
2   &$subref('a','b','c');
3   print "\n";

(Output)
1   abc
2   print "\n";
```

EXPLANATION

1   The scalar *$subref* is assigned an anonymous subroutine by reference. The only function of the subroutine is to print its arguments stored in the *@_* array.
2   The subroutine is called via its reference and passed three arguments.
3   A newline character is passed to the print function.

Closures.   If a reference to an anonymous subroutine is defined at runtime within a particular block along with other lexical variables (*my* variables), the subroutine has access to those variables even if it is called from outside the block and the variables should have gone out of scope. Larry Wall describes closures as just anonymous subroutines with an attitude.[2] Programmers use closures to create **callbacks** (functions that run at some later time), to provide references to methods (subroutines used by objects), and to create functions that create and return functions.

EXAMPLE 12.14

```
(The Script)
1   my $name = "Tommy";

2   { my $name = "Grandfather";
3       my $age = 86;
4       $ref = sub{ return "$name is $age.\n";};   # anonymous subroutine
    }
5   print "\$name is $name\n";
6   print &$ref;

(Output)
5   $name is Tommy
6   Grandfather is 86.
```

---

2.   Wall, L., Christianson, T., and Orwant, J., *Programming Perl, 3rd ed.*, O'Reilly & Associates: Sebastopol, CA, 2000, p. 262.

EXPLANATION

1   The lexical variable *$name* is assigned *Tommy*. The variable is visible from here to the end of the file.

2   A block is entered. A new lexical variable, *$name,* is assigned *Grandfather.* It is visible from here to the end of its block.

3   Another lexical variable, *$age*, is defined. It is visible from here to the end of the enclosing block.

4   An anonymous subroutine is defined within the same block as the two lexical variables (*my* variables), *$name* and *$age*. The address of the subroutine is assigned to *$ref*. The subroutine has access to those variables even if it is called from outside the block.

5   The value of *$name*, *Tommy*, is now visible.

6   The anonymous subroutine is called via the pointer *$ref*. The lexical variables are still available even though they appear to be out of scope. They remain in scope because the reference still needs access to them. Perl doesn't clean up the variables until they are no longer referenced.

EXAMPLE 12.15

```
      # Closure
1   sub paint {
2      my $color = shift;    # @_ array is shifted
3      my $item = sub {      # Pointer to an anonymous subroutine
4           my $thing = shift;
5           print "Paint the $thing $color.\n";
      };
6   return $item;    # Returns a closure
      }

7   my $p1 = paint("red");    #  Creates a closure
8   my $p2 = paint("blue");   #  Creates a closure

9   $p1->("flower");
10  $p2->("sky");
```

```
(Output)
Paint the flower red.
Paint the sky blue.
```

EXPLANATION

1   The subroutine *paint* is declared.
2   The first argument to the *paint* function is shifted from the @_ array and assigned to the lexical scalar, *$color*.
3   A pointer, *$item*, is assigned the address of an anonymous subroutine.
4   The first argument to the function is shifted from the @_ array and assigned to the lexical scalar, *$thing*.
5   When called, the lexical variables are still in scope even though the subroutine was called from outside the blocks where the variables were defined.
6   A pointer to the anonymous subroutine, a *closure*, is returned to the caller.
7   The *paint* function is called with one argument, *red*, and a pointer to the anonymous subroutine, nested in *paint*, is returned and assigned to *$p1*. A closure has been created.
8   The *paint* function is called again with one argument, *blue*, and a pointer to the anonymous subroutine, nested in *paint*, is returned and assigned to *$p2*. Another closure has been created.
9   The anonymous subroutine is called by using the pointer. One argument, *flower*, is passed. The value of *$color, red,* was the first argument to the paint function; it's still visible even though it would seem to be out of scope.
10   The anonymous subroutine is called by using the pointer. One argument, *sky*, is passed. The value of *$color* is still visible.

Subroutines and Passing by Reference.   When passing arguments to subroutines, they are sent to the subroutine and stored in the @_ array. If you have a number of arguments, say an array, a scalar, and another array, the arguments are all flattened out onto the @_ array. It would be hard to tell where one argument ended and the other began unless you also passed along the size of each of the arrays, and then the size would be pushed onto the @_ array and you would have to get that to determine where the first array ended, and so on. The @_ could also be quite large if you are passing a 1,000-element array. So, the easiest and most efficient way to pass arguments, is by address, as shown in Example 12.16.

EXAMPLE 12.16

```
(The Script)
1   @toys = qw(Buzzlightyear  Woody  Bo);
2   $num = @toys;  # Number of elements in @toys is assigned to $num
3   gifts(\$num, \@toys);     # Passing by reference

4   sub gifts {
5       my($n, $t) = @_;   # Localizing the reference with 'my'
6       print "There are $$n gifts: ";
7       print "@$t\n";
8       push(@$t, 'Janey', 'Slinky');
    }
9   print "The original array was changed to: @toys\n";


(Output)
6,7 There are 3 gifts: Buzzlightyear Woody Bo
9   The original array was changed to: Buzzlightyear Woody Bo Janey
    Slinky
```

EXPLANATION

1 The array @*toys* is assigned three values.
2 The scalar $*num* is assigned the number of elements in the @*toys* array. (Remember, a scalar contains only one value, so when you assign an array to a scalar, the number of elements in the array is assigned to the scalar.)
3 The subroutine *gifts* is called with two pointers as parameters.
4 The subroutine is entered.
5 The @_ array contains the two pointer variables. The values of the pointers are copied into two lexical variables, $*n* and $*t*.
6 The pointer to the scalar is de-referenced. It points to the scalar $*n*.
7 The pointer to the array is de-referenced. It points to the array @*toys*.
8 The *push* function adds two new elements to the array pointed to by $*t*.
9 After exiting the subroutine, @*toys* is printed with its new values.

EXAMPLE 12.17

```
(The Script)
    # This script demonstrates the use of hard references
    # when passing arrays. Instead of passing the entire
    # array, a reference is passed.
    # The value of the last expression is returned.

1   my @list1 = (1 .. 100);
2   my @list2 = (5, 10, 15, 20);

3   print "The total is :  ",  &addemup( \@list1, \@list2) , ".\n";
                # Two pointers

4   sub addemup {
5       my($arr1, $arr2) = @_;
                # @_ contains two pointers (references)
6       my ($total1, $total2);
7       print $arr1, "\n" ;
8       print $arr2, "\n";

9       foreach $num (@$arr1){
10          $total1+=$num ;
        }
11      foreach $num (@$arr2) {
12          $total2+=$num ;
        }

13  $total1 + $total2;  # The expression is evaluated and returned
    }

(Output)
7   ARRAY(0x8a62d68)
8   ARRAY(0x8a60f2c)
3   The total is:  5100.
```

EXPLANATION

1   The array *@list1* is assigned a list of numbers between *1* and *100*.
2   The array *@list2* is assigned the list of numbers *5, 10, 15*, and *20*.
3   The *&addemup* subroutine is called. Two parameters are passed. The backslash preceding each of the arrays causes the addresses (pointers) to be passed.
4   The subroutine *&addemup* is declared and defined.
5   The pointers are passed to the @_ array and assigned to *my* variables *$arr1* and *$arr2*, respectively.
6   Two *my* variables, *$total1* and *$total2*, are declared.

EXPLANATION   (CONTINUED)

7, 8   The addresses of the pointers are printed.

9   The *foreach* loop is entered. @*$arr1* de-references the pointer, creating a list of array elements to be processed, one at a time.

10   Each time through the loop, *$total1* accumulates the sum of *$total1* + *$num*.

11, 12   Each time through the *foreach* loop, *$total2* accumulates the sum of *$total2* + *$num*.

13   The sum is returned to where the subroutine was called on line 3. Since the subroutine was called when it was passed as an argument to the *print* function, the results will be printed.

12.1.6   Filehandle References

One of the only ways to pass a filehandle to a subroutine is by reference. You can use a typeglob to create an alias for the filehandle, and then use the backslash to create a reference to the typeglob. Wow...

EXAMPLE 12.18

```
(The Script)
  #!/bin/perl
1  open(README, "/etc/passwd") || die;

2  &readit(\*README);        # Reference to a typeglob

3  sub readit {
4      my ($passwd)=@_;
5      print "\$passwd is a $passwd.\n";
6      while(<$passwd>){
7          print;
       }
8      close($passwd);
   }

9  seek(README,0,0) || die "seek: $!\n";
```

EXAMPLE 12.18 (CONTINUED)

```
(Output)
5   $passwd is a GLOB(0xb0594).
7   root:x:0:1:Super-User:/:/usr/bin/csh
    daemon:x:1:1::/:
    bin:x:2:2::/usr/bin:
    sys:x:3:3::/:
    adm:x:4:4:Admin:/var/adm:
    lp:x:71:8:Line Printer Admin:/usr/spool/lp:
    smtp:x:0:0:Mail Daemon User:/:
    uucp:x:5:5:uucp Admin:/usr/lib/uucp:
    nuucp:x:9:9:uucp Admin:/var/spool/uucppublic:/usr/lib/uucp/uucico
    listen:x:37:4:Network Admin:/usr/net/nls:
    nobody:x:60001:60001:Nobody:/:
    noaccess:x:60002:60002:No Access User:/:
    nobody4:x:65534:65534:SunOS 4.x Nobody:/:
    ellie:x:9496:40:Ellie Quigley:/home/ellie:/usr/bin/csh
9   seek: Bad file number
```

EXPLANATION

1   The */etc/passwd* file is attached to the *README* filehandle and opened for reading.
2   The *readit* subroutine is called. The filehandle is passed by creating a reference to a typeglob. First, the filehandle symbol is globbed with the asterisk. Then, the reference to the typeglob is created by prefixing the typeglob with a backslash.
3   The *readit* subroutine is defined.
4   The @_ variable contains the reference. It is assigned to a local scalar variable called *$passwd*. *$passwd* is a reference to the filehandle.
5   The reference, *$passwd*, when printed shows that it contains the address of a typeglob (alias).
6, 7 The expression in the *while* loop causes a line to be read from the */etc/passwd* file and assigned to the *$_* variable. The line is printed to the screen. The loop will continue until all the lines have been read and printed.
8   The filehandle is closed via the reference. This is probably not a good idea, if the program still wants access to the file without having to reopen it. This is done just to show that the reference is really dealing with the real filehandle.
9   When the subroutine exits, and the program continues execution, the filehandle, *README*, is no longer available. It was closed via the reference. Now, in order to read from the filehandle, it must be reopened. The *seek* function failed.

12.1.7 The *ref* Function

The *ref* function is used to test for the existence of a reference. It returns true if its argument is a reference and the null string if not. The value returned is the type of the thing being referenced. Types that can be returned are

REF

SCALAR

ARRAY

HASH

CODE

GLOB

EXAMPLE 12.19

```
(The Script)
1   sub gifts;       # Forward declaration
2   $num = 5;
3   $junk = "xxx";
4   @toys = qw/ Bud Lightyear Woody Thomas/ ;
5   gifts( \$num, \@toys, $junk );
6   sub gifts {
7       my($n, $t, $j) = @_;
8       print "\$n is a reference.\n" if ref($n);
        print "\$t is a reference.\n" if ref($t);
9       print "\$j is a not a reference.\n" if ref($j);
10      printf "\$n is a reference to a %s.\n", ref($n);
11      printf "\$t is a reference to an %s.\n", ref($t);
    }

(Output)
8   $n is a reference.
    $t is a reference.
9
10  $n is a reference to a SCALAR.
11  $t is a reference to an ARRAY.
```

EXPLANATION

1 The subroutine *gifts* is a forward declaration, allowing Perl to know it is a subroutine defined somewhere in the program. You will not need an ampersand to call the subroutine if it is declared before it is defined.

2 The scalar *$num* is assigned *5*.

3 The scalar *$junk* is assigned the string *xxx*.

EXPLANATION (CONTINUED)

4 The array *@toys* is assigned a list with the *qw* construct.

5 The subroutine *gifts* is called. The first two variables are passed as references by preceding them with a backslash and the last variable, *$junk*, is not passed as a reference.

6 The subroutine *gifts* is defined.

7 The values assigned to the @_ array, in this case, two references (addresses) and one non-reference, will be assigned to *$n*, *$t*, and *$j*, respectively, and made local with the *my* function.

8 The *ref* function is called with a reference, *$n*, as its argument. The line will be printed only if the variable *$n* is a reference.

9 *$j* is not a reference. The return value for the *ref* function is null.

10 The *printf* function prints the value of the data type returned from *ref*, a scalar.

11 The *printf* function prints the value of the data type returned from *ref*, an array.

EXERCISE 12
It's Not Polite to Point!

1. Rewrite *tripper* (from Chapter 10) to take two pointers as arguments and copy the arguments from the @_ in the subroutine into two *my* pointer variables.

2. Create a hash called *employees* with the following three keys:
   Name
   Ssn
   Salary

   The values will be assigned as undefined (*undef* is a built-in Perl function).
   For example:
   Name => undef,

   a. Create a reference to the hash.
   b. Assign values to each of the keys using the reference.
   c. Print the keys and values of the hash using the built-in *each* function and the reference.
   d. Print the value of the reference; in other words, what the reference variable contains, not what it points to.

3. Rewrite the above exercise so that the hash is anonymous and assign the anonymous hash to a reference (pointer). Delete one of the keys from the hash using the reference (use the *delete* function).

4. Write a program that will contain the following structure:

```
$student = { Name => undef,
             SSN => undef,
             Friends => [],
             Grades => { Science => [],
                         Math => [],
                         English => [],
                       }
           };
```

Use the pointer to assign and display output resembling the following:

```
Name is John Smith.
Social Security Number is 510-23-1232.
Friends are Tom, Bert, Nick.
Grades are:
          Science--100, 83, 77
          Math--90, 89, 85
          English--76, 77, 65
```

13

BLESS THOSE THINGS! (OBJECT-ORIENTED PERL)

13.1 The OOP Paradigm

13.1.1 Packages and Modules Revisited

The big addition to Perl 5 is the ability to do object-oriented programming, called OOP for short. OOP is centered around the way a program is organized. Object-oriented languages, such as *C++* and *Java,* bundle up data into a variable and call it an **object**. The object is described to have certain properties, also called **attributes**. For example, a property for a money object might be the amount, the type, the nationality, and so forth. The object's data is normally kept <u>private</u>. Messages are sent to the object through special subroutines called **methods**. These subroutines provide methods to get at the data. The methods are normally <u>public</u>. The only way that a user of the program should access the data is through these public methods. To access the money object, the methods might be *earnit( )*, *findit( )*, *stealit( )*, etc.

The data and the methods are packaged up into a data structure called a **class**. A Perl package will function as a class when using the object-oriented approach. This is not really a new idea for Perl since data is already encapsulated in packages. Recall from our short discussion of packages that a package gives a sense of privacy to your program. Each package has its own symbol table, a hash that contains all the names in the "current" package. This makes it possible to create variables and subroutines that have their own namespace within a package. If other routines are used from another package, the namespaces are kept separate, thus protecting the accidental clobbering of variables of the same name in the program. The idea of hiding data in packages, then, is inherently part of Perl and also happens to be one of the basic tenets of object-oriented programming.

Every Perl program has at least one package called *main,* where Perl statements are internally compiled. The standard Perl library consists of a number of files containing packages. Most of these files are called **modules**. A module is really just a fancy package that is reusable. The reuse of code is accomplished through **inheritance**; that is, a package can inherit characteristics from a parent or base class and thus extend or restrict its own capabilities. The ability to extend the functionality of a class is called **polymorphism**. Hiding data (encapsulation), inheritance, and polymorphism are considered the basic tenets of the object-oriented philosophy.

379

To create a Perl module, you still use the *package* keyword, and the scope is from the declaration of the package to the end of the enclosing block or file. Packages normally are the size of one file. The files can be recognized as modules if their names end with a *.pm* extension and if the first letter of the module is capitalized. **Pragmas** are another special kind of module (the name is spelled in lowercase but still has the *.pm* extension) which directs the compiler to behave in a specified way. Whether the package is called a module or a pragma, it has some special features that differentiate it from an ordinary package. Those special features introduced in Perl 5 give you the ability to model your programs with the object-oriented way of abstract thinking. You can think of procedural languages as action-oriented and OO languages as object-oriented.

Tom Christianson, discussing Perl and objects on his Web page "Easy Perl5 Object Intro," says that people tend to shy away from highly convenient Perl 5 modules because some of them deal with objects. Unfortunately, some problems very much lend themselves to objects. Christianson says that people shouldn't be scared by this because merely knowing enough OO programming to use someone else's modules is not nearly as difficult as actually designing and implementing one yourself.[1] So, if you are not interested in writing programs that take advantage of the OOP features of Perl but still need to use Perl 5 modules that do utilize objects, then you can skip to the end of this chapter and follow the examples provided there in "Using Objects from the Perl Library" on page 427.

13.1.2 Some Object-Oriented Lingo

Object-oriented programming is a huge subject. Thousands of books have been written on OO programming, design, and methodology. Many programmers of the 1990s moved away from traditional top-down structured programming and toward object-oriented programming languages for building complex software. This is not a book on object-oriented design or programming. However, there are some basic key words associated with OOP that should be mentioned before tackling Perl's OOP features. They are listed in Table 13.1.

Table 13.1 Key OOP Words

Word	*Perl Meaning*
Data encapsulation	Hiding data and subroutines from the user, as in a package
Inheritance	The reuse of code, usually from a library where a package inherits from other packages
Polymorphism	Literally "many forms," and specifically, the ability to extend the functionality of a class
Object	A referenced type that knows what class it belongs to; an instance of a class
Method	A special subroutine that manipulates objects
Class	A package that contains data and methods
Constructor	A method that creates and initializes an object
Destructor	A method that destroys an object

---

1. Go to *www.perl.com/CPAN-local/doc/FMTEYEWTK/easy_objects.html* to see Tom Christianson's Web page.

13.2 Classes, Objects, and Methods

13.2.1 Classes and Privacy

A Perl class is just a package. The terms are interchangeable. But if you want to distinguish between the two terms, a class is a package containing special subroutines called **methods** that manipulate objects. A class normally consists of:

1. the data (also called properties or attributes) that belongs in the class; and
2. subroutines that know how to access and manipulate the data in the class.

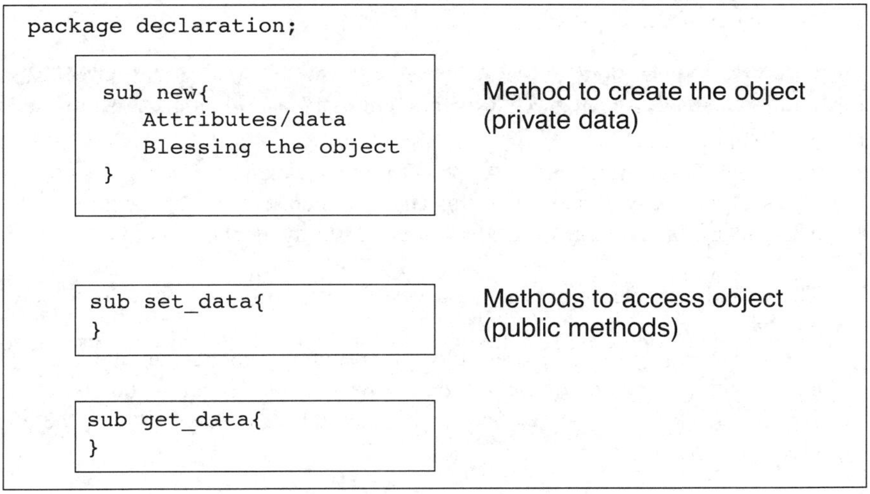

```
package declaration;

    sub new{
        Attributes/data              Method to create the object
        Blessing the object          (private data)
    }



    sub set_data{                    Methods to access object
    }                                (public methods)

    sub get_data{
    }
```

Figure 13.1   What makes up a class? The *.pm* file.

Since a class is really just a package, it has its own symbol table, and yet the data or routines in one class can be accessed in another via the double colon (Perl 5) or the single apostrophe (Perl 4).

Unlike other languages, Perl does not strictly monitor public/private borders within its modules.[2] The *my* function is used to keep variables private. The *my* variables exist only within the innermost enclosing block, subroutine, eval, or file. The *my* variables cannot be accessed from another package by using the double colon (or single apostrophe) because *my* variables are not related to any package; they are not stored in the symbol table of the package in which they are created.

---

2. Wall, L., and Schwartz, R. L., *Programming Perl*, 2nd ed., O'Reilly & Associates: Sebastopol, CA, 1998, p. 287.

EXAMPLE 13.1

```
      #!/bin/perl
1     package main;

2     $name = "Susan";
3     my $birthyear = 1942;

4     package nosy;
5     print "Hello $main::name.\n";
6     print "You were born in $main::birthyear?\n";

(Output)
5     Hello Susan.
6     You were born in ?
```

EXPLANATION

1   The package is *main*.
2   The scalar *$name* is global in scope within this package.
3   The scalar *$birthyear* is local to this and any enclosing inner blocks.
4   The package *nosy* is declared. Its scope is from the declaration to the bottom of the file.
5   The global variable *$name* can be accessed by qualifying it with its package name and two colons.
6   The scalar *$birthyear* is inaccessible to this package via the symbol table. It was declared with the *my* function in a different package, *main*, and is not associated with any symbol table, but stored in a private scratch pad created within the enclosing block.

13.2.2 Objects

To begin with, an object in Perl is created by using a hard reference (pointer). A reference, if you recall, is a scalar that holds the address of some variable. It's a pointer. A reference might also point to a variable or subroutine that has no name, called an anonymous variable. For example, here is a reference called *$ref* to an anonymous hash consisting of two key/value pairs:

```
my $ref   = { Name => "Tom",  Salary => 25000};
```

To access a value in the anonymous hash, the reference (pointer) *$ref* can be de-referenced by using the arrow operator as follows:

```
$ref ->{Name}
```

To make a Perl object, first a reference is created. The reference normally is assigned the address of an anonymous hash (although it could be assigned the address of an array or scalar). The hash will contain the data members of the object. In addition to storing the address of the hash, the reference must know what package it belongs to. This is done by creating the reference and then "blessing" it into a package. The *bless* function acts on the "thing" being referenced into the package, not the reference itself. It creates an internal pointer to track what package the thing (object) belongs to. The object is the thing (usually a hash) that was blessed into the class (package). If the package is not listed as the second argument, the *bless* function assumes the current package. It returns a reference to the blessed object. (See "The bless Function" on page 384 for a complete discussion of *bless*.)

```
my $ref  = {Name => "Tom",  Salary => 25000};   # This is the object
bless($ref, Class);    # The object is blessed into the package named Class
return $ref;           # A reference to the object is returned
```

Once an object has been blessed, you don't have to export symbols with the @EXPORT_OK or @EXPORT arrays. In fact, as a general rule, if the module is trying to be object-oriented, then export nothing.

The Money Class.   Figure 13.2 demonstrates how you might visualize a *Money* class. First you would create a package. This package is called *Money* and is found in a file called *Money.pm*. In OO lingo, the package will now be called a **class**. (Note the class name is the same as the filename without the *.pm* extension.) To illustrate encapsulation, the money bag is drawn around the data that describes the money object. The idea is to encapsulate the money and hide it from the rest of the world. The properties or attributes describe characteristics of the object, such as its shape, color, size, and so forth. In our example, the money properties are *amount*, *currency,* and *name*. In Perl, the object is often described with an anonymous hash, where the key/value pairs are the properties of the object. Outside of the money bag, subroutines are listed. In the OO world, these subroutines are called public methods, and they are the way you get access to the object. In fact, they should be the only way to get into the money bag. One method to get the money might be to earn it, another to find it, another to steal it, and so on. Methods in Perl are just glorified subroutines.

There are no special Perl keywords called *private*, *public,* or *protected* as in other OO languages. Perl's package mechanism makes up the class where the data and subroutines, called methods, are stored. The *my* function keeps variables private to a class, and the *bless* function guarantees that when the object is created, it will know to which class it belongs. The object is usually an anonymous hash or array and is manipulated with a reference that contains its address.

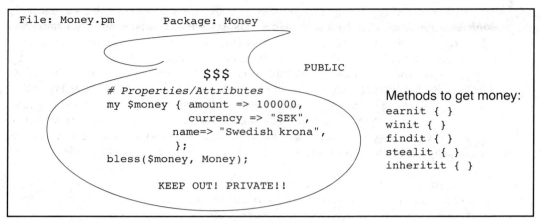

Figure 13.2   Hiding your money.

13.2.3   The *bless* Function

The *bless* function internally tags the object with a reference to the package where it belongs. This is how an **object** is created. If the package (class) is not listed as the second argument, the *bless* function tags the object as belonging to the current package. The *bless* function uses the reference to find the object and returns a reference to the object. Since the blessing associates the object with a particular package (class), Perl will always know to what package the object belongs. An object can be blessed into one class and then *reblessed* into another and then another, and so on, but an object can belong to only one class at a time.

FORMAT

```
bless REFERENCE, CLASSNAME
bless REFERENCE
```

EXAMPLE 13.2

```
my $reference = {};
return bless($reference, $class);
```

Example 13.3 illustrates how to create an anonymous hash, bless it into a package, and then to use the *ref* function to see if it is truly in the package. The reason for doing this will become clearer as we move on.

EXAMPLE 13.3

```
(The Script)
1   package Employee;          # Package declaration

2   my $ref= {name=>"Tom",     # Anonymous hash; data for the package
              salary=>25000,   # Describes how the object will look
             };

3   bless($ref, Employee);
```

```
    # The hash referenced by $ref is the object. It is blessed into
    # the package; i.e., an internal pointer is created to track the
    # package to which it belongs.

4   print "The bless function tags the hash with its package
        name.\n";
5   print "The value of \$ref is: $ref.\n";
6   print "The ref function returns the class (package) name:",
        ref($ref), ".\n";
7   print "The employee's name is $ref->{name}.\n";
                            # Use the reference
```

```
(Output)
4   The bless function tags the hash with its package name.
5   The value of $ref is: Employee=HASH(0x5a08a8).
6   The ref function returns the class (package) name: Employee.
7   The employee's name is Tom.
```

EXPLANATION

1 The *Employee* package is declared.

2 A reference, *$ref*, is assigned the address of an anonymous hash, consisting of two key/value pairs.

3 The *bless* function takes either one or two arguments. The first argument is the reference and the second argument is the name of the package. If the second argument is missing, the current package is assumed.[a] In this example, the current package is called *Employee*. The second argument could have been left out. Now the reference knows that the object it references (the object) is in the *Employee* package.

5 The value of the reference (the address of the object) is printed. It is a reference to a hash in the *Employee* package.

6 The *ref* function returns the name of the package if its argument, a pointer, has been blessed.

7 The pointer to the object is de-referenced.

---

a. It is recommended that the two-argument form for the *bless* function is used, especially with inheritance. (See "Inheritance" on page 407.)

13.2.4 Methods

Definition.   A **method** is a subroutine that operates on an object. It is a special subroutine that belongs to a class and expects its first argument to be either a package name or a reference to an object. Otherwise, it looks like any other subroutine. A method is used primarily to create an object, to assign or change the data in the object, or to retrieve data from an object.[3]

Types of Methods.   There are two types of methods: class (or static) methods and instance (or virtual) methods.[4] The class method expects a class name as its first argument, and the instance method expects an object reference as its first argument.

A **class method** is a subroutine that affects the class as a whole; for example, it can create an object or act on a group of objects. The class method expects a class name as its first argument. In object-oriented programs, a **constructor** function is a class method used to create an object. In Perl, this method is commonly called *new*, although you can call it anything you like. The creation of the object is often called the **instantiation** of the object.

Object-oriented programs use **instance methods** (also called **access methods**) to control the way the object's data is assigned, modified, and retrieved. You can't use an instance method until you have created the object. The method that creates the object is called a constructor. It returns a reference to the object. Once the reference to the newly created object is returned, the instance method uses that reference, often called *$this* or *$self*, to get at the object. The instance method expects a reference to the object as its first argument. It manipulates an object by using the reference to it.

Invoking Methods.   Perl provides a special syntax for invoking methods. Instead of using the *package::function* syntax, methods are invoked in one of two ways: class method invocation or instance method invocation. There are two types of syntax for each method call: **indirect syntax** and **object-oriented syntax**. If you are using objects, either syntax for these method calls is acceptable. The older way of calling methods with the double colons is not recommended.

---

3. Unlike *C++*, Perl doesn't provide any special syntax for a method definition.

4. What you call a method type depends on what book you read. Larry Wall categorizes methods as **class methods**, **instance methods**, and **dual-nature methods**.

Class Method Invocation
Assume the method name is called *new* and the return value, *$ref*, is a pointer to the object.

```
1) $ref = new class(list of arguments);   # indirect syntax
2) $ref = class->new(list of arguments);   # object-oriented syntax
```

If the class is called *Employee*, Perl translates that to

```
$ref = Employee::new(Employee, arguments, ... );
```

Instance Method Invocation
Assume the method name is called *display* and the reference to the object is called *$ref*.

```
1) display $ref(list of arguments);   # indirect syntax
2) $ref->display(list of arguments);   # object-oriented syntax
```

The first example for each method is called the indirect syntax; the second example, using the arrow operator, is called the object-oriented syntax.

When Perl sees one of the above methods being invoked, it knows what class the object belongs to because the object was blessed (an internal pointer is tracking where it is).[5]

If you call either

```
display $ref(arguments...);
```

or

```
$ref->display(arguments...);
```

and *$ref* points to an object in a class called *Employee*, Perl translates that to

```
Employee::display($ref, arguments...);
```

Figure 13.3 illustrates the layout of a typical object-oriented module. The file where the module is created is a *.pm* file. In this example, the *.pm* file is *ClassExample.pm*. The file consists of one package declaration. The package will be called a class; so, this is the *ClassExample* class. The class consists of subroutines, which are now called methods. The first type of method, called *new*, is a constructor method. It is the method that will define and create (construct) the object. When a user of this module calls the method, *new*, he will get back a reference to the newly created object. The *new* method not only creates the object, it also blesses the object so that the object always knows what class (package) it belongs to. (See "The bless Function" on page 384.) The second two methods are called access or instance methods. These are the methods that store and fetch the data from the object. You can't use these methods until you have created an instance of the object. Once you, the user, have a reference to the object, the reference is used to call the instance methods.

---

5. The ability of Perl to call the appropriate module's function is called **runtime binding**, according to Srinivasan, S., *Advanced Perl Programming*, O'Reilly & Associates: Sebastopol, CA, 1997.

Continuing in Fiugre 13.3, we see that the object's data will be described in an empty anonymous hash (although any other data type might be used), and the address of the object will be assigned to a private (*my*) reference. (The object's data will be assigned later with an instance method called *set_data*.) The *bless* function will tag the object with the name of the class where it belongs and return a pointer to the object; i.e., when the user of the module calls the constructor, he gets back a pointer to the newly created object. The constructor is said to "instantiate" the object. Once an instance of the object is created, the instance methods (often called **setters** and **getters**) will be used to access or modify the object. The user calls the instance methods to store data in the object, and to retrieve data from the object. The instance methods **must** have a reference to the object in order to manipulate it. They always take a reference as their first argument.

There are many ways that the module can be designed. This is just one simple approach.

ClassExample.pm (the file)

package ClassExample;   (The class)

```
sub new{
   my $class = shift;
   my $ref = { };  # define the object
   bless($ref, $class);
   return $ref;
}
```
Constructor method
Create the object
Bless the reference to the object
Return the reference to the object

```
sub set_data{
   my  $self = shift;
   $self->{key} = value;
}
```
Access or instance methods

Assign or store the object's attributes

```
sub get_data{
   my $self = shift;
   print $self->{key};
}
1;
```
Get or fetch the object's attributes

User of the Class

```
#!/usr/bin/perl
# package is main

use ClassExample;
$ref_to_obj = ClassExample -> new(args); # Create the object, a pointer is returned;
                              # args refers to any arguments that might be passed

$ref_to_obj -> setdata(args);      # Store or assign data to the object
$ref_to_obj -> getdata(args);      # Fetch data from the object
```

Figure 13.3   The module and the user of the module.

The Class Constructor Method.   **Constructor** is an OOP term for a class method that creates and initializes an object into a class. There is no special syntax for a constructor. It is just a method that is used to get a reference blessed into a package. The first method in a Perl class (i.e., the first subroutine in a package) is normally the one that creates the reference (to the object) and blesses it into the package. This method is often called *new* since it makes a new "thing," but could be called anything you want, such as *create*, *construct*, *initiate*, and so forth.

The object that is blessed into the *new* subroutine is usually an anonymous hash or anonymous array. The anonymous hash or array is assigned the data that describe the object. The data are often described as the **properties** or **attributes** of the object. When referred to collectively, the attributes define the **state** of the object.

EXAMPLE 13.4

```
(The Module: Employee.pm)
1   package Employee;             # Class

2   sub new{                      # Class method called a constructor
3       my $class = shift;
4       my $ref={Name=>undef,     # Attributes of the object
                 Salary=>undef,   # Values will be assigned later
                };
5       bless($ref, $class);
                            # $ref now references an object in this class
6       return $ref;       # A reference to the object is returned
    }
    1;
----------------------------------------
(The User of the Module)
    #!/usr/bin/perl
7   use Employee;
8   my $empref = Employee->new;
    # call the new method and create the object
9   # my $empref = new Employee; another way to call the new method
10  $empref->{Name} = "Dan Savage";   # Use the object
    $empref->{Salary} = 75000;
11  print "\$empref in main belongs to class ", ref($empref),".\n";
12  print "Name is $empref->{Name}.\n";
13  print "Salary is $empref->{Salary}.\n";
```

```
(Output)
11  $empref in main belongs to class Employee.
12  Name is Dan Savage.
13  Salary is 75000.
```

EXPLANATION

1 The package *Employee* is declared. It can be called a class because it contains a method that will manipulate an object.

2 The subroutine *new* is sometimes called a **constructor** in OOP lingo. The primary job of a constructor is to create and initialize an object. In Perl, it doesn't really have any special syntax. This is called a class method since its first argument is the name of the class. It is a subroutine that blesses a referenced "thing" (object) into a class and returns a reference to it. The subroutine can now be called a **method** and the thing it blessed is an **object**. The package is called a **class**.

3 The first argument received by this type of subroutine is the name of the package or class, in this case *Employee*. This is another difference between a method and a subroutine. The first argument of a method is either the name of a class or an object.

4 The reference *$ref* is assigned the address of an anonymous hash (object). The keys are assigned *undef,* meaning the values at this time are undefined and will be defined later.

5 The reference *$ref* is blessed into the class *$class*.

6 When this method is called, it will return a reference to the anonymous hash.

7 This is another script where the module will be used. After the *shbang* line, the *use* statement causes the module *Employee.pm* to be loaded into memory.

8 The *new* method is called with the class/package name *Employee* as its first argument. It returns a reference, *$empref*, which points to the anonymous hash, the object.

9 Perl translates *$empref = Employee–>new()* to *$empref=Employee::new(Employee);* This line is commented out. It demonstrates another way, called the object-oriented syntax, in which to invoke a method. Use either one.

10 A string value *Dan Savage* is assigned to the key *Name* in the associative array pointed to by the reference *$empref*; in other words, the object's data is being assigned a value.

11 The *ref* function returns the name of the class (package) if the reference has been blessed into that class.

12 The *Name* value is accessed through the reference.

13 The *Salary* value is accessed through the reference.

The Class and Instance Methods. To review: The **class methods,** also called **static methods**, are methods or subroutines that don't require the instance of an object in order to function. They are independent functions that act on behalf of the class. A function that calculates a paycheck or gets a list of names from a database is an example of a class method. The most common class method is called a constructor method, a method used to create the object. It takes a class (package) name as its first argument and functions for the entire class.

Object-oriented programs often use **access** or **instance methods** to control the way data is modified, retrieved, and displayed. In order to manipulate an object, the instance or access methods require an **instance** of an object; that is, a reference to an object that has already been created.

If the data need to be represented in a different way in one of the methods, the other methods need not be affected as long as the interface provided to the user remains the same. The instance methods in the following examples are used as access functions that display the data members of the class. Instance methods take an object reference as their first argument.

EXAMPLE 13.5

```perl
      #!/usr/bin/perl
1     package Employee;
2     sub new{           # Class/Static method
3         my $class = shift;
4         my $ref = {};   # Anonymous and empty hash
5         bless($ref);
6         return $ref;
      }
7     sub set_name{      # Instance/Virtual method
8         my $self = shift;
9         print "\$self is a class ", ref($self)," reference.\n";
10        $self->{Name} = shift;
      }
11    sub display_name{
12        my $self = shift;
                    # The object reference is the first argument
13        print $self->{Name},"\n";
      }
      1;


(The Script)
      #!/usr/bin/perl
      # The user of the class
14    use Employee;
15    my $emp = Employee->new;        # Call class method
16    $emp->set_name("Tom Savage");   # Call instance method
17    $emp->display_name;             # Call instance method

(Output)
9     $self is a class Employee reference.
13    Tom Savage
```

EXPLANATION

1   The package *Employee* is declared. This can also be called the class *Employee*.
2   The class method *new* is a constructor. It creates a reference and blesses it into the class *Employee*.
3   The *$class* variable is assigned the name of the class, the first argument in the new constructor.
4   The reference *$ref* is assigned an anonymous, empty hash.
5   The "thing" (anonymous hash) referenced by *$ref* is blessed into the class *Employee*.
6   A reference to the object will be returned to the caller from the *new* method.
7   The instance method *set_name* is defined.
8   A reference to the object is shifted from the @_ array into *$self*. Now the instance method can manipulate the object because it has a reference to it.
9   The return from *ref* is the name of the class *Employee*. The class name is returned by *$ref* only if the object has been blessed.
10 The second argument is shifted from the @_ array. *Tom Savage* is assigned as a value to the key *Name*. This instance method is then used to assign data to the object.
11 The instance method *display_name* is called to access the object's data; in this example, to print the value in *Name* field of the anonymous hash.
12 The object reference is the first argument to the method. It is shifted from the @_ array into *$self*.
13 The value in the key *Name* field is displayed.
14 A new script is started. The program loads *Employee.pm*.
15 The *new* constructor method is called and a reference to the object is returned; that is, a reference to an anonymous hash in the *Employee* class. The constructor method, *new*, always passes at least one argument, the name of the class. *Employee–>new()* translates to *Employee::new(Employee)*.
16 The instance method *set_name* is called with the argument *Tom Savage*. Remember, the first argument passed to an instance method is the reference to the object. *$emp–>set_name ("Tom Savage")* translates to *Employee::set_name($emp, "Tom Savage");*
17 The *display* method is called, which displays the value of the anonymous hash, *Tom Savage*.

Passing Parameters to Constructor Methods.   Instance variables are used to initialize the object when it is created. In this way, each time the object is created, it can be customized. The properties that describe the object may be passed as arguments to the constructor method and assigned to instance variables. They are called **instance variables** because they come into existence when the object is created or instantiated. Either an anonymous hash or an anonymous array is commonly used to hold the instance variables. In the following example, the object "has a" or "contains a" name and a salary.

EXAMPLE 13.6

```
(The Module: Employee.pm)
1    package Employee;
2    sub new{              # Constructor  method
3        my $class = shift;
4        my ($name, $salary) = @_;    # Instance variables
5        my $ref={Name=>$name,        # Instance variables to
                 Salary=>$salary,     # initialize the object
         };
6        bless($ref, $class);
7        return $ref;
     }
8    sub display_object{       # An instance method
9        my $self = shift;        # The name of the object is passed
10       while(($key, $value) = each %$self){
               print "$key: $value \n";
         }
     }
     1;


------------------------------------------------------------------


(The Script)
     #!/usr/bin/perl
     # User of the class; another program
11   use Employee;
     # Documentation explaining how to use the employee
     # package is called the public interface.
     # It tells the programmer how to use the class.

     # To create an Employee object requires two arguments;
     # a name and salary.
     # See "Public User Interface—Documenting Classes" on page 422
     # to create documentation.

     # my $emp1 = new Employee("Tom Savage", 250000);
     # Invoking constructor--two ways.
12   my $emp1  = Employee->new("Tom Savage", 250000);
13   my $emp2 = Employee->new("Devin Quigley", 55000);
     # Two objects have been created.
14   $emp1->display_object;
15   $emp2->display_object;
16   print "$emp1, $emp2\n";

(Output)
14   Name: Tom Savage
     Salary: 250000
15   Name: Devin Quigley
     Salary: 55000
16   Employee=HASH(0x9d450), Employee=HASH(0xa454c)
```

EXPLANATION

1 The package *Employee* is declared.
2 The class method *new* is defined as a constructor.
3 The first argument to the class method is the name of the class (package).
4 The instance variables are created from the remainder of the argument list.
5 The address of an anonymous array is assigned to to the reference, *$ref*. The keys are hard coded and the values are supplied from the instance variables.
6 The "thing" that the reference *$ref* points to is blessed into the class.
7 The value of the reference *$ref* will be returned when the method is called.
8 The subroutine *display_object* is an instance method. It is defined in this class.
9 The first argument to the instance method is the reference to the object.
10 The *while* loop is used with the *each* function to get both keys and values from the hash (object) referenced by *$self*.
11 The user of the class loads *Employee.pm* into his namespace.
12 The *new* method is called with two arguments, *Tom Savage* and *250000*. The only request here is that the name value is the first argument and the salary value is the second argument. There is no error checking. The example simply shows how to pass arguments to a constructor. The value returned to *$emp1* is a reference to the hash object.
13 The *new* method is called again with different arguments, *Devin Quigley* and *55000*. The value returned to *$emp2* is a reference to another object. The *new* method has been used to create two objects. You can create as many objects as you want. They will all have unique addresses, as shown in the output at line 16. Since the objects were blessed in the constructor, Perl knows that the objects are in the *Employee* class.
14 The instance method is called to display the data for the object referenced by *$emp1*.
15 The instance method is called again, but to display the data of the object referenced by *$emp2*.
16 The addresses of the two objects are printed.

Passing Parameters to Instance Methods. The first argument to an instance method is the name of the object reference. In the called method, this value is typically shifted from the @_ array and stored in a *my* variable called *$self* or *$this*, although it doesn't matter what you call the variable. The remaining arguments are then processed as they are in any regular subroutine.

EXAMPLE 13.7

```
     #!/bin/perl
     # Program to demonstrate passing arguments to an instance method.
     # When method is called, user can select what he wants returned.
1    package Employee;

2    sub new{       # Constructor
        my $class = shift;
        my ($name, $salary, $extension) = @_;
        my $ref={ Name=>$name,
                  Salary=>$salary,
                  Extension=>$extension,
              };
        return bless($ref, $class);
     }
3    sub display{             # Instance method
4        my $self = shift;    # Object reference is the first argument
5        foreach $choice ( @_){
6            print "$choice: $self->{$choice}\n";
         }
     }
     1;


     -----------------------------------------------------------------

     (The Script)
        #!/bin/perl
        # User of the class--Another program
7    use Employee;
8    my $emp = new Employee("Tom Savage", 250000, 5433);
9    $emp->display("Name", "Extension");
                        # Passing arguments to instance method

     (Output)
     Name: Tom Savage
     Extension: 5433
```

EXPLANATION

1 The package *Employee* is declared. Since this package deals with blessed references and methods, call it a **class**.

2 The *new* method is a constructor. The object is an anonymous hash consisting of three key/value pairs. The key/value pairs are called the **properties** or **attributes** of the object. The values are passed in as arguments to the constructor. The object, referenced by *$ref*, is blessed into the *Employee* class so that Perl can keep track of the package where the object belongs.

EXPLANATION (CONTINUED)

3   The instance method *display* is defined.
4   The first argument to the *display* instance method is a reference to an *Employee* object. It is shifted and assigned to *$self*.
5   The *foreach* loop iterates through the remaining arguments in the @_ array, one at a time, assigning each argument in turn to the variable *$choice*. The variable *$choice* is a key of the anonymous array.
6   The selected values from the associative array are printed.
7   The user of the class loads the module into his program.
8   The constructor method is called to create a new *Employee* object.
9   The instance method is called with arguments. The first argument sent will be the name of the object's reference, *$emp*, even though you can't see it. The rest of the arguments are in parentheses.

Named Parameters.   If a constructor method is expecting a name, address, and salary to be passed in that order, it would be easy to send the parameters in the wrong order, causing the address to be assigned to the name, or the name to the salary, and so on. Using named parameters provides a method to ensure that parameters can be passed to a method in any order and still result in the values getting assigned to the correct attributes. The arguments are passed by the calling or driver program as key/value pairs (hash) and received by the constructor as a hash. The following example demonstrates how named parameters are passed to a method and by a method.

EXAMPLE 13.8

```
      #!/usr/bin/perl
      # User of Employee.pm--See Example 13.9
1     use Employee;
2     use warnings;
      use strict;
3     my($name, $extension, $address, $basepay, $employee);
4     print "Enter the employee's name. ";
      chomp($name = <STDIN>);
      print "Enter the employee's phone extension. ";
      chomp($extension = <STDIN>);
      print "Enter the employee's address. ";
      chomp($address = <STDIN>);
      print "Enter the employee's basepay. ";
      chomp($basepay = <STDIN>);
```

EXAMPLE 13.8 (CONTINUED)

```
     # Passing parameters as a hash
5    $employee = new Employee( Name=>$name,
                               Address=>$address,
                               Extension=>$extension,
                               PayCheck=>$basepay,
                             );
     print "\nThe statistics for $name are: \n";

6    $employee->get_stats;


(Output)
Enter the employee's name. Daniel Savage
Enter the employee's phone extension. 2534
Enter the employee's address. 999 Mission Ave, Somewhere, CA
Enter the employee's basepay. 2200

The statistics for Daniel Savage are:
Address = 999 Mission Ave, Somewhere, CA
PayCheck = 2200
IdNum = Employee Id not provided!
Extension = 2534
Name = Daniel Savage
```

EXPLANATION

1   The *Employee.pm* module will be used by this program.
2   Warnings will be issued for possible errors and the *strict* pragma will track global and undefined variables, bare words, etc.
3   A list of lexical private variables is created.
4   The user of the program will be asked for the information that will be passed to the *Employee* module.
5   The constructor is called to pass arguments as key/value pairs; that is, a hash is passed to the constructor in the *Employee* module. (See Example 13.9 below.) A reference to the object is returned and assigned to *$employee*.
6   The instance method *get_stats* is called to display the employee's attributes.

EXAMPLE 13.9

```
     # Module Employee.pm--See Example 13.8 to use this module.
1    package Employee;
2    use Carp;
3    sub new{
4       my $class = shift;
5       my(%params)=@_;    # Receiving the hash that was passed
6       my $objptr={
7           Name=>$params{Name} || croak("No name assigned"),
            Extension=>$params{Extension},
8           Address=>$params{Address},
            PayCheck=>$params{PayCheck} || croak("No pay assigned"),
9           ((defined $params{IdNum})?(IdNum=>$params{IdNum}):
                (IdNum=>"Employee's id not provided!"
            )),

        };
10      return bless($objptr,$class);
     }
11   sub get_stats{
12      my $self=shift;
13      while( ($key, $value)=each %$self){
            print $key, " = ", $value, "\n";
        }
        print "\n";
     }
     1;
```

EXPLANATION

1 The class (package) *Employee* is declared.
2 The *Carp* module from the standard Perl library is used to handle error messages.
3 The constructor method *new* is defined.
4 The first argument to the constructor method is the name of the class. It is shifted from the @_ array and assigned to *$class*.
5 The rest of the arguments in the @_ array are assigned to the hash *%params*. They were sent to the constructor as a set of key/value pairs.
6 A reference, *$objptr*, is assigned the address of an anonymous hash.
7 The key, *Name*, is assigned a value, retrieved from the *%params* hash. Error checking is done here. If a corresponding value for the key *Name* is not provided, the *croak* function will be executed, letting the user know that he did not assign a value to the *Name*, and the program will exit.
8 The *Address* property is assigned by getting its value from the *%params* hash.

EXPLANATION (CONTINUED)

9   This is an example of how you can make sure that the user of the module passed the expected arguments. The conditional statement reads: If the *%params* has a key called *IdNum* defined, then get its value and assign it to *IdNum*; otherwise, when the program runs, tell the user he forgot to include this parameter. In the examples using *croak*, the program will die if the user doesn't provide input when asked for it, whereas in this form of checking, the program will continue to run.

10   After assigning properties, a reference to the object is blessed into the class and returned to the caller.

11   The instance method *get_stats* is defined.

12   The first argument is shifted from the @_ array and assigned to *$self*. It is a pointer to the object.

13   The *while* loop is entered. Each key/value pair from the object is returned by the *each* function and displayed.

13.2.5   Polymorphism and Dynamic Binding

Webster's Dictionary defines polymophism as

> polymorphism: *n*. 1. the state or condition of being polymorphous.[6]

There, that should clear things up! Here's another definition:

> Having many forms or the ability to take several forms . . . The same operation may behave differently on different classes.

Polymorphism can be described in many ways, and it's a word that is inherently part of the OO lingo. In Perl, it means that you can provide a method with the same name in different classes and when you call the method, it will do the right thing; in other words, when the reference to the object invokes the method, it will go to the class where the object belongs.

In the following Example 13.10, polymorphism is demonstrated. Two modules, *Cat.pm* and *Dog.pm*, each have three functions with the same names: *new*, *set_attributes*, and *get_attributes*. The driver or user program in Example 13.11 will use both of the modules. A reference to the *cat* or *dog* object is returned when their respective class constructors are called. When the access methods are called with an object reference, Perl knows which subroutine to call and to which class it belongs even though the methods have the same names. Perl determines which class the invoking object belongs to, and looks in that class (package) for the method being called. The ability to call the right method demonstrates polymorphism. Dynamic or **runtime binding** allows the program to defer calling the correct method

---

6. *Webster's Encyclopedic Unabridged Dictionary of the English Language,* Random House Value Publishing: Avenel, NJ, 1996, p. 1500. Reprinted by permission.

until the program is running and, along with polymorphism, to tie the correct method to its associated class without using *if* statements to determine which method to call. This provides a great deal of flexibility and is necessary for inheritance to work properly.

To take advantage of polymorphism and runtime binding, the object-oriented syntax must be used, rather than the *::* syntax. If, for example, you have two classes, *Director* and *Rifleman,* and both classes contain an access method called *shoot*, you can write *$object–>shoot* and Perl will know which class the object belongs to. It determined the correct class at compile time. In this way, the *Director* will not shoot bullets at his cast and the *Rifleman* will not try to take movies of the rifle range. It is also possible to add another class, such as a *BasketballPlayer* class with a different *shoot* method and be sure that the appropriate method will be called for that class. Without runtime binding and polymorphism, the correct class will be determined based on the outcome of some condition, as shown below:

```
if(ref($object) eq "Director") {
    Director::shoot($object);
elsif (ref($object) eq "Rifleman"){
    Rifleman::shoot($object);
else{
    BasketballPlayer::shoot($object);
}
```

EXAMPLE 13.10

```
( File: Cat.pm)
1   package Cat;
2   sub new{        # Constructor
        my $class=shift;
        my $dptr={};
        bless($dptr, $class);
    }
3   sub set_attributes{              # Access Methods
        my $self= shift;
4       $self->{Name} = "Sylvester";
        $self->{Owner} = "Mrs. Black";
        $self->{Type} = "Siamese";
        $self->{Sex} = "Male";
    }
5   sub get_attributes{
        my $self = shift;
        print "-" x 20, "\n";
        print "Stats for the Cat\n";
        print "-" x 20, "\n";
        while(($key,$value)=each( %$self)){
            print "$key is $value. \n";
    }
    print "-" x 20, "\n";
    1;
```

EXAMPLE 13.10 (CONTINUED)

```
(File: Dog.pm)
6    package Dog;
7    sub new{                    # Constructor
         my $class = shift;
         my $dptr = {};
         bless($dptr, $class);
     }
8    sub set_attributes{
         my $self = shift;
9        my($name, $owner, $breed) = @_;
10       $self->{Name} = "$name";
         $self->{Owner} = "$owner";
         $self->{Breed} = "$breed";
     }
11   sub get_attributes{
         my $self = shift;
         print "x" x 20, "\n";
         print "All about $self->{Name}\n";
         while(($key,$value)= each(%$self)){
             print "$key is $value.\n";
         }
         print "x" x 20, "\n";
     }
     1;
```

EXPLANATION

1   This is the package declaration for a class called *Cat* in module, *Cat.pm*.

2   The constructor method for the *Cat* class is called *new*. A *Cat* object is blessed into the class.

3   The access method *set_attributes* will define data properties of the *Cat* object.

4   The object pointer *$self* is used to assign a key/value pair to give the cat a name.

5   Another access method, *get_attributes*, is used to display the *Cat* object.

6   In another file, *Dog.pm*, a package is declared for a class called *Dog*.

7   Like the *Cat* class, the *Dog* class has a constructor called *new*. A *Dog* object is blessed into the class.

8   The access method, *set_attributes*, will define data properties of the *Dog* object.

9   The properties of the *Dog* object are being passed from the driver program and assigned to the @_ array.

10 The object pointer, *$self*, is used to assign a key/value pair to give the dog a name.

11 Like the *Cat* class, another access method, *get_attributes*, is used to display the *Dog* object.

EXAMPLE 13.11

```
(The Script: driver program for Example 13.10)
#!/bin/perl
1  use Cat;   # Use the Cat.pm module
2  use Dog;   # Use the Dog.pm module

3  my $dogref = Dog->new;     # Polymorphism
4  my $catref = Cat->new;

5  $dogref->set_attributes("Rover", "Mr. Jones", "Mutt");
6  $catref->set_attributes;   # Polymorphism

7  $dogref->get_attributes;
8  $catref->get_attributes;

(Output)
xxxxxxxxxxxxxxxxxxx
All about Rover
Owner is Mr. Jones.
Breed is Mutt.
Name is Rover.
xxxxxxxxxxxxxxxxxxx
--------------------
Stats for the Cat
--------------------
Sex is Male.
Type is Siamese.
Owner is Mrs. Black.
Name is Sylvester.
--------------------
```

EXPLANATION

1   The *use* directive loads in the *Cat.pm* module.
2   The *use* directive loads in the *Dog.pm* module. Now we have access to both classes.
3   The *new* constructor method is called.[a] The first argument is the name of the class, *Dog*, which is translated to *Dog::new(Dog)*. A reference to a *Dog* object is returned. Perl knows the reference belongs to the *Dog* class because it was blessed in the constructor method. An instance of a *Dog* object has been created.
4   The *new* constructor method is called. It passes the name of the class as its first argument. A reference to a *Cat* object is returned. Perl translates the method call to *Cat::new(Cat)*. Two classes have used the *new* function, but because Perl knows to which class the method belongs, it always calls the correct version of *new*. This is an example of polymorphism.

a. The new constructor could also be called by using the indirect method, *new Dog*.

EXPLANATION (CONTINUED)

5   Now that we have a reference to the object, we use it to call the access (instance) methods. Perl translates the *$dogref–>set_attributes* method to *Dog::set_attributes($dogref, "Rover", "Mr. Jones", "Mutt")*.

6   This time, the *set_attributes* method for the cat is called. The *Cat* class sets the attributes for the cat.

7   The *get_attributes* method is called to display the data attributes of the *Cat* class.

8   The *get_attributes* method is called to display the data attributes of the *Dog* class.

The :: versus –> Notation.   The –> arrow syntax is used in object-oriented programs that use polymorphism, dynamic binding, and inheritance. The :: syntax is allowed, but it is not flexible and can lead to problems unless conditional statements are used. The following example demonstrates how the :: syntax can be a disadvantage. With the object-oriented syntax, the problem would not occur.

EXAMPLE 13.12

```
# The Cat class
package Cat;
sub new{        # The Cat's constructor
    my $class = shift;
    my $ref = {};
    return bless ($ref, $class);
}
sub set_attributes{   # Giving the Cat some attributes,
                      # a name and a voice
    my $self = shift;
    $self->{Name} = "Sylvester";
    $self->{Talk}= "Meow purrrrrr.... ";
}
sub speak{          # Retrieving the Cat's attributes
    my $self = shift;
    print "$self->{Talk} I'm the cat called $self->{Name}.\n";
}
1;
```

EXAMPLE 13.12 (CONTINUED)

```perl
# The Dog class
package Dog;    # The Dog's Constructor
sub new{
    my $class = shift;
    my $ref = {};
    return bless ($ref, $class);
}
sub set_attributes{    # Giving the Dog some attributes
    my $self = shift;
    $self->{Name} = "Lassie";
    $self->{Talk} = "Bow Wow, woof woof.... ";
}
sub speak {            # Retrieving the Dog's attributes
    my $self = shift;
    print "$self->{Talk} I'm the dog called $self->{Name}.\n";
}
1;
```
```perl
#!/bin/perl
# User Program
# This example demonstrates why to use the object-oriented
# syntax rather than the colon-colon syntax when passing
# arguments to methods.
use Cat;
use Dog;
$mydog = new Dog;    # Calling the Dog's constructor
$mycat = new Cat;    # Calling the Cat's constructor

$mydog->set_attributes;  # Calling the Dog's access methods
$mycat->set_attributes;  # Calling the Cat's access methods

1  $mydog->speak;
2  $mycat->speak;

3  print "\nNow we make a mistake in passing arguments.\n\n";

4  Cat::speak($mydog); # Perl goes Cat class to find the method
                       # even though attributes have been set
                       # for the dog!
```

(Output)
1   Bow Wow, woof woof.... I'm the dog called Lassie.
2   Meow purrrrrr.... I'm the cat called Sylvester.

3   Now we make a mistake in passing arguments.

4   Bow Wow, woof woof.... I'm the cat called Lassie.

EXPLANATION

1   The object-oriented approach of calling the *speak* method guarantees that Perl will bind the method to the class where it was blessed.

A reference to the *Dog* object is passed as the first argument to the *speak* method. It breaks down to *Dog::speak($mydog)*. Perl determines what class to use at compile time so that when the *speak* method is called at runtime, it will be bound the right class.

2   A reference to the *Cat* object is passed as the first argument to the *speak* method. It breaks down to *Cat::speak($mydog)*.

3   The following line passes a dog reference to the *Cat* package. This mistake will not occur when using the object-oriented approach, because Perl will be able to determine to which class the method belongs and make the correct method call. This feature is called **polymorphism** and **runtime binding**.

4   By using the *::* notation, Perl will figure out the class at runtime and use the *speak* method found in the *Cat* class, even though a reference to the *Dog* object is passed. And we wind up with a cat that barks!

13.2.6 Destructors and Garbage Collection

Perl keeps track of the number of references to an object and when the count reaches *0*, the object is automatically destroyed. When your program exits, Perl handles the garbage collection by destroying every object associated with the program and de-allocating any memory that was used. So, you don't have to worry about cleaning up memory.[7] However, you can define a *DESTROY* method in your program to get control of the object just before it goes away.

EXAMPLE 13.13

```
#!/bin/perl
1   package Employee;
    sub new{
        my $class = shift;
        $ref={Name=>undef,
              Salary=>undef,
             };
        bless($ref, $class);
        return $ref;
    }
```

---

7. If you use self-referencing data structures, then you will be responsible for destroying those references.

EXAMPLE 13.13 (CONTINUED)

```
2    sub DESTROY{
         my $self = shift;
3        print "$self->{Name}\n";
4        delete $self->{Name};              # Remove the (object);
5        print "Hash Name entry has been destroyed.
                Bailing out...\n" if ( ! exists $self->{Name});
     }


-------------------------------------------------------------

(The Script)
    #!/usr/bin/perl
    # User of the class
6   use Employee;
7   $empref = new Employee;  # Create the object
    $empref->{Name} = "Dan Savage";
    $empref->{Salary} = 10000;
8   print "Name is $empref->{Name}.\n";
9   print "Salary is $empref->{Salary}.\n";

(Output)
8   Name is Dan Savage.
9   Salary is 10000.
3   Dan Savage
5   Hash Name entry has been destroyed. Bailing out...
```

EXPLANATION

1   The *Employee* class is declared and its constructor method defined.
2   The *DESTROY* method is defined. This method is automatically called when the program ends. Since Perl destroys the objects anyway, this function is unnecessary. You might use it for debugging purposes.
3   The value for the *Name* key in the *Employee* hash is printed.
4   The *Name* key and its associated value are released with *delete*. Its memory is freed for reuse.
5   This message is printed just before the program exits if the hash entry does not exist. Since the entry was deleted, the message is printed. The *exists* tests whether the object exists.
6   Package *main* is declared.
7   The object reference *$empref* is created by calling the constructor method.
8   The value of the hash key *Name* is printed.
9   The value of the hash key *Salary* is printed.

13.3 Inheritance

Inheritance means that a new class can inherit methods from an existing class. The new class can then add to or modify existing code in order to customize the class without having to reinvent what has already been done. The principle is that a class may be subdivided into a number of subclasses that all share common features, but each subclass may provide its own additional features, refining what it borrows to a more specific functionality. The idea of this kind of organization is not new. You may have seen it in a biology class when learning about the plant and animal kingdoms and the breakdown of each phylum, kingdom, class, order, family, species, and variety, or in procedural programs with the use of functions to combine the common elements of a program into specific tasks.

In object-oriented programming, once a class has been written and debugged, it can be stored in a library and reused by other programmers. The programmer can then add features and capabilities to the existing class without rewriting the whole thing. This is done through inheritance, that is, by deriving a new class from an already existing class. The reuse of software and the increased use of library classes where all this software is stored and organized have contributed to the wide popularity of OOP languages. Let's see how Perl implements inheritance.

13.3.1 The @*ISA* Array and Calling Methods

The classes (packages) listed in the @*ISA* array are the **parent** or **base classes** of the current class. This is how Perl implements inheritance. The @*ISA* array contains a list of packages (classes) where Perl will search for a method if it can't find it in the current package (class). If the method still isn't found, then Perl searches for an *AUTOLOAD* function and calls that method instead. And if that isn't found, then Perl searches for the last time in a special predefined package called *UNIVERSAL*. The *UNIVERSAL* class is a global base class for all packages, the highest class in the hierarchy of classes.

The @*ISA* array is not searched in a call to a normal subroutine, but in a call to a subroutine if it is called with the method invocation syntax.

EXAMPLE 13.14

```
    #!/bin/perl
    # Example of attempting inheritance without updating
    # the @ISA array
1   { package Grandpa;
2   $name = "Gramps";
3   sub greetme{
        print "Hi $Child::name I'm your $name from package
    Grandpa.\n";
    }
```

EXAMPLE 13.14 (CONTINUED)

```
4   { package Parent;
    # This package is empty
    }

5   { package Child;
6   $name = "Baby";
7   print "Hi I'm $name in the Child Package here.\n";
8   Parent->greetme();      # Use method invocation syntax
    }
```

```
(Output)
7   Hi I'm Baby in the Child Package here.
8   Can't locate object method "greetme" via package "Parent" at
    inher2 line 23.
```

EXPLANATION

1   The package *Grandpa* is declared.
2   The scalar *$name* is assigned *Gramps* in package *Grandpa*.
3   The subroutine *greetme* is defined and when called, the *print* statement will be exe-
    cuted. *$Child::name* refers to the scalar *$name* in the Child package.
4   The package *Parent* is declared. It is empty.
5   The package *Child* is declared. This package will try to call a method from another
    package. Although objects and methods aren't being used here, the purpose of this
    example is to show you what happens if you try to inherit a method from a class that
    this package doesn't know about.
8   Perl can't find the method *greetme* in package *Parent* and prints the error message.

EXAMPLE 13.15

```
    #!/bin/perl
    # Example of attempting inheritance by updating the @ISA array
1   { package Grandpa;
    $name = "Gramps";
2   sub greetme {
        print "Hi $Child::name I'm your $name from package
    Grandpa.\n";
    }
    }

3   { package Parent;
4   @ISA=qw(Grandpa);    # Grandpa is a package in the @ISA array.
                         # This package is empty.
    }
```

EXAMPLE 13.15 (CONTINUED)

```
5   { package Child;
    $name = "Baby";
6   print "Hi I'm $name in the Child Package here.\n";
7   Parent->greetme();     # Parent::greetme() will fail
    }
```

```
(Output)
6   Hi I'm Baby in the Child Package here.
7   Hi Baby I'm your Gramps from package Grandpa.
```

EXPLANATION

1   The package *Grandpa* is declared.
2   The subroutine *greetme* is defined and, when called, the *print* statement will be executed. *$Child::name* refers to the scalar *$name* in the Child package.
3   The *Parent* package is declared.
4   The *@ISA* array is assigned the name of the package *Grandpa*. Now if a method is called from this *Child* package and Perl can't find it, it will try the *Grandpa* package listed in the *@ISA* array. If you try to call a normal subroutine without method invocation, Perl won't consult the *@ISA* array because it uses the *@ISA* array only when methods are being called. Even though the subroutines used here are not technically methods, by calling *greetme* as a class method, Perl will search the *@ISA* array.
5   The *Child* package is declared.
6   This line will be printed from the *Child* package.
7   The class method *greetme* is called in the *Parent* package. The *@ISA* array tells Perl to look in the *Grandpa* package if the method isn't in the Parent package.

13.3.2   *$AUTOLOAD*, sub *AUTOLOAD*, and *UNIVERSAL*

If a subroutine (or method) cannot be found in the current package or in the *@ISA* array, the *AUTOLOAD* function will be called. The *$AUTOLOAD* variable is assigned the name of the missing subroutine if it is used with the *AUTOLOAD* function. Arguments passed to the undefined subroutine are stored in the *AUTOLOAD* subroutine's *@_* array. If you assign a function name to the *$AUTOLOAD* variable, that subroutine will be called if the *AUTOLOAD* subroutine is provided in place of the missing subroutine. If the *$AUTOLOAD* variable is used with the *AUTOLOAD* subroutine, either the method or regular subroutine syntax can be used. If all fails and Perl still can't find the subroutine, a final package (class) called *UNIVERSAL* is searched for the missing method. The *UNIVERSAL* method contains three methods that all classes inherit. They are *isa()*, *can()*, and *VERSION()*. (See Table 13.2.)

Table 13.2   *UNIVERSAL* Methods

Method	*What It Does*	*Example*
isa	Returns true if one package inherits from another.	*Salesman–>isa("Employee");*
can	Returns true if a package or any of its base classes contain a specified method.	*Salesman–>can("get_data");*
VERSION	Used to check that the correct modules are loaded for that version number. In the example, Perl calls the *UNIVERSAL* method *Salesman–>VERSION(6.1)*	*package Salesman;* *use$VERSION=6.1;*

EXAMPLE 13.16

```
       #!/bin/perl
    1  { package Grandpa;
       $name = "Gramps";
       sub greetme{
    2      print "Hi $Child::name I'm your $name from package
       Grandpa.\n";
       }

    3  { package Parent;
    4  sub AUTOLOAD{
    5      print "$_[0]: $_[1] and $_[2]\n";
    6      print "You know us after all!\n";
    7      print "The unheard of subroutine is called $AUTOLOAD.\n"
       };

    8  { package Child;
       $name = "Baby";
    9  $AUTOLOAD=Grandpa->greetme();
   10  print "Hi I'm $name in the Child Package here.\n";
   11  Parent->unknown("Mom", "Dad");    # Undefined subroutine
       }
```

```
(Output)
    2  Hi Baby I'm your Gramps from package Grandpa.
   10  Hi I'm Baby in the Child Package here.
    5  Parent: Mom and Dad
    6  You know us after all!
    7  The unheard of subroutine is called Parent::unknown.
```

EXPLANATION

1 The package *Grandpa* is declared. It contains one subroutine.
2 This line is printed from the *Grandpa* package.
3 The package *Parent* is declared. It contains an *AUTOLOAD* subroutine. An undefined subroutine is called on line 11. It has two arguments, *Mom* and *Dad*. If Perl can't find this subroutine in the *Child* package, it will look in the @*ISA* array and if it is not there, Perl will look for an *AUTOLOAD* function.
4 The subroutine *AUTOLOAD* is defined.
5 Since this function was called as a class method, the first argument stored in the @_ array is the name of the class. The remaining arguments are *Mom* and *Dad*.
6 This line is printed to show that we got here.
7 The *$AUTOLOAD* variable contains the name of the class and the unnamed subroutine.
8 The package *Child* is declared.
9 If the scalar variable *$AUTOLOAD* is assigned the name of a subroutine, Perl will automatically call that subroutine.
10 This line is printed to show in what order the lines are executed.
11 The *Child* package wants to access a method in the *Parent* package. The *Parent* package does not contain a method or subroutine called *unknown*. It does, on the other hand, contain an *AUTOLOAD* subroutine that will be executed because this subroutine can't be found.

EXAMPLE 13.17

```perl
#!/bin/perl
1   { package Grandpa;
    $name = "Gramps";
2   sub greetme{
        print "Hi $Child::name I'm your $name from package
    Grandpa.\n";
    }

3   { package Parent;
        # This package is empty
    }
4   { package Child;
    $name = "Baby";
5   print "Hi I'm $name in the Child Package here.\n";
6   Parent->greetme();
    }
```

EXAMPLE 13.17 (CONTINUED)

```
7    package UNIVERSAL;
8    sub AUTOLOAD{
9        print "The UNIVERSAL lookup package.\n";
10       Grandpa->greetme();
     }

(Output)
2    Hi I'm Baby in the Child Package here.
9    The UNIVERSAL lookup package.
5    Hi Baby I'm your Gramps from package Grandpa.
```

EXPLANATION

1   The package *Grandpa* is declared.
2   The subroutine *greetme* is defined in this package.
3   The package *Parent* is declared. It is empty.
4   The package *Child* is declared.
5   This line is printed to show the flow of execution in the program.
6   The *greetme* subroutine is called as one of the *Parent* package methods.
7   Since the method could not be found in its own class, or in the @*ISA* array, and an *AUTOLOAD* function is not supplied in the *Parent* package, Perl looks for package *UNIVERSAL* as a last resort. Here the subroutine *AUTOLOAD* calls *greetme*.

13.3.3 Derived Classes

As already discussed, **inheritance** is when one class can inherit methods from an existing class. The existing class is called the **base** or **parent class**, and the new class that inherits it is called the **derived** or **child class**. The base class has capabilities that all its derived classes inherit, and the derived class can then go beyond those capabilities. If a derived class inherits from one base class, it is called **single inheritance**. For example, single inheritance in real life might be that a child inherits his ability to draw from his father. If a derived class inherits from more than one base class, this is called **multiple inheritance**. To continue the analogy, the child inherits his ability to draw from his father and his ability to sing from his mother. In Perl, the derived class inherits methods from its base class (package) and can add and modify these methods when necessary.

The classes are inherited by putting them in the @*ISA* array. The methods to be exported to other modules can be specified in either the @*EXPORTER* or the @*EXPORTER_OK* arrays. The data itself is inherited by referencing keys and values in the anonymous hash where the data was initially assigned. These variables are called **instance variables** and are defined in the constructor method.

In Chapter 11, we looked at modules from the Perl standard library and modules you could create yourself. In order to include a module or pragma into your program, the *use* function was called with the module name (minus the *.pm* extension). The module had the ability to export symbols to other packages that might need to use the module. A special module called *Exporter.pm* handled the details for exporting and importing symbols between modules. This module also needs to be included in the *@ISA* array. If a module functions as a class, then its methods can be called without explicitly listing them in the *@EXPORT* array. Note in the following examples, the class methods and the instance methods are not exported.

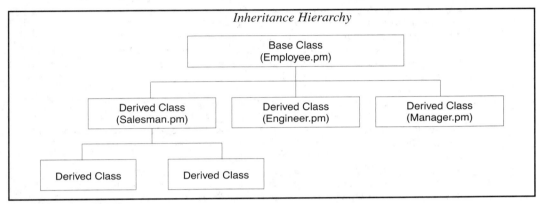

Figure 13.4   Deriving classes from a base class.

The following examples demonstrate inheritance. Example 13.18 is the user of the *Salesman.pm* class. The user program need not make any reference to the base class, *Employee.pm* (see Example 13.19). The *Salesman.pm* class is derived from *Employee.pm*. The *Salesman.pm* class "uses" the *Employee.pm* class.

EXAMPLE 13.18

```
   # The Driver (user) Program
1  use Salesman;
2  use strict;
   use warnings;
   # Create two salesman objects
   print "Entering data for the first salesman.\n";
3  my $salesguy1=Salesman->new;
4  $salesguy1->set_data;
5  print "\nEntering data for the second salesman.\n";

6  my $salesguy2 = Salesman->new;
7  $salesguy2->set_data;

8  print "\nHere are the statistics for the first salesman.\n";
9  $salesguy1->get_data;
10 print "\nHere are the statistics for the second salesman.\n";
11 $salesguy2->get_data;
```

EXAMPLE 13.18 (CONTINUED)

(Output)
```
      The salesman is an employee.
      The salesman can display its properties.
      Entering data for the first salesman.
      Enter the name of the employee. Russ Savage
      Enter the address of Russ Savage. 12 Main St., Boston, MA
      Enter the monthly base pay for Russ Savage. 2200
      Before blessing package is: Employee
      After blessing package is: Salesman
      Enter Russ Savage's commission for this month. 1200
      Enter Russ Savage's bonuses for this month. 500.50
      Enter Russ Savage's sales region. northeast


   5  Entering data for the second salesman.
      Enter the name of the employee. Jody Rodgers
      Enter the address of Jody Rodgers. 2200 Broadway Ave, Chico, CA
      Enter the monthly base pay for Jody Rodgers. 34500
      Before blessing package is: Employee
      After blessing package is: Salesman
      Enter Jody Rodgers's commission for this month. 2300
      Enter Jody Rodgers's bonuses for this month. 1400
      Enter Jody Rodgers's sales region. northwest


   8  Here are the statistics for the first salesman.
      Name = Russ Savage.
      Bonuses = 500.50.
      Commission = 1200.
      BasePay = 2200.
      Address = 12 Main St., Boston, MA.
      PayCheck = 3900.5.
      Region = northeast.



  10  Here are the statistics for the second salesman.
      Name = Jody Rodgers.
      Bonuses = 1400.
      Commission = 2300.
      BasePay = 34500.
      Address = 2200 Broadway Ave, Chico, CA.
      PayCheck = 38200.
      Region = northwest.
```

EXPLANATION

1 This *use* directive loads the *Salesman* module into this package, *main*. The program that contains the user interface is often called the **driver** program. It will be using the *Salesman* module to create a new salesman employee. Even though the *Salesman* class was derived from the *Employee* class, this program doesn't have to know that. All this program needs to do is call the *Salesman* constructor with the correct arguments (if any) and ask the user for input.

2 The *strict* and *warnings* pragmas are turned on to help keep the program from using unsafe constructs and from making compile or runtime errors.

3 The *Salesman* class constructor is called and returns a reference to a salesman object, *$salesguy1*.

4 The *set_data* method is called. The user is asked for input for the first salesman. This method is called from *Salesman.pm*.

6 The constructor method for the *Salesman* module is called. A reference to the new *Salesman* object is returned and assigned to *$salesguy2*.

7 The *set_data* method is called for the second salesman. This method is called from *Salesman.pm*.

9 Inheritance is used here. The *get_data* method is called, but it is not implemented in the *Salesman* module. Perl searches the *@ISA* array in *Salesman.pm* and goes to the base class listed there, *Employee*. Since the *get_data* method is there, it will be called. The statistics for the first salesman are displayed.

11 The *get_data* method is called for the second salesman.

EXAMPLE 13.19

```
    # Module Employee.pm
    # The Base Class
1   package Employee;
2   use strict;
3   use warnings;
    # Constructor method
4   sub new{
5       my $class = shift;
6       my $self = {_Name=>undef,
                    _Address=>undef,
                    _BasePay=>undef,
                   };
7       return bless($self, $class);
    }
```

EXAMPLE 13.19 (CONTINUED)

```
      # Instance/access methods
 8    sub set_data{
 9       my $self = shift;
10           print "Enter the name of the employee. ";
11           chomp($self->{_Name} = <STDIN>);
             print "Enter the address of $self->{_Name}. ";
             chomp($self->{_Address} = <STDIN>);
             print "Enter the monthly base pay for $self->{_Name}. ";
             chomp($self->{_BasePay} = <STDIN>);

         }
12    sub get_data{
13       my $self = shift;
14       my ($key,$value);
15       print "Name = $self->{_Name}.\n";
16       while(($key,$value) = each(%$self)){
17           key =~ s/_//;
18           print "$key = $value.\n" unless $key eq "Name";
         }
         print "\n";
      }
      1;
```

EXPLANATION

1 The package is declared with the same name as the file, *Employee.pm*, minus the *.pm* extension. This is the base class. All employees have some common characteristics. In this example, they all have a name, an address, and a paycheck.

2 The *strict* pragma will do strict error checking; in other words, restrict unsafe constructs such as the use of global variables, bare words, etc.

3 The *warnings* pragma will send warnings for probable compile or runtime errors.

4 The *Employee* constructor method is defined. It is called *new* by convention.

5 The name of the class will be shifted from the @_ array. This is a class method because it acts on behalf of the class and does not require an instance of the object.

6 An anonymous hash will be assigned the attributes/properties for the object as key/value pairs. The values are undefined, to be assigned later. A reference to the hash is returned and assigned to *$self*. (The leading underscore on the keys is a convention used to indicate that this is private data for the object.)

7 The object referenced by *$self* will be blessed into this class, *Employee*, and a reference to it will be returned to the caller.

8 The subroutine, *set_data*, is an access method for the *Employee* class. When called, it will be used to assign data to the object; that is, add values to the keys in the anonymous hash.

9 A reference to the object is shifted from the @_ array and assigned to *$self*.

EXPLANATION (CONTINUED)

10   The user of the module is asked for input.
11   The reference, *$self*, is used to assign values to the keys, *_Name*, *_Address*, *_BasePay*.
12   This access method is used to retrieve and display the object's data.
13   A reference to the object is shifted from the @_ array and assigned to *$self*.
14   Two lexical variables are declared.
15   Because hash values are pulled in random order, this line guarantees that the name of the employee is displayed first.
16   The *while* loop is entered and the *each* function will extract the key/value pairs from the object by using the reference to the object (*$%self*).
17   The leading underscore is removed from the key.
18   The rest of the properties for the object are displayed.

EXAMPLE 13.20

```
      # The Derived Class
1     package Salesman;
2     use strict;
      use warnings;
3     BEGIN{unshift(@INC, "./Baseclass");};
4     our @ISA=qw( Employee);
5     use Employee;
6     print "The salesman is an employee.\n"
              if Salesman->isa('Employee');
7     print "The salesman can display its properties.\n"
              if Salesman->can('get_data');
8     sub new {           # Constructor for Salesman
9        my ($class) = shift;
10       my $emp = new Employee;
11       $emp->set_data;
12       print "Before blessing package is: ", ref($emp), "\n";
         bless($emp, $class);
13       print "After blessing package is: ", ref($emp), "\n";
         return $emp;
      }
```

EXAMPLE 13.20 (CONTINUED)

```
14  sub set_data{
        my $self = shift;
15      my $calc_ptr = sub{ my($base, $comm, $bonus)=@_;
                        return $base+$comm+$bonus; };
16      print "Enter $self->{_Name}'s commission for this month. ";
        chomp($self->{_Commission} = <STDIN>);
        print "Enter $self->{_Name}'s bonuses for this month. ";
        chomp($self->{_Bonuses} = <STDIN>);
        print "Enter $self->{_Name}'s sales region. ";
        chomp($self->{_Region} = <STDIN>);
17      $self->{_PayCheck} = &$calc_ptr( $self->{_BasePay},
                                         $self->{_Commission},
                                         $self->{_Bonuses}
                                       );
    }
    1;
```

EXPLANATION

1 The package (class) *Salesman* is declared.

2 The *strict* and *warnings* pragmas are loaded.

3 The *BEGIN* block is used to make sure the *@INC* array is updated at compile time so that it will be available in the search for the base classes. The *Employee.pm* module is located in a subdirectory called *Baseclass*.

4 The *@ISA* array contains the names of packages that will be used by this package. The *Employee* module is the base class needed by this *Salesman* module. The *our* function makes the *@ISA* array a lexical, global array. Without *our*, the *strict* pragma causes the compiler to abort the script because global variables are not allowed (unless you fully qualify their names with the package name and two colons).

5 The *use* function causes the *Employee* module to be loaded into the program.

6 All packages/classes inherit from the superclass called *UNIVERSAL*, which provides the *isa* method The *isa* method returns true if *Salesman* module inherits from the *Employee* module.

7 All packages/classes also inherit from the super class *UNIVERSAL*, which provides the *can* method. The *can* method returns true if the *Salesman* module or any of its parent classes contain a method called *get_data*, and *undef* if not.

8 The *Salesman* class defines a constructor method called *new*.

9 Arguments passed in are taken from the *@_*. The name of the class is assigned to *$class*.

10 The constructor, *new*, for the *Employee* base class is called. A reference to the object, *$emp*, is returned.

11 The *Salesman* class constructor calls *set_data* to add properties to the object.

12   Before the blessing, the *ref* function returns the name of the class (package) that the object belongs to, the *Employee* base class. The object, with its new properties, is now blessed into the *Salesman* class.

13   After the blessing, the *ref* function returns the name of the class where the object was blessed, *Salesman*. A blessed reference to the object is returned to the caller.

14   The instance method *set_data* is defined for the *Salesman* class.

15   An anonymous subroutine is created to calculate the paycheck; a reference is returned. The subroutine should not be called by a user of the class. Only the class should be able to calculate the paycheck.

16   New properties are added to the *Employee* class.

17   The function to calculate the paycheck is called.

13.3.4   Multiple Inheritance

When a class inherits methods from more than one base or parent class, it is called **multiple inheritance**. In Perl, multiple inheritance is accomplished by adding more than one class to the @*ISA* array.

```
package  Child;
@ISA = qw(Mother Father Teacher);
```

The search is depth-first, meaning that Perl will search for classes in *Mother* and the hierarchy of classes it descends from, then *Father* and the hierarchy of classes it descends from, and finally *Teacher* and all its ancestors.

13.3.5   Overriding a Parent Method

There are times when two classes may have a method with the same name. If a derived class has a method with the same name as the base class, its method will take precedence over the base method. To override the method in the derived class so that you can access the method in the base class, the name of the method must be fully qualified with the class name and two colons.

EXAMPLE 13.21

```perl
1   package Employee;  # Base class
    use strict;
    use warnings;
    sub new{            # Employee's constructor is defined
        my $class = shift;
        my %params = @_;
        my $self = { Name=>$params{"Name"},
                     Salary=>$params{"Salary"},
                   };
        bless($self, $class);
    }
2   sub display{        # Instance method
        my $self = shift;
        foreach $key ( @_){
3           print "$key: $self->{$key}\n";
        }
4       print "The class using this display method is ",
              ref($self),"\n";
    }
    1;
```

```perl
5   package Salesman;  # Derived class
    use strict;
    use warnings;
    use Employee;
6   our @ISA=qw (Exporter Employee);
7   sub new{            # Constructor in derived Salesman class
        my $class = shift;
        my (%params) = @_;
        my $self = new Employee(%params);  # Call constructor
                                           # in base class
        $self->{Commission} = $params{Commission};
        bless($self, $class);    # Rebless the object into
                                 # the derived class
    }
    sub set_Salary{
        my $self = shift;
        $self->{Salary}=$self->{Salary} + $self->{Commission};
    }
8   sub display{        # Override method in Employee class
        my $self = shift;
        my @args = @_;
9       print "Stats for the Salesman\n";
        print "-" x 25, "\n";
10      $self->Employee::display(@args);  # Access to the
                                          # overridden method
    }
    1;
```

EXAMPLE 13.21 (CONTINUED)

```
    # User or Driver Program
    #!/bin/perl
11  use Salesman;
    use strict;
    use warnings;
12  my $emp = new Salesman ( "Name", "Tom Savage",
                             "Salary", 50000,    # Call to constructor
                             "Commission", 1500,
                           );
    $emp->set_Salary;  # Call to the access method
13  $emp->display( "Name" , "Salary", "Commission");
                          # Call Salesman's display method

(Output)
9   Stats for the Salesman
    ------------------------
    Name: Tom Savage
    Salary: 51500
    The class using this display method is Salesman
```

EXPLANATION

1   The class *Employee* is declared. It contains a constructor method called *new* and an instance method called *display*.

2   The *display* access method is defined for the *Employee* class.

3   The attributes for the employee are displayed.

4   The *ref* function returns the name of the class of a blessed object.

5   The *Salesman* class is declared. It will inherit from the *Employee* class and is called a derived class.

6   The *@ISA* array includes the names of the classes it needs: the *Exporter* class and the base class, *Employee*.

7   This is the *Saleman*'s constructor.

8   This *display* method takes precedence here in the derived class because it belongs to class *Salesman*. It is called in the driver program passing a reference to a *Salesman* object.

9   The printout is coming from the derived class (*Salesman*) subroutine, *display*.

10 By qualifying the name of the method to be of class *Employee*, this *display* method will override the current display method in package *Salesman*.

11 This is the driver program. It uses the *Salesman* module.

12 A new *Salesman* object is created, using the indirect method to call the constructor.

13 The *display* method is called. Since there is a *display* subroutine in the *Salesman* class, it is the one that will be called.

13.4 Public User Interface—Documenting Classes

One of the most important phases in creating a useful class is providing the user good documentation describing how the class should be used. This is called the **public user interface**. Whether a module is object-oriented or not, there must be some published user interface—the written documentation—available describing how the programmer (client) should use a class (e.g., what arguments will be passed to a method). The publicly defined interface should not change, even if something in the class is changed. Perl 5 introduced *pod* commands as a way to document modules. This is done by interspersing the program with *pod* (plain old documentation) instructions, similar to embedding HTML or *nroff* instructions within the text of a file. Then the program is run through a Perl filtering program which translates the commands into manual pages in a number of different formats.

13.4.1 *pod* Files

If you look in the standard Perl library, you will find that the modules contain documentation explaining what the module is supposed to do and how to use it. The documentation is either embedded within the program or placed at the end of the program right after the special literal, _ _END_ _. This documentation is called *pod*, short for plain old documentation. A *pod* file is just an ASCII text file embedded with special commands that can be translated by one of Perl's special interpreters, *pod2html*, *pod2latex*, *pod2text*, or *pod2man*. The purpose is to create formatted documents that can be represented in a number of ways. The UNIX *man* pages are an example of documentation that has been formatted with *nroff* instructions. It is now easy to embed a set of *pod* formatting instructions in your scripts to provide documentation in any of the four formats: text, HTML, LaTeX, or nroff.

The first line of the *pod* documentation starts with an equal sign (=) . Each of the words starting with an equal sign are formatting instructions for the *pod* translator. **Each formatting instruction must be followed by a blank line.**

EXAMPLE 13.22

```
(Here is the documentation found at the end of the BigFloat.pm module
    in the standard Perl library, under the subdirectory Math.)

=head1 NAME

Math::BigFloat - Arbitrary length float math package

=head1 SYNOPSIS

  use Math::BigFloat;
  $f = Math::BigFloat->new($string);
```

EXAMPLE 13.22 (CONTINUED)

```
    $f->fadd(NSTR) return NSTR          addition
    $f->fsub(NSTR) return NSTR          subtraction
    $f->fmul(NSTR) return NSTR          multiplication
    $f->fdiv(NSTR[,SCALE]) returns NSTR division to SCALE places
    $f->fneg() return NSTR              negation
    $f->fabs() return NSTR              absolute value
    $f->fcmp(NSTR) return CODE          compare undef,<0,=0,>0
    $f->fround(SCALE) return NSTR       round to SCALE digits
    $f->ffround(SCALE) return NSTR      round at SCALEth place
    $f->fnorm() return (NSTR)           normalize
    $f->fsqrt([SCALE]) return NSTR      sqrt to SCALE places
```

=head1 DESCRIPTION

All basic math operations are overloaded if you declare your big
floats as

    $float = new Math::BigFloat "2.12312312312312312312312312312312";

=over 2

=item number format

canonical strings have the form /[+-]\d+E[+-]\d+/ . Input values can
have inbedded whitespace.

=item Error returns 'NaN'

An input parameter was "Not a Number" or divide by zero or sqrt of
negative number.

=item Division is computed to

C<max($div_scale,length(dividend)+length(divisor))> digits by default.
Also used for default sqrt scale.

=back

=head1 BUGS

The current version of this module is a preliminary version of the
real thing that is currently (as of perl5.002) under development.

=head1 AUTHOR

Mark Biggar

=cut

The preceding text is a *pod* file. It consists of lines starting with an equal sign and a pod command, then a blank line, and text. Perl provides a special translator program that reads the *pod* file and translates it into a readable file, either in plain text, HTML format, nroff text, or LaTeX. The next section describes how to use the *pod* filter programs to make the translation for you.

13.4.2 *pod* Commands

It's easy to embed *pod* instructions in a text file. Commands are placed at the beginning of a line, starting with =*pod* (or any other *pod* command) and ending with =*cut*. Everything after the first =*pod* instruction to the =*cut* instruction will be ignored by the compiler, just as comments are ignored. The nice thing about using the commands is that they allow you to create bold, italic, or plain text, to indent, to create headings, and more. The chart below contains a list of instructions.

Table 13.3   *pod* Commands

Paragraph Commands	What They Do
=*pod*	Marks the start of *pod*, but an equal sign, followed by any pod instruction starts the documentation
=*cut*	Marks the end of *pod*
=*head1 heading*	Creates a level1 heading
=*head2 heading*	Creates a level2 heading
=*item* *	Starts a bulleted list
=*over N*	Moves over *N* number of spaces, usually set to *4*
=*back*	Returns indent back to default, no indent
Formatting Commands	**What They Do**
I*<text>*	Italic text
B*<text>*	Bold text
S*<text>*	Contains text non-breaking spaces
C*<code>*	Contains typed text, literal source code
L*<name>*	Creates a link (cross reference) to name
F*<file>*	Used for listing filenames
X*<index>*	An index entry
Z*<>*	A zero-width character

Table 13.3   *pod* Commands *(continued)*

Filter Specific Commands	What They Do
=for	For HTML-specific commands, e.g., *=for html* *<IMG SRC=file.gif>* *<B>Figure a.>/B>>*
	For text-specific commands, e.g., *=for text* text to represent what the above image means
	For *manpage*-specific commands, e.g., *=for man* *.ce 3* *<center next three lines>*

13.4.3   How to Use the *pod* Interpreters

The *pod* interpreters come with the Perl distribution and are located in the *bin* directory under the main Perl directory; for example, in */usr/bin/perl5/bin*.

The four interpreters are

```
pod2html  (translate to HTML)
pod2text  (translate to plain text)
pod2man    (translate to nroff, like UNIX man pages)
pod2latex (translate to LaTeX)
```

The easiest way to use the interpreters is to copy the one you want into your own directory. For example:

```
$ cp /usr/bin/perl5/bin/pod2text
```

You may also copy the library routine into your directory:

```
$ cp /usr/bin/perl5/lib/BigFloat.pm
```

Now when you list the contents of the directory, you should have both the *pod* interpreter and the library module.

```
$ ls
BigFloat.pm
pod2text
```

13.4.4   Translating *pod* Documentation into Text

To translate the *pod* commands, give the library module to the *pod i*nterpreter and create an output file to save the translated text. If you don't redirect the output to a file, it will simply go to the screen.

```
$ pod2text BigFloat.pm > BigFloat.Text
$ cat BigFloat.Text  (The output file after pod commands have been
                        translated into text.)
```

NAME
    Math::BigFloat - Arbitrary length float math package

SYNOPSIS
```
    use Math::BogFloat;
    $f = Math::BigFloat->new($string);

    $f->fadd(NSTR) return NSTR              addition
    $f->fsub(NSTR) return NSTR              subtraction
    $f->fmul(NSTR) return NSTR              multiplication
    $f->fdiv(NSTR[,SCALE])    returns NSTR  division to SCALE places
    $f->fneg() return NSTR                  negation
    $f->fabs() return NSTR                  absolute value
    $f->fcmp(NSTR) return CODE              compare undef,<0,=0,>0
    $f->fround(SCALE) return NSTR           round to SCALE digits
    $f->ffround(SCALE) return NSTR          round at SCALEth place
    $f->fnorm() return (NSTR)               normalize
    $f->fsqrt([SCALE]) return NSTR          sqrt to SCALE places
```

DESCRIPTION
    All basic math operations are overloaded if you declare your big
    floats as

```
$float = newMath::BigFloat"2.123123123123123123123123123123";
```

    number format
    canonical strings have the form /[+-]\d+E[+-]\d+/ . Input
    values can have inbedded whitespace.

 Error returns 'NaN'
    An input parameter was "Not a Number" or divide by zero or
    sqrt of negative number.

 Division is computed to
    `max($div_scale,length(dividend)+length(divisor))' digits by
    default. Also used for default sqrt scale.

BUGS
    The current version of this module is a preliminary version of
    the real thing that is currently (as of perl5.002) under
    development.

AUTHOR
    Mark Biggar

13.4.5   Translating *pod* Documentation into HTML

To create an HTML document, copy *pod2html* into your directory and type

```
$ pod2html BigFloat.pm > BigFloat.pm.html
```

The *pod2html* translator will create a file called *BigFloat.pm.html*. Now open your browser window and assign *BigFloat.pm.html* to a file protocol in the URL location box; e.g., *<file:/yourdirectory path/BigFloat.pm.html>*.[8]

13.5   Using Objects from the Perl Library

In Chapter 11, "Modularize It, Package It, and Send It to the Library!", we first looked into the standard Perl library that was provided with this distribution, Perl 5.6. In that library there were a number of *.pl* and *.pm* files. The examples covered dealt with packages that did not require knowledge about Perl's use of objects. Those files utilized standard subroutines, not methods. Now that you know how objects and methods are used in Perl, the following examples will demonstrate how to use those modules that require the OOP methodology.

13.5.1   Another Look at the Standard Perl Library

The *@INC* array contains the pathnames to the libraries Perl will search. After looking at the library listings, we will *cd* into the standard Perl library and list the files found there. You'll notice that some of the files end with the *.pm* extension and some end with the *.pl* extension. The files that utilize objects (ending in *.pm*) were introduced in Perl 5 and are the modules that support OOP. The files that do not have an extension are the names of directories where Perl has stored modules that fit into that category. For example, the *File* and *Math* subdirectories contain modules that pertain to those respective subjects.

---

8. If you receive some obscure diagnostic messages, it may be that the documentation for the *.pm* file contains links to some other page that cannot be resolved by the *pod* filter.

EXAMPLE 13.23

```
1   $ perl -e "print join qq/\n/,@INC;"
    c:/Perl/lib
    c:/Perl/site/lib


2   $ ls /Perl/lib
```

AnyDBM_File.pm	Exporter.pm	Symbol.pm	cacheout.pl	newgetopt.pl
AutoLoader.pm	ExtUtils	Sys	charnames.pm	open.pm
AutoSplit.pm	Fatal.pm	Term	chat2.pl	open2.pl
B	Fcntl.pm	Test	complete.pl	open3.pl
B.pm	File	Test.pm	constant.pm	ops.pm
Benchmark.pm	FileCache.pm	Text	ctime.pl	overload.pm
ByteLoader.pm	FileHandle.pm	Thread	diagnostics.pm	perl5db.pl
CGI	FindBin.pm	Thread.pm	dotsh.pl	perllocal.pod
CGI.pm	Getopt	Tie	dumpvar.pl	pwd.pl
CORE	I18N	Time	exceptions.pl	re.pm
CPAN	IO	UNIVERSAL.pm	fastcwd.pl	shellwords.pl
CPAN.pm	IO.pm	User	fields.pm	sigtrap.pm
Carp	IPC	Win32.pod	filetest.pm	stat.pl
Carp.pm	Math	XSLoader.pm	find.pl	strict.pm
Class	Net	abbrev.pl	finddepth.pl	subs.pm
Config.pm	O.pm	assert.pl	flush.pl	syslog.pl
Cwd.pm	Opcode.pm	attributes.pm	ftp.pl	tainted.pl
DB.pm	POSIX.pm	attrs.pm	getcwd.pl	termcap.pl
Data	POSIX.pod	auto	getopt.pl	timelocal.pl
Devel	Pod	autouse.pm	getopts.pl	unicode
DirHandle.pm	SDBM_File.pm	base.pm	hostname.pl	utf8.pm
Dumpvalue.pm	Safe.pm	bigfloat.pl	importenv.pl	utf8_heavy.pl
DynaLoader.pm	Search	bigint.pl	integer.pm	validate.pl
English.pm	SelectSaver.pm	bigrat.pl	less.pm	vars.pm
Env.pm	SelfLoader.pm	blib.pm	lib.pm	warnings
Errno.pm	Shell.pm	bytes.pm	locale.pm	warnings.pm
Exporter	Socket.pm	bytes_heavy.pl	look.pl	

```
3   $ cd Math
4   $ ls
    BigFloat.pm  BigInt.pm    Complex.pm    Trig.pm
```

EXPLANATION

1   The elements of the *@INC* array are printed to ensure that the standard Perl library is included in Perl's library search path.
2   The library routines are listed.
3   Any file not ending in *.pl* or *.pm* is a subdirectory. We change to the *Math* subdirectory.
4   The contents of the directory are listed, showing three *Math* modules.

13.5.2 An Object-Oriented Module from the Standard Perl Library

The following module, *BigFloat.pm*, allows the use of floating-point numbers of arbitrary length. Number strings have the form */[+-]\d*\.?\d*E[+-]\d+/*. When *NaN* is returned, it means that a non-number was entered as input, that you tried to divide by zero, or that you tried to take the square root of a negative number. *BigFloat* uses the *overload* module which allows Perl's built-in operators to be assigned methods that will cause the operators to behave in a new way. The operator is the key and the method assigned is the value. (See *overload.pm* in the standard Perl library.)

EXAMPLE 13.24

```
(The File: BigFloat.pm)

1    package Math::BigFloat;
2    use Math::BigInt;

     use Exporter;  # Just for use to be happy
     @ISA = (Exporter);

3    use overload
4    '+'    =>  sub {new Math::BigFloat &fadd},
     '-'    =>  sub {new Math::BigFloat
                  $_[2]? fsub($_[1],${$_[0]}) : fsub(${$_[0]},$_[1])},
     '<=>'  =>  sub {new Math::BigFloat
                  $_[2]? fcmp($_[1],${$_[0]}) : fcmp(${$_[0]},$_[1])},
     'cmp'  =>  sub {new Math::BigFloat
                  $_[2]? ($_[1] cmp ${$_[0]}) : (${$_[0]} cmp $_[1])},
     '*'    =>  sub {new Math::BigFloat &fmul},
     '/'    =>  sub {new Math::BigFloat
                  $_[2]? scalar fdiv($_[1],${$_[0]}) :
                      scalar fdiv(${$_[0]},$_[1])},
     'neg'  =>  sub {new Math::BigFloat &fneg},
     'abs'  =>  sub {new Math::BigFloat &fabs},
     qw(
         ""     stringify
         0+     numify)    # Order of arguments unsignificant
         ;

5    sub new {
         my ($class) = shift;
         my ($foo) = fnorm(shift);
6        panic("Not a number initialized to Math::BigFloat")
             if $foo eq "NaN";
```

EXAMPLE 13.24 (CONTINUED)

```
7        bless \$foo, $class;
    }

    < Methods continue here. Module was too long to put here>

    # addition
8   sub fadd{ #(fnum_str, fnum_str) return fnum_str
        local($x,$y) = (fnorm($_[$[]),fnorm($_[$[+1]));
        if($x eq 'NaN' || $y eq 'NaN'){
            NaN';
        } else{
            local($xm,$xe) = split('E',$x);
            local($ym,$ye) = split('E',$y);
            ($xm,$x e,$ym,$ye) = ($ym,$ye,$xm,$xe) if ($xe < $ye);
            &norm(Math::BigInt::badd($ym,$xm.('0' x ($xe-$ye))),$ye);
        }
    }


    < Methods continue here>

    # divisionbb
    # args are dividend, divisor, scale (optional)
    # result has at most max(scale, length(dividend),
    # length(divisor)) digits
9   sub fdiv    #(fnum_str, fnum_str[,scale]) return fnum_str
    {
        local($x,$y,$scale) = (fnorm($_[$[]),
                             fnorm($_[$[+1]),$_[$[+2]);
        if ($x eq 'NaN' || $y eq 'NaN' || $y eq '+0E+0') {
            'NaN';
        }else{
            local($xm,$xe) = split('E',$x);
            local($ym,$ye) = split('E',$y);
            $scale = $div_scale if (!$scale);
            $scale = length($xm)-1 if (length($xm)-1 > $scale);
            $scale = length($ym)-1 if (length($ym)-1 > $scale);
            $scale = $scale + length($ym) - length($xm);
            &norm(&round(Math::BigInt::bdiv($xm.('0' x $scale),$ym),
                                        $ym),$xe-$ye-$scale);
        }
    }
```

EXPLANATION

1   The *BigFloat* class is declared. It resides in the *Math* subdirectory of the standard Perl library.
2   The *BigFloat* class also needs to use the *BigInt* module.
3   The *overload* function allows you to change the meaning of the built-in Perl operators. For example, when using *BigFloat.pm*, the +operator is a key and its value an anonymous subroutine that creates an object and calls the &*fadd* subroutine.
4   The + operator is overloaded. See previous explanation.
5   This is *BigFloat*'s constructor method for creating an object.
6   If the value is not a number, this panic message is printed.
7   The object is blessed into the class.
8   This is the subroutine that performs addition on the object.
9   This is the subroutine that performs division on the object.

13.5.3   Using a Module with Objects from the Standard Perl Library

EXAMPLE 13.25

```
1   #!/bin/perl
2   use Math::BigFloat;   # BigFloat.pm is in the Math directory

3   $number = "000.95671234e-21";
4   $mathref = new Math::BigFloat("$number");   # Create the object

5   print "\$mathref is in class ", ref($mathref), "\n";
                  # Where is the object

6   print $mathref->fnorm(), "\n";   # Use methods from the class

7   print "The sum of $mathref + 500 is: ", $mathref->fadd("500"),
                              "\n";
8   print "Division using overloaded operator: ", $mathref / 200.5,
                              "\n";
9   print "Division using fdiv method:", $mathref->fdiv("200.5"),
                              "\n";

10  print "Enter a number ";
    chop($numstr = <STDIN>);

11  if($mathref->fadd($numstr) eq "NaN"){
                  print "You didn't enter a number.\n"};
```

EXAMPLE 13.25 (CONTINUED)

```
# Return value of NaN means the string is not a number,
# or you divided by zero, or you took the square root
# of a negative number.

(Output)
5   $mathref is in class Math::BigFloat
6   +95671234E-29
7   The sum of .00000000000000000000095671234 + 500 is:
    +50000000000000000000000095671234E-29
8   Division using overloaded operator:
    .000000000000000000000004771632618453865336658354114713216957606
9   Division using fdiv method:
    +4771632618453865336658354114713216957606E-63
10  Enter a number hello
11  You didn't enter a number.
```

EXPLANATION

1   The *shbang* line to the Perl interpreter.
2   The *use* function loads the module *BigFloat.pm* into the program. Since this module is in a subdirectory of the library called *Math*, that subdirectory is included by prepending its name to the module with two colons.
3   A large number (*e* notation) is assigned to *$number*.
4   Now the methods from the module are utilized. The *BigFloat* constructor is called. A reference to the object is returned and assigned to *$mathref*.
5   The *ref* function returns the name of the class.
6   The *fnorm* method returns the "normal" value of *$number* in signed scientific notation. Leading zeros are stripped off.
7   The *fadd* method adds *500* to the number.
8   In this example, an overloaded operator is used. The / operator is assigned a class method, *fdiv*, to perform the division. See code from *BigFloat.pm* shown above.
9   This time the *fdiv* method is called directly without using overloading to perform the division. The output is slightly different.
10 The user is asked to enter a number.
11 If *NaN* (not a number) is returned from the *fadd* method, the message is printed. This is a way you could check that user input is a valid numeric value.

EXERCISE 13
What's the Object of This Lesson?

1. Write a module called *Rightnow.pm* that contains three methods:
   a. A constructor called *new*.
   b. A method called *set_time* to set the time. Use the *localtime* function.
   c. A method called *print_time* to print the time. This method will take an argument to determine whether the time is printed in military or standard time; e.g. *print_time("Military")*;
   d. In another Perl script, use the *Rightnow* module to create a *Rightnow* object, and call the *print_time* method to produce output as follows:
   Time now: 2:48:20 PM
   Time now: 14:48:20

   Did you have to use the *Exporter.pm* module? Did you update the *@ISA* array? Did you need to use the *@EXPORT* or *@EXPORT_OK* arrays?

2. Put the *Checking* package in a file called *Checking.pm*. Make it object-oriented. The object will be an anonymous hash and the subroutines will be "methods." The initial balance will be stored in the anonymous hash. Use the *Checking* module in the *myATM* script. All that should remain in that script is code belonging to the *main* package; in other words, the user interface.

   Can you make more than one instance of the checking object and keep track of the balance for each account?

EXERCISE 14
Perls in a Pod

1. Go to the *pod* directory in the standard Perl library. Look for *perlpod.html*. The file contains Larry Wall's user interface for using *pod* commands to document your Perl programs.

   Go to your browser and in the Location box, type:
   `file:/<directory-to -your-library-file>/Pod/pod.html`

   Now you have the instructions for creating *pod* documentation.

2. Create a published interface for your *Checking.pm* module. Embed *pod* commands in your *Checking.pm* script explaining how the module should be used. Follow the guidelines of the modules in the library; for example, there should be a NAME, SYNOPSIS, DESCRIPTION, AUTHOR, etc. Run the *pod* file through the *pod2html* filter and display the documentation in your browser.

14

THOSE MAGIC TIES, DBM STUFF, AND THE DATABASE HOOKS

14.1 Tying Variables to a Class

Normally when you perform some operation on a variable, such as assigning, changing, or printing the value of the variable, Perl performs the necessary operations on that variable internally. For example, you don't need a constructor method just to create a variable and assign a value to it, and you don't have to create access methods to manipulate the variable. The assignment statement $x=5;$ doesn't require any tricky semantics. Perl creates the memory location for x and puts the value 5 in that location.

It is now possible to bind an ordinary variable to a class and provide methods for that variable so that, as if by magic, the variable is transformed when an assignment is made or a value is retrieved from it. A scalar, array, or hash, then, can be given a new implementation. Unlike objects where you must use a reference to the object, tied variables, once created, are treated like any other variable. All of the details are hidden from the user. You will use the same syntax to assign values to the variable and to access the variable as you did before tying.[1] The magic goes on behind the scenes. Perl creates an object to represent the variable and uses predefined method names to construct, set, get, and destroy the object that has been tied to the variable. The programmer who creates the class uses the predefined method names, such as *FETCH* and *STORE,* to include the statements necessary to manipulate the object. The user ties the variable and, from that point on, uses it the same way as he would any other variable in his program.

14.1.1 The *tie* Function

The *tie* function binds a variable to a package or class and returns a reference to an object. All the details are handled internally. The *tie* function is most commonly used with associative arrays to bind key/value pairs to a database; for example, the DBM modules pro-

---

1. DBM databases use the *tie* mechanism to automatically perform database operations on data.

vided with the Perl distribution use tied variables. The *untie* function will disassociate a variable from the class to which it was tied. The format for *tie* follows.

FORMAT

```
$object =  tie variable, class, list;
untie variable;

tie variable, class, list;
$object = tied variable;
```

The *tie* function returns a reference to the object that was previously bound with the *tie* function or undefined if the variable is not tied to a package.

14.1.2 Predefined Methods

Tying variables allows you to define the behavior of a variable by constructing a class that has special methods to create and access the variable. The methods will be called automatically when the variable is used. A variable can't be tied to any class, but must be tied to a class that has predefined method names. The behavior of the variable is determined by methods in the class that will be called automatically when the variable is used. The constructors and methods used to tie (constructor) and manipulate (access methods) the variable have predefined names. The methods will be called automatically when the tied variables are fetched, stored, destroyed, and so on. All of the details are handled internally. The constructor can bless and return a pointer to any type of object. For example, the reference may point to a blessed scalar, array, or hash. But the access methods **must return** a scalar value if *TIESCALAR* is used, an array value if *TIEARRAY* is used, and a hash value if *TIEHASH* is used.

14.1.3 Tying a Scalar

In order to use a tied scalar, the class must define a set of methods that have predefined names. The constructor, *TIESCALAR*, is called when the variable is tied and it creates the underlying object that will be manipulated by the access methods, *STORE* and *FETCH*. Any time the user makes an assignment to the tied scalar, the *STORE* method is called and whenever he attempts to display the tied scalar, the *FETCH* method is called. The *DESTROY* method is not required, but if it is defined, will be called when the tied scalar is untied or goes out of scope. Methods provided for a tied scalar are

```
TIESCALAR $classname, LIST
STORE $self, $value
FETCH $self
DESTROY $self
```

There is also a base module in the standard Perl library for tying scalars that provides some skeletal methods for scalar-tying classes. See the *perltie man* page for a list of the functions required in tying scalar to a package. The basic *Tie::Scalar* package provides a *new* method, as well as methods *TIESCALAR*, *FETCH,* and *STORE*. For documentation of this module, type *perldoc Tie::Scalar.*

Example 14.1 demonstrates tying a scalar and how to access the tied scalar.

EXAMPLE 14.1

```
      # File is Square.pm
      # It will square a number, initially set to 5
1     package Square;
2     sub TIESCALAR{
3        my $class = shift;
4        my $data = shift;
5        bless(\$data,$class);    # Blessing a scalar
      }
6     sub FETCH{
7        my $self = shift;
8        $$self **= 2;
      }
9     sub STORE{
10       my $self = shift;
11       $$self = shift;
      }
      1;
-------------------------------------------------------------------

      # User program
12    use Square;
13    $object=tie $squared, 'Square', 5;   # Call constructor TIESCALAR
14    print "object is $object.\n";
15    print $squared,"\n";       # Call FETCH three times
16    print $squared,"\n";
      print $squared,"\n";
      print "---------------------------\n";

17    $squared=3;                # Call STORE

18    print $squared,"\n";    # Call FETCH
      print $squared,"\n";
      print $squared,"\n";

19    untie $squared;         # Break the tie that binds the
                              # scalar to the object
```

EXAMPLE 14.1 (CONTINUED)

```
(Output)
14  object is Square=SCALAR(0x1a72da8).
15  25
16  625
    390625
    -----------------------------
18  9
    81
    6561
```

EXPLANATION

1   The package/class *Square* is declared. The file is *Square.pm*.

2   *TIESCALAR* is the constructor for the class. It creates an association between the tied scalar and an object. Look at line 13 of this example. This is where the constructor is called. The variable tied to the object is *$squared*.

3   The first argument to the constructor is the name of the class. It is shifted from the @_ array and assigned to *$class*.

4   Look again at line 13. The tied variable, *$squared*, is followed by the name of the class, and then the number 5. The class name is passed first, followed by 5. In the constructor the number 5 is shifted from the @_ array and assigned to *$data*.

5   A reference to the scalar is created and passed to the *bless* function, which creates the object.

6   The *FETCH* method is defined. This access method will retrieve data from the object.

7   The first argument to the *FETCH* method is a reference to the object.

8   The pointer is de-referenced and its value squared.

9   The *STORE* method is defined. It will be used to assign a value to the object.

10 The first argument to the *STORE* method is a reference to the object.

11 The value to be assigned is shifted off the @_ array and assigned to *$$self*.

12 This is the user/driver program. The *Square* module is loaded into the program.

13 The *tie* function automatically calls the constructor *TIESCALAR*. The *tie* function ties the variable, *$squared*, to the class and returns a reference to the newly created object.

14 The reference, *$object*, points to a scalar variable found in the *Square* class.

15 The *FETCH* method is automatically called and the current value of *$squared* is printed.

16 The *FETCH* method is called again. Each time the method is called the current value of the tied variable is squared again and returned.

17 The *STORE* method is automatically called. A new value, 3, is assigned to the tied variable.

18 The *FETCH* method is automatically called and displays the squared value.

19 The *untie* method disassociates the object with the tied variable. If a *DESTROY* method had been defined, it would have been called at this point.

Example 14.2 also ties a scalar, *$cost*, and demonstrates how to access the tied scalar.

EXAMPLE 14.2

```
     # File: MarkUp.pm
1    package MarkUp;
2    sub TIESCALAR {      # Constructor ties a scalar
3        my $class = shift;
4        my  $markup = shift;
         my $cost = 0;
5        my $mcost = [ $markup, $cost ];
                      # Create a reference to an anonymous array
6        return bless ( $mcost, $class);     # Bless the reference
     }

7    sub STORE {
8        my $self = shift;
                      # First argument is a reference to the object
9        my $amount = shift;
                      # Second argument is the value assigned to $cost
10       $self->[1] = $amount * $self->[0];  # Returns a scalar
     }
11   sub FETCH {
12       my $self = shift;
                      # First argument is a reference to the object
13       return $self->[1];
                      # The pointer is derefenced; returns a scalar
     }

14   sub DESTROY {
         print "The object is being destroyed.\n";
     }
     1;


     ----------------------------------------------------------------


     # This is the user/driver program
15   use Markup;
16   $object = tie $cost, 'MarkUp', 1.15;
         # Ties the variable $cost to the MarkUp package
         # Whenever the variable $cost is accessed, it will be passed
         # to the FETCH and STORE methods and its value manipulated by
         # the object it is tied to. A scalar must be returned by
         # FETCH and STORE if tying to a scalar. The constructor
         # can bless a reference to any data type, not specifically
         # a scalar.
17   print "What is the price of the material? ";
18   $cost = <STDIN>;
         # Could have said:  $object->STORE(34)
         # or could have said: (tied $cost)->STORE(34);
```

EXAMPLE 14.2 (CONTINUED)

```
19  printf "The cost to you after markup is %.2f.\n", $cost;
        # Could have said: $object->FETCH
20  untie $cost;   # $cost is now a normal scalar
        # The DESTROY method is called automatically when
        # the program exits

---------------------------------------------------------------

(Output)
17  What is the price of the material? 34
19  The cost to you after markup is 39.10.
20  The object is being destroyed.
```

EXPLANATION

1   A package (class) called *MarkUp* is declared.
2   A predefined method name called *TIESCALAR* is defined and will act as the constructor; it is automatically invoked when the variable is tied.
3   The parameters being passed to the constructor are assigned to the @_ array. See line 13 in the driver program. The first argument shifted off is the name of the class called *Markup*.
4   The second argument shifted off is the value *1.15*.
5   The reference *$mcost* is assigned the address of an anonymous array consisting of two values, *$mcost* and *$class*.
6   The reference is blessed into the class. Note that it doesn't matter whether the reference blessed is to a hash, array, or scalar. The *tie* function only requires that the **access** methods return a scalar if a variable is tied to a scalar as shown in line 13, an array if the variable is tied to an array, and a hash if the variable is tied to a hash. In this example, the value that will be returned by the access methods, *FETCH* and *STORE*, must be a scalar, and they are.
7   *STORE* is an access method used to set or assign values for an object. The name *STORE* is predefined for tied variables.
8   The first argument to the *STORE* method is a reference to the object. It is shifted from the @_ array and assigned to *$self*.
9   The second argument shifted off is the amount spent on the material. (See line 18.)
10   Remember, the reference *$self* points to an anonymous array (the object) that contains two values: the markup cost, and the actual cost of the material. The cost of the material was initialized to *0* in the constructor, *TIESCALAR*. The amount, *$amount*, passed to the *STORE* method is multiplied by the markup price, *$self->[0]*. The result is assigned to *$self->[1]*, the cost of the material after the markup. The tied object has been modified. On line 15 in the driver program, it appears that the only assignment is coming from *STDIN*. As soon as the assignment statement is executed, the *STORE* method is automatically called, behind the user's back, so to speak.

EXPLANATION (CONTINUED)

11 *FETCH* is an access method used to get or retrieve data from an object. The name *FETCH* is predefined for tied variables.

12 The first argument to the *FETCH* method is a reference to the object. It is shifted from the @_ array and assigned to *$self*.

13 The *FETCH* method retrieves and returns the value of the cost after the markup.

14 The *DESTROY* method will be called just before the object is removed, either when it goes out of scope or when the program ends.

15 The *MarkUp* module is loaded into the user's program.

16 The scalar *$cost* is tied to the *MarkUp* class. When *TIESCALAR*, the constructor, is called, it will get the name of the class, *MarkUp*, and 1.15. *$object* is a reference to the object that is tied.

17, 18 The user is asked for input. The *STORE* method is automatically called.

19 FETCH is called and the value of *$cost* is printed.

20 The object is destroyed with *untie*.

14.1.4 Tying an Array

In order to use a tied array, the class must define a set of methods that have predefined names. The constructor, *TIEARRAY*, is called when the variable is tied and it creates the underlying object that will be manipulated by the access methods, *STORE* and *FETCH*. Any time the user makes an assignment to the tied array, the *STORE* method is called, and whenever he attempts to display the tied array, the *FETCH* method is called. The *DESTROY* method is not required, but, if it is defined, will be called when the tied scalar is untied or goes out of scope. There are also a set of optional methods that can be used with tied arrays. *STORESIZE* sets the total number of items in the array, *FETCHSIZE* is the same as using *scalar(@array)* or *$#array + 1* to get the size of the array, and *CLEAR* is used when the array is to be emptied of all its elements. There are also a number of methods, such as *POP* and *PUSH*, that emulate their like-named Perl functions in manipulating the array. Methods provided for an array are

```
TIEARRAY $classname, LIST
STORE $self, $subscript, $value
FETCH $self, $subscript, $value
DESTROY $self
STORESIZE  $self, $arraysize
FETCHSIZE  $self
EXTEND $self, $arraysize
EXISTS $subscript
DELETE $self, $subscript
CLEAR $self
PUSH $self, LIST
```

```
UNSHIFT $self, LIST
POP $self
SHIFT $self
SPLICE $self, OFFSET, LENGTH, LIST
```

There is also a base class called *Tie::Array* in the standard Perl library that contains a number of predefined methods from the above list, making the implementation of tied arrays much easier. To see documentation for this module, type *perldoc Tie::Array*.

EXAMPLE 14.3

```
1   package Temp;
2   sub TIEARRAY {
3       my $class = shift;   # Shifting the @_ array
4       my $obj =  [ ];
5       bless ($obj, $class);
    }
    # Access methods
6   sub FETCH {
7       my $self=shift;
8       my $indx = shift;
9       return $self->[$indx];
    }

10  sub STORE {
11      my $self = shift;
12      my $indx= shift;
13      my $F = shift;      # The Fahrenheit temperature
14      $self->[$indx]=($F - 32) / 1.8;   # Magic works here!

    }
    1;
----------------------------------------------------------------
    #!/bin/perl
    # The user/driver program
15  use Temp;
16  tie @list, "Temp";
17  print "Beginning Fahrenheit: ";
    chomp($bf = <STDIN>);
        print "Ending temp: ";
        chomp($ef = <STDIN>);
    print "Increment value: ";
    chomp($ic = <STDIN>);
    print "\n";
    print "\tConversion Table\n";
    print "\t---------------\n";
```

EXAMPLE 14.3 (CONTINUED)

```
18  for($i=$bf;$i<=$ef;$i+=$ic){
19      $list[$i]=$i;
20      printf"\t$i F. = %.2f C.\n", $list[$i]; }
```

```
(Output)
17  Beginning Fahrenheit: 32
    Ending temp: 100
    Increment value: 5

    Conversion Table
    ----------------
20   2 F. =  0.00 C.
    37 F. =  2.78 C.
    42 F. =  5.56 C.
    47 F. =  8.33 C.
    52 F. = 11.11 C.
    57 F. = 13.89 C.
    62 F. = 16.67 C.
    67 F. = 19.44 C.
    72 F. = 22.22 C.
    77 F. = 25.00 C.
    82 F. = 27.78 C.
    87 F. = 30.56 C.
    92 F. = 33.33 C.
    97 F. = 36.11 C.
```

EXPLANATION

1   This is the package/class declaration. The file is *Temp.pm*.
2   *TIEARRAY* is the constructor for the tied array. It creates the underlying object.
3   The first argument passed into the constructor is the name of the class, *Temp*.
4   A reference to an anonymous array is created.
5   The object is blessed into the class.
6   The access method, *FETCH*, will retrieve elements from the tied array.
7   The first argument shifted off and assigned to *$self* is a reference to the object.
8   The next argument is the value of the subscript in the tied array. It is shifted off and assigned to *$indx*.
9   The value of the array element is returned when the user/driver program attempts to display an element of the tied array.
10 The access method, *STORE*, will assign values to the tied array.
11 The first argument shifted off and assigned to *$self* is a reference to the object.
12 The next argument is the value of the subscript in the tied array. It is shifted off and assigned to *$indx*.

EXPLANATION (CONTINUED)

13   The value of the Fahrenheit temperature is shifted from the argument list. See line 19 where the assignment is being made in the user/driver program. The value being assigned is what will be stored in *$F* in the *STORE* method.

14   The calculation to convert from Fahrenheit to Celsius is made on the incoming tied array element. The user/driver program never sees this calculation, as though it were done by magic.

15   This is the user's program. The *Temp.pm* module is loaded into the program.

16   The *tie* function ties the array to the class, *Temp* and returns an underlying reference to an object that is tied to the array.

17   The user is asked for input. He will provide a beginning Fahrenheit temperature, an ending Fahrenheit temperature, and an increment value.

18   A *for* loop is entered to iterate through the list of temperatures. It charts the Fahrenheit temperature and the corresponding Celsius temperature after the conversion.

19   The magic happens here. When the assignment is made, the *STORE* method is automatically called, where the formula converts the Fahrenheit temperature to Celsius and assigns it to the array. A reference to the tied object and the array index are passed to *STORE*.

20   When *printf* is used, the *FETCH* method will automatically be called and display an element of the tied array. A reference to the tied object and the array index are passed to *FETCH*.

14.1.5 Tying a Hash

In order to use a tied hash, the class must define a set of methods that have predefined names. The constructor, *TIEHASH*, is called when the variable is tied and it creates the underlying object that will be manipulated by the access methods, *STORE* and *FETCH*. Any time the user makes an assignment to the tied hash, the *STORE* method is called, and whenever he attempts to display the tied hash, the *FETCH* method is called. The *DESTROY* method is not required, but, if it is defined, will be called when the tied hash is untied or goes out of scope. There are also a set of optional methods that can be used with tied hashes. *DELETE* removes a key/value pair, *EXISTS* checks for the existence of a key, and *CLEAR* empties the entire hash. If you use Perl's built-in keys, values, or *each* methods, the *FIRSTKEY* and *NEXTKEY* methods are called to iterate over the hash. Methods provided for an associative array are

```
TIEHASH $classname, LIST
FETCH $self, $key
STORE $self, $key
DELETE $self, $key
EXISTS $self, $key
FIRSTKEY $self
NEXTKEY $self, $lastkey
```

```
DESTROY $self
CLEAR $self
```

There is also a base class module called *Tie::Hash* in the standard Perl library that contains a number of predefined methods from the above list, making the implementation of tied arrays much easier. To see documentation for this module, type *perldoc Tie::Hash*.

EXAMPLE 14.4

```
(The Script)
    #!/bin/perl
    # Example using tie with a hash
1   package House;
2   sub TIEHASH {                # Constructor method
3       my $class = shift;       # Shifting the @_ array
        my $price = shift;
        my $color = shift;
        my $rooms = shift;
4       print "I'm the constructor in class $class.\n";
5       my $house = { Color=>$color,     # Data for the tied hash
6                     Price=>$price,
                      Rooms=>$rooms,
                    };
7       bless $house, $class;
    }
8   sub FETCH {                  # Access methods
        my $self=shift;
        my $key=shift;
9       print "Fetching a value.\n";
10      return $self->{$key};
    }
11  sub STORE {
        my $self = shift;
        my $key = shift;
        my $value = shift;
        print "Storing a value.\n";
12      $self->{$key}=$value;
    }
    1;
```

EXAMPLE 14.4 (CONTINUED)

```
     # User/driver program
13   use House;
     # The arguments following the package name are
     # are passed as a list to the tied hash
     # Usage: tie hash, package, argument list
     # The hash %home is tied to the package House.
14   tie %home, "House", 155000, "Yellow", 9;
                      # Calls the TIEHASH constructor
15   print qq/The original color of the house: $home{"Color"}\n/;
                      # Calls FETCH method
16   print qq/The number of rooms in the house: $home{"Rooms"}\n/;
17   print qq/The price of the house is: $home{"Price"}\n/;
18   $home{"Color"}="beige with white trim";   # Calls STORE method
19   print "The house has been painted. It is now $home{Color}.\n";
20   untie(%home);    # Removes the object


(Output)
4    I'm the constructor in class House.
9    Fetching a value.
15   The original color of the house: Yellow
9    Fetching a value.
16   The number of rooms in the house: 9
9    Fetching a value.
17   The price of the house is: 155000
     Storing a value.
     Fetching a value.
     The house has been painted. It is now beige with white trim.
```

EXPLANATION

1   The package/class *House* is declared. The file is *House.pm*.

2   The constructor *TIEHASH* will tie a hash to an object.

3   The first argument is the name of the class, *$class*. The rest of the arguments shifted and all will be assigned as values to the keys of an anonymous hash, the object.

4   The printout shows that the constructor class is called *House*.

5   A reference to an anonymous hash is created and with key/value pairs assigned. They will become the properties of the object.

6   The values assigned to the keys of the anonymous hash were passed to the constructor, *TIEHASH*. (See line 13 in the user program.)

7   The *bless* function returns a reference to the object that is created.

8   The *FETCH* method is an access method that will retrieve a value from the hash object.

9   Each time the user uses the *print* function to display a value from the hash, the *FETCH* method is automatically called and this line will be printed.

10 A value from the hash is returned.

EXPLANATION (CONTINUED)

11   The *STORE* method is an access method that will be called automatically when the
     user attempts to assign a value to one of the keys in the hash.

12   The value to be assigned to the hash came from the argument list passed to the
     STORE method.

13   This is the user/driver program. The *House* module is loaded into the program.

14   The *tie* function calls the *TIEHASH* constructor in *House.pm*. The hash, *%home*, is
     tied to an object in the *House* class. The name of the class, *House*, and three addi-
     tional arguments are passed.

15   This line causes the *FETCH* access method to be called which will display the value
     for the hash key, *Color*.

16   This line causes the *FETCH* access method to be called which will display the value
     for the hash key, *Rooms*.

17   This line causes the *FETCH* access method to be called which will display the value
     for the hash key, *Price*.

18   This line causes the *STORE* access method to be called automatically when a value
     is assigned to one of the hash keys, in this case the key *Color*.

19   The *print* function causes the *FETCH* method to be called automatically to display a
     value for a specified hash key, *Color*.

20   The *untie* function disassociates the hash from the object to which it was tied.

EXAMPLE 14.5

```
     # File is House.pm
1    package House;
2    sub TIEHASH {
         my $class = shift;
         print "I'm the constructor in package $class\n";
         my $houseref = {};
         bless $houseref, $class;
     }
3    sub FETCH {
         my $self=shift;
         my $key=shift;
         return $self->{$key};
     }
4    sub STORE {
         my $self = shift;
         my $key = shift;
         my $value = shift;
         $self->{$key}=$value;
     }
```

EXAMPLE 14.5 (CONTINUED)

```perl
5   sub FIRSTKEY {
        my $self = shift;
6       my $tmp = scalar keys %{$self};
7       return each  %{$self};
    }
8   sub NEXTKEY {
        $self=shift;
        each %{$self};
    }
    1;
```

```perl
    #!/usr/bin/perl
    # File is mainfile
9   use House;
10  tie %home, "House";
    $home{"Price"} = 55000;  # Assign and Store the data
    $home{"Rooms"} = 11;
    # Fetch the data
    print "The number of rooms in the house: $home{Rooms}\n";
    print "The price of the house is: $home{Price}\n";
11  foreach $key (keys(%home)){
12      print "Key is $key\n";
    }
13  while( ($key, $value) = each(%home)){
            # Calls to FIRSTKEY and NEXTKEY
14      print "Key=$key, Value=$value\n";
    }
15  untie(%home);
```

```
(Output)
I'm the constructor in package House
The number of rooms in the house: 11
The price of the house is: 55000
Key is Rooms
Key is Price
Key=Rooms, Value=11
Key=Price, Value=55000
```

EXPLANATION

1   The package/class *House* is declared. The file is *House.pm*.
2   The constructor *TIEHASH* will tie a hash to an object.
3   The *FETCH* method is an access method that will retrieve a value from the hash object.
4   The *STORE* method is an access method that will assign a value to the hash object.

EXPLANATION (CONTINUED)

5   The *FIRSTKEY* method is called automatically if the user program calls one of Perl's built-in hash functions: *keys*, *value*, or *each*.

6   By calling keys in a scalar context, Perl resets the internal state of the hash in order to guarantee that the next time *each* is called it will be given the first key.

7   The *each* function returns the first key/value pair.

8   The *NEXTKEY* method knows what the previous key was (*PREVKEY*) and starts on the next one as the hash is being iterated through a loop in the user program.

9   This is the user/driver program. The *House* module is loaded into the program.

10 The *tie* function calls the *TIEHASH* constructor in *House.pm*. The hash *%home* is tied to an object in the *House* class.

11 The *while* loop is used to iterate through the hash with the *keys* function. The first time in the loop, the *FIRSTKEY* method is automatically called.

12 The value for each key is printed. This value is returned from the access methods, *FIRSTKEY* and *NEXTKEY*.

13 The *while* loop is used to iterate through the hash with the *each* function. The first time in the loop, the *FIRSTKEY* method is automatically called.

14 Each key and value are printed. These values are returned from the access methods, *FIRSTKEY* and *NEXTKEY*.

14.2 DBM Files

The Perl distribution comes with a set of database management library files called DBM, short for database management. The concept of DBM files stems from the early days of UNIX and consists of a set of *C* library routines that allow random access to its records. DBM database files are stored as key/value pairs, an associative array that is mapped into a disk file. There are a number of flavors of DBM support, and they demonstrate the most obvious reasons for using tied hashes.

DBM files are binary. They can handle very large databases. The nice thing about storing data with DBM functions is that the data is persistent; that is, any program can access the file as long as the DBM functions are used. The disadvantage is that complex data structures, indexes, multiple tables, and so forth are not supported, and there is no reliable file locking and buffer flushing, making concurrent reading and updating risky.[2] File locking can be done with the Perl *flock* function, but the strategy for doing this correctly is beyond the scope of this book.[3]

So that you don't have to figure out which of the standard DBM packages to use, the *AnyDBM_File.pm* module will get the appropriate package for your system from the stan-

---

2. Although Perl's *tie* function will probably replace the *dbmopen* function, for now we'll use this function because it's easier than *tie*.

3. For details on file locking, see Descartes, A., and Bunce, T., *Programming the Perl DBI*, O'Reilly & Associates, 2000, p. 35.

dard set in the standard Perl library. The *AnyDBM_File* module is also useful if your program will run on multiple platforms. It will select the correct libraries for one of five different implementations:

Table 14.1   DBM Implementations

odbm	"Old" DBM implementation found on UNIX systems and replaced by NDBM
ndbm	"New" DBM implementation found on UNIX systems
sdbm	Standard Perl DBM, provides cross-platform compatibility, but not good for large databases
gdbm	GNU DBM, a fast, portable DBM implementation; see *www.gnu.org*
bsd-db	Berkeley DB; found on BSD UNIX systems, most powerful of all the DBMs; see *www.sleepycat.com*

The following table comes from the documentation for *AnyDBM_FILE* and lists some of the differences in the various DBM implementations. Type

```
perldoc AnyDBM_File
```

at your command line prompt.

	odbm	ndbm	sdbm	gdbm	bsd-db
	----	----	----	----	------
Linkage comes w/ perl	yes	yes	yes	yes	yes
Src comes w/ perl	no	no	yes	no	no
Comes w/ many unix os	yes	yes[0]	no	no	no
Builds ok on !unix	?	?	yes	yes	?
Code Size	?	?	small	big	big
Database Size	?	?	small	big?	ok[1]
Speed	?	?	slow	ok	fast
FTPable	no	no	yes	yes	yes
Easy to build	N/A	N/A	yes	yes	ok[2]
Size limits	1k	4k	1k[3]	none	none
Byte-order independent	no	no	no	no	yes
Licensing restrictions	?	?	no	yes	no

14.2.1   Creating and Assigning Data to a DBM File

Before a database can be accessed, it must be opened by using the *dbmopen* function or the *tie* function. This binds the DBM file to an associative array (hash). Two files will be created: one file is contains an index directory and has *.dir* as its suffix; the second file, ending in *.pag*, contains all the data. The files are not in a readable format. The *dbm* functions are used to access the data. These functions are invisible to the user.

Data is assigned to the hash, just as with any Perl hash, and an element removed with Perl's *delete* function. The DBM file can be closed with the *dbmclose* or the *untie* function.

FORMAT

```
dbmopen(hash, dbfilename, mode);
tie(hash, Module , dbfilename, flags, mode);
```

EXAMPLE 14.6

```
dbmopen(%myhash, "mydbmfile", 0666);
tie(%myhash,SDBM_File, "mydbmfile", O_RDWR|O_CREAT,0640);
```

Perl's report writing mechanism is very useful for generating formatted data from one of the DBM files. The following examples not only illustrate how to create, add, delete, and close a DBM file, but also how create a Perl-style report.

EXAMPLE 14.7

```
(The Script)
    #!/usr/bin/perl
    # Program name: makestates.pl
    # This program creates the database using the dbm functions
1   use AnyDBM_File;  # Let Perl pick the right dbm for your system
2   dbmopen(%states, "statedb", 0666ᵃ) || die;
                        # Create or open the database
3   TRY: {
4       print "Enter the abbreviation for your state. ";
        chomp($abbrev=<STDIN>);
        $abbrev = uc $abbrev;  # Make sure abbreviation is uppercase
5       print "Enter the name of the state. ";
        chomp($state=<STDIN>);
        lc $state;
6       $states{$abbrev}="\u$state";   # Assign values to the database
7       print "Another entry? ";
        $answer = <STDIN>;
8       redo TRY  if $answer =~ /Y|y/;
    }
9   dbmclose(%states);          # Close the database
--------------------------------------------------------------------
```

EXAMPLE 14.7 (CONTINUED)

```
(The Command line)
10  $ ls
      makestates.pl   statedb.dir   statedb.pag^b
------------------------------------------------------------------
(Output)
4   Enter the abbreviation for your state. CA
5   Enter the name of the state. California
7   Another entry? y
    Enter the abbreviation for your state. me
    Enter the name of the state. Maine
    Another entry? y
    Enter the abbreviation for your state. NE
    Enter the name of the state. Nebraska
    Another entry? y
    Enter the abbreviation for your state. tx
    Enter the name of the state. Texas
    Another entry? n
```

a. Permissions are ignored on Win32 systems.
b. On some versions, only one file with a *.db* extension is created.

EXPLANATION

1   The *AnyDBM_File* module selects the proper DBM libraries for your particular installation.

2   The *dbmopen* function binds a DBM file to a hash. In this case, the database file created is called *statedb* and the hash is called *%states*. If the database does not exists, a valid permission mode should be given. The octal mode given here is *0666*, read and write for all, on UNIX type systems.

3   The labeled block is entered.

4   The user is asked for input, the abbreviation of his state. This input will be used to fill the *%states* hash.

5   The user is asked to enter the name of his state.

6   The value *state* is assigned to the *%states* hash where the key is the abbreviation for the state. The \u escape sequence causes the first letter of the state to be uppercase. When this assignment is made the DBM file will be assigned the new value through a *tie* mechanism that takes place behind the scenes.

7   The user is asked to enter another entry into the DBM file.

8   If the user wants to add another entry to the DBM file, the program will go to the top of the block labeled *TRY* and start over.

9   The *dbmclose* function breaks the tie (by calling the *untie* function), binding the DBM file to the hash *%states*.

10 The listing displays the files that were created with the *dbmopen* function. The first file, *makestates.pl,* is the Perl script. The second file, *statedb.dir,* is the index file, and the last file, *statedb.pg,* is the file that contains the hash data.

14.2.2   Retrieving Data from a DBM File

Once the DBM file has been opened, it is associated with a tied hash in the Perl script. All
details of the implementation are hidden from the user. Data retrieval is fast and easy. The
user simply manipulates the hash as though it were any ordinary Perl hash. Since the hash
is tied to the DBM file, when the data is retrieved, it is coming from the DBM file.

EXAMPLE 14.8

```
(The Script)
    #!/bin/perl
    # Program name: getstates.pl
    # This program fetches the data from the database
    # and generates a report

1   use AnyDBM_File;
2   dbmopen(%states, "statedb", 0666);   # Open the database
3   @sortedkeys=sort keys %states;       # Sort the database by keys
4       foreach $key ( @sortedkeys ){
5       $value=$states{$key};
        $total++;
6       write;
    }
7   dbmclose(%states);      # Close the database

8   format STDOUT_TOP=
    Abbreviation      State
    ==============================
9   .
10  format STDOUT=
    @<<<<<<<<<<<<<@<<<<<<<<<<<<<<<
    $key,           $value

    .
11  format SUMMARY=
    ==============================
    Number of states:@###
                    $total

    .
    $~=SUMMARY;
    write;
```

EXAMPLE 14.8 (CONTINUED)

```
(Output)
  Abbreviation      State
==============================
    AR              Arizona
    CA              California
    ME              Maine
    NE              Nebraska
    TX              Texas
    WA              Washington
==============================
        Number of states:     6
```

EXPLANATION

1   The *AnyDBM_File* module selects the proper DBM libraries for your particular installation.
2   The *dbmopen* function binds a DBM file to a hash. In this case, the database file opened is called *statedb* and the hash is called *%states*.
3   Now that the DBM file has been opened, the user can access the key/value pairs. The *sort* function combined with the *keys* function will sort out the keys in the *%states* hash.
4   The *foreach* loop iterates through the list of sorted keys.
5   Each time through the loop another value is retrieved from the *%states* hash, which is tied to the DBM file.
6   After adding one to the *$total* variable (keeping track of how many entries are in the DBM file), the *write* function invokes the report templates to produce a formatted output.
7   The DBM file is closed; that is, the hash *%states* is disassociated from the DBM file.
8   This is the format template that will be used to put a header on the top of each page.
9   The period ends the template definition.
10 This is the format template for the body of each page printed to standard output. The picture line below is used to format the key/value pairs on the line below the picture.
11 This is the format template that will be invoked at the bottom of the report.

14.2.3   Deleting Entries from a DBM File

To empty the completed DBM file, you can use the *undef* function; for example, *undef %states* would clear all entries in the DBM file created in Example 14.8. Deleting a key/value pair is done simply by using the Perl built-in *delete* function on the appropriate key within the hash that was tied to the DBM file.

EXAMPLE 14.9

```
(The Script)
    #!/bin/perl
    # dbmopen is an older method of opening a dbm file but simpler
    # than using tie and the SDBM_File module provided
    # in the standard Perl library Program name: remstates.pl
1   use AnyDBM_File;
2   dbmopen(%states, "statedb", 0666) || die;
    TRY: {
        print "Enter the abbreviation for the state to remove. ";
        chomp($abbrev=<STDIN>);
        $abbrev = uc $abbrev;  # Make sure abbreviation is uppercase
3       delete $states{"$abbrev"};
        print "$abbrev removed.\n";
        print "Another entry? ";
        $answer = <STDIN>;
        redo TRY  if $answer =~ /Y|y/;  }
4   dbmclose(%states);

(Output)
5   $ remstates.pl
    Enter the abbreviation for the state to remove. TX
    TX removed.
    Another entry? n
6   $ getstates.pl
    Abbreviation      State
    ================================
    AR                Arizona
    CA                California
    ME                Maine
    NE                Nebraska
    WA                Washington
    ================================
    Number of states:   5
7   $ ls
    getstates.pl    makestates.pl    rmstates.pl    statedb.dir
    statedb.pag
```

EXPLANATION

1   The *AnyDBM_File* module selects the proper DBM libraries for your particular installation.

2   The *dbmopen* function binds a DBM file to a hash. In this case, the database file opened is called *statedb* and the hash is called *%states*.

3   Now that the DBM file has been opened, the user can access the key/value pairs. The *delete* function will remove the value associated with the specified key in the *%states* hash tied to the DBM file.

EXPLANATION (CONTINUED)

4   The DBM file is closed; in other words, the hash *%states* is disassociated from the DBM file.

5   The Perl script *remstates.pl* is executed to remove Texas from the DBM file.

6   The Perl script *getstates.pl* is executed to display the data in the DBM file. Texas was removed.

7   The listing shows the files that were created to produce these examples. The last two are the DBM files created by *dbmopen*.

EXAMPLE 14.10

```
1   use Fcntl;
2   use SDBM_File;
3   tie(%address, 'SDBM_File', 'email.dbm', O_RDWR|O_CREAT, 0644)
    || die $!;
4   print "The package the hash is tied to: ",ref tied %address,"\n";

5   print "Enter the email address.\n";
    chomp($email=<STDIN>);
6   print "Enter the first name of the addressee.\n";
    chomp($firstname=<STDIN>);
    $firstname = lc $firstname;
    $firstname = ucfirst $firstname;
7   $address{"$email"}=$firstname;
8   while( ($email, $firstname)=each(%address)){
        print "$email, $firstname\n";
    }
9   untie %address;
```

EXPLANATION

1   The file control module is used to perform necessary tasks on the DBM files.

2   The *SDBM_File* module is used. It is the DBM implementation that comes with standard Perl and works across platforms.

3   Instead of using the *dbmopen* function to create or access a DBM file, this example uses the *tie* function. The hash *%address* is tied to the package *SDBM_File*. The DBM file is called *email.dbm*. If the database doesn't exist, the *O_CREATE* flag will cause it to be created with read/write permissions (*O_RDWR*).

4   The *tied* function returns true if it was successful and the *ref* function returns the name of the package where the hash is tied.

5   In this example, an e-mail address is used as the key in *%address* hash and the value associated with the key will be the first name of the user. Since the keys are always unique, this mechanism will prevent storing duplicate e-mail addresses. The user is asked for input.

EXPLANATION (CONTINUED)

6   The value for the key is requested from the user.

7   Here the database is assigned a new entry. The key/value pair is assigned and stored in the DBM file.

8   The *each* function will pull out both the key and value from the hash *%address*, which is tied to the DBM file. The contents of the DBM file are displayed.

9   The *untie* function disassociates the hash from the DBM file.

15

INTRODUCTION TO PERL DATABASE PROGRAMMING

15.1 Chapter Overview

This chapter explains how to use Perl to do database programming using two technologies, ActiveX Data Objects (ADO) and the Perl database independent interface (DBI), with examples given on two commercial relational database management systems (RDBMS), Microsoft SQL Server (MSS) and Oracle.

The first two examples with each RDBMS use first the DBI and then ADO to do a simple query. They use data source name (DSN) connections and show how to create the DSN.

The next two examples with each RDBMS do more general data definition language (DDL) and data manipulation language (DML) operations including *DROP TABLE, CREATE TABLE, INSERT, UPDATE, DELETE* and more queries with *SELECT*. They also demonstrate using DSN-less connections, which can be useful. Much more detail on Perl and ADO can be found in the book, *ActivePerl with ASP and ADO*, by Tobias Martinsson.

Information is provided about how to obtain free downloads of ActiveState Perl and free evaluation copies of MSS and Oracle RDBMS.

15.1.1 Chapter Contents

The chapter contents are shown here in case the reader chooses to skip some sections.

    Example 15.1: ADO simple query on MSS database using DSN ODBC connection
    Example 15.2: More general DDL and DML with DSN-less ODBC connection

15.2 Perl Database Programming

Perl has powerful procedural programming capabilities, especially text processing. RDBMS are able to efficiently store and retrieve very large amounts of data.

This chapter introduces the reader to marrying the power of Perl and RDBMS capabilities. It shows how to write Perl programs to fetch data from the database management system (DBMS) into the program for any desired processing and how to have the Perl program make changes within the DBMS.

Two technologies are discussed, Perl ADO and DBI database programming. All examples are done for both Microsoft SQL Server and Oracle database management systems.

Some familiarity with SQL programming is assumed.

This is a very brief and simple introduction using both DBI and ADO, and is intended to give enough of a flavor to decide if you want to pursue learning more from a book specifically on the topic. Some such references are listed on the next pages.

15.3 Perl Programming with an RDBMS

The following steps will prepare you to do Perl database programming using ADO and DBI with Microsoft SQL Server and Oracle RDBMS.

1. Install Perl.
2. Install Perl modules for database programming.
3. Install the RDBMS, Microsoft SQL Server, and/or Oracle.
4. Create a DSN, although DSN-less programming is possible and will be illustrated in Examples 15.2 and 15.6.

These steps will be described in detail for a Windows system.

15.3.1   Installing Perl on Windows Systems

1. **Optional:** Download and install UWIN base (at no cost) from
   www.research.att.com/sw/tools/uwin/download.html

   This will give you a Korn shell window, though it isn't required since Perl can be run from a Windows command window (formerly DOS command window).

2. **Required:** Download and install ActiveState Perl (at no cost) from
   www.activestate.com/activeperl/download.htm

   Click on "Windows Intel" and "Save this file to disk." File size is about 8.23 MB. Double-click the downloaded executable and follow the instructions to install.
   After installing, open a Korn shell window or Windows command tool (DOS window) and run *perl -v* from the command line. You may need to first log off and back on.

perl -v.   The output of this command should tell you the version number and that Perl is installed correctly. Read the output and visit the suggested Web sites for more information. If the command doesn't work, reinstall Perl or go back to the Web site for troubleshooting help.
   It will simplify your Perl programming if you create a directory for your Perl scripts such as *C:\bin* and add the directory to your search path. You may need to log off and log back on for the addition to the search path to take effect. Then, create all of your Perl scripts in this directory, naming each script using *.pl* as the filename extension. See the optional example *simple.pl* below.

3. **Optional:** Write and execute a simple Perl program, *simple.pl.*

   You may test the installation of Perl and get some practice programming Perl by typing in and executing the simple program below. The default location for installing the Perl interpreter is *C:\Perl\bin\perl.exe.*[1]

Create and run *simple.pl.*   Create the directory *C:\bin* and add the name to your Windows *PATH* variable. Then create the following file in *C:\bin* using any text editor.

---

1. Note: The installation procedure of ActiveState Perl on Windows automatically adds *C:\Perl\bin* to your search path environment variable and modifies the Registry to link the file extension *.pl* to the Perl executable. When running Perl scripts from the Windows command tool, each Perl script must have an extension *.pl* in order to use this linkage.
   If you install UWIN and run the Perl script from the Korn shell command line, the script must have the usual first line of a UNIX Perl script of the form *#! /c/perl/bin/perl.*
   For generality, I suggest using both the *.pl* extension and the correct first line in Perl scripts on a Windows machine.

File simple.pl

```
#! /usr/bin/perl    ## This line is ignored as a comment on Windows

## simple.pl --

## Simple Perl script to test the installation and demonstrate the
## use of variables and print statements.

print "\nScalar variables must start with \$, for example \$x \n";
print "\tScalar variables may contain a number or a string.\n";
$num = 5;
$str = "This is a string";

print "The value of \$num is: $num \n";
print "The value of \$str is: $str \n";
print "\n";
```

Execute the program from a Windows command tool (DOS window) or a Korn shell window.

```
C:\>  simple.pl
```

Scalar variables must start with $, for example $x. Scalar variables may contain a number or a string. The value of $num is 5. The value of $str is *This is a string.*

15.3.2 Installing Perl Modules Using PPM on Windows Systems

After installing ActiveState Perl, you must install the Perl modules for Perl DBI and ODBC. DBI and ODBC (open database connectivity) are the database interfaces we will use to access Microsoft SQL Server and Oracle databases.

From a command line (either Windows or Korn shell), run

```
C:> ppm        # This will run the Perl Package Manager
               # and give you its prompt:  "PPM>"
```

Make sure your computer is connected to the Internet and enter these commands:

```
PPM>  install  DBD-ODBC   DBD-Oracle   DBI
```

Note: *install* requires current Internet connection.

Enter *y* when prompted for each package name. You may confirm what packages are installed by issuing the command *query.*

```
PPM>    query
DBD-ODBC    [0.28  ] ODBC driver for the DBI module
DBD-Oracle  [1.03  ] Oracle database driver for the DBI module
DBI         [1.13  ] Database independent interface for Perl
....
```

Optionally, you can see a list of all packages available to install by issuing *search*.

```
PPM>    search
```

And *help* gives a summary of PPM commands,

```
PPM>    help
```

though the HTML documentation (see below) is more complete.

Issue *quit* to get back to the command line.

```
PPM>    quit
```

Your Perl installation should now be ready to enter the following programs and run them from the command line.[2]

Start –> Programs –> ActivePerl –> Documentation

ADO.   ADO (ActiveX Data Objects) from Microsoft consists of library routines that access various RDBMS products as well as flat files, spreadsheets, and other data repositories that have OLE DB interface software (provider) written for them. OLE DB is the underlying layer that may be programmed directly from *C++*. ADO sits on top of OLE DB, greatly simplifying the programming which may be done from Perl and Visual Basic, as well as *C* and *C++*.

In Examples 15.1, 15.2, 15.5, and 15.6 we will use the easy ADO interface to communicate to OLE DB, which calls the ODBC driver to reach the data store. This path is shown in bold in Figure 15.1.

If you have OLE DB "provider" (driver) package for your data store then you are able to omit the ODBC layer and improve performance slightly. This is illustrated in Examples 15.2 and 15.6, which are implemented using DSN-less ODBC connections.

But two comment lines also show how to use ADO to OLE DB to RDMBS without going through ODBC. By uncommenting one of these lines and removing one line of the original, the direct OLE DB approach is used.

See Microsoft ADO and OLE DB documentation or a book on the subject such as *ActivePerl with ASP and ADO* by Tobias Martinsson for more details.

---

2. For more information, open Active Perl documentation from Windows and click on PPM near the bottom of the page. An Internet connection is not required.

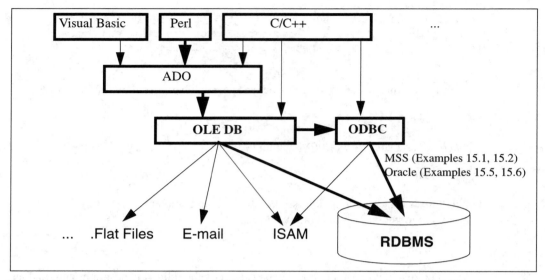

Figure 15.1   Application program using ADO API calls written in Visual Basic, Perl, and C/C++.

DBI.   The DBI is a database interface module for the Perl language. It defines a set of methods, variables, and conventions that provide a consistent database interface independent of the actual database being used.

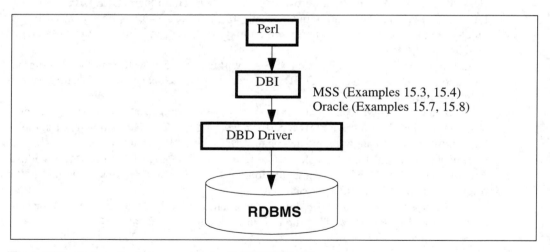

Figure 15.2   Perl application program using Perl DBI API calls.

It is important to remember that the DBI is just an interface, a layer of glue between an application and one or more DBD **database driver** modules. The DBD module is a library with the database-specific code to connect to your target database. For example, to connect to an Oracle database you must load the *DBD-Oracle* module as indicated in the previous section.

For more detail on DBI and the DBD modules, look up DBI in the Module Docs section of the ActivePerl documentation.

15.3.3   Installing an RDBMS

The exercises contained here require installation of the appropriate RDBMS software, Microsoft SQL Server (version 6.5 or later) or Oracle (version 8.0 or later) for their respective exercises.

You can download a free evaluation copy of the RDBMS software from the following sources:

* MSS RDBMS:
  www.microsoft.com/sql/productinfo/evalcd.htm

* Oracle RDBMS:
  www.oracle.com/download

* Oracle Documentation:
  technet.oracle.com/docs/products/oracle8i/doc_index.htm

To install the Microsoft SQL Server (MSS) database after downloading, run *auto-run.exe*. For a non-production database on a practice machine you may just take all the default settings including leaving the *sa* login password as blank. If you change the *sa* password to a non-blank value, you will need to insert that value in the MSS programming Examples 15.1 through 15.4.

To install the Oracle database after downloading, run *setup.exe*. For a non-production database on a practice machine you may just take all the default settings. This includes a sample user named *scott* with password *tiger,* which will be used in the Oracle programming Examples 15.5 through 15.8.

After installing the RDBMS of your choice, you may want to consider doing the non-programming exercises at the end of this chapter.

Exercises 15 and 16 for MSS or Exercises 17 and 18 for Oracle will help you get started with the interactive SQL tools provided with the respective RDBMS, if you are not already familiar with them.

These tools, Query Analyzer for MSS and SQL*Plus for Oracle, can be very helpful to assist in your programming efforts, as they allow you to check the correctness of your SQL statements and the database content by issuing the SQL commands directly to the database and observing the results.

Once your SQL statements are known to be correct, then you can add the Perl program constructs contained in the chapter body to access the database programmatically.

15.3.4   Creating a DSN for MSS Examples

One way to provide your program with the information needed to make a connection to your desired database is to use a DSN.

A DSN contains four vital pieces of information including the DBMS driver (e.g., Microsoft SQL Server) and the server name, user login, and password.

DSN Info Needed for	
Microsoft Access:	C:\datafile.mdb
Microsoft SQL Server:	MSS_servername, user, password
Oracle:	OracleSID, user, password

Here we will need to create a DSN called *MSS_pubs* for Examples 15.1, 15.3, and 15.4. Later we will create a DSN called *ORA_scott* for Examples 15.5, 15.7, and 15.8. DSN-less connections are also possible and are illustrated in Examples 15.2 and 15.6.

Use the following steps to create DSN *MSS_pubs* for Microsoft SQL Server, pubs database:

1. Make sure the database server (Microsoft SQL Server) is installed and running.
2. Open the Control Panel
   Start –> Settings –> Control Panel
3. In the Control Panel, double-click to open the "ODBC Data Sources (32 bit)" icon. (For Windows 2000: In the Control Panel, open the "Administrative Tools" icon and double-click on the icon "Data Sources (ODBC).")

(See Figure 15.3 on next page for the following steps.)

4. Click on "System DSN" tab, then click "Add" near upper right of dialog box. Scroll down, select "SQL Server" and click "Finish." Then enter the following:
   a. Name: **MSS_pubs**
      Description: (optional)
      Server: **(local)**   (May choose from menu)   Click "Next"
   b. Select the second option, "With SQL Server authentication ...", which will already be selected in Windows 98.
      Login ID: **sa**
      Password: <leave blank>   Click "Next"
   c. Check the top box, "Change the default database to:" and enter
      pubs   Click "Next"
   d. Click "Finish"
   e. Click "Test Data Source" and, after seeing the test results, click "OK" twice.

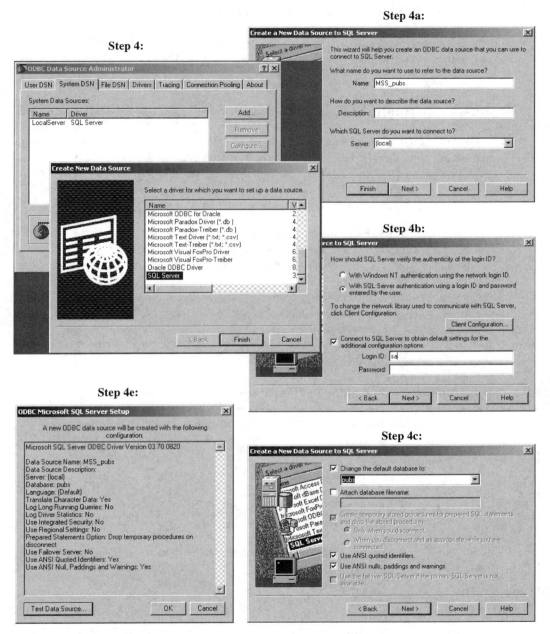

Figure 15.3 Steps in creating the DSN *MSS_pubs* for Microsoft SQL Server.

15.4 Accessing MSS Using ADO and DBI

The most common database operations are doing queries with a *SELECT* statement. The first two examples will use two technologies, ADO and DBI, to do the same simple query on Microsoft SQL Server sample database *pubs*.

15.4.1 Microsoft SQL Server—Query for Examples 15.1 and 15.3

When Microsoft SQL Server RDBMS is installed, it includes a sample database called *pubs* that contains a table called *jobs*. Each row of the *jobs* table may be displayed by executing the following query (*SELECT* statement). The results are shown in the box below.

```
SELECT job_id , job_desc , min_lvl , max_lvl   FROM jobs;
```

Exercise 15 at the end of the chapter shows how to execute this query using the MSS Query Analyzer utility, a client tool provided with the MSS installation. If you haven't used an interactive SQL tool such as MSS Query Analyzer before, it might be useful to do Exercise 15 before proceeding.

This same query will be executed from Perl programs in subsequent examples.

Once the query is executed by the Perl program, the data values are contained in Perl program variables. The programmer may then use the data values in any manner desired, such as saving them to a file, modifying them and putting them back into the database, displaying the values to a user, etc.

Execution of simple query from MSS Query Analyzer:

SQL:	SELECT job_id , job_desc , min_lvl , max_lvl FROM jobs;		
Result:	job_id job_desc	min_lvl	max_lvl
	------ --	-------	-------
	1 New Hire - Job not specified	10	10
	2 Chief Executive Officer	200	250
	3 Business Operations Manager	175	225
	4 Chief Financial Officer	175	250
	5 Publisher	150	250
	6 Managing Editor	140	225
	7 Marketing Manager	120	200
	8 Public Relations Manager	100	175
	9 Acquisitions Manager	75	175
	10 Productions Manager	75	165
	11 Operations Manager	75	150
	12 Editor	25	100
	13 Sales Representative	25	100
	14 Designer	25	100
	(14 row(s) affected)		

The entire result set of the query is contained in what ADO calls a recordset and DBI calls a result set. Notice in the examples how different rows are accessed, as with MoveNext to the next row, and how the individual fields or columns are accessed.

These examples just print the data values to the screen.

15.4.2   Example 15.1: *ex1.pl*
ADO Simple Query on MS SQL Server, DSN

We're ready to write the Perl program to execute the following query on the *jobs* table of the *pubs* database and print the data to the screen.

EXAMPLE 15.1

```
(File ex1.pl)
1  #! /c/perl/bin/perl
2
3  # Perl program accessing Microsoft SQL Server via ADO and ODBC.
4  # First create a DSN named "MSS_pubs" as previously described.
5  # Make sure your database server is running before trying the program.
6  print "hi from $0\n";
7  print ("\t ADO with DSN \"MSS_pubs\" on the local MS SQL Server database \n");
8  print ("\t Execute: SELECT job_id, job_desc, min_lvl, max_lvl FROM jobs \n\n");
9  print "\n";
10 use OLE;
11
12 $conn = CreateObject OLE "ADODB.Connection" ||    # Create ADO auto object
13      die "Error on ADO  CreateObject: $!" ;
14
15 $conn->Open('MSS_pubs');      # Connect to DSN
16
17 if ( $conn->{State}  != 1  )  {    # 1 is adStateOpen , 0 is adStateClosed
18    die ("\t Connection Not Open. Make sure the server is running.\n\n");
19 }
20
21 $sql="SELECT job_id, job_desc, min_lvl, max_lvl FROM jobs"; # SQL Statement to run
22
23 $rs = $conn->Execute($sql);     # Execute the query
24
25 print ("job_id\tjob_desc\t\tmin_lvl\tmax_lvl\n");   # Print header for output
26
27 while( ! $rs->EOF() ) {    # Fetch each row, one at a time until reach end of rs
28    print ( $rs->Fields(job_id)->Value, "\t" );
29    printf( "%-30s\t", $rs->Fields(job_desc)->Value );
30    print ( $rs->Fields(min_lvl)->Value, "\t" );
31    print ( $rs->Fields(max_lvl)->Value, "\n" );
32    $rs->MoveNext;      # Move to the next row of the recordset
33 }
34
35 $rs->Close;         # Close the recordset
36 $conn->Close;       # Close the connection
37 # Last line of file
```

Output—A sample run from the command line looks as follows:

```
C:\> ex1.pl
    ADO with DSN "MSS_pubs" on the local MS SQL Server database
    Execute: SELECT job_id, job_desc, min_lvl, max_lvl FROM jobs

job_id  job_desc                        min_lvl   max_lvl
1       New Hire - Job not specified    10        10
2       Chief Executive Officer         200       250
3       Business Operations Manager     175       225
4       Chief Financial Officer         175       250
5       Publisher                       150       250
6       Managing Editor                 140       225
7       Marketing Manager               120       200
8       Public Relations Manager        100       175
9       Acquisitions Manager            75        175
10      Productions Manager             75        165
11      Operations Manager              75        150
12      Editor                          25        100
13      Sales Representative            25        100
14      Designer                        25        100
```

EXPLANATION

1   See comments on page 461 suggesting the first line shown and the file name having *.pl* extension.
10   Include OLE library, which contain ADO routines.
12   Create an ADO connection object.
15   Open the ADO connection object using the previously defined DSN *MSS_pubs*.
17   Check that the connection is open, *adStateOpen* is *1*.
21   Fill a local string variable *$sql* with the *SELECT* statement to be executed.
23   Call the connection *Execute* method on *$sql* to execute the query in the RDBMS and return the resulting recordset to the local variable *$rs*. This is where data from the database is brought into the Perl program.
25   Print header line for output of the table data.
27–31   Loop through each row of the recordset printing each column (field) value.
27   The *while* condition is (*! $rs->EOF()*), which becomes FALSE after *MoveNext* from the last row.
28–31   Access each column (field) of the row by *$rs->Fields(<column_name>)*.
32   Move to the next row in the recordset.
35   Close the recordset.
36   Close the connection.

15.4.3   Executing DDL and DML Operations

The most common database interaction involves doing queries using the *SELECT* statement as in the previous example.

This section adds other operations using DBI or ADO to execute **pass-through SQL** statements, which means you can construct any legal SQL statement you wish as a string you then pass through to the database server for execution.

This example includes the DDL commands *DROP TABLE* and *CREATE TABLE*, as well DML statements *INSERT, UPDATE, DELETE,* and *SELECT.*

The operations to be performed are listed here:

1. Drop table persons—we want to start fresh
2. Create table persons—gives a new empty table
3. Insert into persons—add two rows of sample data
4. Display all of table persons—to see the results
5. Update a person—to demonstrate a data change
6. Display all of table persons—to see the results
7. Delete a person—to demonstrate a delete
8. Display all of table persons—to see the results

The exact SQL statements are shown in the file *persons.sql* listed in the box below.

persons.sql:

```
/*
      persons.sql
*/
                              —Out with the old to start fresh
DROP TABLE persons;

CREATE TABLE persons (   —In with a new empty table
    personid         INTEGER     PRIMARY KEY,
    pname            VARCHAR(15)  NOT NULL,
    city             VARCHAR(15)
);


INSERT INTO persons VALUES ( 1 , 'Carol Smith' , 'Boston');
INSERT INTO persons VALUES ( 2 , 'Sam Jones' , 'Detroit' );

SELECT personid , pname , city FROM persons;

UPDATE persons SET city = 'Seattle' WHERE personid = 2;
SELECT personid , pname , city FROM persons;

DELETE FROM persons WHERE personid = 1;
SELECT personid , pname , city FROM persons;
```

These SQL statements may be typed into a text file such as *persons.sql* and executed from an SQL tool.

Exercises 16 and 18 at the end of the chapter show how to do this from either MSS Query Analyzer (Exercise 16) or Oracle SQL*Plus (Exercise 18).

15.4.4 Example 15.2: *ex2.pl*
Perl ADO of *persons.sql* on MSS, DSN-less

You need to first install Perl and the DBI modules as described earlier and also have Microsoft SQL Server installed and running, including the sample *pubs* database. Note that in the format for creating a DSN-less connection string, *DSN=;* must be last.

EXAMPLE 15.2

```
(File ex2.pl)
1  #! /c/perl/bin/perl
2
3  # ADO program using pass-through SQL to execute DDL and DML statements.
4
5  use OLE;
6
7  ############## Subroutine PrintPersonsTable();
8  sub PrintPersonsTable{
9      $sql = "SELECT personid , pname , city FROM persons; ";
10
11     $rs = $conn->Execute($sql)  ||  warn "*** SELECT ERROR *** $!";
12
13     print ("   personid\t   pname     \t   city\n");
14     print ("   --------\t -------------\t ---------\n");
15     while (  ! $rs->EOF()  )   # Fetch each row
16     {                          # Print each column value
17         print ("\t", $rs->Fields(personid)->Value , "\t  ");
18         print ( $rs->Fields(pname)->Value , "\t  ");
19         print ( $rs->Fields(city)->Value , "\n");
20         $rs->MoveNext;
21     }
22     $rs->Close;
23     print ("\n");
24  } ############## end Subroutine PrintPersonsTable
25
26 print ("\tADO DSN-Less to pubs database on local MS SQL Server database. \n");
27 print ("\tThis program uses ADO to execute DDL and DML statements \n");
28 print "\n";
29
30 $conn = CreateObject OLE "ADODB.Connection" ||   # Create ADO auto object
31     die "Error on ADO  CreateObject: $!" ;
32
33 $conn->Open("server=(local);driver={SQL Server};UID=sa;PWD=;database=pubs;DSN=;");
34 ## To go directly from OLE DB to MSS, remove the line above and uncomment next line
35 ## $conn->Open("Provider=SQLOLEDB.1;Password=;User ID=sa;Initial Catalog=pubs;Data
       Source=(local)");
36
37 if ( $conn->{State} != 1  ) {     # 1 is adStateOpen , 0 is asStateClosed
38    die  ("\t Connection Not Open. Make sure the server is started.\n\n");
39 }
```

EXAMPLE 15.2 (CONTINUED)

```
40
41 #################################  DROP TABLE persons
42 $sql = "DROP TABLE persons";
43 $conn->Execute($sql)  ||  warn "*** DROP TABLE ERROR *** $!";
44 # Last line of file
45 #################################  CREATE TABLE persons
46 $sql = "CREATE TABLE persons (
47        personidINTEGER PRIMARY KEY ,
48        pname   VARCHAR(15)  NOT NULL,
49        city    VARCHAR(15)
50    );";
51 $conn->Execute($sql)  ||  warn "*** CREATE TABLE ERROR *** $!";
52 #################################  INSERT  2 rows
53 $sql = "INSERT INTO persons VALUES ( 1 , 'Carol Smith' , 'Boston');
54        INSERT INTO persons VALUES ( 2 , 'Sam Jones' , 'Detroit' ); ";
55 $conn->Execute($sql)  ||  warn "*** INSERT ERROR *** $!";
56
57 PrintPersonsTable();
58
59 #################################  UPDATE  1 row
60 $sql = "UPDATE persons SET city = 'Seattle' WHERE personid = 2; ";
61 $conn->Execute($sql)  ||  warn "*** UPDATE ERROR *** $!";
62
63 PrintPersonsTable();
64 #################################  DELETE  1 row
65 $sql = "DELETE FROM persons WHERE personid = 1; ";
66 $conn->Execute($sql)  ||  warn "*** DELETE ERROR *** $!";
67
68 PrintPersonsTable();
   $conn->Close
69 # Last line of file
```

A sample run from the command line is shown here:

```
C:\> ex2.pl
    ADO DSN-less to pubs database on local MS SQL Server database.
    This program uses ADO to execute DDL and DML statements.

    personid   pname              city
    --------   ------------------ ---------
       1       Carol Smith        Boston
       2       Sam Jones          Detroit

    personid   pname              city
    --------   ------------------ ---------
       1       Carol Smith        Boston
       2       Sam Jones          Seattle

    personid   pname              city
    --------   ------------------ ---------
       2       Sam Jones          Seattle
```

15.4.5   Example 15.3: *ex3.pl*
Perl DBI Simple Query on MS SQL Server

This is the same simple query to MSS using a DSN connection, but using the DBI.

EXAMPLE 15.3

```
(File ex3.pl)
1  #! /c/perl/bin/perl
2
3  # Perl program accessing Microsoft SQL Server via DBI and ODBC.
4  # Make sure your database server is running before trying the program.
5
6  print ("\t DBI with DSN \"MSS_pubs\" on the local MS SQL Server database\n");
7  print ("\t Executes: SELECT job_id, job_desc, min_lvl, max_lvl FROM jobs \n\n");
8
9  use DBI;
10
11 my $dbh = DBI->connect('dbi:odbc:MSS_pubs', 'sa', '', 'ODBC')
                                              # dbh=Database Handle
      || die "\tError on DBI->connect.   \n\tMake sure the server is running!!
                               \n\t$DBI::ERRSTR" ;
12
13 $sql = "SELECT job_id, job_desc, min_lvl, max_lvl FROM jobs";
                                              # SQL Statement to run
14
15 my $sth = $dbh->prepare($sql);  # sth = Statement Handle
16
17 $sth->execute();
18
19 my $dat;  # Create a local variable to hold returned row data
20
21 print ("job_id\tjob_desc\t\t\tmin_lvl\tmax_lvl\n");      # Print header for output
22
23 while ( $dat = $sth->fetchrow_hashref )   # Fetch each row
24 {                                         # Print each column value
25   print ("$dat->{job_id}\t");
26   printf("%-30s\t",$dat->{job_desc});     # Could save each column value into
27   print ("$dat->{min_lvl}\t");            # a program variable, e.g.,
28   print ("$dat->{max_lvl}\n");            # $v_jobid = $dat->{job_id}
29 }
30 $sth->finish;
31 $dbh->disconnect
32 # Last line of file
```

Output is same as for *ex1.pl*:

```
C:\> ex3.pl
      DBI with DSN "MSS_pubs" on the local MS SQL Server database
      Executes: SELECT job_id, job_desc, min_lvl, max_lvl FROM jobs

   job_id  job_desc                      min_lvl    max_lvl
   1       New Hire - Job not specified  10         10
   2       Chief Executive Officer       200        250
   3       Business Operations Manager   175        225
   4       Chief Financial Officer       175        250
   5       Publisher                     150        250
   6       Managing Editor               140        225
   7       Marketing Manager             120        200
   8       Public Relations Manager      100        175
   9       Acquisitions Manager          75         175
   10      Productions Manager           75         165
   11      Operations Manager            75         150
   12      Editor                        25         100
   13      Sales Representative          25         100
   14      Designer                      25         100
```

EXPLANATION

1	See comments on page 461 suggesting the first line shown and the file name having *.pl* extension.
9	Include DBI.
11	Open the database connection using the previously defined DSN *MSS_pubs* and return its database handle to local variable *$dbh*.
26	Check that the connection is open.
13	Fill a local string variable *$sql* with the *SELECT* statement to be executed.
15	Prepare the *sql* statement and return the statement handle to local variable *$sth*.
15	Call the connection *Execute* method on *$sql* to execute the query in the RDBMS. The returned data is available through the statement handle method *$sth->fetchrow_hashref,* as shown on line 23.
21	Print header line for output of the table data.
23–28	Loop through each row of the recordset printing each column (field) value.
23	The while condition (*$dat = **$sth->fetchrow_hashref***) becomes NULL when attempting to fetch beyond the last row.
26–28	Access each column (field) of the row by *$dat->{<column_name>}*.
30	Close the recordset.
31	Close the connection.

15.4.6   Example 15.4: *ex4.pl*
Perl DBI of *persons.sql* on MSS

You need to first install Perl and the DBI modules as described earlier and also have
Microsoft SQL Server installed and running, including the sample *pubs* database.

EXAMPLE 15.4

```
File ex4.pl:
1  #! /c/perl/bin/perl
2
3  # DBI program using pass-through SQL to execute DDL and DML statements.
4
5  use DBI;
6
7  print ("\t DBI with DSN \"MSS_pubs\" on the local MS SQL Server database\n");
8  print ("\t This will execute DDL and DML statements using pass-through SQL \n\n");
9
10 ## dbh = Database Handle
11 my $dbh = DBI->connect('dbi:odbc:MSS_pubs', 'sa', '', 'ODBC')
12     || die "\tError on DBI->connect. \n\tMake sure the server is running!!\n\t" ;
13
14 ######## Subroutine PrintPersonsTable();
15 sub PrintPersonsTable{
16     $sql = "SELECT personid , pname , city FROM persons; ";
17     my $sth = $dbh->prepare($sql);
18     $sth->execute()  ||  warn "*** SELECT ERROR *** $!";
19
20     print ("   personid\t   pname     \t   city\n");
21     print ("   --------\t ---------------\t  ---------\n");
22
23     my $dat;  # Create a local variable to hold returned row data
24     while ( $dat = $sth->fetchrow_hashref )  # Fetch each row
       {                                        # Print each column value
         print ("\t$dat->{personid}\t  ");
         print ("$dat->{pname}\t  ");
         print ("$dat->{city}\n");
       }
25     print ("\n");
26 } #### end Subroutine PrintPersonsTable
27
28 ################################## DROP TABLE persons
29 $sql = "DROP TABLE persons";
30 my $sth = $dbh->prepare($sql);  # sth = Statement Handle
31 $sth->execute()  ||  warn "*** DROP TABLE ERROR *** $!";
32
33 ################################## CREATE TABLE persons
34 $sql = "CREATE TABLE persons (
35        personid  INTEGER PRIMARY KEY ,
36        pname     VARCHAR(15)  NOT NULL,
37        city      VARCHAR(15)
38    );";
```

EXAMPLE 15.4 (CONTINUED)

```
39 my $sth = $dbh->prepare($sql);
40 $sth->execute()  ||  warn "*** CREATE TABLE ERROR *** $!";
41 ################################# INSERT 2 rows
42 $sql = "INSERT INTO persons VALUES ( 1 , 'Carol Smith' , 'Boston');
43        INSERT INTO persons VALUES ( 2 , 'Sam Jones' , 'Detroit' ); ";
44 my $sth = $dbh->prepare($sql);
45 $sth->execute()  ||  warn "*** INSERT ERROR *** $!";
46
47 PrintPersonsTable();
48
49 ################################# UPDATE 1 row
50 $sql = "UPDATE persons SET city = 'Seattle' WHERE personid = 2; ";
51 my $sth = $dbh->prepare($sql);  # sth = Statement Handle
52 $sth->execute()  ||  warn "*** UPDATE ERROR *** $!";
53
54 PrintPersonsTable();
55
56 ################################# DELETE 1 row
57 $sql = "DELETE FROM persons WHERE personid = 1; ";
58 my $sth = $dbh->prepare($sql);  # sth = Statement Handle
59 $sth->execute()  ||  warn "*** DELETE ERROR *** $!";
60
61 PrintPersonsTable();
62 $sth->finish;
63 $dbh->disconnect
64 # Last line of file
```

Output is same as for *ex2.pl*:

```
C:\> ex4.pl
        DBI with DSN "MSS_pubs" on the local MS SQL Server database
        This will execute DDL and DML statements using pass-through SQL
        personid   pname                city
        --------   ------------------   ---------
        1          Carol Smith          Boston
        2          Sam Jones            Detroit

        personid   pname                city
        --------   ------------------   ---------
        1          Carol Smith          Boston
        2          Sam Jones            Seattle

        personid   pname                city
        --------   ------------------   ---------
        2          Sam Jones            Seattle
```

15.5 Accessing Oracle Using ADO and DBI

Accessing an Oracle RDBMS instance is quite similar to accessing MSS. The next four examples implement on Oracle what the first four did on MSS.

15.5.1   Oracle—Simple Query for Example 15.5 (ADO) and 15.7 (DBI)

When Oracle RDBMS is installed it includes a sample user named *scott* with a password of *tiger* and several tables including one called *emp*.

Each row of the *emp* table may be displayed by executing the following query (*SELECT* statement). The results are shown in the box below.

```
SELECT ename, empno, job, deptno FROM emp;
```

Exercise 17 at the end of the chapter shows how to execute this query using the Oracle "SQL*Plus" utility, a client tool provided as part of the Oracle installation. If you haven't used an interactive SQL tool such as Oracle SQL*Plus before, it might be useful to do this exercise before proceeding.

Execution of simple query from SQL*Plus window:

SQL:	**SELECT ename, empno, job, deptno FROM emp;**			
Result:	ENAME	EMPNO	JOB	DEPTNO
	----------	---------	---------	--------
	SMITH	7369	CLERK	20
	ALLEN	7499	SALESMAN	30
	WARD	7521	SALESMAN	30
	JONES	7566	MANAGER	20
	MARTIN	7654	SALESMAN	30
	BLAKE	7698	MANAGER	30
	CLARK	7782	MANAGER	10
	SCOTT	7788	ANALYST	20
	KING	7839	PRESIDENT	10
	TURNER	7844	SALESMAN	30
	ADAMS	7876	CLERK	20
	FORD	7902	ANALYST	20
	MILLER	7934	CLERK	10
	JAMES	7900	CLERK	30

This same query will be executed from Perl programs in Example 15.5 using ADO and in Example 15.7 using the DBI.

Once the query is executed by the Perl program, the data values are contained in Perl program variables. The programmer may then use the data values in any manner desired, such as saving them to a file, modifying them and putting them back into the database, displaying the values to a user, etc.

These examples just print the data values to the screen.

15.5.2 Creating a DSN for Oracle Examples

In the default installation of Oracle is a user *scott* with password *tiger*, which contains several tables including *emp* and *dept*. We will use table *emp* in our examples.

Use the following steps to create DSN *ORA_scott* for Oracle RDBMS:

1. Make sure the Oracle database server is installed and running.
2. Open the Control Panel
   Start –> Settings –> Control Panel
3. In the Control Panel, double click to open the "ODBC Data Sources (32 bit)" icon. (For Windows 2000: In the Control Panel, open the "Administrative Tools" icon and double-click on the icon "Data Sources (ODBC)."

(See Figure 15.4 on next page for the following steps.)

4. Click on "System DSN" tab, then click "Add" near upper right of dialog box. Scroll down, select either "Microsoft ODBC Driver for Oracle" or "Oracle ODBC Driver" and click "Finish."[3] Then enter the following:
   a. Data Source Name: **ORA_scott**
      Description: (optional)
      Service Name: **<your Oracle server name>**   (Our Oracle server is *CAT*)
      UserID: **scott/tiger**
      Click "OK" twice

---

3. Either should work, but I've experienced times where only one works. I've had better luck with Microsoft ODBC for Oracle.

Step 4:

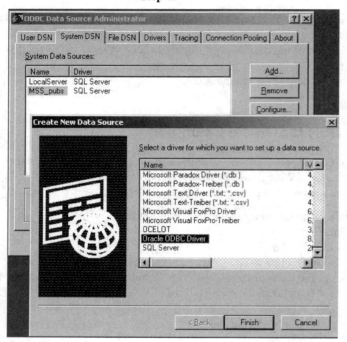

Step 4a:

Figure 15.4 Steps in creating DSN *ORA_scott* for Oracle RDBMS.

15.5.3   Example 15.5: *ex5.pl*
ADO Simple Query on Oracle, DSN

You need to first install Perl and the DBI modules as described earlier, and also have Oracle installed and running, including the sample user *scott/tiger*.

EXAMPLE 15.5

```
(File ex5.pl)
1  #! /c/perl/bin/perl
2
3  # Perl program accessing Oracle via ADO and ODBC.
4  # First create a DSN named "ORA_scott" as previously described.
5  # Make sure your database server is running before trying the program.
6
7  print "hi from $0\n";
8  print ("\t ADO with DSN \"ORA_scott\" on the Oracle server named \"CAT\" \n");
9  print ("\t Execute: SELECT ename, empno, job, deptno FROM emp \n\n");
10 print("\t    ** If connect fails and server is running, change ODBC Driver **\n");
11 print "\n";
12
13 use OLE;
14
15 $conn = CreateObject OLE "ADODB.Connection" ||    # Create ADO auto object
16       die "Error on ADO  CreateObject: $!" ;
17
18 $conn->Open('ORA_scott');      # Connect to DSN
19
20 if ( $conn->{State}  != 1 ) {     # 1 is adStateOpen , 0 is asStateClosed
21    die ("\t Connection Not Open. \n\t Make sure the server is started.\n\n");
22 }
23
24 $sql = "SELECT ename, empno, job, deptno FROM emp";  # SQL Statement to run
25
26 $rs = $conn->Execute($sql);     # Execute the query
27
28 print ("ename\t   empno   job\t\tdeptno\n");
29
30 while( !$rs->EOF() ) {      # Fetch each row, one at a time
31    printf( "%-11s\t", $rs->Fields(ENAME)->Value );
32    print ( $rs->Fields(EMPNO)->Value, "    " );       # Oracle ADO permits lower
33    printf( "%-9s\t", $rs->Fields(JOB)->Value );        # or uppercase column names
34    print ( $rs->Fields(deptno)->Value, "\t" );
35    print ("\n");
36
37    $rs->MoveNext;
38 }
39 $rs->Close;
40 $conn->Close;
41 # Last line of file
```

A sample run from the program line looks as follows:

```
C:\> ex5.pl
    ADO with DSN "ORA_scott" on the Oracle server named "CAT"
    Execute: SELECT ename, empno, job, deptno FROM emp
       ** If connect fails and server is running, change ODBC Driver **

    ename      empno     job             deptno
    SMITH      7369      CLERK           20
    ALLEN      7499      SALESMAN        30
    WARD       7521      SALESMAN        30
    JONES      7566      MANAGER         20
    MARTIN     7654      SALESMAN        30
    BLAKE      7698      MANAGER         30
    CLARK      7782      MANAGER         10
    SCOTT      7788      ANALYST         20
    KING       7839      PRESIDENT       10
    TURNER     7844      SALESMAN        30
    ADAMS      7876      CLERK           20
    JAMES      7900      CLERK           30
    FORD       7902      ANALYST         20
    MILLER     7934      CLERK           10
```

EXPLANATION

1	See comments on page 461 suggesting the first line shown and the filename having *.pl* extension.
13	Include OLE library, which contain ADO routines.
15	Create an ADO connection object.
18	Open the ADO connection object using the previously defined DSN *ORA_scott*.
20	Check that the connection is open, *adStateOpen* is *1*.
24	Fill a local string variable *$sql* with the *SELECT* statement to be executed.
26	Call the connection *Execute* method on *$sql* to execute the query in the RDBMS and return the resulting recordset to the local variable *$rs*. This is where data from the database is brought into the Perl program.
28	Print header line for output of the table data.
30–38	Loop through each row of the recordset printing each column (field) value.
30	The *while* condition is *(! $rs->EOF())* which becomes FALSE after *MoveNext* from the last row.
31–34	Access each column (field) of the row by *$rs->Fields(<column_name>)*.
37	Move to the next row in the recordset.
39	Close the recordset.
40	Close the connection.

15.5.4   Executing DDL and DML Operations in Oracle

These are the same DDL and DML statements previously done with MSS examples. They are repeated here as they will be used next in Examples 15.6 and 15.8. They are also shown in the box below, executed interactively with the Oracle SQL*Plus utility.

The operations to be performed are listed here:

1. Drop table persons—we want to start fresh
2. Create table persons—gives a new empty table
3. Insert into persons—add two rows of sample data
4. Display all of table persons—to see the results
5. Update a person—to demonstrate a data change
6. Display all of table persons—to see the results
7. Delete a person—to demonstrate a delete
8. Display all of table persons—to see the results

Oracle SQL*Plus interactive execution of the statements in *pesons.sql*:

```
SQL> DROP TABLE persons;
Table dropped.
SQL> CREATE TABLE persons (
  2      personid   INTEGER    PRIMARY KEY,
  3      pname   VARCHAR(15)   NOT NULL,
  4      city   VARCHAR(15)
  5      );
Table created.
SQL> INSERT INTO persons VALUES ( 1 , 'Carol Smith' , 'Boston');
1 row created.
SQL> INSERT INTO persons VALUES ( 2 , 'Sam Jones' , 'Detroit' );
1 row created.
SQL> SELECT personid , pname , city FROM persons;
 PERSONID PNAME           CITY
--------- --------------- --------------
        1 Carol Smith     Boston
        2 Sam Jones       Detroit
SQL> UPDATE persons SET city = 'Seattle' WHERE personid = 2;
1 row updated.
SQL> SELECT personid , pname , city FROM persons;
 PERSONID PNAME           CITY
--------- --------------- --------------
        1 Carol Smith     Boston
        2 Sam Jones       Seattle
SQL> DELETE FROM persons WHERE personid = 1;
1 row deleted.
SQL> SELECT personid , pname , city FROM persons;
 PERSONID PNAME           CITY
--------- --------------- --------------
        2 Sam Jones       Seattle
```

The exact SQL statements are shown in the file *persons.sql* shown on page 473.

That series of SQL statements from *persons.sql* is shown here executed interactively using Oracle SQL*Plus.

15.5.5 Example 15.6: *ex6.pl*
Perl ADO of *persons.sql* on Oracle, DSN-less

This program requires Perl and the DBI modules. Also, have Oracle installed and running, including the sample user *scott/tiger*.

EXAMPLE 15.6

```
(File ex6.pl)
1  #! /c/perl/bin/perl
2
3  use OLE;
4
5  ############## Subroutine PrintPersonsTable();
6  sub PrintPersonsTable{
7      $sql = "SELECT personid , pname , city FROM persons ";
8
9      $rs = $conn->Execute($sql)  ||  warn "*** SELECT ERROR *** $!";
10
11     print ("    personid\t    pname    \t   city\n");
12     print ("    --------\t -------------\t  ---------\n");
13     while (  ! $rs->EOF()  )   # Fetch each row
14     {                         #  Print each column value
15         print ("\t", $rs->Fields(PERSONID)->Value , "\t  ");
16         print ( $rs->Fields(PNAME)->Value , "\t  ");  # Oracle ADO permits lower
17         print ( $rs->Fields(city)->Value , "\n");      # or uppercase column names
18         $rs->MoveNext;
19     }
20     $rs->Close;
21     print ("\n");
22 } ############## end Subroutine PrintPersonsTable
23
24 print ("\tADO  DSN-Less to scott/tiger on the Oracle server named \"CAT\" \n");
25 print ("\tThis program uses ADO to execute DDL and DML statements \n\n");
26 print("\t    ** If connect fails and server is running, change ODBC Driver **\n");
27 print "\n";
28
29 $conn = CreateObject OLE "ADODB.Connection" ||   # Create ADO auto object
30         die "Error on ADO  CreateObject: $!" ;
31
32 # Next line uses DSN-less ODBC connection to scott/tiger on the Oracle server "CAT"
33 $conn->Open("server=CAT;driver={Microsoft ODBC for Oracle};UID=scott;
     PWD=tiger;DSN=;");
```

EXAMPLE 15.6 (CONTINUED)

```
34 ## To go directly from OLE DB to MSS, remove line above and uncomment line below
35 ## $conn->Open("Provider=MSDAORA.1;Password=tiger;User ID=scott;Data Source=CAT");
36
37 if ( $conn->{State} != 1  ) {      # 1 is adStateOpen , 0 is asStateClosed
38    die  ("\t Connection Not Open. \n\t Make sure the server is started.\n\n");
39 }
40
41 ####################################  DROP TABLE persons
42 $sql = "DROP TABLE persons";
43 $conn->Execute($sql)  ||  warn "*** DROP TABLE ERROR *** $!";
44 ####################################  CREATE TABLE persons
45 $sql = "CREATE TABLE persons (
46        personid  INTEGER PRIMARY KEY ,
47        pname     VARCHAR(15)  NOT NULL,
48        city      VARCHAR(15)
49     )";
50 $conn->Execute($sql)  ||  warn "*** CREATE TABLE ERROR *** $!";
51
52 ####################################  INSERT 2 rows
53 $sql = "INSERT INTO persons VALUES ( 1 , 'Carol Smith' , 'Boston')";
54 $conn->Execute($sql)  ||  warn "*** INSERT ERROR *** $!";
55
56 $sql = "INSERT INTO persons VALUES ( 2 , 'Sam Jones' , 'Detroit' ) ";
57 $conn->Execute($sql)  ||  warn "*** INSERT ERROR *** $!";
58
59 PrintPersonsTable();
60
61 ####################################  UPDATE  1 row
62 $sql = "UPDATE persons SET city = 'Seattle' WHERE personid = 2 ";
63 $conn->Execute($sql)  ||  warn "*** UPDATE ERROR *** $!";
64
65 PrintPersonsTable();
66
67 ####################################  DELETE   1 row
68 $sql = "DELETE FROM persons WHERE personid = 1 ";
69 $conn->Execute($sql)  ||  warn "*** DELETE ERROR *** $!";
70
71 PrintPersonsTable();
72 $conn->Close
73 # Last line of file
```

A sample run from the command line is shown here:

```
C:\> ex6.pl
        AD0  DSN-less: to scott/tiger on the Oracle server named "CAT"
        This program uses ADO to execute DDL and DML statements
           ** If connect fails and server is running, change ODBC Driver **

        personid  pname              city
        --------  -----------------  ---------
           1      Carol Smith        Boston
           2      Sam Jones          Detroit

        personid  pname              city
        --------  -----------------  ---------
           1      Carol Smith        Boston
           2      Sam Jones          Seattle

        personid  pname              city
        --------  -----------------  ---------
           2      Sam Jones          Seattle
```

15.5.6   Example 15.7: *ex7.pl*
Perl DBI Simple Query on Oracle

Now we're ready to write the Perl program to execute the following query on the *emp* table and print the data to the screen.

EXAMPLE 15.7

```
(File ex7.pl)
1  #! /c/perl/bin/perl
2
3  # Perl program accessing Oracle via DBI and ODBC.
4  # Make sure the database server is running before trying the program.
5
6  print ("\t DBI with DSN \"ORA_scott\" on the Oracle server named \"CAT\" \n");
7  print ("\t Execute: SELECT ename, empno, job, deptno FROM emp \n");
8  print ("\t    ** If connect fails and server is running, change ODBC Driver **\n");
9  print "\n";
10
11 use DBI;
12
13 my $dbh = DBI->connect('dbi:odbc:ORA_scott', 'scott', 'tiger', 'ODBC')
14 || die "***\tError on DBI->connect.Make sure the server is running!!";
                                               # $dbh = Database Handle
15
```

EXAMPLE 15.7 (CONTINUED)

```
16 $sql = "SELECT ename, empno, job, deptno FROM emp";      # SQL Statement to run
17
18 my $sth = $dbh->prepare($sql);                            # $sth = Statement Handle
19
20 $sth->execute();
21
22 my $dat;  # Create a local variable to hold returned row data
23
24 print ("ename\t   empno   job\t\tdeptno\n");              # Print header for output
25
26 while ( $dat = $sth->fetchrow_hashref )                   # Fetch each row
27 {                                                         # Print each column value
28    printf("%-11s", $dat->{ENAME} );                       # In Oracle must use UPPERCASE
29    print ("$dat->{EMPNO}     ");                          # for column names
30    printf("%-9s\t", $dat->{JOB} );
31    print ("$dat->{DEPTNO}\t");
32    print ("\n");
33 }
34 # Last line of file
```

A sample run from the program line is shown here:

```
C:\> ex7.pl
    DBI with DSN "ORA_scott" on the Oracle server named "CAT"
    Execute: SELECT ename, empno, job, deptno FROM emp
        ** If connect fails and server is running, change ODBC Driver **


    ename      empno     job              deptno
    SMITH      7369      CLERK            20
    ALLEN      7499      SALESMAN         30
    WARD       7521      SALESMAN         30
    JONES      7566      MANAGER          20
    MARTIN     7654      SALESMAN         30
    BLAKE      7698      MANAGER          30
    CLARK      7782      MANAGER          10
    SCOTT      7788      ANALYST          20
    KING       7839      PRESIDENT        10
    TURNER     7844      SALESMAN         30
    ADAMS      7876      CLERK            20
    JAMES      7900      CLERK            30
    FORD       7902      ANALYST          20
    MILLER     7934      CLERK            10
```

15.5.7   Example 15.8: *ex8.pl*
Perl DBI of *persons.sql* on Oracle

This program uses pass-through SQL via DBI with DSN to Oracle.

EXAMPLE 15.8

```
(File ex8.pl)
1  #! /c/perl/bin/perl
2
3  use dbi;
4
5  print ("\t DBI with DSN \"ORA_scott\" on Oracle server named \"CAT\" \n");
6  print ("\t This will execute DDL and DML statements using pass-through SQL \n\n");
7
8  ## dbh = Database Handle
9  my $dbh = DBI->connect('dbi:odbc:ORA_scott', 'scott', 'tiger', 'ODBC')
10 || die "***\tError on DBI->connect.   Make sure the server is running!!";
11
12 ######## Subroutine PrintPersonsTable();
13 sub PrintPersonsTable{
14     $sql = "SELECT personid , pname , city FROM persons ";
                                       # No ; SQL terminator in Oracle
15
16     my $sth = $dbh->prepare($sql);
17     $sth->execute()  || warn "*** SELECT ERROR *** \n\t $!";
18
19     print ("   personid\t   pname     \t   city\n");
20     print ("   --------\t -------------\t ---------\n");
21
22     my $dat;  # Create a local variable to hold returned row data
23     while ( $dat = $sth->fetchrow_hashref )  # Fetch each row
24     {                                        # Print each column value
25         print ("\t$dat->{PERSONID}\t  ");
26         print ("$dat->{PNAME}\t  ");         # Remember: UPPERCASE column
                                                # names in Oracle
27         print ("$dat->{CITY}\n");
28     }
29     print ("\n");
30 } #### end Subroutine PrintPersonsTable
31
32 ###################################  DROP TABLE persons
33 $sql = "DROP TABLE persons";
34 my $sth = $dbh->prepare($sql);  # sth = Statement Handle
35 $sth->execute()  || warn "*** DROP TABLE ERROR *** \n\t $!";
36
37 ###################################  CREATE TABLE persons
38 $sql = "CREATE TABLE persons (
39     personid   INTEGER PRIMARY KEY ,
40     pname      VARCHAR(15)  NOT NULL,
41     city       VARCHAR(15)
42     )" ;
```

EXAMPLE 15.8 (CONTINUED)

```
43 my $sth = $dbh->prepare($sql);
44 $sth->execute()  ||  warn "*** CREATE TABLE ERROR *** \n\t $!";
45 #################################### INSERT 2 rows
46 $sql = "INSERT INTO persons VALUES ( 1 , 'Carol Smith' , 'Boston') ";
47 my $sth = $dbh->prepare($sql);
48 $sth->execute()  ||  warn "*** INSERT ERROR *** \n\t $!";
49
50 $sql = "INSERT INTO persons VALUES ( 2 , 'Sam Jones' , 'Detroit' )";
51 my $sth = $dbh->prepare($sql);
52 $sth->execute()  ||  warn "*** INSERT ERROR *** \n\t $!";
53
54 PrintPersonsTable();
55
56 #################################### UPDATE   1 row
57 $sql = "UPDATE persons SET city = 'Seattle' WHERE personid = 2 ";
58 my $sth = $dbh->prepare($sql);  # sth = Statement Handle
59 $sth->execute()  ||  warn "*** UPDATE ERROR *** \n\t $!";
60
61 PrintPersonsTable();
62
63 #################################### DELETE   1 row
64 $sql = "DELETE FROM persons WHERE personid = 1 ";
65 my $sth = $dbh->prepare($sql);  # sth = Statement Handle
66 $sth->execute()  ||  warn "*** DELETE ERROR *** \n\t $!";
67
68 PrintPersonsTable();
69 $sth->finish;
70 $dbh->disconnect
71 # Last line of file
```

A sample run from the command line is shown here:

```
C:\> ex8.pl
        DBI with DSN "ORA_scott" on Oracle server named "CAT"
        This will execute DDL and DML statements using pass-through SQL
```

personid	pname	city
1	Carol Smith	Boston
2	Sam Jones	Detroit

personid	pname	city
1	Carol Smith	Boston
2	Sam Jones	Seattle

personid	pname	city
2	Sam Jones	Seattle

15.6 Exercises: Non-Programming

These are non-programming exercises. (The programming exercises are Examples 15.1 through 15.8.)

These exercises are provided to allow you to become familiar with the interactive SQL tools provided with Microsoft SQL Server (Query Analyzer) and Oracle (SQL*Plus).

These tools can be very valuable to assist in doing database programming as they allow you to issue SQL statements directly to the database to ensure they are correct.

These exercises assume you have installed the appropriate RDBMS software, Microsoft SQL Server (version 6.5 or later) or Oracle (version 8.0 or later).

You can download free evaluation copy of some RDBMS software:

- MSS RDBMS:
  www.microsoft.com/sql/productinfo/evalcd.htm

- Oracle RDBMS:
  www.oracle.com/download

- Oracle Documentation:
  technet.oracle.com/docs/products/oracle8i/doc_index.htm

EXERCISE 15
Introduction to Using MSS

This discussion assumes you have already installed Microsoft SQL Server (MSS) software version 6.5 or later.

1. Open an MSS Query Analyzer as follows:

   Start–>Programs–>Microsoft SQL Server 7.0–>Query Analyzer

2. To login, select "Use SQL Server authentication" and use the following default login information unless you changed it after installation.
   login: **sa**
   password: <leave blank>

3. Maximize the Query Analyzer window or make it large enough to see the "DB" window (upper right corner) and select "pubs" database from the menu. Or, in the upper text edit area type *use pubs* and then execute this command by any one of the following:
   Ctrl-Enter
   F5 key
   Query–>Execute
   right-click on the green arrow

The *use pubs* command is the same as selecting it in the DB window. You must remember each time you start the Query Analyzer to select the correct database.

The *pubs* database is a sample database provided with MSS. There is a table in the *pubs* database called *jobs* whose column structure you can see by executing *sp_help jobs*.

Notice that you may put commands in the top section of the query analyzer and see the output in the bottom section. Run the query to see the data in the *jobs* table by executing the query.

SQL: SELECT job_id , job_desc , min_lvl , max_lvl FROM jobs;

Result:

job_id	job_desc	min_lvl	max_lvl
1	New Hire - Job not specified	10	10
2	Chief Executive Officer	200	250
3	Business Operations Manager	175	225
4	Chief Financial Officer	175	250
5	Publisher	150	250
6	Managing Editor	140	225
7	Marketing Manager	120	200
8	Public Relations Manager	100	175
9	Acquisitions Manager	75	175
10	Productions Manager	75	165
11	Operations Manager	75	150
12	Editor	25	100
13	Sales Representative	25	100
14	Designer	25	100

(14 row(s) affected)

The results should be the same as when executing Perl programs *ex1.pl* and *ex2.pl*.

EXERCISE 16
Executing *persons.sql* in MSS

1. Open an MSS Query Analyzer as described above.

   Start–>Programs–>Microsoft SQL Server 7.0–>Query Analyzer

2. Type in the SQL statements given for *persons.sql* in the upper window of the Query Analyzer.

3. Save the contents to a file you'll name *persons.sql* in some convenient directory of your choice.

persons.sql:

```
/*
    persons.sql
*/


                        —Out with the old to start fresh
DROP TABLE persons;

CREATE TABLE persons (   —In with a new empty table
    personid        INTEGER     PRIMARY KEY,
    pname           VARCHAR(15)  NOT NULL,
    city            VARCHAR(15)
);

INSERT INTO persons VALUES ( 1 , 'Carol Smith' , 'Boston');
INSERT INTO persons VALUES ( 2 , 'Sam Jones' , 'Detroit' );

SELECT personid , pname , city FROM persons;

UPDATE persons SET city = 'Seattle' WHERE personid = 2;
SELECT personid , pname , city FROM persons;

DELETE FROM persons WHERE personid = 1;
SELECT personid , pname , city FROM persons;
```

4. Execute these statements by clicking on the green arrow. The lower window will show the following:

(1 row(s) affected)

(1 row(s) affected)

personid	pname	city
1	Carol Smith	Boston
2	Sam Jones	Detroit

(2 row(s) affected)

(1 row(s) affected)

personid	pname	city
1	Carol Smith	Boston
2	Sam Jones	Seattle

(2 row(s) affected)

(1 row(s) affected)

personid	pname	city
2	Sam Jones	Seattle

(1 row(s) affected)

EXERCISE 17
Introduction to Using Oracle

This discussion assumes you have already installed Oracle software version 8.0 or later.

1. In **Microsoft Windows,** open either an Oracle SQL *Plus window or Oracle Worksheet as follows.

   a. **Oracle SQL *Plus:**
      Start–>Programs–>Oracle For Windows 95 (or NT) –>SQL Plus 8.0

   b. Alternatively, from a Windows (DOS) or a UNIX command line execute:
      ```
      sqlplus  scott/tiger
      ```
      or
      ```
      sqlplus  scott/tiger@servername
      ```

   c. **Oracle SQL Worksheet:**
      (On Oracle 8.0, similar to MSS Query Analyzer)
      Start–>Programs–>Oracle Enterprise Manager–>SQL Worksheet

      If using Oracle SQL Worksheet tool, familiarize yourself with it. The top window is the output window and is read only. The bottom window is where you enter your SQL statements and execute using any one of: Worksheet–>Execute, press function key F5, Ctrl-Enter or click on the middle button to the left of the bottom window (lightning bolt button). Look to see what's under each of the menus at the top. Then hold your mouse pointer over each of the buttons to see what the tool tips say the button is for.

      Log in to your SQL*Plus or SQL Worksheet using the following information:
      Username: scott
      Password: tiger

2. **Execute the Query in your SQL*Plus or SQL Worksheet window:**

   a. In **SQL*PLUS** type the command below at the SQL> prompt and press Enter (if you forget the semicolon, type the semicolon on the second line and press Enter again).

   b. In **SQL Worksheet**, type the command in the lower window and then execute by Ctrl-Enter or F5 or the lightning bolt icon on left or Worksheet –> Execute.

Query:

SQL: SELECT ename, empno, job, deptno FROM emp;

Result:

ENAME	EMPNO	JOB	DEPTNO
SMITH	7369	CLERK	20
ALLEN	7499	SALESMAN	30
WARD	7521	SALESMAN	30
JONES	7566	MANAGER	20
MARTIN	7654	SALESMAN	30
BLAKE	7698	MANAGER	30
CLARK	7782	MANAGER	10
SCOTT	7788	ANALYST	20
KING	7839	PRESIDENT	10
TURNER	7844	SALESMAN	30
ADAMS	7876	CLERK	20
FORD	7902	ANALYST	20
MILLER	7934	CLERK	10
JAMES	7900	CLERK	30

15 rows selected.

The results should be the same as when executing Perl programs *ex5.pl* and *ex6.pl*.

EXERCISE 18
Executing *persons.sql* in Oracle

1. Open an Oracle SQL*Plus window as described previously.
   Start–>Programs–>Oracle For Windows 95 (or NT) –>SQL Plus 8.0

2. Type in the SQL statements given for *persons.sql* in Notepad or another editing
   tool. Save the contents to a file named *persons.sql* in some convenient directory of
   your choice.

persons.sql:

```
/*
     persons.sql
*/


                         —Out with the old to start fresh
DROP TABLE persons;
CREATE TABLE persons (   —In with a new empty table
    personid         INTEGER     PRIMARY KEY,
    pname            VARCHAR(15)   NOT NULL,
    city             VARCHAR(15)
);

INSERT INTO persons VALUES ( 1 , 'Carol Smith' , 'Boston');
INSERT INTO persons VALUES ( 2 , 'Sam Jones' , 'Detroit' );

SELECT personid , pname , city FROM persons;

UPDATE persons SET city = 'Seattle' WHERE personid = 2;
SELECT personid , pname , city FROM persons;

DELETE FROM persons WHERE personid = 1;
SELECT personid , pname , city FROM persons;
COMMIT;
```

3. Execute the statements in the file by entering @ *persons.sql* from the SQL> prompt. You will have to enter the path to *persons.sql* if SQL*Plus is not in the same directory, for example: SQL> @ *C:\Temp\persons.sql*

```
SQL> @persons.sql
DOC> persons.sql
DOC?*/
```

Table dropped.

Table created.

1 row created.

1 row created.

personid	pname	city
1	Carol Smith	Boston
2	Sam Jones	Detroit

1 row updated.

personid	pname	city
1	Carol Smith	Boston
2	Sam Jones	Seattle

1 row deleted.

personid	pname	city
2	Sam Jones	Seattle

Commit complete.

15.7 References

Programming the Perl DBI, Alligator Descartes and Tim Bunce, O'Reilly and Associates, ISBN: 1565926994, 2000.

ActivePerl with ASP and ADO, Tobias Martinsson, John Wiley & Sons; ISBN: 0471383147, 2000.

Learning Perl on Win32 Systems, Randal L. Schwartz et al, O'Reilly and Associates, ISBN: 1565923243, 1997.

Perl by Example, Ellie Quigley, Prentice Hall Computer Books, ISBN 0136556892, 1998.

16

INTERFACING WITH
THE SYSTEM

16.1 System Calls

Those migrating from shell (or batch) programming to Perl often expect that a Perl script is like a shell script—just a sequence of UNIX (or MS-DOS/NT) commands. However, system utilities are not accessed directly in Perl programs as they are in shell scripts. Of course, to be effective there must be some way in which your Perl program can interface with the operating system. Perl has a set of functions, in fact, that specifically interface with the operating system and are directly related to the UNIX system calls so often found in *C* programs. Many of these UNIX system calls are supported by Windows. The ones that are generally not supported are found at the end of this chapter.

A **system call** requests some service from the operating system (kernel) such as getting the time of day, creating a new directory, removing a file, creating a new process, terminating a process, and so on. A major group of system calls deals with the creation and termination of processes, how memory is allocated and released, and sending information (e.g., signals) to processes. Another function of system calls is related to the file system: file creation, reading and writing files, creating and removing directories, creating links, etc.[1]

The UNIX system calls are documented in Section 2 of the UNIX manual pages. Perl's system functions are almost identical in syntax and implementation. If a system call fails, it returns a −1 and sets the system's global variable, *errno,* to a value that contains the reason the error occurred. *C* programs use the *perror* function to obtain system errors stored in *errno*; Perl programs use the special $*!* variable. (See "Error Handling" on page 571.)

The following Perl functions allow you to perform a variety of calls to the system when you need to manipulate or obtain information about files or processes. If the system call you need is not provided by Perl, you can use Perl's *syscall* function, which takes a UNIX system call as an argument. (See"The syscall Function and the h2ph Script" on page 563.)

---

1. System calls are direct entries into the kernel, whereas library calls are functions that invoke system calls. Perl's system interface functions are named after their counterpart UNIX system calls in Section 2 of the UNIX manual pages.

In addition to the built-in functions, the standard Perl library comes bundled with a variety of over 200 modules that can be used to perform portable operations on files, directories, processes, networks etc. If you installed ActiveState, you will also find a collection of Win32 modules in the standard Perl library under C:*perl\site\lib\Win32*.

To read the documentation for any of the modules (filenames with a *.pm* extension) from the standard Perl library, use the Perl built-in *perldoc* function or the UNIX *man* command. ActiveState (Win32) provides online documentation found by pressing the Start button, Programs, and then ActiveState.

EXAMPLE 16.1

```
(At the command line)
1   $ perldoc Copy.pm
```

EXPLANATION

The *perldoc* function takes a module name as its argument (with or without the *.pm* extension). The documentation for the module will then be displayed in a window (Notepad on Win32 platforms). This example displays part of the documentation for the *Copy.pm* module found in the standard Perl library.

```
perldoc1.1000 - Notepad
File  Edit  Format  Help

NAME
     File::Copy - Copy files or filehandles

SYNOPSIS
          use File::Copy;

          copy("file1","file2");
          copy("Copy.pm",\*STDOUT);'
          move("/dev1/fileA","/dev2/fileB");

          use POSIX;
          use File::Copy cp;

          $n=FileHandle->new("/dev/null","r");
          cp($n,"x");'
```

Figure 16.1   *perldoc* and the *Copy.pm* module.

16.1.1   Directories and Files

When walking through a file system, directories are separated by slashes. UNIX file systems indicate the root directory with a forward slash (/), followed by subdirectories separated by forward slashes where, if a filename is specified, it is the final component of the path. The names of the files and directories are case sensitive and their names consist of alphanumeric characters and punctuation, excluding whitespace. A period in a filename has no special meaning, but can be used to separate the base filename from its extension, such as in *program.c* or *file.bak*. The length of the filename varies from different operating systems, with a minimum of 1 character, and on most UNIX type file systems up to 255 characters are allowed. Only the root directory can be named / (slash).[2]

Win32 file systems, mainly FAT, FAT32, and NTFS, use a different convention for specifying a directory path. Basic FAT directories and files are separated by a backslash (\). Their names are case insensitive and start with a limit of 8 characters, followed by a period, and a suffix of no more than 3 characters. (Windows 2000/NT allow longer filenames.) The root of the file system is a drive number, such as *C:* or *D:*, rather than only a slash. In networked environments, the universal naming convention (UNC) uses a different convention for separating the components of a path; the drive letter is replaced with two backslashes, as in *myserver\dir\dir.*

Backslash Issues.   The backslash in Perl scripts is used as an escape or quoting character (*\n, \t,\U, \$500,* etc.), so when specifying a Win32 path separator, two backslashes are often needed, unless a particular module allows a single backslash or the pathname is surrounded by single quote. For example, *C:\Perl\lib\File* should be written *C:\\Perl\\lib\\File.*

The *File::Spec* Module.   The *File::Spec* Module found in the standard Perl library was designed to portably support operations commonly performed on filenames, such as creating a single path out of a list of path components and applying the correct path delimiter for the appropriate operating system or splitting up the path into volume, directory, and filename, etc. A list of *File::Spec* function is provided in Table 16.1.

Since these functions are different for most operating systems, each set of OS-specific routines is available in a separate module, including:

> *File::Spec::UNIX*
> *File::Spec::Mac*
> *File::Spec::OS2*
> *File::Spec::Win32*
> *File::Spec::VMS*

---

2. The Mac OS file system (HFS) is also hierarchical and uses colons to separate path components.

Table 16.1   *File::Spec* Functions

Function	What It Does
abs2rel	Takes a destination path and an optional base path and returns a relative path from the base path to the destination path.
canonpath	No physical check on the file system, but a logical cleanup of a path. On UNIX, eliminates successive slashes and successive "/.".
case_tolerant	Returns a true or false value indicating, respectively, that alphabetic case is or is not significant when comparing file specifications.
catdir	Concatenates two or more directory names to form a complete path ending with a directory, and removes the trailing slash from the resulting string.
catfile	Concatenates one or more directory names and a filename to form a complete path ending with a filename.
catpath	Takes volume, directory, and file portions and returns an entire path. In UNIX, *$volume* is ignored, and directory and file are catenated. A "/" is inserted if necessary.
curdir	Returns a string representation of the current directory. "." on UNIX.
devnull	Returns a string representation of the null device. "*/dev/null*" on UNIX.
file_name_is_absolute	Takes as argument a path and returns true, if it is an absolute path.
join	*join* is the same as *catfile*.
no_upwards	Given a list of file names, strip out those that refer to a parent directory.
path	Takes no argument, returns the environment variable *PATH* as an array.
rel2abs	Converts a relative path to an absolute path.
rootdir	Returns a string representation of the root directory. "/" on UNIX.
splitpath	Splits a path into volume, directory, and filename portions. On systems with no concept of volume, returns *undef* for volume.
tmpdir	Returns a string representation of the first writable directory from the following list or "" if none are writable.
updir	Returns a string representation of the parent directory. ".." on UNIX.

EXAMPLE 16.2

```
1   use File::Spec;
2   $pathname=File::Spec->catfile("C:","Perl","lib","CGI");
3   print "$pathname\n";

(Output)
3   C:\Perl\lib\CGI
```

EXPLANATION

1   If the operating system is not specified, the *File::Spec* module is loaded for the current operating system, in this case *Windows 2000*. It is an object-oriented module, but has a function-oriented syntax as well.

2   A scalar, *$pathname*, will contain a path consisting of the arguments passed to the *catfile* method. The *catfile* function will concatenate the list of path elements.

3   The new path is printed with backslashes separating the path components. On UNIX systems, the path would be printed */Perl/lib/CGI*.

16.1.2   Directory and File Attributes

UNIX.   The most common type of file is a regular file. It contains data, an ordered sequence of bytes. The data can be text data or binary data. Information about the file is stored in a system data structure called an **inode**. The information in the inode consists of such attributes as the link count, the owner, the group, mode, size, last access time, last modification time, and type. The UNIX *ls* command lets you see the inode information for the files in your directory. This information is retrieved by the *stat* system call. Perl's *stat* function also gives you information about the file. It retrieves the device number, inode number, mode, link count, user ID, group ID, size in bytes, time of last access, and so on. (See "The stat and lstat Functions" on page 526.)

A directory is a specific file maintained by the UNIX kernel. It is composed of a list of filenames. Each filename has a corresponding number that points to the information about the file. The number, called an **inode number**, is a pointer to an inode. The inode contains information about the file as well as a pointer to the location of the file's data blocks on disk. The following functions allow you to manipulate directories, change permissions on files, create links, etc.

Directory Entry	
Inode #	Filename

Windows.   Files and directories contain data as well as meta information that describes attributes of a file or directory. The four basic attributes of Win32 files and directories are *ARCHIVE*, *HIDDEN*, *READONLY*, and *SYSTEM*. See Table 16.2.

Table 16.2   Basic File and Directory Attributes

Attribute	Description
ARCHIVE	Set when file content changes
HIDDEN	A file not shown in a directory listing
READONLY	A file that cannot be changed
SYSTEM	Special system files, such as *IO.SYS* and *MS-DOS.SYS*, normally invisible

To retrieve and set file attributes, use the standard Perl extension *Win32::File*. All of the functions return *FALSE (0)* if they fail, unless otherwise noted. The function names are exported into the caller's namespace by request. See Table 16.3.

Table 16.3   *Win32::File* Functions

Function	What It Does
GetAttributes(Filename, ReturnedAttributes)	Gets attributes of a file or directory. *ReturnedAttributes* will be set to the *or*ed combination of the filename attributes.
SetAttributes(Filename, NewAttributes)	Sets the attributes of a file or directory. *newAttributes* must be an *or*ed combination of the attributes.

To retrieve file attributes use *Win32::File::GetAttributes($Path, $Attributes)* and to set file attributes, use *Win32::File::SetAttributes($Path,$Attributes)*. See Table 16.4. The *Win32::File* also provides a number of constants; see Example 16.3.

Table 16.4   *Win32::File* Attributes

Attribute	Description
ARCHIVE	Set when file content changes. Used by backup programs.
COMPRESSED	Windows compressed file, not a zip file. Cannot be set by the user.
DIRECTORY	File is a directory. Cannot be set by the user.
HIDDEN	A file not shown in a directory listing.
NORMAL	A normal file. *ARCHIVE, HIDDEN, READONLY,* and *SYSTEM* are not set.
OFFLINE	Data is not available.
READONLY	A file that cannot be changed.
SYSTEM	Special system files, such as *IO.SYS* and *MS-DOS.SYS*, normally invisible.
TEMPORARY	File created by some program.

EXAMPLE 16.3

```
1   use Win32::File;
2   $File='C:\Drivers';
3   Win32::File::GetAttributes($File, $attr) or die;
4   print "The attribute value returned is: $attr.\n";
5   if ( $attr ){
6       if ($attr & READONLY){
            print "File is readonly.\n";
        }
        if ($attr & ARCHIVE){
            print "File is archive.\n";
        }
        if ($attr & HIDDEN){
            print "File is hidden.\n";
        }
        if ($attr & SYSTEM){
            print "File is a system file.\n";
        }
        if ($attr & COMPRESSED){
            print "File is compressed.\n";
        }
        if ($attr & DIRECTORY){
            print "File is a directory.\n";
        }
        if ($attrib & NORMAL){
            print "File is normal.\n";
        }
        if ($attrib & OFFLINE){
            print "File is normal.\n";
        }
        if ($attrib & TEMPORARY){
            print "File is temporary.\n";
        }
    }
    else{
7       print Win32::FormatMessage(Win32::GetLastError),"\n";
    }
```

```
(Output)
4   The attribute value returned is 18.
    File is hidden.
    File is a directory.
```

EXPLANATION

1   The *Win32::File* module is loaded.

2   The folder *Drivers* on the *C:* drive is assigned to *$File*.

3   The *GetAttributes* function is called with two arguments: the first is the name of the file, and the second is the bitwise *or*ed value of the attribute constants, *READONLY*, *HIDDEN*, etc. This value is filled in by the function *GetAttributes*. Note the *GetAttributes* function is called with a fully qualified package name. That is because it is listed in *@EXPORT_OK* in the *Win32::File* module and must be either specifically requested by the user or given a fully qualified name. If specifically requested, all of the constants would have to be listed as well or they will not be switched to the user's namespace.

4   The value of the *or*ed attributes is printed. If the value is *0*, something is wrong and an error will be formatted and printed from line 7.

5   If one of the attributes for a file or directory is present, the following tests will show which ones were returned describing the file or directory.

6   By bitwise logically *and*ing the value of *$attr* with the value of a constant (in this case, *READONLY*), if the resulting value is true (non-zero), the file is read-only.

7   This function will produce a human-readable error message coming from the last error reported by Windows.

16.1.3   Finding Directories and Files

The *File::Find* module lets you traverse a file system tree for specified files or directories based on some criteria, like the UNIX *find* command or the Perl *find2perl* translator.

FORMAT

```
use File::Find;
find(\&wanted, '/dir1', '/dir2');
sub wanted { ... }
```

The first argument to *find()* is either a hash reference describing the operations to be performed for each file, or a reference to a subroutine. Type: *perldoc File::Find* for details. The *wanted()* function does whatever verification you want for the file. *$File::Find::dir* contains the current directory name, and *$_* is assigned the current filename within that directory. *$File::Find::name* contains the complete pathname to the file. You are *chdir()*ed to *$File::Find::dir* when the function is called, unless *no_chdir* was specified. The first argument to *find()* is either a hash reference describing the operations to be performed for each file or a code reference.

Table 16.5   Hash Reference Keys for *Find::File*

Key	Value
bydepth	Reports directory name after all entries have been reported.
follow	Follows symbolic links.
follow_fast	Similar to *follow* but may report files more than once.
follow_skip	Only processes files (but not directories and symbolic links) once.
no_chdir	Doesn't *chdir* to each directory as it recurses.
untaint	If -*T* (taint mode) is turned on, won't *cd* to directories that are tainted.
untaint_pattern	This should be set using the *qr* quoting operator. The default is set to *qr\^([-+@\w./]+)$|*.
untaint_skip	If set, directories (subtrees) that fail the *untaint_pattern* are skipped. The default is to *die* in such a case.
wanted	Used to call the *wanted* function.

EXAMPLE 16.4

```
(UNIX)
1   use File::Find;
2   find(\&wanted, '/httpd', '/ellie/testing' );

3   sub wanted{
        -d $_ && print "$File::Find::name\n";
    }

(Output)
/httpd
/httpd/php
/httpd/Icons
/httpd/Cgi-Win
/httpd/HtDocs
/httpd/HtDocs/docs
/httpd/HtDocs/docs/images
/httpd/Cgi-Bin
/httpd/Logs
/ellie/testing
/ellie/testing/Exten.dir
/ellie/testing/extension
/ellie/testing/mailstuff
/ellie/testing/mailstuff/mailstuff
/ellie/testing/OBJECTS
/ellie/testing/OBJECTS/polymorph
```

EXPLANATION

1   The *File::Find* module is loaded from the standard Perl library.
2   The first argument to *find()* is a reference to a subroutine called *wanted* followed by two directories to be found.
3   The *wanted* function will check that each name is a directory (*-d*) and list the full pathname of all subdirectories found. *$_* is assigned the name of the current directory in the search.

EXAMPLE 16.5

```
(Windows)
1   use File::Find;
2   use Win32::File;
    # Works on both FAT and NTFS file systems.
3   &File::Find::find(\&wanted,"C:\\httpd", "C:\\ellie\\testing");
4   sub wanted{
5       (Win32::File::GetAttributes($_,$attr)) &&
        ($attr & DIRECTORY) &&
        print "$File::Find::name\n";
    }
```

```
(Output)
C:\httpd
C:\httpd/php
C:\httpd/Icons
C:\httpd/Cgi-Win
C:\httpd/HtDocs
C:\httpd/HtDocs/docs
C:\httpd/HtDocs/docs/images
C:\httpd/Cgi-Bin
C:\httpd/Logs
C:\ellie\testing
C:\ellie\testing/Exten.dir
C:\ellie\testing/extension
C:\ellie\testing/mailstuff
C:\ellie\testing/mailstuff/mailstuff
C:\ellie\testing/OBJECTS
C:\ellie\testing/OBJECTS/polymorph
```

EXPLANATION

1   The *File::Find* module is loaded from the standard Perl library.
2   The *Win32::File* module is loaded from the standard Perl library, from the site-specific directory for Win32 systems. It will be used to retrieve file or directory attributes.
3   The first argument to *find*() is a reference to a subroutine called *wanted* followed by two directories to be found.
4   The *wanted* function is defined.
5   The *wanted* function will check that each name is a directory by calling the *Get-Attributes* function (*Win32::File::GetAttributes*), and will list the full pathname of all subdirectories found. *$_* is assigned the name of the current directory in the search.

16.1.4   Creating a Directory—The *mkdir* Function

UNIX.   The *mkdir* function creates a new, empty directory with the specified permissions (mode). The permissions are set as an octal number. The entries for the . and .. directories are automatically created. The *mkdir* function returns *1* if successful and *0* if not. If *mkdir* fails, the system error is stored in Perl's *$!* variable.

Windows.   If creating a directory at the MS-DOS prompt, the permission mask has no effect. Permissions on Win32 doesn't use the same mechanism as UNIX. For files on FAT partitions (which means all files on Windows 95), you don't have to set permissions explicitly on a file. All files are available to all users and the directory is created with all permissions turned on for everyone.

FORMAT

```
mkdir(FILENAME, MODE);     (UNIX)
mkdir(FILENAME);           (Windows)
```

EXAMPLE 16.6

```
(The Command Line)
1   $ perl -e 'mkdir("joker", 0755);'     # UNIX
2   $ ls -ld joker
    drwxr-xr-x  2 ellie        512 Mar  7 13:43 joker
3   $ perl -e "mkdir(joker);"             # Windows
```

EXPLANATION

1 The first argument to the *mkdir* function is the name of the directory. The second argument specifies the **mode** or permissions of the file. The permissions, *0755*, specify that the file will have read, write, and execute permission for the owner, read and execute for the group, and read and execute for the others. (Remember that without execute permission, you cannot access a directory.)

2 The *ls -ld* command prints a long listing of the directory file with information about the file, the inode information. The leading *d* is for directory, and the permissions are *rwxr-xr-x*.

3 On Win32 systems, the directory is created with all permissions turned on for everyone.

EXAMPLE 16.7

```
    # This script is called "makeit"
1   die "$0 <directory name>  " unless $#ARGV == 0;
2   mkdir ($ARGV[0], 0755 ) || die "mkdir:  $ARGV[0]:  $!\n";

(At The Command Line)
    $ makeit
1   makeit <directory name> at makeit line 3.
    $ makeit joker
2   makeit: joker: File exists
    $ makeit cabinet
    $ ls -d cabinet
    cabinet
```

EXPLANATION

1 If the user doesn't provide a directory name as an argument to the script, the *die* function prints an error message and the script exits.

2 Unless the directory already exists, it will be created.

16.1.5 Removing a Directory—The *rmdir* Function

The *rmdir* function removes a directory, but only if it is empty.

FORMAT

```
rmdir(DIRECTORY);
rmdir DIRECTORY;
```

EXAMPLE 16.8

```
(At the Command Line)
1   $ perl -e 'rmdir("joke") || die qq(joke: $!\n)'      # UNIX
    joke: Directory not empty
2   $ perl -e 'rmdir("joker") || die qq(joker: $!\n)'
    joker: No such file or directory
3   $ perl -e "rmdir(joker) || die qq(joker: $!\n);"      # Windows
    joker: No such file or directory
```

EXPLANATION

1   The directory *joke* contains files. It cannot be removed unless it is empty. The *$!* variable contains the system error, *Directory not empty*.
2   The directory *joker* does not exist; therefore, it cannot be removed. The system error is stored in *$!*.
3   On Win32 systems, *rmdir* works the same way. You just have watch the quotes if you are doing this at the MS-DOS prompt. The directory, *joker*, is not removed because it doesn't exist.

16.1.6 Changing Directories—The *chdir* Function

Each process has its own present working directory. When resolving relative path references, this is the starting place for the search path. If the calling process (e.g., your Perl script) changes the directory, it is changed only for that process, not the process that invoked it, normally the shell. When the Perl program exits, the shell returns with the same working directory it started with.

The *chdir* function changes the current working directory. Without an argument, the directory is changed to the user's home directory. The function returns *1* if successful and *0* if not. The system error code is stored in Perl's *$!* variable.[3]

FORMAT

```
chdir (EXPR);
chdir EXPR;
chdir;
```

---

3. *chdir* is a system call provided with Perl for changing directories. The *cd* command used at the command line is a shell built-in and cannot be used directly in a Perl script.

EXAMPLE 16.9

```
1   $ pwd          # UNIX
    /home/jody/ellie
2   $ perl -e 'chdir  "/home/jody/ellie/perl"; print `pwd`'
    /home/jody/ellie/perl
3   $ pwd
    /home/jody/ellie
4   $ perl -e 'chdir " fooler"  || die "Cannot cd to fooler: $!\n"'
    Cannot cd to fooler: No such file or directory
5   $ cd           # Windows
    C:\ellie\testing
6   $ perl -e "chdir fooler || die qq(Cannot to fooler: $!\n);"
    Cannot cd to fooler: No such file or directory
```

EXPLANATION

1   This is the present working directory for the shell.
2   The directory is changed to */home/jody/ellie/perl*. When the *pwd* command is enclosed in backquotes, command substitution is performed, and the present working directory for this process is printed.
3   Since the Perl program is a separate process invoked by the shell, when Perl changes the present working directory, the directory is changed only while the Perl process is in execution. When Perl exits, the shell returns and its directory is unchanged.
4   If the attempt to change the directory fails, the *die* function prints its message to the screen. The system error is stored in the *$!* variable and then printed.
5   The present working directory is printed at the MS-DOS prompt. *cd* prints the present working directory. (At the UNIX prompt, it is used to change directories.)
6   The attempt to change directory failed as in the UNIX example above. If the directory had existed, the present working directory would be changed.

16.1.7 Accessing a Directory via the Directory Filehandle

The following Perl directory functions are modeled after the UNIX system calls sharing the same name. Although the traditional UNIX directory contained a two-byte inode number and a 14-byte filename (Figure 16.2), not all UNIX systems have the same format. The directory functions allow you to access the directory regardless of its internal structure. The directory functions work the same way with Windows.

Inode	Filename
10	.
22	. .
32	memo
45	mbox
23	notes
12	src

Figure 16.2   A UNIX directory.

The *opendir* Function.   The *opendir* function opens a named directory and attaches it to the directory filehandle. This filehandle has its own namespace, separate from the other types of filehandles used for opening files and filters. The *opendir* function initializes the directory for processing by the related functions *readdir()*, *telldir()*, *seekdir()*, *rewinddir()*, and *closedir()*. The function returns *1* if successful.

FORMAT

```
opendir(DIRHANDLE, EXPR)
```

EXAMPLE 16.10

```
1    opendir(MYDIR, "joker");
```

EXPLANATION

1   The file *joker* is attached to the directory filehandle, *MYDIR*, and is opened for reading. The directory, *joker*, must exist and must be a directory.

The *readdir* Function.   A directory can be read by anyone who has read permission on the directory. You can't write to the directory itself even if you have write permission. The write permission on a directory means that you can create and remove files from within the directory, not alter the directory data structure itself.

When we speak about reading a directory with the *readdir* function, we are talking about looking at the contents of the directory structure maintained by the system. If the *opendir* function opened the directory, in a scalar context, *readdir* returns the next directory entry. The *readdir* function returns the **next** directory entry. In an array context, it returns the rest of the entries in the directory.

FORMAT

```
readdir(DIRHANDLE);
readdir DIRHANDLE;
```

The *closedir* Function.   The *closedir* function closes the directory that was opened by the *opendir* function.

FORMAT

```
closedir (DIRHANDLE);
closedir DIRHANDLE;
```

EXAMPLE 16.11

```
(The Script)
1   opendir(DIR, "..") || die "Can't open: $!\n";
                        # Open parent directory
2   @parentfiles=readdir(DIR);
                        # Gets a list of the directory contents
3   closedir(DIR);      # Closes the  filehandle
4   foreach $file ( @parentfiles )
                        # Prints each element of the array
        { print "$file\n";}

(Output)
.
..
filea
fileb
filec
.sh_history
stories
```

EXPLANATION

1   The *opendir* function opens the directory structure and assigns it to *DIR*, the directory filehandle. The .. (parent) directory is opened for reading.
2   The *readdir* function assigns all the rest of the entries in the directory to the array *@parentfiles*.
3   The *closedir* function closes the directory.
4   The files are printed in the order they are stored in the directory structure. This may not be the order that the *ls* command prints out the files.

The *telldir* Function. The *telldir* function returns the current position of the *readdir()* routines on the directory filehandle. The value returned by *telldir* may be given to *seekdir()* to access a particular location in a directory.

FORMAT

```
telldir(DIRHANDLE);
```

The *rewinddir* Function. The *rewinddir* function sets the position of *DIRHANDLE* back to the beginning of the directory opened by *opendir*. It is not supported on all machines.

FORMAT

```
rewinddir(DIRHANDLE);
rewinddir DIRHANDLE;
```

The *seekdir* Function. The *seekdir* sets the current position for *readdir()* on the directory filehandle. The position is set by the a value returned by *telldir()*.

FORMAT

```
seekdir(DIRHANDLE, POS);
```

EXAMPLE 16.12

```
(The Script)
1   opendir(DIR, ".");   # Opens the current directory
2   while( $myfile=readdir(DIR) ){
3       $spot=telldir(DIR);
4       if ( "$myfile" eq ".login" ) {
            print "$myfile\n";
            last;
        }
    }
5   rewinddir(DIR);
6   seekdir(DIR, $spot);
7   $myfile=readdir(DIR);
    print "$myfile\n";

(Output)
.login
.cshrc
```

EXPLANATION

1   The *opendir* function opens the present working directory for reading.
2   The *while* statement is executed, and the *readdir* function returns the next directory entry from the directory filehandle and assigns the file to the scalar, *$myfile*.
3   After the *readdir* function reads a filename, the *telldir* function marks the location of that read and stores the location in the scalar, *$spot*.
4   When the *.login* file is read, the loop is exited.
5   The *rewinddir* function resets the position of the *DIR* filehandle to the beginning of the directory structure.
6   The *seekdir* function uses the results of the *telldir* function to set the current position for the *readdir* function on the *DIR* filehandle.
7   The **next** directory entry is read by the *readdir* function and assigned to the scalar, *$myfile*.

16.1.8   Permissions and Ownership

UNIX.   There is one owner for every UNIX file. The one benefit the owner has over everyone else is the ability to change the permissions on the file, thus controlling who can do what to the file. A group may have a number of members, and the owner of the file may change the group permissions on a file so that the group will enjoy special privileges.

Every UNIX file has a set of permissions associated with it to control who can read, write, or execute the file. There are a total of 9 bits that constitute the permissions on a file. The first 3 bits control the permissions of the owner of the file, the second set controls the permissions of the group, and the last set controls the rest of the world, that is, everyone else. The permissions are stored in the mode field of the file's inode.

Windows.   Win32 systems do not handle file permissions the way UNIX does. Files are created with read and write turned on for everyone. Files and folders inherit attributes that you can set. By clicking the mouse on a file icon and selecting Properties you can, in a limited way, select permission attributes such as *Archive*, *Read-only*, and *Hidden*. See Figure 16.3.

If your platform is Windows NT, you can set file and folder permissions only on drives formatted to use NTFS[4]. To change permissions, you must be the owner or have been granted permission to do so by the owner. If you are using NTFS, go to Windows Explorer and then locate the file or folder for which you want to set permissions. Right-click the file or folder, click Properties, and then click the Security tab. You will be able to allow, deny, or remove permissions from the group or user.

See the *Win32::FileSecurity* module in the Perl Resource Kit for Win32 if you need to maintain file permissions. To retrieve file permissions from a file or directory, use the

---

4.   NTFS is an advanced file system designed for Windows NT.

Win32::FileSecurity::Get($Path, \%Perms)* extension, where *$Path is the relative or absolute path to the file or directory for which you are seeking permissions, and *\%Perms* is a reference to a hash containing keys representing the user or group and corresponding values representing the permission mask.

Table 16.6   Win32 Extensions to Manage Files and Directories

Extension	*What It Does*
Win32::File	Standard module for retrieving and setting file attributes
Win32::File::GetAtributes(path,attribute)	Retrieves file attributes
Win32::File::SetAttributes(path,attribute)	Sets file attributes
Win32::AdminMisc::GetFileInfo	Retrieves file information fields: CompanyName, FileVersion, InternalName, LegalCopyright, OriginalFileName, ProductName, ProductVersion, LangID, and Language

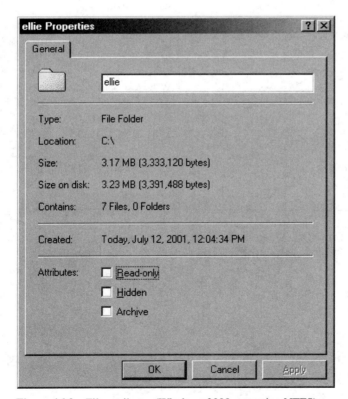

Figure 16.3   File attributes (Windows 2000, not using NTFS).

The *chmod* Function (UNIX).   The *chmod* function changes permissions on a list of files. The user must own the files to change permissions on them.[5] The files must be quoted strings. The first element of the list is the numeric octal value for the new mode. (Today, the binary/octal notation has been replaced by a more convenient mnemonic method for changing permissions. Perl does not use the new method.)

Table 16.7 illustrates the eight possible combinations of numbers used for changing permissions if you are not familiar with this method.

The *chmod* Function (Windows).   ActivePerl supports a limited version of the *chmod* function. However, it can only be used for giving the owner read/write access. (The *group* and *other* bits are ignored.)

The *chmod* function returns the number of files that were changed.

Table 16.7   Permission Modes

Octal	*Binary*	*Permissions*	*Meaning*
0	000	none	All turned off
1	001	--x	Execute
2	010	-w-	Write
3	011	-wx	Write, execute
4	100	r--	Read
5	101	r-x	Read, execute
6	110	rw-	Read, write
7	111	rwx	Read, write, execute

Make sure the first digit is a *0* to indicate an octal number. Do not use the mnemonic mode (e.g., +rx), because all the permissions will be turned off.

---

5. The caller's effective ID must match the owner's user ID of the file, or the owner must be superuser.

FORMAT

```
chmod(LIST);
chmod LIST;
```

EXAMPLE 16.13

```
   (UNIX)
1  $ perl -e '$count=chmod 0755, "foo.p", "boo.p" ;print "$count
        files changed.\n"'
2  2 files changed.
3  $ ls -l foo.p boo.p
   -rwxr-xr-x  1 ellie    0 Mar  7 12:52 boo.p*
   -rwxr-xr-x  1 ellie    0 Mar  7 12:52 foo.p*
```

EXPLANATION

1   The first argument is the octal value *0755*. It turns on *rwx* for the user, *r* and *x* for the group and others. The next two arguments, *foo.p* and *boo.p*, are the files affected by the change. The scalar, *$count*, contains the number of files that were changed.

2   The value of *$count* is *2* because both files were changed to *0755*.

3   The output of the UNIX *ls -l* command is printed, demonstrating that the permissions on files *foo.p* and *boo.p* have been changed to *0755*.

The *chown* Function (UNIX).   The *chown* function changes the owner and group of a list of files. Only the owner or superuser can invoke it.[6] The first two elements of the list must be a numerical *uid* and *gid*. Each authorized UNIX user is assigned a *uid* (user identification number) and a *gid* (group identification number) in the password file.[7] The function returns the number of files successfully changed.

FORMAT

```
chown(LIST);
chown LIST;
```

---

6. On BSD UNIX and some POSIX-based UNIX (Solaris), only the superuser can change ownership.

7. To get the *uid* or *gid* for a user, the *getpwnam* or *getpwuid* functions can be used.

EXAMPLE 16.14

```
(The Script)
1   $ uid=9496;
2   $ gid=40;
3   $number=chown($uid, $gid, 'foo.p', 'boo.p');
4   print "The number of files changed is $number\.n";

(Output)
4   The number of files changed is 2.
```

EXPLANATION

1   The user identification number *9496* is assigned.
2   The group identification number *40* is assigned.
3   The *chown* function changes the ownership on files *foo.p* and *boo.p* and returns the number of files changed.

The *umask* Function (UNIX).   When a file is created it has a certain set of permissions by default. The permissions are determined by what is called the **system mask**. On most systems this mask is *022,* and is set by the login program.[8] A directory has *777* by default (rwxrwxrwx) and a file has *666* by default (rw-rw-rw). The *umask* function is used to remove or subtract permissions from the existing mask.

To take *write* permission away from the "others" permission set, the *umask* value is subtracted from the maximum permissions allowed per directory or file:

777 (directory)	666 (file)
– 002 (umask value)	– 002 (umask value)
775	664

The *umask* function sets the umask for this process and returns the old one. Without an argument, the *umask* function returns the current setting.

FORMAT

```
umask(EXPR)
umask EXPR
umask
```

8. The user can also set the umask in the *.profile* (sh or ksh) or *.cshrc* (csh) initialization files.

EXAMPLE 16.15

```
1   $ perl -e 'printf("The umask is %o.\n", umask);'
    The umask is 22.
2   $ perl -e 'umask 027; printf("The new mask is %o.\n", umask);'
    The new mask is 27.
```

EXPLANATION

1 The *umask* function without an argument prints the current *umask* value.
2 The *umask* function resets the mask to octal *027*.

16.1.9 Hard and Soft Links

UNIX.   When you create a file it has one **hard** link, that is one entry in the directory. You can create additional links to the file, which are really just different names for the same file. The kernel keeps track of how many links a file has in the file's inode. As long as there is a link to the file, its data blocks will not be released to the system. The advantage to having a file with multiple names is that there is only one set of data or master file and that file can be accessed by a number of different names. A hard link cannot span file systems and must exist at link creation time.

   A soft link is also called a **symbolic** link and sometimes a **symlink**. A symbolic link is really just a very small file (it has permissions, ownership, size, etc.). All it contains is the **name** of another file. When accessing a file that has a symbolic link, the kernel is pointed to the name of the file contained in the symbolic link. For example, a link from *thisfile* to */usr/bin/joking/otherfile* links the name *thisfile* to */usr/bin/joking/otherfile*. When *thisfile* is opened, *otherfile* is the file really accessed. Symbolic links can refer to files that do or don't exist and they can span file systems and even different computers. They can also point to other symbolic links.[9]

Windows.   The Win32 system introduced **shortcuts**, special binary files with a *.LNK* extension. A shortcut is similar to a UNIX link, but it is processed by a particular application rather than by the system and is an alias for a file or directory. Shortcuts are icons with a little arrow in a white box in the left corner. See the *Win32::Shortcut* module to create, load, retrieve, save, and modify shortcut properties from a Perl script. (See Figure 16.4.)

---

9. Symbolic links originated in BSD and are supported under many ATT systems. They may not be supported on your system.

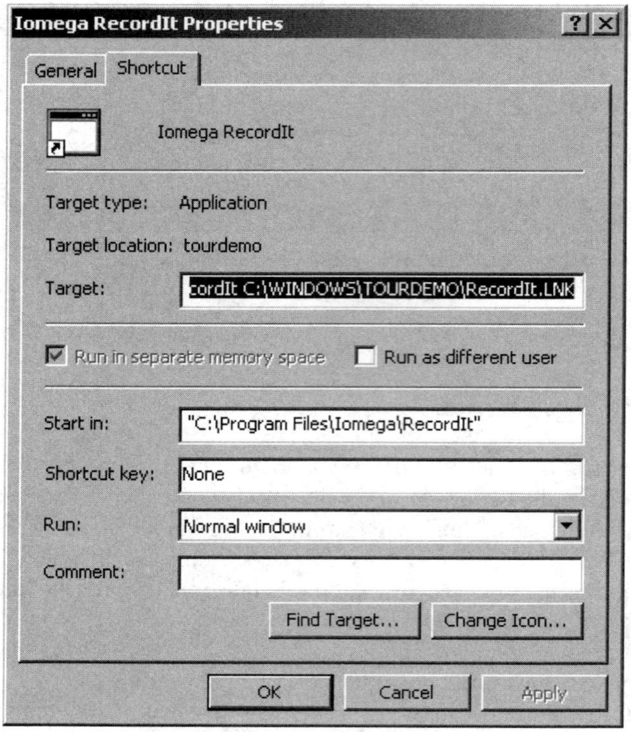

Figure 16.4   Shortcuts and the *.LNK* extension.

The *link* and *unlink* Functions (UNIX).   The *link* function creates a hard link (i.e., two files that have the same name) on UNIX systems. The first argument to the *link* function is the name of an existing file; the second argument is the name of the new file, which cannot already exist. Only the superuser can create a link that points to a directory. Use *rmdir* when removing a directory.

FORMAT

```
link(OLDFILENAME, NEWFILENAME);
```

EXAMPLE 16.16

```
  (UNIX)
1 $ perl -e 'link("dodo", "newdodo");'
2 $ ls -li dodo newdodo
  142726 -rw-r--r--  2 ellie         0 Mar  7 13:46 dodo
  142726 -rw-r--r--  2 ellie         0 Mar  7 13:46 newdodo
```

EXPLANATION

1   The old file *dodo* is given an alternate name, *newdodo*.
2   The *i* option to the *ls* command gives the inode number of the file. If the inode numbers are the same, the files are the same. The old file, *dodo*, started with one link. The link count is now two. Since *dodo* and *newdodo* are linked they are the same file, and changing one will then change the other. If one link is removed, the other still exists. To remove a file, all hard links to it must be removed.

The *unlink* function deletes a list of files on both UNIX and Windows systems, (like the UNIX *rm* command or the MS-DOS *del* command). If the file has more than one link, the link count is dropped by one. The function returns the number of files successfully deleted. To remove a directory, use the *rmdir* function, since only the superuser can unlink a directory with the *unlink* function.

FORMAT

```
unlink (LIST);
unlink  LIST;
```

EXAMPLE 16.17

```
(The Script)
1    unlink('a','b','c') || die "remove: $!\n";
2    $count=unlink <*.c>;
     print "The number of files removed was $count\n";
```

EXPLANATION

1   The files *a*, *b*, and *c* are removed.
2   Any files ending in .c (C source files) are removed. The number of files removed is stored in the scalar, *$count*.

The *symlink* and *readlink* Functions (UNIX).   The *symlink* function creates a symbolic link. The symbolic link file is the name of the file that is accessed if the old filename is referenced.

FORMAT

```
symlink(OLDFILE, NEWFILE)
```

EXAMPLE 16.18

```
1    $ perl -e 'symlink("/home/jody/test/old", "new");'
2    $ ls -ld new
     lrwxrwxrwx  1 ellie    8 Feb 21 17:32 new  -> /home/jody/test/old
```

1   The *symlink* function creates a new filename, *new*, linked to the old filename,
     /home/jody/test/old.
2   The *ls-ld* command lists the symbolically linked file. The symbol —> points to the
     new filename. The *l* preceding the permissions also indicates a symbolic link file.

The *readlink* function returns the value of the symbolic link and is undefined if the file
is not a symbolic link.

```
readlink(SYMBOLIC_LINK);
readlink SYMBOLIC_LINK;
```

EXAMPLE 16.19

```
1    $ perl -e 'readlink("new")';
     /home/jody/test/old
```

1   The file *new* is a symbolic link. It points to */home/jody/test/old*, the value returned by
     the *readlink* function.

16.1.10 Renaming Files

The *rename* Function (UNIX and Windows).   The *rename* function changes the name
of the file, like the UNIX *mv* command. The effect is to create a new link to an existing file
and then delete the existing file. The *rename* function returns *1* for success and returns *0* for
failure. This function does not work across file system boundaries. If a file with the new
name already exists, its contents will be destroyed.

```
rename(OLDFILENAME, NEWFILENAME);
```

EXAMPLE 16.20

```
1    rename ("tmp", "datafile");
```

EXPLANATION

1   The file *tmp* is renamed *datafile*. If *datafile* already exists, its contents are destroyed.

16.1.11 Changing Access and Modification Times

The *utime* Function.   The *utime* function changes the access and modification times on each file in a list of files, like the UNIX *touch* command. The first two elements of the list must be the numerical access and modification times, in that order. The *time* function feeds the current time to the *utime* function. The function returns the number of files successfully changed. The inode modification time of each file in the list is set to the current time.

FORMAT

```
utime (LIST);
utime LIST;
```

EXAMPLE 16.21

```
(The Script--UNIX)
1    print "What file will you touch (create or change time stamp)? ";
     chop($myfile=<STDIN>);
2    $now=time;  # This example makes the file if it doesn't exist
3    utime( $now, $now, $myfile) || open(TMP,">>$myfile");ᵃ

(The Command Line)
     $ ls -l brandnewfile
     brandnewfile: No such file or directory

     $ update.p
1    What file will you touch (create or update time stamp) ?
     brandnewfile

     $ ls -l brandnewfile
2    -rw-r--r-- 1 ellie   0 Mar   6 17:13 brandnewfile
```

a. Wall, L., Christianson, T., and Orwant, J., *Programming Perl*, 3rd ed., O'Reilly & Associates: Sebastopol, CA, 2000.

EXPLANATION

1   The user will enter the name of a file either to update the access and modification times or, if the file does not exist, to create it.
2   The variable, *$now*, is set to the return value of the *time* function, the number of non-leap seconds since January 1, 1970, UTC.
3   The first argument to *$now* is the access time, the second argument is the modification time, and the third argument is the file affected. If the *utime* function fails because the file does not exist, the *open* function will create the file, using *TMP* as the filehandle, emulating the UNIX *touch* command.

16.1.12   File Statistics

The information for a file is stored in a data structure called an **inode**, maintained by the kernel. For UNIX users, much of this information is retrieved with the *ls* command. In C and Perl programs, this information may be retrieved directly from the inode with the *stat* function. See the *File::stat* module, which creates a user interface for the *stat* function. Although the emphasis here is UNIX, the *stat* function also works with Win32 systems.

The *stat* and *lstat* Functions.   The *stat* function returns a 13-element array containing statistics retrieved from the file's inode.The last two fields, dealing with blocks, are defined only on BSD UNIX systems.[10]

The *lstat* function is like the *stat* function, but if the file is a symbolic link, *lstat* returns information about the link itself rather than about the file that it references. If your system does not support symbolic links, a normal *stat* is done.

The special *underscore* file handle is used to provide *stat* information from the file most previously *stat*ed. The 13-element array returned contains the following elements stored in the *stat* structure. (The order is a little different from the UNIX system call, *stat*.)

1. Device number
2. Inode number
3. Mode
4. Link count
5. User ID
6. Group ID
7. For a special file, the device number of the device it refers to
8. Size in bytes, for regular files
9. Time of last access
10. Time of the last modification
11. Time of last file status change
12. Preferred I/O block size for file system
13. Actual number of 512-byte blocks allocated

---

10. Ibid., p. 188.

FORMAT

```
stat(FILEHANDLE);
stat FILEHANDLE;
stat(EXPR);
```

EXAMPLE 16.22

```
(UNIX)
1   open(MYFILE, "perl1") || die "Can't open: $!\n";
2   @statistics=stat(MYFILE);
3   print "@statistics\n";
    close MYFILE;

4   @stats=stat("perl1");
5   printf("The inode number is %d and the uid is %d.\n",
            $stats[1], $stats[4]);
6   print "The file has read and write permissions.\n",
            if -r _ && -w _;

(Output)
3   1819 142441 33261 1 9496 40 -21335 75 761965998 727296409 8192 2
5   The inode number is 142441 and the uid is 9496.
6   The file has read and write permissions.
```

EXPLANATION

1   The file *perl1* is opened via the filehandle *MYFILE*.
2   The *stat* function retrieves information from the file's inode and returns that information to a 13-element array, *@statistics*.
3   The 13-element array is printed. The last two elements of the array are the blocksize and the number of blocks in 512-byte blocks. The size and number of blocks may differ because unallocated blocks are not counted in the number of blocks. The negative number is an NIS device number.
4   This time the *stat* function takes the filename as its argument, rather than the filehandle.
5   The second and fifth elements of the array are printed.
6   The special underscore (_) filehandle is used to retrieve the current file statistics from the previous *stat* call. The file *perl1* was *stat*ed last. The file test operators, *-r* and *-w,* use the current *stat* information of *perl1* to check for read and write access on the file.

EXAMPLE 16.23

```
(Windows)
      # Since UNIX and Windows treat files differently,
      # some of the fields here are
      # blank or values returned are not meaningful
1     @stats = stat("C:\\ellie\\testing");
2     print "Device: $stats[0]\n";
3     print "Inode #: $stats[1]\n";
4     print "File mode: $stats[2]\n";
5     print "# Hard links: $stats[3]\n";
6     print "Owner ID: $stats[4]\n";
7     print "Group ID: $stats[5]\n";
8     print "Device ID: $stats[6]\n";
9     print "Total size: $stats[7]\n";
10    print "Last access time: $stats[8]\n";
11    print "Last modify time: $stats[9]\n";
12    print "Last change inode time: $stats[10]\n";
13    print "Block size: $stats[11]\n";
14    print "Number of blocks: $stats[11]\n";

(Output)
2     Device: 2
3     Inode #: 0
4     File mode: 16895
5     # Hard links: 1
6     Owner ID: 0
7     Group ID: 0
8     Device ID: 2
9     Total size: 0
10    Last access time: 981360000
11    Last modify time: 977267374
12    Last change inode time: 977267372
13    Block size:
14    Number of blocks:
```

16.1.13   Low-Level File I/O

The *read* Function (*fread*).   The *read* function reads a specified number of bytes from a filehandle and puts the bytes in a scalar variable. If you are familiar with *C*'s standard I/O *fread* function, Perl's *read* function handles I/O buffering in the same way. To improve efficiency, rather than reading a character at a time, a block of data is read and stored in a temporary storage area. *C*'s *fread* function and Perl's *read* functions then transfer data, a byte at a time, from the temporary storage area to your program. (The *sysread* function is used to emulate *C*'s low-level I/O *read* function.) The function returns the number of bytes read or an undefined value if an error occurred. If EOF (end of file) is reached, *0* is returned.

In Perl, the *print* function (**not** the *write* function) is used to output the actual bytes returned by the *read* function. Perl's *print* function emulates *C*'s *fwrite* function.

FORMAT

```
read(FILEHANDLE, SCALAR, LENGTH, OFFSET);
read(FILEHANDLE, SCALAR, LENGTH);
```

EXAMPLE 16.24

```
(The Script)
1   open(PASSWD, "/etc/passwd") || die "Can't open: $!\n";
2   $bytes=read (PASSWD, $buffer, 50);
3   print "The number of bytes read is $bytes.\n";
4   print "The buffer contains: \n$buffer";

(Output)
3   The number of bytes is 50.
4   The buffer contains:
    root:YhTLR4heBdxfw:0:1:Operator:/:/bin/csh
    nobody:
```

EXPLANATION

1   The */etc/passwd* file is opened for reading via the *PASSWD* filehandle.
2   The *read* function attempts to read 50 bytes from the filehandle and returns the number of bytes *read* to the scalar, *$bytes*.

The *sysread* and *syswrite* Functions.   The *sysread* function is like *C*'s *read* function. It bypasses the standard I/O buffering scheme and reads bytes directly from the filehandle to a scalar variable. Mixing *read* and *sysread* functions can cause problems, since the *read* function implements buffering and the *sysread* function reads bytes directly from the filehandle.

The *syswrite* function writes bytes of data from a variable to a specified filehandle. It emulates *C*'s *write* function.

FORMAT

```
sysread(FILEHANDLE, SCALAR, LENGTH, OFFSET);
sysread(FILEHANDLE, SCALAR, LENGTH);

syswrite(FILEHANDLE, SCALAR, LENGTH, OFFSET);
syswrite(FILEHANDLE, SCALAR, LENGTH);
```

The *seek* Function.   Perl's *seek* function is the same as the *fseek* standard I/O function in *C*. It allows you to randomly access a file. It sets a position in a file, measured in bytes from the beginning of the file, where the first byte is byte *0*. The function returns *1* if successful, *0* if not.

FORMAT

```
seek(FILEHANDLE, OFFSET, POSITION);
```

POSITION = The absolute position in the file where
    0 = Beginning of file
    1 = Current position in file
    2 = End of file

OFFSET = Number of bytes from *POSITION*. A positive offset advances the position forward in the file. A negative offset moves the position backward in the file. A negative *OFFSET* sets the file position for *POSITION* 1 or 2.

EXAMPLE 16.25

```
(The Script)
1   open(PASSWD, "/etc/passwd") || die "Can't open: $!\n";
2   while ( chomp($line = <PASSWD>) ){
3       print "---$line---\n" if $line =~ /root/;
    }
4   seek(PASSWD, 0, 0) || die "$!\n"; # Start back at the beginning
                                      # of the file at first byte
5   while(<PASSWD>){print if /ellie/;}
6   close(PASSWD);

(Output)
3   ---root:YhTLR4heBdxfw:0:1:Operator:/:/bin/csh---
5   ellie:aVD17JSsBMyGg:9496:40:Ellie Savage:/home/jodyellie:/bin/csh
```

EXPLANATION

1 The */etc/passwd* file is opened via the *PASSWD* filehandle.
2 The *while* statement loops through the *PASSWD* filehandle, reading a line at a time until end of file is reached.
3 The line is printed if it contains the regular expression *root*.
4 The *seek* function sets the file position at position *0*, the beginning of the file, byte offset *0*. Since the filehandle was not closed, it remains opened until closed with the *close* function.
5 The *while* statement loops through the file.
6 The *PASSWD* filehandle is officially closed.

The *tell* Function.   The *tell* function returns the current byte position of a filehandle for a regular file. The position can be used as an argument to the *seek* function to move the file position to a particular location in the file.

FORMAT

```
tell (FILEHANDLE);
tell FILEHANDLE;
tell;
```

EXAMPLE 16.26

```
(The Script)
1   open(PASSWD, "/etc/passwd") || die "Can't open: $!\n";
    while ( chomp($line = <PASSWD>) ){
        if ( $line =~ /sync/){
2           $current = tell;
            print "---$line---\n";
        }
3   printf "The position returned by tell is %d.\n", $current;
4   seek(PASSWD, $current, 0);
    while(<PASSWD>){
5       print;
    }


(Output)
2   --sync::1:1::/:/bin/sync--
3   The position returned by tell is 296.
5   sysdiag:*:0:1:Old System Diagnostic:/usr/diag/sysdiag/sysdiag
    sundiag:*:0:1:System Diagnostic:/usr/diag/sundiag/sundiag
    ellie:aVD17JSsBMyGg:9496:40:Ellie Savage:/home/jodyellie:/bin/csh
```

EXPLANATION

1   The */etc/passwd* file is opened via the *PASSWD* filehandle.
2   When the line containing the regular expression, *sync*, is reached, the *tell* function will return the current byte position to the scalar *$current*. The current position is the next byte after the last character read.
3   The byte position returned by the *tell* function is printed.
4   The *seek* function locates the current position starting from the beginning of the file to the offset position returned by the *tell* function.

16.1.14   Packing and Unpacking Data

Not all files are text files. Some files, for example, may be packed into a binary format to save space, store images, or in a uuencoded format to facilitate sending a file through the mail. These files are not readable as is the text on this page. The *pack* and *unpack* functions can be used to convert the lines in a file from one format to another.

The *pack* and *unpack* Functions.   The *pack* and *unpack* functions have a number of uses. These functions are used to pack a list into a binary structure and then expand the packed values back into a list. When working with files, you can use these functions to create uuencode files, relational databases, and binary files.

The *pack* function converts a list into a scalar value that may be stored in machine memory. The template is used to specify the type of character and how many characters will be formatted. For example, the string *c4* or *cccc* packs a list into 4 unsigned characters and *a14* packs a list into a 14-byte ASCII string, null padded. The *unpack* function converts a binary formatted string into a list. The opposite of *pack* puts a string back into Perl format.

Table 16.8   The Template *pack* and *unpack*—Types and Values

Template	Description
a	An ASCII string (null padded)
A	An ASCII string (space padded)
b	A bit string (low-to-high order, like *vec*)
B	A bit string (high-to-low order)
c	A signed *char* value
C	An unsigned *char* value
d	A double-precision float in the native format
f	A single-precision float in the native format
h	A hexadecimal string (low nybble first, to high)
H	A hexadecimal string (high nybble first)
i	A signed integer
I	An unsigned integer
l	A signed long value
L	An unsigned long value
n	A short in "network" (big-endian) order
N	A long in "network" (big-endian) order
p	A pointer to a null-terminated string
P	A pointer to a structure (fixed-length string)
q	A signed 64-bit value
Q	An unsigned 64-bit value
s	A signed short value (16-bit)
S	An unsigned short value (16-bit)
u	A uuencoded string
v	A short in "VAX" (little-endian) order
V	A long in "VAX" (little-endian) order
w	A BER compressed unsigned integer in base 128, high bit first
x	A null byte
X	Back up a byte
@	Null fill to absolute position

FORMAT

```
$string=pack(Template, @list );
@list = unpack(Template, $string );
```

EXAMPLE 16.27

```
(The Script)
1   $bytes=pack("c5", 80,101,114, 108, 012);
2   print "$bytes\n";
```

```
(Output)
Perl
```

EXPLANATION

1   The first element in the list, the template (see Table 16.8), is composed of the type and the number of values to be packed, in this example, four signed characters. The rest of the list consists of the decimal values for characters *P*, *e*, *r*, and *l* and the octal value for the newline. This list is packed into a binary structure. The string containing the packed structure is returned and stored in *$bytes*. (See your ASCII table.)

2   The four-byte character string is printed.

EXAMPLE 16.28

```
(Script)
1   $string=pack("A15A3", "hey","you");   # ASCII string, space padded
2   print "$string";
```

```
(Output)
2   hey            you
```

EXPLANATION

1   Two strings, *hey* and *you*, are packed into a structure using the template *A15A3*. *A15* will convert the string *hey* into a space-padded ASCII string consisting of 15 characters. *A3* converts the string *you* into a 3-character space-padded string.

2   The strings are printed according to the pack formatting template. They are left justified.

EXAMPLE 16.29

```
(The Script)
    #!/bin/perl
    # Program to uuencode a file and then uudecode it
1   open(PW, "/etc/passwd") || die "Can't open: $!\n";
2   open(CODEDPW, ">codedpw") || die "Can't open: $!\n";

3   while(<PW>){
4       $uuline=pack("u*", $_);
5       print CODEDPW $uuline;
    }
    close PW;
    close CODEDPW;

6   open(UUPW, "codedpw") || die "Can't open: $!\n";
    while(<UUPW>){
7       print;
    }
    close UUPW;
    print "\n\n";

8   open(DECODED, "codedpw") || die;
9   while(<DECODED>){
10      @decodeline = unpack("u*", $_);
11      print "@decodeline";
    }
```

```
(Output)
7   E<F]O=#IX.C`Z,3I3=7!E<BU5<V5R.B\Z+W5S<B]B:6X08W-H"@``
    19&%E;6]N.G@Z,3HQ.CHO.@H`
    58FEN.G@Z,CHR.CHO=7-R+V)I;CH*
    .<WES.G@Z,SHS.CHO.@H`
    :861M.G@Z-#HT.D%D;6EN.B]V87(0861M.@H`
    L;'`Z>#HW,3HX.DQI;F4@4')I;G1E<B!!9&UI;CHO=7-R+W-P;V]L+VQP.@H`
    ?<VUT<#IX.C`Z,#I-86EL($$1A96UO;B!5<V5R.B\Z"@!R
    E=75C<#IX.C4Z-3IU=6-P($%D;6EN.B]U<W(O;&EB+W5U8W@`Z"@!L
    M;G5U8W@`Z>#HY.CDZ75C<<"!!9&UI;CHF%R+W-
    P;V]L+W5U8W@!P=6)L:6,Z,Z
    5+W5S<B]L:6(O=75C<<"]U=6-I8V\*
    J;&ES=&5N.G@Z,S<Z-#I.971W;W)K($$D;6EN.B]U<W(O;F5T+VYL<SH*
    ?;F]B;V1Y.G@Z-C`P,#H<$Z-#`P,#H#80F]D>2!#
    I;F]A8V-E<W,@,C>#HV,#`P,#HV,#`P,#HV86-C.;R!5<V5R.@H`
    J;F]B;V]B;V1Y-#IX.C8U-3,T+3,T+30T.D5N;VYE;G0N5-UT9V5R<2
    M96QL:64Z>#HY-
    #DV.C0P.D5L+;&EE(%%U<6-;Y:+VAO;64O;F]A8V-E<W,
    *<B]B:6X08W-H"@!C
```

EXAMPLE 16.29 (CONTINUED)

```
11   root:x:0:1:Super-User:/:/usr/bin/csh
     daemon:x:1:1::/:
     bin:x:2:2::/usr/bin:
     sys:x:3:3::/:
     adm:x:4:4:Admin:/var/adm:
     lp:x:71:8:Line Printer Admin:/usr/spool/lp:
     smtp:x:0:0:Mail Daemon User:/:
     uucp:x:5:5:uucp Admin:/usr/lib/uucp:
     nuucp:x:9:9:uucp Admin:/var/spool/uucppublic:/usr/lib/uucp/uucico
     listen:x:37:4:Network Admin:/usr/net/nls:
     nobody:x:60001:60001:Nobody:/:
     noaccess:x:60002:60002:No Access User:/:
     nobody4:x:65534:65534:SunOS 4.x Nobody:/:
     ellie:x:9496:40:Ellie Quigley:/home/ellie:/usr/bin/csh
```

EXPLANATION

1 The local *passwd* file is opened for reading.
2 Another file called *codepw* is opened for writing.
3 Each line of the filehandle is read into *$_* until the end of file is reached.
4 The *pack* function uuencodes the line (*$_*) and assigns the coded line to the scalar, *$uuline*. uuencode is often used to convert a binary file into an encoded representation that can be sent using e-mail.
5 The uuencoded string is sent to the filehandle.
6 The file containing the uuencoded text is opened for reading and attached to the *UUPW* filehandle.
7 Each line of uuencoded text is printed.
8 The uuencoded file is opened for reading.
9 Each line of the file is read from the filehandle and stored in *$_*.
10 The *unpack* function converts the uuencoded string back into its original form and assigns it to *@decodeline*.
11 The uudecoded line is printed.

EXAMPLE 16.30

```
(The Script)
    #!/bin/perl
1   $ints=pack("i3", 5,-10,15);
2   open(BINARY, "+>binary" ) || die;
3   print BINARY "$ints";
4   seek(BINARY, 0,0) || die;
    while(<BINARY>){
5       ($n1,$n2,$n3)=unpack("i3", $_);
6       print "$n1 $n2 $n3\n";
    }


(Output)
6    5 -10 15
```

EXPLANATION

1   The three integers, *5* , *–10*, and *15*, are packed into 3 signed integers. The value returned is a binary structure assigned to *$ints*.
2   The *BINARY* filehandle is opened for reading and writing.
3   The packed integers are sent to the file. This file is compressed and totally unreadable. To read it, it must be converted back into an ASCII format. This is done with *unpack*.
4   The *seek* function puts the file pointer back at the top of the file at byte position *0*.
5   We're reading from the file one line at a time. Each line, stored in *$_*, is unpacked and returned to its original list of values.
6   The original list values are printed.

16.2 Processes

Your Perl script is a program that resides on disk. When the program is placed in memory and starts execution, it is called a **process**. Each process has a number of attributes that are inherited from its parent, the **calling process**. Perl has a number of functions that will allow you to retrieve the information about the process. Before examining these functions, a short discussion about processes may help you to understand (or recall) the purpose of some of Perl's system calls.

16.2.1 UNIX Processes

Every process has a unique process ID, a positive integer called the *pid*. Every process has a **parent** except process 0, the swapper. The first process *init*, *pid* 1, is the ancestor of all future processes, called **descendants**, or more commonly, **child** processes.

In the following diagram, the Perl process is a descendant of the shell (*sh*).

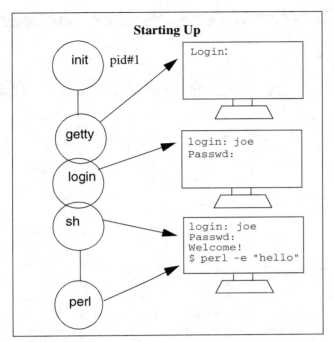

Figure 16.5   The Perl process as a descendant of the shell.

Each process also belongs to a **process group**, a collection of one or more processes used for job control and signal handling. Each process group also has a unique *pid* and a process leader. When you log on, the process group leader may be your login shell. Any process created from your shell will be a member of this process group. The terminal opened by the process group leader is called the controlling terminal, and any processes it spawns inherits it. Any signals sent to the process will be sent to all processes in the group. That is why, when you press <Ctrl>-c, the process you are running and any of its children will terminate. Perl provides functions to obtain the process group ID and to set the process group.

When a process is created, it is assigned four numbers, indicating who owns the process. They are the real and effective user ID, and the real and effective group ID. The user ID, called the real *uid*, is a positive integer that is associated with your login name. The real *uid* is the third field in the */etc/passwd* file. When you log on, the first process created is called the *login* shell, and it is assigned the user ID. Any processes spawned from the shell also inherit this *uid*. Any process running with the *uid* of zero is called a **root** or **superuser** process with special privileges.

There is also a group ID number,called the real *gid*, which associates a group with your login name. The default *gid* is the fourth field in the password file, and it is also inherited by any child process. The system administrator can allow users to become members of other groups by assigning entries in the */etc/group* file.

The following is an entry from the *passwd* file, illustrating how the *uid* and *gid* values are stored (fields are separated by colons).

EXAMPLE 16.31

```
(Entry from /etc/passwd)
   john:aYD17IsSjBMyGg:9495:41:John Doe:/home/dolphin/john:/bin/ksh
```

EXPLANATION

(The Fields)
1   login name
2   encrypted password
3   uid
4   gid
5   gcos
6   home directory
7   login shell

The **effective *uid* (*euid*)** and **effective *guid* (*guid*)** of a process are normally set to the same number as the real *uid* and real *gid* of the user who is running the process. UNIX determines what permissions are available to a process by the effective *uid* and *gid*. If the *euid* or *guid* of a file is changed to that of another owner, when you execute a program, you essentially become that owner and get his access permissions. Programs in which the effective *uid* or effective *gid* have been set are called **set user ID** programs or *setuid* programs. When you change your password, the */bin/passwd* program has a *setuid* to *root*, giving you the privilege to change your password in the *passwd* file, which is owned by *root*.

16.2.2   Win32 Processes

The process model for Windows differs from UNIX systems, and since Perl was originally designed for UNIX, a number of library routines were added to the standard Perl library to accommodate the Windows world. The Win32 directory (*C:/Perl/site/lib/Win32*) is a site-specific directory that comes with Windows versions of Perl and contains a number of modules for creating, suspending, resuming, and killing processes. The *Win32::Process* module contains a number of functions to manipulate processes. Below is a listing from the Win32 directory:

```
AuthenticateUser.pm    Internet.pm        Registry.pm
ChangeNotify.pm        Mutex.pm           Semaphore.pm
Client.pl              NetAdmin.pm        Server.pl
Clipboard.pm           NetResource.pm     Service.pm
Console.pm             ODBC.pm            Shortcut.pm
Event.pm               OLE                Sound.pm
EventLog.pm            OLE.pm             Test.pl
File.pm                PerfLib.pm         TieRegistry.pm
FileSecurity.pm        Pipe.pm            WinError.pm
IPC.pm                 Process.pm         test-async.pl
```

16.2.3 The Environment (UNIX and Windows)

When you log on, your shell program inherits a set of environment variables initialized by either the login program or one of shell's startup files (*.profile* or *.login*). These variables contain useful information about the process, such as the search path, the home directory, the user name, and the terminal type. The information in environment variables, once set and exported, is inherited by any child processes that are spawned from the process (parent) in which they were initialized. The shell process will pass the environment information on to your Perl program.

The special associative array *%ENV* contains the environment settings. If you change the value of an environment setting in your Perl script, it is set for this process and any of its children. The environment variables in the parent process, normally the shell, will remain untouched.

EXAMPLE 16.32

```
(The Script)
(UNIX)
1   foreach $key (keys(%ENV)){
2           print "$key\n";}
3   print "Your login name is $ENV{'LOGNAME'}\n";
4   $pwd=$ENV{'PWD'};
    print "/The present working directory is $pwd, "\n";

(Output)
2   OPENWINHOME
    MANPATH
    FONTPATH
    LOGNAME
    USER
    TERMCAP
    TERM
    SHELL
    PWD
    HOME
    PATH
    WINDOW_PARENT
    WMGR_ENV_PLACEHOLDER
3   Your login name is ellie
4   The present working directory is /home/jody/ellie
```

EXPLANATION

1 The *keys* function is used to get all the currently set environment variables from the *%ENV* array. These variables were inherited from the parent process, the shell.
2 Each environment variable is printed.
3 The value of *LOGNAME*, the user name, is printed.
4 The value of *PWD*, the present working directory, is assigned to *$pwd* and printed.

EXAMPLE 16.33

```
(Windows)
    while(($key,$value)=each(%ENV)){
        print "$key: $value\n" if $key =~ /^P/;
    }

(Output)
1   PROMPT: $p$g
    PROCESSOR_IDENTIFIER: x86 Family 6 Model 5 Stepping 2,
        GenuineIntel
    PATH: c:\Oracle\Ora81\bin;"C:\PROGRAM FILES
        \OCLE\JRE\1.1.7\BIN";C:\ORAWIN95\BIN;C:\PERL\BIN\;
        C:\MKSNT;C:\WINDOWS;C:\WINDOW
    PATHEXT: .pl;.COM;.EXE;.BAT;.CMD;.VBS;.VBE;.JS;.JSE;.WSF;.WSH
    PROGRAMFILES: C:\PROGRA~1
    PROCESSOR_ARCHITECTURE: x86
    PROCESSOR_REVISION: 0502
    PERL5LIB: C:\Perl\lib
    PROCESSOR_LEVEL: 6
```

EXPLANATION

1 The *each* function is used to get all the currently set environment variables from the *%ENV* array. These variables were inherited from the parent process, the MS-DOS shell.

16.2.4 Processes and Filehandles

As discussed in Chapter 9, "Getting a Handle on Files," processes can be opened in Perl via either an input or output filehandle. For example, if you want to see all the currently running processes on your machine, you could create a filehandle for the UNIX *ps* command. (See Chapter 9 for details. See also "The system Function" on page 567.)

EXAMPLE 16.34

```
(The Script)
    # UNIX ps command
1   open(PROC, "ps -aux  |" ) || die "$!\n";
                    # If running System V, use ps -ef
2   print STDOUT <PROC>;
```

```
(Output)
2  ellie  3825  6.4  4.5  212  464 p5  R 12:18  0:00 ps -aux
   root      1  0.0  0.0   52    0 ?  IW Feb 5  0:02 /sbin/init
   root     51 10.0  0.0   52    0 ?  IW Feb 5  0:02 portmap
   root      2 10.0  0.0   52    0 ?   D Feb 5  0:02 pagedaemon
   root     90 10.0  0.0   52    0 ?  IW Feb 5  0:02 rpc.statd

                    <more processes here>

   ellie  1383  0.8  8.4  360  876 p4  S Dec 26 11:34 /usr/local/OW3/bin/xview
   ellie   173  0.8 13.4 1932 1392 co  S Dec 20389:19 /usr/local/OW3/bin/xnews
   ellie   164  0.0  0.0  100    0 co IW Dec 20  0:00 -c

                <some of the output was cut to save space>

   ellie  3822  0.0  0.0    0    0 p5  Z Dec 20  0:00 <defunct>
   ellie  3823  0.0  1.1   28  112 p5  S 12:18  0:00 sh -c ps -aux | grep '^'
   ellie  3821  0.0  5.6  144  580 p5  S 12:18  0:00 /bin/perl checkon ellie
   ellie  3824  0.0  1.8   32  192 p5  S 12:18  0:00 grep ^ellie
```

EXPLANATION

1   The *PROC* filehandle is opened for reading. It is called an **input filter**. The output from the *ps* command is piped to Perl via the *PROC* filehandle.

2   The contents of the filter are printed to *STDOUT*.

Login Information—The *getlogin* Function.   The *getlogin* function returns the current login from */etc/utmp*. If *null* is returned from *getlogin*, use *getpwuid*. The *getpwuid* function takes the *uid* of the user as an argument and returns an entry from the password file associated with that *uid*.

The *$<* variable evaluates to the real *uid* of this process.

FORMAT

```
getlogin;
```

EXAMPLE 16.35

```
(The Script)
1   $loginname=getlogin || (getpwuid($<))[0]|| die "Not a user here!!";
2   print "Your loginname is $loginname.\n";

(Output)
2   Your loginname is john.
```

EXPLANATION

1   The *getlogin* function returns the login name from */etc/utmp* and, if that fails, retrieves it from the password file with the *getpwuid* function. The *$<* variable contains the real *uid* of this process.

2   The scalar *$loginname* contains the user's login name, the first entry of the password file.

Special Process Variables (*pid, uid, euid, gid, euid*). Perl provides some special variables that store information about the Perl process executing your script. If you want to make your program more readable, you can use the *English* module in the standard Perl library to represent these variables in English.

$$ The process ID of the Perl program running this script
$<   The real *uid* of this process
$>   The effective *uid* of this process
$(The real *gid* of this process
$)   The effective *gid* of this process

The Parent Process ID—The *getppid* Function and the *$$* Variable. Each process on the system is identified by its process identification number (*pid*), a positive integer. The special variable *$$* holds the value of the *pid* for this process. This variable is also used by the shell to hold the process ID number of the current process.

The *getppid* function returns the process ID of the parent process.

EXAMPLE 16.36

```
(The Script)
1   print "The pid of this process is $$\n";
2   print "The parent pid of this process is ", getppid,"\n";

(Output)
1   The pid of this process is 3304
2   The parent pid of this process is 2340

(At the Command Line)
3   $ echo $$
    2340
```

EXPLANATION

1 The process identification number (*pid*) for this process, this Perl script, is printed.
2 The process that spawned this process is ordinarily the shell, the parent process. The parent's *pid* is called the *ppid*.
3 After the Perl script exits, the *$$* is used to print the *pid* of the shell. The *ppid* for the Perl script was *2340*, the value of its parent's *pid*, that of the shell.

The Process Group ID—The *pgrp* Function.   The *pgrp* function returns the current group process for a specified *pid*. Without an argument or with an argument of *0*, the process group ID of the current process is returned.

FORMAT

```
getpgrp(PID);
getpgrp PID;
getpgrp;
```

EXAMPLE 16.37

```
(The Script)
1   print "The pid of the Perl program running this script is ", $$;
2   printf "The ppid, parent's pid (Shell) , is %d\n", getppid;
3   printf "The process group's pid is %d\n", getpgrp(0);

(Output)
1   The pid of the Perl program running this script is 6671
2   The ppid, parent's pid (Shell), is 6344
3   The process group's pid is 6671
```

16.2.5   Process Priorities and Niceness

The kernel maintains the scheduling priority selected for each process. Most interactive and short-running jobs are favored with a higher priority. The UNIX *nice* command allows you to modify the scheduling priority of processes (BSD, pre-System V). On moderately or heavily loaded systems, it may be to your advantage to make CPU-intensive jobs run slower so that jobs needing higher priority get faster access to the CPU. Those jobs that don't hog the processor are called *nice*.

The *nice* value is used in calculating the priority of a process. A process with a positive *nice* value runs at a low priority, meaning that it receives less than its share of the CPU time. A process with a negative *nice* value runs at a high priority, receiving more than its share of the processor. The *nice* values range from *–20* to *19*. Most processes run at priority zero, balancing their access to the CPU. (Only the superuser can set negative *nice* values.)

The following functions, *getpriority* and *setpriority*, are named for the corresponding system calls, found in Section 2 of the UNIX *man* pages.

The *getpriority* Function.   The *getpriority* function returns the current priority (nice value) for a process, process group, or a user. Not all systems support this function. If not implemented, *getpriority* produces a fatal error. *WHICH* is one of three values: *0* for the process priority, *1* for the process group priority, and *2* for the user priority. *WHO* is interpreted relative to the process identifier for the process priority, process group priority, or user priority. A value of zero represents the current process, process group, or user.

FORMAT

```
getpriority(WHICH, WHO);
```

EXAMPLE 16.38

```
(The Script)
1   $niceval = getpriority( 0,0);
2   print "The priority, nice value, for this process is $niceval\n";

(Output)
2   The priority, nice value, for this process is 0.
```

EXPLANATION

1   The *getpriority* function will return the *nice* value for the current process.
2   The *nice* value for this process is zero. This gives the process no special favor when taking its share of time from the CPU.

The *setpriority* Function (*nice*).   The *setpriority* function sets the current priority (*nice* value) for a process, a process group, or a user. It modifies the scheduling priority for processes. If the *setpriority* system call is not implemented on your system, *setpriority* will return an error.

WHICH is one of three values: *0* for the process priority, *1* for the process group priority, and *2* for the user priority. *WHO* is interpreted relative to the process identifier for the process priority, process group priority, or user priority. A value of zero represents the current process, process group, or user. *NICEVALUE* is the *nice* value. A low *nice* value raises the priority of the process and a high *nice* value decreases the priority of the process. (Confusing!)

Unless you have superuser privileges, you cannot use a negative *nice* value. Doing so will not change the current *nice* value.

FORMAT

```
setpriority(WHICH, WHO, NICEVALUE);
```

EXAMPLE 16.39

```
(The Script)
1   $niceval = getpriority(0,0);
2   print "The nice value for this process is $niceval.\n";
3   setpriority(0,0, ( $niceval + 5 ));
4   print "The nice value for this process is now", getpriority(0,0);
```

```
(Output)
2   The nice value for this process is 0.
4   The nice value for this process is now 5.
```

EXPLANATION

1   The *getpriority* function will return the nice value for the current process.
2   The *nice* value is printed.
3   The *setpriority* function adds *5* to the *nice* value of the current process. The process will have a lower priority. It is being "nice."
4   The new *nice* value returned by the *getpriority* function is *5*.

16.2.6   Password Information

UNIX.   The following functions iterate through the */etc/passwd* file and retrieve information from that file into an array. These functions are named for the same functions found in the system library (Section 3 of the UNIX manual) and perform the same tasks. If you are interested in obtaining information about the */etc/group* file, the Perl functions *getgrent, getgrgid,* and *getgrnam* all return a four-element array with information about group entries. A description of these functions can be found in the UNIX manual pages. Here is an example of an */etc/passwd* file:

```
root:YhTLR4heBdxfw:0:1:Operator:/:/bin/csh
nobody:*:65534:65534::/:
sys:*:2:2::/:/bin/csh
bin:*:3:3::/bin
uucp:*:4:8::/var/spool/uucppublic:
news:*:6:6::/var/spool/news:/bin/csh
sync::1:1::/:/bin/sync
ellie:aVD17TSsBMfYg:9496:40:Ellie Shellie:/home/jody/ellie:/bin/ksh
```

Windows.   Windows 2000 and NT store information about users in a binary database called *SAM* (Security Accounts Manager), part of the Registry. Because the data is stored in binary format, normal Perl read operations won't work. It is better to use the Win32 extensions to get user information. *Win32::NetAdmin* is bundled with ActiveState under

\perl\site\lib\win32. (See Table 16.9.) A user account can be manipulated with two functions of this module: *UserGetAttributes()* and *UserSetAttributes*. Another good extension is David Roth's *Win32::AdminMisc* found at *www.roth.net*.

The Win 32 *net.exe* command also displays information about the user and the system.

EXAMPLE 16.40

```
1  C:\  net help
   The syntax of this command is:

   NET HELP command
      -or-
   NET command /HELP


   Commands available are:

   NET ACCOUNTS              NET HELP              NET SHARE
   NET COMPUTER              NET HC:\ELPMSG        NET START
   NET CONFIG                NET LOCALGROUP        NET STATISTICS
   NET CONFIG SERVER         NET NAME              NET STOP
   NET CONFIG WORKSTATION    NET PAUSE             NET TIME
   NET CONTINUE              NET PRINT             NET USE
   NET FILE                  NET SEND              NET USER
   NET GROUP                 NET SESSION           NET VIEW

   NET HELP SERVICES lists the network services you can start.
   NET HELP SYNTAX explains how to read NET HELP syntax lines.
   NET HELP command | MORE displays Help one screen at a time.

2  C:\ net user

   User accounts for \\HOMEBOUND

   -------------------------------------------------------------------

   Administrator           Ellie Quigley            Guest
   SQLAgentCmdExec
   The command completed successfully.
```

Table 16.9 *Win32::NetAdmin* Extensions

Win32::NetAdmin::UserGetAttributes(*$Machine,*
$UserName,
$Password,
$PasswordAge,
$Privilege,
$Homedir,
$Comment,
$Flags,
$ScriptPath);

Win32::NetAdmin::UserSetAttributes(*$Machine,*
$UserName,
$Password,
$PasswordAge,
$Privilege,
$Homedir,
$Comment,
$Flags,
$ScriptPath);

EXAMPLE 16.41

```
1   use Win32::NetAdmin qw(GetUsers UserGetAttributes) ;
2   GetUsers("", FILTER_NORMAL_ACCOUNT,\%hash)or die;
3   foreach $key(sort keys %hash){
        print "$key\n";
    }

(Output)
Administrator
Ellie Quigley
Guest
SQLAgentCmdExec
```

Encrypted passwords cannot be transferred from UNIX to Win32 systems and vice versa. They are cryptologically incompatible. To manage passwords, use the *Win32::AdminMisc* or the *Win32::NetAdmin* module extension.

Table 16.10   Win32 Password Extensions

Win32::AdminMisc::UserCheckPassword($Machine, $User, $Password)

Win32::AdminMisc::SetPassword($Machine | $Domain), $User, $NewPassword);

Win32::AdminMisc::UserChangePassword($Machine | $Domain), $User, $OldPassword, $NewPassword);

Win32::NetAdmin::UserChangePassword(($Machine | $Domain), $User, $OldPassword, $NewPassword);

For Windows user, the following functions for obtaining group and user information have not been implemented by ActiveState as of this printing:

```
endgrent(), endpwent(), getgrent(), getgrgid(), getgrnam(),
getpwent(), getpwnam(), getpwuid(), setgrent(), setpwent()
```

Getting a Password Entry (UNIX)—The *getpwent* Function.   The *getpwent* function retrieves information from the */etc/passwd* file. The return value from *getpwent* is a nine-element array consisting of:

1. Login name
2. Encrypted password
3. User ID
4. Group ID
5. Quota
6. Comment
7. Gcos (user information)
8. Home directory
9. Login shell

FORMAT

```
($name, $passwd, $uid, $gid, $quota, $comment, $gcos, $dir,
    $shell )=getpwent;
```

EXAMPLE 16.42

```
(The Script)
1   while( @info=getpwent) {
2       print "$info[0]\n" if $info[1]=~/\*+/;
    }

(Output)
2   nobody
    daemon
    sys
    bin
    uucp
```

EXPLANATION

1   The *getpwent* function gets a line from the */etc/passwd* file and stores it in the array, *@info*. The loop continues until *getpwent* cannot read another entry from */etc/passwd*.

2   If the second element of the array contains at least one star (*), the first element, the user name, is printed.

Getting a Password Entry by Username—The *getpwnam* Function.   The *getpwnam* function takes the user name as an argument and returns a nine-element array corresponding to that user's name field in the */etc/passwd* file.

FORMAT

```
getpwnam(loginname);
```

EXAMPLE 16.43

```
(The Script)
    #!/bin/perl
1   foreach $name ( "root", "bin", "ellie" ){
2       if (($login, $passwd, $uid)=getpwnam($name)){
3           print "$login--$uid\n";
        }
    }

(Output)
3   root--0
    ellie--9496
    bin--3
```

1   The *foreach* loop contains login names in its list, each to be processed in turn.
2   The *getpwnam* function retrieves information from */etc/passwd* and stores the first
    three fields of information in the array elements *$login, $passwd,* and *$uid*, respec-
    tively.
3   The *login* name and the *uid* are printed.

Getting a Password Entry by *uid*—**The** *getpwuid* **Function.**   The *getpwuid* function
takes a numeric user ID (*uid*) as an argument and returns a nine-element array corresponding to that user's *uid* entry in the */etc/passwd* file.

FORMAT

```
getpuid(UID)
```

EXAMPLE 16.44

```
(The Script)
1   foreach $num ( 1 .. 10 ){
2       if (($login, $passwd, $uid)=getpwuid($num)){
3       print "$login--$uid\n";}
    }

(Output)
3   daemon--1
    sys--2
    bin--3
    uucp--4
    news--6
    ingres--7
    audit--9
```

EXPLANATION

1   The *foreach* loop contains a range of *uid* numbers from *1* to *10* in its list, each to be
    processed in turn.
2   The *getpwuid* function retrieves information from */etc/passwd* and stores the first
    three fields of information in the array elements, *$login, $passwd,* and *$uid*, respec-
    tively.
3   The *login* name and its corresponding *uid* are printed.

16.2.7   Time and Processes

When working in a computer environment, programs often need to obtain and manipulate
the current date and time. UNIX systems maintain two types of time values: calendar time
and process time.

The calendar time counts the number of seconds since 00:00:00 January 1, 1970, UTC (Coordinated Universal Time, which is a new name for Greenwich Mean Time).

The process time, also called CPU time, measures the resources a process utilizes in clock time, user CPU time, and system CPU time. The CPU time is measured in clock ticks per second.

Perl has a number of time functions that interface with the system to retrieve time information.

The *times* function.   The *times* function returns a four-element array consisting of the CPU time for a process, measured in:

- User time—Time spent executing user's code
- System time—Time spent executing system calls
- Children's user time—Time spent executing all terminated child processes
- Children's system time—Time spent executing system calls for all terminated child processes

FORMAT

```
($user, $system, $cuser, $csystem) = times;
```

EXAMPLE 16.45

```
(The Script)
    #!/bin/perl
1   printf "User time in this program %2.3f seconds\n", (times)[0];
2   printf "System time in this program %2.3f seconds\n", (times)[1];

(Output)
3   User time in this program 0.217 seconds
4   System time in this program 0.600 seconds
```

EXPLANATION

1   The *time* function returns a four-element array and the first element is printed, the user time.
2   The *time* function returns a four-element array and the second element is printed, the system time.

The *time* Function (UNIX and Windows).   The *time* function returns the number of non-leap seconds since January 1, 1970, UTC. Its return value is used with the *gmtime* and *localtime* functions (see below) to put the time in a human readable format. The *stat* and *utime* functions also use the *time* functions when comparing file modification and access times.

The *gmtime* Function. The *gmtime* function converts the return value of the *time* function to a nine-element array consisting of the numeric values for the UTC. If you are a *C* programmer, you will recognize that these values are taken directly from the *tm structure* found in the header file, */usr/include/time.h.* (See Table 16.11.)

FORMAT

```
gmtime(EXPR);
gmtime EXPR;
($sec, $min, $hour, $monthday, $month, $year, $weekday,
        $yearday, $isdaylight)=gmtime;
```

Table 16.11   Return Values for the *gmtime* Function

List Element	Meaning
$sec	Seconds after the minute: [0, 59]
$min	Minutes after the hour: [0, 59]
$hour	Hour since midnight: [0, 23]
$monthday	Day of the month: [1, 31]
$month	Months since January: [0, 11]
$year	Years since 1900
$weekday	Days since Sunday: [0, 6]
yearday	Days since January 1: [0, 365]
isdaylight	Flag for daylight saving time

EXAMPLE 16.46

```
(The Script)
    #!/bin/perl
1   ($sec, $min, $hour, $monthday, $month, $year, $weekday, $yearday,
       $isdaylight) = gmtime;
2   print "The weekday is $weekday and the month is $month.\n";
3   print "The time in California since midnight is ",
       `date "+%H:%M"`;
4   print "The Coordinated Univeral Time is $hour:$min
        since midnight\n";
5   print "Daylight saving is in effect.\n" if $isdaylight;
```

EXAMPLE 16.46 (CONTINUED)

```
(Output)
2   The weekday is 2 and the month is 6.
3   The time in California since midnight is 20:35.
4   The Coordinated Univeral Time is 3:35 since midnight.
5   <no output>
```

EXPLANATION

1   The *gmtime* function returns an array as defined in the table above.
2   The weekday and the month are printed for Coordinated Universal Time.
3   The time in California is printed by utilizing the UNIX *date* command.
4   The Coordinated Universal Time is printed.
5   If daylight savings is in effect, the value of *$isdaylight* is set to non-zero. Daylight time is not in effect, so nothing prints.

The *localtime* Function.   The *localtime* function converts the UTC to a nine-element array with the local time zone.

FORMAT

```
localtime(EXPR);
localtime EXPR;
($sec, $min, $hour, $mday, $mon, $year, $wday, $yday,
        $isdst)=localtime(time);
```

EXAMPLE 16.47

```
(At the Command Line)
1   $ perl -e "print scalar (localtime);"
    Fri Nov  3 15:26:16 2000

(In Script)
2   $localtime=localtime;
    print $localtime;
```

EXPLANATION

1   If the *localtime* function is use in scalar context, its return value is output similar to the UNIX/Win32 *date* command. The *scalar* function forces scalar context.
2   Assigning the return value of *localtime* to a scalar.

EXAMPLE 16.48

```
(The Script)
    #!/bin/perl
1   ($sec, $min, $hour, $mday, $mon, $year, $wday, $yday, $isdst)=
           localtime(time);
2       % weekday=(
        "0"=>"Sunday",
        "1"=>"Monday",
        "2"=>"Tuesday",
        "3"=>"Wednesday",
        "4"=>"Thursday",
        "5"=>"Friday",
        "6"=>"Saturday",
    );
    if ( $hour > 12 ){
3       print "The hour is ", $hour - 12 ," :$min: o'clock.\n";
        }
    else {
        print "The hour is $hour:$min o'clock.\n";
        }
4       print qq/The day is $weekday{"$wday"}.\n/;
                            # day starts at zero
5       printf "The year is %d.\n", 1900+$year;
6       print "The isdst is $isdst.\n";
    }

(Output)
3   The hour is 9:52 o'clock.
4   The day is Wednesday.
5   The year is 2001.
6   The isdst is 0.
```

EXPLANATION

1 The *localtime* function converts the return of the time function to the local time.
2 An associative array, *%weekday*, associates a number of the weekday with the string
   for the day of the week.
3 The hour and the minutes are printed.
4 The scalar *$wday* returned from the localtime function is a number. It is used as an
   index into the associative array *%weekday* to get the string *Wednesday*.
5 The year is printed.
6 The *$isdt* element of the array prints *0* if daylight saving is not in effect.

16.2.8 Process Creation UNIX

What happens when your Perl program starts executing? Here is a brief sketch of what goes on. Normally, the Perl program is executed from the shell command line. You type the name of your script (and its arguments) and then press the Enter key. At that point, the shell starts working. It first creates (*fork*s) a new process called the **child process**. The child is essentially a copy of the shell that created it. There are now two processes running, the parent and child shell. After the child process is created, the parent shell normally sleeps (*wait*s) while its child process gets everything ready for your Perl program, that is, handles redirection (if necessary) pipes, background processing, etc. When the child shell has completed its tasks, it then executes (*exec*s) your Perl program in place of itself. When the Perl process completes, it exits (*exit*s) and its exit status is returned to the waiting parent process, the shell. The shell wakes up, and a prompt appears on the screen. If you type in a UNIX command, this whole process is repeated.

It's conceivable that your Perl program may want to start up a child process to handle a specific task, for example, a database application or a client/server program.

The *fork* Function.   The *fork* function is used to create processes on UNIX systems. The *fork* function is called once and returns twice. It creates a duplicate of the parent (calling) process. The new process is called the child process. The child process inherits its environment, open files, real and user IDs, masks, current working directory, signals, and so on. Both processes, parent and child, execute the same code, starting with the instruction right after the *fork* function call.

The *fork* function lets you differentiate between the parent and child because it returns a different value to each process. It returns *0* to the child process and the *pid* of the child to the parent process. It is not guaranteed which process will execute first after the call to the *fork* function.

Normally the *wait, exec,* and *exit* functions work in conjunction with the *fork* function so that you can control what both the parent and the child are doing. The parent, for example, waits for the child to finish performing some task, and after the child exits, the parent resumes where it left off.

Figure 16.6 illustrates how the UNIX shell uses the *fork* system call to create a new process. After you type the name of your Perl program at the shell prompt, the shell forks, creating a copy of itself called the child process. The parent shell sleeps (*wait*s). The child shell executes (*exec*s) the Perl process in its place. The child never returns. Note that *ENV* variables, standard input, output, and standard error are inherited. When the Perl program completes, it exits and the parent shell wakes up. The shell prompt reappears on your screen. The Perl program could use the *fork* function to spawn off another application program.

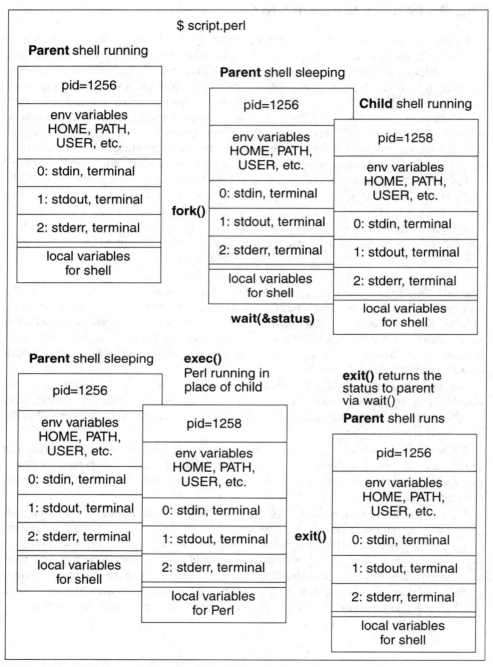

Figure 16.6 Perl process creation from the shell.

FORMAT

```
fork;
```

EXAMPLE 16.49

```
(The Script)
1   $return_val=fork;
2   if ( $return_val == 0 ){
        print "This is the child process; return value
            is $return_val.\n";
    }
3   elsif ( defined $return_val ){
        print "This is the parent process; return value
            is $return_val.\n";
    }
    else{
4       die "fork error: $!\n";
    }

(Output)
2   This is the child process; return value is 0.
3   This is the parent process; return value is 3512.
```

EXPLANATION

1   The *fork* function is called to create a copy of this process.
2   The return value is checked. If the return value is *0*, the child's code is in execution.
3   If the return value is non-zero, the parent process is executing.
4   This statement is executed if the *fork* function fails. It might fail if the process table is full; that is, if the system has reached its maximum number of allowed processes.

The *exec* Function.   Whereas *fork* creates a brand new process, the *exec* function is used to initiate a new program in place of the currently running program. Normally, the *exec* function is called after *fork*. Perl inherits attributes from the shell, and a process that is executed from within Perl also inherits Perl's attributes, such as *pid*, *gid*, *uid*, signals, directories, etc. If, then, the *exec* function is called directly (no *fork*) from within a Perl script, the new program executes in place of the currently running Perl program. When that program completes, you do not return to your Perl program. Since *exec* does not flush the output buffer, the *$|* variable needs to be set to ensure command buffering.

The filehandles *STDIN*, *STDOUT*, and *STDERR*, remain open following a call to the *exec* function.

At the system level there are six different *exec* functions used to initiate new programs. Perl calls the *C* library function *execvp* if more than one argument is passed to the *exec* function. The arguments are the name of the program to execute and any other arguments that will be passed to that program. If a single scalar is passed to the *exec* function and it contains any shell metacharacters, the shell command, */bin/sh -c*, is passed the command for interpretation.

FORMAT

```
exec(UNIX COMMAND);
exec UNIX COMMAND;
```

EXAMPLE 16.50

```
(The Script)
1   exec 'echo hi there you!';
2   print "hello";

(Output)
1   hi there you

(The Script)
1   exec 'ls *.c';
2   print "hello.";

(Output)
file1.c file2.c file3.c
```

EXPLANATION

1   In both examples, the *exec* function will execute the UNIX command.
2   In both examples, the *print* statement will not be executed because *exec* never returns. The UNIX commands were executed **in place** of the Perl program.

The *wait* and *waitpid* Functions.   The *wait* function waits for a child process to finish execution. After a *fork* call, both processes, parent and child, execute. The *wait* function forces the parent to wait until its child is finished and returns the *pid* of the child process to the parent. If there are no child processes, *wait* returns a −1.[11]

FORMAT

```
wait;
```

---

11. The *waitpid* function also waits for a child process to finish execution, but it can specify which child it will wait for, and it has special flags that control blocking.

EXAMPLE 16.51

```
(The Script)
1   $return_val=fork;
2   if ( $return_val == 0 ){          # In child
        print "This is the child process; return value
            is $return_val.\n";
3       exec "/bin/date" || die "exec failed: $!\n";
    }
4   elsif ( defined $return_val ){    # In parent
        print "This is the parent process; return value is $pid.\n";
5       $pid = wait;
        print "Back in parent process.\n";
        print "The deceased child's pid is $pid.\n";
    }
    else{
6       die "fork error: $!\n";
    }

(Output)
4   This is the parent process; return value is 3530.
2   This is the child process; return value is 0.
3   Wed Mar 26 23:57:18 PST 2001.
5   Back in the parent process.
    The deceased child's pid is 3530.
```

EXPLANATION

1   The *fork* function creates a copy of the current process. Now there are two processes running, the parent Perl process and the child Perl process. They are both executing the code directly following the *fork* call. The return value is assigned *0* in the child and the *pid* of the child in the parent.

2   If in the child process, the *if* statement block is executed.

3   The *exec* function executes the UNIX *date* command and does not return.

4   If in the parent process, the *elsif* statement block is executed. The value of *$return_val* is the *pid* of the child process.

5   The *wait* function is called by the parent, who waits for the child to finish. The *pid* of the deceased child is returned.

6   If the *fork* failed (no more processes?), the *die* function will print the error message and the program will exit.

The *exit* Function.   The *exit* function causes the program to exit. It can be given an integer argument ranging from values between zero and 255. The exit value is returned to the parent process via the *wait* function call. By convention, UNIX programs exiting with a zero status are successful, and those exiting with non-zero failed in some way. (Of course, the criteria for success for one programmer may not be the same as those for another.)

FORMAT

```
exit (Integer);
exit Integer;
```

EXAMPLE 16.52

```
(The Script)
    # The name of the script is args.p
1   exit 12 if $#ARGV == 0;

(Output)
1   $ args.p
2   $ echo $?
    12
```

EXPLANATION

1   The script is missing an argument.
2   The shell's *$?* variable contains the exit status of the Perl program. If using *C* shell,
     the exit status is stored in *$status*.

16.2.9   Process Creation Win32

You can use the *system* and *exec* functions, and backquotes on Win32 systems just the same
as you would with UNIX.

The *start* Command.   The Perl *system* function is used by both Windows and UNIX to
start a operating system command. The *system* function executes a program and doesn't
return until that program finishes. If the Windows *start* command is given as an argument
to the Perl system function, a new application will run, and your script will also continue to
run.

EXAMPLE 16.53

```
    use warnings;
1   $return_value = system ("start /Program
    Files/Netscape/Communicator/Program/netscape.exe");

2   print "Program continues; Netscape is running.\n";
3   print "The return_value from system is $return_value.\n";

(Output)
Program continues; Netscape is running.
The return_value from system is 0.
```

EXPLANATION

1 The Perl *system* function starts a new process. By using the Win32 *start* command, you can start a new process, and the Perl script will continue to run, rather than waiting for the new process to complete. If the process starts up successfully, a return value of *0* is returned by the *system* function.

2 Netscape Communicator has started up and will continue to run, until its window is closed.

3 The return value from the *system* function is printed.

The *Win32::Spawn* Module. The *Win32::Spawn* function behaves like the *system* function and the Windows *start* menu.

FORMAT

```
use Win32;
Win32::Spawn($ProgramName, $CommandLine,$ProcessID);
```

EXAMPLE 16.54

```
1   use warnings;
2   use Win32;
3   $|=1;
4   $Application="C:/mksnt/date.exe";
5   $CommandLine="date +%D";
6   $status=Win32::Spawn($Application, $CommandLine, $ProcessID);
7   if ($status != 0){
8       print "pid is $ProcessID.\n";
    }
    else{
9       print "Didn't spawn $Application.\n";
10      print Win32::FormatMessage(Win32::GetLastError);
    }
```

```
(Output)
8 pid is 448.
11/01/00
```

EXPLANATION

1 The *warnings* pragma will send syntactic warnings, unitialized values, etc., to help with possible problems that may occur in the program.

2 The *Win32* module is loaded. This is a module that comes with ActiveState and is found in standard Perl library under the *site/lib/Win32* directory. It contains a number of useful modules for Windows programmers to handle servers, clients, registries, events, network administration, processes, and more.

3 The special scalar *$|* is assigned the value *1*. It ensures that the output buffers will be flushed immediately when the *print* function is used.

EXPLANATION (CONTINUED)

4 The application is the MSK toolkit[a], found on the *C:* drive. This toolkit contains *.exe* files that emulate UNIX commands. The *date.exe* file produces the today's date.

5 The command line consists of any arguments that will be passed to the application.

6 The *Win32::Spawn* function is called with three arguments. Two of them have been given values, but *$ProcessID* is not known. It will be given a value after the application is started.

7 If the status returned from the *Win32::Spawn* function is not *0*, the process ID number will be printed.

8 The process ID number is *448*.

9 *Didn't spawn C:/mksnt/date.exe.* is displayed if the *.exe* file doesn't exist.

10 If the process couldn't be started because the application doesn't exist, the *GetLastError* function prints:

The system cannot find the file specified.
Program continues to run....

This is a Windows-generated error caused when the operating system failed to start the program. The *FormatMessage* function creates a readable printout of the error.

a. MSK Toolkit for Windows NT and Windows 95 Release 6.1, Mortice Kern Systems Inc.

The *Win32::Process* Module.   Another extension you can use to launch Windows applications is the object-oriented *Win32::Process* module. It provides a number of methods for creating and managing processes. Processes can be suspended, resumed, and killed with this module.

Table 16.12   *Win32::Process* Methods

Method	What It Does
Create($Obj, $AppName, $CommandLine, $Inherit, $CreateFlags, $InitialDir);	Creates the process object
$Obj->GetExitCode($ExitCode);	Gets the exit code of the process
$Obj->GetPriorityClass($Class);	Gets the proceds priority class
$ProcessObj->GetProcessID()	Returns the process ID
$Obj->Kill($ExitCode);	Kills the process with exit code
$Obj->Resume();	Resumes a suspended process
$Obj->SetPriorityClass($Class);	Sets the process affinity mask (NT)
$Obj->Suspend();	Suspends the process
$Obj->Wait($Timeout);	Waits for the process to die

EXAMPLE 16.55

```
1   use Win32::Process;
2   use Win32;
3   sub ErrorReport{
        print Win32::FormatMessage( Win32::GetLastError() );
    }

4   Win32::Process::Create($ProcessObj,
        "C:\\windows\\notepad.exe", "notepad myfile.txt", 0,
        NORMAL_PRIORITY_CLASS, ".") || die ErrorReport();
    print "Notepad has started\n";
5   print "The exit code is:
        ",$ProcessObj->GetExitCode($ExitCode),"\n";
```

(Output)
Notepad has started
The exit code is: 1

EXPLANATION

1   The *Win32::Process* module is loaded. It is used to launch Windows applications.
2   The Win32 module is loaded.
3   The *ErrorReport* function will send a formatted error message for the last system error that occured, if there was one.
4   The *Create* function creates a process. The first argument, *$ProcessObj*, is a container for the process object, followed by the full pathname of the application, command line arguments, and required flags.
5   The exit code of the process is returned.

16.3   Other Ways to Interface with the Operating System

If the system functions are still not enough, Perl offers a number of alternate ways to deal with the operating system. You can use the *syscall* function, command substitution, the *system* function, and the *here document* to get system information.

16.3.1   The *syscall* Function and the *h2ph* Script

The *syscall* function calls a specified system call with its arguments. If the *C* system call is not implemented, a fatal error is returned. The first argument is the name of the system call preceded by *&SYS_*. The remaining arguments are the actual parameters that are required by the real system call. If the argument is numeric, it is passed as a *C* integer. If not, the pointer to the string value is passed. You may have to coerce a number to an integer by adding *0* to it if it is not a literal and cannot be interpreted by context.

Before using the *syscall* function, you should run a script called *h2ph* (*h2ph.bat* on Windows) that comes with the Perl distribution. At the bottom of the *h2ph* script (after _ _END_ _) are the manual pages for *h2ph*, including an explanation on how to run the script. This script converts the proper *C* header files to the corresponding Perl header files. These files must be added to the Perl library if you are using functions that require them. All the files created have the *.ph* extension. After running the *h2ph* script, make sure that the @*INC* array in your program includes the path to these library functions.[12]

FORMAT

```
syscall (&SYS_NAME, LIST);
```

EXAMPLE 16.56

```
(UNIX: At the Command Line)
1   $ cd /usr/include; /usr/local/bin/perl/h2ph  *  sys/*

(In Script)
    #!/bin/perl
    # The name of the script is args.p
2   push(@INC, "/usr/local/lib");
3   require "syscall.ph";
4   $bytes=syscall(&SYS_getpagesize);
5   printf "The pagesize for this Sparc Sun Workstation is %d
            bytes \n",$bytes;

(Output)
5   The pagesize for this Sparc Sun Workstation is 4096 bytes.
```

EXPLANATION

1   *h2ph* is executed so that the necessary *C* header files are converted to Perl header files. The files created will be placed in */usr/local/lib* and end with a *.ph* extension.
2   The directory containing the *.ph* files is pushed onto the @*INC* array.
3   The file *syscall.ph* is required for using *C* system calls.
4   The Perl *syscall* function will call the *getpagesize* system call. The prefix &*SYS_* is necessary Perl syntax. It must be prepended to the real system call name.
5   The page size for this Sun4c is *4096* bytes.

---

12. See also the *h2xs* script that comes with Perl 5 distribution, for building a Perl extension from any *C* header file.

16.3.2   Command Substitution—The Backquotes

Although we have already discussed command substitution and backquotes in Chapter 4, "What's in a Name," a quick review might be in order here because command substitution is yet another way for Perl to interface with operating system commands.

Backquotes are used by the UNIX shells (not Windows) to perform command substitution and are implemented in Perl scripts pretty much the same way. For example, the command line: *echo The present working directory is `pwd`* will cause the command in backquotes to be executed and its results substituted into the string. **Like** the UNIX shell, enclosing a command in backquotes causes it to be executed. **Unlike** the shell, if double quotes surround the backquoted string, command substitution will **not** occur. The output resulting from executing the command is saved in a scalar variable.

EXAMPLE 16.57

```
(The Script)
    #!/bin/perl
1   print "The hour is ",`date`;

2   @d=`date`;
3   print $d[0]'

4   @d=split(/ /,`date`);
5   print "$d[0]\n"
6   $machine=`uname -n`;
7   print "$machine\n"'

(Output)
1   The hour is Thu Mar 27 20:47:17 PST 2001
3   Thu Mar 27 20:59:11 PST 2001
5   Thu
7   dolphin
```

EXPLANATION

1   The UNIX *date* command is enclosed in backquotes. It is executed and appended to the string *The hour is*.
2   The array *@d* is set to the output of the *date* command. The output is stored as a single string, unlike the shells, where the output is stored as a list.
3   Since the output of the command is stored as a single string, *$d[0]* is the entire string.
4   The *split* command creates a list from the output returned from the *date* command.
5   Now the first element of the array is the first word in the list, *Thu*.
6   The scalar, *$machine*, is assigned the value of the UNIX command, *uname -n*, which contains the name of the host machine (*hostname* on BSD).
7   The name of the host machine is printed.

16.3.3   The *Shell.pm* Module (Perl 5)

This module lets you use UNIX commands that you normally type at the shell prompt in a Perl script. The commands are treated like Perl subroutines. Arguments and options are passed to the commands as a list of strings.

EXAMPLE 16.58

```
(The Script)
    #!/bin/perl
1   use Shell qw(pwd ls date);    # Shell commands listed
2   print "Today is ", date();
3   print "The time is ", date("+%T");
4   print "The present working directory is ", pwd;
5   $list=ls( "-aF");
6   print $list;


(Output)
2   Today is Fri Mar 28 13:41:56 PST 2001
3   The time is 13:41:57
4   The present working is /home/ellie/sockets
6   ./
    ../
    sh.test*
    shellstuff
    timeclient*
    timeclient5*
    timeserver*
    timeserver5*
```

EXPLANATION

1   The *Shell.pm* module will be used in this program. The three UNIX shell commands, *pwd, ls,* and *date* will be treated as ordinary Perl subroutines.
2   The *date* command is executed as a subroutine. This is an alternative to using back-quotes.
3   Arguments passed to the *date* command are strings enclosed in quotes.
4   The *pwd* command is executed.
5   The output of the *ls* command is assigned to scalar *$list*. The argument is passed to the function as a single string.
6   The output of *ls -aF* is a list of files in the present working directory. The *-a* switch includes the dot files and the *F* causes the executable scripts to be marked with an asterisk (*) and the directories with a /.

16.3.4   The *system* Function

Like its *C* counterpart, the *system* function takes a system command as its argument, sends the command to the system shell for interpretation, and returns control back to the calling program, your script. This is just like the *exec* functions, except that a *fork* is done first, so that control is returned to the Perl script. Because it does not flush the output buffer, the special Perl variable $| is set to *1* to force a flush of the buffer after *print* or *write* statements.[13]

```
system("system command");
system "system command";
```

EXAMPLE 16.59

```
(UNIX: The Command Line)
1   system("cal 1 2001");
    print "Happy New  Year!\n";'

(Output)
      January 2001
Su   Mo   Tu   We   Th   Fr   Sa
 1    2    3    4    5    6
 7    8    9   10   11   12   13
14   15   16   17   18   19   20
21   22   23   24   25   26   27
28   29   30   31
    Happy New Year!


(Windows)
2   system("notepad.exe");
```

EXPLANATION

1   The *system* function executes the UNIX *cal* command to print out the calendar for the month of January, 2001.
2   The *system* function executes the Windows *notebook.exe* command and starts up a session of Notepad.

---

13. A *fork* is done, the script waits for the command to be executed, and control is then returned to the script.

EXAMPLE 16.60

```
(The Script)
1   print "Hello there\n";
2   print "The name of this machine is ";
3   system ("uname -n");        # Buffer is not flushed
4   print "The time is ", `date`;

(Output)
1   Hello there
3   jody
2,4 The name of this machine is The time is Fri Mar 28 13:39:35 PST 2001
```

EXPLANATION

1 The first *print* statement is executed as expected.
2 Since Perl depends on the default I/O buffering mechanism, the buffer may not be flushed immediately after the *print* statement; the results of the *system* function, executed by the shell, are printed first.
3 The *system* function causes the shell to execute the UNIX command, *uname -n*.
4 This *print* statement is printed directly after the *print* statement in line 2.

EXAMPLE 16.61

```
(The Script)
    #!/bin/perl
1   $|=1;       # Set special variable to flush the output buffer
2   print "Hello there\n";
3   print "The name of this machine is ";
    system ("uname -n");
4   print "The time is ", 'date';

(Output)
2   Hello there
3   The name of this machine is jody
4   The time is Tue Jan 26 13:43:54 PST 2001
```

EXPLANATION

1 The $| special variable, when set to non-zero, forces the output buffer to be flushed after every *write* or *print*.

16.3.5   *here documents*

The Perl *here document* is derived from the UNIX shell *here document*. As in the shell, the Perl *here document* is a line-oriented form of quoting, requiring the << operator followed by an initial terminating string. There can be no spaces after the <<. If the terminating string is not quoted or double-quoted, variable expansion is performed. If the terminating string is single-quoted, variable expansion is not performed. Each line of text is inserted between the first and last terminating string. The final terminating string must be on a line by itself, with no surrounding whitespace.

Perl, unlike the UNIX shell, does not perform command substitution (backquotes) in the text of a *here document*. Perl, on the other hand, does allow you to execute commands in the *here document* if the terminator is enclosed in backquotes.

EXAMPLE 16.62

```
(The Script)
    #!/bin/perl
    $price=100;
1   print <<EOF;     # No quotes around terminator EOF are same
                     # as double quotes
2   The price of $price is right.    # Variables are expanded
3   EOF


4   print <<'FINIS';
5   The price of $price is right.
                    # The variable is not expanded
                    # if terminator is enclosed in single quotes

6   FINIS


7   print << x 4;   # Prints the line 4 times
8   Christmas is coming!
        # Blank line is necessary here as terminating string
9   print <<`END`;  # If terminator is in backquotes,
                    # will execute UNIX commands

10  echo hi there
11  echo -n "The time is "
12  date
13  END


(Output)
2   The price of 100 is right.
5   The price of $price is right.
8   Christmas is coming!
    Christmas is coming!
    Christmas is coming!
    Christmas is coming!
10  hi there
    The time is Fri Nov  3 17:03:46 PST 2000
```

16.3.6   Globbing (Filename Expansion and Wildcards)

If you have worked at the UNIX or MS-DOS command line, you have been introduced to the shell metacharacters used to expand filenames. The asterisk (*) is used to match all characters in a filename, the question mark (?) to match one character in a filename, and brackets ([ ]) to match one of a set of characters in a filename. The process of expanding these shell metacharacters to a filename is called **globbing**.

Perl supports globbing if the filenames are placed within angle brackets, the read operators. There is also a Perl 5 function for globbing, as explained below.

EXAMPLE 16.63

```
(The Script)
    #!/bin/perl
1   @myfiles=<*.[1-5]>;
2   print "@myfiles\n";
3   foreach $file ( <p??l[1-5]*>){
4       print "$file\n" if -T $file;
    }

(Output)
2   exer.3 exer.4 exer.5 fileter.1 format.1 format.2 format.3 perl.4
    perl.4.1
4   perl1
    perl2
    perl3
    perl4
    perl4.1
    perl5
```

EXPLANATION

1   In an array context, after the globbing is performed, a list of all the matched files is returned, and returned to the array *@myfiles*. The list consists of any files that start with zero or more of any character, followed by a period, and ending with a number between *1* and *5*.

2   The list of matched files is printed.

3   The *foreach* loop is entered. Each time through the loop, the scalar *$file* is set to the next file that is successfully globbed, that is, any file starting with a *p*, followed by any two characters, followed by an *l*, followed by a number between *1* and *5*, and ending in zero or more of any character.

4   If the file is a text file (*-T*), its name is printed.

The *glob* Function.   The *glob* function does the same thing as the <*> operator. It expands the filename metacharacters just as the shell does and returns the expanded filenames.

EXAMPLE 16.64

```
(Command Line)
1   $ perl -e 'while(glob("p???[1-5]")) {print "$_\n";}'
    perl1
    perl2
    perl3
    perl4
    perl5

(In Script)
2   while ( glob("p???[1-5]")){
3       print "$_\n";
    }

(Output)
3   perl1
    perl2
    perl3
    perl4
    perl5
```

EXPLANATION

1   At the command line, the *glob* function will "glob" onto any files in the current working directory whose name begins with a *p*, followed by any three characters (*???*), followed by any number between *1* and *5* (*[1–5]*). Each filename that matches the expression is assigned to *$_* and then printed.
2   This time, *glob* is being used in a script. The behavior is exactly the same as in the first example.
3   The expanded filenames are printed.

16.4 Error Handling

There are a number of occasions when a system call can fail; for example, when you try to open a file that doesn't exist, or remove a directory when it still contains files, or when you try to read from a file for which you do not have read permission. Although we have used the *die* function in earlier examples, now we will go into more detail about error handling and functions you can use to handle errors. The functions are the *die* function, the *warn* function, and the *eval* function.

- The *die* function is used to quit the Perl script if a command or filehandle fails.
- The *warn* function is like the *die* function, but it does not exit the script.
- The *eval* function has multiple uses, but it is primarily used for exception handling.

You may remember that the *short-circuit* operators, && and ||, evaluate the operands on the left and then evaluate the operands on the right. If the operand to the left of the && is *true*, the right-hand side is evaluated. If the operand to the left of the || is *false*, the right-hand side is evaluated.

The *Carp.pm* Module.   There are many ways to die. Perl 5's *Carp* module extends the functionality of *die* and *warn*. (See Example 11.10 on page 343.)

16.4.1   The *die* Function

If a system call fails, the *die* function prints a string to *STDERR* and exits with the current value of *$!*. The *$!* variable yields the current value of *errno*, the UNIX global variable containing a number indicating a system error. The only time that *errno* is updated is when a system call **fails**. When a system call fails, a code number is assigned to *errno* to indicate the type of error. If the newline is omitted in the string, the message is printed with its line number. (See */usr/include/sys* for a complete list.)

Here is an example from */usr/include/sys/errno.h*:

```
#define EPERM     1    /* Not owner */
#define ENOENT    2    /* No such file or directory */
#define ESRCH     3    /* No such process */
#define EINTR     4    /* Interrupted system call */
#define EIO       5    /* I/O error */
...
```

Win32 error codes differ from UNIX error codes, making it impossible to rely on the value returned in *$!*. There are a number of Win32 extensions that provide their own error functions to give more meaningful results. See the documentation for *Win32::GetLastError* in the standard Perl library included with ActiveState.

FORMAT

```
die(LIST)
die LIST
die
```

EXAMPLE 16.65

```
(In Script)
1   die "Can't cd to junk: $!\n" unless chdir "/usr/bin/junk";

(Output)
1   Can't cd to junk: No such file or directory
```

EXPLANATION

1   The *chdir* failed. The *$!* contains the error message from *errno*. The newline causes the string after the *die* function to be printed with the value of the *$!* variable.

EXAMPLE 16.66

```
(In Script)
1   die unless chdir '/plop' ;

(Output)
1   Died at croak.perl line 4.
```

EXPLANATION

1   The *chdir* function failed. This time the *$!* was not included in the *die* string. The line where the error took place is printed.

EXAMPLE 16.67

```
(In Script)
1   chdir '/plop' or die "Stopped";

(Output)
1   Stopped at croak.perl line 4.
```

EXPLANATION

1   This example produces the same output as the previous example, but using a different syntax. If *chdir* fails, the *die* function to the right of *or* is executed.

16.4.2   The *warn* Function

The *warn* function (operator) is just like the *die* function except that the program continues to run. If the *die* function is called in an *eval* block, the argument string given to *die* will be assigned to the special variable *$@*. After a *die*, this variable can be passed as an argument to *warn*, and the output sent to *STDERR*. (See "The eval Function," below.)

16.4.3   The *eval* Function

The *eval* function is used for exception handling, that is, catching errors. The block following *eval* is treated and parsed like a separate Perl program, except that all variable settings and subroutine and format definitions remain after *eval* is finished.

The value returned from the *eval* function is that of the last expression evaluated. If there is a compile or runtime error, or the *die* statement is executed, an undefined value is returned and a special variable, *$@*, is set to the error message. If there is no error, *$@* is a null string.

Evaluating Perl Expressions with *eval*

EXAMPLE 16.68

```
(The Script)
    #!/bin/perl
    # The eval function will evaluate each line you type
    # and return the result. It's as though you are
    # running a little independent Perl script.
    # Script name: plsh

1   print "> ";            # Print the prompt
2   while(<STDIN>){
3       $result=eval ;    # eval evaluates the expression $_
4       warn $@ if $@;    # If an error occurs, it will be assigned to $@
5       print "$result\n if $result";
6       print "> ";        # Print the prompt
    }

(Output)
(The Command line)
    $ plsh
2   > hello
5   hello
2   > bye
5   bye
2   > 5 + 4
5   9
2   > 8 / 3
5   2.66666666666667
2   > 5 / 0
4   Illegal division by zero at (eval 5) line 3, <STDIN> line 5.
    > "Oh I see
    Can't find string terminator '"' anywhere before EOF at (eval 6)
        line 1,   <STDIN> line
    > exit
```

EXPLANATION

1   This line prints a prompt for the user. This program is like a little Perl shell. It can help you in evaluating an expression before putting it in a program, especially if you're not sure how Perl will handle it.

2   The *while* loop is entered. Each time the loop is entered it will read a line of input from the user and assign it to *$_*.

3   The *eval* function, without an argument, will evaluate the expression in *$_* and assign the result of the evaluation to *$result*.

4   If the *eval* finds a syntax error or a system error results from the evaluation of the expression, the error message returned will be assigned to the *$@* variable. If there is no error, the *$@* variable is assigned a null string.

5   If the expression was successfully evaluated, the result will be printed.

6   The prompt is displayed and the loop re-entered.

Using *eval* to Catch Errors in a Program

EXAMPLE 16.69

```
(In Script)
    #!/bin/perl
    print "Give me a number.";
    chop($a=<STDIN>);
    print "Give me a divisor.";
    chop($b=<STDIN>);
1   eval{ die unless $answer = $a/$b ; };
2   warn $@ if $@;
3   printf "Division of %.2f by %.2f is %.2f.\n",$a,$b,
            $answer if $answer ;
4   print "I'm here now. Good-day!\n";

(Output)
    Give me a number.45
    Give me a divisor.6
3   Division of 45.00 by 6.00 is 7.50.
4   I'm here now. Good-day!

(Output)
    Give me a number.5
    Give me a divisor.0
2   Illegal division by zero at ./eval.p line 8, <STDIN> line 2.
4   I'm here now. Good-day!
```

EXPLANATION

1   The *eval* function will evaluate the division (*$a/$b*) and store the result in *$answer*. Note that *$answer* is first used inside the *eval* function. It remains after *eval* is finished.

2   If all went well, and the division was completed, this line is ignored. If there was an error (e.g., division by zero), the *$@* variable is set to the system error. The *warn* function then prints the message to *STDERR*, and the program resumes. If the *die* function is called in an *eval* block, the program does not exit but continues execution after the *eval* block exits.

3   The result of the division is printed, if successful.

4   This line is printed just to show you that the program continued execution even after a failure, since the *warn* function does not cause the script to exit.

The *eval* Function and the *Here Document*

EXAMPLE 16.70

```
(The Script)
    #!/bin/perl
1   eval<<"EOF";
2       chdir "joker" || die "Can't cd: $!\n";
3   EOF
4   print "The error message from die: $@";
5   print "Program $0 still in progress.\n";

(Output)
4   The error message from die: Can't cd: no such file or directory
5   Program ./eval4.p still in progress.
```

EXPLANATION

1 The *here document* is like a special form of quoting. The *eval* function will get everything between the first EOF to the terminating EOF.
2 If the *chdir* function fails the *die* function is called and the program resumes after the last EOF of the *here document*.
3 EOF terminates the *here document*.
4 The error message from the *die* function is stored in the *$@* variable.
5 The program continues.

16.5 Signals

A signal sends a message to a process and normally causes the process to terminate, usually due to some unexpected event, such as illegal division by zero, a segmentation violation, bus error, or a power failure. The kernel also uses signals as timers, for example, to send an alarm signal to a process. The user sends signals when he hits the BREAK, DELETE, QUIT, or STOP keys.

The kernel recognizes 31 different signals, listed in */usr/include/signal.h*. You can get a list of signals by simply typing *kill -l* at the UNIX prompt. (See Table 16.13.)

Table 16.13 Signals (BSD)*

Name	Number	Default	Description
SIGHUP	1	Terminate	Hangup
SIGINT	2	Interrupt	Interrupt
SIGQUIT	3	Terminate	Quit/produces core file
SIGILL	4	Terminate	Terminate

*This is a partial listing of the signals.

Catching Signals.   Signals are asynchronous events, that is, the process doesn't know when a signal will arrive. Programmatically you can ignore certain signals coming into your process or set up a signal handler to execute a subroutine when the signal arrives. In Perl scripts, any signals you specifically want to handle are set in the *%SIG* associative array. If a signal is ignored, it will be ignored after *fork* or *exec* function calls. (For a real application, see Appendix B.)

A signal may be ignored or handled for a segment of your program and then reset to its default behavior. See Example 16.71 below.

FORMAT

```
$SIG{'signal'};
```

EXAMPLE 16.71

```
(The Script)
    #!/bin/perl
1   sub handler{
2       local($sig) = @_;       # First argument is signal name
3       print "Caught SIG$sig--shutting down\n";
4       exit(1);
    }
5   $SIG{'INT'} = 'handler';  # Catch <Ctrl>-c
6   $SIG{'HUP'}='IGNORE';
7   print "Here I am!\n";
    sleep(10);
8   $SIG{'INT'}='DEFAULT';ᵃ
```

```
(Output)
7   Here I am
        < <Ctrl>-c is pressed while the process sleeps >
3   Caught SIGINT--shutting down
```

a. Wall, L., and Schwartz, R. L., *Programming Perl*, 2nd ed., O'Reilly & Associates:Sebastopol, CA, 1998.

EXPLANATION

1   The subroutine called *handler* is defined.
2   The *local* function sets the first argument, the signal name, to the scalar *$sig*.
3   If the signal arrives, the handler routine is executed and this statement is printed.
4   The program exits with a value of *1*, indicating that something went wrong.
5   A value for the *$SIG* associative array is set. The key is the name of the signal without the *SIG* prefix. The value is the name of the subroutine that will be called. If *<Ctrl>-c*, the interrupt key, is pressed during the run of the program, the handler routine is called.
6   *IGNORE* will ignore the hangup signal.
7   The *print* statement is executed and the process sleeps for 10 seconds. If the signal, *<Ctrl>-c*, arrives, the signal handler routine is called.
8   The *SIGINT* signal is reset to its default state, which is to terminate the process when *<Ctrl>-c* is pressed.

Sending Signals to Processes—The *kill* **Function.**   If you want to send a signal to a process or list of processes, the *kill* function is used. The first element of the list is the signal. The signal is a numeric value or a signal name if quoted. The function returns the number of processes that received the signal successfully. A process group is killed if the signal number is negative. You must own a process to kill it, that is, the effective *uid* and real *uid* must be the same for the process sending the *kill* signal and the process receiving the *kill* signal.

For complex signal handling, see the POSIX module in the Perl standard library.

FORMAT

```
kill(LIST);
kill LIST;
```

EXAMPLE 16.72

```
1   $ sleep 100&
2   $ jobs -l
    [1] + 6505 Running     sleep 100&
3   $ perl -e 'kill 9, 6505'
    [1]      Killed      sleep 100
```

EXPLANATION

1   At the UNIX shell prompt, the *sleep* command is executed in the background. The *sleep* command causes the shell to pause for 100 seconds.
2   The *jobs* command lists the processes running in the background. The *sleep* process *pid* is *6505*.
3   Perl is executed at the command line. The *kill* function takes two arguments. The first one, signal *9*, guarantees that the process will be terminated. The second argument is the *pid* of the *sleep* process.

The *alarm* **Function.**   The *alarm* function tells the kernel to send a *SIGALARM* signal to the calling process after some number of seconds. Only one alarm can be in effect at a time. If you call *alarm* and an alarm is already in effect, the previous value is overwritten.

FORMAT

```
alarm (SECONDS);
alarm SECONDS;
```

EXAMPLE 16.73

```
(The Script)
1   alarm(1);
2   print "In a Forever Loop!";
3   for (; ;){ printf "Counting...%d\n", $x++;}

(Output)
2   In a Forever Loop!
3   Counting...0
    Counting...1
    Counting...2
    Counting...3
    Counting...4
       ...
    Counting...294
    Counting...295
4   Alarm Clock
```

EXPLANATION

1   A *SIGALARM* signal will be sent to this process after one second.
2   This statement is printed.
3   The loop starts. We wait for one second. The resolution on the actual second may be off. The *syscall* function can be used to call other functions, for example, *setitimer (2)* and *getitimer (2)*, with better timing resolution.
4   When the alarm goes off, the message *Alarm Clock* is printed by the function.

The *sleep* Function.   The *sleep* function causes the process to pause for a number of seconds or forever if a number of seconds is not specified. It returns the number of seconds that the process slept. You can use the *alarm* function to interrupt the sleep.

FORMAT

```
sleep(SECONDS);
sleep SECONDS;
sleep;
```

EXAMPLE 16.74

```
(The Script)
   #!/bin/perl
1  $|=1          # flush output buffer
2  alarm(5);
   print "Taking a snooze...\n";
3  sleep 100;
4  print "\07 Wake up now.!\n";


(Output)
2  Taking a snooze...   # Program pauses now for 5 seconds
4  (Beep) Wake up now.
```

EXPLANATION

1   The *$|* variable forces the output buffer to be flushed after it writes and prints.
2   The *alarm* function tells the kernel to send a *SIGALARM* signal to the process in 5 seconds.
3   The process goes to sleep for 100 seconds or until a signal is sent to it.
4   The *\07* causes a beep to sound before the statement *Wake up now!*

Attention Windows Users!   For those using ActivePerl on Win32 systems, the following functions have not been implemented. Primary among these is *alarm()*, which is used in a few Perl modules. Because they're missing in ActivePerl, you can't use those modules. Here is a complete list of unimplemented functions:

Functions for processes and process groups:
   alarm(), fork(), getpgrp(), getppid(), getpriority(), setpgrp(), setpriority()

Functions for fetching user and group info:
   endgrent(), endpwent(), getgrent(), getgrgid(), getgrnam(), getpwent(), getpwnam(), getpwuid(), setgrent(), setpwent()

System V interprocess communication functions:
   msgctl(), msgget(), msgrcv(), msgsnd(), semctl(), semget(), semop(), shmctl(), shmget(), shmread(), shmwrite()

Functions for filehandles, files, or directories:
   link(), symlink(), chroot()

Input and output functions:
   syscall()

Functions for fetching network info:
 getnetbyname( ), getnetbyaddr( ), getnetent( ), getprotoent( ),
 getservent( ), sethostent( ), setnetent( ), setprotoent( ),
 setservent( ), endhostent( ), endnetent( ), endprotoent( ),
 endservent( ), socketpair( )

See the *perlport* and *perlwin32* documentation pages for more information on the portability of built-in functions in ActivePerl.

17

REPORT WRITING WITH PICTURES

Perl is the Practical Extraction and Report Language. After you have practically extracted and manipulated all the data in your file, you may want to write a formatted report to categorize and summarize this information. If you have written reports with the *awk* programming language, you may find Perl's formatting a little peculiar at first.

17.1 The Template

In order to write a report, Perl requires that you define a template to describe visually how the report will be displayed, that is, how the report is to be formatted. Do you want left-justified, centered, or right-justified columns? Do you have numeric data that needs formatting? Do you want a title on the top of each page or column titles? Do you have some summary data you want to print at the end of the report?

We'll start with a simple template for a simple report and build on that until we have a complete example.

A format template is structured as follows:

FORMAT

```
format FILEHANDLE=

    picture line
    value line (text to be formatted)


write;
```

17.1.1 Steps in Defining the Template

The steps for defining a template are as follows:

1. Start the format with the keyword *format*, followed by the name of the output filehandle and an equal sign. The default filehandle is *STDOUT*, the screen. The template definition can be anywhere in your script.

   ```
   format FILEHANDLE=
   ```

2. Although any text in the template will be printed as is, the template normally consists of a **picture line** to describe how the output will be displayed. The picture
   consists of symbols that describe the type of the fields (see Table 17.1). The fields
   are either centered, left justified, or right justified (see Table 17.2). The picture line
   can also can be used to format numeric values.

Table 17.1   Field Designator Symbols

Field Designator	*Purpose*
@	Indicates the start of a field
@*	Used for multiline fields
^	Used for filling fields

Table 17.2   Field Display Symbols

Type of Field Symbol	*Type of Field Definition*
<	Left justified
>	Right justified
|	Centered
#	Numeric
.	Indicates placement of decimal point

3. After the field designator, the @ symbol, the *type* of field symbol is repeated as
   many times as there will be characters of that type. This determines the size of the
   field. If >>>>>> is placed directly after the @ symbol, it describes a seven-character right-justified field.[1] Strange, huh? Any real text is not placed directly after
   the @ symbol, or the field type is not interpreted.
4. After the picture line, which breaks the line into fields, comes the *value line*, text
   that will be formatted as described by the picture. Each text field is divided by a
   comma and corresponds, one to one, with the field symbol in the picture line. Any
   whitespace in the value line is ignored.

---

1. Even though there are only six > symbols, the @ field designator counts as one, making the total character
   width seven.

5. When you are finished creating the template, **a period (.) on a line by itself terminates** the template definition.
6. After the template has been defined, the *write* function invokes the format and sends the formatted records to the specified output filehandle. For now, the default filehandle is *STDOUT*.

EXAMPLE 17.1

```
(The Script)
    #!/bin/perl
1   $name="Tommy";
    $age=25;
    $salary=50000.00;
    $now="03/14/97";
    # Format Template
2   format STDOUT=
3   --------------------REPORT-------------------------
4   Name: @<<<<<< Age:@##Salary:@#####.## Date:@<<<<<<<<<
5       $name,        $age,        $salary,        $now
6   .       # End Template

7   write;
8   print "Thanks for coming. Bye.\n";

(Output)
    --------------------REPORT-------------------------
    Name: Tommy   Age: 25 Salary: 50000.00 Date:03/14/97
    Thanks for coming. Bye.
```

EXPLANATION

1   Variables are assigned.
2   The keyword *format* is followed by *STDOUT*, the default and currently selected filehandle, followed by an equal sign.
3   This line will be printed as is. Any text in the format that is not specifically formatted will print as is.
4   This line is called the **picture line**. It is a picture of how the output will be formatted. The @ defines the start of a field. There will be four fields. The first one is a left-justified seven-character field, preceded by the string *Name:* and followed by the string *Age:*. The second field consists of two digits followed by *Salary:*; The third field consists of eight digits with a decimal point inserted after the sixth digit, followed by the string *Date*.
5   These are the variables that are formatted according to the picture. Each variable is separated by a comma and corresponds to the picture field above it.
6   The dot ends the template definition.
7   The *write* function will invoke the template to display the formatted output to *STDOUT*.

17.1.2   Changing the Filehandle

If you want to write the report to a file, instead of to the screen, the file is assigned to a filehandle when it is opened. This same filehandle is used for the format filehandle when defining the template. To invoke the format, the *write* function is called with the name of the output filehandle as an argument.

EXAMPLE 17.2

```
      #!/bin/perl
 1    $name="Tommy";
      $age=25;
      $salary=50000.00;
      $now="03/14/94";

 2    open(REPORT, ">report" ) || die "report: $!\n";
      # REPORT filehandle is opened for writing
 3    format REPORT=    # REPORT is also used for the format filehandle
      -----------------------
         | EMPLOYEE INFORMATION |
      -----------------------
 4    Name: @<<<<<<
 5        $name
      -----------------------
      Age:@###
          $age
      -----------------------
      Salary:@#####.##
          $salary
      -----------------------
      Date:@>>>>>>>>>
          $now
      -----------------------
 6    .
 7    write REPORT;        # The write function sends output to the file
                           # associated with the REPORT filehandle
      ------------------------------------------------------------------
```

EXAMPLE 17.2 (CONTINUED)

```
(Output)
---------------------
| EMPLOYEE INFORMATION |
---------------------
Name: Tommy
---------------------
Age: 25
---------------------
Salary: 50000.00
---------------------
Date:   03/14/94
---------------------
```

EXPLANATION

1 Variables are defined.
2 The file *report* is opened and attached to the *REPORT* filehandle.
3 The *format* keyword is followed by the output filehandle, *REPORT*.
4 The picture line describes the text string *Name:* , followed by a six-character left-justified field.
5 The scalar variable, *$name*, will be formatted as described in the picture line corresponding to it (see above).
6 The dot ends the format template definition.
7 The *write* function will invoke the format called *REPORT* and write formatted output to that filehandle. If the filehandle is not specified, the filehandle *REPORT* does not receive the formatted output because the *write* function has not been told where the output should go.

17.1.3 Top-of-the-Page Formatting

In the following example, the title, *EMPLOYEE INFORMATION*, is printed each time the format is invoked. It might be preferable to print only the title at the top of each page. Perl allows you to define a **top-of-the-page format** that will be invoked only when a new page is started. The default length for a page is 60 lines. After 60 lines are printed, Perl will print the top-of-the-page format at the top of the next page. (The default length can be changed by setting the special variable *$=* to another value.) In the following example, the *write* function sends all output to *STDOUT* each time the *while* loop is entered.

The example is shown before top-of-the-page formatting is applied.

EXAMPLE 17.3

```
(The File)
    $ cat datafile
    Tommy Tucker:55:500000:5/19/66
    Jack Sprat:44:45000:5/6/77
    Peter Piper:32:35000:4/12/93

(The Script)
    #!/bin/perl
1   open(DB, "datafile" ) || die "datafile: $!\n";
2   format STDOUT=
    ----------------------
    | EMPLOYEE INFORMATION |
    ----------------------
    Name: @<<<<<<<<<<<
        $name
    ----------------------
    Age: @##
        $age
    ----------------------
    Salary: @#####.##
        $salary
    ----------------------
    Date: @>>>>>>>>>
        $start
    .
3   while(<DB>){
4       ($name, $age, $salary, $start)=split(":");
5       write ;
    }

(Output)
----------------------
| EMPLOYEE INFORMATION |
----------------------
Name: Tommy Tucker
----------------------
Age: 55
----------------------
Salary: 50000.00
----------------------
Date: 5/19/66
```

EXAMPLE 17.3 (CONTINUED)

```
-----------------------
| EMPLOYEE INFORMATION |
-----------------------
Name: Jack Sprat
-----------------------
Age: 44
-----------------------
Salary: 45000.00
-----------------------
Date: 5/6/77
-----------------------
| EMPLOYEE INFORMATION |
-----------------------
Name: Peter Piper
-----------------------
Age: 32
-----------------------
Salary: 35000.00
-----------------------
Date: 4/12/54
```

EXPLANATION

1   The file, *datafile*, is opened for reading via the *DB* filehandle.
2   The format for *STDOUT* is created with picture lines and data.
3   The *while* loop reads one line at a time from the *DB* filehandle.
4   Each line is split by colons into an array of scalars.
5   The *write* function invokes the *STDOUT* format and sends the formatted line to *STDOUT*.

The format for top-of-the-page formatting follows.

FORMAT

```
format STDOUT_TOP=

    picture line
    value line (text to be formatted)

.(End of template)
```

Chapter 17 • Report Writing with Pictures

The keyword *format* is followed by the name of the filehandle appended with an underscore and the word *TOP*. If a picture line is included, the value line consists of the formatted text. Any text not formatted by a picture is printed literally. The period (.) terminates the top-of-page format template.

The *$%* is a special Perl variable that holds the number of the current page.

The following example shows the results of top-of-the-page formatting.

EXAMPLE 17.4

```
(The Script)
    #!/bin/perl
1   open(DB, "datafile" ) || die "datafile: $!\n";
2   format STDOUT_TOP=
3       -@||-
4       $%
    -----------------------
5   | EMPLOYEE INFORMATION |
    -----------------------
6   .
7   format STDOUT=

    Name: @<<<<<<<<<<<<
        $name
    -----------------------
    Age: @##
        $age
    -----------------------
    Salary: @#####.##
        $salary
    -----------------------
    Date: @>>>>>>>
        $start
    .
8   while(<DB>){
9       ($name, $age, $salary, $start)=split(":");
10      write ;
    }
```

EXAMPLE 17.4 (CONTINUED)

```
(Output)
            -  1  -
-----------------------
| EMPLOYEE INFORMATION |
-----------------------
Name: Tommy Tucker
-----------------------
Age: 55
-----------------------
Salary: 50000.00
-----------------------
Date: 5/19/66

Name: Jack Sprat
-----------------------
Age: 44
-----------------------
Salary: 45000.00
-----------------------
Date: 5/6/77

Name: Peter Piper
-----------------------
Age: 32
-----------------------
Salary: 35000.00
-----------------------
Date: 4/12/93
```

EXAMPLE 17.5

```
(The Script)
    #!/bin/perl
1   open(DB, "datafile" ) || die "datafile: $!\n";
2   open(OUT, ">outfile" )|| die "outfile: $!\n";
3   format OUT_TOP=    # New filehandle

4       -@||-
5       $%
    -----------------------
    | EMPLOYEE INFORMATION |
    -----------------------
    .
```

EXAMPLE 17.5 (CONTINUED)

```
    format OUT=
    Name: @<<<<<<<<<<<<
        $name
    -----------------------
    Age: @##
        $age
    -----------------------
    Salary: @#####.##
        $salary
     -----------------------
    Date: @>>>>>>>
          $start
    -----------------------
      .
    while(<DB>){
        ($name, $age, $salary, $start)=split(":");
6       write OUT;
    }
```

```
(Output)
$ cat outfile
        -  1 -
-----------------------
| EMPLOYEE INFORMATION |
-----------------------
Name: Tommy Tucker
-----------------------
Age: 55
-----------------------
Salary: 50000.00
-----------------------
Date: 5/19/66
-----------------------
Name: Jack Sprat
-----------------------
Age: 44
-----------------------
Salary: 45000.00
-----------------------
Date: 5/6/77
-----------------------
Name: Peter Pumpkin
-----------------------
Age: 32
-----------------------
Salary: 35000.00
-----------------------
Date: 4/12/93
-----------------------
```

17.1.4   The *select* Function

The *select* function is used to set the default filehandle for the *print* and *write* functions. When you have **selected** a particular filehandle with the *select* function, the *write* or *print* functions do not require an argument. The selected filehandle becomes the default when a format is invoked or when the *print* function is called.

The *select* function returns the scalar value of the *previously* selected filehandle.

If you have a number of formats with different names, the *$~* variable is used to hold the name of the report format for the currently selected output filehandle. The *write* and *print* functions will send their output to the currently selected output filehandle.

The *$^* variable holds the name of the top-of-page format for the currently selected output filehandle.

The *$.* variable holds the record number (similar to the *NR* variable in *awk*).

EXAMPLE 17.6

```
(The Script)
    #!/usr/bin/perl
    # Write an awklike report
1   open(MYDB, "> mydb") || die "Can't open mydb: $!\n";
2   $oldfilehandle= select(MYDB);
                    # MYDB is selected as the filehandle for write
3   format MYDB_TOP =
                    DATEBOOK INFO

    Name            Phone           Birthday        Salary

    .

4   format MYDB =
    @<<<@<<<<<<<<<<<<<<<<@<<<<<<<<<<<<@|||||||||@#######.##
    $.,         $name,          $phone,       $bd,        $sal
    .

5   format SUMMARY =

6   The average salary for all employees is $@#######.##.
                                            $total/$count
    The number of lines left on the page is @###.
                                            $-
    The default page length is @###.
                            $=
```

EXAMPLE 17.6 (CONTINUED)

```
7   .
    open(DB,"datebook") || die "Can't open datebook: $!\
    while(<DB>){
        ( $name, $phone, $address, $bd, $sal )=split(/:/);
8       write ;
        $count++;
        $total+=$sal;
    }
    close DB;

9   $~=SUMMARY;      # New report format for MYDB filehandle
10  write;

11  select ($oldfilehandle); # STDOUT is now selected for further
                             # writes or prints
12  print "Report Submitted On" , `date`;

(Output)
16  Report Submitted On Sat Mar 26 11:52:04 PST 2001

(The Report)
    $ cat mydb
                        DATEBOOK INFO
        Name            Phone            Birthday        Salary
1       Betty Boop      245-836-8357     6/23/23         14500.00
2       Igor Chevsky    385-375-8395     6/18/68         23400.00
3       Norma Corder    397-857-2735     3/28/45         245700.00
                 . . .
25      Paco Gutierrez  835-365-1284     2/28/53         123500.00
26      Ephram Hardy    293-259-5395     8/12/20         56700.00
27      James Ikeda     834-938-8376     12/1/38         45000.00
    The average salary for all employees is $82572.50.
    The number of lines left on the page is 32.
    The default page length is 60.
```

EXPLANATION

1   The filehandle *MYDB* is opened for writing.
2   The *select* function sets the default filehandle for the *write* and *print* functions to the filehandle, *MYDB*. The scalar *$oldfilehandle* is assigned the value of the **previously** assigned filehandle. The previously defined filehandle, in this example, is the default, *STDOUT*.
3   The top-of-the-page template is defined for filehandle *MYDB*.
4   The format for the body of the report is set for filehandle *MYDB*.
5   Another format template is defined with a new name, *SUMMARY*. This format can be invoked by assigning the format name *SUMMARY* to the special variable *$~*. (See line 9.)

6 The picture line is defined.

7 The format template is terminated.

8 The format is invoked and output is written to the currently selected filehandle, *MYDB*.

9 The *$~* variable is assigned the new format name. This format will be used for the currently selected filehandle, *MYDB*.

10 The *write* function invokes the format *SUMMARY* for the currently selected filehandle, *MYDB*.

11 The *select* function sets the filehandle to the value of *$oldfilehandle*, *STDOUT*. Future *write* and *print* functions will send their output to *STDOUT* unless another output filehandle is selected.

12 This line is sent to the screen.

17.1.5 Multiline Fields

If the value line contains more than one newline, the @ * variable is used to allow multiline fields. It is placed in a format template on a line by itself, followed by the multiline value.

EXAMPLE 17.7

```
(The Script)
    #!/bin/perl
1   $song="To market,\n
    to market, \nto buy a fat pig.\n";
2   format STDOUT=
3   @*
4   $song
5   @*
6   "\nHome again,\nHome again,\nJiggity, Jig!\n"

    .
    write;

(Output)
To market,
to market,
to buy a fat pig.
Home again,
Home again,
Jiggity, Jig!
```

EXPLANATION

1   The scalar *$song* contains newlines.
2   The format template is set for *STDOUT*.
3   The @ * fieldholder denotes that a multiline field will follow.
4   The value line contains the scalar *$song*, which evaluates to a multiline string.
5   The @ * fieldholder denotes that a multiline field will follow.
6   The value line contains a string embedded with newline characters.
7   End template definition.

17.1.6   Filling Fields

The caret (^) fieldholder allows you to create a filled paragraph containing text that will be placed according to the picture specification. If there is more text than will fit on a line, the text will wrap to the next line, etc., until all lines are printed in a paragraph block format. Each line of text is broken into words. Perl will place as many words as will fit on a specified line. The value line variable can be repeated over multiple lines. Only the remaining text for each line is printed rather than reprinting the entire value over again. If the number of value lines is more than the actual number of lines to be formatted, blank lines will appear.

Extra blank lines can be suppressed by using the special tilde (~) character, called the **suppression indicator**. If two consecutive tildes are placed on the value line, the field that is to be filled (preceded by a ^) will continue filling until all text has been blocked in the paragraph.

EXAMPLE 17.8

```
(The Script)
    #!/bin/perl
    $name="Hamlet";
    print "What is your favorite line from Hamlet? ";
1   $quote = <STDIN>;
2   format STDOUT=
3   Play: @<<<<<<<<<    Quotation:     ^<<<<<<<<<<<<<<<<<<<
4         $name,                       $quote
5                                      ^<<<<<<<<<<<<<<<<<<<
                                       $quote
                                       ^<<<<<<<<<<<<<<<<<<<
                                       $quote
6   ~                                  ^<<<<<<<<<<<<<<<<<<<
                                       $quote

    .
    write;
```

EXAMPLE 17.8 (CONTINUED)

```
(Output)
What is your favorite line from Hamlet? To be or not to be, that is
the question:
Whether 'tis nobler in the mind to suffer the slings and arrows of
outrageous fortune...

Play: Hamlet        Quotation: To be or not to be, that is the
                               question: Whether 'tis nobler in the
                               mind to suffer the slings and arrows
                               of outrageous fortune...
```

EXPLANATION

1   The user is asked for input and should type a line from Shakespeare's *Hamlet*. (The line wraps.)

2   The format template for *STDOUT* is defined.

3   The picture line contains two fields, one for the name of the play, *$name,* or *Hamlet*, and one for the line of user input, *$quote*. The ^ fieldholder is used to create a filled paragraph. The quote will be broken up into words that will fit over four lines. If there are more words than value lines, they will not be formatted. If there are less words than lines, blank lines will be suppressed due to the ~ character preceding the last picture line.

4   The value line contains the variables to be formatted according to the picture above them.

5   The second line contained in *$quote* is placed here if all of it did not fit on the first line.

6   If we run out of text after formatting three lines, the blank line will be suppressed.

EXAMPLE 17.9

```
(The Script)
    #!/bin/perl
    $name="Hamlet";
    print "What is your favorite line from Hamlet? ";
    $quote = <STDIN>;
    format STDOUT=
    Play: @<<<<<<<<<<   Quotation:   ^<<<<<<<<<<<<<<<<<<
1         $name,                     $quote
2         ~~                         ^<<<<<<<<<<<<<<<<<<
                                     $quote

    .
3   write;
```

EXAMPLE 17.9 (CONTINUED)

```
(Output)
What is your favorite line from Hamlet? To be or not to be, that is
the question:
Whether 'tis nobler in the mind to suffer the slings and arrows of
outrageous fortune...

Play: Hamlet          Quotation: To be or not to be,
                                 that is the
                                 question: Whether
                                 'tis nobler in the
                                 mind to suffer the
                                 slings and arrows of
                                 outrageous fortune...
```

EXPLANATION

1   The value line is set. It will contain the name of the play and the quotation.
2   Using two tildes (suppression indicators) tells Perl to continue filling the paragraph until all of the text in *$quote* is printed or a blank line is encountered.
3   The *write* function invokes the format.

18

SEND IT OVER THE NET AND SOCK IT TO 'EM!

18.1 Networking and Perl

Because sharing information and transferring files among computers are so integral to everything we do, Perl offers a number of functions to obtain network information in your program. In order to write programs utilizing interprocess communication (sockets, message queues, etc.), it is essential to understand some of the basic terminology associated with the network. The following discussion is merely an introduction to some of the common networking vernacular, so that when you try to dissect or write Perl programs that require these functions, you will not have to search through all your *C* books or wade through the manual pages to figure out what is going on.

18.2 Client/Server Model

Most network applications use a client/server model. The server provides some service to one or more clients. The client may request a service from a server on the same machine or on a remote machine. Server programs provide such services as e-mail, Telnet, and FTP. In order for the client and server to talk to each other, a connection is made between the two processes, often by utilizing sockets. Today, one of the most well-known client/server models is the client (browser)/server (Web server) model used by the Web.

18.3 Network Protocols (TCP/IP)

When sending data over a network, there must be some reliable way to get the data from one machine to another. In order to facilitate this complicated process, networks are organized in a series of layers, each layer offering a specific networking service to the next layer. The layers are independent and have clearly defined interfaces for supplying functions to the next layer. A high layer passes data and information to the layer below it, until the bottom layer is reached. At the bottom layer, two machines can physically communicate with each other. The rules and procedures used for one network layer on a machine to communicate with its counterpart network layer on another machine are called **protocols**. The most popular software networking protocols in UNIX are Ethernet, IP, TCP, and UDP.

18.3.1   Ethernet Protocol (Hardware)

The Ethernet layer is the physical layer of the network. Any host connected to the Ethernet bus has physical access to data sent over the network. The Ethernet protocol prepares the data for transmission across a wire. It organizes the data in frames using 48-bit Ethernet source and destination addresses. The Ethernet layer, the lowest layer, represents the transfer of data on the physical network.

18.3.2   Internet Protocol (IP)

The IP layer is above the Ethernet layer; it prepares the data for routing on independent networks. IP uses a 4-byte Internet protocol address (IP address), and data is organized in pieces of information called **packets**. A packet contains an IP header with source and destination addresses, a protocol type, and a data portion. Although the IP protocol is more complicated than the Ethernet protocol, it is connectionless and unreliable in delivering packets. It doesn't guarantee how or even that the data will be received, but if the data being sent is too large, IP will break it down into smaller units. The IP protocol hides the underlying differences among the different networks from the user.

18.3.3   Transmission Control Protocol (TCP)

Although the IP layer provides some flow control, it is not guaranteed to be reliable; that is, the data may not be received in the same order it was sent or it may never get to its destination at all. The TCP protocol provides a reliable end-to-end service and flow of control analogous to making a phone call. Once the connection is made, both sides can communicate with each other, and even if they talk at the same time, the messages are received in the same order they were sent. Programs that use TCP are *rlogin*, *rsh*, *rcp*, and *telnet*.

18.3.4   User Datagram Protocol (UDP)

UDP is an alternative to TCP. It is used in applications that do not require a continuous connection and are sending short messages periodically with no concern whether some of the data is lost. A UDP datagram is similar to sending a letter in the mail: Each packet has an address, there is no guaranteed delivery time or sequencing, and duplicate packets may be sent.[1] This method prevents programs from hanging when a return is expected. Examples of programs that use this protocol are *rwho* and *ruptime*.

---

1. Rieken, B., and Weiman, L., *Adventures in Unix, Network Applications Programming*, John Wiley & Sons, Wiley Professional Computing: New York, 1992, p. 7.

18.4 Network Addressing

Networks consist of a number of interconnected machines called **hosts**. The system administrator assigns the hostname when a new machine is added to the network. Each host on a TCP/IP/Ethernet network has a name and three types of addresses: an Ethernet address, an IP address, and a TCP service port number. When information is passed from one layer to another in a network, the packet contains header information, including the addresses needed to send the packet to its next destination.

18.4.1   The *pack* and *unpack* Functions

Often, the addresses returned by the networking functions are in a binary format. In order to convert those addresses into an ASCII format, the Perl's *unpack* function can be used. Conversely, in order to pack an array or list into a binary format, the *pack* function is used. Before getting into all the details, let's review how the *pack* function works. (See "The pack and unpack Functions" on page 531.)

FORMAT

```
pack(Template, Array);
```

EXAMPLE 18.1

```
(The Script)
1   $bytes=pack("c4", 80,101,114,108);
2   print "$bytes\n";

(Output)
Perl
```

EXPLANATION

1   The first element in the list, the Template (see Table 18.1), is composed of the type and the number of values to be packed, in this example, four signed characters. The rest of the list consists of the decimal values for characters *P*, *e*, *r*, and *l*. This list is packed into a binary structure. The string containing the packed structure is returned and stored in *$bytes* (see your ASCII table).

2   The four-byte character string is printed.

Table 18.1   The Template *pack* and *unpack*—Types and Values

Template	Description
a	An ASCII string (null padded)
A	An ASCII string (space padded)
b	A bit string (low-to-high order, like *vec*)
B	A bit string (high-to-low order)
c	A signed *char* value
C	An unsigned *char* value
d	A double-precision float in the native format
f	A single-precision float in the native format
h	A hexadecimal string (low nybble first, to high)
H	A hexadecimal string (high nybble first)
i	A signed integer
I	An unsigned integer
l	A signed long value
L	An unsigned long value
n	A short in "network" (big-endian) order
N	A long in "network" (big-endian) order
p	A pointer to a null-terminated string
P	A pointer to a structure (fixed-length string)
q	A signed 64-bit value
Q	An unsigned 64-bit value
s	A signed short value (16-bit)
S	An unsigned short value (16-bit)
u	A uuencoded string
v	A short in "VAX" (little-endian) order
V	A long in "VAX" (little-endian) order
w	A BER compressed unsigned integer in base 128, high bit first
x	A null byte
X	Back up a byte
@	Null fill to absolute position

18.4.2   Ethernet Addresses

Since the Ethernet address is usually burned into the PROM when the machine is manufactured, it is not a number that is assigned by a system administrator. It is simply used to identify that particular piece of hardware. The */etc/ethers* (UCB) file contains the Ethernet addresses and hostnames for a particular network.

18.4.3   IP Addresses

The IP address is a 32-bit number assigned by the system administrator to a particular host on the network. If a host is connected to more than one network, it must have an IP address for each of the networks. It consists of a set of four decimal numbers (often called a four-octet address) separated by dots (e.g., 129.150.28.56). The first part of the address identifies the network to which the host is connected, and the rest of the address represents the host. The addresses are divided into classes (A through C). The classes determine exactly what part of the address belongs to the network and what part belongs to the host. The */etc/hosts* file contains the address of your host machine, the host's name, and any aliases associated with it. (See the *gethostent* and related functions.)

18.4.4   Port Numbers

When serving a number of user processes, a server may have a number of clients requesting a particular service that use either the TCP or UDP protocol. When delivering information to a particular application layer, these protocols use a 16-bit integer **port number** to identify a particular process on a given host. TCP and UDP port numbers between 0 and 255, called **well-known ports**, are reserved for common services. (Some operating systems reserve additional ports for privileged programs.)[2] The most common services are Telnet and FTP with TCP port numbers 23 and 21, respectively. If you write a server application that will use either the TCP or UDP protocols, the application must be assigned a unique port number. This port number should be some number outside the range of the special reserved port numbers. The */etc/services* file contains a list of the well-known port numbers.

18.4.5   Perl Protocol Functions

The following Perl functions allow you to retrieve information from the */etc/protocols* file. The functions are named after the system calls and library functions found in Sections 2 and 3 of the UNIX manual pages.

The *getprotoent* Function.   The *getprotoent* function reads the next line from the network protocols database, */etc/protocol,* and returns a list. The entries are the official names of the protocols, a list of aliases or alternate names for the protocol, and the protocol num-

---

2. Stevens, W. R., Wright, G. R., *TCP/IP Illustrated, Volume 1: The Protocols*, Addison Wesley Longman, 1993, p. 13.

ber. The *setprotoent* function opens and rewinds the */etc/protocols* file. If *STAYOPEN* is non-zero, the database will not be closed after successive calls to the *getprotoent*. The *endprotoent* function closes the database.

FORMAT

```
getprotoent;
setprotoent (STAYOPEN);
endprotoent;
```

EXAMPLE 18.2

```
(The Script)
1   while (($name,  $aliases, $proto ) = getprotent){
2   printf "name=%-5s,aliases=%-6sproto=%-8s\n",
            $name, $aliases, $proto;
    }

(Output)
2    name=ip,     aliases=IP     proto=0
     name=icmp,   aliases=ICMP   proto=1
     name=igmp,   aliases=OGMP   proto=2
     name=ggp,    aliases=GGP    proto=3
     name=tcp,    aliases=TCP    proto=6
     name=pup,    aliases=PUP    proto=12
     name=udp,    aliases=IDP    proto=17
```

EXPLANATION

1   The *getprotoent* function gets an entry from the */etc/protocols* file. The loop will read through the entire file. The name of the protocol, any aliases associated with it, and the protocol number are retrieved.
2   Each entry and its values are printed.

The *getprotobyname* Function.   The *getprotobyname* function is similar to the *getprotoent* above in that it gets an entry from the */etc/protocols* file. *getprotobyname* takes the protocol name as an argument and returns its name, any aliases, and its protocol number.

FORMAT

```
getprotobyname(NAME);
```

EXAMPLE 18.3

```
(The Script)
1   ($name,  $aliases, $proto ) = getprotobyname('tcp');
    print "name=$name\taliases=$aliases\t$protocol number=$proto\n";

(Output)
name=tcp      aliases=TCP     protocol number=6
```

EXPLANATION

1   The name of the protocol, any alias name, and the protocol number are retrieved from the */etc/protocols* function. The name of the protocol, *tcp*, is passed as the *NAME* argument.

The *getprotobynumber* Function.   The *getprotobynumber* function is similar to the *getprotoent* function above in that it gets an entry from the */etc/protocols* file. The *getprotobynumber* takes the protocol number as an argument and returns the name of the protocol, any aliases, and its protocol number.

FORMAT

```
getprotobynumber(NUMBER);
```

EXAMPLE 18.4

```
(The Script)
1   ($name,  $aliases, $proto) = getprotobynumber(0);
    print "name=$name\taliases=$aliases\t$protocol number=$proto\n";

(Output)
name=ip     aliases=IP    protocol number=0
```

EXPLANATION

1   *getprotobynumber* retrieves an entry from the */etc/protocols* file based on the protocol number passed as an argument. It returns the name of the protocol, any aliases, and the protocol number.

18.4.6   Perl's Server Functions

These functions let you look up information in the network services file, */etc/services*.

The *getservent* Function.   The *getservent* function reads the next line from the */etc/services* file. If *STAYOPEN* is non-zero, the */etc/services* file will not be closed after each call.

FORMAT

```
getservent;
setservent (STAYOPEN);
endservent;
```

EXAMPLE 18.5

```
(The Script)
1   setservent(1 );
2   ($name, $aliases, $port, $proto) = getservent;
3   print
    "Name=$name\nAliases=$aliases\nPort=$port\nProtocol=$protocol\n";
            < program continues here >

4   ($name, $aliases, $port, $proto) = getservent;
                    # Retrieves the next entry in /etc/services
5   print
    "Name=$name\nAliases=$aliases\nPort=$port\nProtocol=$protocol\n";
6   endservent;

(Output)
3   Name=tcpmux
    Aliases=
    Port=1
    Protocol=tcp
5   Name=echo
    Aliases=
    Port=7
    Protocol=tcp
```

EXPLANATION

1   The *setservent* function guarantees that the */etc/services* file remains open after each call if the *STAYOPEN* flag is non-zero.
2   The *getservent* function returns the name of the service, any aliases associated with the services, the port number, and the network protocol.
3   The retrieved values are printed.
4   The second call to *getservent* retrieves the next line from the */etc/services* file.
5   The retrieved values are printed.
6   The *endservent* function closes the network file.

The *getservbyname* Function.   The *getservbyname* function translates the service port name to its corresponding port number.

FORMAT

```
getservbyname(NAME, PROTOCOL);
```

EXAMPLE 18.6

```
($name,$aliases,$port,$protocol)=getservbyname('telnet', 'tcp');
```

EXPLANATION

The name of the service is *telnet* and the protocol is *tcp*. The service name, aliases, the port number, and the protocol are returned.

The *getservbyport* Function.   The *getservbyport* function retrieves information from the */etc/services* file.

FORMAT

```
getservbyport(PORT, PROTOCOL);
```

EXAMPLE 18.7

```
(The Script)
   #!/bin/perl
   print "What is the port number? ";
   chop($PORT=<>);

   print "What is the protocol? ";
   chop($PROTOCOL=<>);

1  ($name,  $aliases, $port, $proto ) = getservbyport(
                                        $PORT, $PROTOCOL);
   print "The getservbyport function returns:
      name=$name
      aliases=$aliases
      port number=$port
      prototype=$protocol \n";
```

EXAMPLE 18.7 (CONTINUED)

```
(Output)
What is the port number?  517
What is the protocol?  udp
The getservbyport function returns:
    name=talk
    aliases=talk
    port number=517
    prototype=udp
```

EXPLANATION

1   The well-known port number, *517*, and the protocol name, *udp*, are passed to the *getservbyport* function. The name of the service, any aliases, the port number, and the protocol name are returned.

18.4.7   Perl's Host Information Functions

These functions allow you to retrieve information from the */etc/hosts* file. They are named after the system library routines found in Section 3 of the UNIX *man* pages.

The *gethostent* Function.   The *gethostent* function returns a list consisting of the next line from the */etc/hosts* file. The entries are the official name of the host machine; a list of aliases or alternate names for the host; the type of address being returned; the length, in bytes, of the address; and a list of network addresses, in byte order, for the named host.

FORMAT

```
gethostent;
sethostent(STAYOPEN);
endhostent;
```

EXAMPLE 18.8

```
(The Script)
   #!/bin/perl
1  while ( ($name, $aliases, $addrtype, $length, @addrs) =
           gethostent ){
2      ($a, $b, $c, $d) = unpack ( 'C4', $addrs[0]);
3      print "The name of the host is $name.\n";
4      print "Local host address (unpacked) $a.$b.$c.$d\n";
   }
```

EXAMPLE 18.8 (CONTINUED)

```
(Output)
3    The name of the host is localhost.
4    Local host address (unpacked) 127.0.0.1
     The name of the host is jody.
     Local host address (unpacked) 129.150.28.56
```

EXPLANATION

1 The *gethostent* function retrieves the next entry from the */etc/hosts* file.
2 The raw address returned by the *gethostent* function is unpacked into four bytes (*C4*) so that it can be printed.
3 The name of the host, *jody*, is printed.
4 The local host's IP address is printed.

The *gethostbyaddr* Function. The *gethostbyaddr* function translates a network address to its corresponding names. It retrieves the information from the */etc/hosts* file for a host by passing a raw address as an argument. The entry consists of the official name of the host machine; a list of aliases or alternate names for the host; the type of address being returned; the length, in bytes, of the address; and a list of network addresses, in byte order, for the named host.

FORMAT

```
gethostbyaddr(ADDRESS, DOMAIN_NUMBER);
```

EXAMPLE 18.9

```
(The Script)
     #!/bin/perl
1    $address=pack("C4", 127,0,0,1);
2    ($name, $aliases, $addrtype, $length, @addrs) = gethostbyaddr
        ($address,2);
3    ($a, $b, $c, $d) = unpack ( 'C4', $addrs[0]);
4    print "Hostname Is $name and the Internet address Is
        $a.$b.$c.$d.\n";

(Output)
Hostname is localhost and the Internet address is 127.0.0.1.
```

1 The Internet address is *127.0.0.1*. It is packed into 4 bytes and this address is used by the *gethostbyaddr* function.
2 The raw address and the value of *AF_INET* (found in */usr/lnclude/sys/socket.h*) are passed to the *gethostbyaddr* function.
3 The raw address is unpacked into 4 bytes.
4 The name of the host and Internet address are printed.

The *gethostbyname* Function. The *gethostbyname* function returns an entry from the */etc/hosts* file for the name of a specific host passed as an argument. The entry consists of the official name of the host machine; a list of aliases or alternate names for the host; the type of address being returned; the length, in bytes, of the address; and a list of network addresses, in byte order, for the named host.

FORMAT

```
gethostbyname(NAME);
```

EXAMPLE 18.10

```
($name, $aliases, $addtrtype, $length,
     @addrs)=gethostbyname("dolphin");
```

EXPLANATION

(See the *gethostent* function, above, for explanation.)

18.5 Sockets

Sockets were first developed at the University of California, Berkeley, in 1982 in order to support interprocess communication on networks. The client/server model is used for interprocess communication through sockets. Not all operating systems support sockets. If your system is one of these, the socket examples shown here will not work.

Sockets are a software abstraction representing the endpoints between two communicating processes, a server and a client; in other words, sockets allow processes talk to each other. The communicating processes can be on the same machine or on different machines. The server process creates the socket. The client process knows the socket by name. In order to ensure where the data is coming from or going to on a network, the socket uses IP and port addresses. A program using a socket opens the socket (similar to opening a file), and once the socket is opened, I/O operations can be performed for reading and writing information to the communicating processes. When a file is opened, a file descriptor is returned. When a socket is opened, a socket descriptor is returned to the server and one is returned to the client. The socket interface, however, is much more complex than working with files, since communication is often done across networks.

Remote login and file transfer programs are common utilities that communicate across a network through the use of sockets.

18.5.1   Types of Sockets

Every socket has a type of communication path to identify how the data will be transferred through the socket. The two most common types of sockets, *SOCK_STREAM* and *SOCK_DGRAM*, utilize the TCP and UDP protocols, respectively.

There are other less common types of sockets, such as *SOCK_SEQPACKET* and *SOCK_RAW*, but we will not discuss those here.

Stream Sockets.   The *SOCK_STREAM* type of stream socket provides a reliable, connection-oriented, sequenced, two-way service. It provides for error detection and flow control, and it removes duplicate segments of data. The underlying protocol is TCP. (See "Network Protocols (TCP/IP)" on page 599.)

Datagram Sockets.   The *SOCK_DGRAM* type of datagram socket provides a connectionless service. Packets sent may be received in any order or may not be received on the other end at all. There is no guarantee of delivery and packets may be duplicated. The underlying protocol is UDP. (See "User Datagram Protocol (UDP)" on page 600.)

18.5.2   Socket Domains

When a socket is opened, a number of system calls are issued describing how the socket is to be used. The process must specify a communication domain, also called an **address family**, to identify the way the socket is named and what protocols and addresses are needed in order to send or receive data. The domain of a socket identifies where the server and client reside—on the same machine, on the Internet, or on a Xerox network.

The two standard domains are the **UNIX domain** and the **Internet domain**. When using sockets for interprocess communication, the UNIX domain is used for processes communicating on the same machine, whereas the Internet domain is used for processes communicating on remote machines using the TCP/IP protocols. (The *AF_NS* **domain** is used for processes on a Xerox network.)

The UNIX Domain and the *AF_UNIX* **Family.**   If the communication is between two processes on a local machine, the address family (AF) is called *AF_UNIX*. The UNIX domain supports the *SOCK_STREAM* socket type and the *SOCK_DGRAM* socket type. The *SOCK_STREAM* type in the UNIX domain provides a bidirectional communication between processes, similar to the *pipe* facility. *SOCK_STREAM* is a reliable byte-stream transfer between processes. The datagram sockets are unreliable, not often used, and cause the socket to behave like message queues or telegrams.

Sockets in the UNIX domain have pathnames in the UNIX file system. The *ls -l* command lists the file as a socket if the first character is an *s* (see Example 18.11). In the system file */usr/include/sys/socket.h*, the *AF_UNIX* family is assigned the constant value, *1*.

EXAMPLE 18.11

```
$ ls -1F greetings
srwxrwxrwx                   1 ellie     0 Apr 26 09:31  greetings=
```

The Internet Domain and the *AF_INET* Family.   The Internet domain sockets, identified as *AF_INET*, are used for interprocess communication between processes on different computers. The Internet domain also supports the socket types *SOCK_STREAM* and *SOCK_DGRAM*.

The Internet socket is defined by its IP address to identify the Internet host and its port number to identify the port on the host machine.

The underlying protocol for *SOCK_STREAM* is TCP. The underlying protocol for *SOCK_DGRAM* is UDP. In the system file */usr/include/sys/socket.h*, the *AF_INET* family is defined as the constant *2*.

Socket Addresses.   A socket, once created, needs an address so that data can be sent to it. In the *AF_UNIX* domain, the address is a filename, but in the *AF_INET* domain it is an IP address and a port number.

18.5.3 Creating a Socket

The *socket* function creates the socket and returns a filehandle for the socket. In the server this socket is called the rendezvous socket.

FORMAT

```
socket(SOCKET_FILEHANDLE, DOMAIN, TYPE, PROTOCOL);
```

EXAMPLE 18.12

```
    $AF_UNIX=1;
    $SOCK_STREAM=1;
    $PROTOCOL=0;

1   socket(COMM_SOCKET, $AF_UNIX, $SOCK_STREAM, $PROTOCOL);
```

EXPLANATION

1   In this example, the *socket* function creates a filehandle called *COMM_SOCKET*. The domain or family is UNIX, the socket type is *STREAM*, and the protocol is assigned *0*, which allows the system to choose the correct protocol for this socket type.

18.5.4 Binding an Address to a Socket Name

The *bind* Function. The *bind* function attaches an address or a name to a *SOCKET* filehandle. (See Example programs at the end of this chapter.)

FORMAT

```
bind(SOCKET_FILEHANDLE, NAME);
```

EXAMPLE 18.13

```
1   bind(COMM_SOCKET, "/home/jody/ellie/perl/tserv");
2   bind(COMM_SOCKET, $socket_address);
```

EXPLANATION

1   When using the UNIX domain, the socket filehandle *COMM_SOCKET* is bound to a UNIX pathname.
2   When using the Internet domain, the socket filehandle *COMM_SOCKET* is bound to the packed address for the socket type.

18.5.5   Creating a Socket Queue

The *listen* Function.   The *listen* function waits for *accepts* on the socket and specifies the number of connection requests to be queued before rejecting further requests. Imagine having call waiting on your phone with up to five callers queued.[3] If the number of client requests exceeds the queue size, an error is returned. The function returns true if successful, false otherwise. The error code is stored as *$!*.

FORMAT

```
listen(SOCKET_FILEHANDLE, QUEUE_SIZE);
```

EXAMPLE 18.14

```
listen(SERVERSOCKET, 5);
```

EXPLANATION

The number of waiting connections in the queue is set to *5*. The *listen* function queues the incoming client requests for the *accept* function (see below).

18.5.6   Waiting for a Client Request

The *accept* Function.   The *accept* function in the server process waits for a request from the client to arrive. If there is a queue of requests, the first request is removed from the queue when a connection is made. The *accept* function then opens a new socket filehandle with the same attributes as the original or **generic** socket, also called the **rendezvous socket,** and attaches it to the client's socket. The new socket is ready to communicate with the client socket. The generic socket is now available to accept additional connections. The *accept* function returns true if successful, false otherwise. The error code is stored as *$!*.

FORMAT

```
accept(NEWSOCKET, GENERICSOCKET);
```

---

3. Wall, L., and Schwartz, R. L., *Programming Perl*, 2nd ed., O'Reilly & Associates: Sebastopol, CA, 1998,
    p. 158.

EXAMPLE 18.15

```
accept (NEWSOCK, RENDEZ_SOCK );
```

EXPLANATION

The server process uses the *accept* function to accept requests from clients. It takes the first pending request from the queue and creates a new socket filehandle, *NEWSOCK*, with the same properties as *RENDEZ_SOCK* filehandle, also called the generic or rendezvous socket.

18.5.7 Establishing a Socket Connection

The *connect* Function. The *connect* function uses the socket filehandle and the address of the server socket to which it will connect. It makes a rendezvous with the *accept* function in the server. After the connection is made, data can be transferred. If the UNIX domain is used, the pathname of the UNIX file is provided. If the Internet domain is used, the address is a packed network address of the proper type for the server. It returns true if successful, false otherwise. An error code is stored as *$!*.

FORMAT

```
connect(SOCKET, ADDRESS);
```

EXAMPLE 18.16

```
1   connect(CLIENTSOCKET, "/home/joe/sock" );
2   connect(CLIENTSOCKET, $packed_address);
```

EXPLANATION

1   In the UNIX domain, a UNIX pathname is attached to the filehandle, *CLIENT-SOCKET*.

2   In the Internet domain, a packed network address is attached to the filehandle, *CLIENTSOCKET*. The address is obtained from the *gethostbyname* function and is packed with the Perl *pack* function. For example:
    $hostname="houston";
    $port=9876;
    $AF_INET=2;
    $SOCK_STREAM=1;
    ($name, $aliases, $type, $len, $address)=gethostbyname($hostname);
    $packed_address=pack(S n a4 x8, $AF_INET, $port, $address);

18.5.8   Socket Shutdown

The *shutdown* function.   The *shutdown* function shuts down a socket connection as specified. If the *HOW* argument is *0*, further *receives* on the socket will be refused. If the *HOW* argument is *1*, further *sends* on the socket will be refused, and if the argument is *2*, all *sends* and *receives* are stopped.

FORMAT

```
shutdown(SOCKET, HOW);
```

EXAMPLE 18.17

```
shutdown(COMM_SOCK, 2);
```

EXPLANATION

The socket filehandle *COMM_SOCK* will disallow further *sends* or *receives*. It is shut down.

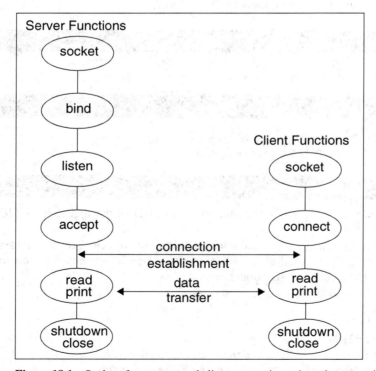

Figure 18.1   Sockets for a server and client connection-oriented communication.

18.6 Client/Server Programs

The sample programs shown here were tested on Sun workstations running SunOS 4.1.3 and SunOS 5.3. These programs are examples of stream sockets for the UNIX and Internet domains. Although datagrams (UDP) are supported, they are unreliable and delivery of packets is not guaranteed. They are used in the Internet domain by programs such as *rwho* and *ruptime*, but are rarely used in the UNIX domain.

18.6.1 Connection-Oriented Sockets on the Same Machine

The following scripts are very simple examples of the client/server model utilizing stream sockets for communication endpoints. Both client and server reside on the same machine, and the client simply reads a greetings message from the server and prints the message on the screen. There is little error checking or signal handling. The programs are simple demonstrations of how the above-named socket functions are used. (For socket functions not included in this chapter, see Table A.1 in Appendix A.)

The Server Program

EXAMPLE 18.18

```
(The Script)
   #!/bin/perl

   # The server and the client are on the same machine.
   print "Server Started.\n";
1  $AF_UNIX=1;      # The domain is AF_UNIX
2  $SOCK_STREAM=1;  # The type is SOCK_STREAM
3  $PROTOCOL=0;     # Protocol 0 is accepted as the "correct
                    # protocol" by most systems.

4  socket(SERVERSOCKET, $AF_UNIX, $SOCK_STREAM, $PROTOCOL) ||
       die " Socket $!\n";
   print "socket OK\n";
5  $name="./greetings";  # The name of the socket is associated
                         # within the file system
   unlink "./greetings" || warn "$name: $!\n";

6  bind(SERVERSOCKET, $name) || die "Bind $!\n";
   print "bind OK\n";

7  listen(SERVERSOCKET, 5) || die "Listen $!\n";
   print "listen OK\n";

   while(1){
```

EXAMPLE 18.18 (CONTINUED)

```
8       accept(NEWSOCKET, SERVERSOCKET ) || die "Accept $!\n";
        # Accept client connection

9       $pid=fork || die "Fork: $!\n";
10      if ($pid == 0 ){
11          print (NEWSOCKET "Greetings from your server!!\n";

12          close(NEWSOCKET);
            exit(0);
        }
        else{
13          close (NEWSOCKET);
        }
    }
```

EXPLANATION

1   The domain is set to UNIX. The client and server are on the same machine.
2   The socket type is *SOCK_STREAM*, a connection-oriented, byte-stream type of communication.
3   The *protocol* is set to *0*. This value is handled by the system if set to *0*.
4   The *socket* function is called. The filehandle *SERVERSOCKET* is created in the server.
5   The pathname of the file *greetings* is the name in the file system the socket *SERVERSOCKET* will be associated with. It will be the real name to which the socket filehandle is attached. If the file already exists, it will be removed with the *unlink* function.
6   The socket filehandle is bound to the UNIX file *greetings*.
7   The *listen* function allows the process to specify how many pending connections it will accept from the client. The requests are queued and the maximum number that can be queued is five.
8   The *accept* function waits for a client request and creates a new socket filehandle, *NEWSOCKET*, with the same attributes as the original filehandle, *SERVERSOCKET* (also called the rendezvous socket). *NEWSOCKET* is the socket that actually communicates with the client. The rendezvous socket remains available to accept future connections.
9   A child process is created with the *fork* function. Now both parent and child are in execution.
10 If the *pid* returned is zero, the child is in execution. If the pid is non-zero, the parent is in execution.
11 If the child process is in execution (pid is zero), the greetings message is written to the socket, *NEWSOCKET*. The server is communicating with its client.
12 The *NEWSOCKET* filehandle is closed by the child and the child exits.
13 The *NEWSOCKET* filehandle is closed by the parent so that it can receive more client requests.

The Client Program

EXAMPLE 18.19

```
(The Script)
    #!/usr/bin/perl
    print "Hi I'm the client\n";

1   $AF_UNIX=1;
2   $SOCK_STREAM=1;
3   $PROTOCOL=0;

4   socket(CLIENTSOCKET, $AF_UNIX, $SOCK_STREAM, $PROTOCOL);
5   $name="./greetings";

    do{
        # Client connects  with server
6       $result = connect(CLIENTSOCKET, "$name" );
        if ($result != 1 ){
            sleep(1);
        }
7   }while($result !=  1 );  # Loop until a connection is made
8   read(CLIENTSOCKET, $buf, 500);
9   print STDOUT "$buf\n";
10  close (CLIENTSOCKET);
    exit(0);
```

EXPLANATION

1   The domain is *AF_UNIX*. The client and server reside on the same machine. The value assigned to the scalar is the value that is assigned to the *AF_UNIX* macro in the system file */usr/include/sys/socket.h*. The *socket* function requires these values as arguments in order to create a socket.

2   The type of socket is *SOCK_STREAM*, a sequenced, reliable, bidirectional method of communication between the client and server. The value assigned to the scalar is the value that is assigned to the *SOCK_STREAM* macro in the system file */usr/include/sys/socket.h*. The *socket* function requires these values as arguments in order to create a socket.

3   The protocol value is handled by the system calls involved in creating the socket. It determines how the socket is implemented at a low level. By assigning *0* as the protocol value, the *socket* function considers this the "correct protocol"; that is, you don't have to worry about the details.

EXPLANATION (CONTINUED)

4 The *socket* function creates a socket filehandle called *CLIENTSOCKET*.

5 The socket filehandle *CLIENTSOCKET* will be associated with the UNIX file *greetings*.

6 The *connect* function connects the *CLIENTSOCKET* filehandle to the UNIX file *greetings* so that the client can communicate with the server. The return from the function is true if it succeeded, and false otherwise.

7 Until the connection is made, the program loops.

8 Now that the connection has been made, the client reads as many as 500 bytes from the server socket and stores the bytes in the scalar, *$buf*.

9 The contents of *$buf* are printed to *STDOUT*.

10 The *CLIENTSOCKET* filehandle is closed. For more control, the *shutdown* function should be used.

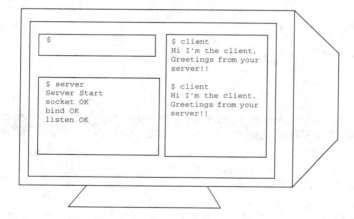

Figure 18.2   The output.

18.6.2   Connection-Oriented Sockets on Remote Machines (Internet Clients and Servers)

The following program was executed on two Sun workstations. The server's hostname is *scarecrow*, running SunOS 5.3, and the client's hostname is *houston*, running SunOS 4.1.3. In this program, the client on one machine asks the server on another machine for the time. The server sends the time to the client socket, and the client prints the time in readable format to the screen. These examples do not take advantage of Perl 5's *Socket.pm* module in the standard library. All values are hardcoded and therefore are not necessarily portable from one machine to another. (See "The Socket.pm Module" on page 625.)

EXAMPLE 18.20

```perl
#!/usr/bin/perl  -T
# timeserver -- a Time Server program,
# opens a Rendezvous Socket on port 9876
# and waits for a client to connect.
# When each client connects, this server determines the machine
# time on its host and writes the value on the communication
# socket to the client.
#
#                      Usage: timeserver [port number]
#
use strict;
use warnings;
1   ($port)=@ARGV;
2   $port=9876 unless $port;
3   $AF_INET=2;
4   $SOCK_STREAM = 1;
5   $sockaddr = 'S n a4 x8';
6   ($name,$aliases,$proto)=getprotobyname('tcp');
7   if($port !~ /^\d+$/){
8       ($name, $aliases, $port)=getservbyport($port,'tcp');
    }
    print "Port = $port\n";
9   $this = pack($sockaddr, $AF_INET, $port, "\0\0\0\0");
10  select(COMM_SOCK); $| = 1; select (STDOUT);
        # Create R_SOCKET, the rendezvous socket descriptor
11  socket(R_SOCKET, $AF_INET, $SOCK_STREAM, $proto ) ||
            die "socket: $!\n";
        # Bind R_SOCKET to my address, $this
12  bind(R_SOCKET, $this) || die "bind: $!\n";
13  listen(R_SOCKET, 5) || die "connect: $!\n";
        # Infinite loop - wait until client connects,
        # then serve the client
    while(1){
14      accept(COMM_SOCK, R_SOCKET) || die "$!\n";
15      $now = time;
16      print COMM_SOCK $now;
    }
```

EXPLANATION

1 A hostname may be passed as a command line argument (see line 7).

2 If the *ARGV* array is empty, the scalar *$port* is assigned the value *9876*. This port number is assigned by the programmer to a number outside the reserved port numbers. On a Sun system, port numbers through *1024* are reserved. The port number *9876* is also called an *ephemeral port*, i.e., it is short-lived.

3 The scalar *$AF_INET* is assigned the value *2*, the constant value assigned to the macro *AF_INET* in */usr/include/sys/socket.h*. This number represents the Internet domain, *AF_INET*.

4 The type of socket is *SOCK_STREAM*, assigned the value of *1* in */usr/include/ sys/socket.h*.

5 The *pack* function will use this format for the socket address.

6 The *getprotobyname* function returns the official protocol name, any aliases, and the protocol number using the *tcp* protocol as the name.

7 If the scalar *$port* is not an assigned number, but the name of the server machine was passed in at the command line, the *getservbyport* function will return the correct port number for the server using the *tcp* protocol.

8 The *port number* is printed.

9 The address for this Internet domain and port number is packed into a binary structure consisting of an unsigned short, a short in "network" order, four ASCII characters, and 8 null bytes. In comparable *C* programs, you will note that the method for getting addresses is by using a *sockaddr* (see line 5) structure (see */usr/include/ sys/socket.h*). Perl handles most of this for you.

10 The *socket* filehandle is selected as the current default handle for output. The *$|* special variable is set to *1*, forcing buffers to be flushed on every *write* or *print*. The *stdout* filehandle is normally line buffered when sending output to a terminal and block buffered otherwise. When output is going to a pipe or socket, the buffers will be flushed.

11 The *socket* function creates the rendezvous socket filehandle, *R_SOCKET*.

12 The *bind* function binds the socket filehandle to the correct address for the server.

13 The *listen* function sets the queue limit to *5*, the maximum for pending requests from the client.

14 The *accept* function waits for a client request, and when it gets one, accepts it by creating a new socket filehandle called *COMM_SOCK* with all the same attributes as *R_SOCKET*. *COMM_SOCK* is the server socket that will communicate with the client.

15 The *time* function returns the number of non–leap-year seconds since Jan. 1, 1970, UTC.

16 The *time* is sent to the socket filehandle, *COMM_SOCK*.

EXAMPLE 18.21

```
        #!/usr/local/bin/perl
        # timeclient--a client for the Time Server program,
        # creates a socket and connects it to the server on port 9876.
        # The client then expects the server to write the server's
        # host time onto the socket. The client simply does
        # a read on its socket, SOCK, to get the server's time.
        #
        #            Usage:  timeclient [server_host_name]
        #
        print "Hi, I'm in Perl program \'client\' \n";
1       ($them) = @ARGV;
2       $them = 'localhost' unless $them;
3       $port = 9876 ;          # timeserver is at this port number
4       $AF_INET = 2;
5       $SOCK_STREAM = 1;
6       $sockaddr = 'S n a4 x8';
7       ($name, $aliases, $proto) = getprotobyname('tcp');
8       ($name,$aliases, $port, $proto)=getservbyname($port, 'tcp')
            unless $port =~ /^\d+$/;

9       ($name,$aliases, $type, $len, $thataddr)=gethostbyname($them);
10      $that = pack($sockaddr, $AF_INET, $port, $thataddr);
        # Make the socket filehandle
11      if ( socket(SOCK, $AF_INET, $SOCK_STREAM, $proto ) ){
            print "Socket ok.\n";
        }
        else { die $!; }
        # Call up the server
12      if(connect(SOCK, $that)){
            print "Connect ok.\n";
        }
        else { die $!;}
        # Set socket to be command buffered
13      select(SOCK); $| = 1; select (STDOUT);
        # Now we're connected to the server, let's read her host time
14      $hertime = <SOCK>;
        close(SOCK);
        print "Server machine time is: $hertime\n";
15      @now = localtime($hertime);
        print "\t$now[2]:$now[1] ", $now[4]+1,"/$now[3]/$now[5]\n";
```

EXPLANATION

1 The server's hostname may be passed as a command line argument.
2 If the *ARGV* array is empty, the hostname is set to *localhost*.
3 To identify the server process, the client needs to know the server's port number.
4 The domain is *Internet*.
5 The type of socket is *SOCK_STREAM*, assigned the value of *1* in */usr/include/ sys/socket.h.*
6 The *pack* function will use this format for the socket address.
7 The *getprotobyname* function returns the official protocol name, any aliases, and the protocol number, using the *tcp* protocol as the name.
8 The *getservbyname* function returns the name of the official name of the server, any aliases, the port number, and the protocol name, unless *$port* contains already assigned digits.
9 The raw network address information is obtained from the host by *gethostbyname*.
10 The address for the server's Internet domain and port number is packed into a binary structure consisting of an unsigned short, a short in "network" order, four ASCII characters, and 8 null bytes. In comparable *C* programs, you will note that the method for getting addresses is by using a *sockaddr* structure (see */usr/include/sys/socket.h*).
11 The *socket* function creates an Internet domain, connection-oriented socket filehandle, *SOCK*.
12 The *connect* function connects the client's socket to the server's address.
13 The *SOCK* filehandle is selected. Buffers will be flushed after prints and writes.
14 Perl reads from the *SOCK* filehandle. The server's time is retrieved.
15 The time is converted to local time and printed.

Server Machine

```
$ uname -n
scarecrow
$ timeserver
9876
```

Client Machine

```
$ hostname
houston
$ timeclient
Hi I'm the Perl program 'client'
Socket ok.
Connect ok.
Server machine time is:
   981415699 15:28 5/2/01
```

Figure 18.3   Connection-oriented sockets on remote machines.

18.7 The *Socket.pm* Module

Although sockets were originally an idea started at Berkeley for UNIX systems, they are now supported on many other operating systems. Perl 5 introduced a special module, called *Socket.pm,* to deal with sockets. This makes it much easier to port programs from one machine to another, because the necessary functions and constants needed for your machine are handled in the module, thus allowing you to get away from hard coding values into the program as seen in the examples above. However, a caveat: You must understand the way the *Socket* module works before using it. The names of constants are not intuitive and the later versions of Perl 5 have introduced more functionality to the module.

The following examples demonstrate how to write the previous TCP/IP server and client programs by taking advantage of *Socket.pm* and some of the other pragmas offered in Perl 5 to better secure the programs when used on a network.

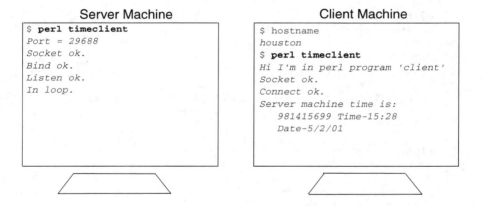

Figure 18.4   Server/client and *Socket.pm*, discussed in the following examples.

The Server

EXAMPLE 18.22

```
(The Server Script)
1   #!/bin/perl  -Tw
2   require 5.6;
3   use strict;
4   use Socket;
5   use FileHandle;

    # timeserver --  a Time Server program, opens a rendezvous
    # socket on port 29688 and waits for a client to connect.
    # When each client connects, this server determines the machine
    # time on its host and writes the value on the communication
    # socket to the client.
    #
    #                       Usage: timeserver
    #
6   my($this, $now);
7   my $port = shift || 29688;

8   $this = pack('Sna4x8', AF_INET, $port, "\0\0\0\0");
    print "Port = $port\n";
9   my $prototype = getprotobyname('tcp');
10  socket(SOCKET, PF_INET, SOCK_STREAM, $prototype) ||
                           die "socket: $!\n";
    print "Socket ok.\n";

11  bind(SOCKET, $this) || die "bind: $!\n";
    print "Bind ok.\n";

12  listen(SOCKET, SOMAXCONN) || die "connect: $!\n";
    print "Listen ok.\n";

13  COMM_SOCKET->autoflush;
    SOCKET->autoflush;

    # Infinite loop -- wait until client connects,
    # then serve the client
14  while(1){
        print "In loop.\n";
15      accept(COMM_SOCKET, SOCKET) || die "$!\n";
        print "Accept ok.\n";
16      $now = time;
17      print COMM_SOCKET $now;
    }
```

EXPLANATION

1 The *-w* switch sends diagnostics to *STDERR* if an identifier is mentioned only once, a scalar is used before being set, a non-number is used as a number, etc. The *-T* switch turns on taint checking to prevent data coming into your program from affecting something inside your program. If using a directory path, the taint mode checks to see if the directory is writeable by others, and it checks arguments coming into the program. Once tainted, the data (or any variable that references the tainted data) cannot be used in any command that invokes a subshell. It is suggested that taint checking be turned on for server programs and CGI scripts, that is, programs that are run by someone else.

2 The *require* uses the version number as an argument. This ensures that Perl versions prior to 5.6 will abort.

3 The *strict* pragma ensures that your program does not use unsafe constructs. It disallows symbolic references, and barewords, and variables must be declared using the *my* function.

4 The *Socket* module will be used in this program. The module is designed to make the use of sockets more portable.

5 The *FileHandle* module is used here to take advantage of its method *autoflush,* which will force the proper flushing of buffers when writing to the socket.

6 These variables will be used later in the program. They must be declared with *my* because the *strict* pragma enforces this as a safety feature.

7 A hostname may be passed as a command line argument and shifted into the *$port* variable. If the *ARGV* array is empty, the scalar *$port* is assigned the value *9688*, a number well outside the range of reserved port numbers.

8 *AF_INET* is a constant defined in the *Socket* module to represents the Internet domain. The *pack* function packs the IP address and port number for the server socket into *$this*.

9 The *getprotobyname* function returns the official protocol name, any aliases, and the protocol number, using the *tcp* protocol as the name.

10 The *socket* function creates the rendezvous socket filehandle, *SOCKET*.

11 The *bind* function binds the socket filehandle to the correct address for the server.

12 The *listen* function sets the queue limit to *SOMAXCONN*, the maximum for pending requests from the client (usually 5).

13 The *autoflush* method from the *FileHandle* class forces buffers to be flushed as soon as something is written to the socket.

14 An infinite loop is started. The server is now waiting for a client request.

15 The *accep*t function waits for a client request, and when it gets one, accepts it by creating a new socket filehandle called *COMM_SOCK*, with all the same attributes as *SOCKET*.

16 The server calls the *time* function to get the current time and assigns that value to *$now.*

17 The server sends the time to *COMM_SOCK*. Client will get it at its end.

The Client

EXAMPLE 18.23

```
   #!/usr/local/bin/perl -Tw
   require 5.6.0;
1  use Socket;
   use FileHandle;
2  use strict;
3  my($remote, $port, @thataddr, $that,$them, $proto,@now,
       $hertime);

   # timeclient --  a client for the Time Server program,
   # creates a socket and connects it to the server on
   # port 29688.
   # The client then expects the server to write server's
   # host time onto the socket, so the client simply does
   # a read on its socket, SOCK, to get the server's time
   #
   #
   #              Usage:  timeclient [server_host_name]
   #
   print "Hi, I'm in perl program \'client\' \n";
4  $remote = shift || 'localhost' ;
5  $port =  29688 ;     # timeserver is at this port number
6  @thataddr=gethostbyname($remote);

7  $that = pack('Sna4x8', AF_INET, $port, $thataddr[4]);

8  $proto = getprotobyname('tcp');

   # Make the socket filehandle

9  if ( socket(SOCK, PF_INET, SOCK_STREAM, $proto ) ){
       print "Socket ok.\n";
   }
   else { die $!; }

   # Call up the server
10 if (connect(SOCK, $that)) {
       print "Connect ok.\n";
   }
   else { die $!;}

   # Set socket to be command buffered
11 SOCK->autoflush;

   # Now we're connected to the server, let's read her host time
12 $hertime = <SOCK>;
13 close(SOCK);
```

EXAMPLE 18.23 (CONTINUED)

```
14   print "Server machine time is: $hertime\n";
15   @now = localtime($hertime);
16   print "\tTime-$now[2]:$now[1] ",
             "Date-",$now[4]+1,"/$now[3]/$now[5]\n";
```

```
(Output)
$ perl timeserver
Port = 29688
Socket ok.
Bind ok.
Listen ok.
In loop.


$ perl timeclient
Hi, I'm in perl program 'client'
Socket ok.
Connect ok.
Server machine time is: 981415699
        Time-15:28 Date-2/5/01
```

EXPLANATION

1   The *Socket* module will be used in this program.
2   The *strict* pragma is used to ensure that variables used in this program are "safe."
3   These variables will be used later in the program. They must be declared with *my* because the *strict* pragma enforces this as a safety feature.
4   A server's hostname may be passed as a command line argument and shifted into the *$port* variable. If the *ARGV* array is empty, the scalar *$port* is assigned *localhost*.
5   The client gets the server's port number if it was assigned a value.
6   Now the client gets the server's official address. The raw network address information is obtained by *gethostbyname*.
7   The address for the server's Internet domain and port number is packed into a binary structure consisting of an unsigned short, a short in "network" order, four ASCII characters, and eight null bytes.
8   The *tcp* protocol information is returned.
9   The *socket* function creates an Internet domain, connection-oriented socket filehandle, *SOCK*.
10 The *connect* function connects the client's socket to the server's address.
11 The *autoflush* method forces the socket's buffers to be flushed after prints and writes.
12 Perl reads from the *SOCK* filehandle. The server's time is retrieved via the socket.
13 The socket is closed.
14 The time value (number of non–leap-year seconds since 1/1/1970, UTC) retrieved from the server is printed.
15 The time is converted to local time and assigned to array *@now*.
16 The converted time is printed.

19

CGI AND PERL:
THE HYPER DYNAMIC DUO

19.1 What Is CGI?

Now that the informational spider web called the Internet has become a commercial shop-ping center, it seems that everyone has a home page hanging out there. And if you don't have one now, you probably will by the time this book gets out on the market. There are zillions of books and software programs on how to navigate, surf, master Web sites, design Web pages, unleash HTML, Java, XML, Perl, and any other topic related to the Internet. What do you need to get started with all this? Well, as you know, you need a computer hooked up to a phone line; a browser program such as Netscape, Mosaic, or Internet Explorer; and access to a server program such as Apache, CERN, or Netscape. After con-necting to the Internet, you learn rather quickly how to navigate your way around and unless you have a job or some other life, you could surf around forever and never see it all.

So what makes up a Web page? A Web page is a file that contains HTML tags and text, formatting instructions, and underlined phrases called **links** that connect you to other doc-uments either on the same machine or on some other machine on the network. The docu-ment (called a **hypertext document**) tells the browser on your system how to display the document; for example, whether or not it has a blue background with big white letters or a white background with pink borders and a photograph of your face, an order form for buy-ing a new computer, a registration form for a local college, or an image of you dancing around in your living room to old Beatles songs. The page may contain what is called **hypermedia**, which includes images, sound, movies, and hotlinks to other documents. A Web page is created in a text editor and the resulting HTML file is called the **source file**. So that the browser recognizes the file, its name ends in either *.html* or *.htm*. The HTML tags tell the browser how to display the document on your screen. Learning the basics of HTML is not difficult, but developing an artistic and interesting design is another story, and now there are companies devoted to creating these masterpieces for other companies doing competitive business over the Web.

There are two types of pages: **static** pages and **dynamic** pages. Static pages do not require interaction with the user. The most they can do is send already existing documents to users. They are analagous to a page in a book, and usually describe the services some individual or company offers. They can be very artistic and interesting, but they can't handle information on demand. Dynamic pages, on the other hand, are "alive." They can accept and retrieve information from the user, produce specialized and customized content, search through text, query databases, and generate documents on the fly. They can manage information that is constantly changing, based on the requests of different users. These dynamic pages require more than an HTML text file. They are driven by programs or scripts that interact with the Web server, which then transfers information to your browser. To send the information back and forth between the program and the server, a gateway program is used. The server itself relays user requests to a program, which in turn manages the information, such as retrieving data from a file or database as a result of a user request and then sending it back to the server. The CGI (Common Gateway Interface) protocol defines how the server communicates with these programs. Its function is to allow the WWW server to go beyond its normal boundaries for retrieving and accessing information from external databases and files. It is, then, a specification that defines how data can be transferred from the script to the server and from the server to the script. Gateway programs, called **CGI scripts**, can be written in any programming language, but Perl has become the de facto standard language, mainly because it is flexible and easy to use.

If you have read the previous chapters, you know that the Perl interpreter is easy to obtain. You know that it is portable. And you know about Perl's ability to handle regular expressions, files, sockets, and I/O. Once you know Perl, writing CGI scripts is relatively easy. The critical part is making sure the server and Perl have been properly installed and that your scripts are placed in the directory where the server will look for them. The pathnames must also be set correctly so that the server knows where you are storing the scripts and how to reach the necessary libraries. All efforts are for nothing if any of the necessary steps from installation to implementation are incorrect in any way. It is very frustrating to see the browser whining about not finding a requested file or server or scolding that you are forbidden to run a program, or that your document contains no data when you know it does.

This chapter is not written to make you a master Web designer; it is to give you some understanding of how Perl fits into the CGI scheme and how dynamic pages for the Web are created. Sometimes, seeing the overall picture is the key to understanding the purpose and plan of the more detailed design. There is a plethora of Web information available on the Internet and in trade books to fill in the details.

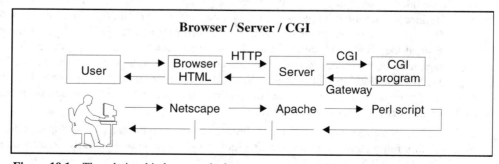

Figure 19.1   The relationship between the browser, server, and CGI program.

19.2 Internet Communication Between Client and Server

19.2.1   The HTTP Server

We discussed the client/server model and the TCP/IP protocols for regulating network operations in Chapter 18, "Send It Over the Net and Sock It To 'Em!". On the Internet, communication is also handled by a TCP/IP connection. The Web is based on this model. The server side responds to client (browser) requests and provides feedback by sending back a document, by executing a CGI program, or by issuing an error message. The network protocol that is used by the Web so that the server and client know how to talk to each other is the Hypertext Transport Protocol, or HTTP. This does not preclude the TCP/IP protocol being implemented. HTTP objects are mapped onto the transport data units, a process that is beyond the scope of this discussion; it is a simple, straightforward process that is unnoticed by the typical Web user. (See *www.cis.ohio-state.edu/cgi-bin/rfc/rfc2068.html* for a technical description of HTTP.) The HTTP protocol was built for the Web to handle hypermedia information; it is object-oriented and stateless. In objectoriented terminology, the documents and files are called **objects** and the operations that are associated with the HTTP protocol are called **methods**. When a protocol is stateless, neither the client nor the server stores information about each other, but manages its own state information.

Once a TCP/IP connection is established between the Web server and client, the client will request some service from the server. Web servers are normally located at well-known TCP port 80. The client tells the server what type of data it can handle by sending *Accept* statements with its requests. For example, one client may accept only HTML text, whereas another client might accept sounds and images as well as text. The server will try to handle the request (requests and responses are in ASCII text) and send back whatever information it can to the client (browser).

EXAMPLE 19.1

```
(Client's (Browser) Request)
GET /pub HTTP/1.0
Connection: Keep-Alive
User-Agent: Mozilla/4.0 Gold
Host: severname.com
Accept: image/gif, image/x-xbitmap, image/jpeg, image/pjpeg,*/*
```

EXAMPLE 19.2

```
(Server's Response)
HTTP/1.1 200 OK
Server: Apache/1.2b8
Date: Mon, 22 Jan 2001  13:43:22 GMT
Last-modified: Mon, 01 Dec 2000 12:15:33
Content-length: 288
Accept-Ranges: bytes
Connection: close
Content-type: text/html

<HTML><HEAD><TITLE>Hello World!</TITLE>
        ---continue with body---
</HTML>
Connection closed by foreign host.
```

The response confirms what HTTP version was used, the status code describing the results of the server's attempt (did it succeed or fail?), a header, and data. The header part of the message indicates whether the request is okay, what type of data is being returned (for example, the content type may be *html/text*), and how many bytes are being sent. The data part contains the actual text being sent.

The user then sees a formatted page on the screen, which may contain highlighted hyperlinks to some other page. Regardless of whether the user clicks on a hyperlink, once the document is displayed, that transaction is completed and the TCP/IP connection will be closed. Once closed, a new connection will be started if there is another request. What happened in the last transaction is of no interest to either client or server; in other words, the protocol is stateless.

HTTP is also used to communicate between browsers, proxies, and gateways to other Internet systems supported by FTP, Gopher, WAIS, and NNTP protocols.

19.2.2   HTTP Status Codes and the Log Files

When the server responds to the client, it sends information that includes the way it handled the request. Most Web browsers handle these codes silently if they fall in the range between 100 and 300. The codes within the 100 range are informational, indicating that the server's request is being processed. The most common status code is 200, indicating success, which means the information requested was accepted and fulfilled.

Check your server's access log to see what status codes were sent by your server after a transaction was completed.[1] The following example consists of excerpts taken from the Apache server's access log. This log reports information about a request handled by the server and the status code generated as a result of the request. The error log contains any standard error messages that the program would ordinarily send to the screen, such as syntax or compiler errors.

---

1. For more detailed information on status codes, see
   www.w3.org/Protocols/HTTP/HTRESP.html

Table 19.1   HTTP Status Codes

Status	CodeMessage
100	Continue
200	Success, OK
204	No Content
301	Document Moved
400	Bad Request
401	Unauthorized
403	Forbidden
404	Not Found
500	Internal Server Error
501	Not Implemented
503	Service Unavailable

EXAMPLE 19.3

```
(From Apache's Access log)
1    susan - - [06/Jul/1997:14:32:23 -0700] "GET /cgi-bin/hello.cgi
     HTTP/1.0" 500 633
2    susan - - [16/Jun/1997:11:27:32 -0700] "GET /cgi-bin/hello.cgi
     HTTP/1.0" 200 1325
3    susan - - [07/Jul/1997:09:03:20 -0700] "GET /htdocs/index.html
     HTTP/1.0" 404 170
```

EXPLANATION

1   The server hostname is *susan*, followed by two dashes indicating unknown values, such as user ID and password. The time the request was logged, the type of request is *GET* (see "The GET Method" on page 660), and the file accessed was *hello.cgi*. The protocol is HTTP/1.0. The status code sent by the server was 500, *Internal Server Error,* meaning that there was some internal error, such as a syntax error in the program, *hello.cgi*. The browser's request was not fulfilled. The number of bytes sent was 633.

2   Status code 200 indicates success! The request was fullfilled.

3   Status code 404, *Not Found*, means that the server found nothing matching the URL requested.

19.2.3   The URL (Uniform Resource Locator)

URLs are what you use to get around on the Web. You click on a hotlink and you are transported to some new page, or you type a URL in the browser's Location box and a file opens up or a script runs. It is a virtual address that specifies the location of pages, objects, scripts, etc. It refers to an existing protocol such as HTTP, Gopher, FTP, mailto, file, Telnet, or news (see Table 19.2). A typical URL for the popular Web HTTP protocol looks like this:

```
http://www.comp.com/dir/text.html
```

Table 19.2   Web Protocols

Protocol	Function	Example
http:	Hyper Text Transfer Protocol	http://www.nnic.noaa.gov/cgi-bin/netcast.cgi open Web page or start CGI script
ftp:	File Transfer Protocol	ftp://jague.gsfc.nasa.gov/pub
mailto:	Mail protocol by e-mail address	mailto:debbiej@aol.com
file:	Open a local file	file://opt/apache/htdocs/file.html
telnet:	Open a Telnet session	telnet://nickym@netcom.com
news:	Opens a news session by news server	news:alt.fan.john-lennon Name or Address

The two basic pieces of information provided in the URL are the protocol *http* and the data needed by the protocol, *www.comp.com/dir/files/text.html*. The parts of the URL are further defined in Table 19.3.

Table 19.3   Parts of a URL

Part	Description
protocol	Service such as HTTP, Gopher, FTP, Telnet, news, etc.
host/IP number	DNS host name or its IP number
port	TCP port number used by server, normally port 80
path	Path and filename reference for the object on a server
parameters	Specific parameters used by the object on a server
query	The query string for a CGI script
fragment	Reference to subset of the object

The default HTTP network port is 80; if an HTTP server resides on a different network port, say *12345* on *www.comp.com*, then the URL becomes

```
http://www.comp.com.12345/dir/text.html
```

Not all parts of a URL are necessary. If you are searching for a document in the Locator box in the Netscape browser, the URL may not need the port number, parameters, query, or fragment parts. If the URL is part of a hotlink in the HTML document, it may contain a relative path to the next document, that is, relative to the root directory of the server. If the user has filled in a form, the URL line may contain information appended to a question mark in the URL line. The appearance of the URL really depends on what protocol you are using and what operation you are trying to accomplish.

EXAMPLE 19.4

```
1   http://www.cis.ohio-state.edu/htbin/rfc2068.html
2   http://127.0.0.1/Sample.html
3   ftp://oak.oakland.edu/pub/
4   file://opt/apache_1.2b8/htdocs/index.html
5   http://susan/cgi-bin/form.cgi?string=hello+there
```

EXPLANATION

1   The protocol is *http*.
    The hostname *www.cis.ohio-state.edu/htbin/rfc2068.html* consists of[a]
        The hostname translated to an IP address by the Domain Name Service, DNS.
        The domain name is *ohio-state.edu*.
        The top-level domain name is *edu*.
        The directory where the HTML file is stored is *htbin*.
        The file to be retrieved is *rfc20868.html*, an HTML document.
2   The protocol is *http*.
    The IP address is used instead of the hostname; this is the IP address for a local host.
    The file is in the server's document root. The file consists of HTML text.
3   The protocol is *ftp*.
    The host *oak.oakland*.
    The top-level domain is *edu*.
    The directory is *pub*.
4   The protocol is file. A local file will be opened.
    The hostname is missing. It then refers to the local host.
    The full path to the file *index.html* is listed.

5   The information after the question mark is the query part of the URL, which may
    have resulted from submitting input into a form. The query string is URL encoded.
    In this example, a plus sign has replaced the space between *hello* and *there*. The serv-
    er stores this query in an environment variable called *QUERY_STRING*. It will be
    passed on to a CGI program called from the HTML document. (See "The GET Meth-
    od" on page 660.)

a. Most Web severs run on hostnames starting with *www*, but this is only a convention.

File URLs and the Server's Root Directory.   If the protocol used in the URL is *file*, the
server assumes that file is on the local machine. A full pathname followed by a filename is
included in the URL. When the protocol is followed by a server name, all pathnames are
relative to the document root of the server. The document root is the directory defined in
the server's configuration file as the main directory for your Web server. The leading slash
that precedes the path is not really part of the path as with the UNIX absolute path, which
starts at the root directory. Rather, the leading slash is used to separate the path from the
hostname. An example of a URL leading to documents in the server's root directory:

```
http://www.myserver/index.html
```

The full UNIX pathname for this might be

```
/usr/bin/myserver/htdocs/index.html
```

   A shorthand method for linking to a document on the same server is called a partial or
relative URL. For example, if a document at *http://www.myserver/stories/webjoke.html*
contains a link to *images/webjoke.gif*, this is a relative URL. The browser will expand the
relative URL to its absolute URL, *http://www.myserver/stories/images/webjoke.gif*, and
make a request for that document if asked.

19.3 Creating a Web Page with HTML

In order to write Web pages, you must learn at least some of what makes up the HTML language. There are volumes written on this subject. Here we will cover just enough to intro-
duce you to HTML and give you the basics so that you can write some simple dynamic pages
with forms and CGI scripts. See Appendix D for a succinct tutorial on HTML.
   As previously stated, Web pages are written as ASCII text files in HTML. HTML consists of a set of instructions called **tags** that tell your Web browser how to display the text
in the page.[2] When you type in the URL or click on a hyperlink in a page, the browser (cli-

2. If you have ever used the UNIX programs *nroff* and *troff* for formatting text, you'll immediately recognize the
    tags used for formatting with HTML.

ent) communicates to the server that it needs a file and the file is sent back to the browser. The file contains HTML content that may consist of plain text, images, audio, video, and hyperlinks. It's the browser's job to interpret the HTML tags and display the formatted page on your screen. (To look at the source file for a Web page, you can use the View Document menu under View in the Netscape browser, or using Internet Explorer select the View menu and then select Source to see the HTML tags used to produce the page.)

Creating Tags.   The HTML source file can be created with any text editor. Its name ends in *.html* or *.htm* to indicate it is an HTML file. The HTML tags that describe the way the document looks are enclosed in angle brackets < >. The tags are easy to read. If you want to create a title, for example, the tag instruction is enclosed in brackets and the actual text for the title is sandwiched between the marker that starts the instruction, *<TITLE>*, and the tag that ends the instruction, *</TITLE>*. The following line is called a **TITLE element**, consisting of the *<TITLE>* start tag, the enclosed text, and the *</TITLE>* end tag. A tag may also have attributes to further describe its function. For example, a text input area may allow a specified number of rows and columns, or an image may be aligned and centered at the top of the page. The elements and attributes are case-insensitive.

```
<TITLE>War and Peace</TITLE>
```

When the browser sees this instruction, the title will be printed in the bar at the top of the browser's window as a title for the page. To put comments in the HTML document, the commented text is inserted between <!-- and -->.

Because HTML is a structured language, there are rules about how to place the tags in a document. These rules are discussed below.

A Simple HTML Document.   The following HTML file is created in your favorite text editor and consists of a simple set of tagged elements.

EXAMPLE 19.5

```
(The HTML Text File)
1    <HTML>
2    <HEAD>
3    <TITLE>Hyper Test</Title>
4    </HEAD>
5    <BODY>
6    <H1>Hello To You and Yours!</H1>
7    <H2 ALIGN="center">Welcome
8    </H2>
9    <P>Life is good. Today is <I>Friday.</I></P>
10   </BODY>
11   </HTML>
```

EXPLANATION

1   All of the text for the HTML document is between the *<HTML>* start tag and the *</HTML>* end tag. Although HTML is the standard language for creating Web pages, there are other markup languages that look like HTML; The HTML element identifies this as an HTML document. You can omit these tags and your browser will not complain. It is just more official to use them.

2   Between the *<HEAD>* tag and *</HEAD>* tag information about the document is inserted, such as the title. This information is not displayed with the rest of the document text. The *<HEAD>* tag always comes right after the *<HTML>* tag.

3   The *<TITLE>* tag is used to create the title shown at the top of the browser window.

4   This is the closing tag for the *<HEAD>* tag.

5   The main part of the document appears in the browser's window, and is enclosed between the *<BODY>* start tag and *</BODY>* end tag.

6   A level 1 heading is enclosed between the *<H1>* and *</H1>* start and end tags.

7   This is a level 2 heading. The *ALIGN* attribute tells the browser to center the heading on the page.

8   This is the end tag for a level 2 heading.

9   The *<P>* starts a new paragraph. The string *Friday* will be printed in italicized text. *</P>* marks the end of the paragraph.

10   This tag marks the end of the body of the document.

11   This tag marks the end of the HTML document.

Figure 19.2   The HTML document from Example 19.5, as displayed in Internet Explorer.

Table 19.4   Simple HTML Tags and What They Do

Tag Element	Function
<!-- text -->	Commented text; nothing is displayed.
<BASE HREF="http://www.bus.com/my.html">	Where this document is stored.
*<HTML>*document*</HTML>*	Found at the beginning and end of the document, indicating to a browser that this is an HTML document.
*<HEAD>*headinginfo*</HEAD>*	First element inside the document. Contains title, metatags, JavaScript, and CSS. Only the title is displayed directly.
*<TITLE>*title of the document*</TITLE>*	Title of the document; displayed outside the document text in a window frame or top of the screen. Can be placed in the bookmark list.
*<BODY>*document contents*</BODY>*	Contains all the text and other objects to be displayed.
*<H1>*heading type*</H1>*	Creates boldface heading elements for heading levels 1 through 6. The levels elements are: H1, H2, H3, H4, H5, and H6. The largest, topmost heading is H1.
*<P>*text*</P>*	Paragraph tag. Marks the beginning of a paragraph. Inserts a break after a block of text. Can go anywhere on the line. Ending paragraph tags are optional. Paragraphs end when a *</P>* or another *<P>* (marking a new paragraph) is encountered.
*<B>*text*</B>*	Bold text.
*<I>*text*</I>*	Italic text.
*<TT>*text*</TT>*	Typewriter text.
*<U>*text*</U>*	Underlined text.
* *	Line break.
<HR>	Horizontal shadow line.
<UL>	Start of an unordered (bulleted) list.
<LI>	An item in a list.

Table 19.4   Simple HTML Tags and What They Do *(continued)*

Tag Element	*Function*
<LI>	Another item in a list.
</UL>	The end of the list.
<OL>	Start of an ordered list.
<DL>	Descriptive list.
<DT>	An item in a descriptive list
<DT>	Another item in a descriptive list.
</DL>	End of the descriptive list.
<STRONG>	Bold text.
<EM>	Italic text.
<BLOCKQUOTE>text</BLOCKQUOTE>	Italicized blocked text with spaces before and after quote.
<A HREF SRC="URL">	Creates a hotlink to a resource at address in URL on the Web.
<IMG SRC="URL">	Loads an image into a Web page. URL is the address of the image file.

19.4 How HTML and CGI Work Together

As previously discussed, HTML is the markup language used to determine the way a Web page will be displayed. CGI is a protocol that allows the server to extend its functionality. A CGI program is executed on behalf of the server mainly to process forms such as a registration form or a shopping list. If you have purchased a book or CD from Amazon.com, you know what a form looks like. When a browser (client) makes a request of the server, the server examines the URL. If the server sees *cgi-bin* as a directory in the path, it will go to that directory, open a pipe, and execute the CGI program. The CGI program gets its **input from the pipe** and sends its **standard output back though the pipe** to the server. **Standard error** is sent to the server's **error log**. If the CGI program is to talk to the server, it must speak the Web language, since this is the language that is ultimately used by the browser to display a page. The CGI program then will format its data with HTML tags and send it back to the HTTP server. The server will then return this document to the browser where the HTML tags will be rendered and displayed to the user.

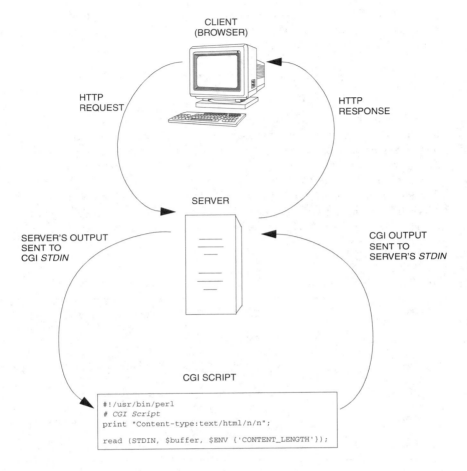

Figure 19.3   The client/server/CGI program relationship.

19.4.1   A Simple CGI Script

The following Perl script consists of a series of *print* statements, most of which send HTML output back to *STDOUT* (piped to the server). This program is executed directly from the CGI directory, *cgi-bin*. Some servers require that CGI script names end in *.cgi* or *.pl* so that they can be recognized as CGI scripts. After creating the script, the execute permission for the file must be turned on. For UNIX systems, at the shell prompt type

```
chmod 755 <scriptname>
```

 or

```
chmod +x <scriptname>
```

The URL entered in the browser Location window includes the protocol, the name of the host machine, the directory where the CGI scripts are stored, and the name of the CGI script. The URL will look like this:

```
http://servername/cgi-bin/perl_script.pl
```

The HTTP headers. The first line of output for most CGI programs is an HTTP header that tells the browser what type of output the program is sending to it. Right after the header line, there must be a blank line and two newlines. The two most common types of headers, also called **MIME** types (which stands for multipurpose Internet extension), are "Content-type: text/html\n\n" and "Content-type: text/plain\n\n." Another type of header is called the **Location** header, which is used to redirect the browser to a different Web page. And finally, **Cookie** headers are used to set cookies for maintaining state; that is, keeping track of information that would normally be lost once the transaction between the server and browser is closed.

Table 19.5   HTTP Headers

Header	Type	Value
Content-type:	text/plain	Plain text
Content-type:	text/html	HTML tags and text
Content-type:	image/gif	GIF graphics
Location:	http://www....	Redirection to another Web page
Set-cookie: NAME=VALUE...	Cookie	Set a cookie on a client browser

Right after the header line, there must be a blank line. This is accomplished by ending the line with \n\n in Perl.

EXAMPLE 19.6

```
1   #!/bin/perl
2   print "Content-type: text/html\n\n";      # The HTTP header
3   print "<HTML><HEAD><TITLE> CGI/Perl First Try</TITLE></HEAD>\n";
4   print "<BODY BGCOLOR=Black TEXT=White>\n";
5   print "<H1><CENTER> Howdy, World! </CENTER></H1>\n";
6   print "<H2><CENTER> It's ";
7   print "<!--comments -->";    # This is how HTML comments are
    included
8   print `date`;    # Execute the UNIX date command
9   print "and all's well.\n";
10  print "</H2></BODY></HTML>\n";
```

EXPLANATION

1   This first line is critical. Many Web servers will not run a CGI script if this line is missing. This tells the server where Perl is installed.

2   This line is called the **MIME header**. No matter what programming language you are using, the first output of your CGI program must be a MIME header followed by two newlines. This line indicates what type of data your application will be sending. In this case, the CGI script will be sending HTML text back to the server. The \n\n cause a blank line to be printed. The blank line is also crucial to success of your CGI program.

3   The next lines sent from Perl back to the server are straight HTML tags and text. This line creates the header information, in this case, a title for the document.

4   This defines the background color as black and the textual material as white.

5   *<H1>* is a level 1 heading. It is the largest of the headings and prints in bold text. *Howdy, World!* will be formatted as a level 1 heading and centered on the page.

6   All text from this point until line 10 will be formatted as a level 2, centered heading.

7   This is how comments are inserted into an HTML document. They are not displayed by the browser.

8   The UNIX *date* command is executed and its output is included as part of the centered, second-level heading. A better way to get the date so that your program is portable is to use *localtime*, a Perl built-in. Try changing line 9 to

$now = localtime;
print "$now\n";)

9   This line is printed as part of heading level 2.

10 These tags end the second level heading, the body of the document and the HTML document itself.

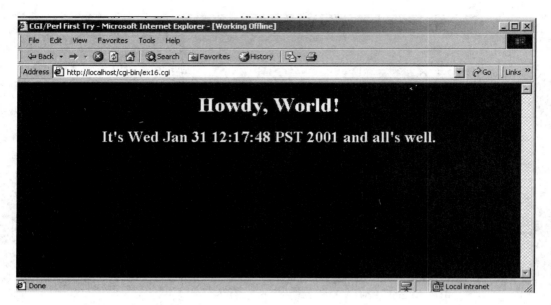

Figure 19.4   Output from the CGI program in Example 19.6.

19.5 Log Files

Error Logs and *STDERR*.   Normally, error messages are sent to the terminal screen (*STDERR*) when something goes wrong in a Perl script, but when launched by a server as a CGI script, the errors are not sent to the screen, but to the server's error log file. In the browser you may see "Empty Document" or "Internal Server Error," which tells you nothing about what went wrong in the program.

Always check your syntax at the shell command line with the -*c* switch before handing the script to the server. Otherwise, you will not see your error messages unless you check the log files. **Check the syntax of your Perl scripts with the -*c* switch.**

EXAMPLE 19.7

```
(At the Command line)
1  perl -c perlscript
2  perlscript syntax OK
```

EXAMPLE 19.8

```
(Perl syntax errors shown in the Apache server's error log)

    [Mon Jul 20 10:44:04 1998] access to /opt/apache_1.2b8/
        cgi-bin/submit-form failed for susan, reason: Premature end
        of script headers
    [Mon Sep 14 11:11:32 1998] httpd: caught SIGTERM, shutting down
    [Fri Sep 25 16:13:11 1998] Server configured -- resuming normal
        operations
1   Bare word found where operator expected at welcome.pl line 21,
        near "/font></TABLE"
    (Missing operator before TABLE?)
2   syntax error at welcome.pl line 21, near "<TH><"
    syntax error at welcome.pl line 24, near "else"
    [Fri Sep 25 16:16:18 1998] access to /opt/apache_1.2b8/
        cgi-bin/visit_count.pl failed for susan, reason:
        Premature end of script headers
```

Access Logs and Status Codes.   Check your server's access log to see what status codes were sent by your server after a transaction was complete.[3] The following example consists of excerpts taken from the Apache server's access log. This log reports information about a request handled by the server and the status code generated as a result of the request.

Table 19.6   HTTP Status Codes

Status	*Message Code*
100	Continue
200	Success, OK
204	No Content
301	Document Moved
400	Bad Request
401	Unauthorized
403	Forbidden
404	Not Found
500	Internal Server Error
501	Not Implemented
503	Service Unavailable

---

3. For more detailed information on status codes, see
    www.w3.org/Protocols/HTTP/HTRESP.html

EXAMPLE 19.9

```
(Status codes from the Apache server's access log)

1   susan - - [08/Oct./1999:10:45:36 -0700]
    "GET /cog-bin/visit_count.pl HTTP/1.0" 500 388
2   susan - - [08/Oct./1999:10:45:59 -0700]
    "GET /cgi-bin/visit_count.pl HTTP/1.0" 200 426
```

19.6 Where to Find CGI Applications

There are a number of Web sites that provide online resources to help you get started in writing your own CGI scripts. Most house prebuilt scripts that you can freely download, examine, and modify. Browsing through some of following sites can also give you a good idea of how Web pages are designed.

Table 19.7 Web Sites for CGI Beginners and Developers (Just a few of thousands!)

The Web Site	What It Is
www.virtualville.com/library/cgi.html	An introduction to CGI
www.virtualville.com/library/scripts.html	Scripts to Go. A collection of CGI scripts
www.worldwidemart.com/scripts/	Matt's Script Archive
www.extropia.com	Open-source Web software, formerly Selena Sol's Public Domain CGI Script Archive
www.perl.com/CPAN/	The Comprehensive Perl Archive Network
cgi-lib/berkeley.edu	The cgi-lib.pl Home Page
www.yahoo.com/Computers_and_Internet/Internet/ World_Wide_Web/CGI_Common_Gateway_Interface/	Yahoo CGI Resources

19.7 Getting Information Into and Out of the CGI Script

The server and the CGI script communicate in four major ways. Once the browser has sent a request to the server, the server can then send it on to the CGI script. The CGI script gets its input from the server as:

1. Environment variables
2. Query strings
3. Standard input
4. Extra path information

After the CGI program gets the input from the server it parses and processes it, and then formats it so that the server can relay the information back to the browser. The CGI script sends output through the gateway by

1. Generating new documents on the fly
2. Sending existing static files to the standard output
3. Using URLs that redirect the browser to go somewhere else for a document

19.7.1   CGI Environment Variables

The CGI program is passed a number of environment variables from the server. The environment variables are set when the server executes the gateway program, and are set for all requests. The environment variables contain information about the server, the CGI program, the ports and protocols, path information, etc. User input is normally assigned to the *QUERY_STRING* environment variable. In the following example, this variable has no value because the user never was asked for input; that is, the HTML document has no INPUT tags.

The environment variables are set for all requests and are sent by the server to the CGI program. In a Perl program, the environment variables are assigned to the *%ENV* hash as key/value pairs. They are shown in Table 19.8.

Table 19.8   CGI Environment Variables

Name	*Value*	*Example*
AUTH_TYPE	Validates user if server supports user authentication	
CONTENT_TYPE	The MIME type of the query data	*text/html*
CONTENT_LENGTH	The number of bytes passed from the server to CGI program	*Content-Length=55*
DOCUMENT ROOT	The directory from which the server serves Web documents	/opt/apache/htdocs/index.html
GATEWAY_INTERFACE	The revision of the CGI used by the server	CGI/1.1
HTTP_ACCEPT	The MIME types accepted by the client	image/gif, image/jpeg, etc
HTTP_CONNECTION	The preferred HTTP connection type	Keep-Alive

Table 19.8   CGI Environment Variables *(continued)*

Name	*Value*	*Example*
HTTP_HOST	The name of the host machine	susan
HTTP_USER_AGENT	The browser (client) sending the request	Mozilla/3.01(X11;I; Sun05.5.1 sun4m)
PATH_INFO	Extra path information passed to a CGI program	
PATH_TRANSLATED	The *PATH_INFO* translated to its absolute path	
QUERY_STRING	The string obtained from a *GET* request from the URL (information following the *?* in the URL)	*http://susan/cgi-bin/ form1.cgi?Name=Christian+ Dobbins*
REMOTE_HOST	The remote hostname of the user making a request	*eqrc.ai.mit.edu*
REMOTE_ADDR	The IP address of the host making a request	*192.100.1.11*
REMOTE_PORT	The port number of the host making a request	*33015*
REQUEST_METHOD	The method used to get information to the CGI program	*GET, POST*, etc
SCRIPT_FILENAME	The absolute pathname of the CGI program	*/opt/apache/cgi-bin/hello.cgi*
SCRIPT_NAME	The relative pathname of the CGI program; a partial URL	*/cgi-bin/hello.cgi*
SERVER_ADMIN	E-mail address of the system administrator	*root@susan*
SERVER_NAME	The server's hostname, DNS alias, or IP address	*susan, 127.0.0.0*
SERVER_PROTOCOL	The name and version of the protocol	*HTTP/1.0*
SERVER_SOFTWARE	Name and version of the server software	*Apache/1.2b8*

An HTML File with a Link to a CGI Script.   The following example is an HTML file that will allow the user to print out all the environment variables. When the browser displays this document, the user can click on the hotlink *here* and the CGI script, *env.cgi*, will then be executed by the server. In the HTML document the string *here* and the URL *http://susan/cgi-bin/env.cgi* are enclosed in the *<A></A>* anchor tags. If the hotlink is ignored by the user, the browser displays the rest of the document. The following example is the HTML source file that will be interpreted by the browser. The browser's output is shown in Figure 19.5.

EXAMPLE 19.10

```
(The HTML file with a hotlink to a CGI script)
1    <HTML>
2    <HEAD>
3    <TITLE>TESTING ENV VARIABLES</TITLE>
     </HEAD>
     <BODY>
     <P>
     <H1> Major Test </H1>
4    <P> If you would like to see the environment variables<BR>
     being passed on by the server, click .
5    <A HREF="http://localhost/cgi-bin/env.cgi">here</A>
     <P>Text continues here...
     </BODY>
     </HTML>
```

EXPLANATION

1   The *<HTML>* tag says this document is using the HTML protocol.
2   The *<HEAD>* tag contains the title and any information that will be displayed outside the actual document.
3   The *<TITLE>* tag is displayed in the top bar of the browser window.
4   The *<P>* tag is the start of a paragraph. The *
* tag causes the line to break.
5   The *<A>* tag is assigned the path to the CGI script, *env.cgi*, on server *localhost*. The word *here* will be displayed by the browser in blue underlined letters. If the user clicks on this word, the CGI script will be executed by the server. The script will print out all of the environment variables passed to the script from the server. This is one of the ways information is given to a CGI script by a Web server. The actual CGI script is shown below, in Example 19.11.

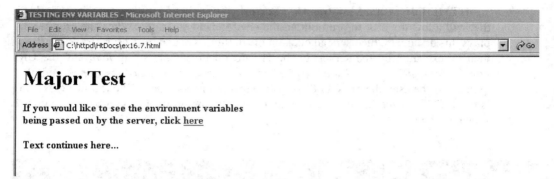

Figure 19.5   The output of the HTML file in Example 19.10. It contains a hotlink to the CGI script.

EXAMPLE 19.11

```
(The CGI Script)
1   #!/bin/perl
2   print "Content type: text/plain\n\n";
3   print "CGI/1.1 test script report:\n\n";
4   # Print out all the environment variables

5   while(($key, $value)=each(%ENV)){
6       print "$key = $value\n";
    }
```

EXPLANATION

1   The *#!* line is important to your server if your server is running on a UNIX platform. It is the path to the Perl interpreter. The line must be the correct pathname to your version of perl or you will receive the following error message from your server: *Internal Server Error ...*

2   The first line generated by the CGI script is a valid HTTP header, ending with a blank line. The header contains a content type (also called a MIME type) followed by *text/plain*, meaning that the document will consist of plain text. If the script were to include HTML tags, the content type would be *text/html*.

3   The version of the Common Gateway Interface used by this server is printed.

4   This is a Perl comment line.

5   The *%ENV* hash contains environment variables (keys and values) passed into the Perl script from the server. The *each* function will return both the key and the value and store them in scalars, *$key* and *$value*, respectively.

6   The *$key/$value* pairs are printed back to *STDOUT*, which has been connected to the server by a pipe mechanism.

Figure 19.6   The environment variables displayed by the CGI script in Example 19.11.

19.8 Processing Forms with CGI

Processing user input is one of the most common reasons for using a CGI script. This is normally done with forms. The form offers you a number of methods, called **virtual input devices**, with which to accept input. These include radio buttons, check boxes, pop-up menus, and text boxes. All forms are in HTML documents and begin with a *<FORM>* tag and end with a *</FORM>* tag. A method attribute may be assigned. The method attribute indicates how the form will be processed. The *GET* method is the default and the *POST* method is the most commonly used alternative. The *GET* method is preferable for operations that will not affect the state of the server; that is, simple document retrieval and database lookups, etc., whereas the *POST* method is preferred for handing operations that may change the state of the server, such as adding or deleting records from a database. These methods will be described in the next section. The *ACTION* attribute is assigned the URL of the CGI script that will be executed when the data is submitted by pressing the Submit button.

The browser gets input from the user by displaying fields that can be edited. The fields are created by the HTML *<INPUT TYPE=key/value>* tag. These fields might take the form of check boxes, text boxes, radio buttons, etc. The data that is entered into the form is sent to the server in an encoded string format in a name/value pair scheme. The value represents the actual input data. The CGI programmer must understand how this input is encoded in order to parse it and use it effectively. First let's see how input gets into the browser by looking at a simple document and the HTML code used to produce it. The user will be able to click on a button or enter data in the text box. The input in this example won't be processed, thereby causing an error to be sent to the server's error log when the Submit button is selected. Nothing will be displayed by the browser. The default for obtaining input is the *GET* method.

A summary of the steps in producing a form is

1. START: Start the form with the HTML *<FORM>* tag.
2. ACTION: The *ACTION* attribute of the *<FORM>* tag is the URL of the CGI script that will process the data input from the form.
3. METHOD: Provide a method on how to process the data input. The default is the *GET* method.
4. CREATE: Create the form with buttons and boxes and whatever looks nice using HTML tags and fields.
5. SUBMIT: Create a Submit button so that the form can be processed. This will launch the CGI script listed in the *ACTION* attribute.
6. END: End the form and the HTML document.

19.8.1 Input Types for Forms

Table 19.9 Form Input Types

Input Type	*Attributes*	*Description*
CHECKBOX	NAME, VALUE	Displays a square box that can be checked. Creates name/value pairs from user input. Multiple boxes can be checked.
FILE	NAME	Specifies files to be uploaded to the server. MIME type must be multipart/form-data.
HIDDEN	NAME, VALUE	Provides name/value pair without displaying an object on the screen.

Table 19.9   Form Input Types *(continued)*

Input Type	Attributes	Description
IMAGE	SRC, VALUE, ALIGN	Same as the Submit button, but displays an image instead of text. The image is in a file found at SRC.
PASSWORD	NAME, VALUE	Like a text box but input is hidden. Asterisks appear in the box to replace characters typed.
RADIO	NAME, VALUE	Like check boxes, except only one box (or circle) can be checked at a time.
RESET	NAME, VALUE	Resets the form to its original position; clears all input fields.
SELECT	NAME, OPTION SIZE, MULTIPLE	Provides pop-up menus and scrollable lists. Only one can be selected. Attribute *MULTIPLE* creates a visibly scrollable list. A *SIZE* of *1* creates a pop-up menu with only one visible box.
SUBMIT	NAME, VALUE	When pressed, executes the form; launches CGI.
TEXT	NAME SIZE, MAXLENGTH	Creates a text box for user input. *SIZE* specifies the size of the text box. *MAXLENGTH* specifies the maximum number of characters allowed.
TEXTAREA	NAME, SIZE ROWS, COLS	Creates a text area that can take input spanning multiple lines. *ROWS* and *COLUMNS* specify the size of the box.

19.8.2   Creating an HTML Form

A Simple Form with Text Fields, Radio Buttons, Check Boxes, and Pop-up Menus. First let's see how input gets into the browser by looking at a simple document and the HTML code used to produce it. The user will be able to click on a button, or enter data in the text box. The input in this example won't be processed, thus causing an error to be sent to the server's error log when the Submit button is selected. Nothing will be displayed by the browser. The HTML file is normally stored under the server's root in a directory called *htdocs*. If the HTML file is created on the local machine, then the *file:///* protocol is used in the Location box with the full pathname of the HTML file, which would normally end with an *.html* or *.htm* extension.

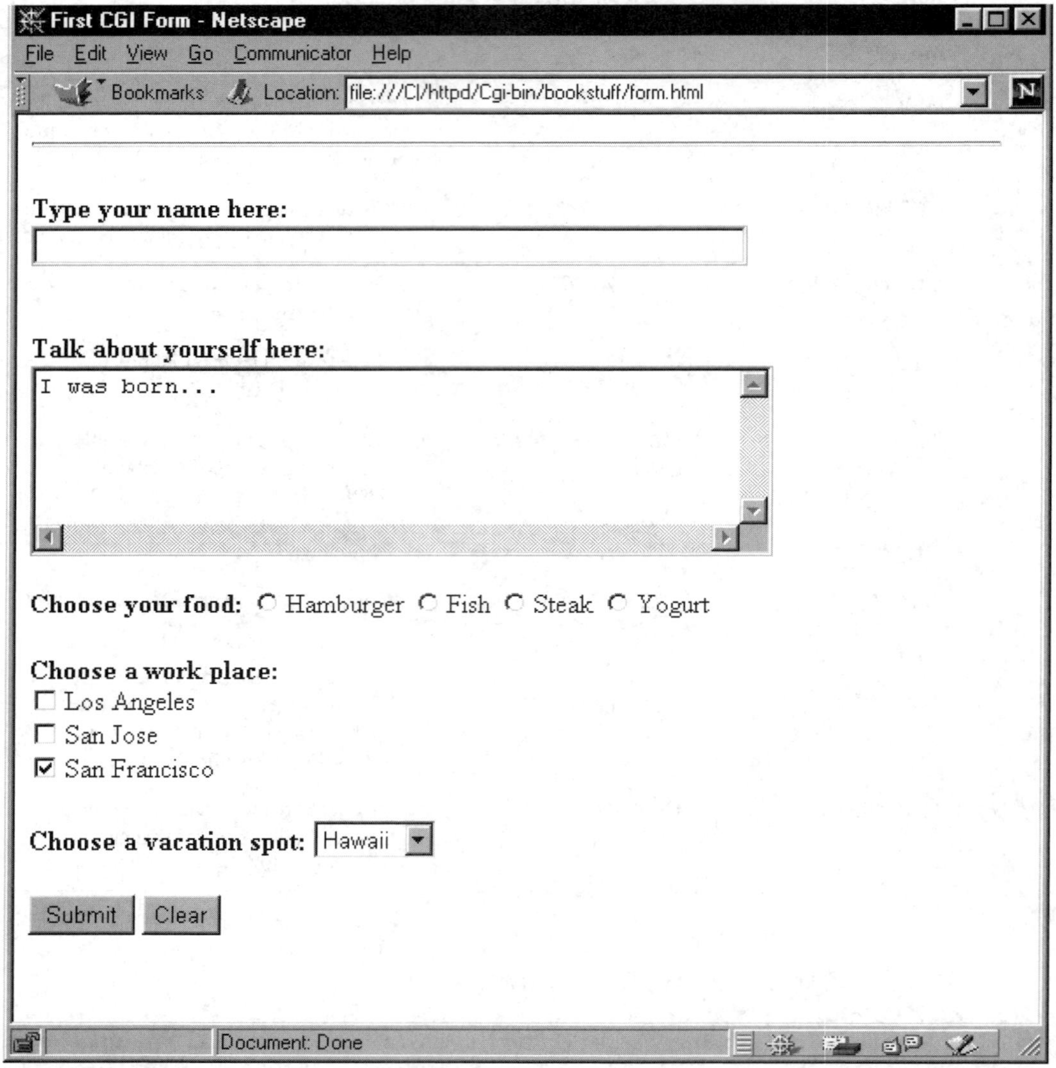

Figure 19.7   A form as it is initially displayed.

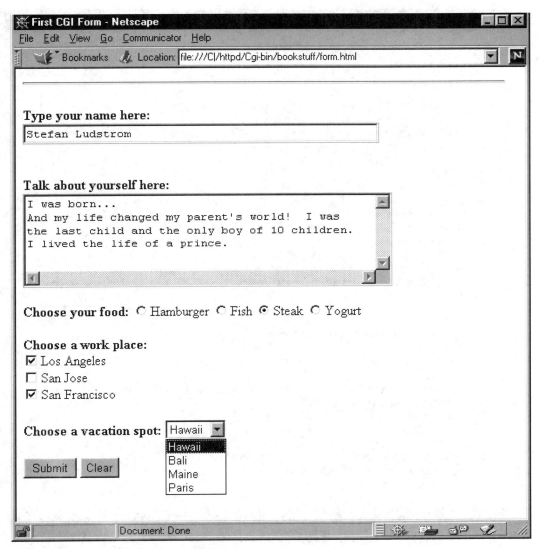

Figure 19.8   A form filled with user input.

EXAMPLE 19.12

```
(The HTML Form Source File)
1    <HTML><HEAD>
2    <TITLE>First CGI Form</TITLE></HEAD>
     <HR>
3    <FORM ACTION="/cgi-bin/bookstuff/form1.cgi" >
4    <P><B> Type your name here:
5    <INPUT TYPE="text" NAME="namestring" SIZE=50>
6    <P><BR> Talk about yourself here: <BR>
7    <TEXTAREA NAME="comments" ROWS=5 COLS=50>I was born...
     </TEXTAREA>
     </B>
8    <P> Choose your food:
9    <INPUT TYPE="radio" NAME="choice" VALUE="burger">Hamburger
     <INPUT TYPE="radio" NAME="choice" VALUE="fish">Fish
     <INPUT TYPE="radio" NAME="choice" VALUE="steak">Steak
     <INPUT TYPE="radio" NAME="choice" VALUE="yogurt">Yogurt
     <P> <B>Choose a work place:</B> <BR>
10   <INPUT TYPE="checkbox" NAME="place" VALUE="LA">Los Angeles
     <BR>
     <INPUT TYPE="checkbox" NAME="place" VALUE="SJ">San Jose
     <BR>
     <INPUT TYPE="checkbox" NAME="place" VALUE="SF" Checked>San
     Francisco
     <P>
11   <B>Choose a vacation spot:</B>
12   <SELECT NAME="location"> <OPTION SELECTED VALUE="hawaii"> Hawaii
     <OPTION VALUE="bali">Bali
     <OPTION VALUE="maine">Maine
     <OPTION VALUE="paris">Paris
     </SELECT> <P>
13   <INPUT TYPE="SUBMIT" VALUE="Submit">
14   <INPUT TYPE="RESET" VALUE="Clear">
     </FORM> </HTML>
```

EXPLANATION

1 This tag says that this is the start of an HTML document.
2 The *<TITLE>* tag; the title appears outside of the browser's main window.
3 The beginning of a *<FORM>* tag, which specifies where the browser will send the input data and the method that will be used to process it. The default method is the *GET* method. When the data is submitted, the CGI script will be executed by the server. The CGI script is located under the server's root directory in the *cgi-bin* directory, the directory where CGI scripts are normally stored. In this example, the *cgi* script is stored in a directory called *bookstuff,* below the *cgi-bin* directory.

EXPLANATION (CONTINUED)

4   The *<P>* tag starts a new paragraph. The *<B>* tag says the text that follows will be in bold type. The user is asked for input.

5   The input type is a text box that will hold up to 50 characters. When the user types text into the text box, that text will be stored in the user-defined *NAME* value, *namestring*. For example, if the user types *Stefan Lundstom*, the browser will assign *namestring=Stefan Lundstrom* to the query string. If assigned a *VALUE* attribute, the text field can take a default; i.e., text that appears in the text box when it is initially displayed by the browser.

6   The user is asked for input.

7   The text area is similar to the text field, but will allow input that scans multiple lines. The *<TEXTAREA>* tag will produce a rectangle (name comments) with dimensions in rows and columns (5 rows by 50 columns) and an optional default value (*I was born...*).

8   The user is asked to pick from a series of menu items.

9   The first input type is a list of radio buttons. Only one button can be selected. The input type has two attributes: a *TYPE* and a *NAME*. The value of the *NAME* attribute *choice*, for example, will be assigned *burger* if the user clicks on the *Hamburger* option. *choice=burger* is passed onto the CGI program. And if the user selects *Fish*, *choice=fish* will be assigned to the query string, and so on. These key/value pairs are used to build a query string to pass onto the CGI program after the Submit button is pressed.

10 The input type this time is in the form of check boxes. More than one check box may be selected. The optional default box is already checked. When the user selects one of the check boxes, the value of the *NAME* attribute will be assigned one of the values from the *VALUE* attribute such as *place=LA* if *Los Angeles* is checked.

11 The user is asked for input.

12 The *<SELECT>* tag is used to produce a pop-up menu (also called a drop-down list) or a scrollable list. The *NAME* option is required. It is used to define the name for the set of options. For a pop-up menu, the *SIZE* attribute is not necessary; it defaults to 1. The pop-up menu initially displays one option and expands to a menu when that option is clicked. Only one selection can be made from the menu. If a *SIZE* attribute is given, that many items will be displayed. If the *MULTIPLE* attribute is given (e.g., *SELECT MULTIPLE NAME=whatever*), the menu appears as a scrollable list, displaying all of the options.

13 If the user clicks the Submit button, the CGI script listed in the form's *ACTION* attribute will be launched. In this example, the script wasn't programmed to do anything. An error message is sent to the server's error log and to the browser.

14 If the *Clear* button is clicked, all of the input boxes are reset back to their defaults.

19.8.3   The *GET* Method

The simplest and most widely supported type of form is created with what is called the *GET* method. It is used every time the browser requests a document. If a method is not supplied, the *GET* method is the default. It is the only method used for retrieving static HTML files and images.

Since HTML is an object-oriented language, you may recall that a method is a name for an object-oriented subroutine. The *GET* method passes data to the CGI program by appending the input to the program's URL, usually as a URL-encoded string. The *QUERY_STRING* environment variable is assigned the value of the encoded string.

Servers often have size limitations on the length of the URL. For example, the UNIX size is limited to 1240 bytes. If a lot of information is being passed to the server, the *POST* method should be used.

Figure 19.9   The HTML form created in the following Example 19.13.

EXAMPLE 19.13

```
HTML Source File with a Form Tag and ACTION Attribute
---------------------------------------------------------------
      <HTML><HEAD><TITLE>First CGI Form</TITLE></HEAD>
      <HR>
1     <FORM ACTION="/cgi-bin/form1.cgi" METHOD=GET>
      <! When user presses "submit", cgi script is called to process
      input >
2     Please enter your name: <BR>
3     <INPUT TYPE="text" SIZE=50 NAME="Name">
      <P>
      Please enter your phone number: <BR>
4     <INPUT TYPE="text" SIZE=30 NAME="Phone">
      <P>
5     <INPUT TYPE=SUBMIT VALUE="Send">
      <INPUT TYPE=RESET VALUE="Clear">
6     </FORM>
      </HTML>
```

EXPLANATION

1   The *<FORM>* tag specifies the URL and method that will be used to process a form. When a user submits the form, the browser will send all the data it has obtained from the browser to the Web server. The *ACTION* attribute tells the server to call a CGI script at the location designated in the URL and send the data on to that program to be processed. The *METHOD* attribute tells the browser how the input data is to be sent to the server. The *GET* method is the default, so it does not need to be assigned here. The CGI program can do whatever it wants to with the data and, when finished, will send it back to the server. The server will then relay the information back to the browser for display.

2   The user is asked for input.

3   The input type is a text box that will hold up to 50 characters. The *NAME* attribute is assigned the string *Name*. This will be the key part of the key/value pair. The user will type something in the text box. The value entered by the user will be assigned to the *NAME* key. This *NAME=VALUE* pair will be sent to the CGI script in that format; for example, *Name=Christian*.

4   The *NAME* attribute for the input type is *Phone*. Whatever the user types in the text box will be sent to the CGI program as *Phone=VALUE*; for example, *Phone=510-456-1234*

5   The *SUBMIT* attribute for the input type causes a Submit button to appear with the string *Send* written on the button. If this box is selected, the CGI program will be executed. The input is sent to the CGI program. The *RESET* attribute allows the user to clear all the input devices by clicking on the *Clear* button.

6   The *</FORM>* tag ends the form.

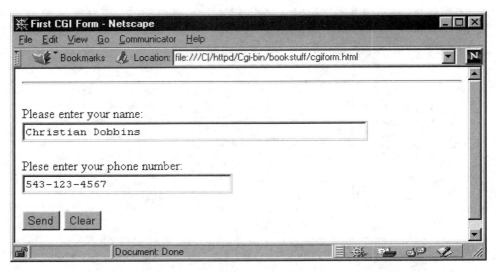

Figure 19.10   Filling out the form from Example 19.13.

EXAMPLE 19.14

```
(The CGI Script)
1   #!/bin/perl
    # The CGI script that will process the form information sent
    # from the server
2   print "Content-type: text/html\n\n";

    print "First CGI form :\n\n";
    # Print out only the QUERY_STRING environment variable

3   while(($key, $value)=each(%ENV)){
4       print "<H3>$key = <I>$value</I></H3><BR>"
                    if $key eq "QUERY_STRING";
    }
```

EXPLANATION

1   The *#!* line tells the server where to find the Perl interpreter.
2   Perl's output goes to the browser rather than the screen. The content type (also called the MIME type) is *text/html* text since there are HTML tags in the text.
3   Perl's input comes from the server. The *while* loop is used to loop through all of the environment variables in the *%ENV* hash. These variables were passed into the Perl script from the Web server.
4   This line will be printed only when the value of the *QUERY_STRING* environment variable is found. It wasn't really necessary to loop through the entire list. It would have been sufficient to just type *print "$ENV{QUERY_STRING}
";*.

19.8.4   Processing the Form

The Encoded Query String.   When using the *GET* method, information is sent to the CGI program in the environment variable, *QUERY_STRING*.[4] The string is URL-encoded. In fact, all data contained in an HTML form is sent from the browser to the server in an encoded format. When the *GET* method is used, this encoded data can be seen on the URL line in your browser preceded by a question mark. The string following the *?* will be sent to the CGI program in the *QUERY_STRING* environment variable. Each key/value pair is separated by an ampersand (*&*) and spaces are replaced with plus signs (+). Any non-alphanumeric values are replaced with their hexadecimal equivalent, preceded by a percent sign (%). After pressing the Submit button in the previous example, you would see the input strings in your browser's Location box (Netscape), appended to the URL line and preceded by a question mark. The highlighted part in the following example is the part that will be assigned to the environment variable, *QUERY_STRING*. The *QUERY_STRING* environment variable will be passed to your Perl script in the *%ENV* hash. To access the key/value pair in your Perl script, add a *print* statement: *print $ENV{QUERY_STRING};*

EXAMPLE 19.15

```
1    What you see in the Location box of the browser:

http://servername/cgi-bin/
     form1.cgi?Name=Christian+Dobbins&Phone=543-123-4567

2    What the server sends to the browser in the ENV hash value,
     QUERY_STRING:

QUERY_STRING=Name=Christian+Dobbins&Phone=543-123-4567
```

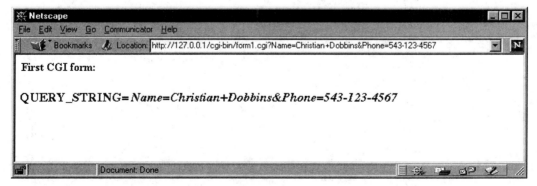

Figure 19.11   Output of the CGI script from Example 19.13.

---

4. When using the *POST* method, input is assigned to a variable from *STDIN* and encoded the same way.

Decoding the Query String with Perl.   Decoding the query string is not a difficult task because Perl has such a large number of string manipulation functions, such as *tr, s, split, substr, pack,* etc. Once you get the query string from the server into your Perl program, you can parse it and do whatever you want with the data. For removing &, +, and = signs from a query string, use the substitution command, *s,* the *split* function, or the translate function, *tr.* To deal with the hexadecimal-to-character conversion of those characters preceded by a % sign, the *pack* function is normally used.

Table 19.10   Encoding Symbols in a Query String

Symbol	Function
&	Separates key/value pairs.
+	Replaces spaces.
%xy	Represents any ASCII character with a value of less than 21 hexadecimal (33 decimal), or greater than 7f (127 decimal) and special characters ?, &, %, +, and = . These characters must be escaped with a %, followed by the hexadecimal equivalence (xy) of that character, e.g., %2F represents a forward slash, and %2c represents a comma.

Table 19.11   URL Hex-Encoded Characters

Character	Value
Tab	%09
Space	%20
!	%21
"	%22
#	%23
$	%24
%	%25
&	%26
(	%28
)	%29
,	%2C

Table 19.11   URL Hex-Encoded Characters *(continued)*

Character	Value
.	%2E
/	%2F
:	%3A
;	%3B
<	%3C
=	%3D
>	%3E
?	%3F
@	%40
[	%5B
\	%5C
]	%5D
^	%5E
`	%60
{	%7B
|	%7C
}	%7D
~	%7E

Parsing the Form's Input with Perl.   After the Perl CGI script gets the input from the form, it will be decoded. This is done by splitting up the key/value pairs and replacing special characters with regular text. Once parsed, the information can be used to create a guest book, a database, send e-mail to the user, and so on.

The routines for parsing the encoded string can be stored in subroutines and saved in your personal library, or you can take advantage of the *CGI.pm* library module, part of Perl's standard distribution, which eliminates all the bother.

Decoding the Query String. Steps to decode are handled with Perl functions. The following shows a URL-encoded string assigned to *$ENV{QUERY_STRING}*.

```
Name=Christian+Dobbins&Phone=510-456-1234&Sign=Virgo
```

The key/pair values show that the URL has three pieces of information separated by the ampersand (&): *Name*, *Phone*, and *Sign*:

```
Name=Christian+Dobbins&Phone=510-456-1234&Sign=Virgo
```

The first thing to do would be to split up the line and create an array (see step 1 below). After splitting up the string by ampersands, remove the + with the *tr* or *s* functions and split the remaining string into key/value pairs with the split function using the = as the split delimiter (see step 2 below).

```
1.  @key_value = split(/&/, $ENV{QUERY_STRING});
    print "@key_value\n";

2.  Output:
    Name=Christian+Dobbins   Phone=510-456-1234   Sign=Virgo
```

The @key_value array created by splitting the query string:

Name=Christian+Dobbins	Phone=510-456-1234	Sign=Virgo

```
3.  foreach $pair ( @key_value){
        $pair =~ tr/+/ /;
        ($key, $value) = split(/=/, $pair);
        print "\t$key: $value\n";
         }

4.  Output:
    Name: Christian Dobbins
    Phone: 510-456-1234
    Sign: Virgo
```

EXAMPLE 19.16

```
(Another URL-Encoded String assigned to $ENV{QUERY_STRING})

1   $input="string=Joe+Smith%3A%2450%2c000%3A02%2F03%2F77";
2   $input=~s/%(..)/pack("c", hex($1))/ge;
3   print $input,"\n";

    Output:
    string=Joe+Smith:$50,000:02/03/77
```

EXPLANATION

1   This string contains ASCII characters that are less than 33 decimal and greater than 127, the colon, the dollar sign, the comma, and the forward slash.

2   The *pack* function is used to convert hexadecimal-coded characters back into character format.

3   The search side of the substitution, */%(..)/*, is a regular expression that contains a literal percent sign followed by any two characters (each dot represents one character) enclosed in parentheses. The parentheses are used so that Perl can store the two characters it finds in the special scalar, *$1*.

     On the replacement side of the substitution, the *pack* function will first use the *hex* function to convert the two hexadecimal characters stored in *$1* to their corresponding decimal values and then pack the resulting decimal values into an unsigned character. The result of this execution is assigned to the scalar, *$input*.

     Now you will have to remove the + sign.

19.8.5   Putting It All Together

The *GET* Method.   Now it is time to put together a form that will be processed by a Perl CGI program using the *GET* method. The CGI program will decode the query string and display the final results on the HTML page that is returned after the form was filled out and the Submit button pressed.

The following examples demonstrate

1. The HTML fill-out form

2. The HTML source file that produced the form

3. The form after it has been processed by the CGI script

4. The Perl CGI script that processed the form

EXAMPLE 19.17

```
(The HTML source file)

    <HTML><HEAD><TITLE>CGI Form</TITLE></HEAD><BODY>
    <HR>
1   <FORM ACTION="http://127.0.0.1/cgi-bin/getmethod.cgi" METHOD=GET>
    <!When user presses "submit", cgi script is called to process
    input >
2   Please enter your name: <BR>
3   <INPUT TYPE="text" SIZE=50 NAME=Name>
    <P>
    Plese enter your salary ($####.##): <BR>
    <INPUT TYPE="text" SIZE=30 NAME=Salary>
    <P>
    Plese enter your birth date (mm/dd/yy): <BR>
    <INPUT TYPE="text" SIZE=30 NAME=Birthdate>
    <P>
4   <INPUT TYPE=SUBMIT VALUE="Submit Query">
    <INPUT TYPE=RESET VALUE="Reset">
5   </FORM>
    </BODY></HTML>
```

EXPLANATION

1   The form is started with the *<FORM>* tag. When the user presses the Submit button on the form, the *ACTION* attribute is triggers the HTTP server on this machine (local host is IP address 127.0.0.1) to start up the script called *getmethod.cgi* found under the server's root in the *cgi-bin* directory.
2   The user is asked for information.
3   The user will fill in the text boxes with his name, salary, etc.
4   When the user presses the Submit button, the CGI script assigned to the *ACTION* attribute will be activated.
5   This is the end of the form tag.

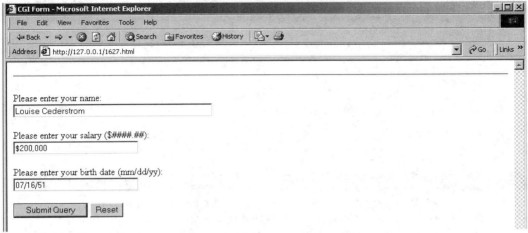

Figure 19.12   The HTML form from Example 19.17.

EXAMPLE 19.18

```perl
#!/usr/bin/perl
# The CGI script that processes the form shown in Figure 19.12.
1   print "Content-type: text/html\n\n";
    print "<H2><U>Decoding the query string</U></H2>";

    # Getting the input
2   $inputstring=$ENV{QUERY_STRING};
    print "<B>Before decoding:</B><BR>";
    print "<H3>$inputstring</H3>";

    # Translate + signs to space
3   $inputstring =~ tr/+/ /;

    # Decoding the hexadecimal characters
4   $inputstring=~s/%(..)/pack("C", hex($1))/ge;

    # After decoding %xy
    print "-" x 80, "<BR>";
    print "<B>After decoding <I>%xy</I>:</B>";
5   print "<H3>$inputstring</H3>";
    # Extracting & and creating key/value pairs
6   @key_value=split(/&/, $inputstring);
7   foreach $pair ( @key_value){
        ($key, $value) = split(/=/, $pair);
```

EXAMPLE 19.18(CONTINUED)

```
8    %input{$key} = $value;     # Creating a hash
       }
     # After decoding
     print "-" x 80, "<BR>";
     print "<B>After decoding + and &:</B>";
9    while(($key, $value)=each(%input)){
10      print "<H3>$key: <I>$value</I></H3>";
     }
     print "<B>Now what do we want to do with this information?"
```

EXPLANATION

1. This MIME header line describes the format of the data returned from this program to be HTML text. The two newlines (required!) end the header information.
2. The *%ENV* hash contains the key/value pairs sent to this Perl program by the Web server. The value of the *QUERY_STRING* environment variable is assigned to a scalar, *$inputstring*.
3. The *tr* function translates all + signs to spaces.
4. The *pack* function converts any hexadecimal numbers to their corresponding ASCII characters.
5. The value of the scalar *$inputstring* is sent from the Perl script to the server and then on to the browser.
6. The scalar *$inputstring* is now split by ampersands. The output returned is stored in the three-element array, *@key_value*, as:
   Name=Louise Cederstrom&Salary=$200,000&Birthdate=7/16/51
7. The *foreach* loop is used to iterate through the *@key_value* array. The resulting key/value pairs are created by splitting each array element by the = sign.
8. A new hash called *%input* is created with corresponding key/value pairs.
9. The *while* loop is used to iterate through the hash.
10. The new key/value pair is printed and sent back to the Web server. The browser displays the output. Now that the Perl script has parsed and stored the input that came from the form, it is up to the programmer to decide what to do with this data. He may send back an e-mail to the user, store the information in a database, create an address book, etc. The real work is done!

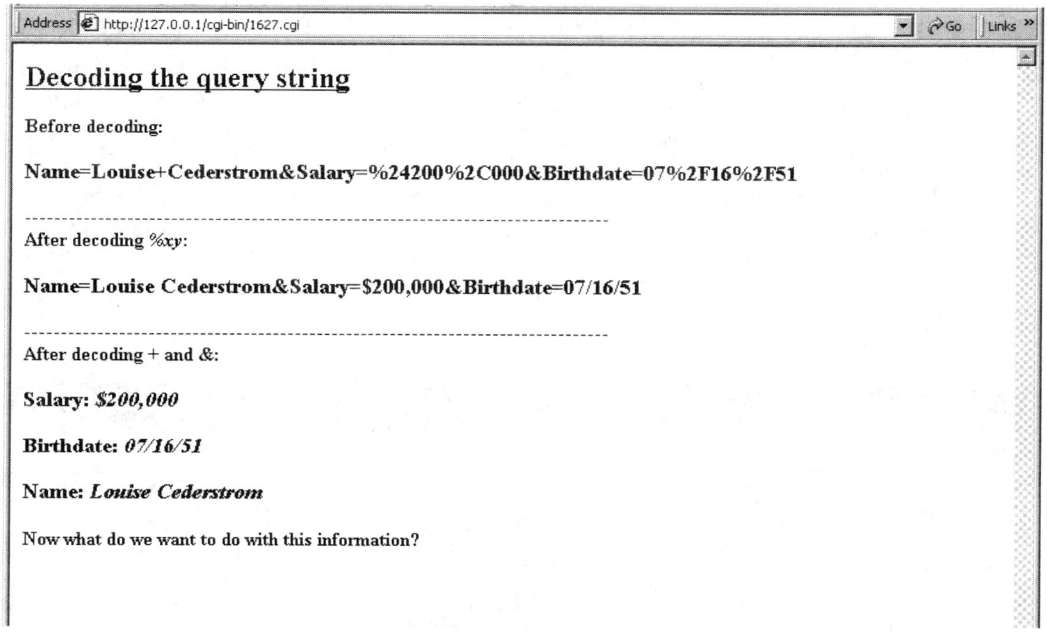

Address 🔘 http://127.0.0.1/cgi-bin/1627.cgi   ▾ ⟳ Go   Links »

Decoding the query string

Before decoding:

Name=Louise+Cederstrom&Salary=%24200%2C000&Birthdate=07%2F16%2F51

After decoding %xy:

Name=Louise Cederstrom&Salary=$200,000&Birthdate=07/16/51

After decoding + and &:

Salary: $200,000

Birthdate: 07/16/51

Name: Louise Cederstrom

Now what do we want to do with this information?

Figure 19.13   Output after CGI/Perl processing, Example 19.18.

The *POST* Method.   The only real difference between the *GET* and *POST* methods is the way that input is passed from the server to the CGI program. When the *GET* method is used, the server sends input to the CGI program in the *QUERY_STRING* environment variable.

When the *POST* method is used, the CGI program gets input from standard input, *STDIN*. Either way, the input is encoded in exactly the same way. One reason for using the *POST* method is that some browsers restrict the amount of data that can be stored in the *QUERY_STRING* environment variable. The *POST* method doesn't store its data in the query string. Also, the *GET* method displays the input data in the URL line in the Location box of the browser, whereas the *POST* method hides the data. Since the *POST* method does not append input to the URL, it is often used in processing forms where there is a lot of data being filled into forms.

In an HTML document, the *<FORM>* tag starts the form. The *ACTION* attribute tells the browser **where** to send the data that is collected from the user, and the *METHOD* attribute tells the browser **how** to send it. If the *POST* is method used, the output from the browser is sent to the server and then to the CGI program's standard input, *STDIN*. The amount of data, that is, the number of bytes taken as input from the user, is stored in the *CONTENT_LENGTH* environment variable.

Rather than assigning the input to the *QUERY_STRING* environment variable, the browser sends the input to the server in a message body, similar to the way e-mail messages are sent. The server then encapsulates all the data and sends it on to the CGI program.

The CGI program reads input data from the *STDIN* stream via a pipe.

The Perl *read* function reads the *CONTENT_LENGTH* amount of bytes, saves the input data in a scalar, and then processes it the same way it processes input coming from the query string. It's not that the format for the input has changed; it's just **how** it got into the program. Note that after the *POST* method has been used, the browser's Location box does not contain the input in the URL as it did with the *GET* method.

EXAMPLE 19.19

```
      (The HTML source file)
      <HTML>
      <HEAD>
      <TITLE>CGI Form</TITLE>
      <HR>
1     <FORM ACTION="http://127.0.0.1/cgi-bin/postmethod.cgi"
      METHOD=POST>
      <!When user presses "submit", cgi script is called to process
      input >
2     Please enter your name: <BR>
3     <INPUT TYPE="text" SIZE=50 NAME=Name>
      <P>
      Please enter your salary ($####.##): <BR>
      <INPUT TYPE="text" SIZE=30 NAME=Salary>
      <P>
      Please enter your birth date (mm/dd/yy): <BR>
      <INPUT TYPE="text" SIZE=30 NAME=Birthdate>
      <P>
4     <INPUT TYPE=SUBMIT VALUE="Submit Query">
      <INPUT TYPE=RESET VALUE="Reset">
5     </FORM>
      </HTML>
```

EXPLANATION

1   The *<FORM>* tag starts the form. The *ACTION* attribute is assigned the URL of the CGI script, *postmethod.cgi*, that will be executed whent the Submit button is pressed by the user, and the *METHOD* attribute is assigned *POST* to indicate how the data coming from the form will be handled.
2   The user is asked for input.
3   Text Fields are created to hold the user's name, salary, and birth date.
4   The Submit button is created.
5   The form is ended.

EXAMPLE 19.20

```perl
(The CGI Script)
    #!/bin/perl
    # Scriptname: postmethod.cgi
1   print "Content-type: text/html\n\n";
    print "<H2><U>Decoding the query string</U></H2>";

    # Getting the input
2   if ( $ENV{REQUEST_METHOD} eq 'GET'){
3       $inputstring=$ENV{QUERY_STRING};
        }
    else{
4       read(STDIN, $inputstring, $ENV{'CONTENT_LENGTH'});
    }
5   print "<B>Before decoding:</B><BR>";
    print "<H3>$inputstring</H3>";

    # Replace + signs with spaces
6   $inputstring =~ tr/+/ /;

    # Decoding the hexadecimal characters
7   $inputstring=~s/%(..)/pack("C", hex($1))/ge;
    # After decoding %xy
    print "-" x 80, "<BR>";
8   print "<B>After decoding <I>%xy</I>:</B>";
    print "<H3>$inputstring</H3>";

    # Extracting the & and = to create key/value pairs

9   @key_value=split(/&/, $inputstring);
10  foreach $pair ( @key_value){
11      ($key, $value) = split(/=/, $pair);
12      %input{$key} = $value;    # Creating a hash to save the data
    }
    # After decoding
    print "-" x 80, "<BR>";
    print "<B>After decoding + and &:</B>";
13  while(($key, $value)=each(%input)){
        # Printing the contents of the hash
        print "<H3>$key: <I>$value</I></H3>";
    }
    print "<B>Now what do we want to do with this information?";
```

EXPLANATION

1   The content being sent to the browser is text interspersed with HTML tags.
2   One of the environment variables sent by the server to the script is *$ENV{REQUEST_METHOD}*, which will have a value of either *GET* or *POST*.
3   If the value of the *$ENV{REQUEST_METHOD}* variable is *GET*, the scalar, *$inputstring* will be assigned the value of the query string, *$ENV{QUERY_STRING}*.
4   If the value of the *$ENV{REQUEST_METHOD}* variable is *POST*, the scalar, *$inputstring* will be assigned the input coming from the standard input stream via the *read* function. The amount of data read is found in the environment variable, *$ENV{CONTENT-LENGTH}*.
5   The value of *$inputstring* is printed with the URL encoding still in place; for example, a space is represented by a + sign, the key/value pairs are separated with an &, and the % sign is followed by the hexadecimal value of the character it represents.
6   All + signs are translated to single spaces.
7   This line replaces the hexadecimal characters with their corresponding ASCII values.
8   After decoding the % hex values, the value of *$inputstring* is printed.
9   The *split* function uses the & as a field separator.
10 The *foreach* loop iterates through array, assigning each element, in turn, to *$pair*.
11 Key/value pairs are created by splitting the string at = signs.
12 A hash, *%input*, is being created on the fly. It will consist of key/value pairs created by splitting up the input string.
13 The *each* function extracts the key/value pairs from the *%input* hash. Each time through the loop the next key/value pair is extracted and displayed in the browser.

Figure 19.14   The HTML input form from Example 19.19.

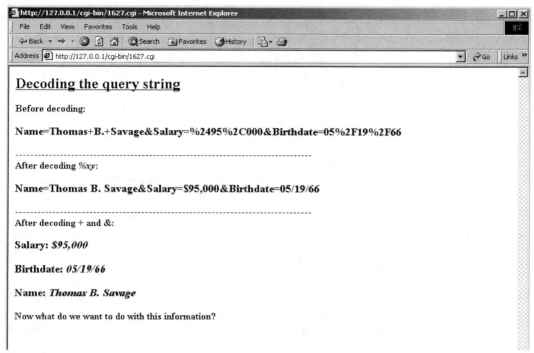

Figure 19.15   The output from the CGI script in Example 19.20.

19.8.6 Handling E-mail

The SMTP Server.   When processing a form, it is often necessary to send e-mail before exiting. You may be sending e-mail to the user and/or to yourself with the submitted form data. E-mail cannot be sent over the Internet without a valid SMTP (Simple Mail Transfer Protocol) server. [5]

The SMTP server is an instance of a mail daemon program that listens for incoming mail on Port 25. SMTP is a TCP-based client/server protocol where the client sends messages to the server. UNIX systems commonly use a mail program called *sendmail* to act as the SMTP server listening for incoming mail. Normally you would run *sendmail* at the command line with the recipient's name as an argument. To end the e-mail message, a period is placed on a line by itself. In a CGI script, the mail will not be sent interactively, so you will probably want to use the *sendmail* options to control these features. See Table 19.12.

---

5. The format for Internet mail messages is defined by RFC822.

Table 19.12 *sendmail* Options

Option	What It Does
-o	A *sendmail* option follows
-t	Reads headers *To*, *From*, *Cc*, and *Bcc* information from message body
-f "email address"	Message is from this e-mail address
-F "name"	Message is from *name*
-i	Periods will be ignored if on a line by themselves
-odq	Queues up multiple e-mail messages to be delivered asynchronously

For Windows, two programs similar to *sendmail* are *Blat,* a public domain Win32 console utility that sends e-mail using the SMTP protocol *(see www.interlog.com/~tcharron/ blat.html),* and *wSendmail,* a small utility that can send e-mail from programs, the command line, or directly from an HTML form (see *www.kode.net/wsendmail.html or www.softseek.com/ Internet/E_Mail/E_Mail_Tools*). Go to CPAN and find the *MailFolder* package, which contains modules such as *Mail::Folder, Mail::Internet,* and *Net::SMTP,* to further simplify the sending and receiving e-mail. For a complete discussion on *sendmail,* see *www.networkcomputing.com/unixworld/tutorial008.*

EXAMPLE 19.21

```
(From the HTML form where the e-mail information is collected)

<FORM METHOD="post" ACTION="http://127.0.0.1/cgi-bin/submit-form">
<INPUT TYPE="hidden" NAME="xemailx"
        VALUE="elizabeth@ellieq.com">
<INPUT TYPE="hidden" NAME="xsubjext"
        VALUE="Course Registration">
<INPUT TYPE="hidden"  NAME="xgoodbyex"
        VALUE="Thank you for registering.">
<P>
<A NAME="REGISTRATION">
<TABLE CELLSPACING=0 CELLPADDING=0>
<TR>
    <TD ALIGN=right><B>First Name:</B></TD>
    <TD ALIGN=left><INPUT TYPE=text NAME="first_name*" VALUE="">
    </TD>
</TR>
```

EXAMPLE 19.21 (CONTINUED)

```
<TR> <TD ALIGN=right><B>Last Name:</B></TD>
    <TD ALIGN=left><INPUT TYPE=text NAME="last_name*"
        VALUE=""></TD>
</TR>
<TR>
    <TD ALIGN=right><B>Company:</B></TD>
    <TD ALIGN=left><INPUT TYPE=text SIZE=30 NAME="company*"
        VALUE=""></TD>
</TR>
<TR>
    <TD ALIGN=right><B>Address1:</B></TD>
    <TD ALIGN=left><INPUT TYPE=text SIZE=30
        NAME="address1*" VALUE=""></TD>
</TR>
<TR>
    <TD ALIGN=right><B>Address2:</B></TD>
    <TD ALIGN=left><INPUT TYPE=text SIZE=30 NAME="address2"
        VALUE=""></TD>
</TR>
<TR>
    <TD ALIGN=right><B>City/Town:</B></TD>
    <TD ALIGN=left><INPUT TYPE=text SIZE=30 NAME="city*"
        VALUE=""></TD>
</TR>
<TR>
    <TD ALIGN=right><B>State/Province:</B></TD>
    <TD ALIGN=left><INPUT TYPE=text SIZE=10 NAME="state"
        VALUE=""><FONT SIZE=-1> Abbreviation or code</TD></TR>
<TR>
    <TD ALIGN=right><B>Postal/Zip Code:</B></TD>
    <TD ALIGN=left><INPUT TYPE=text SIZE=10 NAME="zip"
        VALUE=""></TD>

</TR>

-------------------------------------------------------------

<continues here>
```

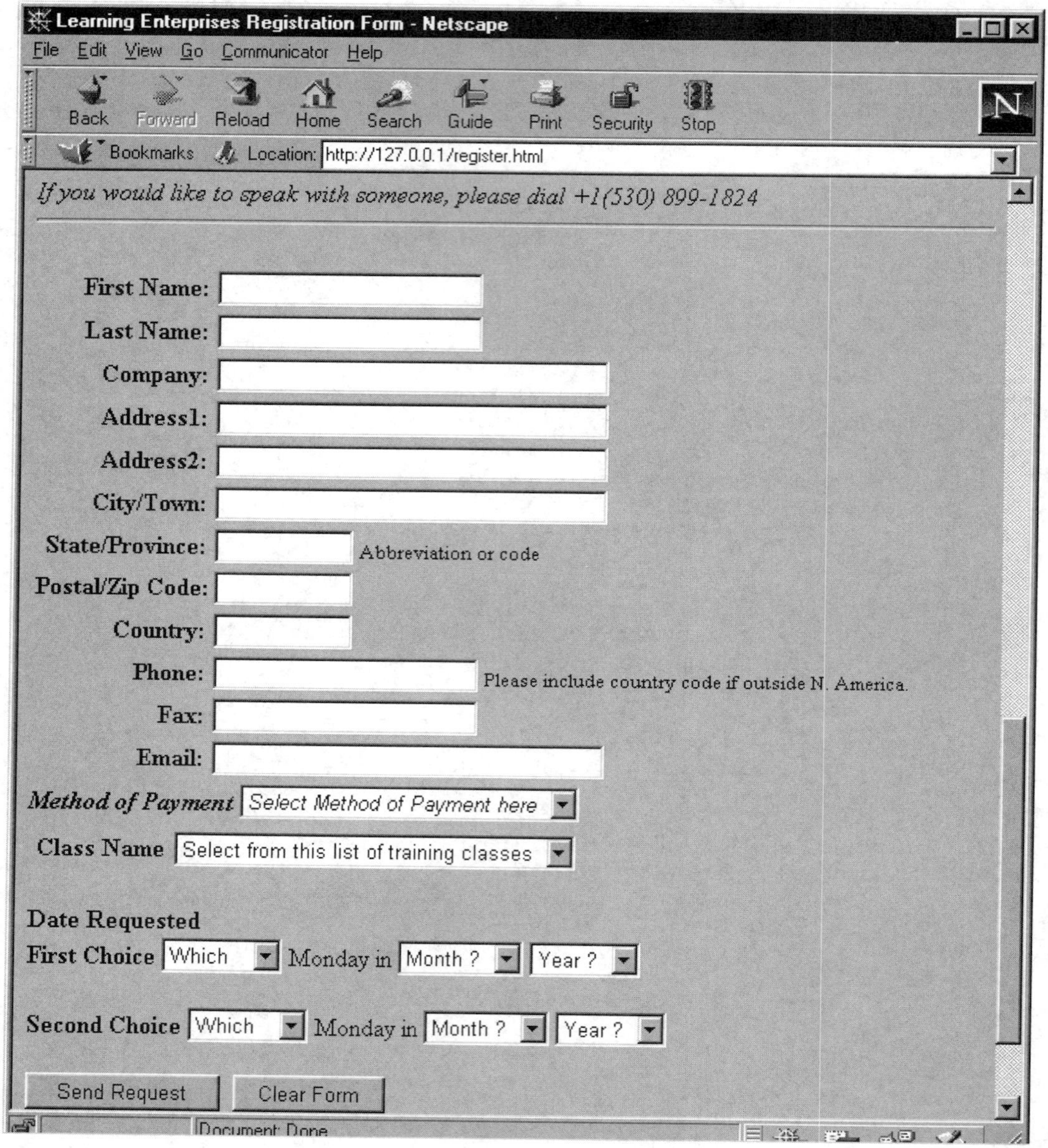

Figure 19.16 Portion of the HTML registration form from Example 19.21.

EXAMPLE 19.22

```
(From a CGI script)
# An HTML Form was first created and processed to get the name of the
# user who will receive the e-mail, the person it's from, and the
# subject line.
1   $mailprogram="/usr/lib/sendmail";   # Your mail program goes here
2   $sendto="$input{xemailx}";          # Mailing address goes here
3   $from="$input{xmailx}";
4   $subject="$input{xsubjext}";

5   open(MAIL, "|$mailprogram -t  -oi") || die "Can't open mail
        program: $!\n";
    # -t option takes the headers from the lines following the mail
    # command -oi options prevent a period at the beginning of  a
    # line from meaning end of input
6   print MAIL "To: $sendto\n";
    print MAIL "From: $from\n";
    print MAIL "Subject: $subject\n\n";

7   print MAIL <<EOF;     # Start a "here document"

    Registration Information for $input{$first_name}
        $input{$last_name}:
    Date of Registration: $today
    ------------------------------------------------
    First Name:           $input{$first_name}
    Last Name:            $input{$last_name}
    Street Address:       $input{$address}
    City:                 $input{$city}
    State/Province:       $input{$state}

    <Rest of message goes here>

8   EOF
9   close MAIL;  # Close the filter
```

EXPLANATION

1   The name of the mail program being used here is *sendmail*, located in the UNIX sub-directory, */usr/lib*.
2   This line will be assigned to the *To:* header in the e-mail document.
3   This line will be assigned to the *From:* header in the e-mail document.
4   And this line is the *Subject:* header in the e-mail document.

EXPLANATION (CONTINUED)

5   Perl is going to open a filter called *MAIL* that will pipe the user's e-mail message to the *sendmail* program. The *-t* option tells *sendmail* to scan the e-mail document for the *To:*, *From:*, and *Subject:* lines (instead of from the command line) and the *-i* option tells the mail program to ignore any period that may be found on a line by itself.

6   These are the header lines indicating to whom the mail is going, where it's going, and the subject of the mail. These values were pulled from the form.

7   A *here document* is started. The text between EOF and EOF is sent to the sendmail program via the *MAIL* filter.

8   EOF marks the end of the *here document*.

9   The *MAIL* filter is closed.

The *Mail::Mailer* Perl Module.   *Mail::Mailer* provides a simple interface for sending Internet mail with *sendmail* and *mail* or *mailx*.

EXAMPLE 19.23

```
(From a CGI script)
1   use Mail::Mailer;
2   my $mailobj = new Mail::Mailer("smtp", Server=>"www.ellieq.com");
3   $mailer -> open( {
            To => $emailaddress,
            From => $sender,
            Subject => "Testing email..."
    } );
    # The mail message is created in a here document
4   print $mailobj << EOF;
    This is a test to see if the Mail::Mailer module is working for
    us. Thankyou for participating in this little experiment!
    EOF

5   close $mailobj;
```

EXPLANATION

1   After downloading *Mail::Mailer* from CPAN, it is to be used in the CGI script.
2   The constructor *new* is called with the name of the SMTP server passed as the first argument. Mail will use the *Net::SMTP* Perl module to send the mail. The server will relay the message on to the e-mail address listed in the *To:* header. A pointer to the mail object is returned.
3   The *Mail::Mailer*'s *open* method is called with an anonymous hash as an argument, consisting of three attributes: the *To:* field with the recipient's address, the *From:* field with the sender's address, and the *Subject:* field. The *open* method creates a Perl output filter. Output from the script will go as input to mail program.
4   A *here document* is created to send the e-mail message.
5   The object is closed; that is, the mail filter is closed.

E-mail and the *mailto:* Protocol.   HTML anchors can be used to create links to files and to e-mail adresses. When a user selects the e-mail hyperlink, their e-mail program starts an e-mail message to the address specified in the *HREF* attribute. The *mailto:* protocol is followed by the valid e-mail address.

EXAMPLE 19.24

```
(Portion of the HTML form showing the e-mail hyperlink)
</MENU>
<P>
Students unable to send appropriate payment information will be
    dropped from the class unceremoniously.
<P>
<I>
If you would like to speak to one of our staff, please dial
    +1(530)899-1824.
<BR>
If you have a question , <A HREF="mailto:elizabeth@ellieq.com">click
    here.</A>
<BR>
<I><FONT SIZE=2>Provide as much detail in your request as possible,
    so that we may reply quickly and as informative as possible.</I>
</TD>
</TR>
<BR>
<BR>If you would like to speak with someone, please dial +1(530) 899-
    1824
<HR>

-----------------------------------
```

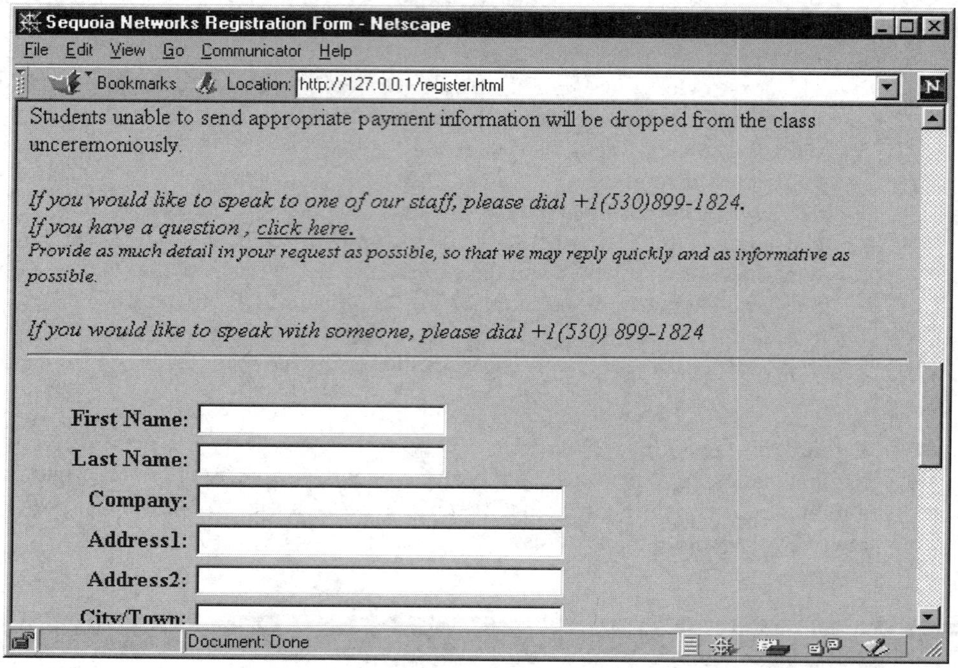

Figure 19.17   The HTML form and hyperlink to an e-mail address, from Example 19.24.

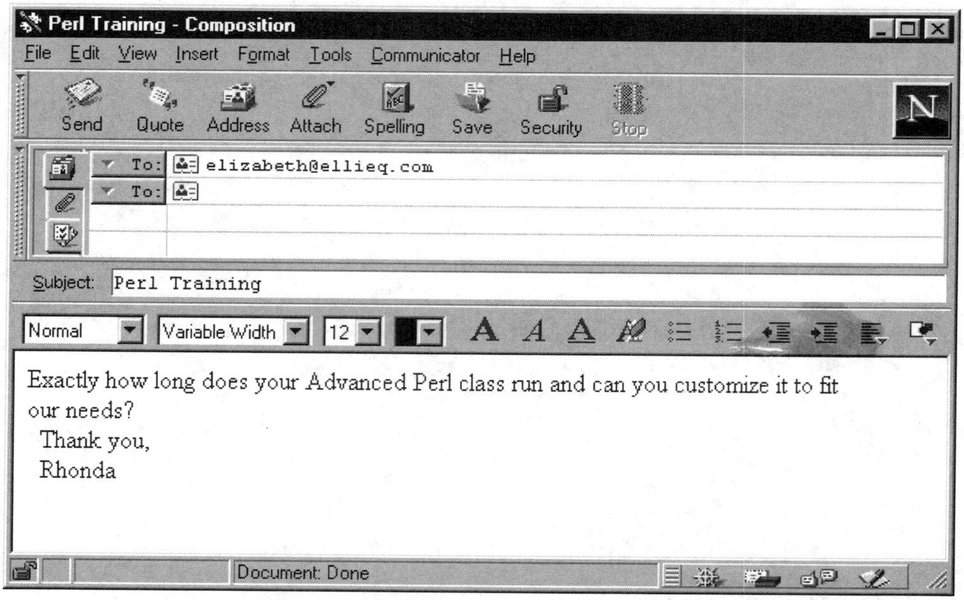

Figure 19.18   E-mail window that appears after clicking on the hyperlink, from Example 19.24.

19.8.7   Extra Path Information

Information can also be provided to the CGI script by appending some extra path information to the URL of the HTML document. The path information starts with a forward slash (/) so that the server can identify where the CGI script ends and the new information begins. The information can then be processed in the CGI script by parsing the value of the *PATH_INFO* environment variable where this extra information is stored.

If the information appended is a path to another file, the *PATH_TRANSLATED* environment variable is also set, mapping the *PATH_INFO* value to the document root directory. The document root directory is found in the *DOCUMENT_ROOT* environment variable. The pathname is treated as relative to the root directory of the server.

EXAMPLE 19.25

```
(The HTML Document)

1   <HTML>
2   <HEAD>
    <Title>Testing Env Variables</title>
    </HEAD>
    <BODY>
    <P>
    <H1> Major Test </h1>
    <P> If You Would Like To See The Environment Variables<Br>
    Being Passed On By The Server, Click .

3   <A Href="Http://susan/cgi-bin/pathinfo.cgi/color=red/
    size=small">here</a>
    <P>
    Text Continues Here...
    </BODY>
    </HTML>
```

EXAMPLE 19.26

```
(The CGI Script)

    #!/bin/perl

1   print "Content type: text/html\n\n";

    print "CGI/1.0 test script report:\n\n";

    print "The argument count is ", $#ARGV + 1, ".\n";
    print "The arguments are @ARGV.\n";
    # Print out all the environment variables

2   while(($key, $value)=each(%ENV)){
3       print "$key = $value\n";
    }

    print "=" x 30, "\n";
4   print "$ENV{PATH_INFO}\n";
5   $line=$ENV{PATH_INFO};
6   $line=~tr/\// /;
7   @info = split(" ", $line);
8   print "$info[0]\n";
9   eval "\$$info[0]\n";
10  print $color;
```

EXPLANATION

1 The content type is *text/html*.
2 The loop iterates through each of the *ENV* variables, assigning the key to *$key* and the corresponding value to *$value*.
3 Each key and value is printed.
4 The value for the *$ENV{PATH_INFO}* environment variable is printed.
5 The value of *$ENV{PATH_INFO}* variable is assigned to the scalar *$line*.
6 All forward slashes are replaced with spaces. */color=red/size=small* will become *color=red size=small* and assigned to *$line*.
7 The *split* function splits the scalar *$line* into an array, using spaces as the separator.
8 The first element of the array, *color=red*, is printed.
9 The *eval* function evaluates the expression and assigns *red* to *$color*.
10 When the scalar *$color* is printed, the value is *red*.

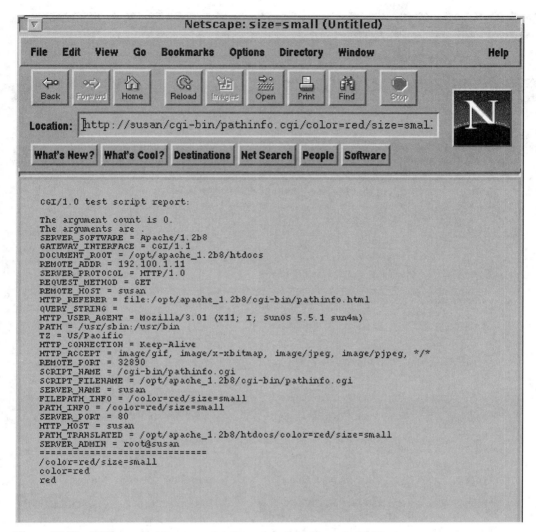

Figure 19.19   CGI output with extra path information, from Example 19.26.

19.8.8   Server Side Includes

It is not always necessary to produce a full-blown CGI script just to get a small amount of
data on the fly from a static HTML document. If you just wanted to know the name of a
remote server, the current file, or the date and time, etc., it would seem silly to have to write
a CGI script. Now most servers support a shortcut feature that allows the HTML document
to output these small amounts of information without requiring an HTTP header. The feature is called *SSI*, short for Server Side Includes, which are really just HTML directives that
are inserted into the HTML document; this type of file normally ends with *.shtml*.

FORMAT

```
<!--command option=value -->
```

EXAMPLE 19.27

```
<!--#exec cgi="/cgi-bin/joker/motto"-->
```

EXPLANATION

Executes the CGI program enclosed in quotes as though it was called from an anchor link.

Table 19.13 Some Common SSI Commands

Command	*Example*	*Meaning*
config	<!-- #config sizefmt="bytes" -->	Sets the format for display size of the file in bytes
echo	<!-- #echo var="DATE_GMT" -->	Prints the date in Greenwich Mean Time (same as UTC); other values are shown in Example 19.28
exec	<!-- #exec cmd="finger" -->	Executes shell command *finger*
flastmod	<!-- $flastmod file="test.html" -->	Inserts a file in the current directory or in a subdirectory
fsize	<!-- #fsize file="test.html" -->	Prints the size of the file
include	<!-- #include file="myfile.html" -->	Inserts a file in the current directory or in a subdirectory

The following example is the HTML source test file from an *OmniHTTPd* Web server.

EXAMPLE 19.28

```
        <HTML>
        <HEAD>
        <Meta Http-equiv="Pragma" Content="No-cache">
        <Title>CGI And SSI Test</title>
        </head>
        <Body Bgcolor="#ffffff">
        <H1>CGI And SSI Test</h1>

        <Hr>
        <H2>standard CGI Test</h2>
        You Are Visitor # <Img Src="/cgi-bin/visitor.exe"><P>
        <Hr>

1       <H2>Server Side Includes</h2>
        If Server Side Includes Are Enabled, You Will See Data Values
        Below:
        <P>
2       The Date Is: <!--#echo Var="Date_local"--><Br>
3       The Current Version Of The Server Is:
            <!--#echo Var="Server_software"--><Br>
4       The CGI Gateway Version Is:
            <!--#echo Var="Gateway_interface"--><Br>
5       The Server Name Is:   <!--#echo Var="Server_name"--><Br>
6       This File Is Called: <!--#echo  Var="Document_name"--><Br>
7       This File's Uri Is: <!--#echo Var= "Document_uri"--><Br>
8       The Query String Is:
            <!--# Echo Var="Query_string_unescaped"--><Br>
9       This File Was Last Modified:
            <!--#echo Var="Last_modified"--><Br>
10      The Size Of The Unprocessed File Is
            !--#fsize Virtual="/test.shtml"--><Br>
11      You Are Using <!--#echo Var="Http_user_agent"--><Br>
12      You Came From <!--#echo Var="Http_referer"--><P>
        <Br>
        <Input Type="Submit" Value="Go!">
        </FORM>
        <HR>
        </BODY>
        </HTML>
```

EXPLANATION

1   Server side includes is enclosed in heading tags to print. If server side includes are enabled, you will see data values below:

2   The date is: *Jul 22 1999*
3   The current version of the server is: *OmniHTTPd/2.0a2(Win32;i386)*
4   The CGI gateway version is: *CGI/1.1*
5   The server name is: *ellie.Learn1.com*
6   This file is called: *C:\HTTPD\HTDOCS\test.shtml*
7   This file's URI is: */test/shtml*
8   The query string is:
9   This file was last modified: *Jun24 1997*
10 The size of the unprocessed file is *1989*
11 You are using Mozilla/2.01KIT *(Win95; U)*
12 You came from *http://127.0.0.1/default.htm*

An Object-Oriented Perl/CGI Program.   If you would like to study a complete CGI program, written by a professional Web developer, go to Appendix B.

19.9 The *CGI.pm* Module

19.9.1 Introduction

The most popular Perl 5 library for writing dynamic CGI programs such as guestbooks, page counters, feedback forms, etc., is the *CGI.pm* module written by Lincoln Stein; it is included in the standard Perl library starting with version 5.004. The most recent version of *CGI.pm* can be found at *www.perl.com/CPAN*. *CGI.pm* not only takes advantage of the object-oriented features that were introduced in Perl 5, it also provides methods (*GET* and *POST*) to interpret query strings, handle forms, and hide the details of HTML syntax.

Lincoln Stein has also written *Official Guide to Programming with CGI.pm*[6] (*www.wiley.com/compbooks/stein*), an excellent, easy-to-read guide from which much of the following information was gleaned.

---

6. Stein, L., *Official Guide to Programming with CGI.pm, The Standard for Building Web Scripts*, Wiley Computer Publishing, 1998.

19.9.2   Advantages

1. *CGI.pm* allows you to keep a fillout form (HTML) and the script that parses it, all in one file under the *cgi-bin* directory. In this way your HTML file (that holds the form) and your CGI script (that reads, parses, and handles the form data) are not so far apart.[7]

2. After the user has filled out a form, the results appear on the same page; in other words, the user doesn't have to backpage to see what was on the form and the fill-out form does not lose data, it maintains its state. Data that doesn't disappear is called "sticky." To override stickiness, see "The override Argument" on page 719.

3. All the reading and parsing of form data is handled by the module.

4. Methods are used to replace HTML tags for creating text boxes, radio buttons, menus, etc. to create the form, as well as for assigning standard tags such as headers, titles, paragraph breaks, horizontal rule lines, breaks, etc.

5. To see what HTML tags are produced by the *CGI.pm* module, from the View menu, select Source (in Internet Explorer) after the form has been displayed.

6. Accepting uploaded files and managing cookies is easier with the *CGI.pm* module.

19.9.3   Two Styles of Programming with *CGI.pm*

The Object-Oriented Style.   Using the object-oriented style, you create one or more CGI objects and then use object **methods** to create the various elements of the page. Each CGI object starts out with the list of named parameters that were passed to your CGI script by the server. You can modify the objects and send them to a file or database. Each object is independent; it has its own parameter list. If a form has been filled out, its contents can be saved from one run of the script to the next; that is, it maintains its **state**. (Normally the HTML documents are **stateless**, in other words, everything is lost when the page exits.)

EXAMPLE 19.29

```
1   use CGI;
2   $obj=new CGI;   # Create the CGI object
3   print $obj->header,      # Use functions to create the HTML page
4   $obj->start_html("Object oriented syntax"),
5   $obj->h1("This is a test..."),
    $obj->h2("This is a test..."),
    $obj->h3("This is a test..."),
6   $obj->end_html;
```

---

7. Ibid.

EXPLANATION

The following output can be seen by viewing the source from the browser. It demonstrates the HTML output produced by the *CGI.pm* module.

```
<!DOCTYPE html
PUBLIC "-//W3C//DTD XHTML 1.0 Transitional//EN"
"DTD/xhtml1-transitional.dtd">
<html xmlns="http://www.w3.org/1999/xhtml" lang="en-US">
<head><title>Object oriented syntax</title></head><body>
<h1>This is a test...</h1>
<h2>This is a test...</h2>
<h3>This is a test...</h3>
</body>
</html>
```

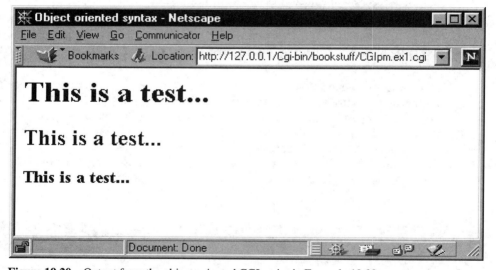

Figure 19.20   Output from the object-oriented CGI script in Example 19.29.

Function-Oriented Style.   The function-oriented style is easier to use than the object-oriented style, because you don't create or manipulate the CGI object directly. The module creates a default CGI object for you. You use the same built-in functions to manipulate the object, pass parameters to the functions to create the HTML tags, and retrieve the information passed into the form.

Although the function-oriented style provides a cleaner programming interface, it limits you to using one CGI object at a time.

The following example uses the function-oriented interface. The main differences are that the *:standard* functions must be imported into the program's namespace, and you don't create a CGI object. It is created for you.[8]

EXAMPLE 19.30

```
    #!/usr/bin/perl
1   use CGI qw(:standard);      # Function-oriented style uses a set of
                                # standard functions
2   print header,
3   start_html("Function oriented syntax"),
4   h1("This is a test..."),
    h2("This is a test..."),
    h3("This is a test..."),
5   end_html;
```

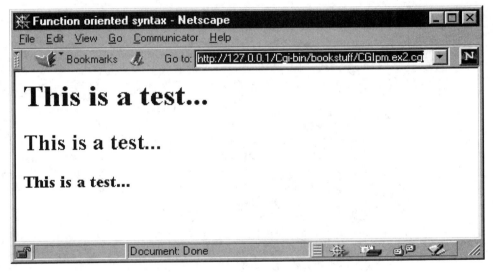

Figure 19.21   Output from the function-oriented CGI script in Example 19.30.

19.9.4   How Input from Forms Is Processed

A CGI script consists of two parts: the part that creates the form that will be displayed in the browser, and the part that retrieves the input from the form, parses it, and handles the information by sending it back to the browser, to a database, to e-mail, etc.

---

8. A default object called *$CGI::Q* is created, which can be accessed directly if needed.

Creating the HTML Form.   Methods are provided to simplify the task of creating the HTML form. For example, there are methods to start and end the HTML form, methods for creating headers, check boxes, pop-up menus, radio buttons, Submit and Reset buttons, etc. Table 19.14 lists the most used of the HTML methods provided by *CGI.pm*.

When passing arguments to the *CGI.pm* methods, two styles can be used:

- **Named arguments**—passed as key/value pairs. Argument names are preceded by a leading dash and are case insensitive.

EXAMPLE 19.31

```
(Named Arguments)
1   print popup_menu(-name=>'place',
                     -values=>['Hawaii','Europe','Mexico', 'Japan' ],
                     -default=>'Hawaii',
                    );
2   print popup_menu(-name=>'place',
                     -values=> \@countries,
                     -default=>'Hawaii',
                    );
```

EXPLANATION

1   The arguments being passed to the *popup_menu* method are called **named parameters** or **argument lists**. The argument names in this examples are *-name*, *-values*, and *-default*. These arguments are always preceded by a leading dash and are case insensitive. If the argument name might conflict with some built-in Perl function or reserved word, quote the argument. Note that the arguments are passed to the method as a set of key/value pairs. The *-values* key has a corresponding value consisting of an anonymous array of countries.

2   This is exactly like the previous example, except that the value for the *-values* key is a reference to an array of countries. Somewhere else in the program, the array *@countries* was created and given values.

- **Positional arguments**—passed as strings, they represent a value. They are used with simple HTML tags. For example, *CGI.pm* provides the *h1()* method to produce the HTML tags, *<H1>* and *</H1>*. The argument for *h1()* is the string of text that is normally inserted between the tags. The method is called as follows:

```
print  h1("This is a positional argument");
```

which translates to

```
<H1>This is a positional argument</H1>
```

If using HTML attributes,[9] and the first argument is a reference to an anonymous hash, the attribute and its values are added after the leading tag into the list. For example:

```
print h1({-align=>CENTER}, "This heading is centered");
```

translates to

```
<H1 ALIGN="CENTER">This heading is centered</H1>
```

If the arguments are a reference to an anonymous list, each item in the list will be properly distributed within the tag. For example:

```
print li( ['apples', 'pears', 'peaches'] );
```

translates to three bulleted list items:

```
<LI>apples</LI> <LI>pears</LI> <LI>peaches</LI>
```

whereas

```
print li( 'apples', 'pears', 'peaches' );
```

translates to one bulleted list item:

```
<LI>apples pears peaches</LI>
```

EXAMPLE 19.32

```
(The CGI script)
     # Shortcut calling styles with HTML methods
     use CGI qw(:standard);  # Function-oriented style print header
1    start_html("Testing arguments"),
     b(),
2    p(),
3    p("red", "green", "yellow"),
4    p("This is a string"),
5    p({-align=>center}, "red", "green", "yellow"),
6    p({-align=>left}, ["red","green","yellow"]),
     end_html;
```

----

9. Attributes do not require a leading dash.

EXAMPLE 19.32 (CONTINUED)

```
(Output produced by CGI.pm methods)
1   Content-Type: text/html; charset=ISO-8859-1<!DOCTYPE html
    PUBLIC "-//W3C//DTD XHTML 1.0 Transitional//EN"
    "DTD/xhtml1-transitional.dtd">
    <html xmlns="http://www.w3.org/1999/xhtml" lang="en-US">
    <head><title>Testing arguments</title></head>
    <body>
    <b />
2   <p />
3   <p>red green yellow</p>
4   <p>This is a string</p>
5   <p align="center">red green yellow</p>
6   <p align="left">red</p> <p align="left">green</p>
    <p align="left">yellow</p>
    </body>
    </html>
```

EXPLANATION

1   The function-oriented style of the *CGI.pm* module is used. The *START_HTML* method generates the header information and starts the body of the HTML document.
2   The *p()* (paragraph method) generates a paragraph tag that takes no arguments. It is a start tag only.
3   The quoted list of comma-separated arguments produces a single string argument. The paragraph's text is displayed as one line on the brower: *red green yellow*. It consists of a start tag, the arguments as a single string, and an end tag.
4   The string is also displayed as a single string. It consists of a start tag, the string, and and end tag.
5   The string is a centered paragraph. This paragraph tag consists of a start tag, attributes, arguments, and an end tag.
6   This paragraph tag displays each word, left-justified, on a line by itself. It consists of a start tag, with the attributes for left alignment distributed across each of the listed arguments. The arguments are listed as a reference to an anonymous array.

To avoid conflicts and warnings (*-w* switch), enclose all arguments in quotes.

Table 19.14   HTML Methods

Method	What it Does	Attributes
a( )	Anchor tag *<A>*	*-href, -name, -onClick, -onMouseOver,* *-target*
applet( ) (:html3 group)	Embedding applets *<APPLET>*	*-align, -alt, -code, -codebase, -height,* *-hspace, -name, -vspace, -width*
b( )	Bold text *<B>*	
basefont( ) (:html3)	Set size of base font *<FONT>*	*-size* (sizes 1–7)
big (:netscape group)	Increase text size *<BIG>*	
blink (:netscape group)	Creates blinking text *<BLINK>*	
br( )	Creates a line break * *	
button( )	Creates a push button to start a JavaScript event handler when pressed	*-name, -onClick, -value, -label*
caption (:html3)	Inserts a caption above a table *<CAPTION>*	*-align, -valign*
center( ) (:netscape group)	Center text *<CENTER>*	Doesn't seem to work Use the *<CENTER>* tag.
cite( )	Creates text in a proportional italic font *<CITE>*	
checkbox( )	Creates a single named check box and label	*-checked, -selected, -on, -label, -name,* *-onClick, -override, -force, -value*
checkbox_group( )	Creates a set of check boxes linked by one name	*-columns, -cols, -colheaders, -default,* *-defaults, -labels, -linebreak, -name,* *-nolabels, -onClick, -override, -force,* *-rows, -rowheaders, -value, -values*
code( )	Creates text in a monospace font *<CODE>*	
dd( )	Definition item of definition list *<DD>*	

Table 19.14   HTML Methods *(continued)*

Method	*What it Does*	*Attributes*
defaults( )	Creates a fill-out button for submitting a form as though for the first time; clears the old parameter list	
dl( )	Creates a definition list *<DL>*; see *dd( )*	*-compact*
dt( )	Term part of definition list *<DT>*	
em( )	Emphatic (italic) text	
end_form( ), endform( )	Terminate a form *</FORM>*	
end_html( )	Ends an HTML document *</BODY></HTML>*	
font( ) (:netscape group)	Changes font	*-color, -face, -size*
frame( ) (:netscape group)	Defines a frame	*-marginheight, -marginwidth, -name, -noresize, -scrolling, -src*
frameset( ) (:netscape group)	Creates a frameset *<FRAMESET>*	*-cols, -rows*
h1( )...h6( )	Creates heading levels 1–6 *<H1>, <H2> ... <H6>*	
hidden( )	Creates a hidden, invisible text field, uneditable by the user	
hr( )	Creates a horizontal rule *<HR>*	*-align, -noshade, -size, -width*
i( )	Creates italic text *<I>*	
img( )	Creates an inline image *<IMG>*	*-align, -alt, -border, -height, -width, -hspace, -ismap, -src, -lowsrc, -vrspace, -usemap*
image_button( )	Produces an inline image that doubles as a form submission button	*-align, -alt.-height, -name, -src, -width*
kbd( )	Creates text with keyboard style	

Table 19.14   HTML Methods *(continued)*

Method	*What it Does*	*Attributes*
li( )	Creates list item for an ordered or unordered list	*-type, -value*
ol( )	Start an ordered list	*-compact, -start, -type*
p( )	Creates a paragraph *<P>*	*-align, -class*
password_field( )	Creates a password field; text entered will be stars	
popup_menu( )	Creates a pop-up menu *<SELECT><OPTION>*	*-default, -labels, -name, -onBlur, -onChange, -onFocus, -override, -force, -value, -values*
pre( )	Creates preformatted typewriter text for maintaining line breaks, etc. *<PRE>*	
radio_group( )	Creates a set of radio buttons all linked by one name	*-columns, -cols, -colheaders, -default, -labels, -linebreak, -name, -nolabels, -onClick, -override, -force, -rows, -rowheaders, -value, -values*
reset( )	Creates form's Reset button	
scrolling_list( )	Controls a scrolling list box form element	*-default, -defaults, -labels, -multiple, -name, -onBlur, -onChange, -onFocus, -override, -force, -size, -value, -values*
Select( )	Creates a select tag; Note the uppercase "S" to avoid conflict with Perl's built-in *select* function. *<SELECT>*	
small( ) (:netscape group)	Reduce size of text	
start_form( ),startform( )	Starts an HTML form *<FORM>*	
start_multipart_form( ),	Just like *start_form*, but used when uploading files	
strong( )	Bold text	
submit( )	Creates a Submit button for a form	*-name, -onClick, -value, -label*

Table 19.14   HTML Methods *(continued)*

Method	*What it Does*	*Attributes*
sup( ) (:netscape group)	Superscripted text	
table( ) (:html3 group)	Creates a table	*-align,bgcolor, -border, -bordercolor, -bordercolor-dark, -bordercolorlight, -cellpadding, -hspace, -vspace, -width*
td( ) (:html3 group)	Creates a table data cell *<TD>*	*-align, -bgcolor, -bordercolor, -bordercolorlight,-bordercolordark, -colspan, -nowrap, -rowspan, -valign, -width*
textarea( )	Creates a multiline text box	*-cols, -columns, -name, -onChange, -onFocus,OnBlur, -onSelect, -override, -force, -value, -default, -wrap*
textfield( )	Produces a one-line text entry field	*-maxLength, -name, -onChange, -onFocus, -onBlur, -onSelect, -override, -force, -size, -value, -default*
th( ) (:html3 group)	Creates a table header *<TH>*	
Tr( ) (:html3 group)	Defines a table row; Note the uppercase "T" to avoid conflict with Perl's *tr* function. *<TR>*	*-align,bgcolor, -bordercolor, -bordercolordark, -bordercolorlight, -valign*
tt( )	Typewriter font	
ul( )	Start unordered list	

Processing the Form's Data with *param().*   After the user has filled in a form, *CGI.pm* will take the input from the form and store it in name/value pairs. The names and values can be retrieved with the *param( )* function. When *param( )* is called, if null is returned, then the form has not yet been filled out. If the *param( )* function returns true (non-null), then the form must have been filled out, and the *param( )* function can be used to retrieve the form information. If you want an individual value, the *param( )* can retrieve it by its name. The following example illustrates the two parts to the CGI program: the HTML form, and how to get the information with the *param( )* function. For a list of other methods used to process parameters, see Table 19.16.

EXAMPLE 19.33

```perl
     #!/usr/bin/perl
1    use CGI qw(:standard);
2    print header;
3    print start_html(-title=>'Using the Function-Oriented Syntax',
                       -BGCOLOR=>'yellow');
4    print img({-src=>'/Images/GreenBalloon.gif', -align=LEFT}),
5        h1("Let's Hear From You!"),
         h2("I'm interested."),

6        start_form,
7        "What's your name? ", textfield('name'),
8        p,
         "What's your occupation? ", textfield('job'),
         p,
9        "Select a vacation spot. ", popup_menu(
             -name=>'place',
             -values=>['Hawaii','Europe','Mexico', 'Japan' ],
                                         ),
         p,
10           submit,
11       end_form;

     print hr;

12   if ( param() ){    # If the form has been filled out,
                        # there are parameters
13       print "Your name is ", em(param('name')),
         p,
             "Your occupation is ", em(param('job')),
         p,
             "Your vacation spot is", em(param('place')),
         hr;
     }
```

EXPLANATION

1   The *use* directive says that the *CGI.pm* module is being loaded and will import the *:standard* set of function calls, which use a syntax new in library versions 1.21 and higher. This syntax allows you to call methods without explicitly creating an object with the *new* constructor method; that is, the object is created for you. The *Official Guide to Programming with CGI.pm* by Lincoln Stein contains a complete list of shortcuts.

2   The header method *header* returns the *Content-type: header*. You can provide your own MIME type if you choose, otherwise it defaults to *text/html*.

3   This will return a canned HTML header and the opening *<BODY>* tag. Parameters are optional and are in the form *-title*, *-author*, and *-base*. Any additional parameters, such as the Netscape unofficial *BGCOLOR* attribute, are added to the *<BODY>* tag; for example, *BGCOLOR=>yellow*.

EXPLANATION (CONTINUED)

4   The *img* method allows you to load an image. This GIF image is stored under the document's root in a directory called *Images*. It is aligned to the left of the text. Note: The *print* function here does not terminate until line 11. All of the CGI functions are passed as a comma-separated list to the *print* function.

5   This will produce a level 1 heading tag. It's a shortcut and will produce the *<H1>* HTML tag.

6   This method starts a form. The defaults for the form are the *ACTION* attribute, assigned the URL of this script, and the *METHOD* attribute, assigned the *POST* method.

7   The *textfield* method creates a text field box. The first parameter is the *NAME* for the field, the second parameter representing the *VALUE* is optional. *NAME* is assigned *name* and *VALUE* is assigned "".

8   The *p* is a shortcut for a paragraph *<P>*.

9   The *popup_menu* method creates a menu. The required first argument is the menu's name (*-name*). The second argument, *-values,* is an array of menu items. It can be either anonymous or named.

10 The *submit* method creates the Submit button.

11 This line ends the form.

12 If the *param* method returns non-null, each of the values associated with the parameters will be printed.

13 The *param* method returns the value associated with *name*; in other words, what the user typed as input for that parameter.

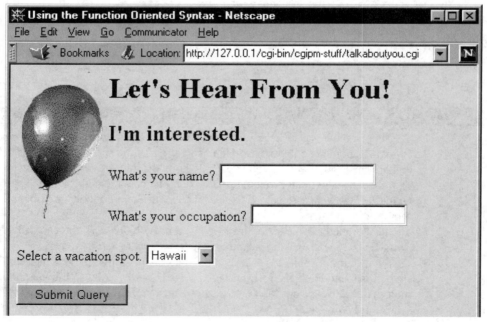

Figure 19.22   Output from lines 1–11 in Example 19.33 before filling out the form.

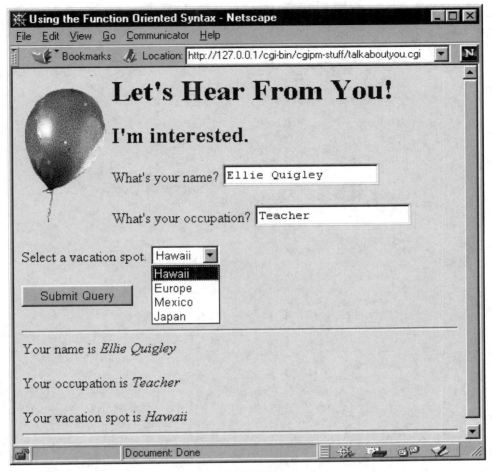

Figure 19.23   The completed form and result of *CGI.pm* processing.

Checking the Form at the Command Line.   If you want to see the HTML tags generated by the *CGI.pm* form, you can run your script at the command line, but you will probably see the following error message:

```
(Offline mode: enter name=value pairs on standard input)
```

You can handle this by typing in key/value pairs and then pressing *<Ctrl>-d* (UNIX) or *<Ctrl>-z* (Windows) or by passing an empty parameter list. When the parameter list is empty, the output will let you see the HTML tags that were produced without any values assigned. See Example 19.34.

EXAMPLE 19.34

```
(At the Command Line)
1  $ perl talkaboutyou.pl
   (Offline mode: enter name=value pairs on standard input)
   name=Dan
   job=Father
   place=Hawaii
   <Now press Ctrl-d or Ctrl-z>

(Output)
   Content-Type: text/html

   <!DOCTYPE HTML PUBLIC "-//IETF//DTD HTML//EN">
   <HTML><HEAD><TITLE>Using the Function Oriented Syntax</TITLE>
   </HEAD><BODY BGCOLOR="yellow">
   <H1>Let's Hear From You!</H1>
   <H2>I'm internested.</H2>
   <FORM METHOD="POST"  ENCTYPE="application/x-www-form-urlencoded">
       What's your name? <INPUT TYPE="text" NAME="name"
       VALUE="Dan"><P>What's your occupation? <INPUT TYPE="text"
       NAME="job" VALUE="Father"><P>Select a vacation spot.
       <SELECT NAME="place">
   <OPTION SELECTED VALUE="Hawaii">Hawaii
   <OPTION   VALUE="Europe">Europe
   <OPTION   VALUE="Mexico">Mexico
   <OPTION   VALUE="Japan">Japan
   </SELECT>
   <P><INPUT TYPE="submit" NAME=".submit"></FORM>
       <HR>Your name is <EM>Dan</EM><P>Your occupation is <EM>Father
       </EM><P>Your vacation spot is <EM>Hawaii</EM><HR>

(At the Command Line)
2  $ perl talkaboutyou.pl < /dev/null  or perl talkaboutyou.pl ' '
   Content-Type: text/html

(Output)
   <!DOCTYPE HTML PUBLIC "-//IETF//DTD HTML//EN">
   <HTML><HEAD><TITLE>Using the Function Oriented Syntax</TITLE>
   </HEAD><BODY BGCOLOR="yellow">
   <H1>Let's Hear From You!</H1>
   <H2>I'm interested.</H2><FORM METHOD="POST"
       ENCTYPE="application/x-wwwform-urlencoded">
       What's your name? <INPUT TYPE="text" NAME="name"
       VALUE=""><P>What's your occupation? <INPUT TYPE="text"
       NAME="job" VALUE=""><P>Select a vacation spot.
       <SELECT NAME="place">
   <OPTION   VALUE="Hawaii">Hawaii
   <OPTION   VALUE="Europe">Europe
   <OPTION   VALUE="Mexico">Mexico
   <OPTION   VALUE="Japan">Japan
   </SELECT>
   <P><INPUT TYPE="submit" NAME=".submit"></FORM><HR>Your name is
       <EM><P>Your occupation is <EM><P>Your vacation spot is <EM><HR>
```

EXPLANATION

1   When running in offline mode, you can enter the key/value pairs as standard input. You need to check the form so that you get the right keys and then supply the values yourself. In this example, *name=Dan, job=Father, place=Hawaii* were supplied by the user. After pressing *<Ctrl>-d* (UNIX) or *<Ctrl>-z* (Windows), the input will be processed by *CGI.pm*.

2   By passing an empty parameter list, you can see the HTML output as it appears without the values assigned. If using UNIX, */dev/null* is the UNIX bit bucket (black hole), and reading from that directory is the same as reading from an empty file. By supplying a set of empty quotes as an argument, the effect is the same.

19.9.5   *CGI.pm* Form Elements

Table 19.15   CGI Methods

Method	Example	What It Does
append	$query–>append(-name=>'value');	Appends values to parameter
checkbox	$query–>checkbox(-name=>'checkbox_name', -checked=>'checked', -value=>'on', -label=>'clickme');	Creates a standalone check box
checkbox_group	$query–>checkbox_group(-name=> 'group_name', -values=>[list], -default=>[sublist], -linebreak=>'true', -labels=>\%hash);	Creates a group of check boxes
cookie	$query–>cookie(-name=>'sessionID', -value=>'whatever', -expires=>'+3h', -path=>'/', -domain=>'ucsc.edu', -secure=>1);	Creates a Netscape cookie
defaults	$query–>defaults;	Creates a button that resets the form to its defaults
delete	$query–>delete('param');	Deletes a parameter
delete_all	$query–>delete;	Deletes all parameters; clears $query, the object
endform	$query–>endform;	Ends the *<FORM>* tag
header	$query–>header(-cookie=>'cookiename');	Puts a cookie in the HTTP header
hidden	$query–>hidden(-name=>'hidden', -default=>[list]);	Creates a hidden-from-view text field
image_button	$query–>image_button(-name=>'button', -src=>'/source/URL', -align=>'MIDDLE');	Creates a clickable image button
import_names	$query–>import_names('namespace');	Imports variables into namespace

Table 19.15   CGI Methods *(continued)*

Method	*Example*	*What It Does*
keywords	@*keywords* = $*query*–>*keywords;*	Obtains parsed keywords from the *Isindex* input string and returns an array
new	$*query* = *new CGI;*	Parses input and puts it in object $*query* for both the *GET* and *POST* methods
	$*query* = *new CGI(INPUTFILE);*	Reads contents of form from previously opened filehandle
param	@*params* = $*query*–>*param(-name=>'name',* *-value=>'value');*	Returns an array of parameter names passed into the script
	$*value* = $*query*–>*('arg');*	Returns a value (or list of values) for the @*values* = $*query*–>*('arg')* parameter passed
password_field	$*query*–>*password_field(-name=>'secret'* *-value=>'start', -size=>60, -maxlength=>80);*	Creates a password field
popup_menu	$*query*–>*popup_menu(-name=>'menu'* *-values=>@items, -defaults=>'name',* *-labels=>\%hash);*	Creates a pop-up menu
radio_group	$*query*–>*radio_group(-name=>'group_name',* *-values=>[list], -default=>'name',* *-linebreak=>'true', -labels=>\%hash);*	Creates a group of radio buttons
reset	$*query*–>*reset;*	Creates the Reset button to clear a form boxes to former values
save	$*query*–>*save(FILEHANDLE);*	Saves the state of a form to a file
scrolling_list	$*query*–>*scrolling_list(-name=>'listname',* *-values=>[list], -default=> [sublist],* *-multiple=>'true', -labels=>\%hash);*	Creates a scrolling list
startform	$*query*–>*startform(-method=> -action=>,* *-encoding);*	Returns a *<FORM>* tag with optional method, action, and encoding
submit	$*query*–>*submit(-name=>'button',* *-value=>'value');*	Creates the *Submit* button for forms
textarea		Same as text field, but includes multiline text entry box
textfield	$*query*–>*textfield(-name=>'field',* *-default=>'start', -size=>50, -maxlength=>90);*	Creates a text field box

Table 19.16   CGI Parameter Methods

Method	What It Does	Example
delete(), Delete()	Deletes a named parameter from parameter list. Delete must be used if you are using the function-oriented style of *CGI.pm*.	$obj–>delete('Joe'); $obj–>delete(-name=>'Joe'); Delete('Joe'); Delete(-name=>'Joe');
delete_all(), Delete_all()	Deletes all CGI parameters.	$obj–>delete_all(); Delete_all();
import_names()	Imports all CGI parameters into a specified namespace.	
param()	Retrieves parameters from a fillout form in key/value pairs. Can return a list or a scalar.	print $obj–>param(); @list=$obj–>param(); print param('Joe'); $name=$obj–>param(-name=>'Joe');

Methods For Generating Form Input Fields.   The following examples use the object-oriented style, and can easily be replaced with the function-oriented style by removing all object references. The *print_form* subroutine will cause the form to be displayed in the browser window and the *do_work* subroutine will produce output when the *param* method returns a true value, meaning that the form was filled out and processed.

The texfield() Method

The *textfield* method creates a text field. The text field allows the user to type in a single line of text into a rectangular box. The box dimensions can be specified with the *-size* argument, where the size is the width in characters, and *-maxlength* (a positive integer) sets an upper limit on how many characters the user can enter. If *-maxlength* is not specified, the default is to enter as many characters as you like. With the *-value* argument, the field can be given a default value, text that will appear in the box when it is first displayed.

FORMAT

```
print $obj->textfield('name_of_textfield');
print $obj->textfield(
    -name=>'name_of_textfield',
    -value=>'default starting text',
    -size=>'60',          # Width in characters
    -maxlength=>'90');    # Upper width limit
```

EXAMPLE 19.35

```perl
   #!/usr/bin/perl
1  use CGI;
2  $query = new CGI;
   # Create a CGI object
3  print $query->header;
4  print $query->start_html("Forms and Text Fields");
5  print  $query->h2("Example: The textfield method");

6  &print_form($query);
7  &do_work($query) if ($query->param);
   print $query->end_html;

8  sub print_form{
9      my($query) = @_;
10     print $query->startform;
       print "What is your name? ";
11     print $query->textfield('name');   # A simple text field
       print  $query->br();

12     print "What is your occupation? ";
13     print $query->textfield(-name=>'occupation',   # Giving values
                               -default=>'Retired',   # to the
                               -size=>60,             # text field
                               -maxlength=>120,
                              );
       print $query->br();
14     print $query->submit('action', 'Enter ');
15     print $query->reset();
16     print $query->endform;
       print $query->hr();
   }
17 sub do_work{
       my ($query) = @_;
       my (@values, $key);
       print $query->("<H2>Here are the settings</H2>");
18     foreach $key ($query->param){
           print "$key: \n";
19         @values=$query->param($key);
           print join(", ",@values), "<BR>";
       }
   }
```

EXPLANATION

1   The *CGI.pm* module is loaded. It is an object-oriented module.

2   The CGI constructor method, called *new*, is called and a reference to a CGI object is returned.

3   The HTML header information is printed; for example, *Content-type: text/html*.

4   The *start_html* method produces the HTML tags to start HTML, the title *Forms and Textfields*, and the body tag.

5   The *h2* method produces an *<H2>*, heading level 2, tag.

6   This user-defined *print_form* function is called, with a reference to the CGI object is passed as an argument.

7   The *do_work* function is called with a reference to the CGI object passed as an argument. This is a user-defined function that will only be called if the *param* function returns true, and *param* returns true only if the form has been filled out.

8   The *print_form* function is defined.

9   The first argument is a reference to the CGI object.

10   The *startform* method produces the HTML *<FORM>* tag.

11   The *textfield* method produces a text box with one parameter, *name*. Whatever is assigned to the text box will be assigned to *name*.

12   The user is asked to provide input into the text box.

13   This *textfield* method is sent arguments as key/value hash pairs to further define the text field. The default will show in the box. See the output of this example in Figure 19.24.

14   The *submit* method creates a Submit button with the text *Enter* in the button.

15   The *reset* method creates a Reset button with the default text *Reset* in the the button.

16   The *endform* method creates the HTML *</FORM>* tag.

17   This is the user's *do_work* function that is called after the user fills out the form and presses the Submit (*Enter*) button. It processes the information supplied in the form with the *param* function.

18   The *param* function returns a key and a list of values associated with that key. The key is the name of the parameter for the input form and the values are what were assigned to it either by the user or in the form. For example, the key named *occupation* was filled in by the user as *jack of all trades,* whereas the *action* key in the Submit button was assigned *Enter* within the form before it was processed.

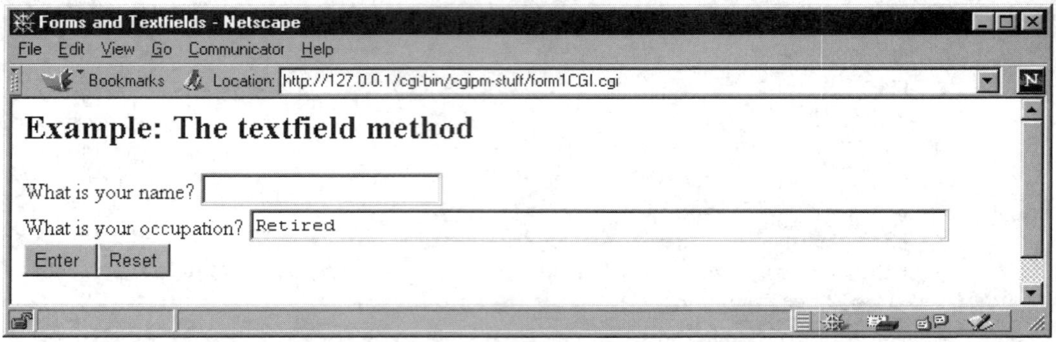

Figure 19.24   Output for text field form, Example 19.35.

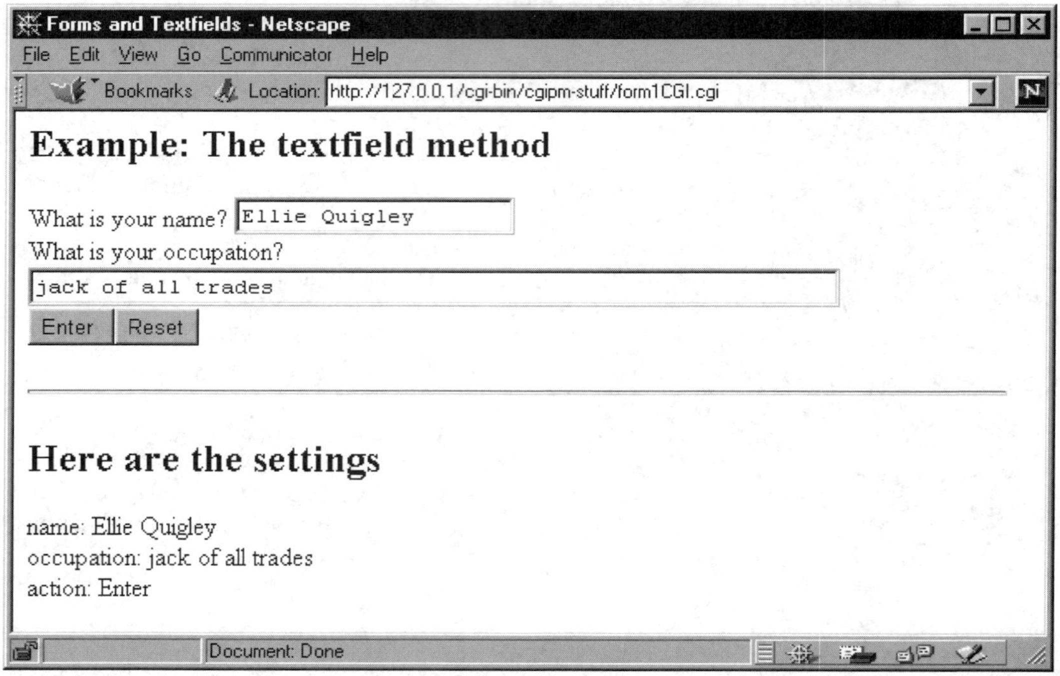

Figure 19.25   Output after the form was filled out and processed, Example 19.35.

Figure 19.26   The HTML source that was produced by *CGI.pm*.

The checkbox() Method

The *checkbox()* method is used to create a simple check box for a *yes* or *no* (Boolean) response. The check box has *NAME* and *VALUE* attributes, where *-name* gives the CGI parameter a name and *-value* contains one item or a reference to a list of items that can be selected. If the *-checked* is assigned *1*, the box will start as checked. If *-label* assigned a value, it will be printed next to the check box; if not, the *-name* value of the check box will be printed. If not selected, the check box will contain an empty parameter.

The *checkbox_group()* method creates a set of check boxes all linked by a single name. The options are not mutually exclusive; that is, the user can check one or more items. If *-linebreak* is assigned a non-zero number, the options will be vertically aligned. Ordinarily, the options would be displayed in a horizontal row. (See Example 19.36.)

FORMAT

```
    print $obj->checkbox(-name=>'name_of_checkbox',
                         -checked=>1,
                         -value=>'ON'
                         -label=>'Click on me'
                        );


%labels = ('choice1'=>'red',
           'choice2'=>'blue',
           'choice3'=>'yellow',
          );
    print $obj->checkbox_group(-name=>'name_of_checkbox',
                               -values=>[ 'choice1', 'choice2',
                                          'choice3', 'green',...],
                               -default=>[ 'choice1', 'green' ],
                               -linebreak => 1,
                               -labels=>\%labels
                              );
```

EXAMPLE 19.36

```
     #!/usr/bin/perl
     use CGI;
     $query = new CGI;
     print $query->header;
     print $query->start_html("The Object Oriented CGI and Forms");
     print "<H2>Example using Forms with Checkboxes</H2>\n";

     &print_formstuff($query);
     &do_work($query) if ($query->param);

     print $query->end_html;
     sub print_formstuff{
         my($query) = @_;
1        print $query->startform;

         print "What is your name? ";
         print $query->textfield('name');    # A simple text field
         print "<BR>";

         print "Are you married? <BR>";
2        print $query->checkbox(-name=>'Married',
                                 -label=>'If not, click me' );
                                 # Simple checkbox
         print "<BR><BR>";
         print "What age group(s) do you hang out with? <BR>";
3          print $query->checkbox_group(-name=>'age_group',
                                       -values=>[ '12-18', '19-38',
                                                  '39-58','59-100' ],
                                       -default=>[ '19-38' ],
                                       -linebreak=>'true',
                                     );
4        print $query->submit('action', 'Select');
5        print $query->reset('Clear');
         print $query->endform;
         print "<HR>\n";
     }

6    sub do_work{
         my ($query) = @_;
         my (@values, $key);
         print "<H2>Here are the settings</H2>";
7        foreach $key ($query->param){
             print "$key: \n";
8            @values=$query->param($key);
             print join(", ",@values), "<BR>";
         }
     }
```

EXPLANATION

1   The *startform* method produces the HTML *<FORM>* tag.

2   The is the simplest kind of check box. If the user is not married, he should click the box. The name of the check box is *Single*, the label, *If not, click me* is displayed next to the check box. If *-checked* is assigned *1*, the box will be checked when it is first displayed.

3   This an example of a check box group where a set of related check boxes are linked by a common name, *age_group*. The *-values* argument is assigned a reference to a list of options that will appear to the right of each of the check boxes. If *-labels* were used it would contain a hash consisting of key/value pairs that would be used as the labels on each of the check boxes. The *-default* argument determines which boxes will be checked when the check boxes are first displayed. The *-linebreak* argument is set to a non-zero value, true, which will cause the options to be displayed as a vertical list.

4   When the user presses the Submit button, labeled *Select*, the form will be processed.

5   The Reset button clears the screen only if the user has not yet submitted the form. To override "stickiness," that is, to set the check boxes back to original default values, set the *-override* argument to a non-zero value.

6   The *do_work* function is called when the form is submitted. This is where all the reading and parsing of the form input is handled.

7   Each of the parameters that came in from the form (key/value pairs) are printed.

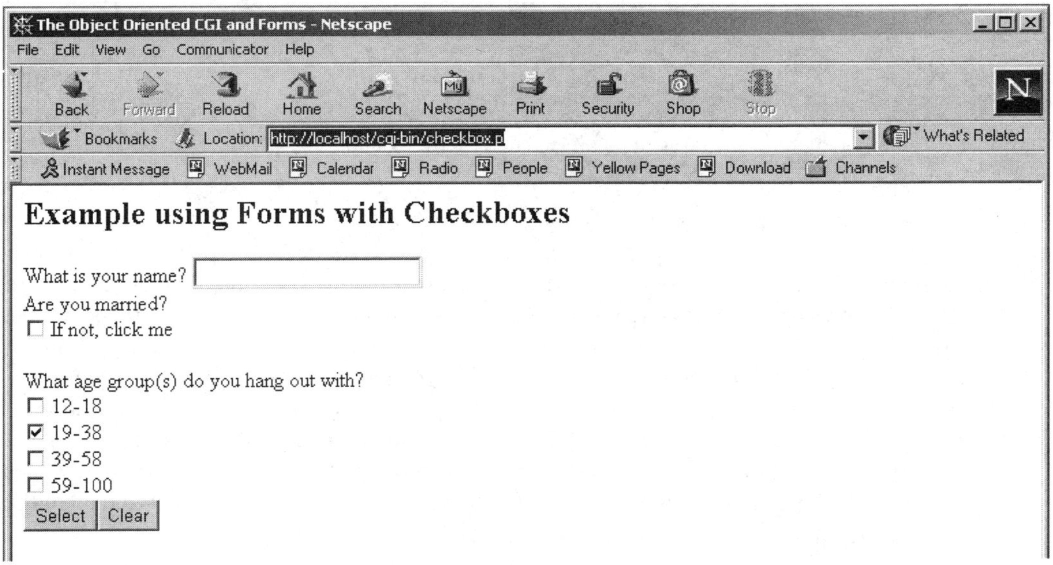

Figure 19.27   Output for check box form in Example 19.36.

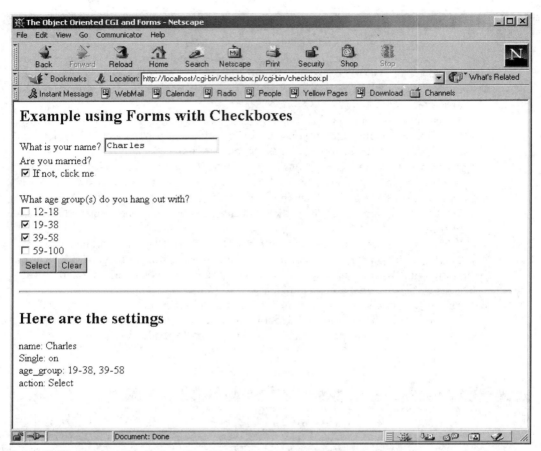

Figure 19.28   Output after the form was filled out and processed, Example 19.36.

The radio_group() and popup_menu() Methods

To select among a set of mutually exclusive choices, you can use radio buttons or pop-up menus. Radio button groups allow a small number of choices to be grouped together to fit in the form; for a large number of choices, the pop-up menu is better. They both have arguments consisting of name/value pairs. Since the value argument consists of more than one selection, it takes a reference to an array. The *-default* argument is the value that is displayed when the menu first appears. The optional argument *-labels* is provided if you want to use different values for the user-visible label inside the radio group or pop-up menu and the value returned to your script. It's a pointer to an associative array relating menu values to corresponding user-visible labels. If a default isn't given, the first item is selected in the pop-up menu.

FORMAT

```
%labels = ('choice1'=>'red',
           'choice2'=>'blue',
           'choice3'=>'yellow',
          );
print $obj->radio_group(-name=>'name_of_radio_group',
                        -values=>['choice1','choice2',
                                   'choice3', 'green', ...],
                        -default=>[ 'choice1', 'green' ],
                        -linebreak => 1,
                        -labels=>\%labels
                       );


%labels = ('choice1'=>'red',
           'choice2'=>'blue',
           'choice3'=>'yellow',
          );
print $obj->popup_menu(-name=>'name_of_popup_menu',
                       -values=>['choice1','choice2','choice3',
                                  'green',...],
                       -default=>[ 'choice1', 'green' ],
                       -linebreak => 1,
                       -labels=>\%labels
                      );
```

EXAMPLE 19.37

```
   #!/bin/perl
1  use CGI;
   $query = new CGI;
   print $query->header;
   print $query->start_html("The Object-Oriented CGI and Forms");
   print "<H2>Example using Forms with Radio Buttons</H2>\n";
   &print_formstuff($query);
   &do_work($query) if ($query->param);
   print $query->end_html;

   sub print_formstuff{
   my($query) = @_;
   print $query->startform;
   print "What is your name? ";
   print $query->textfield('name');   # A simple text field
   print "<BR>";
   print "Select your favorite color? <BR>";
```

EXAMPLE 19.37 (CONTINUED)

```
2    print $query->radio_group(-name=>'color',
                               -values=>[ 'red', 'green',
                                          'blue','yellow' ],
                               -default=>'green',
                               -linebreak=>'true',
                              );
     print $query->submit('action', 'submit');
     print $query->reset('Clear');
     print $query->endform;
     print "<HR>\n";
     }
     sub do_work{
         my ($query) = @_;
         my (@values, $key);
         print "<H2>Here are the settings</H2>";
3        foreach $key ($query->param){
             print "$key: \n";
4            @values=$query->param($key);
             print join(", ",@values), "<BR>";
         }
     }
```

EXPLANATION

1   The *CGI.pm* module is loaded.
2   A radio group is created in the form by calling the CGI *radio_group* method with its arguments. The values of the individual radio buttons will be seen to the right of each button. The default button that will be checked when the form is first displayed is *green*. The *-linebreak* argument places the buttons in a vertical position rather than in a horizontal line across the screen.The user can select only **one** button.
3   After the user has filled out the form and pressed the Submit button, the *param* method will return the keys and values that were sent to the CGI script.
4   The key/value pairs are displayed.

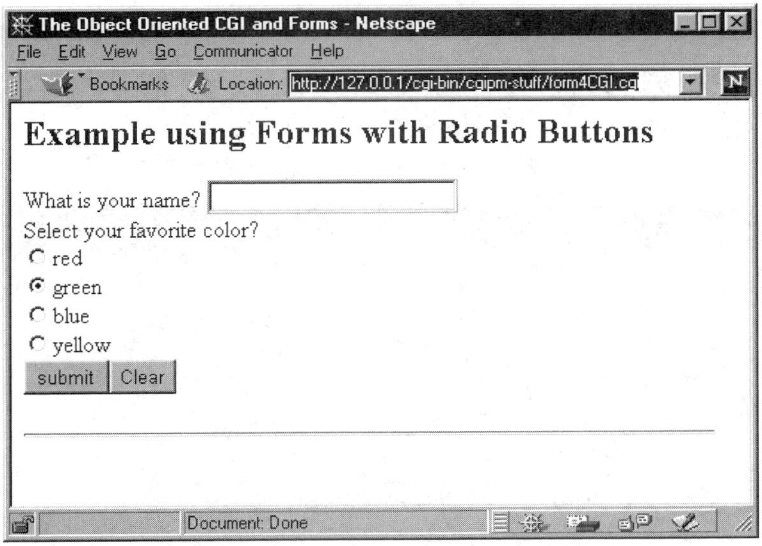

Figure 19.29   Output for radio button form, Example 19.37.

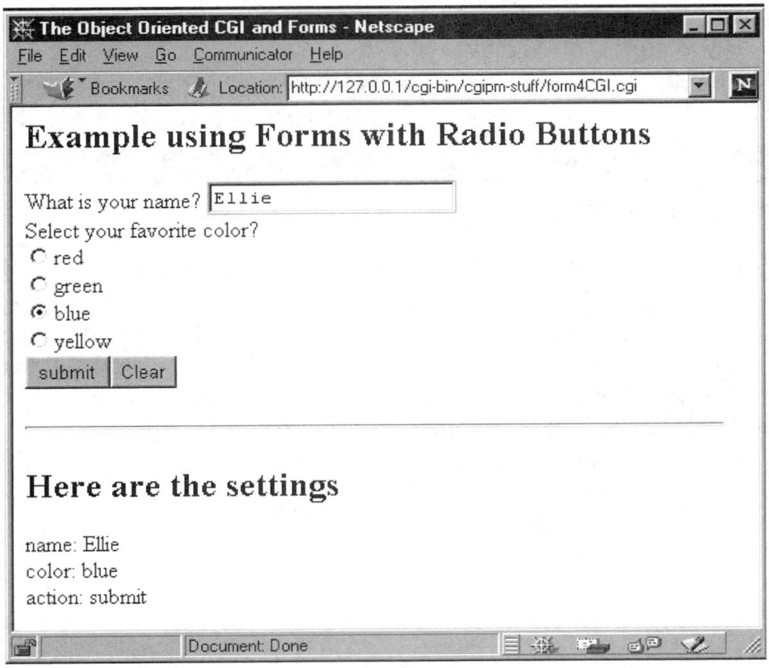

Figure 19.30   Output after form was filled out and processed, Example 19.37.

Labels

Labels allow the buttons to have user-friendly names that are associated with different corresponding values within the program. In the following example, the labels *stop*, *go*, and *warn* will appear beside radio buttons in the browser window. The values returned by the *param* method will be *red, green,* and *yellow*, respectively.

EXAMPLE 19.38

```
( The -labels Parameter -- Segment from CGI script)
    print $query->startform;
    print "What is your name? ";
    print $query->textfield('name');    # A simple text field
    print "<BR>";
    print "We're at a cross section. Pick your light.<BR>";
1   print $query->radio_group(-name=>'color',
2                             -values=>[ 'red', 'green', 'yellow' ],
                              -linebreak=>'true',
3                             -labels=>{red=>'stop',
                                        green=>'go',
                                        yellow=>'warn',
                                        },
4                             -default=>'green',
                              );
    print $query->submit('action', 'submit');
    print $query->reset('Clear');
    print $query->endform;
    }
```

EXPLANATION

1   The *radio_group* method is called with its arguments. Only one value can be selected.
2   The values that the *params* function returns will be either *red, green,* or *yellow.*
3   The labels are what actually appear next to each radio button. The user will see *stop, go,* and *warn* in the browser, but the CGI parameters associated with those labels are *red, green,* and *yellow,* respectively. If, for example, the user clicks on the *stop* button, the key/value pair passed to the script will be *color=>red.*
4   The default button is to have the button labeled *go* checked.

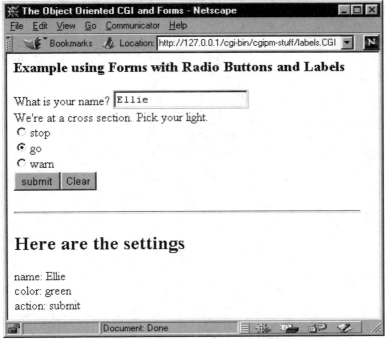

Figure 19.31 Output for labels form after being filled out and processed, Example 19.38.

The popup_menu() Method

The **pop-up menu** is also referred to as a **drop-down list**. It is a list of selections that will be displayed when the user clicks on the scrollbar icon to the right of the text. Only one selection can be made.

EXAMPLE 19.39

```
#!/usr/bin/perl
use CGI;
$query = new CGI;
print $query->header;
print $query->start_html("The Object-Oriented CGI and Forms");
print "<H2>Example using Forms with Pop-up Menus</H2>\n";
&print_formstuff($query);
&do_work($query) if ($query->param);
print $query->end_html;
```

EXAMPLE 19.39 (CONTINUED)

```perl
sub print_formstuff{
my($query) = @_;
print $query->startform;
print "What is your name? ";
print $query->textfield('name');  # A simple text field
print "<BR>";
print "Select your favorite color? <BR>";
print $query->popup_menu(-name=>'color',
                         -values=>[ 'red', 'green', 'blue',
                                    'yellow' ],
                         -default=>'green',
                         -labels=>'\%labels',
                        );
print $query->submit('action', 'submit');
print $query->reset('Clear');
print $query->endform;
print "<HR>\n";
}

sub do_work{
    my ($query) = @_;
    my (@values, $key);
        print "<H2>Here are the settings</H2>";
        foreach $key ($query->param){
            print "$key: \n";
            @values=$query->param($key);
            print join(", ",@values), "<BR>";
    }
}
```

Figure 19.32   Output for pop-up menu form, Example 19.39.

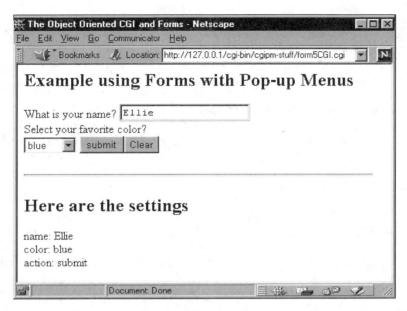

Figure 19.33   Output for pop-up menu form after being filled out and processed, Example 19.39.

The submit() and reset() Methods

The *submit()* method creates a button that, when pressed, sends form input to the CGI script. If given an argument, you can label the button, often for the purpose of distinguishing it from other buttons if several Submit buttons are used.

The *reset()* method is used to clear all the entries in a form. It restores the form to the state it was in when last loaded, not to its default state. (See "The defaults Method," below.)

Clearing Fields

The override Argument

Note that if you press the Reset button or restart the same form, the previous information is sticky; in other words, the input box is not cleared. You can force the entry to be cleared by using the *-override* or *-force* argument with a non-zero value; for example:

```
textfield(-name=>'name', -override=>1);
```

The defaults Method

The *defaults()* method clears all entries in the form to the state of the form when it was first displayed in the browser window; that is, the parameter list is cleared. To create a user-readable button, call the defaults method; for example:

```
print defaults(-name=>'Clear All Entries');
```

Error Handling

When your *CGI.pm* script contains errors, the error messages are normally sent by the server to error log files configured under the server's root. If the program aborts, the browser will display "Document contains no data" or "Server Error." These messages are not very helpful.

The carpout and fatalsToBrowser Methods

CGI.pm provides methods, not only to store errors in your own log file, but also to see fatal error messages in the browser's window. The *carpout* function is provided for this purpose. Since is not exported by default, you must import it explicitly by writing:

```
use CGI::Carp qw(carpout);
```

The *carpout* function requires one argument, a reference to a user-defined filehandle where errors will be sent. It should be called in a *BEGIN* block at the top of the CGI application so that compiler errors will be caught. To cause fatal errors from *die*, *croak*, and *confess* to also appear in the browser window, the *fatalsToBrowser* function must also be imported.

EXAMPLE 19.40

```
   #!/usr/bin/perl
1  use CGI;
2  BEGIN{ use CGI::Carp qw(fatalsToBrowser carpout);
3      open(LOG,">>errors.log") ||die "Couldn't open log file\n";
4      carpout(LOG);
   }
   $query = new CGI;
   <Program continues here>
```

EXPLANATION

1   The *CGI.pm* module is loaded.
2   The *CGI::Carp* module is also loaded. This *Carp* module takes two arguments: *fatalsToBrowser* and *carpout*. The first argument, *fatalstobrowswer*, sends Perl errors to the browser and *carpout* makes it all possible by redirecting the standard error from the screen to the browser and error log.
3   A file called *errors.log* is opened for creation/appending. This log file will contain the error messages that will also be seen in the browser.
4   The *carpout* function will send errors to the *errors.log* file. Here is a line from that file:

[Thu Feb 8 18:59:04 2001] C:\httpd\CGI-BIN\carpout.pl: Testing error messages from CGI script.

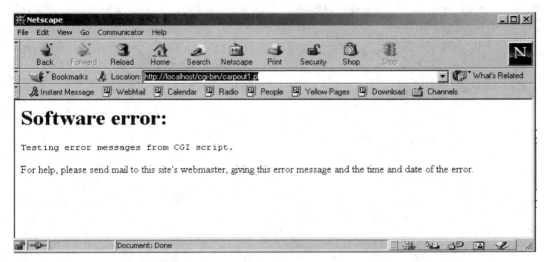

Figure 19.34   Redirecting errors with *carpout* and *fatalsToBrowser*.

Changing the Default Message.   By default, the software error message is followed by a note to contact the Webmaster by e-mail with the time and date of the error. If you want to change the default message, you can use the *set_message* method, which must be imported into the programs namespace.

FORMAT

```
use CGI::Carp qw(fatalsToBrowser set_message);
set_message("Error message!");
set_message(\reference_to_subroutine);
```

EXAMPLE 19.41

```
1   use CGI;
2   BEGIN{ use CGI::Carp qw(fatalsToBrowser carpout);
3       open(LOG,">>errors.log") ||die "Couldn't open log file\n";
4       carpout(LOG);
5       sub handle_errors {
6           my $msg = shift;
7           print "<h1>Software Error Alert!!</h1>";
            print "<h2>Your program sent this error:<br><I>
                $msg</h2></I>";
        }
    }
8   set_message(\&handle_errors);
9   die("Testing error messages from CGI script.\n");
```

EXPLANATION

1   The *CGI.pm* module is loaded.

2   The *CGI::Carp* module is also loaded. The *Carp.pm* module takes two arguments: *fatalsToBrowser* and *carpout*. The first argument, *fatalsToBrowser* sends Perl errors to the browser and *carpout* makes it all possible by redirecting the standard error from the screen to the browser and error log.

3   A file called *errors.log* is opened for creation/appending. This log file will contain the error messages that will also be seen in the browser.

4   The *carpout* function will send errors to the *errors.log* file.

5   A user-defined subroutine called *handle_errors* is defined. It will produce a customized error message in the user's browser window.

6   The first argument to *handle_errors* subroutine is the error message coming from a *die* or *croak*. In this example, the *die* message on line 9 will be be assigned to *$msg*, unless the *die* on line 3 happens first. This message will also be sent to the log file, *errors.log*.

7   This error message will be sent to the browser.

8   The *set_message* method is called with a reference to the user-defined subroutine *handle_errors*, passed as an argument. *handle_errors* contains the customized error message.

9   The *die* function will cause the program to exit, sending its error message to the *handle_errors* subroutine via *set_message*.

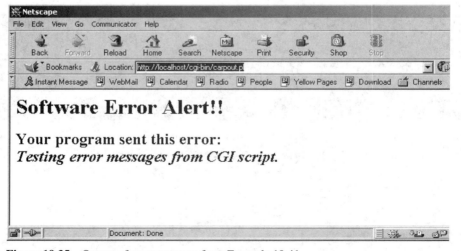

Figure 19.35   Output of error message from Example 19.41.

EXAMPLE 19.42

```
(Contents of the errors.log file created by carpout)
carpout.pl syntax OK
[Thu Feb  8 18:27:48 2001] C:\httpd\CGI-BIN\carpout.pl: Testing err
rom CGI script.
[Thu Feb  8 18:30:01 2001] C:\httpd\CGI-BIN\carpout.pl: <h1>Testing
es from CGI script.
[Thu Feb  8 18:55:53 2001] C:\httpd\CGI-BIN\carpout.pl: Undefined s
in::set_message called at C:\httpd\CGI-BIN\carpout.pl line 11.
[Thu Feb  8 18:55:53 2001] C:\httpd\CGI-BIN\carpout.pl: BEGIN faile
n aborted at C:\httpd\CGI-BIN\carpout.pl line 12.
[Thu Feb  8 18:56:49 2001] carpout.pl: Undefined subroutine &main::
alled at carpout.pl line 11.
[Thu Feb  8 18:56:49 2001] carpout.pl: BEGIN failed--compilation ab
out.pl line 12.
```

Cookies.   The HTTP protocol, by design, is stateless in order to keep the connections brief. After a transaction is completed, the connection is lost and the browser and server have no recollection of what transpired from one session to the next. But now that the Internet is used as a huge shopping center, it is often necessary to keep track of users and what they have purchased, their preferences, registration information, etc. Netscape introduced **cookies** in order to establish a persistent state; that is, keep information around that would normally be lost at the end of a transaction. Cookies offer a way to keep track of visitors and their preferences after they have visited a site.

The cookie is a piece of data that is sent by the server from your CGI script to the visitor's browser where it is stored in a file (often called *cookie.txt* or just *cookie*) for as long as you specify. It is a string assigned to an HTTP header that gets entered into the memory of the browser (client) and then stored in a file on the hard drive. The browser maintains a list of cookies on disk that belong to a particular Web server and returns them back to the Web server via the HTTP header during subsequent interactions. When the server gets the cookie it assigns the cookie values (name/value pairs) to the *HTTP_COOKIE* environment variable. The cookie, then, is passed back and forth between the browser and the server. The CGI program can set the cookie in a cookie response header (*Set-Cookie*) and retrieve values from the cookie from the environment variable, *HTTP_COOKIE*.

By default, the cookie is short-term and expires when the current browser session terminates, but it can be made persistent by setting an expiration date to some later time, after which it will be discarded. The path decides where the cookie is valid for a particular server. If not set, it defaults to the location of the script that set the cookie. The path it refers to is the server's path, where the server's root is */*. The domain name is the domain where the cookie is valid; that is, the current domain as in *127.0.0.1* or *www.ellieq.com*.

Cookies are set in the HTTP cookie header as follows:

```
Set-Cookie:  Name=Value; expires=Date; path=Path; domain=Domainname; secure
```

EXAMPLE 19.43

```
#!/bin/perl
# A simple CGI script to demonstrate setting and retrieving a cookie.
# Run the program twice:  the first time to set the cookie on the
# client side, and second to retrieve the cookie from the browser
# and get its value from the environment variable,
# $ENV{HTTP_COOKIE, coming from the server.

1   my $name = "Ellie";
2   my $expiration_date = "Friday, 17-Feb-01 00:00:00: GMT";
3   my $path = "/cgi-bin";

4   print "Set-Cookie: shopper=$name, expires=$expiration_date,
        path=$path\n";
    print "Content-type: text/html\n\n";

5   print <<EOF;
    <html><head><Title>Cookie Test</Title></Head>
    <body>
    <h1>Chocolate chip cookie!!</h1>
    <h2>Got milk?</h2>
    <hr>
    <p>
    What's in the HTTP_COOKIE environment variable?
    <br>
6   $ENV{HTTP_COOKIE}
    <p>
    <hr>
    </body></html>
    EOF
```

EXPLANATION

1 The variable is set for the shopper's name.
2 The expiration date is set for when the cookie will be deleted.
3 This is the path on the server where the cookie is valid.
4 This is the HTTP header that is assigned the information that will be stored in the cookie file in the browser.
5 This is the start of the *here document* that will contain the HTML tags to be rendered by the browser.
6 The value of the *HTTP_COOKIE* environment variable displays the cookie information that was retrieved and sent back to the server from the browser in an HTTP header.

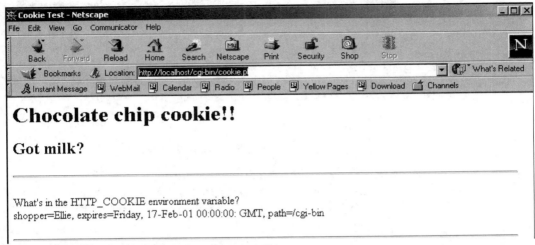

Figure 19.36   The *HTTP_Cookie* environment variable.

Table 19.17   Cookie Values

Name	Name of the cookie. The term *Name* is the actual name of the cookie; for example, it could be *preference=blue* where *preference* is the name of the cookie and *blue* is the data assigned to the cookie.
Value	Data assigned to the cookie; spaces, semicolons, commas, not allowed.
Date	When the cookie will expire: s = seconds; m = minutes; h = hours; d = days; *now*, M = months; y = years; *Fri,15-Mar-00 12:35:33 GMT*; e.g., *+30m* is 30 minutes from now; *-1d* is yesterday; *+2M* is two months from now; and *now* is now.
Path	Path where cookie is valid.
Domain	Domain name refers to the domain where the script is running and the cookie is valid.
Secure	Makes the cookie invalid unless a secure connection is established.

The values of the cookie are stored in the *HTTP_COOKIE* environment variable. Netscape limits the number of cookies to *300*. *CGI.pm* makes it easy to use cookies. See the following Example 19.44.

EXAMPLE 19.44

```perl
    #!/usr/bin/perl
1   use CGI;
2   $query = new CGI;
3   if ( $query->param && $query->param('color') ne ""){
4       $color=$query->param('color') ;     # Did the user pick a color
    }
5   elsif ( $query->cookie('preference')){      # Is there a cookie
                                                # already?
6       $color=$query->cookie('preference');  # Then go get it!
    }
    else{
7   $color='yellow';}  # Set a default background color if
                       # a cookie doesn't exist, and the user didn't
                       # select a preference
8   $cookie=$query->cookie(-name=>'preference',
                          -value=>"$color",  # Set the cookie values
                          -expires=>'+30d',
                          );
9   print $query->header(-cookie=>$cookie);
                    # Setting the HTTP cookie header

10  print $query->start_html(-title=>"Using Cookies",
                            -bgcolor=>"$color",
                            );
    print $query->h2("Example: Making Cookies");

    &print_prompt($query);
    &do_work($query) if ($query->param);

    print $query->end_html;

11  sub print_prompt{
        my($query) = @_;
        print $query->startform;
        print "What is your name? ";
        print $query->textfield(-name=>'name',
                                -size=>30);  # A simple text field
        print "<BR>";
        print "What is your occupation? ";
        print $query->textfield(-name=>'occupation',  # Giving values
                                -default=>'Retired',   # to text field
                                -size=>30,
                                -maxlength=>120
                                );
```

EXAMPLE 19.44 (CONTINUED)

```
            print "<BR>";
            print "What is your favorite color? ";
            print $query->textfield(-name=>'color');   # Giving values
            print $query->br();
            print $query->submit('action', 'Enter');
            print $query->reset();
            print $query->endform;
            print $query->hr();
        }
12  sub do_work{
            my ($query) = @_;
            my (@values, $key);
            print "<H2>Here are the settings</H2>";
13          foreach $key ($query->param){
            print "$key: \n";
            @values=$query->param($key);
            print join(", ",@values), "<BR>";
            }
        }
```

EXPLANATION

1   The module is loaded into this script.
2   The CGI module's constructor, *new*, is called and a reference to a CGI object is returned and assigned to *$query*. We will be using the object-oriented form of *CGI.pm* in this example.
3   If the form was filled out and if the user selected a color, the *param* function will return true; in other words, if *param* is not a null string, the value of the selected color will be assigned to the scalar, *$color*.
4   If the form has been filled out, and a cookie was sent back to the server, the value of the cookie will be retrieved and store it in the scalar, *$color*.
5   If the user didn't select a color, and there was no cookie, then the default background will be set to *yellow*.
6   If a cookie was set, retrieve the value of the preference from the cookie. The *cookie* method will extract the value of the *HTTP_COOKIE* environment variable.
7   If this is the first time this script has been run, a default value of *yellow* will be set for the background color.
8   Key/value pairs for the cookie are set. The cookie is set to expire after *30* days. If no expiration date is set, the cookie is only good for the current session of the browser.
9   The *header* method creates the HTTP cookie.
10 The background color for the HTML page is set by the *start_html* method.
11 The method that displays the HTML form is defined.
12 The method that parses the form after it has been filled out is defined.
13 Each of the key/value pairs produced by the *param* method are displayed.

EXAMPLE 19.45

```
(What the Cookie HTTP header looks like)

Set-Cookie: preference=yellow; path=/form1CGI.cgi; expires=Sun,
17-Sep-2000 09:46:26 GMT
```

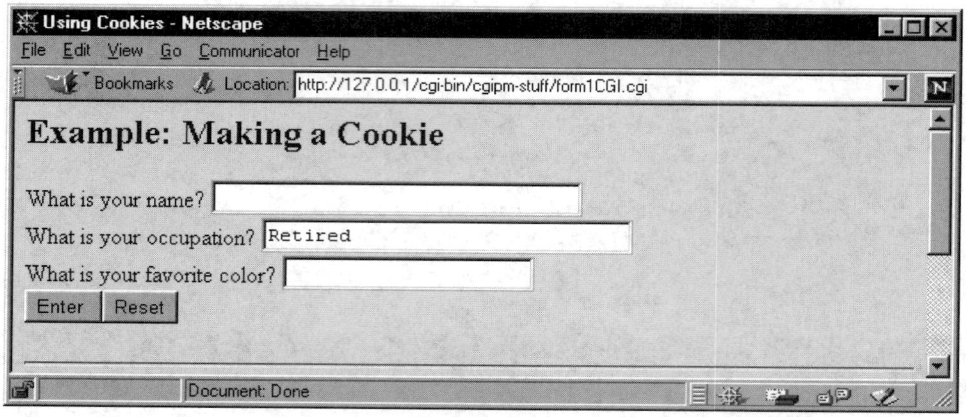

Figure 19.37   The default background color was set to *yellow*.

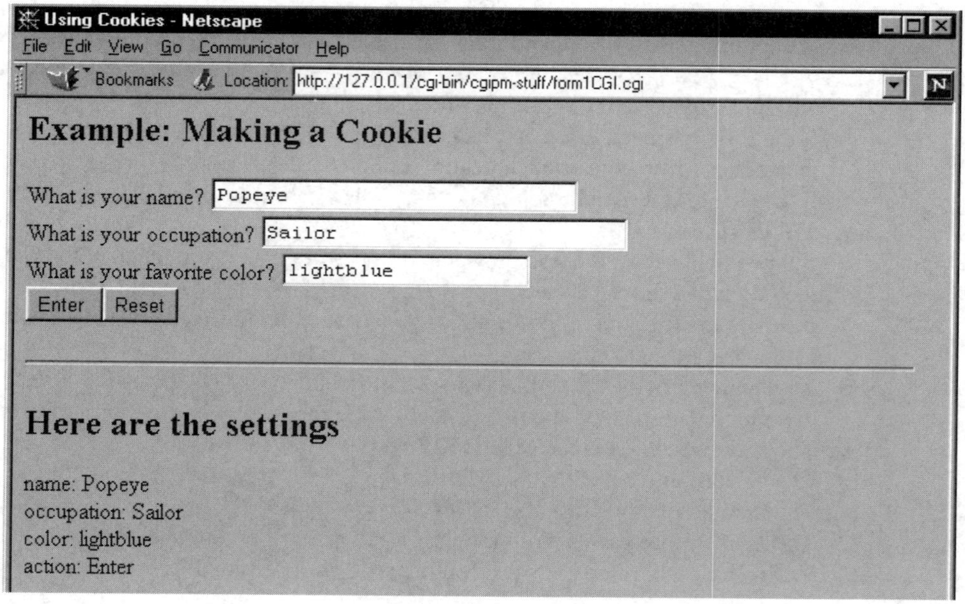

Figure 19.38   The user's preference, *lightblue*, is stored in a cookie.

19.9.6   HTTP Header Methods

The cookie is assigned to an HTTP header as shown in the previous example. Table 19.18 lists other methods that can be used to create and retrieve information from HTTP headers.

Table 19.18   HTTP Header Methods

HTTP Header Method	What It Does
accept( )	Lists MIME types or type
auth_type( )	Returns authorization type for the current session
cookie( )	Creates and retreives cookies
header( )	Returns a valid HTTP header and MIME type
https( )	Returns information about SSL for a session
path_info( )	Sets and retrieves addtional path information
path_translated( )	Returns additional path information
query_string( )	Returns the URL encoded query string
raw_cookie( )	Returns a list of unprocessed cookies sent from the browser
redirect( )	Generates an HTTP header with a redirection request to the browser to load a page at that location
referer( )	Returns the URL of the page the browser displayed before starting your script
remote_addr( )	Returns the IP address of the remote host, possibly a proxy server
remote_ident( )	Returns remote user's login name if the identity daemon is activiated
remote_host( )	Returns the DNS name of the remote host
remote_user( )	Returns the account name used to authenticate a password
request_method( )	Returns the HTTP method, *GET*, *POST*, or *HEAD*
script_name( )	Returns the URL of this script relative to the server's root
self_url( )	Returns the URL of the CGI script: protocol, host, port, path, additional path info, and parameter list; can be used to reinvoke the current script
server_name( )	Returns the name of the Web server
server_software( )	Returns the name and version of the Web server
server_port( )	Returns the port number for the current session (usually 80)
url( )	Returns URL of the current script without additional path information and query string
user_agent( )	Returns browser information
user_name( )	Returns remote user's name if it can
virtual_host( )	Returns the name of the virtual host being accessed by the browser

EXAMPLE 19.46

```
    #!/usr/bin/perl
    use CGI qw(:standard);
1   print header;
2   print start_html(-title=>'Using header Methods'),
    h1("Let's find out about this session!"),
    p,
3   h4 "Your server is called ", server_name(),
    p,
4   "Your server port number is ", server_port(),
    p,
5   "This script name is: ", script_name(),
    p,
6   "Your browser is ", user_agent(), "and it's out of date!",
    p,
7   "The query string looks like this: ", query_string(),
    p,
8   "Where am I? Your URL is: \n", url(),
    p,
9   "Cookies set: ", raw_cookie();

10  print end_html;
```

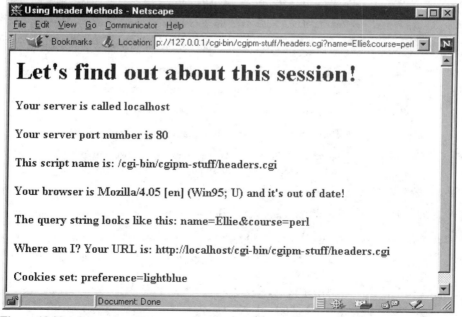

Figure 19.39 Output from Example 19.46.

EXERCISE 19
Surfing for Perls

1. **The Environment Variables and CGI**
   Create a CGI script that will print to the browser:
   The name of the server is: <Put the values here.>
   The gateway protocol is:
   The client machine's IP address:
   The client machine's name:
   The document root is:
   The CGI script name is:
   (Hint: Use the *%ENV* hash.)

2. **Creating A CGI Program**
   a. Write a CGI script called *town_crier* that will contain HTML text and Perl statements.
   b. The script will contain two subroutines: *&welcome* and *&countem*.
   c. The *welcome* subroutine will print *Welcome Sir Richard!!*. Use a blue font that blinks the welcome. (Note: Internet Explorer ignores *blink*.) The subroutine will also print today's date. (Use the *ctime* library function.)
   d. The subroutine called *countem* will be written in a file called *countem.pl*. The *town_crier* script will call *countem* passing its name (*town_crier*) as an argument to the subroutine. Remember, the name of the script is stored in the *$0* variable, e.g., *&countem ($0);*. The subroutine will return the number of times the page has been visited.
   e. See Figure 10.40 for an idea of how this script will display its output in the browser's window.
   f. The *countem* function should be designed to
   • Take an argument—the name of the file that called it. Unless there is a file called *town_crier.log* already in the directory, the file will be created. Either way, the file will be opened for reading and writing. (If the *countem* function were called from another Perl script, then the log file created would have the name of that script, followed by the *.log* extension.)
   • If the log file is empty, *countem* will write the value *1* into the file; otherwise a line will be read from the file. The line will contain a number. The number will be read in and stored in a variable. Its value will be incremented by *1*. Each time *town_crier* is executed, this function is called.
   • The new number will sent back to the file, overwriting the number that was there.
   • The log file will be closed.
   • The *countem* subroutine will return the value of the number to the calling program. (In the example, I put the number in a cell of an HTML table and sent the whole string back to the *town_ crier*. Don't bother to try to create the table if you don't have time. Just send back the number.)

- If running on a UNIX system, use the *flock* function to put an exclusive lock on the log file while you are using it and will remove the lock when you are finished.

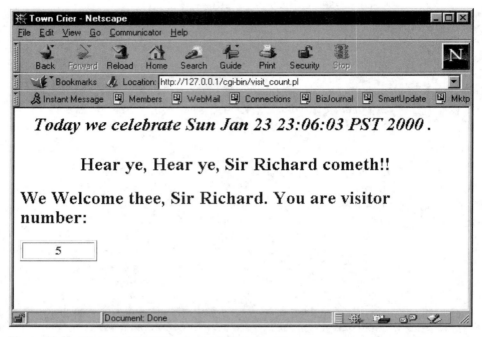

Figure 19.40   Output of the CGI program in Exercise 19.

EXERCISE 20
Let's Use *CGI.pm*

1. **Creating Forms—HTML**
   a. Create a Web page called Stirbucks that contains a form to order coffee, similar to the order form in Figure 19.41.
   b. In the *action* attribute of the initial *<FORM>* tag, specify a URL that directs the server to a CGI script using the default *GET* method.
   c. Test your file in a browser.
   d. The CGI script will print the value of the *QUERY_STRING* environment variable.

2. **Processing Forms—CGI**

   a. Write a CGI script that will send back to the user an HTML page that thanks him for his order and tells him the coffee he selected will be delivered to his shipping address. Use the *GET* method. After getting the information from the form, write your own fuction to parse the input.

   b. Redesign the form to include the *POST* method. The program will test which method was used and call the parse function.

   c. Create a DBM file that keeps a list of the e-mail addresses submitted. When a user submits an order, his e-mail address will be listed in the DBM file. Make sure there are no duplicates. Design a function to do this.

   d. The CGI script will handle e-mail. Send e-mail to yourself confirming the information that was submitted. Design another function to handle e-mail.

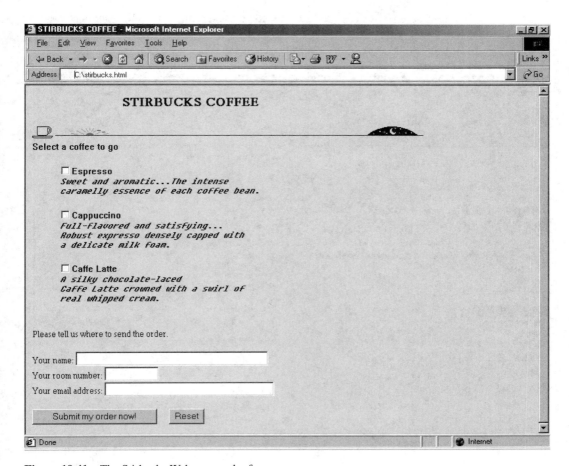

Figure 19.41 The Stirbucks Web page order form.

3. Rewrite the *Stirbucks* program so that the HTML form and the CGI script are in one CGI program created with the *CGI.pm* module. Use the function-oriented style.

4. Add to the *Stirbucks* program a cookie that will save the user's preferences so that each time he orders coffee, he will get a free sweet. If he doesn't state a preference, he will get a bagel with his coffee. The bagel or the alternate choice for a free sweet is saved in a Netscape cookie. The cookie should not expire for 1 week. (See Figure 19.42.)

5. Write a CGI script (with the *CGI.pm* module) that will replace the *ATM* script you wrote in Chapter 11. The new CGI script will provide a form in the browser that will produce a menu of items; that is, deposit, withdraw, balance, etc. Use the object-oriented CGI methods to create the HTML form. In the same script, the *param* function will check which selection was checked, and, based on the selection, the appropriate method will be called from *Checking.pm*. After the form has been filled out and submitted, the results of processing will appear on the same page.

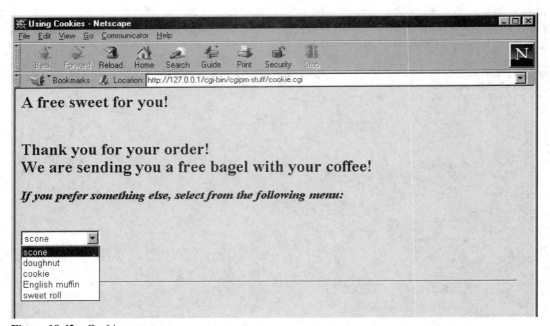

Figure 19.42   Cookie output.

PERL BUILT-INS, PRAGMAS, MODULES, AND THE DEBUGGER

A.1 Perl Functions

The following is a complete list of Perl functions and a short description of what they do. Note: The text in parentheses is a reference to the like-named UNIX system call found in Section 2 of the UNIX manual pages. The like-named UNIX library functions are found in Section 3 of the UNIX manual pages.

Table A.1 Perl Functions

Function	*Description*
abs	*abs VALUE* Returns the absolute value of its argument (*$_* is the default). Ignores signs.
accept	*accept(NEWSOCKET, GENERICSOCKET)* Accepts a socket connection from clients waiting for a connection. *GENERICSOCKET*, a filehandle, has been previously opened by the *socket* function, is bound to an address, and is listening for a connection. *NEWSOCKET* is a filehandle with the same properties as *GENERICSOCKET*. The *accept* function attaches *GENERICSOCKET* to the newly made connection. See accept(2).
alarm	*alarm(SECONDS)* *alarm SECONDS* Sends a *SIGALARM* signal to the process after a number of *SECONDS*. See alarm(3).
atan2	*atan2(X,Y)* Returns the arctangent of X/Y in the range <pi>.

Table A.1   Perl Functions *(continued)*

Function	Description
bind	*bind(SOCKET, NAME)* Binds an address, *NAME*, to an already opened unnamed socket, *SOCKET*. See bind(2).
binmode	*binmode(FILEHANDLE)* *binmode FILEHANDLE* For operating systems that distinguish between text and "binary" mode (not UNIX). Prepares the *FILEHANDLE* for reading in binary mode.
bless	*bless(REFERENCE, CLASS)* *bless REFERENCE* Tells the object referenced by *REFERENCE* that it is an object in a package (*CLASS*) in the current package if no *CLASS* is specified. Returns the reference.
caller	*caller(EXPR)* *caller EXPR* *caller* Returns an array with information about the subroutine call stack, including the package, filename, and line number. With *EXPR*, a number, the function seeks backwards *EXPR* stack frames before the current one.
chdir	*chdir(EXPR)* *chdir EXPR* *chdir* Changes the present working directory to *EXPR*. If *EXPR* is omitted, changes directory to home directory. See chdir(2).
chmod	*chmod(MODE, LIST)* *chmod MODE, LIST* Changes permissions of a list of files; first argument is the permission *MODE* number (octal); the remaining arguments are a list of filenames. Returns the number of files changed. See chmod(2).
chomp	*chomp(LIST)* *chomp(VARIABLE)* *chomp VARIABLE* *chomp* Chops off the last character of a string, *VARIABLE*, or the last character of each item in a *LIST* if that character corresponds to the current value of $/,which is by default set to the newline. Unlike *chop* (see below), it returns the number of characters deleted.

Table A.1 Perl Functions *(continued)*

Function	Description
chop	*chop(LIST)* *chop(VARIABLE)* *chop VARIABLE* *chop* Chops off the last character of a string, *VARIABLE*, or the last character of each item in a *LIST* and returns the chopped value. Without an argument, chops the last character off *$_*.
chown	*chown(LIST)* *chown LIST* Changes the owner and group IDs of a list of files. First two elements in the list are the numerical *uid* and *gid*, respectively. The rest of the list are the names of files. Returns the number of files changed. See chown(2).
chr	*chr NUMBER* Returns the ASCII value for *NUMBER*, e.g., *chr(66)* returns *B*.
chroot	*chroot(FILENAME)* *chroot FILENAME* Changes root directory for the current process to *FILENAME*, which is the starting point for pathnames starting with /. Must be superuser to do this. See chroot(2).
close	*close(FILEHANDLE)* *close FILEHANDLE* Closes the file, socket, or pipe associated with *FILEHANDLE*.
closedir	*closedir(DIRHANDLE)* *closedir DIRHANDLE* Closes a directory structure opened by *opendir*. See directory(3).
connect	*connect(SOCKET, NAME)* Connects a process with one that is waiting for an *accept* call. *NAME* is a packed network address. See connect(2).
cos	*cos(EXPR)* *cos EXPR* Returns the cosine of *EXPR* (in radians).
crypt	*crypt(PLAINTEXT, SALT)* The password encryption function where *PLAINTEXT* is the user's password and *SALT* is a two-character string consisting of characters in the set [*a–zA–Z./*]. See crypt(3).

Table A.1   Perl Functions *(continued)*

Function	*Description*
dbmclose	*dbmclose(%ASSOC_ARRAY)* *dbmclose %ASSOC_ARRAY* Breaks the binding between a DBM file and an associative array. Only useful with NDBM, a newer version of DBM, if supported. See *untie*. See dbm(3).
dbmopen	*dbmopen(%ASSOC_ARRAY, DBNAME, MODE)* Binds a DBM or NDBM file to an associative array. Before a database can be accessed, it must be opened by *dbmopen*. The files *file.dir* and *file.pag* must exist. *DBNAME* is the name of the file without the *.dir* and *.pag* extension. If the database does not exist and permission *MODE* is specified, the database is created. See *tie*. See dbminit(3).
defined	*defined(EXPR)* *defined EXPR* Returns a Boolean value *1* if *EXPR* has a real value. Returns a Boolean value *0* if *EXPR* does not have a real value. *EXPR* may be a scalar, array, hash, or subroutine. For a hash, checks only whether the value (not key) is defined.
delete	*delete $ASSOC{KEY}* Deletes a value from an associative array. If successful, returns the deleted value; otherwise, returns an undefined value. If a value in *%ENV* is deleted, the environment will be modified. The *undef* function can also be used and is faster.
die	*die(LIST)* *die LIST* *die* Prints the *LIST* to *STDERR* and exits with the value of *$!*, the system error message (*errno*). When in an *eval* function, sets the $@ value to the error message, and aborts *eval*. If the value of *LIST* does not end in a newline, the name of the current script, the line number, and a new line are appended to the message.
do	*do BLOCK* *do SUBROUTINE(LIST)* *do EXPR* *do BLOCK* returns the value of the last command in the *BLOCK*. *do SUBROUTINE(LIST)* calls a *SUBROUTINE* that has been defined. *do EXPR* uses *EXPR* as a filename and executes the contents of the file as a Perl script. Used primarily to include subroutines from the Perl subroutine library.

Table A.1   Perl Functions *(continued)*

Function	*Description*
dump	*dump LABEL* Causes an immediate binary image core dump. The *undump* command, used for undumping a core file, is not part of the Perl 5.6.0 distribution.
each	*each(%ASSOC_ARRAY)* *each %ASSOC_ARRAY* Returns a two-element array, the key and value for the next value of an associative array, in random order.
eof	*eof(FILEHANDLE)* *eof( )* *eof* Returns *1* if the next read on *FILEHANDLE* indicates the end of file. If *FILEHANDLE* is omitted, it returns the end of file for the last file read.
eval	*eval(EXPR)* *eval EXPR* Evaluates *EXPR* as a Perl program in the context of the current Perl script. Often used for trapping otherwise fatal errors. Syntax errors or runtime errors or those coming from the *die* function are returned to the *$@* variable. The *$@* variable is set to NULL if there are no errors. The value returned is the value of the last expression evaluated.
exec	*exec(LIST)* *exec LIST* Executes a system command *LIST* in context of the current program. Never returns. If *LIST* is scalar, checks for *shell* metacharacters and *passes* them to */bin/sh*. Otherwise, arguments are passed to the *C* function call, *execvp*. Does not flush output buffer.
exists	*exists EXPR* Returns TRUE if a specified key from an associative array exists, even if its corresponding value is undefined.
exit	*exit(INTEGER)* *exit INTEGER* Exits with script with status value of *INTEGER*. If *INTEGER* is omitted, exits with *0*, meaning the program exits with successful status. A non-zero status implies that something went wrong in the program.
exp	*exp(EXPR)* *exp EXPR* The exponential function. Returns *e* to the power of *EXPR*.

Table A.1   Perl Functions *(continued)*

Function	*Description*
fcntl	*fcntl(FILEHANDLE, FUNCTION, SCALAR)* Changes properties on an open file. Requires *sys/fcntl.ph*. The *FUNCTION* can duplicate an existing file descriptor, get or set file descriptor flags, get or set file status flags, get or set asynchronous I/O ownership, and get or set record locks. *SCALAR* is an integer for flags. See fcntl(2).
fileno	*fileno(FILEHANDLE)* *fileno FILEHANDLE* Returns the integer file descriptor for *FILEHANDLE*. Descriptors start with *STDIN, STDOUT, STDERR, 0, 1*, and *2*, respectively. May not be reliable in Perl scripts if a file is closed and reopened. See ferror(3).
flock	*flock(FILEHANDLE, OPERATION)* Applies or removes advisory locks on files. *OPERATION* specifies an operation on a lock for a file, shared locks, exclusive locks, or nonblocking locks. The *OPERATION* to remove a file is *unlock*. See flock(2).
fork	*fork* Creates a new (child) process. The child is a copy of the parent process. Both child and parent continue execution with the instruction immediately following the *fork*. Returns *0* to the child process and the *pid* of the child to the parent.

format	*format NAME =*
	    picture line
	    value list
	       ...
	.
	Declares a set of picture lines to describe the layout of corresponding values. The *write* function uses the specified format to send output to a named filehandle represented by *NAME*. If *NAME* is omitted, the default is *STDOUT*.

formline	*formline PICTURE, LIST* An internal function used by *format* to format a list of values according to the picture line. Can also be called directly in a program.
getc	*getc(FILEHANDLE)* *getc FILEHANDLE* *getc* Returns the next character from the input file associated with *FILEHANDLE*. Returns a NULL string at EOF. If *FILEHANDLE* is omitted, reads from *STDIN*.

Table A.1   Perl Functions *(continued)*

Function	*Description*
getgrent	*getgrent* *setgrent* *endgrent* Iterates through */etc/group* and returns an entry from */etc/group* as a list, including group name, password, group ID (*gid*), and members. See getgrent(3).
getgrgid	*getgrgid(GID)* Returns a group entry file by group number. See getgrgid(3).
getgrnam	*getgrnam(NAME)* Returns a group file entry by group name. See getgrent(3).
gethostbyaddr	*gethostbyaddr(ADDRESS, AF_INET)* Translates a network address to its corresponding names and alternate addresses. Returns the hostname, aliases, address type, length, and unpacked raw addresses. *AF_INET* is always 2. See gethostbyaddr(3).
gethostbyname	*gethostbyname(HOSTNAME)* Translates a hostname to an entry from the */etc/hosts* file as a list, including the hostname, aliases, addresses. In scalar context, returns only the host address. See gethostbyname(3).
gethostent	*gethostent* *sethostent(STAYOPEN)* *endhostent* Iterates through */etc/hosts* file and returns the entry as a list, including name, aliases, addresss type, length, and alternate addresses. Returns a list from the network host database, */etc/hosts*. See gethostent(3).
getlogin	*getlogin* Returns the current login from */etc/utmp*, if there is such a file. If *getlogin* does not work, try *$loginname = getlogin || (getpwuid($<))[0] || die "Not a user here"* See getlogin(3).
getnetbyaddr	*getnetbyaddr(ADDR, ADDRESSTYPE)* Translates a network address to its corresponding network name or names. Returns a list from the network database, */etc/networks*. In scalar context, returns only the network name. See getnetent(3).

Table A.1   Perl Functions *(continued)*

Function	Description
getnetbyname	*getnetbyname(NAME)* Translates a network name to its corresponding network address. Returns a list from the network database, */etc/networks*. In scalar context, returns only the network address. See getnetent(3).
getnetent	*getnetent* *setnetent(STAYOPEN)* *endnetent* Iterates through the */etc/networks* file and returns the entry as a list. Returns a list from the network database, */etc/networks*. In scalar context, returns only the network name. See getnetent(3).
getpeername	*getpeername(SOCKET)* Returns the packed *sockaddr* address of other end of the *SOCKET* connection. See getpeername(2).
getpgrp	*getpgrp(PID)* *getpgrp PID* Returns the current process group for the specified *PID* (*PID 0* is the current process). Without *EXPR*, returns the process group of the current process. See getpgrp(2).
getppid	*getppid* Returns the *pid* of the parent process. If *1* is returned, that is the *pid* for *init*. *Init* adopts a process whose parent has died. See getpid(2).
getpriority	*getpriority(WHICH, WHO)* Returns the current priority, nice value, for *WHICH*—a process, a process group, or a user. *WHO* is relative to *WHICH* group. A *WHO* value of zero denotes the current process, process group, or user. See getpriority(2).
getprotobyname	*getprotobyname(NAME)* Translates a protocol *NAME* to its corresponding number and returns a list including the protocol name, aliases, and the protocol number. Returns a line from the network protocol database, */etc/protocols*. See getprotoent(3).
getprotobynumber	*getprotobynumber(NUMBER)* Translates a protocol *NUMBER* to its corresponding name and returns a list including the protocol name, aliases, and the protocol number. Returns a line from the network protocol database, */etc/protocols*. See getprotoent(3).

Table A.1   Perl Functions *(continued)*

Function	*Description*
getprotoent	*getprotoent* *setprotent(STAYOPEN)* *endprotoent* Returns a list from the */etc/protocols* database, including the protocol name, aliases, and the protocol number. If the *STAYOPEN* flag is non-zero, the database will not be closed during subsequent calls. The *endprotoent* function closes the file. In scalar context, returns the protocol name. See getprotoent(3).
getpwent	*getpwent* *setpwent* *endpwent* Iterates through the */etc/passwd* file and returns the entry as a list, username, password, *uid*, *gid*, quotas, comment, gcos field, home directory, and startup *shell*. The *endpwent* function closes the file. In scalar context, returns the username. See getpwent(3).
getpwnam	*getpwnam(NAME)* Translates a username to the corresponding entry in */etc/passwd* file. Returns a list, including the username, password, *uid*, *gid*, quotas, comment, gcos field, home directory, and startup *shell*. In scalar context, returns the numeric user ID. See getpwent(3).
getpwuid	*getpwuid(UID)* Translates the numeric user ID to the corresponding entry from the */etc/passwd* file. Returns a list, including the username, password, *uid*, *gid*, quotas, comment, gcos field, home directory, and startup shell. In scalar context, returns the username. See getpwent(3).
getservbyname	*getservbyname(NAME, PROTOCOL)* From */etc/services* database, translates a port name to its corresponding port number as a scalar and, returns as an array, the service name, aliases, port where service resides, and protocol needed, from the */etc/services* database. In scalar context, returns only the service port number. See getservent(3).
getservbyport	*getservbyport(PORT_NUMBER, PROTOCOL)* From */etc/services* database, translates a port number to its corresponding port name as a scalar and returns as an array the service name, aliases, port where service resides, and protocol needed, from the */etc/services* database. In scalar context, returns only the service port number. See getservent(3).

Table A.1   Perl Functions *(continued)*

Function	*Description*
getservent	*getservent* *setservent(STAYOPEN)* *endservent* Iterates through the */etc/services* database, returning the service name, aliases, port where service resides, and protocol needed. If *STAYOPEN* flag is non-zero, the database will not be closed during subsequent calls and *endservent* closes the file. In scalar context, returns only the service port name. See getservent(3).
getsockname	*getsockname(SOCKET)* Returns the packed sockaddr address of the local end of the *SOCKET* connection. See getsockname(2).
getsockopt	*getsockopt(SOCKET, LEVEL, OPTNAME)* Returns the requested options, *OPTNAME*, associated with *SOCKET* at the specified protocol *LEVEL*. See getsockopt(2).
glob	*glob EXPR* Performs filename expansion on *EXPR* as the *shell* does. Without *EXPR*, *$_* is used. Uses the internal < *> operator.
gmtime	*gmtime(EXPR)* *gmtime EXPR* Converts the results of the *time* function to a 9-element array with the Greenwich Mean Time zone, including the second, minute, hour, day of the month, month, year, day of the week, day of the year, and *1* if daylight standard time is in effect. See ctime(3) and *timegm( )* in the Perl library module *Time::Local*.
goto	*goto LABEL* *goto EXPR* *goto &NAME* Program branches to the LABEL and resumes execution. Cannot *goto* any construct that requires intialization, such as a subroutine or *foreach* loop. *Goto* never returns a value. The form *goto &NAME* substitutes the currently running subroutine with a call to *NAME* (used by the *AUTOLOAD* subroutine).
grep	*grep(EXPR, LIST)* *grep BLOCK LIST* Returns to a new array, any element in *LIST* where *EXPR* matches that element. Returns a scalar, the number of matches.

Table A.1   Perl Functions *(continued)*

Function	*Description*
hex	*hex(EXPR)* *hex EXPR* Returns the decimal value of *EXPR* interpreted as a hexadecimal string. Without *EXPR*, uses *$_*.
import	*import CLASSNAME LIST* *import CLASSNAME* Not a built-in function, but a class method defined by modules that will export names to other modules through the *use* function.
index	*index(STR, SUBSTR, POSITION)* *index(STR, SUBSTR)* Returns the position of the first occurrence of *SUBSTR* in *STR*. *POSITION* specifies a starting position for the substring in the string starting with base 0.
int	*int(EXPR)* *int EXPR* Returns the integer portion of *EXPR*. Without *EXPR*, *$_* is used.
ioctl	*ioctl(FILEHANDLE, FUNCTION, SCALAR)* Used to control I/O operations, mainly terminal I/0. Requires *sys/ioctl.ph*. *FUNCTION* is an I/O request. *SCALAR* will be read or written depending on the request. See ioctl(2).
join	*join(EXPR, LIST)* Returns a single string by joining the separate strings of *LIST* into a single string where the field separator is specified by *EXPR*, a delimiter.
keys	*keys(%ASSOC_ARRAY)* *keys %ASSOC_ARRAY* Returns a normal array consisting of all the keys in the associative array.
kill	*kill(SIGNAL, PROCESS_LIST)* *kill PROCESS_LIST* Sends a *SIGNAL* to a list of processes. The *SIGNAL* can either be a number or a signal name (signal name must be quoted). (Negative *SIGNAL* number kills process group.) See kill(2).
last	*last LABEL* *last* The last command is comparable to *C*'s *break* command. It exits the innermost loop, or, if the loop is labeled last *LABEL*, exits that loop.
lc	*lc EXPR* Returns *EXPR* in lowercase. Same as \L \E escape sequence.

Table A.1   Perl Functions *(continued)*

Function	*Description*
lcfirst	*lcfirst EXPR* Returns *EXPR* with the first character in lowercase. Same as \l \E sequence.
length	*length(EXPR)* *length EXPR* Returns the length in characters of scalar *EXPR*, or if *EXPR* is omitted, returns length of *$_*. Not used to find the size of an array or associative array.
link	*link(OLDFILE, NEWFILE)* Creates a hard link. *NEWFILE* is another name for *OLDFILE*. See link(2).
listen	*listen(SOCKET, QUEUESIZE)* Listens for connections on a *SOCKET* with a *QUEUESIZE* specifying the number of processes waiting for connections. See listen(2).
local	*local(LIST)* Makes variables in *LIST* local for this block, subroutine, or *eval*.

localtime	*localtime(EXPR)*
	localtime EXPR
	Converts the time returned by the *time* function to a 9-element array for the local timezone. The array consists of
	    seconds
	    minutes
	    hours
	    day of the month
	    number of the month (0 is January)
	    years since 1990
	    day of the week (0 is Sunday)
	    day of the year (0 is January 1)
	    isdst (true if daylight savings is on)
	See ctime(3).

lock	*lock THING* Places a lock on a variable, subroutine, or object referenced by *THING* until the lock goes out of scope. Used only with threads if they are enabled.
log	*log(EXPR)* *log EXPR* Returns the logarithm (base *e*) of *EXPR*. If *EXPR* is omitted, returns *log($_)*.

Table A.1   Perl Functions *(continued)*

Function	*Description*

lstat	*lstat(FILEHANDLE)*
	 lstat FILEHANDLE
	 lstat(EXPR)
	 Returns a 14-element array consisting of file statistics on a symbolic link, rather than the file the symbolic link points to. The array consists of
	    device
	    file inode number
	    file mode
	    number of hard links to the file
	    user ID of owner
	    group ID of owner
	    raw device
	    size of file
	    file last access time
	    file last modify time
	    file last status change time
	    preferred blocksize for file system I/O actual number of blocks allocated
	 See stat(2).

m	*/PATTERN/* *m/PATTERN/* *m* is the match operator that interprets *PATTERN* as a regular expression and is used when alternate delimeters are needed, such as *m!PATTERN!*.
map	*map(BLOCK LIST)* *map(EXPR, LIST)* Evaluates *BLOCK* or *EXPR* for each element of *LIST* and returns the list value containing the results of the evaluation. The following example translates a list of numbers to characters: *@chars = map chr, @numbers*
mkdir	*mkdir(NAME, MODE)* Creates a directory, *NAME*, with *MODE* permissions (octal). See mkdir(2).
msgctl	*msgctl(MSGID, CMD, FLAGS)* Calls the *msgctl* system call, allowing control operations on a message queue. Has weird return codes. Requires library files *ipc.ph* and *msg.ph*. See System V IPC. See also msgctl(2).
msgget	*msgget(KEY, FLAGS)* Calls *msgget* system call. Returns the message queue ID number, or if undefined, an error. See System V IPC. See also msgget(2).

Table A.1 Perl Functions *(continued)*

Function	*Description*
msgrcv	*msgrcv(MSGID, VAR, MSG_SIZE, TYPE, FLAGS)* Calls the *msgrv* system call. Receives a message from the message queue, stores the message in *VAR*. *MSG_SIZE* is the maximum message size and *TYPE* is the message type. See System V IPC. See also msgrcv(2).
msgsnd	*msgsnd(ID, MSG, FLAGS)* Calls the *msgsnd* system call. Sends the message *MSG* to the message queue. *MSG* must begin with the message type. The *pack* function is used to create the message. See System V IPC. See also msgsnd(2).
my	*my TYPE EXPR : ATTRIBUTES* *my EXPR : ATTRIBUTES* *my TYPE EXPR* *my EXPR* Variables declared with the *my* function are made private, i.e., they exist only within the innermost enclosing block, subroutine, eval, or file. Only simple scalars, complete arrays, and hashes can be declared with *my*. *TYPE* and *ATTRIBUTES* optional and experimental at this time.
new	*new CLASSNAME LIST* *new CLASSNAME* Not a built-in function, but a constructor method defined by the *CLASSNAME* module for creating *CLASSNAME* type objects. Convention taken from *C++*.
next	*next LABEL* *next* Starts the next iteration of the innermost or loop labeled with *LABEL*. Like the *C continue* function.
no	*no Module LIST* If a pragma or module has been imported with *use,* the *no* function says you don't want to use it anymore.
not	*not EXPR* Logically negates the truth value of *EXPR*.
oct	*oct(EXPR)* *oct EXPR* *oct* Returns the decimal value of *EXPR*, an octal string. If *EXPR* contains a leading *0x*, *EXPR* is interpreted as hex. With no *EXPR*, *$_* is converted.

Table A.1   Perl Functions *(continued)*

Function	*Description*
open	*open(FILEHANDLE, EXPR)* *open(FILEHANDLE)* *open FILEHANDLE* Opens a real file, *EXPR*, and attaches it to *FILEHANDLE*. Without *EXPR*, a scalar with the same name as *FILEHANDLE* must have been assigned that filename. read "FILEHANDLE" write ">FILEHANDLE" read/write "+>FILEHANDLE" append ">>FILEHANDLE" pipe out "| UNIX Command" pipe in "UNIX Command |"
opendir	*opendir(DIRHANDLE, EXPR)* Opens a directory structure named *EXPR* and attaches it to *DIRHANDLE* for functions that examine the structure. See directory(3).
ord	*ord(EXPR)* *ord* Returns the unsigned numeric ASCII values of the first character of *EXPR*. If *EXPR* is omitted, *$_* is used.
our	*our TYPE EXPR : ATTRIBUTES* *our EXPR : ATTRIBUTES* *our TYPE EXPR* *our EXPR* Declares one or more variables to be valid globals within the enclosing block, file, or eval. Like *my* for globals but does not create a new private variable. Useful when the *strict* pragma is turned on and a global variable is wanted.
pack	*$packed=pack(TEMPLATE, LIST)* Packs a list of values into a binary structure and returns the structure. *TEMPLATE* is a quoted string containing the number and type of value. *TEMPLATE* is a An ASCII string, null padded A An ASCII string, space padded b A bit string, low-to-high order B A bit string, high-to-low order h A hexadecimal string, low nybble first H A hexadecimal string, high nybble first c A signed char value C An unsigned char value

Table A.1   Perl Functions *(continued)*

Function	*Description*
pack (cont.)	s A signed short value S An unsigned short value i A signed integer value I An unsigned integer value l A signed long value L An unsigned long value n A short in "network" order N A long in "network" order f A single-precision float in native format d A double-precision float in native format p A pointer to a string x A null byte X Back up a byte @ Null-fill to absolute precision u A uuencoded string
package	*package NAMESPACE* A package declaration creates a separate namespace (symbol table) for *NAMESPACE*, the Perl way of creating a class. The *NAMESPACE* belongs to the rest of the innermost enclosing block, subroutine, *eval* or file. If the package declaration is at the same level, the new one overrides the old one.
pipe	*pipe(READHANDLE, WRITEHANDLE)* Opens a pipe for reading and writing, normally after a *fork*. See pipe(2).
pop	*pop(ARRAY)* *pop ARRAY* Pops and returns the last element of the array. The array will have one less element.
pos	*pos(SCALAR)* *pos SCALAR* Returns the offset of the character after the last matched search in *SCALAR* left off, i.e., the position where the next search will start. Offsets start at 0. If the *$scalar* is a signed *"hello"* and the search is *$scalar =~ m/l/g*, the *pos* function would return the position of the character after the first *l*, position 3.
print	*print(FILEHANDLE LIST)* *print(LIST)* *print FILEHANDLE LIST* *print LIST* *print* Prints a string or a comma separated list of strings to *FILEHANDLE*, or to the currently selected *FILEHANDLE*, or to *STDOUT*, the default. Retuns *1* if successful, *0* if not.

Table A.1 Perl Functions *(continued)*

Function	*Description*
printf	*printf(FILEHANDLE FORMAT, LIST)* *printf(FORMAT, LIST)* Prints a formatted string to *FILEHANDLE* or, if *FILEHANDLE* is omitted, to the currently selected output filehandle. *STDOUT* is the default. Similar to C's *printf*, except * is not supported. See printf(3).
prototype	*prototype FUNCTION* Returns the prototype of a function as a string, where *FUNCTION* is the name of the function. Returns *undef* if there is no prototype.
push	*push(ARRAY, LIST)* Pushes the values in *LIST* onto the end of the *ARRAY*. The array will be increased. Returns the new length of *ARRAY*.
q, qq, qw, qx	*q/STRING/* *qq/STRING/* *qw/LIST/* *qx/COMMAND/* An alternative form of quoting. The *q* construct treats *STRING* as if enclosed in single quotes. The *qq* construct treats *STRING* as if enclosed in double quotes. The *qw* construct treats each element of *LIST* as if enclosed in single quotes, and the *qx* treats *COMMAND* as if in backquotes.
quotemeta	*quotemeta EXPR* Returns the scalar value of *EXPR* with all regular expression metacharacters backslashed.
rand	*rand(EXPR)* *rand EXPR* *rand* Returns a random fractional number (scalar) between 0 and *EXPR*, where *EXPR* is a positive number. Without *srand* generates the same sequence of numbers. If *EXPR* is omitted, returns a value between 0 and 1. See rand(3).
read	*read(FILEHANDLE, SCALAR, LENGTH, OFFSET)* *read(FILEHANDLE, SCALAR, LENGTH)* Reads *LENGTH* number of bytes from *FILEHANDLE*, starting at position *OFFSET*, into *SCALAR* and returns the number of bytes read, or *0* if EOF. (Similar to *fread* system call.) See fread(3).
readdir	*readdir(DIRHANDLE)* *readdir DIRHANDLE* Reads the next entry of the directory structure, *DIRHANDLE*, opened by *opendir*. See directory(3).

Table A.1   Perl Functions *(continued)*

Function	Description
readline	*readline FILEHANDLE* Reads and returns a line from selected *FILEHANDLE;* e.g., *$line = readline(STDIN).*
readlink	*readlink(EXPR)* *readlink EXPR* Returns the value of a symbolic link. *EXPR* is the pathname of the symbolic link, and if omitted, $_ is used. See readlink(2).
readpipe	*readpipe scalar EXPR* *readpipe LIST(proposed)* An internal function that implements the *qw//* quote construct or backquotes for command subsitution; e.g., to print the output of the UNIX *ls* command, type *print reapipe(ls).*
recv	*recv(SOCKET, SCALAR, LEN, FLAGS)* Receives a message of *LEN* bytes on a socket into *SCALAR* variable. Returns the address of the sender. See recv(2).
redo	*redo LABEL* *redo* Restarts a loop block without reevaluting the condition. If there is a continue block, it is not executed. Without *LABEL*, restarts at the innermost enclosing loop.
ref	*ref EXPR* Returns a scalar TRUE value, the data type of *EXPR,* if *EXPR* is a reference, else the NULL string. The returned value depends on what is being referenced, a *REF, SCALAR, ARRAY, HASH, CODE,* or *GLOB.* If *EXPR* is an object that has been blessed into a package, the return value is the package (class) name.
rename	*rename(OLDNAME, NEWNAME)* Renames a file *OLDNAME* to *NEWNAME.* Does not work across filesystem boundaries. If *NEWNAME* already exists, it is destroyed. See rename(2).
require	*require(EXPR)* *require EXPR* *require* Includes file *EXPR* from the Perl library by searching the *@INC* array for the specified file. Also checks that the library has not already been included. *$_* is used if *EXPR* is omitted.

Table A.1   Perl Functions *(continued)*

Function	*Description*
reset	*reset(EXPR)* *reset EXPR* *reset* Clears variables and arrays or, if *EXPR* is omitted, resets *??* searches.
return	*return LIST* Returns a value from a subroutine. Cannot be used outside of a subroutine.
reverse	*reverse(LIST)* Reverses the order of *LIST* and returns an array.
rewinddir	*rewinddir(DIRHANDLE)* *rewinddir DIRHANDLE* Rewinds the position in *DIRHANDLE* to the beginning of the directory structure. See directory(3).
rindex	*rindex(STRING, SUBSTR, OFFSET)* *rindex(STRING, SUBSTR)* Returns the last position of *SUBSTR* in *STRING* starting at *OFFSET*, if *OFFSET* is specified like *index* but returns the last position of the substring rather than the first.
rmdir	*rmdir(FILENAME)* *rmdir FILENAME* Removes a directory, *FILENAME*, if empty.
s	*s/SEARCH_PATTERN/REPLACEMENT/[g][i][e][o]* Searches for *SEARCH_PATTERN* and, if found, replaces the pattern with some text. Returns the number of substitutions made. The *g* option is global across a line. The *i* option turns off case sensitivity. The *e* option evaluates the replacement string as an expression, e.g., *s/\d+/$&+5/e*
scalar	*scalar(EXPR)* Forces *EXPR* to be evaluated in a scalar context.
seek	*seek(FILEHANDLE, POSITION, WHENCE)* Positions a file pointer in a file, *FILEHANDLE*, from some position, relative to its postition in the file, *WHENCE*. If *WHENCE* is *0*, starts at the beginning of the file; if WHENCE is *1*, starts at the current position of the file, and if *WHENCE* is *2*, starts at the end of the file. *POSITION* cannot be negative if *WHENCE* is *0*.
seekdir	*seekdir(DIRHANDLE, POSITION)* Sets the *POSITION* for the *readdir* function on the directory structure associated with *DIRHANDLE*. See directory(3).

Table A.1 Perl Functions *(continued)*

Function	*Description*
select	*select(FILEHANDLE)* *select* Returns the currently selected filehandle if *FILEHANDLE* is omitted. With *FILEHANDLE*, sets the current default filehandle for *write* and *print*. See Formatting.
select	*select(RBITS, WBITS, EBITS, TIMEOUT)* Examines the I/O file descriptors to see if descriptors are ready for reading, writing, or have exceptional conditions pending. Bitmasks are specified and *TIMEOUT* is in seconds. See select(2).
semctl	*semctl(ID, SEMNUM, CMD, ARG)* Calls the *semctl* system call, allowing control operations on semaphores. Has weird return codes. Requires library files *ipc.ph* and *sem.ph*. See System V IPC. See also semctl(2).
semget	*semget(KEY, NSEMS, SIZE, FLAGS)* Returns the semaphore ID associated with *KEY*, or undefined if an error. Requires library files *ipc.ph* and *sem.ph*. See System V IPC. See also semget(2).
semop	*semop(KEY, OPSTRING)* Calls the *semop* system call to perform operations on a semaphore identified by *KEY*. *OPSTRING* must be a packed array of *semop* structures. Requires library files *ipc.ph* and *sem.ph*. See System V IPC. See also semop(2).
send	*send(SOCKET, MSG, FLAGS,TO)* *send(SOCKET, MSG, FLAGS)* Sends a message on a *SOCKET*. See send(2).
setpgrp	*setpgrp(PID, PGRP)* Sets the current process group for the specified process, process group, or user. See getpgrp(2).
setpriority	*setpriority(WHICH,WHO, PRIORITY)* Sets the current priority, *nice* value, for a process, process group, or user. See getpriority(2).

Table A.1   Perl Functions *(continued)*

Function	*Description*
setsockopt	*setsockopt(SOCKET, LEVEL, OPTNAME, OPTVAL)* Sets the requested socket option on *SOCKET*. See getsockopt(2).
shift	*shift(ARRAY)* *shift ARRAY* *shift* Shifts off the first value of the *ARRAY* and returns it, shortening the array. If *ARRAY* is omitted, the *@ARGV* array is shifted, and if in subroutines, the *@_* array is shifted.
shmctl	*shmctl(ID, CMD, ARG)* Calls the *shmctl* system call, allowing control operations on shared memory. Has weird return codes. Requires library file *ipc.ph* and *shm.ph*. See System V IPC. See also shmctl(2).
shmget	*shmget(KEY, SIZE, FLAGS)* Returns the shared memory segment ID associated with the *KEY*, or undefined if an error. The shared memory segment created is of at least *SIZE* bytes. Requires *ipc.ph* and *shm.ph*. See System V IPC. See also shmget(2).
shmread	*shmread(ID, VAR, POS, SIZE)* Reads from the shared memory *ID* starting at position *POS* for *SIZE*. *VAR* is a variable used to store what is read.The segment is attached, data is read from, and the segment is detached. Requires *ipc.ph* and *shm.ph*. See System V IPC. See also shmat(2).
shmwrite	*shmwrite(ID, VAR, POS, SIZE)* Writes to the shared memory *ID* starting at position *POS* for *SIZE*. *VAR* is a variable used to store what is written. The segment is attached, data is written to, and the segment is detached. Requires *ipc.ph* and *shm.ph*. See System V IPC. See also shmat(2).
shutdown	*shutdown(SOCKET, HOW)* Shuts down a *SOCKET* connection. If *HOW* is 0, further receives will be disallowed. If *HOW* is *1*, further sends will be disallowed. If *HOW* is 2, then further sends and receives will be disallowed. See shutdown(2).

Table A.1   Perl Functions *(continued)*

Function	*Description*
sin	*sin(EXPR)* *sin* Returns the sine of *EXPR* (expressed in radians). If *EXPR* is omitted, returns sine of *$_*.
sleep	*sleep(EXPR)* *sleep EXPR* *sleep* Causes program to sleep for *EXPR* seconds. If *EXPR* is omitted, program sleeps forever. See sleep(3).
socket	*socket(SOCKET, DOMAIN, TYPE, PROTOCOL)* Opens a socket of a specified type and attaches it to filehandle, *SOCKET*. See socket(2).
socketpair	*socketpair(SOCKET, SOCKET2, DOMAIN, TYPE, PROTOCOL)* Creates an unnamed pair of connect sockets in the specified domain, of the specified type. See socketpair(2).
sort	*sort(SUBROUTINE LIST)* *sort(LIST)* *sort SUBROUTINE LIST* *sort LIST* Sorts the *LIST* and returns a sorted array. If *SUBROUTINE* is omitted, sorts in string comparison order. If *SUBROUTINE* is specified, gives the name of a subroutine that returns an integer less than, equal to, or greater than 0, depending on how the elements of the array are to be ordered. The two elements compared are passed (by reference) to the subroutine as *$a* and *$b*, rather than *@_*. *SUBROUTINE* cannot be recursive. See Array Functions.
splice	*splice(ARRAY, OFFSET, LENGTH,LIST)* *splice(ARRAY, OFFSET, LENGTH)* *splice(ARRAY, OFFSET)* Removes elements designated starting with *OFFSET* and ending in *LENGTH* from an array, and if *LIST* is specified, replaces those elements removed with *LIST*. Returns the elements removed from the list. If *LENGTH* is not specified, everything from *OFFSET* to the end of *ARRAY* is removed.

Table A.1   Perl Functions *(continued)*

Function	*Description*
split	*split(/PATTERN/, EXPR, LIMIT)* *split(/PATTERN/, EXPR)* *split(/PATTERN/)* *split* Splits *EXPR* into an array of strings and returns them to an array. The *PATTERN* is the delimiter by which *EXPR* is separated. If *PATTERN* is omitted, whitespace is used as the delimiter. *LIMIT* specifies the number of fields to be split.
sprintf	*$string=sprintf(FORMAT, LIST)* Returns a string rather than sending output to *STDOUT* with the same formatting conventions as the *printf* function. See printf(3).
sqrt	*sqrt(EXPR)* *sqrt EXPR* Returns the square root of *EXPR*. If *EXPR* is omitted, the square root of $_ is returned.
srand	*srand(EXPR)* *srand EXPR* *srand* Sets the random seed for the *rand* function. If *EXPR* is omitted, the seed is the *time* function. See rand(3).
stat	*stat(FILEHANDLE)* *stat FILEHANDLE* *stat(EXPR)* Returns a 13-element array consisting of file statistics for *FILEHANDLE* or file named as *EXPR*. The array consists of the device the file inode number file mode number of hard links to the file user ID of owner group ID of owner raw device size of file file last access time file last modify time file last status change time preferred blocksize for file system I/O actual number of blocks allocated See stat(2).

Table A.1   Perl Functions *(continued)*

Function	Description
study	*study(SCALAR)* *study SCALAR* *study* Uses a linked list mechanism to increase efficiency in searching for pattern matches that are to be repeated many times. Can only study one *SCALAR* at a time. If *SCALAR* is omitted, *$_* is used. Most beneficial in loops where many short constant strings are being scanned.
sub	*sub NAME BLOCK* *sub NAME* *sub BLOCK* *sub NAME PROTO BLOCK* *sub NAME PROTO* *sub PROTO BLOCK* The first two declare the existence of named subroutines and return no value. Without a block, *sub NAME* is a forward declaration. The *sub BLOCK* is used to create an anonymous subroutine. The last three are like the first three, except they allow prototypes to describe how the subroutine will be called. A prototype will notify the compiler that a subroutine definition will appear at some later time and can tell the compiler what type and how many arguments the subroutine expects. For example, *sub foo ($$@)* declares that the subroutine *foo* will take three arguments, two scalars and an array. An error will occur if, for example, fewer than three arguments are passed.
substr	*substr(EXPR, OFFSET, LENGTH)* *substr(EXPR, OFFSET)* Returns a substring after extracting the substring from *EXPR* starting at position *OFFSET* and, if *LENGTH* is specified, for that many characters from *OFFSET*. If *OFFSET* is negative, starts from the far end of the string.
symlink	*symlink(OLDFILE, NEWFILE)* Creates a symbolic link. *NEWFILE* is symbolically linked to *OLDFILE*. The files can reside on different partitions. See symlink(2).
syscall	*syscall(LIST)* *syscall LIST* Calls the system call specified as the first element in *LIST*, where the system call is preceded with *&SYS_* as in *&SYS_system* call. The remaining items in *LIST* are passed as arguments to the system call. Requires *syscall.ph*.

Table A.1   Perl Functions *(continued)*

Function	*Description*
sysopen	*sysopen(FILEHANDLE, FILENAME, MODE)* *sysopen(FILEHANDLE, FILENAME, MODE, PERMS)* Opens *FILENAME* using the underlying operating system's version of the *open* call, and assigns it to *FILEHANDLE*. The file modes are system dependent and can be found in the Fcntl library module. 0 means read-only, 1 means write-only, and 2 means read/write. If *PERMS* is omitted, the default is 0666. See open(2).
sysread	*sysread(FILEHANDLE, SCALAR, LENGTH, OFFSET)* *sysread(FILEHANDLE, SCALAR, LENGTH)* Reads *LENGTH* bytes into variable *SCALAR* from *FILEHANDLE*. Uses the *read* system call. See read(2).
sysseek	*sysseek(FILEHANDLE, POSITION, WHENCE)* Sets *FILEHANDLE*'s system position using the syscall *lseek* function, bypassing standard I/O. The values of *WHENCE* are *0* to set the new position to *POSITION*, *1* to set it to the current position plus *POSITION*, and *2* to set it to EOF plus *POSITION* (often negative). See *lseek(2)*.
system	*system(LIST)* *system LIST* Executes a shell command from a Perl script and returns. Like the *exec* function, except forks first, and the script waits until the command has been executed. Control then returns to script. The return value is the exit status of the program and can be obtained by dividing by 256 or right-shifting the lower 8 bits. See system(3).
syswrite	*syswrite(FILEHANDLE, SCALAR, LENGTH, OFFSET)* *syswrite(FILEHANDLE, SCALAR, LENGTH)* *syswrite(FILEHANDLE, SCALAR)* Returns the number of bytes written to *FILEHANDLE*. Writes *LENGTH* bytes from variable *SCALAR* to *FILEHANDLE*, starting at position *OFFSET*, if *OFFSET* is specified. Uses the *write* system call. See write(2).
tell	*tell(FILEHANDLE)* *tell FILEHANDLE* *tell* Returns the current file position, in bytes (starting at byte 0), for *FILEHANDLE*. Normally the returned value is given to the *seek* function in order to return to some position within the file. See lseek(2).

Table A.1   Perl Functions *(continued)*

Function	*Description*
telldir	*telldir(DIRHANDLE)* *telldir DIRHANDLE* Returns the current position of the *readdir* function for the directory structure, *DIRHANDLE*. See directory(3).

tie	*tie(VARIABLE, CLASSNAME, LIST)*
	Binds a *VARIABLE* to a package (*CLASSNAME*) that will use methods to provide the implemenation for the variable. *LIST* consists of any additional arguments to be passed to the new method when constructing the object. Most commonly used with associative arrays to bind them to databases. The methods have predefinednames to be placed within a package. The predefined methods will be called automatically when the tied variables are fetched, stored, destroyed, etc.
	The package implementing an associative array provides the following methods:
	    TIEHASH $classname, LIST
	    DESTROY $self
	    FETCH $self, $key
	    STORE $self, $key
	    DELETE $self, $key
	    EXISTS $self, $key
	    FIRSTKEY $self
	    NEXTKEY $self, $lastkey
	Methods provided for an array are:
	    TIEARRAY $classname, LIST
	    DESTROY $self
	    FETCH $self, $subscript
	    STORE $self, $subscript, $value
	Methods provided for a scalar are:
	    TIESCALAR $classname, LIST
	    DESTROY $self
	    FETCH $self
	    STORE $self, $value
	
	Example:
	<pre>$object = tie %hash, Myhashclass
	   while($key, $value)=each (%hash){
	   print "$key, $value\n" # invokes the FETCH method
	$object = tie @array, Myarrayclass
	   $array[0]=5 # invokes the STORE method
	$object = tie $scalar, Myscalarclass
	   untie $scalar # invokes the DESTROY method</pre>

Table A.1   Perl Functions *(continued)*

Function	*Description*
tied	*tied VARIABLE* Returns a reference to the object that was previously bound with the *tie* function or undefined if *VARIABLE* is not tied to a package.
time	*time* Returns a four-element array of non-leap seconds since January 1, 1970, UTC. Used with *gmtime* and *localtime* functions. See ctime(3).
times	*times* Returns a four-element array giving the user and system CPU times, in seconds, for the process and its children. See times(3).
tr	*tr/SEARCHPATTERN/REPLACEMENT/[c][d][e]* *y/SEARCHPATTERN/REPLACEMENT/[c][d][e]* Translates characters in *SEARCHPATTERN* to corresponding character in *REPLACEMENT*. Similar to UNIX *tr* command.
truncate	*truncate(FILEHANDLE, LENGTH)* *truncate(EXPR, LENGTH)* Truncate *FILEHANDLE* or *EXPR* to a specified *LENGTH*. See truncate(2).
uc	*uc EXPR* Returns *EXPR* (or *$_* if no *EXPR*) in uppercase letters. Same as *U* *E* escape sequences.
ucfirst	*ucfirst EXPR* Returns the first character of *EXPR* (or *$_* if no *EXPR*) in uppercase. Same as *u* escape sequence.
umask	*umask(EXPR)* *umask EXPR* *umask* Sets the *umask* (file creation mask) for the process and returns the old *umask*. With *EXPR* omitted, returns the current *umask* value. See umask(2).
undef	*undef(EXPR)* *undef EXPR* *undef* Undefines *EXPR*, an lvalue. Used on scalars, arrays, hashes, or subroutine names (&subroutine) to recover any storage associated with it. Always returns the undefined value. Can be used by itself when returning from a subroutine to determine if an error was made.

Table A.1   Perl Functions *(continued)*

Function	*Description*
unlink	*unlink(LIST)* *unlink LIST* *unlink* Removes a *LIST* of files. Returns the number of files deleted. Without an argument, unlinks the value stored in *$_*. See unlink(2).
unpack	*unpack(TEMPLATE, EXPR)* Unpacks a string representing a structure and expands it to an array value, returning the array value, using *TEMPLATE* to get the order and type of values. Reverse of *pack*. See pack.
unshift	*unshift(LIST)* *unshift* Prepends *LIST* to the beginning of an array. Returns the number of elements in the new array.
untie	*untie VARIABLE* Breaks the binding (unties) between a variable and the package it is tied to. Opposite of *tie*.
use	*use MODULE VERSION LIST* *use MODULE LIST* *use MODULE* *use MODULE()* *use pragma* A compiler directive that imports subroutines and variables from *MODULE* into the current package. *VERSION* is the current version number of Perl. *LIST* consists of specific names of the variables and subroutines the current package will import. Use empty parameters if you don't want to import anything into your namespace. The *-m* and *-M* flags can be used at the command line instead of *use*. Pragmas are a special kind of module that can affect the behavior for a block of statements at compile time. Three common pragmas are *integer, subs*, and *strict*.
utime	*utime(LIST)* *utime LIST* Changes the access and modification times on a list of files. The first two elements of *LIST* are the numerical access and modification times.
values	*values(%ASSOC_ARRAY)* *values ASSOC_ARRAY* Returns an array consisting of all the values in an associative array, *ASSOC_ARRAY* in random order.

Table A.1   Perl Functions *(continued)*

Function	*Description*
vec	*vec(EXPR, OFFSET, BITS)* Treats a string, *EXPR*, as a vector of unsigned integers. Returns the value of the element specified. *OFFSET* is the number of elements to skip over in order to find the one wanted, and *BITS* is the number of bits per element in the vector. *BITS* must be one of of a power of two from 1 to 32, e.g., 1, 2, 4, 8, 16, or 32.
wait	*wait* Waits for the child process to terminate. Returns the *pid* of the deceased process and *−1* if there are no child processes. The status value is returned in the *$?* variable. See wait(2).
waitpid	*waitpid(PID, FLAGS)* Waits for a child process to terminate and returns true when the process dies, or *−1* if there are no child processes, or if *FLAGS* specify non-blocking and the process hasn't died. *$?* gets the status of the dead process. Requires *sys/wait.ph*. See wait(2).
wantarray	*wantarray* Returns true if the context of the currently running subroutine wants an array value, i.e., the returned value from the subroutine will be assigned to an array. Returns false if looking for a scalar. Example: *return wantarray ? () : undef*
warn	*warn(LIST)* *warn LIST* Sends a message to *STDERR*, like the *die* function, but doesn't exit the program.
write	*write(FILEHANDLE)* *write FILEHANDLE* *write* Writes a formatted record to *FILEHANDLE* or currently selected *FILEHANDLE* (see *select*), i.e., when called, invokes the format (picture line) for the *FILEHANDLE*, with no arguments. Either goes to *STDOUT* or to the *FILEHANDLE* currently selected by the *select* call. Has nothing to do with the *write*(2) system call. See syswrite.
y	*y/SEARCHPATTERN/REPLACEMENT/[c][d][e]* Translates characters in *SEARCHPATTERN* to corresponding characters in *REPLACEMENT*. Also known as *tr* and similar to UNIX *tr* command or *sed* *y* command.

A.2   Special Variables

Table A.2   Filehandles

Variable	What It Does
$|	If non-zero, forces buffer flush after every write and print on the currently selected filehandle
$%	Current page number of currently selected filehandle
$=	Current page length of currently selected filehandle
$–	Number of lines left on the page for currently selected filehandle
$~	Name of current report format for currently selected filehandle
$^	Name of current top-of-page format for currently selected filehandle

Table A.3   Local to Block

Variable	What It Does
$1.. $9	Contains remembered subpatterns that reference a corresponding set of parentheses. Same as \1..\9
$&	The string matched by the last pattern match. (Like *sed* editor)
$`	The string preceding what was matched in the last pattern match
$'	The string that follows whatever was matched by the last pattern match
$+	The last pattern matched by the last search pattern

EXAMPLE A.1

```
$str="old and restless";

print "$&\n" if $str =~ /and/;
print "$'\n" if $str =~ /and/;
print "$'\n" if $str =~ /and/;
print "\nold string is: $str\n";
$str=~s/(old) and (restless)/$2 and $1/;
print "new string is: $str\n";
print "\nlast pattern matched: $+\n";

(Output)
and
old
restless
old string is: old and restless
new string is: restless and old
last pattern matched is: restless
```

Table A.4   Global

Variable	What It Does
$_	Default input and pattern-searching space.
$.	Current input line number of last filehandle that was read; must close the filehandle to reset line numbers for next filehandle.
$/	Input record separator, newline by default. (like RS in *awk.*)
$\	Output record separator for the print function. Does not print a newline unless set: $\="\n"
$,	Output field separator for the print function. Normally delimiter is not printed between comma separated strings unless set: $,=" ".
$"	Same as $, but applies to printing arrays when in double quotes. Default is space.
$#	Output format for numbers printed with the print function. (Like OMFT in *awk.*)
$$	The process ID number of the Perl program running this script.
$?	Status returned by last pipe closed, command in backquotes, or system function.
$*	Default is *0*. If set to *1*, does a multiline match within a string; *0* for a match within a single line.
$0	Name of this Perl script.
$[	Index of first element of an array, and first character in a substring. Default is *0*.
$]	The first part of the string is printed out when using *perl -v* for version information.
$;	The subscript separator for multidimensional array emulation. Default is \034. (Like *SUBSEP* in *awk.*)
$!	Yields the current value of *errno* (system error number) if numeric, and the corresponding system error string.
$@	Error message from the last *eval*, *do*, or *require* function.
$<	The real *uid* of this process.
$>	The effective *uid* of this process.
$(	The real *gid* of this process.
$)	The effective *gid* of this process.

Table A.4 Global *(continued)*

Variable	What It Does
$:	The set of characters after which a string may be broken to fill continuation lines (starting with ^) in a format. Default is \n- to break on whitespace, newline, or colon.
$^A	The accumulator for *formline* and *write* operations.
$^C	TRUE if Perl is run in compile-only mode using command line option -c.
$^D	Perl's debug flags when -D switch is used.
$^E	Operating-system–dependent error information.
$^F	Maximum file descriptor passed to subprocess, usually two.
$^H	The current state of syntax checks.
$^I	Current value of inplace-edit extension when -i switch is used. Use *undef* to disable inplace editing.
$^L	Formfeed character used in formats.
$^M	Emergency memory pool.
$^O	Name of the operating system.
$^P	Internal Perl debugging flag.
$^S	State of the Perl interpreter.
$^T	Time of day when script started execution. Used by -A, -C, and -M test operators and be set to any number value returned by *time* to perform file tests relative to the current time.
$^V	The Perl version.
$^W	The current value of the warning switch.
$^X	The full pathname by which this Perl was invoked.
_	An underscore. The special designator for file testing when stating files.
ARGV	The special filehandle array for looping over line arguments.
$ARGV	The variable containing the name of the current file when reading from <ARGV>.
@ARGV	The array containing command line arguments.
DATA	Special filehandle referring to anything following _ _END_ _.

Table A.4   Global *(continued)*

Variable	What It Does
@F	The array into which input lines are autosplit when the *-a* switch is used.
@INC	Array containing pathnames where *require* and *do* functions look for files that are to be included in this script.
%INC	Associative array containing entries for files that have been included by calling *do* or *require*. The key is the filename and the value is its location.
%ENV	Associative array containing the current environment.
@EXPORT	Default symbols to be exported.
@EXPORT_OK	Symbols to be exported upon request by the user.
%EXPORT_TAGS	Used by *Exporter.pm* to collectively name sets of symbols.
%SIG	Associative array used to set signal handlers.
STDERR	Special filehandle for standard error.
STDIN	Special filehandle for standard input.
STDOUT	Special filehandle for standard output.

A.3   Perl Pragmas

A pragma is a special "pseudo" module that hints how the compiler should behave. The *use declaration* allows the importation of compiler directives called pragmas into your Perl program. Pragmas determine how a block of statements will be compiled. They are lexically scoped; the scope is limited to the current enclosing block and can be turned off with the *no* directive. Pragma names are conventionally lowercase. Here is a partial list.

Table A.5   Perl Pragmas

Pragma	What It Does
use autouse	Provides a mechanism for runtime demand loading of a module only when a function from that module gets called.
use base	Lets a programmer declare a derived class based upon listed parent classes at compile time and eliminates the need for *require*; e.g., *use base qw(A B);* is equivalent to *BEGIN{ require A; require B;;* *push(@ISA, qw(A B));}*

Table A.5   Perl Pragmas *(continued)*

Pragma	What It Does
use bytes	Prior to Perl 5.6, all strings were treated as a sequence of bytes. Now strings can contain characters wider than a byte that are represented as numbers. The *bytes* pragma allows you to specify that the code is using the older byte-oriented semantics.
use constant	Declares the named symbol to be a constant with a given scalar or list; For example: *use constant BUFFER_SIZE => 4096; use constant OS=> 'Solaris';*
use diagnostics	Forces verbose warning messages beyond the normal diagnostics issued by the Perl compiler and interpreter. Since it affects only the innermost block, the pragma is normally placed at the beginning of the program. Cannot use *no diagnostics.*
use integer	A lexically scoped pragma that tells the compiler to handle all mathmatical operations as integer math and truncates the fractional part of floating point numbers when performing such operations.
use locale	A lexically scoped pragma that tells the compiler to enable or disable the use of POSIX locales when dealing with regular expressions, built-in operations, character conversions, etc.
use open	Declares one or more default disciplines for I/O operations; the two disciplines currently supported are *:raw* and *:crlf.*
use overload	Used to redefine the meanings of built-in operations when using objects. See *Math::BigFloat* in the standard Perl library for examples of overloaded operators.
use strict 'vars'	With *'vars'* as an argument, must use lexical (*my*) variables or fully qualified variable names with the package name and the scope operator or imported variables. If not adhered to, will cause a compilation error.
use strict 'ref'	Generates a runtime error if symbolic references are used, such as typeglobs.
use strict 'subs'	Generates a compile-time error if a bare word is used and it is not a predeclared subroutine or filehandle.
use strict	Generates compile-time errors if symbolic references are used, if non-lexical variables are declared, or if bare words that are not subroutines or filehandles are used.
use vars qw(list)	Used to declare global variables before *our* was introduced.
use warnings	A lexically scoped pragma that permits flexible control over Perl's built-in warnings like the *-w* switch or *$^W* variable.

Table A.5   Perl Pragmas *(continued)*

Pragma	*What It Does*
use lib 'library path'	Loads in the library at compile time, not run time.
use sigtrap 'signal names'	Initializes a set of signal handlers for the listed signals. Without an argument for a set of default signals. Prints a stack dump of the program and issues an *ABRT* signal.
use subs qw(subroutine list)	Predeclares a list of subroutines allowing the subroutines listed to be called without parentheses and overrides built-in functions.
no integer	To turn off or unimport the pragma, the pragma name is preceded with *no*.

A.4   Perl Modules

Table A.6   General Programming

Module	*Description*
Benchmark	Checks and compares the speed of running code in CPU time
Config	Accesses Perl configuration options from the *%Config* hash
Env	Converts the *%ENV* hash to scalars containing environment variables, e.g., *$ENV{HOME}* becomes *$HOME*
English	Provides scalars in English or *awk* names for special variables, e.g., *$0* can be represented as *$PROGRAM_NAME*
Getopt	Provides for processing of command line options and switches with arguments
Shell	Used to run shell commands within Perl scripts by treating the commands as subroutines, e.g., *$today=date();*
Symbol	Generates anonymous globs with *gensym()* and qualifies variable names with *qualify()*

Table A.7   CGI

Module	Description
CGI	CGI (Common Gateway Interface) class
CGI::Apache	Used with *CGI.pm* and the Perl-Apache API
CGI::Carp	Handles HTTP error messages and creates error log files
CGI::Cookie	Interfaces with Netscape cookies
CGI::Fast	Interfaces with Fast CGI
CGI::Pretty	Produces pretty formatted HTML code
CGI::Push	Simple interface to server push

Table A.8   Error Handling

Module	Description
Carp	Generates *die*-like error messages to report line numbers of the calling routine where the error occurred. The subroutines that can be called from this module are *carp()*, *croak()*, and *confess()*.
Errno	Loads the *libc errno.h* defines.
Sys::Syslog	Provides a Perl interface to the UNIX *syslog(3)* library calls.

Table A.9   File Handling

Module	Description
Cwd	Gets the pathname of the current working directory. Produces an error message if used with the *-w* switch.
DirHandle	Provides an object-oriented interface for directory handles.
Fcntl	Loads the *libc fcntl.h* (file control) defines.
File::Basename	Splits a filename into components or extracts a filename or a directory from full directory path.
File::CheckTree	Runs file tests on a collection of files in a directory tree.
File::Copy	Used to copy files or filehandles.
File::DosGlob	Does DOS-like globbing.
File::Find	Used to traverse a UNIX file tree.

Table A.9   File Handling *(continued)*

Module	Description
File::Finddepth	Searches depth-first through a file system.
File::Glob	Does UNIX filename globbing.
File::Path	Creates and removes a list of directories.
File::Spec	Performs portable operations on filenames.
FileCache	Allows more files to be opened than permitted by the system.
FileHandle	Provides an object-oriented interface to filehandle access methods.
SelectServer	Saves and restores a selected filehandle.
flush.pl	Writes any data remaining in the filehandle's buffer or prints an expression and then flushes the buffer.
pwd.pl	Sets the *PWD* environment variable to the present working directory after using *chdir*.
stat.pl	Puts the values returned by the stat function into scalars—*$st_dev*, *$st_ino*, *$st_mode*, *$st_nlink*, *$st_uid*, *$st_rdev*, *$st_atime*, *$st_mtime*, *$st_ctime*, *$st_blksize*, *$st_blocks*.

Table A.10   Text Processing

Module	Description
Pod::Text	Converts *pod* documentation to ASCII-formatted text.
Search::Dict	Searches for a string in a dictionary (alphabetically ordered) file and sets the file pointer to the next line.
Term::Complete	Provides a filename-completion–like interface for prompting a user for partial input that can be completed by pressing a tab key or a complete list of choices by pressing <Ctrl>-d.
Text::Abbrev	Creates an abbreviation table, a hash consisting of key/value pairs from a list. The key is the abbreviation and the value is the string that was abbbreviated, e.g., *ma/mail, mo/more.*
Text::ParseWords	Parses a line of text into a list of words like the *shell* does, stripping leading whitespace.
Text::Soundex	Maps words to four character length codes that roughly correspond to how the word is pronounced or sounds.
Text::Tabs	Expands tabs into spaces and unexpands tabs to spaces.
Text::Warp	Wraps text into a paragraph.

Table A.11   Database Interfaces

Module	Description
AnyDBM_File	A UNIX-based module providing framework for multiple DBMs.
DB_File	Provides access to Berkeley DB manager. See *ftp//ftp.cs.berkeley.edu/ucb/4bsd.*
DBI	Returns a list of DBs and drivers on the system, and functions to interact with the database.
GDBM_File	Provides access to the GNU database manager. See *ftp://prep.ai.mit.edu/pub/gnu.*
NDBM_File	A UNIX-based module providing an interface to NDBM files.
ODBM_File	A UNIX-based module providing an interface to ODBM files.
SDBM_File	A UNIX-based module providing an interface to SDBM files

Table A.12   Math

Module	Description
bigrat.pl	Enables infinite precision arithmetic on fractions.
Math::BigFloat	Supports arbitary-sized floating-point arithmetic.
Math::BigInt	Supports arbitrary-sized integer arithmetic.
Math::Complex	Supports complex numbers to demonstrate overloading.
Math::Trig	Supports trigonometric functions.

Table A.13   Networking

Module	Description
chat2.pl	Allows Perl to manipulate interactive network services such as FTP.
comm.pl	Newer than *chat2.pl.* Allows Perl to manipulate interactive services.
IPC::Open2	Opens a process for reading and writing to allow data to be piped to and from an external program.
IPC::Open3	Opens a process for reading,writing, and error handling so that data can be piped to and from an external program.

Table A.13   Networking *(continued)*

Module	Description
Net::Ping	Checks whether a remote machine is up.
Socket	Creates sockets and imports socket methods for interprocess communication and loads *socket.h* header file.
Sys::Hostname	Gets the hostname for the system.

Table A.14   Time and Locale

Module	Description
I18N::Collate	Compares 8-bit scalar data according to the current locale.
Time::gmtime	An interface to Perl's built-in *gmtime*() function.
Time::Local	Computes the UNIX time (the number of non-leap year seconds since January 1, 1970) from local and GMT (UTC) time.
Time::localtime	An interface to Perl's built-in *localtime()* function.

Table A.15   Terminals

Module	Description
Term::Cap	Provides low-level functions to manipulate terminal configurations as a terminal interface to the *termcap* database.

Table A.16   Object-Oriented Module Functions

Module	Description
Autoloader	For large modules, loads in only needed sections of a module.
AutoSplit	Splits module into bite-sized chunks for autoloading.
Devel::SelfStubber	Generates stubs for self-loading modules to ensure that if a method is called, it will get loaded.
DynaLoader	Used to automatically and dynamically load modules.
Exporter	Used by other modules to make methods and variables available through importation.
overload	Used to overload mathmatical operations.
Tie::Hash	Provides methods for tying a hash to a package.

Table A.16   Object-Oriented Module Functions *(continued)*

Module	Description
Tie::Scalar	Provides methods for tying a scalar to a package.
Tie::SubstrHash	Provides a hash-table–like interface to an array with constant key and record size.

Table A.17   Language Extension

Module	Description
ExtUtils::Install	For installing and deinstalling platform-dependent Perl extensions.
ExtUtils::Liblist	Determines what libraries to use and how to use them.
ExtUtils::MakeMaker	Creates a *Makefile* for a Perl extension in the extension's library.
ExtUtils::Manifest	Automates the maintenance of *MANIFEST* files, consisting of a list of filenames.
ExtUtils::Miniperl	Writes *C* code for *perlmain.c* that contains the bootstrap code for making archive libraries needed by modules available from within Perl.
ExtUtils::Mkbootstrap	Is called from the extension's *Makefile* to create a bootstrap file needed to do dynamic loading on some systems.
ExtUtils::Mksysmlists	Writes *linker* option files used by some linkers during the creation of shared libraries for dynamic extensions.
ExtUtils::MM_OS2	Overrides the implementation of methods, causing UNIX behavior.
ExtUtils::MM_Unix	To be used with *MakeMaker* to provide methods for both UNIX and non-UNIX systems.
ExtUtils::MM_VMS	Overrides the implementation of methods, causing UNIX behavior.
Fcntl	Translates the *C fcntl* header file.
POSIX	Provides the Perl interface to IEEE std 1003.1 identifiers.
Safe	Provides private compartments where unsafe Perl code can be evaluated.
Test::Harness	Used by *MakeMaker* to run test scripts for Perl extensions and produce diagnostics.

A.5   Command Line Switches

Table A.18   Command Line Switches

Switch	Description
-0	Specify a record separator.
-a	Turns on autosplit mode when used with *-n* or *-p*, performing implicit split on whitespace. Fields are put in *@F* array. ```date	perl -ane 'print "$F[0]\n";```
-c	Checks Perl syntax without executing script.
-d	Turns on Perl debugger for script.
-D	Sets Perl debugging flags. (Check your Perl installation to make sure debugging was installed). To watch how Perl executes a script, use *-D14*.
-e command	Used to execute Perl commands at the command line rather than in a script.
-Fpattern	Specifies a pattern to use when splitting the input line. The pattern is just a regular expression enclosed in slashes, single or double quotes. For example, *-F/:+/* splits the input line on one or more colons. Turned on if *-a* is also in effect.
-h	Prints a summary of Perl's command line options.
-iextension	Enables in-place editing when using <> to loop through a file. If extension is not specified, modifies the file in place. Otherwise renames the input file with the extension (used as a backup), and creates an output file with the original filename which is edited in place. This is the selected filehandle for all *print* statements.
-Idirectory	Used with *-P* to tell the *C* preprocessor where to look for included files, by default */usr/include* and */usr/lib/perl* and the current directory.
-ldigits	Enables automatic line-ending processing. Chops the line terminator if *-n* or *-p* are used. Assigns *$\\* the value of digits (octal) to add the line terminator back on to *print* statements. Without digits specified, sets *$* to the current value of *$/*. (See Table A.2, "Special Variables").
-m[-]module	
-M[-]module	
-M[-]'module'	
-[mM]module=arg[,arg]...	
-mmodule	Executes the *use* module before executing the Perl script.

Table A.18   Command Line Switches *(continued)*

Switch	Description
-Mmodule	Executes the *use* module before executing the Perl script. Quotes are used if extra text is added. The dash shown in square brackets means that the use directive will be replaced with *no*.
-n	Causes Perl to implicitly loop over a named file, printing only lines specified.
-p	Causes Perl to implicitly loop over a named file, printing all lines in addition to those specified.
-P	Causes script to be run through the C preprocessor before being compiled by Perl.
-s	Enables switch parsing after the script name but before filename arguments removing any switches found there from the *@ARGV* array. Sets the switch names to a scalar variable of the same name and assigns *1* to the scalar, e.g., *-abc* becomes *$abc* in the script.
-S	Makes Perl use the *PATH* environment variable to search for the script if the *#!/usr/bin/perl* line is not supported.
-T	Forces "taint" checks to be turned on for testing a script, which is ordinarily done only on *setuid* or *setgid* programs. Recommended for testing CGI scripts.
-u	Causes a core dump of script after compilation. (UNIX based).
-U	Allows Perl to do unsafe operations, e.g., unlinking directories if superuser.
-v	Prints Perl version information. (UNIX based).
-V	Prints a summary of the most important Perl configuration values and the current value of the *@INC* array.
-V:NAME	Prints the value of *NAME*, where *NAME* is a configuration variable.
-W	Enables all warnings even if disabled locally using *no warnings*.
-w	Prints warnings about possible misuse of reserved words, filehandles, subroutines, etc.
-xdirectory	Any text preceding the *#!/usr/bin/perl* line will be ignored. If a directory name is provided as an argument to the *-x* switch, Perl will change to that directory before execution of the script starts.
-X	Disables all warnings.

A.6   Debugger

1. Getting Information About the Debugger

Information on how to use the debugger is found by typing at your command line:

```
perldoc perldebug
```

Here is a sample of the output:

NAME
    perldebug - Perl debugging

DESCRIPTION
    First of all, have you tried using the -w switch?

The Perl Debugger
    If you invoke Perl with the -d switch, your script runs under the Perl
    source debugger. This works like an interactive Perl environment,
    prompting for debugger commands that let you examine source code, set
    breakpoints, get stack backtraces, change the values of variables, etc.
    This is so convenient that you often fire up the debugger all by itself
    just to test out Perl constructs interactively to see what they do. For
    example:

```
$ perl -d -e 42
```

    In Perl, the debugger is not a separate program the way it usually is in
    the typical compiled environment. Instead, the -d flag tells the
    compiler to insert source information into the parse trees it's about to
    hand off to the interpreter. That means your code must first compile
    correctly for the debugger to work on it. Then when the interpreter
    starts up, it preloads a special Perl library file containing the
    debugger.

    The program will halt **right before** the first runtime executable
    statement (but see below regarding compile-time statements) and ask you
    to enter a debugger command. Contrary to popular expectations, whenever
    the debugger halts and shows you a line of code, it always displays the
    line it's **about** to execute, rather than the one it has just executed.

    Any command not recognized by the debugger is directly executed
    (*eval*'d) as Perl code in the current package. (The debugger uses the
    DB package for keeping its own state information.)

For any text entered at the debugger prompt, leading and trailing whitespace is first stripped before further processing. If a debugger command coincides with some function in your own program, merely precede the function with something that doesn't look like a debugger command, such as a leading ; or perhaps a +, or by wrapping it with parentheses or braces.

<continues here>

----

2. Entering and Exiting the Debugger

To invoke the Perl debugger, use the -d switch. It allows you to examine your program in an interactive-type environment after it has successfully compiled. After each line, the script will stop and ask for a command. The line you will be looking at is the next line that will be executed, not the previous one. The prompt contains the current package, function, file and line number, and the current line. Following is a list of the debug commands.

Once you start the debugger, all the debugging commands are listed by typing h at the debug prompt or h h if you can't read what is displayed.

To exit the debugger, type q for quit or R for restart.

```
$ perl -d exer.1

Loading DB routines from $RCSfile: perldb.pl,v $$Revision: 4.0.1.2
    $$Date: 91/11/05 17:55:58 $
Emacs support available.
Enter h for help.
main'(exer.1:3):          print "Today is ", `date`;
  DB<1> h
T                         Stack trace.
s                         Single step.
n                         Next, steps over subroutine calls.
r                         Return from current subroutine.
c [line]                  Continue; optionally inserts a one-time-only
                          breakpoint at the specified line.
<CR>                      Repeat last n or s.
l min+incr                List incr+1 lines starting at min.
l min-max                 List lines.
l line                    List line.
l                         List next window.
-                         List previous window.
w line                    List window around line.
l subname                 List subroutine.
f filename                Switch to filename.
/pattern/                 Search forwards for pattern; final / is optional.
?pattern?                 Search backwards for pattern.
L                         List breakpoints and actions.
S                         List subroutine names.
t                         Toggle trace mode.
```

b [line] [condition]	Set breakpoint; line defaults to the current execution line; condition breaks if it evaluates to true, defaults to 1.
b subname [condition]	Set breakpoint at first line of subroutine.
d [line]	Delete breakpoint.
D	Delete all breakpoints.
a [line] command	Set an action to be done before the line is executed. Sequence is: check for breakpoint, print line if necessary, do action, prompt user if breakpoint or step, evaluate line.
A	Delete all actions.
V [pkg [vars]]	List some (default all) variables in package (default current).
X [vars]	Same as "V currentpackage [vars]".
< command	Define command before prompt.
> command	Define command after prompt.
! number	Redo command (default previous command).
! -number	Redo numberth-to-last command.
H -number	Display last number commands (default all).
q or ^D	Quit.
p expr	Same as "print DB'OUT expr" in current package.
= [alias value]	Define a command alias, or list current aliases.
command	Execute as a Perl statement in current package.

```
    DB<1> l
3:      print "Today is ", `date`;
4:      print "The name of this \uperl script\e is $0.\n";
5:      print "Hello. The number we will examine is 125.5.\n";
6:      printf "The \unumber\e  is %d.\n", 125.5;
7:      printf "The \unumber\e  is %d.\n", 125.5;
8:      printf "The following number is taking up 20 spaces and is
        right-justified.\n";
9:      printf "|%-20s|\n", 125;
10:     printf "\t\tThe number in hex is %x\n", 125.5;
11:     printf "\t\tThe number in octal is %o\n", 125.5;
12:     printf "The number in scientific notation is %e\n", 125.5;
    DB<1> q      (quit)
```

3. Debugger Commands

Getting help:

h	Lists help messages for all debugger commands.
h p	Lists a help message for debugger command *p*.

Listing parts of a script:

l	Lists 10 lines of the program.
l 8	Lists line 8.
l 5–10	Lists lines 5 through 10.
l greetme	Lists statements in subroutine, *greetme.*
L	Lists the next line to execute.

w7	Lists a window of lines containing specified line 7. Lists 3 lines before the specified lines and fills the window with lines after it.
/^abc/	Searches forward for regular expression *abc,* where *abc* is at the beginning of the line.
?abc?	Searches backward for regular expression *abc.*
S	Lists all subroutines in the program by package name, two colons and the name of the subroutine.
r	Executes the remainder of statements in the current subroutine and then displays the line immediately after the subroutine call.

Stepping line by line:

s	Single step a line at a time through the script.
n	Like *s* but executes subroutine calls without stepping through them.
Enter	Pressing the Enter key causes the previous *s* or *n* command to be repeated.
.	Repeats the last line executed.
–	Repeats all lines preceding the current one.
r	Conitinues until the currently executing subroutine returns and displays the return value and type after returning.

Getting out of the debugger:

q	Quit the debugger.
<Ctrl>-d	Quit the debugger.
R	Restart the debugger and a new session.

Breakpoints:
Breakpoints allow you to set a place where the program will stop so that you can examine what's going on. They must be set on lines that start an executable statement.

b 45	Sets break point to line 45. Type *c* to continue and the program will stop execution at line 45.
c	Continue execution.
b greetme	Sets break point to subroutine *greetme.*
b $x > 10	Triggers a breakpoint only if the condition is true.
w	Creates a window around the breakpoint and marks the line where the breakpoint is found; e.g., *10==>b* (breakpoint is at line 10).
d	Deletes the breakpoint on the line about to execute.
d 12	Deletes the breakpoint at line 12.
D	Deletes all breakpoints.

Printing variable values:

X name	Displays the value of any variables called *name.* Variable names are NOT preceded by their identifying funny character; e.g., use *x* rather than *$x* or *@x.*
V package	Displays all variables within a package.
p $x + 3	Evaluates and prints the expression.

Tracing:

T   Produces a stack backtrace listing of what subroutines were called.

t   Toggles trace mode.

Aliases:

=   Lists all aliases.

=   *ph print "$hashref->{Science}->{Lou}"*   *ph* is an alias for printing a hash value.

B

SOME HELPFUL SCRIPTS

Before I joined them, the group I work with had become accustomed to having their upcoming schedules charted, but this was a time-consuming task that the manager was doing manually. All of the information had to be transferred from the central database to a text file by hand. I took on the project of automating the task with a shell script.

The original program was a *C* shell script to access the database and create the text file containing the charted schedule. For security reasons I wanted the programs displaying the chart to have a different user identity from my own, but the program to access the database had to run as an authorized user. These requirements led to the use of the *set user-id* shell script.

The original *C* shell script was about one thousand lines and took around ten minutes to execute. Then I found Perl and thought I would convert the program and see if this new scripting language was any good. Admittedly, I didn't translate all of the error checking from the *C* shell script to the Perl program (most of it was redundant or unnecessary), but the size difference was remarkable—the first fully functioning Perl program was around five hundred lines of code. The difference in size was not nearly as exciting as the reduction in execution time. The script that took ten minutes with the *C* shell took ten seconds as a Perl program! And it isn't even pre-interpreted object code.

Since the original security requirements for user identity were still in place, running the Perl script with *set user-id* was needed. But since standard Perl will not work with *set user-id*, *taintperl* was required. A couple of features from the original script had to be altered so that *taintperl* would accept the script. For instance, the *PATH* environment variable had to be set within the Perl script rather than externally. *Taintperl* seems to require that command paths or program names used with system calls all be defined within the program to prevent any trojan horses from being referenced.

With few exceptions (usually programmer error or database problems), this Perl script to build the schedule chart has been working maintenance-free for almost three years. This may not be the most efficient program for performing the desired task, but I was learning Perl while I was writing this program, and for a reasonably complex goal as a first attempt at writing a Perl program, I think it came out pretty good.

B.1 *taintperl* Script by Mark Houser

```
#! /usr/local/bin/taintperl
#
# This program will generate an input list of the form:
#
#  Loc  Course Start   #    Instructor  Lab       Room      Class#    First
#  MPTS SA-135 Apr 11  12   Lastname    MPLAB-4   MPLAB-5   12345     First
#
# as generated by an ISQL database query, sorted by Start date,
# Location, and Course number, then convert the information to
# a chart similar to the following:
#
#                                          Created:  9:07am, April 11, 1994
#
#          1994
#          April              May                                         J
#         | 11   | 18   | 25   | 2    | 9    | 16   | 23   | 30   |
#=============================================================================
#First   | SA-135|      |      | Course| Course|      | Course|      |
#Lastname| 5/4   |      |      | Rm/Lab| Rm/Lab|      | Rm/Lab|      |
#        |       |      |      |       |       |      |       |      |
#---------+-------+-------+-------+-------+-------+-------+-------+-------+
#
# NOTES:
#
# The original input list was based on a query used by management, in order
# reduce the amount of ISQL design necessary. The ISQL queries for the
# list already existed.
#
# For simplicity, the program is itself run from a shell script which
# checks the validity of certain arguments (like month names), although
# many of these checks have been incorporated here as well.
#
# taintperl is used since the program was designed to run as a set-uid
# program, and regular perl will not run as a set-uid program.
#
#
#
# taintperl does not like any external or environment variables,
# therefore all needed environment variables are defined internally.
#
# Make sure command paths for necessary commands are defined
$ENV{'PATH'} = '/usr/ucb:/usr/bin';
#
# Set up the database access environment variables
#
$ENV{'SYBASE'} = '/usr/sybase';
$ENV{'DSQUERY'} = 'YALE';
#
# Check for arguments
#
```

```
if ( $#ARGV > 1 )
    {
    print STDERR "Usage: maker [ month [ date ] ]\n";
    exit (3);
    }
#
# Define array of last names
#
@instr_last_name = ( "Lastname", "LastnameA", "LastnameB", "LastnameC",
            "LastnameD", "LastnameE", "LastnameF" );
#
# Define associative array of first names, indexed by last names
#
%instr_first_name =
    (
    "Lastname", "First",
    "LastnameA", "FirstA",
    "LastnameB", "FirstB",
    "LastnameC", "FirstC",
    "LastnameD", "FirstD",
    "LastnameE", "FirstE",
    "LastnameF", "FirstF",
    "Others", ""
    );
#
# Define month names
#
@monthnames = ( "January", "February", "March", "April", "May", "June",
    "July", "August", "September", "October", "November", "December");
#
# Define month lengths
#
@monthlen = ( 31, 28, 31, 30, 31, 30, 31, 31, 30, 31, 30, 31 );
#
# Define associative array to determine month number (0-11) from
# abbreviated month name.
#
%monthabrs =
    (
    "Jan", 0,
    "Feb", 1,
    "Mar", 2,
    "Apr", 3,
    "May", 4,
    "Jun", 5,
    "Jul", 6,
    "Aug", 7,
    "Sep", 8,
    "Oct", 9,
    "Nov", 10,
    "Dec", 11
    );
#
# Define Location expansions based on location code using associative array
#
```

```
%locations =
    (
    'ANDV', 'Andover',
    'ATLN', 'Atlanta',
    'BALT', 'Baltimo',
    'CHIG', 'Chicago',
    'DALL', 'Dallas',
    'DENV', 'Denver',
    'DETR', 'Detroit',
    'HOUS', 'Houston',
    'LOSA', 'LosAngl',
    'MILW', 'Milwauk',
    'MPTS', 'Milpita',
    'NYNY', 'NewYork',
    'OFFA', 'OffSite',
    'OFFB', 'OffSite',
    'OFFM', 'OffSite',
    'OHIO', 'Columbu',
    'ORCO', 'OrangCo',
    'ORLA', 'Orlando',
    'SEAL', 'Seattle',
    'STLO', 'StLouis',
    'UNKN', 'Unknown'
    );
#
# Define correction values to add/subtract to date to determine the
# date of the next/previous Monday from a certain day of the week.
#
@adj2monday = ( 1, 0, -1, -2, -3, 3, 2);
#
# Retreive the current time from the system
#
@localtime = localtime(time);
#
# Break out the wanted pieces from the current system time
#
($lmin,$lhour,$lmday,$lmonth,$lyear,$lwday) = @localtime[1..6];

#
# Subroutine mondays is used to find the mondays for the particular
# month and year passed as arguments
#
sub mondays
    {
    # define the local variables
    local ($month, $year) = @_;
    local (@mondays);
    # increment month for use with the cal command
    $month ++;
    # use the cal command to get the dates for the given month and year
    open (CALIN, "/usr/bin/cal $month $year |");
    # count is used to count the number of input lines seen
    $count = 0;
    # while the cal command provides input ...
```

```perl
    while ( <CALIN> )
        {
        $count ++;
            # chop off the return at the end of the line
        chop;
            # break up the line
        @y = split;
            # remove the first empty entry, if one exists, created by
            # leading spaces
        shift (@y) if ("$y[0]" == "");
        if (($#y > 4) && ($count == 3))
                # the first week of the month (the 3rd line of output from
                # the cal command) may not have a Monday, but if it does
                # there are at least 4 other dates, too, and we'll have to
                # count backwards to find the Monday to add to the list.
            {
            push (@mondays,$y[$#y-5]);
            }
        elsif ($#y > 0 && $count > 3)
                # every other week of the month, the monday is always the
                # second date of the week.
            {
            push (@mondays,$y[1]);
            }
        }
    return (@mondays);
    }

#
# A quick subroutine to determine if the passed year is a leap year
#
sub leapyear
    {
    local ($year) = @_;
    ((!($year % 4)) && (!(!(($year % 100) || (!($year % 400))))));
    }


#
# subroutine leapmonth returns true if the month is February and
# it is also a leap year
#
sub leapmonth
    {
    local ($month, $year) = @_;
    (($month == 1) && (&leapyear($year)));
    }

if ( $#ARGV >= 0 )
    {
    # get the month from the command line (if given)
    $month = shift (@ARGV);
    # starting year is the current year
    $syear = $lyear;
    # convert month and check
```

```perl
if ( $month =~ /^[0-9]+$/ && ($month < 1 || $month > 12))
        # handle invalid month numbers first
    {
    print STDERR "I only understand month numbers between 1 and 12.\n";
    exit 3;
    }
if ( $month =~ /^[1-9]$|^1[0-2]$/ )
        # valid month numbers may be 1 to 12, but will be used as 0 to 11
    {
    $smonth = $month - 1;
    }
else
        # determine the month from the month name
    {
        # only the first three letters of the month name are significant
    $tmp_month = substr($month,0,3);
        # and those will be made all lowercase ...
    $tmp_month =~ tr/A-Za-z/a-za-z/;
        # ... except for the first letter
    substr ($tmp_month,0,1) =~ tr/a-z/A-Z/;
        # look up the name number in the associative array
    $smonth = $monthabrs{$tmp_month};
    if ( "$smonth" eq "" )
            # the month name given can't be found in the associative array
        {
        print STDERR "I don't understand the month of $month.\n";
        exit 3;
        }
    }
# if the starting month is more than 5 months in the past, let's make
# it next year instead ...
$syear ++ if (($lmonth - $smonth) > 5);
# ... or it could be last year
$syear -- if (($lmonth - $smonth) < -5);
# get them mondays for the staring month and year
@mondays = &mondays ($smonth, "19$syear");
# if there are still more arguments, it has to be a date
if ( $#ARGV >= 0 )
    {
    $date = shift (@ARGV);
    if ($date =~ /^[0-9]+$/)
        {
        if ($date > $monthlen[$smonth] +
                &leapmonth($smonth,$syear))
                # date too high for specified month, such as April 31
                # or February 30 (Feb. 29 is valid some years).
            {
            print STDERR "Error: $monthnames[$smonth] only has ";
            print STDERR $monthlen[$smonth] +
                &leapmonth($smonth,$syear);
            print STDERR " days";
            print STDERR " in 19$syear" if ($smonth == 1 );
            print STDERR ".\n";
            exit 4;
            }
```

```
             $is_a_monday = 0;
                 # compare the date provided with the mondays of the
                 # starting month
             foreach $tmp_ (@mondays)
                 {
                 $is_a_monday = 1 if ($date == $tmp_);
                 }
             if ( ! $is_a_monday )
                 # only deal with mondays
                 {
                 print STDERR "Date provided is not a Monday.\n";
                 exit 4;
                 }
             $sdate = $date;
             }
        else
             # date provided was not a number
             {
             print STDERR "I don't understand the date of $date.\n";
             exit 4;
             }
        }
    else
         # if date is not provided on command line, take first monday of
         # the provided month
         {
         $sdate = $mondays[0];
         }
    }
else
    # otherwise starting point is "nearest" Monday to today
    {
    $syear = $lyear;
    $smonth = $lmonth;
    # use Monday of this week until Friday, then use next Monday
    # (see adj2monday array definition)
    $sdate = $lmday + $adj2monday[$lwday];
    if ( $sdate <= 0 )
         # adjustment could move us back to last month ...
         {
         $smonth --;
         if ( $smonth < 0 )
             # ... and that could move us back to last year ...
             {
             $syear --;
             $smonth = 11;
             }
         # ... correct the start date accordingly
         $sdate += ($monthlen[$smonth] + &leapmonth($smonth, "19$syear"));
         }
    elsif ( $sdate > ($monthlen[$smonth] + &leapmonth($smonth, "19$syear")) )
         # adjustment could move us into next month ...
         {
         # ... correct the date ...
```

```
        $sdate -= ($monthlen[$smonth] + &leapmonth($smonth, "19$syear"));
        $smonth ++;
        if ( $smonth > 11 )
                # ... adjustment could move us into next year
            {
            $syear ++;
            $smonth = 0;
            }
        }
    }

# perl indexes starting at 0, isql (and most everything else outside perl)
# tends to index starting with 1, so we'll adjust when needed to have the
# right values for the outside world
$tmp_month = $smonth+1;

# isql uses leading zeros, so they're added when needed
$imonth = ($tmp_month < 10) ? 0.${tmp_month} : $tmp_month;
$idate = ($sdate < 10) ? 0.${sdate} : $sdate;
$iyear = $syear;

$isql_date = "${imonth}/${idate}/${iyear}";

# run the isql query, saving to output in a temporary file
# Note: the isql query is actually being performed by another user-id, and
#       this is the reason the program is run as a set-uid program and that
#       taintperl is needed
open (QUERY, "| /usr/sybase/bin/isql -Uisqluser -P password > /tmp/query$$");

# all standard output will go to the isql query we just opened
select (QUERY);
print "print ''\n";
print "select\n";
print "  Loc=convert(char(4),clstloc),\n";
print "  Course=convert(char(8),counumb),\n";
print "  Date=convert(char(7),(convert(char(3),datename(month,clstart))+' '+\n";
print "  convert(char(2),datename(day,clstart)))),\n";
print "  Enr=convert(char(3),clsenro),\n";
print "  Instr=convert(char(12),inslnam),\n";
print "  labcode,\n";
print "  crmcode,\n";
print "  Class#=convert(char(6),clsnumb),\n";
print "  FName=convert(char(8),insfnam)\n";
print "\n";
print "from class, course, instructor, laboratory, classroom\n";
print "\n";
print "where clscour = counumb and\n";
print "  crmcode = clsclrm and\n";
print "  clsinst = insnumb and\n";
print "  clslabr = labcode and\n";
print "  clstart between '$isql_date' and dateadd(week, 8, '$isql_date') and\n";
print "  clsstat != 'CANC' and\n";
print "  (counumb like 'SG%' or\n";
print "   counumb like 'SI%' or\n";
```

```perl
print "    counumb like 'SP%' or\n";
print "    counumb like 'SL%' or\n";
print "    counumb like 'SM%' or\n";
print "    counumb like 'PM%' or\n";
print "    counumb like 'SA%' or\n";
print "    counumb like 'IN%' or\n";
print "    counumb like 'SC%' or\n";
print "    counumb like 'FR%' or\n";
print "    counumb like 'OA%' or\n";
print "    counumb like 'EU%')\n";
print " \n";
print "order by clstart, clstloc, clscour\n";
print "go\n";
select (STDOUT);

# isql query is closed and standard output is back where it belongs
close(QUERY);

# open the query file generated by the isql
# Note: given an input file of appropriate form (see above), all of the
#       isql query could be replaced by just an open statement like this
open (QUERY, "/tmp/query$$");
while (<QUERY>)
    # foreach entry in the list generated by the isql query ...
    {
    # ... get rid of the carriage return
    chop;
    # break up the line into an array
    @class_entry = split;
    if ( ( "$instr_first_name{$class_entry[6]}" ne "" ) &&
        ( "$instr_first_name{$class_entry[6]}" eq "$class_entry[10]" ) )
            # check that the instructor name is known in the associative array
            # and that the first names (in the associative array and the isql
            # query) match [check of the first names was added in a late
            # revision when more than one instructor had the same last name];
            # if so ...
        {
            # ... put the relavant information for that instructor into
            # colon (:) separated lists
        $name = $class_entry[6];
        $class_instr{$name} .= ":$name";
        $class_site{$name} .= ":$class_entry[1]";
        $class_title{$name} .= ":$class_entry[2]";
        $class_month{$name} .= ":$class_entry[3]";
        $class_date{$name} .= ":$class_entry[4]";
        $class_lect{$name} .= ":$class_entry[8]";
        $class_lab{$name} .= ":$class_entry[7]";
        $class_number{$name} .= ":$class_entry[9]";
        }
    elsif ("$class_entry[1]" eq "MPTS" || "$class_entry[1]" eq "OFFM")
            # otherwise this may be a contract instructor, in which case ...
        {
        if ( "$class_entry[2]" =~ /^EU|^SA/ &&
```

```
          ! ("$class_entry[2]" =~ /^EU-10[123]/ ))
             # ... we're only interested in certain classes, but we still
             # need to save the relavant information ...
          {
             # ... and we'll put that information in the lists for Others
          $class_instr{'Others'} .= ":$class_entry[6]";
          $class_site{'Others'} .= ":$class_entry[1]";
          $class_title{'Others'} .= ":$class_entry[2]";
          $class_month{'Others'} .= ":$class_entry[3]";
          $class_date{'Others'} .= ":$class_entry[4]";
          $class_lect{'Others'} .= ":$class_entry[8]";
          $class_lab{'Others'} .= ":$class_entry[7]";
          $class_number{'Others'} .= ":$class_entry[9]";
          }
       }
    }

# query file created with isql is no longer needed
system ("rm -f /tmp/query$$");

foreach $name (@instr_last_name, 'Others')
    # for every known instructor and any other instructor
    {
    # delete the initial colon (:) from the lists
    # print statemennts are for debugging (note that they're commented)
    #print "${name}:\n";
    substr ($class_instr{$name},0,1) = "";
    #print "\t$class_instr{$name}\n";
    substr ($class_site{$name},0,1) = "";
    #print "\t$class_site{$name}\n";
    substr ($class_title{$name},0,1) = "";
    #print "\t$class_title{$name}\n";
    substr ($class_month{$name},0,1) = "";
    #print "\t$class_month{$name}\n";
    substr ($class_date{$name},0,1) = "";
    #print "\t$class_date{$name}\n";
    substr ($class_lect{$name},0,1) = "";
    #print "\t$class_lect{$name}\n";
    substr ($class_lab{$name},0,1) = "";
    #print "\t$class_lab{$name}\n";
    substr ($class_number{$name},0,1) = "";
    #print "\t$class_number{$name}\n";
    }

# open another file for output of the chart ...
open (CHART, "> /tmp/chart_$$" );
# ... and make standard output go to that file
select (CHART);
# output file creation time ...
print " " x 40, "Created: ";
# ... and the time should be on a 12 hour clock with am and pm
if ($lhour == 0)
    # midnight is 12am
    {
```

```
        $lhour = 12;
        $ampm = "am";
        }
elsif ($lhour < 12)
        {
        $ampm = "am";
        }
elsif ($lhour == 12)
        # noon is 12pm
        {
        $ampm = "pm";
        }
else
        {
        $lhour -= 12;
        $ampm = "pm";
        }
# display the adjusted time ...
printf ("%2d:%02d%s", $lhour, $lmin, $ampm);
# ... and date
print ", $monthnames[$lmonth] $lmday, 19$lyear\n";
# display the headers, including the year(s) covered
$year_line = " " x 11 . "19$syear      ";;
# and prepare for the months headings line
$month_line = " " x 76;
substr ($month_line, 11, 0) = "$monthnames[$smonth]";
# and prepare the Monday of the week heading line
$date_line = " " x 10 . "|";
$count = 0;
$tmp_year = $syear;
$tmp_month = $smonth;
$tmp_date = $sdate;
#
# the chart will cover 8 weeks, so we'll alter the heading lines to contain
# the appropriate info ...
#
while ( $count < 8 )
        {
        $count ++;
        push (@weeks, "${tmp_year}:${tmp_month}:${tmp_date}");
        $date_line .= sprintf (" %2d    |", $tmp_date);
        $tmp_date += 7;
        $year_line .= "           ";
        if ($tmp_date > $monthlen[$tmp_month] + &leapmonth($tmp_month, "19$tmp_year"))
            {
            $tmp_date -= ($monthlen[$tmp_month] + &leapmonth($tmp_month,"19$tmp_year"));
            $tmp_month ++;
            if ( $tmp_month > 11 )
                {
                $tmp_year ++;
                $tmp_month = 0;
                substr ($year_line, -8, 4) = "19$tmp_year";
                }
            $real_pos = 11 + ($count * 8);
```

```perl
        if ( substr($month_line, $real_pos, 1) ne " " )
            {
            $real_pos ++;
            while ( (substr($month_line, $real_pos, 1) ne " ") &&
                ($real_pos < 80) )
                {
                $real_pos ++;
                }
            }
        substr ($month_line, $real_pos, 0) = $monthnames[$tmp_month];
        }
    }
print "\n";
# cut off any extra stuff that may have been added to the line
$month_line = substr($month_line, 0, 76);
substr($month_line, -1, 1) =
    (substr($month_line, -1, 1) eq " ") ? "" : substr($month_line, -1, 1);
# cut off the last 8 chars of the year header
substr($year_line, -8, 8) = "";
# finally display the heading lines
print "$year_line\n";
print "$month_line\n";
print "$date_line\n";
# end of the headers, display a separator
print "=" x 75, "\n";;

foreach $instructor ( @instr_last_name, "Others" )
    {
    #
    # prepare for the posibility that the instructor may be assigned
    # more than once in the same week -- especially true of Others
    #
    $pass = 0;
    # debugging print statement ...
    #print "Before loop:  $class_instr{$instructor} $pass\n";
    $more_instr = "";
    while ( ("$more_instr" ne "") || ($pass < 1) )
            {
    # ... commented prints to STDERR are also used for debugging
    # [early versions of the program did not use STDERR for debugging
    #  print statements; debugging print statements in later revisions
    #  added the STDERR due to standard output being directed to a file.]
    #print STDERR "TEST:  Inside loop:  $class_instr{$instructor} $pass\n";
            $pass ++;
            #
            # reset the display variables
            #
        $instr_display = "";
        $title_display = "";
        $site_display = "";
        $number_display = "";
        $more_instr = "";
        $more_sites = "";
        $more_title = "";
```

```perl
$more_month = "";
$more_date = "";
$more_lect = "";
$more_lab = "";
$more_number = "";
    #
    # make arrays of information for this instructor
    #
@instr_list = split (/:/, $class_instr{$instructor});
@site_list = split (/:/, $class_site{$instructor});
@title_list = split (/:/, $class_title{$instructor});
@month_list = split (/:/, $class_month{$instructor});
@date_list = split (/:/, $class_date{$instructor});
@lect_list = split (/:/, $class_lect{$instructor});
@lab_list = split (/:/, $class_lab{$instructor});
@number_list = split (/:/, $class_number{$instructor});
foreach $week ( @weeks )
    {
        # get the "current" time for display
    ($curr_year, $curr_month, $curr_date) = split (/:/,$week);
    #print "Checking week for $monthnames[$curr_month] ",
    #     "$curr_date, 19$curr_year\n";
    $test_range = -1;
        # determine if the instructor is assigned during "current"
        # week
    if ($curr_month == $monthabrs{$month_list[0]})
        {
        $test_range = $date_list[0] - $curr_date;
        }
    elsif (($curr_month - $monthabrs{$month_list[0]}) == -1 ||
        ($curr_month - $monthabrs{$month_list[0]}) == 11 )
        {
        $test_range = (($monthlen[$curr_month] +
               &leapmonth($curr_month,"19$curryear")) -
               $curr_date) + $date_list[0];
        }
    #
    # if the class start date is within 4 days of the beginning
    # of the week, the instructor is assigned to that class
    #
    if ( $test_range >= 0 && $test_range < 5 )
        {
        #print STDERR "TEST:  $instructor teaches this week!\n";
        #
        # get the information from the array, and remove
        # from the array for the next pass through the loop
        # use sprintf for formatting
        #
        $instr = shift @instr_list;
        $title_display .= sprintf ("%7.7s|", shift @title_list);
        $site = shift @site_list;
        $number_display .= sprintf ("%7.7s|", shift @number_list);
        #
        # lecture and lab locations retreived with the isql
```

```perl
    # query have something in front of the room number,
    # the following will get only the desired numbers
    #
     $lect = shift @lect_list;
     $lect =~ s/\D+0*(\d+)$/\1/;
     $lab = shift @lab_list;
     $lab =~ s/\D+0*(\d+)$/\1/;
    # get the class/lab combination ready
     $clslab = "$lect/$lab";
    # center the information
     $fill = (7 - length ($clslab)) / 2;
     $clslab .= " " x $fill;
     if ( "$site" eq "MPTS" )
    # if the location is in Milpitas (CA) than we'll
    # display the classroom/lab location
        {
         $site_display .= sprintf ("%7.7s|", $clslab);
        }
     else
       # otherwise the city location...
        {
       # ... if known ...
        $site = "UNKN"
            if ("$locations{$site}" eq "");
       # ... is displayed
        $site_display .= sprintf ("%7.7s|",
            $locations{$site});
        }
    # make an class with no instructor assigned
    # look better
     $instr = "N/A" if (("$instr" eq "Not_assigned") ||
            ("$instr" eq "Assigned_Not"));
    # fill it for centering
     $fill = (7 - length ($instr)) / 2;
    # add to display
     $instr_display .= ( $instr ne $instructor ) ?
        sprintf ("%7.7s|", $instr . " " x $fill) :
        " " x 7 . "|" ;
     shift @month_list;
     shift @date_list;
    #
    # double check to see if the next class is
    # assigned to the same week -- test code from
    # above repeats ...
    #
    #print STDERR "TEST:  Entering test loop...\n";
    #print STDERR "TEST:  month_list = @month_list\n";
    #print STDERR "TEST:  date_list = @date_list\n";
    #print STDERR "TEST:  dates left = $#date_list\n";
     while ( (($test_range >= 0) && ($test_range < 5)) &&
            ( $#date_list >= 0) )
        {
        $test_range = -1;
#print STDERR "TEST:  Range reset to $test_range\n";
```

```
#print STDERR "TEST:  Current Month = $curr_month\n";
#print STDERR "TEST:  Checking Month
# $monthabrs{$month_list[0]}\n";
        if ($curr_month == $monthabrs{$month_list[0]})
            {
            $test_range = $date_list[0] - $curr_date;
            }
        elsif (($curr_month - $monthabrs{$month_list[0]}) == -1 ||
            ($curr_month - $monthabrs{$month_list[0]}) == 11 )
                {
                $test_range = (($monthlen[$curr_month] +
                        &leapmonth($curr_month,"19$curryear")) -
                        $curr_date) + $date_list[0];
            }
#print STDERR "TEST:  New Range = $test_range\n";
#
# this instructor is assigned to more than one class
# "this" week ...
        if ( $test_range >= 0 && $test_range < 5 )
            {
#print STDERR "TEST:  Range = $test_range\n";
            if ( "$instructor" eq "Others" )
# ... which is OK if the instructor is Other ...
                {
                $more_instr .= ":$instr_list[0]";
                $more_sites .= ":$site_list[0]";
                $more_title .= ":$title_list[0]";
                $more_month .= ":$month_list[0]";
                $more_date .= ":$date_list[0]";
                $more_lect .= ":$lect_list[0]";
                $more_lab .= ":$lab_list[0]";
                $more_number .= ":$number_list[0]";
    }
    else
        # ... but otherwise it means something is wrong,
        # so flag it in the display
        {
        substr ( $title_display,
            length($title_display)-8,
            length($title_display)) = "Multi- |";
        substr ( $site_display,
            length($site_display)-8,
            length($site_display)) = " Assign|";
        substr ( $instr_display,
            length($instr_display)-8,
            length($instr_display)) = "^^^^^^^|";
        }
#
# shift the list for the next pass through the loop
#
            shift @instr_list;
            shift @site_list;
            shift @title_list;
            shift @month_list;
```

```
                         shift @date_list;
                         shift @lect_list;
                         shift @lab_list;
                         shift @number_list;
                         }
                #print STDERR "TEST:  End of test loop...\n";
                #print STDERR "TEST:  month_list = @month_list\n";
                #print STDERR "TEST:  date_list = @date_list\n";
                #print STDERR "TEST:  dates left = $#date_list\n";
                 }
         }
    else
        # otherwise the instructor is not assigned to that week
        # so we'll just fill the display
        {
        $instr_display .= (" " x 7 . "|");
        $title_display .= (" " x 7 . "|");
        $site_display .= (" " x 7 . "|");
        $number_display .= (" " x 7 . "|");
        }
    }
#
# finally display the lines for this instructor
#
printf "%-10s|", substr($instr_first_name{$instructor},0,10);
print "$title_display\n";
printf "%-10s|", substr($instructor,0,10);
print "$site_display\n";
printf "%10s|", "";
print "$instr_display\n";

    # Extra stuff for display of class number, which is not needed
    # for common use

    # For Management Use:
#print " " x 10, "|", "$number_display\n";

print "-" x 10, "+", "-------+" x 8, "\n";

if ( "$more_instr" ne "" )
    # another pass needs to be done for this instructor (Others)
    {
    #
    # strip off the initial colon (:) from each list
    #
    substr ($more_instr,0,1) = "";
    substr ($more_sites,0,1) = "";
    substr ($more_title,0,1) = "";
    substr ($more_month,0,1) = "";
    substr ($more_date,0,1) = "";
    substr ($more_lect,0,1) = "";
    substr ($more_lab,0,1) = "";
    substr ($more_number,0,1) = "";
    #
```

```
                    # reset the lists for the instructor for the next pass
                    #
             $class_instr{$instructor} = $more_instr;
             $class_sites{$instructor} = $more_sites;
             $class_title{$instructor} = $more_title;
             $class_month{$instructor} = $more_month;
             $class_date{$instructor} = $more_date;
             $class_lect{$instructor} = $more_lect;
             $class_lab{$instructor} = $more_lab;
             $class_number{$instructor} = $more_number;
             }
        }
    }

# close the output file
close (CHART);

# reset the location of standard output to normal
select (STDOUT);

# open the previously created output file
open (CHART, "/tmp/chart_$$" );

# display the file
# this was done so that we don't see the program think -- it just shows
# the final chart all at once
print <CHART>;

# output file is no longer needed -- clean up
system ("rm -f /tmp/chart_$$");
```

B.2   *maxpstat* by John J. Nouveaux

```
#!/usr/bin/perl
#
# maxpstat
#
# Usage:
#   maxpstat   [interval [ count ]]
#
# Where:
#   interval = Interval, in seconds, between "pstat" checks (default = 60).
#   count = Number of reports before quitting (default = infinite ).
#
#
# Description:
#   This script runs the "pstat" system command every interval seconds,
#   comparing the output from previous "pstat" runs, and
#   saves the maximum values for the "process", "files", and "inodes"
#   output fields.
#
```

```
#    When a new maximum value for any field is discovered it is immediately
#    reported, and when the script has finished a summary report is printed.
#    If the script is interrupted via a control-c, or a TERM signal ( see
#    signal (3V)), the summary report is immediately printed. Other signals
#    are ignored by the script.
#
#    See the pstat(8) man page for details of that command.
#
# Written by:
#    John J. Nouveaux
#    Copyright, 1992
#
# History:
#        May 13th, 19921.0 - initial release.
#
# Version:
#    1.0


# Define external references.

require 'ctime.pl';    # Displays time in readable format

# Set up signal processing, currently catching only interrupt and terminate
# signals.

$SIG{'HUP'} = 'IGNORE';#1
$SIG{'INT'} = 'sighandler';#2
$SIG{'QUIT'}= 'IGNORE';#3
$SIG{'ILL'} = 'IGNORE';#4
$SIG{'TRAP'}= 'IGNORE';#5
$SIG{'ABRT'}= 'IGNORE';#6
$SIG{'EMT'} = 'IGNORE';#7
$SIG{'FPE'} = 'IGNORE';#8
$SIG{'KILL'}= 'IGNORE';#9
$SIG{'BUS'} = 'IGNORE';#10
$SIG{'SEGV'}= 'IGNORE';#11
$SIG{'SYS'} = 'IGNORE';#12
$SIG{'PIPE'}= 'IGNORE';#13
$SIG{'ALRM'}= 'IGNORE';#14
$SIG{'TERM'}= 'sighandler';#15
$SIG{'URG'} = 'IGNORE';#16
$SIG{'STOP'}= 'IGNORE';#17
$SIG{'TSTP'}= 'IGNORE';#18
$SIG{'CONT'}= 'IGNORE';#19
$SIG{'CHLD'}= 'IGNORE';#20
$SIG{'TTIN'}= 'IGNORE';#21
$SIG{'TTOU'}= 'IGNORE';#22
$SIG{'IO'}  = 'IGNORE';#23
$SIG{'XCPU'}= 'IGNORE';#24
$SIG{'XFSZ'}= 'IGNORE';#25
$SIG{'VTALRM'}= 'IGNORE';#26
$SIG{'PROF'}= 'IGNORE';#27
$SIG{'WINCH'}= 'IGNORE';#28
$SIG{'LOST'}= 'IGNORE';#29
```

```perl
$SIG{'USR1'}= 'IGNORE';#30
$SIG{'USR2'}= 'IGNORE';#31

# Define local variables.

$counterr = "count";              # for error processing
$intervalerr = "interval";        # for error processing
$pstat = "/usr/etc/pstat -T";     # path to "pstat" command
@DoW = ( 'Sun', 'Mon', 'Tue', 'Wed', 'Thu', 'Fri', 'Sat' );
@MoY = ( 'Jan', 'Feb', 'Mar', 'Apr', 'May', 'Jun',
            'Jul', 'Aug', 'Sep', 'Oct', 'Nov', 'Dec' );

# Set defaults.

$interval = 60;
$count = 9999999999;              # infinity (actually 316+ years)

# Process input parameters (if any).

if (@ARGV) {

# Set the interval parameter.

        $interval = shift (@ARGV);

# If the interval is non-numeric, print a usage error and exit.

    if ($interval =~ /\D+/) {
        &usage ($intervalerr, $interval);
    }

# Set the count parameter.

    if (@ARGV){
        $count = shift (@ARGV);


# If the count is non-numeric, print a usage error and exit.

      if ($count =~ /\D+/) {
          &usage ($counter, $count);
      }
    }
 }

# Initialize starting date/time (used in final report).

 $starttime = time;
 ($startsec, $startmin, $starthour, $startmday, $startmon, $startyear, $startwday,
  $startyday, $startisdst) = localtime ($starttime);

# Add leading zeros as appropriate.
```

```
if ($starthour < 10) {
  $starthour = "0" . "$starthour";
}

if ($startmin < 10) {
  $startmin = "0" . "$startmin";
}

if ($startsec < 10) {
  $startsec = "0" . "$startsec";
}

# Get "pstat" system table sizes (this is configured into the kernel).

open (PSTAT, "$pstat |");
$currentfiles        = <PSTAT>;    # Raw input lines
$currentinodes       =<PSTAT>;
$currentprocesses    = <PSTAT>;

if ($currentfiles =~ m".*/(\d*)") {
   $filetabsize = $1;             # Size of files table
}


if ($currentinodes =~ m".*/(\d*)") {
   $inodetabsize = $1;            # Size of inode cache
}

if ($currentprocesses =~ m".*/(\d*)") {
   $proctabsize = $1;            # Size of process table
}

close (PSTAT);

# Check parameters as specified in command arguments.

for ($loopindex = $count; $loopindex != 0; $loopindex--){

# Get "pstat" input via a named-pipe filehandle.

   open (PSTAT, "$pstat |");
   $currentfiles      = <PSTAT>; # Raw input lines
   $currentinodes     = <PSTAT>;
   $currentprocesses  = <PSTAT>;
   close(PSTAT);

# Extract current count for each category.

  if ($currentfiles =~ m"\s*(\d*)/") {
     $currentfiles = $1;         # current number of opened files
  }

  if ($currentinodes =~ m"\s*(\d*)/") {
     $currentinodes = $1;        # current number of cached inodes
  }
```

```perl
   if ($currentprocesses =~ m"\s*(\d*)/") {
      $currentprocesses = $1;     # current number of active processes
   }

# If the current counter for any of the categories exceeds
# the stored maximum replace the stored maximum with the current
# value and print a message.

   if ($currentfiles > $maxfiles) {
      $maxfiles = $currentfiles;
      $filepercent = int (((100*$maxfiles)/$filetabsize) + .5);

      print ("$maxfiles files out of $filetabsize or $filepercent percent.\n");
   }

   if ($currentinodes > $maxinodes) {
      $maxinodes = $currentinodes;
      $inodepercent = int (((100*$maxinodes)/$inodetabsize) + .5);
      print ("$maxinodes inodes out of $inodetabsize or $inodepercent percent.\n");
   }

   if ($currentprocesses > $maxprocesses) {
      $maxprocesses = $currentprocesses;
      $procpercent = int (((100*$maxprocesses)/$proctabsize) + .5);
      print ("$maxprocesses processes out of $proctabsize or $procpercent percent.\n");
   }

# Sleep until next interval.

   sleep ($interval);

} # end while


# Final output processing (presuming we've fallen through the above loop.
# Note: Control-c's and kill's are caught in the signal handler.

&finalreport;

exit;

# Subroutine.

sub finalreport{

# This routine generates the final report giving summary
# information about the maximum values observed.

# Set ending date/time.

   $endtime = time;

# Duration is initially set to the number of seconds this report ran.
```

```perl
    $duration = $endtime - $starttime;

# Divide duration by number of seconds in a day to get
# the number of days.

    $enddays = int ($duration / (60 * 60 * 24 ));

# Divide remainder of duration by number of seconds in an hour to get
# number of hours.

    $duration = $duration - ($enddays * 60 * 60 * 24);
    $endhours = int ($duration / (60 * 60));

# Divide remainder of duration by number of seconds in a minute to get
# number of minutes.

    $duration = $duration - ($endhours * 60 * 60 * 24);
    $endmins = int ($duration / (60 * 60));


# Write the final report.

    write;

}

sub sighandler {

# This routien is used to process ALL signals received by this script
# and is called internally by perl whenever a signal is received.
#
# Called:
#    sighandler = (signal);
#
# Where:
#   signal = signal received (see signal(3V))

 local ($signal) = @_;

# print "Signal $signal received\n";      # for debug purposes

# Process signals of interest.

  if ("$signal" eq "INT" || "$signal" eq "TERM" ) {
    &finalreport;
    exit;
  }
}


# Usage processing.

sub usage {

# Called:
```

```
#    usage (msgtext, value)
#
# Where:
#    msgtext = parameter name to be inserted into the error message
#    value = illegal value for that parameter name

# Assign input parameters.

   ($msgtext, $value) = $@;
   local ($usage);

# Print error message, based upon input parameters.

   $usage =
    "The $msgtext parameter you specified, contained a non-numeric value:
     $value\n",
    "Please try again.\n",
    "\n",
    "Usage: maxpstat [interval [count]]\n" ,
    "  Where: interval = the number of seconds between checks\n",
    "              count = the number of times to check the pstat values\n",
    "   interval has a default value of 60 (seconds)\n",
    "   count has a default value of infinity (you must type ctl-c to\n",
    "      stop the checking\n";

   die $usage;

}

# Output report file format specification.

format STDOUT =

This script started on @<< @<< @<, @<<< at @<:@<:@<
$DoW[$startwday], $MoY[$startmon], $startmday, $startyear+1900, $starthour,
              $startmin, $startsec
and ran for @>> days, @> hours, and @> minutes.
              $enddays, $endhours,      $endmins
During that time the following maximum usage was observed:

@>>> out of @>>> files    or @>> percent of the file table
$maxfiles, $filetabsize,  $filepercent
@>>> out of @>>> inodes    or @>> percent of the inode table
$maxinodes, $inodetabsize,  $inodepercent
@>>> out of @>>> processes or @>> percent of the process table
$maxprocesses, $proctabsize,  $procpercent.
```

B.3 *randomize* by John J. Nouveaux

```perl
#!/usr/bin/perl
#
# randomize
#
# This script randomizes the order of lines in an input file.
#
#
# Usage:
#  randomize
#
# Written by: John J. Nouveaux
#
# History:   V1.0 (3/19/92) - initial release.

# Set local variables.

$INPUTFILE = "$ENV{'HOME'}/education/ASA/rev.d/ta.sorted";
# Input file

$OUTPUTFILE = "$ENV{'HOME'}/education/ASA/rev.d/ta.random";
#  customers report file

# Set window header.

print "Reading input file\n";

# Open input file.

open ( INPUTFILE, "<$INPUTFILE" );

# Copy input file to internal array.

$numinlines = 1;
while ( <INPUTFILE> ){
  $inarray [$numinlines] = $_;
  $numinlines++;
} # end while

close ( INPUTFILE );
$numinlines--;

# Generate random number sequence.

print "Generating random numbers\n";

srand (time);
$outindex = 2 * $numinlines;
while ( $outindex != 0 ){

# Generate pairs of random numbers, and switch those array entries.
```

```
    $ran1 = int ( rand ($numinlines)) + 1;
    $ran2 = $ran1;
    while ( $ran2 == $ran1 ) {
      $ran2 = int ( rand ($numinlines)) + 1;
    } # end while

    $tmp = $inarray [$ran1];
    $inarray [$ran1] = $inarray [$ran2];
    $inarray [$ran2] = $tmp;
    $outindex--;
} # end while

# Generate randomized output file.

print "Writing output file\n";

open ( OUTPUTFILE, ">$OUTPUTFILE" )|| die "Can't open $!\n";
$index = $numinlines;
while ( $index != 0 ) {
  print  OUTPUTFILE "$inarray[$index]";
  print "$inarray[$index]";
  $index--;
} # end while

# Done.

print "Finished\n";
exit;
```

C

AN OBJECT-ORIENTED PERL/CGI PROGRAM

by Charles Dalsass

I started working with Perl because I was amazed by the speed with which a programmer could put together complex applications using Perl. I believe that no other language offers Perl's productivity for a developer at the application level. The reason for this has less to do with the language itself, than with its developer network and CPAN. You can really appreciate the speed of development over Java or Python (a better comparison) when you reach that critical juncture where a common algorithm is needed to complete a certain part of the project. The Java or Python programmer writes the code from scratch, and since an application programmer's expertise lies in users and sessions and screens and search results (and not algorithms or network intricacies), the code suffers bugs and misses some things completely. The Perl programmer simply downloads the code from CPAN.

Contrary to what you might read, CGI will be in use for a long time. We all know the arguments against it. Mainly, that CGI's architecture is hundreds of times slower than embedded interpreters such as IIS/ASP. This is true, especially with the large footprint of CGI/Perl. However, nothing beats CGI/Perl's simplicity, portability, and robustness. Those qualities will continue to make it an attractive development choice for certain tasks. The recent expansion in the use of inexpensive UNIX-based solutions such as Linux for Web hosting and Internet services will further this as well.

My company (Neptune Web) has developed one of the world's highest-trafficked Perl-based Web sites (see our clients list at *www.neptuneweb.com* for more info). During its growth, we've proven again and again that for certain types of Web sites, there is nothing more cost effective for our clients than the Perl/CGI combination (our production site uses *mod_perl*, while the development site uses regular Perl/CGI). We also believe that while certain types of applications work very well with this architecture, others do not. For example, Web sites that are dynamic but don't require extensive third-party libraries fit the "Web page programming" metaphor well, and seldom interact with the system (other than a database and e-mail); these are best suited for IIS/ASP, PHP, or Cold Fusion. For small-business customers, this is often the best choice, since the ISPs that host these customers' sites typically already have this software installed. For larger projects that have very specialized needs (for example, high traffic, extensive use of third-party software, reduced licensing costs, server farm etc.), we've found that the Perl/CGI architecture is the most productive and cost-effective architecture.

The log-file analyzer was originally written to determine the most popular greeting cards being sent from our client's Web site. For the example you see, I've generalized the program and taken out the code specific to our client's site. The simple CGI interface prompts the user for the number of results to display, the sort order of the results, and a regular expression to match URLs against. The output appears after a few headers have been printed to the screen. The format is a fixed-width columnar one, with item number, hit count, URL, bytes sent, 200s (request returned successfully), 304s (returned not modified), and 302s (request redirected elsewhere).

The power of the program comes from its simple OO structure, which gives you the ability create a customized version to meet your specific needs. As you can probably tell by the columnar output, the program can be easily converted to a command line interface. (Actually, the CGI wrapper was added later on for the purpose of the example.)

The program uses two general modules *basic.pm* and *basicList.pm*. *basic.pm* is a "base-level" object that should be inherited from by all other objects. *basic.pm* is essentially a wrapper around a hash. Since all objects in your code inherit from the *basic.pm* class, your code can make certain assumptions about the objects it manipulates—providing a level of abstraction. *basicList.pm* inherits from *basic.pm* and contains the functionality for a list of any type of object (as long as the objects inherit from *basic.pm*). Finally, *analyzerList.pm* inherits from *basicList.pm* and provides the functionality for analyzing log files that we need in the log file analyzer program. (The program also uses a trivial HTML form and a CGI wrapper—*analyze.cgi*). These classes separate out the code that is general (applies to all programs you might write in the future) and code that is specific to this program. For example *basic.pm* and *basicList.pm* should have nothing to do with analyzing log files, but *analyzerList.pm* is all about log files.

The most important point of this example is for you to realize code reuse. Every time you write code, you should try to fit that code into a framework that will be around the next time you need to do something similar. This will allow you to build a library of general use functions that get better with age.

C.1 The *analyze.cgi* Program and Associated Files

This example is intended to demonstrate aspects of OO design using a real-world problem. It is not intented to be used as is. The concepts are

    a. Inheritance
    b. Separating general from application specific code
    c. Use of a configuration file to separate out differences between development and production environments

The code consists of the following files:

html/realtime.htm   This is a trivial HTML form for submitting queries to the log-file analyzer program. Although many of the Perl gurus recommend using *CGI.pm* to generate HTML, I feel this is a bad idea. This practice has given Perl/CGI a bad name because the interface is so closely integrated with the code. For dynamic HTML pages (this page is not dynamic), I recommend using many of the available template facilites so that the HTML code can be edited by a non-programmer.

cgi-bin/analyze.cgi   This is the main log-file analyzer program invoked as a CGI program. This program contains all of the CGI-specific code and ties the code from the libraries together. Notice that I've tried to make a logical separation between the code that depends on *CGI.pm* and code that doesn't. Separating the CGI and non-CGI–based code allows you to reuse the libraries you've created. For example, you might later decide to turn the program into a command line program, or need to run the log analyzer from *cron*. This code is the least reusable of the Perl code shown in this example.

/cgi-bin/analyze.cfg   The configuration file separates out the differences between the production and development environments. Some people prefer to include any variable that requires change (such as an e-mail address) into the configuration file. This is valid, although it may clutter the config file and probably belongs somewhere else.

The configuration file consists of a block of Perl that will be *eval*ed when the program runs. The great thing about using the notation I have presented here is that you can use any variety of nested hashes, arrays, etc. to represent very complex configurations. Although I've only used the top level in an anonymous hash, you can add all kinds of other things. For example:

```perl
$main::config = {
    logfile => "/home/logfile/cgi-bin/samplelog",
    librarypath => "/home/logfile/cgi-bin/libs",
    urltoqueryform => "/realtime.htm",
    urlstoignore => [
        { url=>"empty.gif", type=>"ignorecompletely" },
        { url=>"nothing.htm", type=> "ignorefirstonly"},
    ]
};
```

Here, I've added a new configuration item *urlstoignore,* which is an anonymous array (ref) that contains an anonymous hash (refs).

/cgi-bin/libs/analyzerList.pm   This library provides all of the application-specific code. Its superclass is *basicList* because *basicList* contains much of the code used for the application. This code is less reusable than *basic.pm* and *basicList.pm* (since this library will only be used if you need to analyze log files), but much more reusable than *analyze.cgi.*

/cgi-bin/libs/basic.pm   This is a generic object based on a hash. Its primary members are *getAttr* and *setAttr* which are used to set internal attributes of the object. This library and *basicList.pm* are generic code (do not contain any code specific to this—or any—application). They are both designed for maximum reuse.

/cgi-bin/libs/basicList.pm   This is a generic list object. Its members allow you to append arbitrary objects to the list, sort the list, display the list, and iterate through the list.

```
Sample logfile from the server
--------------------
202.155.44.233 - - [16/Feb/2001:04:02:01 -0600] "GET / HTTP/1.0" 200 41266
194.170.1.69 - - [16/Feb/2001:04:02:01 -0600] "GET /popupwindow/popwindow.js HTTP/1.0" 304 -
61.11.18.217 - - [16/Feb/2001:04:02:03 -0600] "GET /images/GoldRoses.gif HTTP/1.1" 200 1957
216.236.202.26 - - [16/Feb/2001:04:02:03 -0600] "GET /images/smiley2.gif HTTP/1.0" 304 -
203.177.22.130 - - [16/Feb/2001:04:02:03 -0600] "GET /audio/dear.mid HTTP/1.0" 200 14838
203.197.123.111 - - [16/Feb/2001:04:02:04 -0600] "GET /images/smiley2.gif HTTP/1.1" 200 4219
61.9.112.210 - - [16/Feb/2001:04:02:04 -0600] "GET /fun/fun304a.htm HTTP/1.0" 200 7506
202.169.129.72 - - [16/Feb/2001:04:02:04 -0600] "GET /images/birthbeartile.jpg HTTP/1.1" 200 9941
203.197.73.209 - - [16/Feb/2001:04:02:04 -0600] "GET /popupwindow/popwindow.js HTTP/1.0" 200 3690
216.147.132.110 - - [16/Feb/2001:04:02:04 -0600] "GET /images/rrose.gif HTTP/1.0" 200 1165
--------------------


Output of running the analyzer program

analyzing log file...

complete. begin sorting results...

complete. begin tallying...

complete. begin display...
Click here to query the log files again.
Status Codes
-------
200: request sent
304: request was reported as 'not modified' and was not sent.
302: request was redirected
```

Item	Hits	Page	Bytes Sent	200's	304's	302's
1	12	/audio/hugyou.wav	761112	12	0	0
2	28	/tellformpost.htm	410583	27	0	0
3	25	/tellform.htm	371577	25	0	0
4	9	/	330128	8	1	0
5	69	/logotopa.gif	312125	55	14	0
6	4	/valentine/images/anitaz.gif	267762	3	1	0
7	4	/valentine/images/cupidangels.jpg	235453	2	2	0
8	4	/audio/angeldst.wav	229410	4	0	0
9	5	/images/friend1.gif	223430	5	0	0
10	5	/audio/crying.mid	211490	5	0	0
11	1	/valentine/images/aniBuq6.gif	175655	1	0	0
12	60	/popupwindow/popwindow.js	173430	47	13	0
13	5	/contest/hawaii/entry.htm	172192	5	0	0

14	12	/audio/kiss.wav	168384	12	0	0
15	10	/banners/ban3.gif	164772	9	1	0
16	4	/images/bearhugz.gif	147712	4	0	0
17	3	/valentine/images/redsatinbg.gif	143913	3	0	0
18	2	/valentine/images/kathrt.jpg	138072	2	0	0
19	3	/audio/Kissmeqk.mid	137685	3	0	0
20	8	/contest/hawaii/Palmtree24.jpg	131381	5	2	0
21	2	/valentine/images/wearinghrt.jpg	128426	1	1	0
22	3	/images/perfectrose.jpg	122746	2	1	0
23	11	/banners/ban6.gif	121304	8	3	0
24	3	/images/redliquid2.jpg	117564	3	0	0
25	7	/list/list1.htm	110411	7	0	0
26	3	/valentine/images/valbear.gif	102146	2	1	0
27	13	/banners/ban1.jpg	101552	11	2	0
28	10	/banners/ban4.jpg	101182	8	1	0
29	1	/images/strawpinkblos.jpg	95202	1	0	0
30	3	/audio/be_roman.mid	92940	3	0	0
31	5	/valentine.htm	92535	5	0	0
32	5	/reading.htm	87435	5	0	0
33	3	/audio/adicted-to-love.mid	84630	2	1	0
34	3	/audio/FriendsForever.mid	84390	2	1	0
35	3	/images/collieandkitten.jpg	84027	3	0	0
36	4	/images/dancaave01.gif	82044	3	1	0
37	3	/audio/rockinrobin.mid	81966	3	0	0
38	3	/letters/index5.htm	81606	3	0	0
39	7	/funnews.htm	74186	7	0	0
40	8	/banners/ban2.jpg	73956	6	2	0
41	1	/audio/daydream.mid	71859	1	0	0
42	7	/main.gif	71080	5	2	0
43	2	/images/beautifulval.jpg	69908	2	0	0
44	1	/audio/MyRomance.mid	69480	1	0	0
45	2	/valentine/audio/redredwine.mid	66158	2	0	0
46	6	/images/friendtile1.jpg	64068	6	0	0
47	2	/images/lovepoem2.gif	62534	2	0	0
48	5	/fun/fun440.htm	62515	5	0	0
49	1	/audio/inlove.mid	61000	1	0	0
50	5	/images/lovedog.gif	59465	5	0	0
51	1	/audio/UnderTheSea.mid	57286	1	0	0
52	2	/images/sweetangel3.jpg	56748	2	0	0
53	1	/valentine/audio/illstillbelovingyou.mid	55992	1	0	0
54	26	/freereply.htm	54184	26	0	0
55	1	/images/woodwalk.jpg	52498	1	0	0
56	3	/audio/furelise.mid	49896	3	0	0
57	11	/funnews20.gif	49620	10	1	0
58	1	/audio/baker.mid	48546	1	0	0
59	1	/images/crystaltrees640.jpg	46079	1	0	0
60	2	/audio/peacefuldream.mid	45674	2	0	0
61	1	/audio/closetoyou.mid	45446	1	0	0
62	3	/audio/dear.mid	44514	3	0	0
63	20	/freenews.htm	44340	20	0	0
64	1	/images/animabear.gif	43845	1	0	0
65	3	/images/img00069.gif	43053	3	0	0
66	3	/fun/fun419.htm	42363	3	0	0
67	3	/images/love006.gif	42258	3	0	0
68	1	/valentine/audio/AnyOtherWay.mid	41269	1	0	0
69	4	/island.jpg	40752	4	0	0
70	1	/valentine/images/kathrttile2.jpg	39691	1	0	0

71	1	/fun/fun31.htm	39195	1	0	0
72	1	/images/pandapickingflowani.gif	38792	1	0	0
73	1	/audio/Onlyhaveeyesforyou.mid	38429	1	0	0
74	1	/images/cucumberdog.jpg	37514	1	0	0
75	3	/fun/fun465.htm	36807	3	0	0
76	1	/images/1319749.jpg	35761	1	0	0
77	1	/images/bspinredrose.gif	35514	1	0	0
78	1	/audio/stayingalive.mid	35494	1	0	0
79	3	/valentine/html/valentine24.htm	35406	3	0	0
80	1	/audio/almostparadise.mid	35358	1	0	0
81	3	/valentine/html/valentine4.htm	35112	3	0	0
82	4	/fun/fun344.htm	34881	3	1	0
83	1	/images/Godtile.jpg	34823	1	0	0
84	1	/images/piratestar.gif	34441	1	0	0
85	1	/images/brown_romeo.jpg	34277	1	0	0
86	1	/images/yelrosewbutani.gif	33866	1	0	0
87	2	/audio/happyjoy.mid	33724	2	0	0
88	1	/images/mtnview.jpg	33543	1	0	0
89	1	/audio/tango.mid	33337	1	0	0
90	2	/letters/index10.htm	32904	2	0	0
91	1	/audio/walking_on_the_sun.mid	32864	1	0	0
92	2	/images/starback.gif	32864	2	0	0
93	1	/images/lizardcard.jpg	32413	1	0	0
94	1	/images/loversinlargerose2.jpg	30536	1	0	0
95	2	/images/img00069a.gif	28652	2	0	0
96	2	/letters/index3.htm	28136	2	0	0
97	1	/images/Dj020.jpg	26480	1	0	0
98	3	/valentine/audio/canufeellovetonite.mid	25764	2	1	0
99	1	/images/fcatanim.gif	25364	1	0	0
100	1	/images/skeleton786.gif	24984	1	0	0
	1000		11538598	840	133	6

The Program Files

```
package basicList;
use strict;
@basicList::ISA = qw(basic);


=head1 NAME

basicList - A general class to represent list of objects which inherit from basic.

=head1 AUTHOR

Charles M. Dalsass<lt>cdalsass@neptuneweb.com>

=cut

=head1 SYNOPSIS

$a = new basicList;
$a->append( new basic({ fname => "charlie",
```

```
                lname => "dalsass"
                }) );
$a->append( new basic({ fname => "john",
                lname => "doe"
                }) );
$a->dump();

=cut



# this function will return the object at the numeric index. 0 is the
# first object.

sub getObjectAtIndex {
    my($self,$index) = @_;
    my @objects = @{$self->{objects}};
    return $objects[$index];
}

# This function is an accessor function to the objects within the
# basicList which lets you overwrite the objects in the list. The
# param must be an array ref.  This function should be called in "new"
# in case it needs to be subclassed (e.g. for an index).

sub setObjects {
    my($self,$list) = @_;
    $self->{objects} = $list;
}

# sortSingleColumn($column,$order) sort the basicList according the
# given column in the order 'asc' or 'desc'

sub sortBySingleColumn {
    my($self,$column,$order,$forcenumeric) = @_;
    my @sorted;
    if ($forcenumeric) {
    @sorted = sort { $a->getAttr($column) <=> $b->getAttr($column)  }
                                      @{$self->{objects}};
    } else {
    @sorted = sort { $a->getAttr($column) cmp $b->getAttr($column)  }
                                      @{$self->{objects}};
    }
    if($order =~ /^DESC$/i) {
    @sorted = reverse (@sorted);
    }
    $self->{objects} = \@sorted;
}


# reduceToSplice($start, $items) delete everything except $start to
# $end items in the list.

sub reduceToSplice {
    my($self,$start,$items) = @_;
    my @objects = splice(@{$self->{objects}}, $start , $items );
    $self->{objects} = \@objects;
}
```

```
# insertAtOffset($obj, $offset) insert an object at a point in the
# list where 0 is the beginning of the list.

sub insertAtOffset {
    my($self,$obj,$offset) = @_;
    splice(@{$self->{objects}}, $offset , 0, $obj );
}

# prepend($obj) this function puts an object at the beginning of the list. works
# just like append.

sub prepend {
    my($self,$obj) = @_;
    unshift(@{$self->{objects}},$obj);
}

# obtainMaxColumnWidths($columns) need to know how wide the object's
# attributes are in your list? (e.g. for printing out) this function
# returns a hash containing the name of the column as a key and the
# maximum column width as the value in the hash. Pass in an arrayref
# of columns to look at only at certain columns.

sub obtainMaxColumnWidths {
    my ($self,$columns) = @_;
    my($curObj, %maxColHash, $key);
    $self->resetIter();
    while ($curObj =  $self->nextObject()) {
    foreach $key ($curObj->keys()) {
        $maxColHash{$key} = length($curObj->getAttr($key)) unless
                        exists($maxColHash{$key}) and  $maxColHash{$key} >
                        length($curObj->getAttr($key))   ;
    }
    }
    return \%maxColHash;
}

# renderAsFixedWidthColumns($params) Print out a list in a fixed width
# manner. params is a hash of parameters to pass into the function.
# this function is designed so that you can pass in the hash of max
# columns widths (which you might have gotten from a call to
# obtainMaxColumnWidths). This way, you can "cache" that calculation.

sub renderAsFixedWidthColumns {
    my ($self,$params) = @_;
    my $columns = $params->{columns} if $params->{columns};
    my %maxWidthHash = $params->{maxwidthhash} ? %{$params->{maxwidthhash}} :
                    %{$self->obtainMaxColumnWidths(@$columns)};
    my $curObj;
    $self->resetIter();

# loop through the objects printing each as a fixed width.
# Use the previously recorded maxWidthHash to determine
# how to format each column

    while($curObj =  $self->nextObject()) {
    if ($columns) {
```

```
        foreach my $col (@$columns) {
        # use the "-" to left justify the columns, specify an integer
        # precision to tell how to pad the columns with whitespace
        printf("%-" . $maxWidthHash{$col} . "s",$curObj->getAttr($col));
        }
    }
    else {
        foreach my $col ($curObj->keys()) {
        printf("%-" . $maxWidthHash{$col} . "s",$curObj->getAttr($col));
        }
    }
    print "\n";
    }
}



# new($input) Create a new basicList. Input is a hashref. the
# attribute "$input" may contain a list of objects.

sub new {
    my($type,$input) = @_;
    my($list,$self);
    # if input is a hash, then expect some params to go with it
    $list = $input;
    if (!$list) {$list = [];}
    my($self) = {};
    bless $self,$type;
    $self->{objects} = $list;
    $self->resetIter();
    $self->{attr} = {} unless $self->{attr};
    return ($self);
}

# resetIter resets the current iteration variable to 1. call this
# function before looping through the entries in a basicList.

sub resetIter {
    my($self) = @_;
    $self->{currentItem} = 1;
}

# dump prints out all of the objects in the list in a human readable
# format.

sub dump {
    my($self) = @_;
    my($curObj);
    $self->resetIter();
    while($curObj = $self->nextObject()) {
    print "--------------\n";
    $curObj->dump();
    }
    print $@;
}
```

```perl
# nextObject: obtain the next object from the list based on the
# internal interation variable. Return undef when finished.

sub nextObject {
    my($self) = @_;
    my(@objects,$obj);
    @objects = @{$self->{objects}};
    if ($self->{currentItem} <= $self->getLength()) {
    $obj = $objects[$self->{currentItem} - 1];
    } else {
    $obj = undef;
    }
    $self->{currentItem}++;
    return $obj;
}


# getLength: return the length of the list (number of objects)

sub getLength {
    my($self) = @_;
    my(@list) = @{$self->{objects}};
    return ($#list + 1);
}


# append($obj): add a new object to the end of the list.

sub append {
    my($self,$obj) = @_;
    push(@{$self->{objects}},$obj);
}



# numberItems ($field, $startnum) set an entry with the given field
# name to a number starting with (optional) $startnum for each item in
# the list. The numbering will start at 1 if $startnum is not
# provided.

sub numberItems {
    my($self,$field,$startnum) = @_;
    my($item);
    $startnum = 1 unless  $startnum;
    foreach $item (@{$self->{objects}}) {
    $item->setAttr($field,$startnum++);
    }
}


1;
```

```
--------------------
package basic;
use strict;


=head1 NAME

basic - A general class to represent an object. All other objects
within this framework should inherit from this class.

=head1 AUTHOR

Charles M. Dalsass<lt>cdalsass@neptuneweb.com>

=cut

=head1 SYNOPSIS

$a = new basic;
$a->setAttr("name","charlie");
print "name = " . $a->getAttr("name");
$a->dump();

=cut

# new

sub new {
    my($type,$hash) = @_;
    my($self) = {};
    bless $self,$type;
    $self->{attr} = $hash;
    return($self);
}

# getAttr: fundamental method. May be overriden in a base class.
sub getAttr {
    my($self,$name) = @_;
    return ($self->{attr}->{$name});
}

# setAttr: fundamental method to set an attribute. May be overriden in
# a base class.

sub setAttr {
    my($self,$name,$value) = @_;
    if (!$name) {
    return();
    }
    $self->{attr}->{$name} = $value;
}

# dump($pad) pretty print the object.
sub dump {
    my($self,$pad) = @_;
    my($key);
    foreach $key (@{$self->getAttrNames()}) {
```

```
        print "$pad$key=".$self->getAttr($key)."\n";
        }
}

# keys: return the keys or Attribute names of the object.
sub keys {
    my($self) = @_;
    return keys (%{$self->{attr}});
}

1;
```

HTML DOCUMENTS: A BASIC INTRODUCTION

by Joan Murray

D.1   Intro to the Intro

The progress of HTML (HyperText Markup Language) in the age of the Internet and the World Wide Web has unfolded much in the way of classic Alpine skiing and X-treme skiing. Even people who don't ski know about the rules: bend the knees, hold onto the poles, stay on the trails, and follow a curved path down the slope. There is no mention of snowboarding, hot-dogging, playing catch on skis, or combining skiing with sky-diving. What used to be a winter pastime of country folk now requires special equipment, clothing, accessories, lodging, and transportation. Like skiing, HTML started out simply and can still be used simply, but if you follow the trail to the big time you'll find all the fancy and dangerous complications involved in fashionable pursuits, which is how HTML got mixed up with a scripting language like Perl in the first place.

D.2   What Is HTML?

HTML is described in various ways:

1. A subset of SGML (Standard Generalized Markup Language), the standard for markup languages
2. A collection of platform-independent styles defining various components of a WWW (World Wide Web) document.
3. Put simply, HTML documents are plain-text (ASCII) files with markup (identifier) tags

D.2.1   HTML: It Used to Be as Easy as Falling Off a Log

The basics still apply, but modern technology, new standards, and the Great Browser Wars have made inroads. This overview covers what endures, though that too may change. Our secret weapon is using commercially available Web tools to keep up with the changes. Each

821

section of the overview will contain an update where changes have crept (and in some cases galloped) in.

The introduction of Web site building software like FrontPage and Dreamweaver might make you think that knowing HTML is no longer necessary. However, even the best product doesn't always produce desired results, so you need to be able to tweak where necessary. That brings us to the question:

Why learn HTML code?

1. To know what you're looking at and know how it's done, and, what's better, to be able to do the same yourself
2. To help judge WYSIWYG (what you see is what you get) software products used to create Web pages
3. To get by when you don't have the high-tech tools—even a basic knowledge of HTML will enable you to create a presentable Web site

Why did "They" think this up in the first place?

The Internet had existed for a decade or two as a way to send and receive messages and other documents when someone decided that since monitors had replaced teletype as standard output it might be nice to be able to read material in an orderly fashion on the monitor. One of the results was the invention of a system of embedded codes that would make this possible. The rules set up for HTML reflect the original interested parties, the military and universities, using the system and the state of personal computing devices at the time. They reveal themselves in the default colors, sizes, fonts, and text types and order.

D.3   HTML Tags

The nice part about the basic HTML is that it is easy to do. It is time-consuming and complicated, but it is not difficult. Everything you need is contained in the tags, which are the code identifying an HTML document and the various parts of its contents to a browser.

The tags all follow a set form—start and stop:

* Left angle bracket (<), tag name, right angle bracket (>) for start tag
* Left angle bracket (<), slash (/), tag name, right angle bracket (>) for stop tag

These are usually paired in start/stop set (e.g.,*<H1>* and *</H1>*). These tags define various parts of the HTML document. Only a small set of tags is required; the others are advisable to make the document easier for the user to read.

D.3.1   Required Elements

\<HTML\>, \</HTML\>	Defines the HTML document
\<HEAD\>, \</HEAD\>	Defines the part of the document for the browsers use
\<TITLE\>, \</TITLE\>	Identifies the document to the Web
\<BODY\>, \</BODY\>	Defines the part of the document we see and use

Believe it or not, this is all that is required in an HTML document. The head and title part are required for use by the browser. Unless they peek behind the scene, users see only what is presented between the two body tags.

D.3.2   The Order of the Required Elements and Their Tags

\<HTML\>
\<HEAD\>
\<TITLE\> \</TITLE\>
\</HEAD\>
\<BODY\>
\</BODY\>
\</HTML\>

D.3.3   The Elements: What They Are and How They Are Used

\<HTML\>

This tag tells the browser the file contains HTML-coded information. The file extension *.html* identifies an HTML document. With DOS-based files use *.htm*; Windows- and Mac-based files can use *.htm* or *.html*. Currently, UNIX files should use only *.html*.

\<HTML\> UPDATE!

There now are *.shtml*, *.stm*, *.asp*, and *.xml* Web pages, to name a few. UNIX servers undoubtedly recognize these also, but they are beyond the scope of this overview.

\<HEAD\>

This tag identifies first part of HTML-coded document. It contains the title. (This does not appear on the page itself.)

\<TITLE\>

This tag contains the document title. It is displayed on a browser window only and is not visible on the page itself. On the Web, it identifies a page subject to search engine criteria. It is used as a "hotlist," "favorites," or "bookmark" entry. It should be short, descriptive, and unique.

<HEAD> UPDATE!

Most Web page heads contain more than titles. The following are examples of what can be found there.

    Metatags: make site topics known to (some) search engines

    Style sheets/cascading style sheets (CSS): define aspects of the body

    Java scripts and JavaScript: add jazzy elements to the body of the document

<BODY>

This tag contains content of the document organized into various units:

    Headings (*<H1>* to *<H6>*)

    Paragraphs *<P>*

    Lists, which can be ordered *<OL>* or unordered *<UL>*

    Preformatted text *<PRE>*

    Addresses *<ADDRESS>*

    Space dividers *
*, *<HR>*

    Graphic items

<BODY> UPDATE!

Preformatted text is rarely used unless you want something to look like a typed page. Tables replace preformatted text in most cases. The address portion is now often replaced by a reply form or e-mail address. Many of the interactive elements such as reply forms use CGI (Common Gateway Interface) scripts, usually written in Perl.

D.4   The Minimal HTML Document

```
<HTML>
<HEAD>
<TITLE>A Simple HTML Document. Only the browser sees this title </TITLE>
</HEAD>
<BODY>
<H1>Sample Heading -- You and I see this heading</H1>
<P>This is a sample text representing a paragraph. It will ignore
spaces and keep on being one paragraph <P>This is another paragraph
</BODY>
</HTML>
```

D.4.1   Headings

Don't confuse these with *<HEAD>*, which is not visible to the end user. The heading is at the top of the Web document. Think "Headline." There are six heading tags ordered by size: *<H1>* is the largest and *<H6>* the smallest. According to the original rules it isn't fair to pick and choose headings by appearance. *<H1>* is a primary heading *<H2>* a secondary heading, etc. Those who have been doing this a long time claim it is virtually impossible to distinguish between *<H4>*, *<H5>*, and *<H6>*.

There are a million ways to solve the heading problem. In some fonts, *<H1>* is so huge you would only use it for something of great importance, such as "War is Declared." Because HTML now interacts with Web tools like Java and XML, the *<P>* tag now requires a matching *</P>* tag. Strictly speaking, this is not an HTML requirement because it is not HTML that is having trouble knowing that the paragraph has finished.

D.4.2   Tags to Separate Text

NOTE: Formerly these did NOT require end tags.

<P>
This tag separates text into paragraphs—a hard return with space (line feed). Originally this tag came after the paragraph, but since we use monitors and not actual print devices we don't need to signal a hard return. So now *<P>* indicates to the browser that what follows is a paragraph.

*
*
This breaks text into lines—a hard return with no space between lines.

<HR>
This is a horizontal rule—a graphic representation of a line to separate text areas.

D.4.3   Lists

Lists are perennial favorites of organizations. When the Web began, they represented ways to break up text in a helpful fashion. They could (and still can) be used for definitions, tables of contents, or just plain lists. The numbered list is a favorite of the academic community; the bulleted list that of the military; otherwise, they are really self-explanatory.

There are two types of lists:

1. Ordered (numbered) list
   <OL>
   <LI> Item number one
   <LI> Item number two
   </OL>
2. Unordered (bulleted) list
   <UL>
   <LI> First item
   <LI> Next item
   </UL>

Lists are old fashioned. Use them with discretion. Avoid long lists; instead block topics as subpage(s). Use tables or links (or both) where possible.

The *<LI>* tag has suffered the same fate as the *<P>* tag. You must use an *</LI>* tag to be truly up to date. Originally there were several subcategories of lists, but they've pretty much done away with most of them.

D.4.4   Tables for Fun and Profit

Tables are scary when you look behind the scene and see all those tags and indents. To make a table, use the same principle as the traveler on the 1,000-mile journey: one step at a time. This overview covers simple tables, the kind that replaced preformatted *<PRE>* text. Though complicated they are no more exasperating than counting all the spaces between words in preformatted text to make the results come out even.

The Basic Table Tags:

<TABLE> </TABLE>   Defines table
<TR> </TR>   Defines table row
<TD> </TD>   Defines table cell (data)

The principle is the same as with the HTML document as a whole: The table *<TABLE>* contains rows *<TR>*, which contain data cells *<TD>*.

Tailoring Tables:

<TABLE ALIGN="CENTER">
<TABLE BORDER ALIGN="CENTER">
<TABLE BGCOLOR="#FEFEFF">, <TABLE BGCOLOR="AQUA">

You can use many of the same tag elements you use to tweak other page elements. The *ALIGN=* command puts items including tables to left, right, or center on page.

Some browsers allow you to add color to the background (Netscape, Internet Explorer). The same is true of background images, but Netscape and IE treat them differently.

Similar rules guide formatting of table rows and cells. You can adjust text position and background in these units.

How Table Tags Are Used:

This will yield a simple table with two rows and two cells.

<TABLE>
<TR><TD>data</TD><TD>more data</TD></TR>
<TR><TD>data</TD><TD>maybe a picture</TD></TR>
</TABLE>

By adding spacing, alignment, color, and other tags, you can manipulate tables. You can enlarge the table by increasing the number of rows or data cells. You can specify header rows, make data cells span more than one row and/or column, put background colors, borders, and more. It's all in the details.

D.5 Character Formatting

There are two ways to indicate text formatting:

1. Logical—according to its meaning
2. Physical—according to its appearance

As you familiarize yourself with both of these, you can see the committee mentality at work. Either two groups already had different codes in place, or someone wanted to go home.

Many pages use physical tags even though logical tags are standard. The rule is, BE CONSISTENT.

WYSIWYGs like FrontPage and Dreamweaver, which don't require a lot of text entry, use the logical tags. (If you don't have to type *<STRONG></STRONG>* again and again, you don't really care that the software package chose to use it over *<B></B>*.)

Cascading style sheets (more on them later) will make font/text tags even more interesting than they are now.

D.5.1 Logical Tags

<EM>	For emphasis—usually *italics*
<STRONG>	For strong emphasis—usually **bold**
<CODE><KBD>	Various—`Fixed-width font`

D.5.2 Physical Tags

<B>	**Bold text**
<I>	*Italic text*
<TT>	`Typewriter Text`

D.6 Linking

This is what makes hypertext hyper. It is also the reason to use HTML in the first place. If you like to read, get a book. If you need to connect to various references, hypertext is the way to go. HTML links text and/or images to other documents or other parts of the same document using anchors.

The hypertext tag is *<A>* for anchor; the reference part of tag is *HREF="File"*. The hypertext reference contains the pathname (relative or absolute) of the document (file) you are trying to access.

D.6.1 Creating a Link

If you can get this next bit, you have mastered the magic of hypertext. Notice that the cue to the user does not have to be the pathname to the link. (When the Web was young, site builders did not understand this and often would spell out the path on the Web page, thus causing anxiety in the user.) In the example below, *newfile.html* is referred to in the text as *My Special Page*.

All hypertext link tags take this form:

<A HREF="filename.html">Hot Link</A>

Sample reference:

<A HREF="newfile.html">My File</A>

Put whatever you wish here leading to <u>My Special Page</u>. The same deal over here.

D.6.2   Links to a URL (Uniform Resource Locator)

The hypertext link tag is the same form for a URL as for any other link:

<A HREF="URLname.html">Hot Link</A>

The *URLname* portion is written exactly as it appears in the browser's URL window:

http://host.domain/path/filename

D.7   Adding Comments

Form for comments:

<!-- Put Comment Here -->

"Commenting out" questionable code is considered bad form in HTML. Use commenting only for real comments except as directed to hide Java, JavaScript, XML, CSS, and other scripts from the browser.

D.8   Case Sensitivity

HTML per se is not case sensitive. The following tags are only three examples that are all the same to HTML:

<Body>
<BODY>
<body>

UNIX ties are case sensitive:
"Escape sequences" (*&gt*)
Filenames (*HooXd.u*)
<A HREF="jones.html">Jones &amp Co.</A>

XML, Java, JavaScript, and CSS all have to be just right.

Sometime during the great parade that the World Wide Web has become, someone noticed that HTML was the only unit that was not in step with the march of progress. So, beginning with HTML 4.0, all tags are to be in lowercase to conform with the other elements that make up part of modern Web sites. You can still build a simple Web site without worrying about case sensitivity, but once you start using the sophisticated tools of Web building, lowercase will be the rule. (In this review I will stick to UPPERCASE for tags so that they are more visible, but don't try this at home.)

D.9   Graphics and Images

D.9.1   Creating an Inline Image

To include an image inline (next to text) or otherwise, use the form:

<IMG SRC="ImageName">

Graphic files are usually *.gif* or *.jpg*. *.jpg* appears as *.jpeg* in Windows environments. While the *.jpg* extension can be used on Windows, most UNIX environments currently do not support *.jpeg*.

D.9.2   The Complex Tag

The coding used to create and place images introduces complexity to the tag. The opening anchor tag *<A>* for a hyperlink uses this complexity to identify the link (HREF). The image tag *<IMG>* adds SRC to identify the image. Since images on a page create complexity (increased load time, increased file size), complex, not to say complicated, tags become the norm. You use this complex tag form to define other elements of the Web page such as headings, paragraphs, and tables.

D.9.3   Sizing and Placing the Image

The warring factions of the Web world are constantly debating what a Web site should be. Much of the debate centers on images and their effect on page loading time. While many points of the image debate are beyond the scope of this overview, one is not: the image size attributes. Everyone agrees that it is best to include the width and height of an image to speed page loading. The browser window can give you the information if you know what to do and where to look. We will use Netscape directions for our example.

Launch Netscape, click on **File** in the text menu bar, select **Open Page**, then **Choose File** in the pop-up window, and locate the image on your computer. **NOTE:** make sure the "Types of Files" bar is set to "All Files (*.*)." Select the image whose dimensions you want to know and click the **OK** button. The blue bar at the very top of the browser window contains the measurements in pixels: width then height.

<IMG SRC=picture.gif WIDTH="40" HEIGHT="100" >

You position the image on the page by adding *ALIGN="LEFT"* (or *"RIGHT"* or *"CEN-TER"*) inside the image tag.

D.9.4 Creating a Text Alternative for an Image

Not all browsers support graphics; LYNX, one of the oldest, does not.

Some users turn image-loading off, and most graphics are impractical for sight-impaired users. Using a text label to identify graphic images is good manners and practical. The ALT tag inside the *<IMG>* tag identifies text alternatives for graphics.

<IMG SRC="UpArrow.gif" ALT="UP">

The portion identifying the image does not have to be one word or a repeat of the image filename. Newer Browsers show ALT text when you "mouse over" the image, and inserting a user-friendly phrase such as *View of downtown Rochester, 1948* or *Back to Top* rather than *photo_main_47.jpg* and *arrow.gif* can provide additional information to Web spiders that the image would otherwise conceal.

D.9.5 Where Do I Find Graphics?

The Web has many sites full of free graphics. You need to use discretion since some folks think that if butterflies are free, so are Bugs Bunny, Snoopy, Homer Simpson, and the Nike Swoosh, and there they all are on their "free graphics" Web site. The most useful graphics are part of the 4 B's: buttons, bars, ball, and backgrounds. They used to be very easy to find; every free Web graphics site had them, but with the new Web tools the trend is toward the "unique" (read baroque). One site that has the old reliables is the All Free Original Clipart page. Their URL is *http://www.free-graphics.com/*. The site is well organized so it is easy to review the small graphic objects you want. To get to the type of item you want, choose a category from the menu on the left side of the page. Each section has directions on how to download the image you want to use. When you work on the exercise to create a page of images you may want to use selections from this site.

D.9.6   Background Graphics

All but the earliest versions of Netscape and Microsoft Internet Explorer support background graphics, colors, and textures. You can get images from a Web graphic site such as the one listed above. Since some early browsers (and they're still out there) don't support background images, you can include code in the tag for a background color as well. The browser will pick up the color. This is useful, too, for those users who turn graphics off.

D.9.7   Creating Backgrounds

Since a background color or image can be included in as an attribute, the *<BODY>* tag can become quite complex. For a background image the form is the following:

<BODY BACKGROUND="filename.gif">

Background color is a bit tricky; it uses hexadecimals, but there are several sites on the Web that list these, and Web building tools include these codes. Basically, *000000* represents black and *FFFFFF* represents white. The form for background color follows:

<BODY BGCOLOR="#FF90CB">

To simplify things, there are some standard colors you can add using their name only. The current HTML standard names 16 of these colors; aqua, black, blue, fuchsia, gray, green, lime, maroon, navy, olive, purple, red, silver, teal, yellow, and white.

D.9.8   Default Colors

When the standards for the Web were first created, color monitors were VGA at best, and modems were 300 to 1200 baud. So, the default colors are rather mundane. The default background, referred to as light gray, is more of a battleship gray. Regular text is black. For hotlinks, "Unvisited" hotlink text is blue, an "Active" hotlink text is red, and "Visited" hotlink text is violet. Additionally, All hotlinks are underlined.

Now in the time of streaming media, monitors capable of displaying thousands of colors, and 56K modems, backgrounds can be anything, and an Active link changes so quickly to Visited it hardly matters what color it is. For best contrast on background, try white (*FFFFFF*) or black (*000000*). Experiment with near misses; word on the street is that off-white or black is easier on the eyes.

Besides the 16 named colors there are 216 "Web-safe" colors that work on most browsers without doing strange things. Most graphics tools have a Web-safe palette option.

Hotlinks should be obvious to the user. Purists say stick to the default blue and purple for unvisited and visited. Newer browsers can disable hotlink underline. Leave the underline intact when you build a site and let the user decide.

D.9.9   Bars, Bullets, and Icons

You can get these simple graphics from the *All Free Graphics* Web site to spruce up your page. The temptation is to use a lot of them because you can; don't yield to it. Be especially careful with animated GIFs. An envelope or mailbox constantly opening and closing at the bottom of a Web page can be mighty irritating.

Use bars in place of *<HR>* (hard rule) separators. Position them carefully.

> *<P ALIGN="CENTER"><IMG SRC="somebar.gif"><P>*

Bullets are used to attract attention. (NEW!) is always popular. Small balls fall into the bullet category.

Icons, those small graphical representations, make great clickable images (links to other files). The image replaces the text that identifies the hotlink. This is the principle behind all those "Click here for…" banner graphics you see on every Web site.

> *<A HREF="Some.html"><IMG SRC="icon.gif"></A>*

To eliminate the "hot" blue border around a linked icon, add *BORDER="0"* to the image tag.

> *<A HREF="Some.html"><IMG SRC="icon.gif" BORDER ="0"></A>*

D.9.10   Graphics Update

Flash 5—Need I say more? Types of graphics fall in and out of favor. The understated look is always good.

D.9.11   External Sights 'n' Sounds

You can use anchor and reference to link to an image as a separate entity. This will open a page to a stand-alone image. Many sites use this device to keep slow loading, large graphics below the main page.

<A HREF="Image.gif">link anchor</A>

The syntax is the same for a sound (*.au*, *.wav*) or movie (*.mov*, *.mpg*)

NOTE: Sound and movies are slow loaders and not everyone can access these.

D.10 Troubleshooting

Even pages put seamlessly together using WYSIWYG software can turn out not quite as expected. Usually the problem is something involving fancier HTML elements. (FrontPage is notorious for constantly trying to second-guess the author.) For those who are drawers of water and hewers of HTML, the problems are much more mundane. The following covers the most common errors. Believe me when I say everybody who has written HTML has done all of these.

1. Watch out for overlapping tags:
   *<B>*Example of *<I>*overlapping*</B>* tags*<I>*
   <!-- here the author wants the last two words in italics, and everything but the last word to be bold. -->
   *<B>*It should be *<I>*this*</I></B><I>* instead*</I>*
   <!-- That's what keeps them buying FrontPage -->

2. Make sure all the tags are matched.
   *<H1>*Win a million dollars! *</H1>*
   Forgetting to stop an action can result in interesting effects such as *an entire page in italics* or headline sized type.

3. Be sure there are no missing parts to a tag (/, <, >, or ").

4. Embed only anchors and character tags inside defining tags.
   <H1><A HREF="file.html">Hot Stuff</A> </H1>

5. Watch out for misspellings such as HREP or Hl (letter el) for H1 (one).

D.10.1 Ask Heloise!

The more popular browsers will correct most errors they detect. That doesn't mean that your page doesn't look hosed on someone else's browser. If that person is trying to get some useful information, the error may thwart his efforts.

Ideally, all pages should be validated. This process checks for missing parts, overlapping tags, unmatched tags, and other problems. The W3 consortium has a validator on its site at *www.w3.org.*

Check your code against more than one browser. Only standard-issue HTML works on both Netscape and IE, and the latest standard may not work on earlier browser versions. Metatags and style sheets, the norm by today's standards, have to be commented out because the earlier browsers will print them code and all, right on the user's screen.

To be safe put all tag content after the equal sign in double quotes.

<BODY BGCOLOR="aqua" BACKGROUND="grandma.jpg">
<P ALIGN="RIGHT">

Sometimes browsers get cranky and won't recognize a qualifier even when it's a clone of a tag you've used countless times with no trouble.

Even if you use a WYSIWYG editor double check all your ALT tags. The WYSIWYG will put in *ALT="00187.gif"* or *"fzzypic1.jpg"* because that's what the image source is called. If you can't figure out how to make them more user friendly using the WYSIWYG side, add them on the HTML side. Dreamweaver files can be opened in Notepad, and FrontPage has a nice HTML source code page incorporated in it.

D.10.2   Some Sites that Help You with HTML

www.w3c.org

World Wide Web Consortium—This is the authority on all things involving the Web.

hotwired.lycos.com/webmonkey

WebMonkey—Full of hip tutorials on all sorts of Web-related topics.

www.ncsa.uiuc.edu/General/Training

National Center for Supercomputing—the home of Mosaic.

www.ncsa.uiuc.edu/General/Training/HTMLIntro/HTML.Help.html

The ultimate beginner's manual: read it online and print it out for future reference.

www.htmlgoodies.com

HTML Goodies—excellent tutorials by Joe Burns, Ph.D.; subscribe to his newsletters.

D.11 Metatags, Cascading Style Sheets, and Java

These are some topics that you should know about.

* Metatags: more than you want anyone to know about your site but really need to tell them
* Cascading style sheets: giving a "pulled together" look to even the largest sites
* Java scripts and JavaScript: where the action is

D.11.1   Metatags Example (Part 1)

Metatags are a study in themselves. Each part of the following example shows you the most common tags used. Some sites put the tags in Part 1 of the example first, followed by the *TITLE* tag and then the real metatag meat. They all follow the complex tag form seen below. The *META NAME* portion stays the same. You change the part in quotes after the *CONTENT=* to fit your situation. The first part is standard. You can copy it verbatim except for the *CONTENT* portion of the *META NAME="Author"* tag.

```
<HEAD>
<TITLE>Simon Says Put the Title First</TITLE>
<META NAME="Author" CONTENT="myownwebpage.com">
<META NAME="distribution" CONTENT="global">
<META NAME="resource-type" CONTENT="document">
```

```
<META NAME="language" CONTENT="en">
</HEAD>
```

D.11.2   Metatags Example (Part 2)

The second part illustrates the keywords that identify your site to some search engines. Notice the great variety of keywords used by this site. Most of them are common to many sites. It's not so much a case of trying to be different but of giving the people what they want. The trick is to pick words that match what your audience is looking for (note the word "free"), which explains why a Web search can lead to some very strange results indeed.

META NAME="Keywords" CONTENT="SHOPPING, JOB BANK, Sign Up!, Find-A-Job, Post-A-Job, CLASSIFIEDS, Search Ads, Place Ad, Change Ad, Delete Ad, Cool Notify, Hot List, DIRECTORIES, ActiveX, ASP, C/C++, CGI, Databases, Emerging Tech, HTML/DHTML, Intranets, Java, JavaScript, Middleware, Perl, Visual Basic, XML, What's Cool, What's New, Japanese Pages, REFERENCE, Online Reference Library, LEARNING CENTER, Course Catalog, Tutorials, Experts Q&A, JOURNAL, Tech Focus, Tech Workshop, Staff Picks, Users' Choice, Profiles, NEWS CENTRAL, Archive, DOWNLOADS, Free Graphics, Free Scripts, COMMUNITY, Discussions, J.D.A., Whos Who, CALENDAR, Online Events, Industry Events, Conferences, ABOUT US, Who We Are, What We Do, News About Us, Advertising Info, Vendor Info, Job Openings, Awards, FAQs, email, highlights, developers, Current issues">

D.11.3   Metatags Example (Part 3)

This tag describes your site and your purpose. When users do a Web search the description is what the search engine retrieves and prints (together with the title) in the search results.

<META NAME="description" CONTENT="myownwebpage.com is the leading online service for novice Web page developers. It includes So Help Me Mama, the unofficial and utterly useless directory for Java, as well as news, information, tutorials, and directories for other Internet technologies including ActiveX, JavaScript, Perl, VRML, Java Beans, push technologies, and other Internet and intranet technologies. myownwebpage.com is also the home of Really Cheap Software, the Unprofessional Developer's Store, where naïve developers can purchase and download thousands of Web, authoring, and other development products at some of today's highest prices.**">

D.11.4   Style Sheet Example

Originally, Web pages were all about information and not about formatting; certainly not about style. Discreet additions of color and subtle graphics were one thing but spinning, screaming, flashing page parts quite another. Not only was this not dignified, but the variety of colors and styles meant more work for the developer maintaining the Web site. As things got more complicated, style sheets were introduced as a way to create a look without so much hand tweaking.

The site developer puts the requirements for color and text elements in one of three places, and these determine the look of the site. For special cases you can define the requirements inside a tag, such as the body tag. For a simple site with few pages to maintain you can define the requirements in the *<HEAD>* portion of each page. (See the example below.) For a large site or one that keeps changing its look you can define the requirements in a separate document. The cascading part of CSS (cascading style sheets) comes from the way style requirements are prioritized. Local (inside tag) requirements take precedence over document (inside the head portion) requirements, which take precedence over global (separate document) requirements. In this introductory overview we will use as an example the within-document form. NOTE: this is not as straightforward as old-fashioned HTML. It doesn't use the traditional start/stop tags except to identify the section as style.

Because older browsers can't deal with style sheets, everything defining the style must be placed between comment tags and contained in a section surrounded by *<STYLE>* tags. Various elements are defined using an identifier and its qualifiers. You must put these attributes inside curly braces. A qualifier (such as font size or font family) is followed by a colon and a specifier (such as 24 pt or sans serif). A semicolon separates sets of attributes for each element you choose to define. The example shown uses standard elements and suggested attributes.

```
<HEAD>
<TITLE>You call that a style sheet?</TITLE>
<STYLE="text/css">
<!--
BODY {background: #FFFFFF}
H1 {font-size: 24pt; font-family: arial}
H2 {font-size: 18pt; font-family: braggadocio}
H3 {font size: 14pt; font-family: sans-serif}
-->
</STYLE>
</HEAD>
```

D.11.5 JavaScript Example

JavaScript adds action to a Web page. Its advantages are that it is not compiled and doesn't have to run on a server. Web developers use JavaScript to create small "events" such as pop-up windows (see the example below) and image rollovers. As with style sheets older browsers can't handle JavaScript so it must be hidden inside comment tags. The example shown causes three pop-up windows to appear successively on a Web page when you launch it. Like every other special effect on the Web, this sort of thing can be overdone.

```
<head> <title>First Exercise</title>
<script language="JavaScript">

<!-- hide me

alert("Here's a little script");
alert("Just to show");
```

```
alert("That I know JavaScript!");

// end hide -->

</script>
</head>
```

D.12   Looking Behind the Scenes (or, What Did We Do Before the Right-Click?)

To borrow source code or download graphics use your right mouse button to open a menu of selections. If you wish to view source code, right-click on a clear area of the background. Good old IE launches a separate Notepad document you can save with a new filename to examine at your leisure. If you are interested in capturing an image, right-click on the image. Choose "save image/picture as." It's usually good to rename the file, especially if it's called something like *0018dr.jpg*.

To capture some text, highlight it with your mouse and copy it using <Ctrl>-c. Paste it into a document using <Ctrl>-v.

D.13   What About Frames?

The way things are going, frames, like sex, politics, and religion, will be a topic that one may not discuss in polite company. People either love them or loath them. WebMonkey has several tutorials on frames. Go to *hotwired.lycos.com/webmonkey/authoring* and click on the frames topic.

D.14   Some Final Thoughts

Consider how your page will be used. If people have to read a lot, they don't want attention-getting elements distracting them. Finally, here are a few general tips to keep in mind:

- The current standard for HTML tags is lowercase.
- Container is the jazzy new word for any HTML element (*<P>*, *<TD>*).
- With the advent of style sheets, *<DIV>* is the hip new tag. Its main use is as a container to identify style elements you've created and named yourself versus the standard type shown in the style example. It's one of those complex tags with parts. Check out online tutorials from HTML Goodies or WebMonkey to learn more about this.
- If you are going to create a table, draw it first. Write the necessary code in those fields that will need special tabs, and use the annotated sketch as a reference for coding.

- Visible e-mail addresses can attract spam (junk e-mail); CGI forms offer more control.
- Check Web sites devoted to HTML to learn of the latest developments (see "Some Sites that Help You with HTML" on page 834).
- Examine the source code on pages you like to help you develop your own pages.

About the Author of This Tutorial

I work for the Navy in Monterey, California. In 1996 my employer, Fleet Numerical Meteorology and Oceanography Center, which supplies weather data for the Navy's ships and planes, was preparing to launch a Web site for its users. No adequate software package was available, but the job had to be done. As part of a "train the trainer" endeavor, I took a class on the Internet and the information superhighway at the nearby Naval Postgraduate School. One project, building a Web page using HTML, led me to create and teach a class in HTML basics that helped provide talented co-workers with the knowledge to launch our first Internet pages. Even though we now use more sophisticated Web-building tools, I've taught that basic class many times.

— *Joan Murray*

INDEX

ABOUT THE AUTHOR

Ellie Quigley is the author of *Perl by Example*, *UNIX Shells by Example*, and now *Linux Shells by Example*. She is also the creator of the world's number one interactive Perl course, *Perl Multimedia Cyber Classroom*. A leading instructor and trainer, her courses in Perl and UNIX shell programming at the University of California Santa Cruz Extension Program and at Sun Microsystems have become legendary throughout Silicon Valley.

ABOUT THE CD-ROM

Welcome to *Perl by Example*, third edition. This CD-ROM contains Perl scripts and batch files to correspond with the examples shown in the book. If you already have Perl installed on your computer, the scripts are ready to run on your machine. If you don't already have Perl, it's available at no cost from *www.perl.com*.

Installing and Running the Scripts

Installation of these examples is merely a copying of the appropriate (Linux or Windows) directory tree to your hard drive. The scripts provided here are intended to be run from the command line in a terminal/console window or emulator.

- On Windows, they will be run through an MS-DOS application window. Just type the name of the script at the command line:

```
> example15.pl
```

If Perl has not been associated with the *.pl* extension on your system, then you should go to the file explorer window and set up the association. If Perl's directory is included in your PATH environment variable, you can also call Perl directly as follows:

```
> perl example15.pl
```

- On Linux/UNIX, they will be run through a command shell. Just type the name of the script at the command line:

```
> example15
```

If the system complains about not finding the file, you may need to modify your shell environment so that PATH includes your current directory. Either that or call the script explicitly as follows:

```
> ./example15
```

If the system does not recognize it as an executable Perl script, then run the Perl command on it:

```
> perl example15
```

- The Perl scripts provided for UNIX or Windows should also work fine on a Mac OS. The batch scripts will not work unless you are running some kind of Windows or UNIX emulator on your Mac. If you are running Perl directly on the Mac, most of the steps included in the batch scripts can be accomplished by dragging and dropping icons on your desktop.

The chapter directories on the CD correspond with the chapters in the book, and the example numbers on the files correspond as much as possible with the example numbering in the book. The majority of the files in each chapter directory are Perl scripts. For Windows, these all have the extension *.pl*. On UNIX, the *.pl* extension is left out for the example scripts. However, there are some auxiliary Perl scripts that are called from batch file examples, and these occasionally have a *.p* or *.pl* extension.

Many of the examples are batch files instead of Perl scripts. On Windows, these files have names that end with the extension *.bat*, while on UNIX, these files must be distinguished by looking at their first line (which consists of the special comment *#! /bin/sh*). The README file for each chapter specifically indicates which examples are batch files.

The other key type of file found in these chapter directories is the input file. Input files are plain text files, and their filenames always begin with the word "input." On Windows, these files also end with a *.txt* extension, to indicate that they are plain text.

System Requirements

- Windows 95 or later (or any UNIX/Linux OS or emulator)
- 16 MB RAM
- 3 MB hard drive space
- OS must recognize filenames longer than 8 bytes
- 2x CD-ROM drive
- Perl version 5.003 or later installed on your system

In addition, it is highly recommended that you have at least Perl version 5.6.0 on your system, to get the most of all the latest features described in the book. Some of the later chapters have specific system needs in order to run.

License Agreement

Use of the software accompanying *Perl by Example* is subject to the terms of the License Agreement and Limited Warranty, found on the previous page.

Technical Support

Prentice Hall does not offer technical support for the contents of this CD-ROM. However, if the CD-ROM is damaged, you may obtain a replacement copy by sending an e-mail that describes the problem to *disc_exchange@prenhall.com*.